IBM® WebSphere® Portal Primer

Second Edition

IBM® WebSphere® Portal Primer

Second Edition

Foreword by Robert Will
Distinguished Engineer, IBM Corporation,
Chief Architect of WebSphere Portal

Ashok K. Iyengar, Venkata V. Gadepalli, Bruce R. Olson

IBM Press
MC Press Online, LP
Lewisville, Texas

IBM Press Program Manager: Tara B. Woodman, Ellice Uffer
Cover Design: IBM Corporation
Published by MC Press Online, LP
Publishing as IBM Press

IBM WebSphere Portal Primer: 2nd Edition
Foreword by Robert Will
Ashok Iyengar, Vishy Gadepalli, and Bruce Olsen

IBM Press offers excellent discounts on this book when ordered in quantity for bulk purchases or special sales, which may include electronic versions and/or custom covers and content particular to your business, training goals, marketing focus, and branding interests. For more information, please contact:

MC Press
Corporate Offices:
125 N. Woodland Trail
Lewisville, TX 75077
817.961.0660

MC Press Online, LP

Sales and Customer Service
P.O. Box 4300
Big Sandy, TX 75755-4300
www.mcpressonline.com/ibmpress

ISBN: 1-931182-23-X
Printed in Canada, at WebCom, Toronto, Ontario.
First printing: June, 2005
Second printing: October 2006

Acknowledgments

The authors would like to say thank you to the subject matter experts who reviewed our manuscript:

> *Robert Will, Don Jones, Ron Lynn, Kirk Davis, Eric Martinez de Morentin, Stacy Joines, Jonathan Brunn, Varadarajan Ramamoorthy, Daniel Collins, and Varaprasad Bhatta.*

Your constructive criticism, attention to the technical details, and insights were invaluable and did a lot to improve the content of the book. We would also like to thank members of the WebSphere Portal development team and WebSphere Enablement team for answering questions and allowing us to bounce ideas off them. Robert Will's foreword sets the tone of the book and gives readers his vision for the WebSphere Portal product.

Special thanks to Tara Woodman, the point person in the IBM Press program for her consistent support.

We can't say enough about the folks at MC Press; we wonder if other publishers are as tolerant and flexible. Thanks to Merrikay Lee for managing it all; Jeff Phillips for accommodating all those cover changes; Dan DiPinto, the graphic artist, for creating our vision; and Joann Woy for doing a marvelous job of copy editing.

Finally, a huge debt of gratitude to Carol Jones, who was our mentor during the first edition.

Ashok Iyengar

The rewards of writing a book that might be useful to others make it all worthwhile. And needless to say, it is not possible without the support of a whole lot of people—people at work, family members, friends, and my co-authors, Vishy and Bruce.

Special thanks to my managers, Robert Freeman and Tom Kristek, and the management team at IBM for all the encouragement and flexibility they have provided. It is wonderful to work for such supportive managers.

Speaking of family, this one is for the three individuals who influenced me during my formative years—my sister, Siri, who kept me honest; my brother, Prakash, whom I always looked up to; and my quiet sister, Pushpa.

I would be amiss not to mention the three individuals who currently influence me—Radha, Sameer, and Siddharth. Thank you for supporting me in all my efforts.

Venkata Gadepalli

First of all, I would like to thank my co-authors, Ashok Iyengar and Bruce Olson, for keeping us on track and for all their efforts in making the publishing of this book come true.

I am also thankful for all the sacrifices my wife Radhika and my son Siddharth had to make during the writing of this book. I am also very grateful for the great support of my parents and my extended family of uncles and aunts and cousins, who keep encouraging me.

Last, but not least, I would like to thank my managers at IBM, Ken Hygh and Tom Kristek, for all the encouragement and support they provided in this endeavor.

I would like to dedicate this book to the memory of my grandparents, who had a great influence on me as I was growing up.

Bruce R. Olson

I would like to thank my co-authors, Ashok Iyengar and Venkata Gadepalli, for asking me to participate in the second edition of this book. They are good friends and a pleasure to work with. Special thanks to Ashok for being the driving force in making this book a reality.

As always, I am thankful for the support of my wife Diane, and my sons John and Cory. I also want to thank my parents and brothers, as well as all of my friends who have been there for me. I would especially like to thank my brother David, Brian Cheng, and Kevin Williams. Finally, I would like to thank my managers at IBM, Ken Hygh and Tom Kristek, for their support.

I would like to dedicate this book to the memory of my Uncle Ralph. He had a huge influence early in my career in the field of computer science. He was always a source of inspiration and encouragement throughout my personal and professional life.

Contents

Foreword

Portals have evolved at an amazing pace. The early leaders provided little more than a collection of static content and bookmarks. When we began work on WebSphere Portal, we had a much broader vision than most of the other products out there. We saw portals as a unique opportunity to make users more productive. Whether the users were employees managing their expense accounts or customers learning how to put together the bicycle they bought, we saw portals as a way for businesses to deliver applications and information to people in ways that were beneficial to the users of the portal and efficient for the business.

While we could see the potential, we didn't know everything that was needed. We've evolved the WebSphere Portal vision by working closely with our customers, listening to what they were trying to do, providing assistance in the short term with custom services, and then rolling these ideas into the product stream. Ashok Iyengar, Venkata Gadepalli, and Bruce Olson have been and still are on the front lines of portal deployments, working with our customers on a daily basis. The insights they bring back to the lab are invaluable. With this second edition, they bring these insights to you while explaining how to best leverage WebSphere Portal's capabilities today.

As WebSphere Portal has evolved, we've learned that simple integration of the web UI is not enough. WebSphere Portal provides a framework for integration across multiple dimensions. We provide services for user experience integration, user profile and security integration, content integration, business process and application integration, and "people integration" with services to help users collaborate to get their job done. We've evolved our vision, and made the implementations better through our interactions with our customers and the input from our services team.

The product team has worked to make WebSphere Portal both powerful and consumable. But there is an incredible amount of capability "in the box," and learning about it and then leveraging it effectively can take some time. Where do you start? What is the best path for what you're trying to do? Ashok, Vishy, and Bruce have created a dynamic book that will help you get the most out of WebSphere Portal, and to get you on the right track. They've done it before with many, many customers, solving real life business problems. And they've done an incredible job of distilling their experiences into this practical, step-by-step guide that will help you get the most out of WebSphere Portal.

Whether you received this book from your boss or bought it on your own, you're taking your first step in learning about the future of software development. I have worked with the authors and learned from them, and I am sure that in reading this book, you will too.

Robert Will
Distinguished Engineer, IBM Corporation
Chief Architect of WebSphere Portal

Introduction

The dictionary defines a portal as a door or entrance; hence, that picture on the cover. In this book, you will learn why the word *portal* has become a major buzzword in the world of information technology (IT). Most of the major software vendors have a portal server product or aspire to have one. Not to be outdone, enterprises big and small are clamoring to put up portal presences on the Web.

A recent report from Forrester Research states, "IT executives expect eBusiness spending to drop, but more than one-third of Global 3500 firms plan to purchase portal servers. Why do enterprise portal projects get funding while IT budgets shrink?"

What Are Portals?

In IT, portals are defined as doorways into the vast Internet world. If you do not know it yet, Web sites are passé; we are already into the second generation of portals. Organizations like Yahoo, Netscape, CNN, and MSNBC have been serving up information via portals for some time. It is like a Web supermarket, where you buy or view just what you want. Portals are fast becoming gateways to the corporate world, delivering information in a way that seems tailored to each employee.

A portal lets you do four things with online information:

- *Organize*—Portals let you organize online information for personal and competitive advantage. For example, you can set up a portal to send a message to your mobile phone when a critical stock price is reached.
- *Search*—By organizing information, a portal enables you to quickly search through that information to find answers quickly. Portals also offer the ability to send the information you find to others.
- *Personalize*—The biggest benefit of portals is their ability to personalize information. You can select the topics you want information on, keep track of the stocks you own, know the weather in your area, and have it presented in the format you like. This feature involves two prerequisites: The user has to log in, and the portal has to store user-profile information.
- *Collaborate*—More and more portals are offering users the ability to communicate and collaborate with each other in real-time. E-mail started as a way to reduce paper mail. Now, we look to reduce e-mail, and collaboration plays a part in doing that. The ability to chat with people online, or share a document via e-meetings, is a powerful feature that portals can provide.

Portal Servers

Enterprises want to know how portals can be set up, what kind of expertise is required to put them into production, and how many kinds of portals exist. At the center of portal technology is a piece of software called the *portal server*. IBM was one of the first major software companies to market a portal server. Some are stand-alone portal servers, and others are deeply integrated with an application server. IBM's WebSphere Portal falls into the latter category. It is integrated with the award-winning WebSphere Application Server. As part of the IBM WebSphere family, it is Java-based and J2EE compliant.

Most other major software vendors, such as Oracle, Microsoft, Sun, BEA, and SAP, have portal servers. Smaller, specialized software companies, such as Plumtree and Vignette, also market their own portal servers, but these typically run on other application servers.

Portal Types

Three different types of portals exist: business-to-business (B2B), business-to-employee (B2E), and business-to-consumer (B2C). These can encompass the Internet, an intranet, and/or an extranet.

B2B Portal

A simple definition of *B2B* is any business process between two companies that uses digital technology. The business process could represent one or more functions that provide information, facilitate transactions, execute transactions, or completely integrate shared business processes into separate, existing systems. This is known as *e-commerce*. B2B concerns itself primarily with supply-chain management. B2B portals allow businesses to deal directly with their suppliers and distributors, allowing online transfers of orders, invoices, and even payments.

Although B2B processes were in existence before portals arrived on the scene, the two are made for each other. Traditionally, B2B portals were hosted by third parties with specialized software, and maintenance used to be a mammoth undertaking. With the advent of industrial-strength portal servers like WebSphere Portal, however, enterprises can host from the same site a regular portal for Internet and intranet users, and a B2B portal, without compromising service or security.

Many experts think that B2B portals will far outpace B2C portals in the coming years. Over the next four to five years, B2B is expected to have a compound annual growth of 41%. The Gartner Group estimates that the worldwide B2B Internet commerce market will be $8.5 trillion in 2005. Business relationships and interbusiness processes will drastically change in the next couple years, giving rise to new methodologies, standards, and the refinement of B2B portals.

A report by ActivMedia Research finds that companies with an online presence attribute one-sixth of their revenue to online sales. In addition to taking orders, the report finds that the main goals of many B2B Web sites are to:

- Forge new customer relationships and bolster existing ones with product and sales data
- Collect qualified sales leads for follow-up
- Enhance post-sales services

B2E Portal

A B2E portal (also sometimes called a "people portal"), answers questions like these:

- What training is available for me, as an employee?
- Where can I get some leadership coaching, so I can advance my career?
- How does a huge corporation effectively communicate its benefits, bonuses, and other information to its employees worldwide?

A fine distinction exists between an intranet and a B2E portal. An intranet focuses on the company. On an intranet, you expect to find things like hiring policies, the employee directory, and a CEO's message. You can find much of this information on the B2E portal, but you'll also find personal information, such as links to how your retirement plan is doing and the details of your current health benefits.

A B2E portal has three distinguishing characteristics, according to searchCIO.com:

- A single point of entry: one URL for everyone within an organization
- A mixture of organization-specific and employee-defined components
- The potential to be highly customized and easily altered to suit the particular employee

In a broad sense, B2E encompasses everything that businesses do to attract and retain well-qualified staff in a competitive market, such as aggressive recruiting tactics, benefits, education opportunities, flexible hours, bonuses, and employee empowerment strategies. Thus, a B2E portal is more focused on the employee as an individual.

Figure I.1 shows w3.ibm.com which is an example of a well laid-out B2E portal. A B2E portal should be the one place that every employee can turn to, anywhere, anytime.

Figure I.1: Example of a B2E portal.

B2C Portal

Commonly known as "e-tailing Web sites," B2C portals are geared toward the consumer. The exchange of services, information, and/or products from a business to a consumer defines B2C. With their use of personalization, recommendations, and search engines, B2C portals create a very personalized experience, making it easy for consumers to shop online. Another way to look at a B2C portal is as an intermediary site that links customers to suppliers. Amazon, eBay (shown in Figure I.2), and ZDNet are popular examples of B2C portals.

The eSpending Report, compiled by market research companies, shows that online shopping sales have exhibited phenomenal increases from the previous year. For example, during the 2004 holiday season, sales jumped to $23.2 billion. This reflects a 25 percent increase from the $18.5 billion spent online during the same timeframe in 2003. On a related note, eMarketer, another market research company, claims that online advertisement revenues from display, sponsorship, and rich media advertising will grow by 21% in 2005. Two key factors drive this growth: Consumers want the convenience that e-shopping provides, and multichannel retailers are bolstering their online presences.

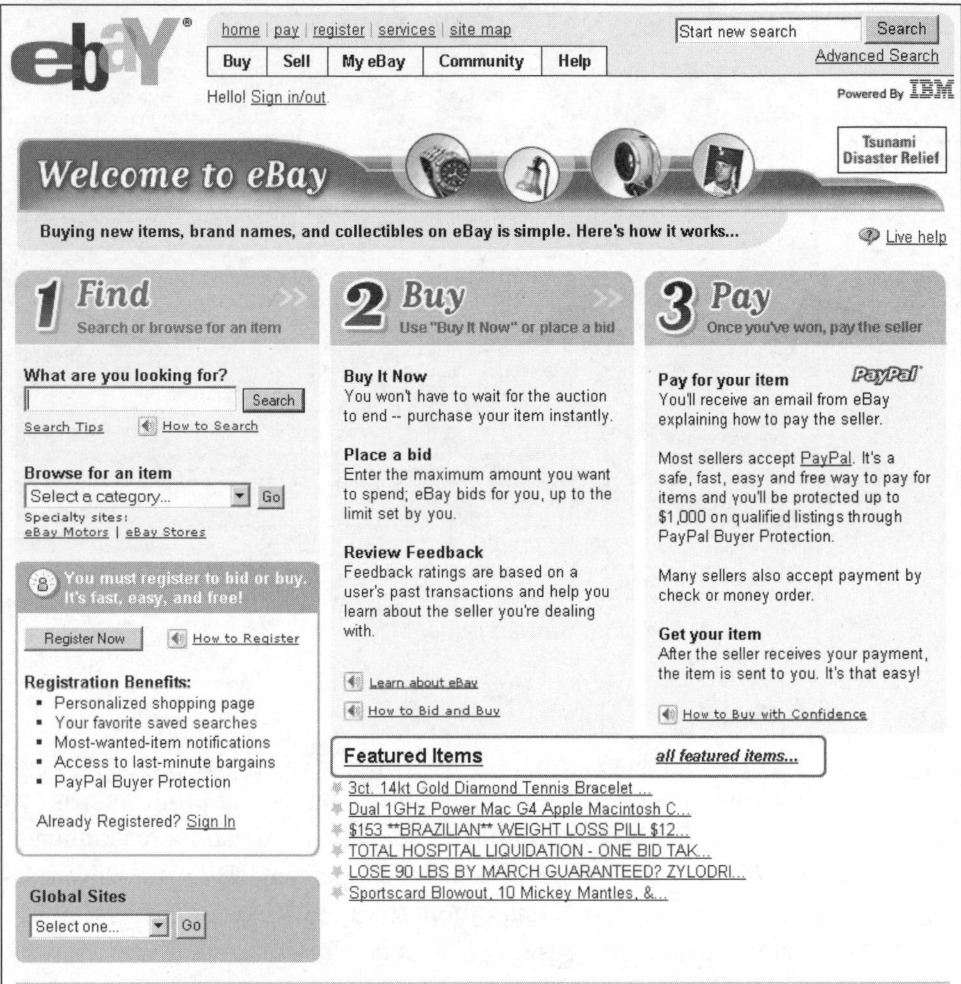

Figure I.2: The popular eBay site is an example of a B2C portal.

What's in the Book?

This book assumes you have little or no prior experience with portals. It does not assume you have extensive experience with Java programming, J2EE, HTML,

Web Services, or XML, but neither does it provide an exhaustive description of these technologies.

The book is organized as follows:

- Chapter 1 introduces the WebSphere Portal product and discusses the different components that make up WebSphere Portal server.
- Chapter 2 explains the concepts, definitions, standards, and architecture in the WebSphere platform.
- Chapter 3 deals with planning, installing, and configuring the WebSphere Portal software on the Windows, Solaris, Linux, and AIX platforms.
- Chapter 4 shows how to establish a portal site's unique look and feel, which includes customized banners, color schemes, and page layout.
- Chapter 5 deals with personalizing the portal. All aspects of Personalization Server are covered here, so the user gets that feeling of having visited "my portal."
- Chapter 6 has many code samples, and appropriately so. It introduces the Portlet API and takes you through several different portlet-programming samples.
- Chapter 7 talks about security, explains the issues involved in securing a portal, and describes the different ways of achieving single sign-on.
- Chapter 8 discusses some of the advanced components of WebSphere Portal, such as Search and Site Analyzer. A discussion is also included of WebSphere Portal Application Integrator and the newest topic—process portals.
- Chapter 9 deals with Collaboration and Content Management. This entails working with Lotus components that really differentiate WebSphere Portal from other portal servers.
- Chapter 10 shows how to go from a simple Web site to a portal. Some out-of-box portlets are described, and this chapter also illustrates portlet-to-portlet communication and internationalization.

The book ends with some appendices containing information on installing WebSphere Portal, tracing the working of Portal Server, and finding additional sources of information. One particularly useful source is the IBM WebSphere Portlet Catalog.

Who Are We?

We are part of a small but highly technical group at IBM known as the WebSphere Enablement Team. Venkata Gadepalli and Bruce Olson are based in Raleigh, North Carolina, and Ashok Iyengar works out of the San Diego, California office.

The team's reporting chain includes WebSphere Services and the Software Group. The team's charter is to make WebSphere Software succeed at customer sites, primarily in the pre-sales cycle. We do this by way of proofs of concept (PoCs), technical demonstrations of the software products, architecture and design, mentoring, and even some post-sales activities, such as installation and writing custom code. Most of our work is done at customer locations, which include enterprises around the world. Thus, we provide you with tips and recommendations based on actual experiences.

For the past four years, we have focused on WebSphere Portal and components related to portal technology (such as Personalization Server, portlet programming, Web Content Management, Directory Server, and collaboration). Before that, we worked with the WebSphere Application Server. It has been a great ride—not only have we seen the WebSphere Portal product evolve and mature into one of the premier portal servers on the market, but we also have seen our customers embrace the portal concept, learn about it, and become very sophisticated with its functionality. Actually, customers are taking portal to the next level, using it to create process portals. We see this as the third generation of Internet portals.

Comments?

We hope this book, like the previous edition, will be useful not only as a guide to WebSphere Portal, but also as a text on portal servers in general. We hope you enjoy reading it as much as we enjoyed writing it.

Please help us improve future editions of this book by reporting any inaccuracies, misleading or confusing statements, and plain old typographical errors that you might find. E-mail your reports and comments to us in care of this publisher.

Door Closings

Internet portals are exciting, cutting-edge technology. The very essence of a portal is that users should not know that they are entering one, but once there, they should have access to a plethora of features. The theme throughout this book is that the portal is a doorway, as depicted on the cover.

But how does one go about building a portal? What are these things called *portlets*? Isn't a portal just another Web site? We answer these questions, and many others, in this book. Our vehicle is the market-leading WebSphere Portal offering. The ensuing chapters talk about this product, show how to install and configure it, review its salient features, and take you through its typical usage scenarios.

Note: The official name of the product is IBM WebSphere Portal for Multiplatforms V5.1. Throughout this book it is referred to as WebSphere Portal. When talking about the portal server in itself, it is referred to as WebSphere Portal server.

Chapter 1
Enter the Portal

A couple of years ago, a customer mentioned "integration at the glass"—a phrase that we had not heard before. Now, everybody in the IT world seems to talk about it, and we have Enterprise Portals to thank for that new phrase. What started off as simple Web-based interfaces are now powerful content management and collaboration centers. Portals in general have become the Web interface of choice to provide business users—and the emphasis here is on business users—rapid access to the information and services they need to be more efficient. "Integration at the glass" might seem superfluous, but that is hardly the case. Integration happens at all levels, and the real benefit of the portal stems from the fact that real integration takes place in the backend, and the results are aggregated and presented "at the glass."

So, if you want to be able to integrate with existing backend systems and have a Web interface that provides personalized content along with e-mail and collaboration functionality, you need a framework. IBM WebSphere Portal is one such portal framework that gives individuals the freedom to create virtual desktops and gives enterprises the ability to have "integration at the glass."

This chapter includes a technical introduction to IBM WebSphere Portal. For those who are already familiar with the WebSphere Portal product suite, Chapter 3 is where the in-depth technical discussions start.

The WebSphere Platform

Based on the Java 2 Platform, Enterprise Edition (J2EE), IBM WebSphere Application Server is firmly established as the premier platform in e-business computing. WebSphere scales well and provides enterprises with a comprehensive set of integrated e-business solutions. The current release of WebSphere Application Server is Version 6 but Version 5.1 supports WebSphere Portal V5.1. The three different facets of the WebSphere platform are shown in Figure 1.1. They are *Business Portals, Business Integration*, and *Foundation & Tools*. By utilizing each side of the WebSphere pyramid, you can create and operate a dynamic, reliable, and secure e-business.

Three elements make up the Foundation & Tools portion of WebSphere:

- IBM WebSphere Application Server
- IBM WebSphere MQ, the messaging middleware component
- IBM Rational Application Developer, the Eclipse-based pluggable application-development toolset that supercedes WebSphere Studio Application Developer

The Business Integration side of the product suite pyramid is also known as *Business Process Management*, or *BPM*. BPM deals with business modeling, B2B integration, process automation, and message integration. These products are geared to help businesses streamline their operations and save money.

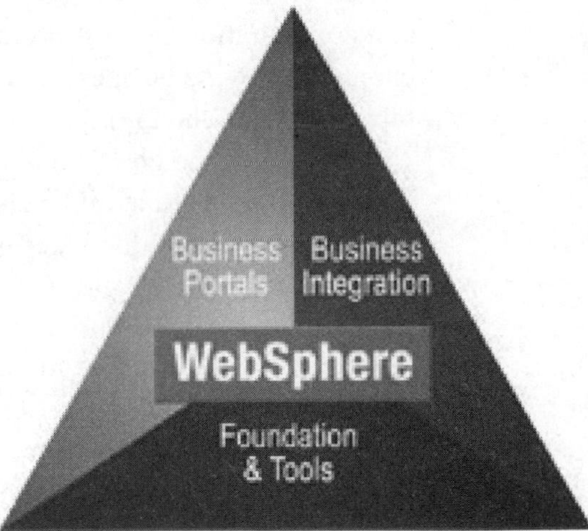

Figure 1.1: The WebSphere platform pyramid.

Finally, the Business Portals part of the suite pyramid encompasses products like Portal Server, WebSphere Commerce Server, Tivoli Web Site Analyzer, WebSphere Voice Server, and WebSphere Translation Server. This book covers the IBM WebSphere Portal for Multiplatforms, which is IBM's official name for this product.

WebSphere Portal

WebSphere Portal is software for building and deploying enterprise portals, big and small. It provides an extensible framework for delivering access to enterprise applications and information. As portals enter their third generation of maturity, WebSphere Portal has introduced new concepts of delegated administration, cascading page layouts, portal federation through Web services, advanced portlet applications, business process integration, and advanced personalization.

WebSphere Portal is available in two different offerings known as editions: *Enable* and *Extend*. These editions are cumulative in function and components. For example, Extend includes all functionality available in Enable, plus additional functionality. Table 1.1 shows the software components that are packaged in each WebSphere Portal offering. Another version of the software is called WebSphere Portal *Express*, which is just like the Enable edition but is licensed on per-user basis.

Table 1.1: WebSphere Portal Editions

Enable Edition

Components	Brief Description
Portal Server	Provides presentation, user management, security, and other services for constructing the portal site.
Personalization	Provides the following personalization technologies for targeting Web content to meet user needs and preferences: • Rules-based personalization, where the business manager defines a set of business rules that determine which Web content is displayed for a particular user. • Recommendations, using advanced statistical models and other matching techniques to extract trends from the behavior of Website visitors. This approach adapts to changing trends in visitor interests without creating new business rules. • Campaign management, for e-mail and Web-based promotions, such as product introductions and enrollment offers.
Document Manager	Allows users to have a central document repository that is lightweight and database independent for team collaboration.
Lotus Collaborative Services	These UI-neutral API methods and tag libraries portlet developers add Lotus Software collaborative functionality. They leverage features of Domino, Lotus Team Workplace, Lotus Instant Messaging, and Web Conferencing.

Table 1.1: WebSphere Portal Editions (continued)

Enable Edition

Components	Brief Description
WebSphere Application Server products	This includes WebSphere Application Server, WebSphere Business Integration Server Foundation (WBISF), and WebSphere Application Server Network Deployment. Together they provide J2EE services that include containers for Java portlets, JavaBeans, JavaServer Pages (JSPs), Enterprise JavaBeans (EJBs), Java Server Faces (JSF), and Struts used in the WebSphere Portal environment.
WebSphere Member Manager	This component is responsible for accessing user registries for managing users and groups. User registries can be LDAP servers, a Custom User Registry, or the Member Manager database.
WebSphere Translation Server	A machine translation (MT) engine that removes all language barriers, thus providing content to users in their native language. It is designed for scalability and uses remote method invocation (RMI) and Java protocols to communicate. A User Dictionary is also included.
Web Content Management	Delivers end-to-end Web content management while leveraging content in back-end systems. With Lotus Workplace Web Content Management, one can manage the content and design of pages; framework and navigation; and the creation, editing, approval, and publication of a Web site's content.
Databases	Cloudscape database is a file-based lightweight database that stores configuration, user identities, credentials, and permissions for accessing portal resources. DB2 Universal Database Enterprise Edition is a highly scalable relational database.
IBM Tivoli Directory Server	A Lightweight Directory Access Protocol (LDAP) directory that stores, updates, and retrieves user-specific data relating to authentication, users, and groups.
IBM Rational Application Developer	An integrated development environment (IDE) for building, testing, and deploying J2EE applications. Provides professional developer tools for creating, testing, debugging, and deploying portlets, JSPs, servlets, EJBs, and other assets related to portals and Web applications. It includes numerous wizards, templates, and sample portlets.

Table 1.1: WebSphere Portal Editions (continued)

Extend Edition	
Components	**Brief Description**
All products in Enable edition	
IBM Lotus Domino Enterprise Server	Popularly known as Domino, this is an integrated messaging and Web application server. It includes Notes, which is groupware software that provides e-mail, messaging, and collaboration features, and Domino Directory, which can be used as the LDAP Server
Lotus Collaboration Center	An integrated framework for finding, connecting, and working with people. It includes the People Finder portlet, My Lotus Team Workplaces (LTW) portlet, and Lotus Web Conferencing portlet. These components make employee interaction speedier and improve personal and organizational productivity.
Lotus Collaboration Components	Provides a series of collaborative service components for the portal that include: Instant messaging (IM) and online awareness based on IBM Lotus IM and Web conferencing technology. Virtual team rooms based on IBM Lotus Team Workplace technology; these can be used as secure workplaces meant for colleagues, suppliers, partners, and/or customers.
IBM Lotus Extended Search	Provides a parallel, distributed, heterogeneous searching capability. Searches Lotus Notes databases; legacy data stores; Web search sites; Microsoft Index Server, Site Server and Exchange 2000; as well as multiple Lotus Notes domains.
IBM Tivoli Site Analyzer	Analyzes Web content integrity and site performance, provides usage statistics, and analyzes portal server logs. Reports from Site Analyzer reveal information that can be used to improve the portal performance for a better user experience.

WebSphere Portal server

WebSphere Portal server provides common services such as application connectivity, integration, administration, and presentation that are required across portal environments. It is installed as another application within WebSphere Application Server, with its own Web and Enterprise JavaBean (EJB) container. Since it is part of the WebSphere Application Server, it provides the same benefits of management, cloning, and scaling. The main components running within the Portal Server's Web container are portlets and portlet applications.

Portlets

A portlet is a small portal application that is displayed as a rectangular area on a Web page. This rectangular area is akin to a miniature browsing area. Portlets are the heart of a portal. They are independent, reusable components that provide access to applications, Web-based content, and other resources. Web pages, services, applications, and syndicated-content feeds can be accessed through portlets.

Portlets are written in Java, utilizing a Portlet Application Programming Interface (API). A standard API now exists, as explained in Chapter 6. Portlets are developed, deployed, managed, and displayed independently of each other. However, you can create special portlets that communicate with each other. Figure 1.2 is a screen shot of one of the default screens of WebSphere Portal server, which is really a portal page entitled *Productivity*. This page is one of three pages under the page group called *My Work,* and it contains three portlets—*Reminder*, *My ToDos*, and *Bookmarks*. (You'll learn more about the concepts of pages, page groups, and portlets in later chapters.)

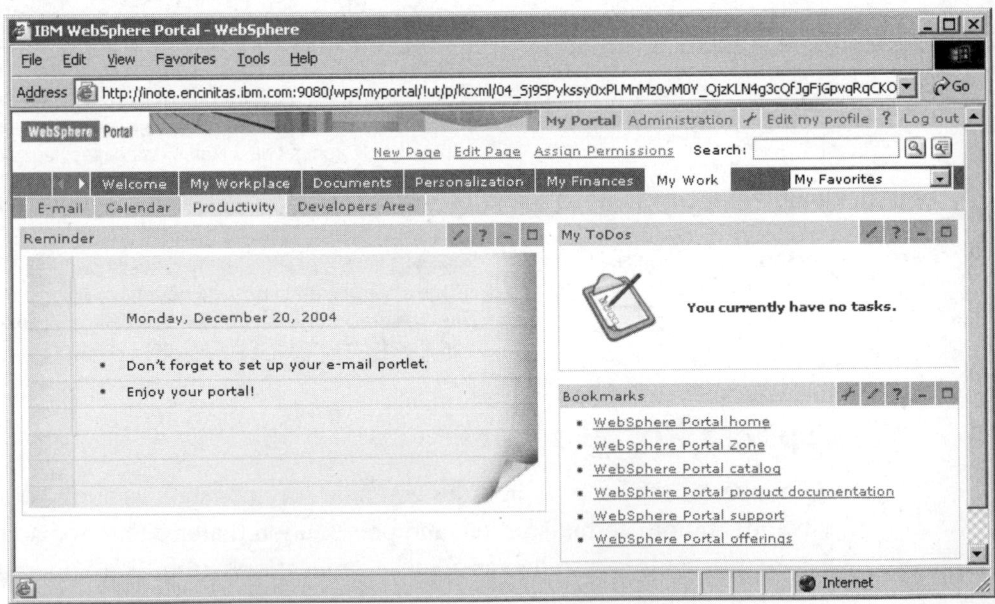

Figure 1.2: A sample portal page in WebSphere Portal.

Portlets are becoming prevalent in the IT world. Enterprises can create their own portlets or select from a portlet catalog that has portlets made available from IBM and other third-party vendors. Now that a standard Portlet API exists, a portlet written for one portal server can conceivably work in another vendor's portal server without modifications.

Note: The term *portlet* is used by IBM, Oracle, BEA, and Sun. Other vendors use terms like *gadgets* and *Web parts.*

The IBM portlet catalog is available at http://catalog.lotus.com/wps/portal/portlet/catalog. Many of the more than 500 plus portlets are freely downloadable, but some are written by third-party software vendors and require a usage or license fee. Make sure you download and use portlets meant for your particular version of WebSphere Portal server, because portlets written for older versions of WebSphere Portal might not work correctly with the current version 5.1.

Portlet Applications

Portlets, in fact, can be parts of complete applications. A portlet application can contain one or more portlets and follow the *model-view-controller* (*MVC*) design. Portlet applications are packaged as Web Archive (.war) files, per the J2EE specifications for Web applications.

Like servlets, portlets run inside a Web container that is part of the portal server. As in the case of servlets, the Web container provides a runtime environment in which portlets are instantiated, used, and finally destroyed. Portlets rely on the portal infrastructure to access user profile information, participate in window and action events, communicate with other portlets, access remote content, look up credentials, and store persistent data.

Portlets, however, are administered more dynamically than servlets. For example, a portlet application consisting of several portlets can be installed or removed while the server is running. An existing portlet can even be dynamically updated with a newer version.

The Portlet API

Portlets are assembled into a larger portal page, with multiple instances of the same portlet displaying different data for each user. Portlets rely on the portal infrastructure for their functionality. Since they are very similar to servlets, it makes sense that IBM portlets are a special subclass of HttpServlet, with properties that allow them to easily plug into and run in the portal server. The portlet Application Programming Interface (API) provides standard interfaces for the portlets' functionality.

The portlet API defines a common base class and interfaces for portlets, in order to cleanly separate a portlet from the portal infrastructure. In most respects, the portlet API is an extension of the servlet API, except that the Portlet API restricts certain functions to a subset of the full servlets API. This makes sense for portlets running in the context of a portal. For example, unlike servlets, portlets may not send errors or redirects as a response. This is done only by the portal itself, which controls the overall response page.

Normally, one or more portlets are invoked in the course of handling a single request, from a user, each one contributing its content to the overall page display. Some portlets can be rendered in parallel, so that the portal server assembles all the markup fragments when all the portlets finish or time-out. Portlets that are not considered thread-safe will be rendered sequentially.

The markup fragments that portlets produce may contain links, actions, and other content. The portlet API defines URL-rewriting methods that allow portlets to transparently create links, without needing to know how URLs are structured in the particular portal. (The portlet API and its usage in creating portlet applications are discussed in more detail in Chapter 6.)

Portal Architecture

WebSphere Portal is a third-generation portal server with a lot of components, and it offers one of the most comprehensive portal solutions. This is possible because WebSphere Portal server mirrors the proven MVC architecture of the WebSphere Application Server. With its own robust portlet API, plus support for the new JSR 168 portlet API, WebSphere Portal not only integrates well with existing backend components, but also is easily extendable.

Enterprises can use existing security systems by using *Trust Association Interceptors* to achieve portal authentication. You can delegate the authorization decisions out to external security management systems. WebSphere Portal has a

Document Manager that is used for collaboration and a Web Content Management component that makes it easy to develop, manage, and publish content to the portal. If enterprises already have third-party content-management systems, WebSphere Portal toolkits are available to interface with many of them.

WebSphere Portal gets installed as a set of J2EE enterprise applications in WebSphere Application Server. Like every other J2EE application, it is comprised of Web Applications and EJBs. Some of the major Enterprise Applications related with WebSphere Portal server are:

- WebSphere Member Management or WMM (wmmApp.ear)
- WPS Enterprise Application (wps.ear)
- WebSphere Content Management or WCM (wcm.ear)
- Personalization applications (PZN_Utilities.ear, pznpublish.ear, pznscheduler.ear)
- Business Process application (BPEContainer.ear)
- Portal Document Management or PDM (pdmauthor.ear, pdmsearchadapter.ear)

In addition to these enterprise applications, about 95 portlets get installed. When you view the WebSphere Application Server Administrative Console, as shown in Figure 1.3, you will see numerous Enterprise Applications, all running on one or more nodes of the WebSphere Application Server. Keep in mind that you can start with the base WebSphere Portal Enable and then add components in the future to move up to the Extend edition.

WebSphere Portal Components

Table 1.2 shows the products and components that are packaged in each WebSphere Portal offering. The rest of this chapter gives you an overview of the major components. Although some of these components either were or still are stand-alone products, they are very nicely integrated with Portal Server.

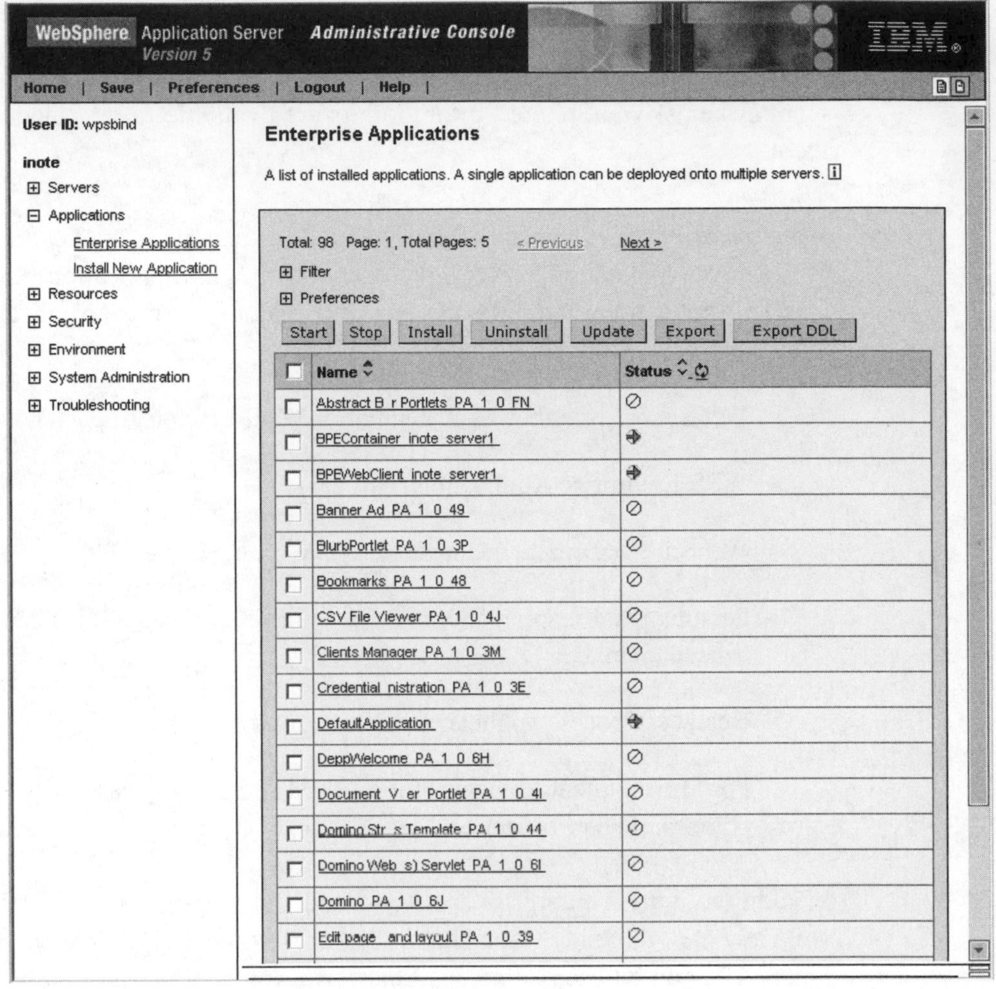

Figure 1.3: WebSphere Portal enterprise applications.

Table 1.2: WebSphere Portal Product and component matrix

Product or Component	Enable	Extend
WebSphere Portal	x	x
WebSphere Translation Server	x	x
WebSphere Application Server products	x	x

Table 1.2: WebSphere Portal Product and component matrix (continued)

Product or Component	Enable	Extend
IBM Lotus Domino Enterprise Server		x
IBM Lotus Extended Search		x
IBM Lotus Instant Messaging and Web Conferencing		*
IBM Lotus Team Workplace		*
IBM Lotus Workplace Web Content Management	x	x
IBM Rational Application Developer	x	x
IBM Tivoli Directory Server	x	x
IBM Tivoli Web Site Analyzer		x
Cloudscape Database	x	x
DB2 Universal Database Enterprise Edition	x	x
Document Manager	x	x
Lotus Collaboration Center		x
Lotus Collaborative Services	x	x
Member Manager	x	x
Portal Personalization	x	x

* Lotus Instant Messaging and Web Conferencing and Lotus Team Workplace are limited to portal use only.

Personalization

A major point of confusion in the marketplace is the distinction between *customization* and *personalization*. Optimizing each user's experience of the portal is one of the key goals of WebSphere Portal. To this end, Portal Server provides end-user and administrative interfaces for creating and modifying the content of portal pages, as well as adjusting the look and layout of the pages. With these tools, users can customize their own pages by selecting portlets and customizing the settings of each one.

WebSphere Portal also comes with the Personalization Server. The purpose of this server is to select content for users, based on information in their profiles and on business logic. It provides facilities that allow subject-matter experts to select content suited to the unique needs and interests of each portal visitor. To enable either Personalization Server or WebSphere Portal to perform these types of functions, the content must have metadata describing one or more categories.

The Personalization Server and portal server share a common user profile and a common content model. This model is based on the WebSphere resource framework interfaces classes. Thus, personalization rules can be added easily to portlets to select portal content and target it to the portal's registered users. (Personalization is covered in more detail in Chapter 5.)

Search

WebSphere Portal provides integrated text-search capabilities, including a search portlet, a crawler, and a document indexer. The search service can search the portal's document repository as well as Internet content.

Customers seeking support for large document collections or support for searching a wide range of document types and data sources should consider using IBM's Lotus Extended Search (included with the WebSphere Portal Extend offering), or IBM's Enterprise Information Portal, now known as WebSphere Information Integrator for Content.

The default search portlet that works with the Portal Search Engine (PSE) is deployed during the installation of WebSphere Portal. However, specific portlets are available that work with the other advanced search engines. (Search concepts are discussed in more detail in Chapter 8.)

Site Analyzer

Tivoli Web Site Analyzer is a software component that comes with the Extend edition of WebSphere Portal. Both technical and business users can use Site Analyzer (SA) to monitor and maintain a very effective portal site.

Portal administrators and site developers can obtain overall usage statistics, such as logins and logouts, enrollments, and error conditions. Site developers can get portlet and page usage statistics, including portlet actions, number of views, and modifications. The business sponsors can measure the effectiveness of the business rules and campaigns, and use visitors' profiles to market products more effectively via the portal. (Site Analyzer is discussed in more detail in Chapter 8.)

Collaborative Components

Lotus Domino Server, Lotus Instant Messaging and Web Conferencing (formerly Sametime), Lotus Team Workplace (formerly QuickPlace), and Domino Document Manager are the building blocks for the Collaborative Components In WebSphere Portal. They provide Java API methods and tags for Java Server Pages (JSPs) for extending the functionality of Lotus' collaborative portlets. Using the Collaborative Services not only hides the complexities of integrating with these components, but also manages the security context. Lotus Software Collaborative Services are listed in Table 1.3.

Table 1.3: WebSphere Portal Collaborative Services

Service	Brief Description
People Service	Retrieves information about a specified person from the configured Directory Server.
Domino Service	Provides access to Domino data, including views, documents, and directory-related information. This service is used to locate Domino servers, create and edit documents, and work with views.
Discovery Server Service	Provides methods that provide Discovery Server functionality, such as Search APIs, Discovery Server Objects API, and APIs for use in user interface.
QuickPlace Service	Provides methods for working with Lotus Team Workplaces.
Sametime Service	Set of methods that provides standardized access to the Lotus Instant Messaging and Web Conferencing server.

Note: Lotus Discovery Server is no longer included with WebSphere Portal V5.1, but the Collaborative Services API continues to support Discovery Server and its service.

All the Collaborative Components, except the People Services are UI-neutral. That means, portlet developers can design the user interface for the collaborative features they are implementing. (Collaboration is covered in more detail in Chapter 9.)

Content Management

When companies deploy portals, they are focused primarily on content aggregation, especially the delivery of personalized content. WebSphere Portal meets the portal's content-delivery needs by supporting syndicated content, by integrating with Web content-management systems, and by providing built-in content-organizing portlets.

Content syndication is about delivering fresh, personalized, and filtered content from multiple sources to subscribers. Typically, the content is related to news, finance, and entertainment. Companies are embracing syndication concepts and standards to automate the publishing of electronic catalogs and other internal information and to make this information available to workers through enterprise portals.

Web content management deals with creating, approving, and publishing Web content from content creators to Web servers. This process involves defining content types, roles, publication options, destination specifications, and workflow processes. Lotus Workplace Web Content Management delivers end-to-end Web content management through Internet, intranet, extranet, and portal sites. In addition, Lotus Workplace Web Content Management leverages content in back-end systems and reduces development and implementation time.

Translation Server

Based on IBM machine translation (MT) technology, the Translation Server helps enterprises remove language as a barrier to global communication and e-commerce. Enterprises can use it to provide Web pages, e-mail messages, and instant-messaging conversations in multiple languages, in real time. Specifically designed for enterprise use, the Translation Server allows companies to leverage their existing Web infrastructure to provide content to users in their native language, at a fraction of the cost of professional translation. Translation servers typically have a language translation engine and a dictionary.

Door Closings

The allure of portals lies in the fact that their value is tangible and can be "seen" by business users and sponsors. You can collaborate in real-time with colleagues, experts, peers, business partners, and even customers from anywhere at any time. The notion that business users can be empowered to contribute their own content to the company portal makes the concept of portals very compelling. In short, WebSphere Portal provides a framework on which to build enterprise, marketplace, consumer, and workspace portals, accessible from a wide variety of desktop and mobile devices.

Chapter 2
A Portal Blueprint

This chapter provides you with the concepts, definitions, standards, and architecture that form the basis on which all Java-based portal server software is built. Many of these concepts, definitions, standards, and architectures hold equally true for both WebSphere Application Server V5.x and WebSphere Portal server V5.x.

Concepts are basically good computing paradigms. *Definitions* are defined by the IT industry at large. *Standards* are based on widely accepted Java standards, some of which relate to portal servers. *Architecture*, though specific to WebSphere Portal, is really dictated by a combination of the portal server's software, the available hardware, and the goals of an enterprise.

J2EE Architecture in WebSphere Portal

This section introduces J2EE and gives you an overview of the J2EE runtime environment, just to reinforce some of the concepts. Since WebSphere Portal is based on Java, its architecture closely follows the J2EE architecture. As such, the terminology and concepts will seem familiar to those who already know the Java language.

If you are interested in simply using and working with WebSphere Portal, you may choose to skip this section. If, on the other hand, you want a more detailed description of the Java-based standard, please refer to the information at the following Web sites:

- Java 2 Platform, Enterprise Edition home page, http://java.sun.com/j2ee
- IBM WebSphere Developer Domain, http://www.ibm.com/websphere/developer
- Portlet API JSR #168, http://www.jcp.org/jsr/detail/168.jsp

What Is J2EE?

Java 2 Platform, Enterprise Edition defines the standard for developing multitier enterprise applications. J2EE simplifies enterprise applications by basing them on standardized, modular components; by providing a complete set of services to those components; and by handling many details of application behavior automatically, without complex programming.

These modular components are servlets, Java Server Pages (JSPs), and Enterprise Java Beans (EJBs). The set of services is provided by the containers in which these components operate, such as the Web server or the EJB container. As such, the architecture shown in Figure 2.1 lets a client indirectly access back-end enterprise applications while protecting enterprise-sensitive data.

J2EE comes with a standard application model and platform. It not only comes with a reference implementation, but also a compatibility test suite for products wanting to achieve J2EE certification.

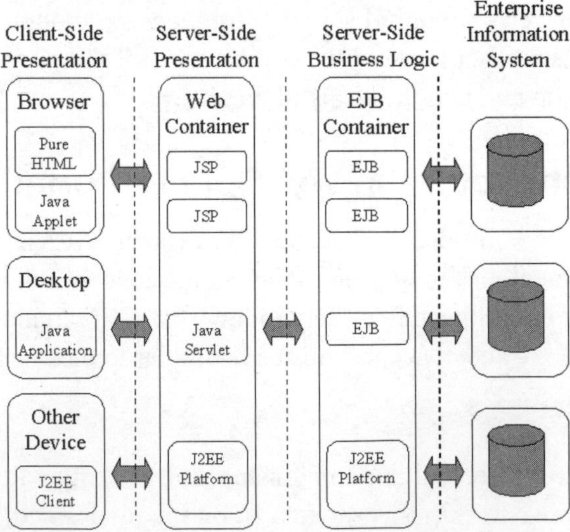

Figure 2.1: General J2EE architecture.

Although the J2EE architecture in Figure 2.1 does not show it, we recommend using the Model-View-Container (MVC) paradigm with respect to Portal. In that regard, the Web Server really is the Web Container. This is explained in a later section in this chapter.

J2EE Application Model

As mentioned, the J2EE programming model has four types of application components:

- Java application clients
- Applets
- Servlets and Java Server Pages (JSPs)
- Enterprise Java Beans (EJBs)

Each application component executes in a well-defined container, which is an execution environment within whose scope components run. Containers are built on the Java 2 Platform, Standard Edition (J2SE), and provide the runtime support. By having a container between the application component and the set of services, J2EE can provide a federated view of the APIs for the application components.

The primary component in a portal server application is the portlet. A portlet is a reusable component that provides access to Web-based content, applications, and other resources. Since a portlet is really an extension of a servlet, portlets run in the Web container, along with servlets and JSPs.

Table 2.1 lists the application components and the containers in which they run. The table also refers to JAR, WAR, and EAR files. These file types stand for "Java Archive," "Web Archive," and "Enterprise Archive," respectively. They are covered in detail later in this chapter.

Table 2.1: Application Components and Containers

Application Components	J2EE Containers	Container Notes
Application client	Application Client container	Packed as JAR files. Not required to manage transactions.
Applets	Applet container	Communicate over HTTP in a browser; can also use serialized objects.

Table 2.1: Application Components and Containers (continued)

Application Components	J2EE Containers	Container Notes
Portlets,servlets,JSPs	Web container	Create portlet/servlet instances, load and unload portlet/servlet, create and manage request and response objects. Packaged as WAR files.
EJBs	EJB container	Packaged as EAR files. Provide threading, transaction support, and data storage management.

Figure 2.2 shows the J2EE containers and the data flow from a portal server perspective. It shows the four kinds of containers that provide all the required services for the components they support, namely the Applet container, Application Client container, Web container, and EJB container. The components and containers are the same, with the additional component, a portlet, shown residing in the Web container.

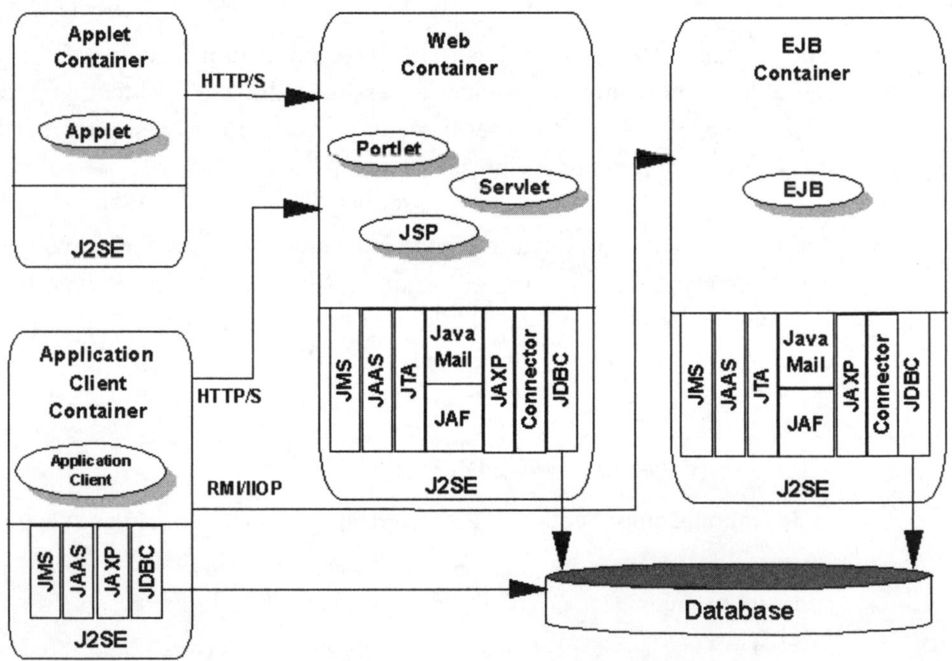

Figure 2.2: J2EE application model.

In addition to providing support for EJBs, servlets, and JSPs, the J2EE specification defines a number of standard services for use by J2EE components. Services provide integration with existing systems, including JDBC for database connectivity, Java Messaging Service (JMS), JavaMail, Java Authentication and Authorization Service (JAAS), Java API for XML Processing (JAXP), Java IDL, and Java Transaction Architecture (JTA). These services not only help Java and Web clients communicate with back-end legacy systems, they also can be configured to handle reliable and secure business transactions.

Figure 2.3 takes a step back, to look at the entire Java platform. You can see how the various components and services fit along with the Java 2 SDK (Software Development Kit).

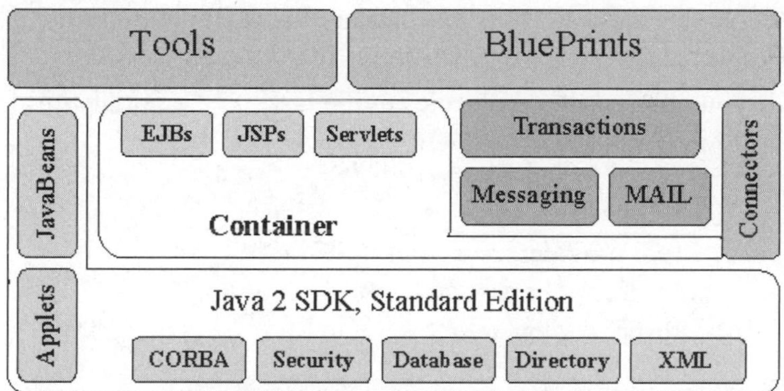

Figure 2.3: J2SE component and service model.

You get a simplified architecture, based on standard components, services, and clients, that takes advantage of Java's write-once-run-anywhere technology. This architecture offers scalability to meet the computing demands of even the largest configuration. It also offers a unified, flexible security model, which is critical to many enterprises.

This passing reference to Java 2 SDK does not do justice to the revolutionary Java platform introduced by Sun, Inc. Suffice to say that it is a stable, secure, and feature-complete development and deployment environment that provides software developers a cross-platform compatible and rapid application development platform. More information on J2SE can be obtained from http://java.sun.com/j2se.

J2EE Platform Roles

The J2EE platform defines six distinct roles for use during the application development lifecycle:

- Product provider
- Tool provider
- Application component provider
- Application assembler
- Application deployer
- System administrator

Product providers and tool providers have a product focus. Application component providers and application assemblers focus on the application. Application deployers and system administrators focus on the runtime.

If you mapped the J2EE roles to the tasks in the portal world, you would have the following categories:

- Product provider
- Tool provider
- Portlet application assembler
- Portlet deployer
- Portal Administrator

The roles are similar, but not identical, because in the portal world, they help identify the tasks that need to be performed by the people working on a Java application, namely the portal. There is no role corresponding to Application component provider because portals integrate existing applications. Roles are analogous to privileges within the portal. Users are grouped together. Then, individual users or groups are assigned certain privileges via Access Control Lists (ACLs).

J2EE Compliance

WebSphere Application Server V5.x is fully J2EE certified. Since WebSphere Application Server serves as the engine or the platform for WebSphere Portal server, which is an application within the application server, all the benefits of J2EE compliance are available for Portal Server. WebSphere V5.0 also provides Web Services support, Connector Architecture, and JMS/XA interface to IBM MQ

Series. The Connector Architecture and Java Messaging Support (JMS) are useful in middleware space. Web Services helps with creating and accessing portlets on remote systems and communicating with components running on non-Java systems like .Net.

Table 2.2 lists the various API levels supported by the base version of WebSphere Application Server V5.x. The basic tenet of the Portlet API is that it will be based on the Servlet specification. It is also envisioned that the Developer API will be similar to the Servlet API. In reality, the Portlet API will be something of a subset of the Servlet API.

Table 2.2: WebSphere Portal and J2EE Compliance

J2EE Items	APIs	WebSphere Portal V5.1
Components	Portlet*	JSR168
	Servlet	2.2
	JSP	1.1
	EJB	1.1
Services	JDBC	2.0
	JTA/JTS	1.1
	JNDI	1.2.1
	JAF	1.0
	XML4J	3.1.1
	XSL	2.0
Communication	RMI/IIOP	1.0
	JMS	1.0.1
	JavaMail	1.1

**The Portlet API submitted as Java Specification Request (JSR) 168 has been accepted as a standard. More information can be obtained at* http://www.jcp.org/jsr/detail/168.jsp.

MVC Paradigm and Architecture

The programming model for portlets, servlets, and JSPs is based on the model-view-controller (MVC) model. In the MVC model, the data itself (the model), the presentation of the data (the view), and the logic manipulating the data (the controller) are designed to be independent. If the view needs to change, the business logic and the data are not affected. If the data interface changes, the controller can be updated without affecting the view.

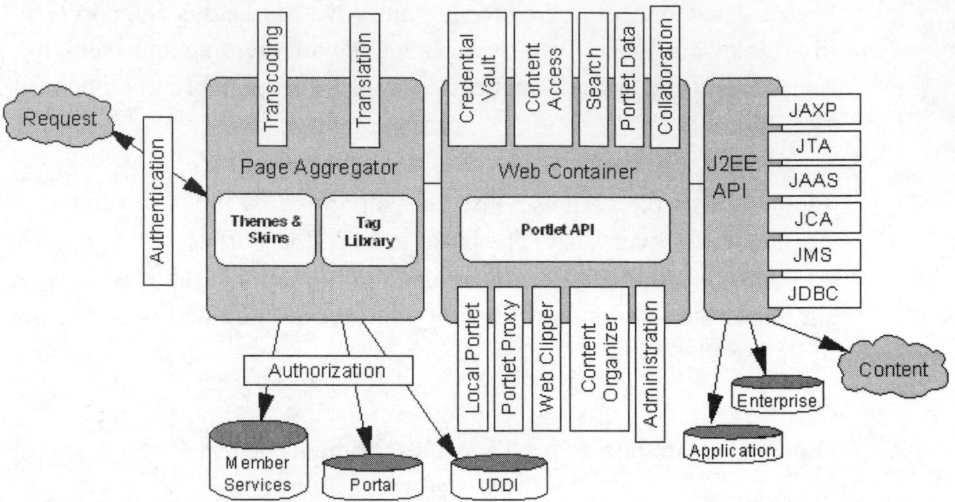

Figure 2.4: Overall portal architecture.

The overall portal architecture is shown in Figure 2.4. In keeping with the J2EE architecture, separation is present between the presentation or view layer (the Page Aggregator), the controller layer (the Web container, where the portlets reside), and the model layer (the J2EE API, which really deals with integrating with the back-end systems).

In the MVC model, the portlet receives a request from a Web client, accesses the data through a set of reusable components (beans or EJBs), and invokes a JSP component to display the results of the request. The sequence of events and data flow is shown in Figure 2.5.

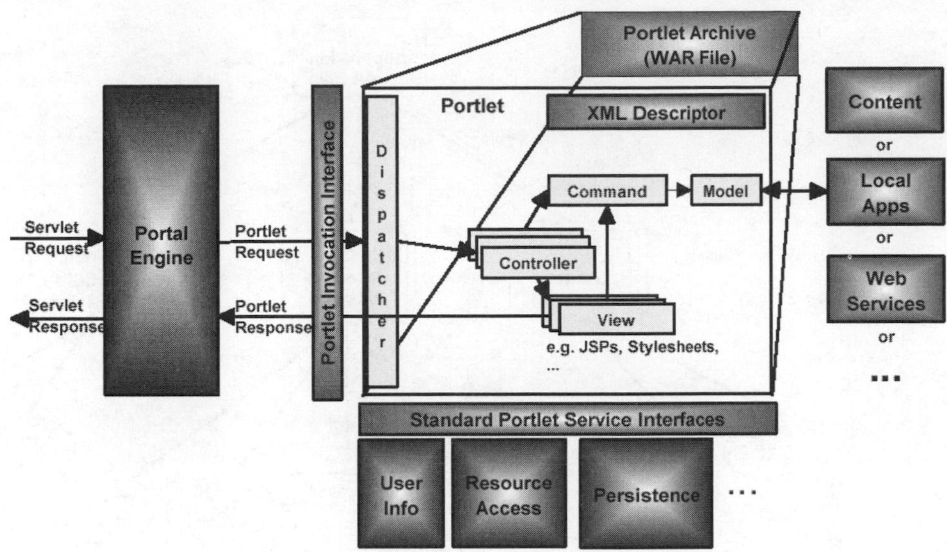

Figure 2.5: Portlet execution cycle.

Packaging J2EE Applications

Earlier in this chapter, we mentioned Java Archive (JAR) files. J2EE components, like servlets and portlets, are packaged into modules. Modules are then packaged into applications, and applications are then deployed. Each module and application contains a J2EE Deployment Descriptor (DD), and is packaged up as an archive file. A DD basically lists the contents of an archive file and contains the entire file structure. Software development and assembly tools use Deployment Descriptors to validate a package.

Figure 2.6 shows the file structure of a J2EE enterprise application. It is commonly known as an Enterprise Archive (EAR) file. The arrows in Figure 2.6 show what is contained at each level. An EAR file can contain one or more JAR files, and/or one or more Web applications. Web applications are packaged as Web Archive (WAR) files. These files show up in the UNIX and Windows file systems with the file extensions *.ear*, *.jar*, and *.war*.

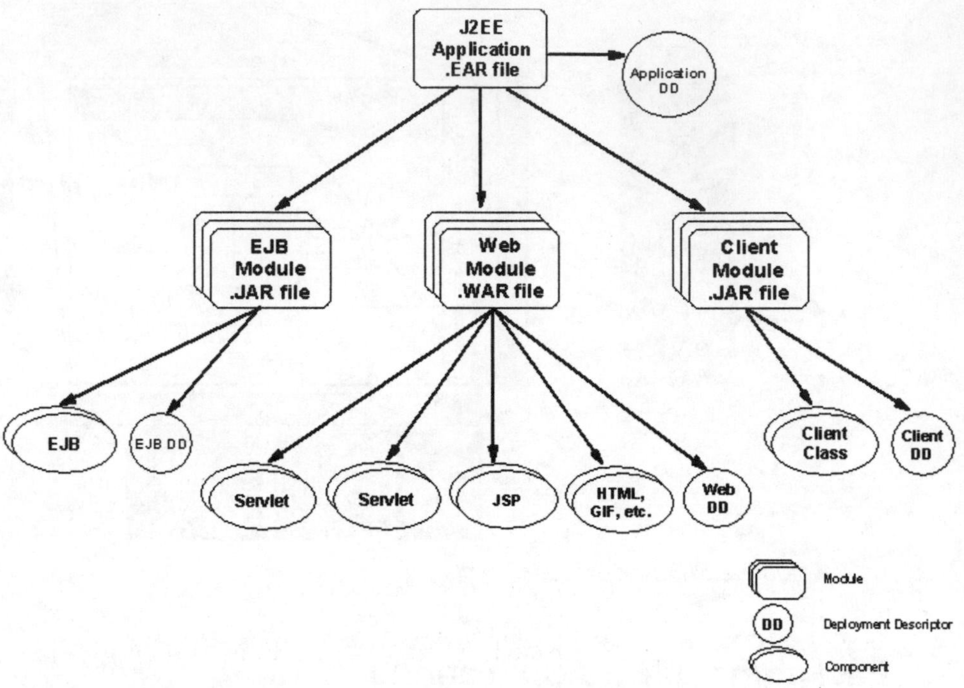

Figure 2.6: J2EE Application Archive file structure.

In the case of a portal application, one or more portlets (possibly JSPs), and/or servlets and accompanying image files make up the application. These portal applications or portlets are packaged up as a WAR file. The Deployment Descriptor for the portlet application is in a file called *web.xml*. Table 2.3 lists the contents of a sample WAR file.

Table 2.3: Sample Portlet WAR File Contents

File	Description
/PORTLET.war/META-INF/MANIFEST.MF	Standard JAR file manifest
/PORTLET.war/WEB-INF/web.xml	Web application descriptor is a mandatory item in a J2EE Web archive. It provides the application server with information about the Web resources in the application.

Table 2.3: Sample Portlet WAR File Contents (continued)	
/PORTLET.war/WEB-INF/portlet.xml	The portlet deployment descriptor provides the portal server with information about the portlet resources in the application, including configuration, support characteristics, and localized titles.
/PORTLET.war/WEB-INF/lib	Directory containing required JAR files
/PORTLET.war/WEB-INF/classes/MYPORTLET.class	Portlet class file
/PORTLET.war/PORTLET/MYJSP.jsp	JSP file or files
/PORTLET.war/images/MYIMAGE.gif	Image file

The Portlet Application Programming Interface (API) is explained in detail in Chapter 5. That chapter shows how to code portlets, build portlet applications, construct Deployment Descriptors, and package it all.

Topologies

"Topology," in the context of this chapter, refers to the mapping of software components to available computer hardware. Other than cost, the primary factors that affect topology are:

- Performance
- Availability
- Security
- Maintainability

WebSphere Portal is another application running within WebSphere Application Server, so all the things to watch out for and the numerous benefits about the various WebSphere Application Server topologies apply. The topologies presented in this section should look very similar to the WebSphere Application Server V5.1 topologies. WebSphere Portal topologies typically involve tier 2. These come in one-node, two-node, and three-node configurations. Tier 2 is where the Web container, with the portlets, logically resides.

Note: WebSphere Portal V5.1 needs WebSphere Application Server V5.1 to run on the same machine.

The following abbreviations are used in the topology diagrams:

- WAS – WebSphere Application Server
- PZN – Personalization Server
- WPS – WebSphere Portal server
- BPC – Business Process Container
- LDAP – Lightweight Directory Access Protocol
- JSP – Java Server Page
- EJB – Enterprise Java Bean
- DB – Database
- LIMWC – Lotus Instant Messaging and Web Conferencing (formerly Sametime)
- LWWCM – Lotus Workplace Web Content Management
- LTW – Lotus Team Workplace (formerly QuickPlace)

The topology diagrams depict the middle tier hosting the application server with a "shadow" box. This suggests that more than one application server could be running on the same machine. In fact, the additional server or servers might be identical copies of the original server, known as *clones*.

One-Node Configuration

Figure 2.7 shows the simplest configuration. All software components are installed on a very powerful multi-CPU machine, with at least 2 GB of memory and a minimum of 6 GB of storage. Please refer to the WebSphere Portal server performance tuning guide from IBM for not only memory and disk requirements but for key tuning parameters.

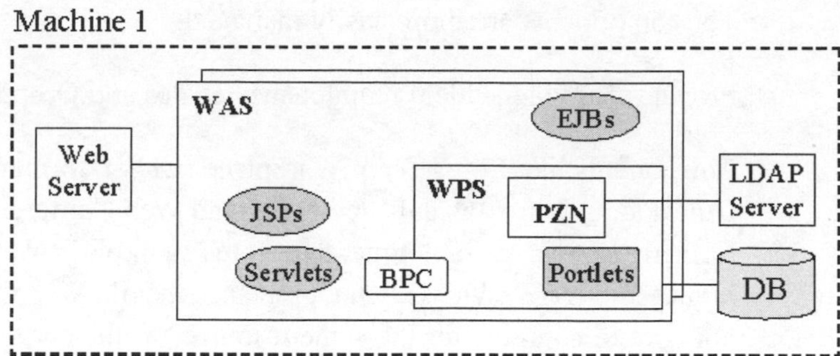

Figure 2.7: WebSphere Portal configuration on one node.

This one-node configuration works well as a development or test environment, it would not be robust enough for a mission-critical production environment. This hardware setup is easy to configure, and it does provide for software process isolation.

Although you get full utilization of the machine's computing power in this configuration, the application server, database server, and directory server will be competing for CPU and memory. Therefore, in a production environment, we highly recommended that you separate the middle tier (the application server) from the backend servers. This helps in system scaling and management and can be used to set up a failover configuration.

Most enterprises will already have a database server and/or a LDAP directory server. A portal server would be an addition to this environment. That would suggest having the database server separate from the application and portal servers. Putting not only the LDAP server on a separate node but even running the database on a separate server is highly recommended.

Note: If your configuration uses Domino Server, we suggest that you install the Domino components on a separate machine. It is a good idea to separate the old Sametime (LIMWC) and QuickPlace (LTW) servers.

Figure 2.8 shows a variation of the basic "everything-on-one-node" configuration. In this example, all of the Domino components are on one or more physical machines, separate from the other servers. Isolating the Domino components provides the following benefits:

- The components are more easily managed.
- Provides for independent maintenance cycles and OS patch levels.
- Components like Lotus Team Workplace (LTW), formerly known as QuickPlace; Lotus Instant Messaging and Web Conferencing (LIMWC), formerly known as Sametime; and Lotus Workplace Web Content Management (LWWCM), which replaces the old Web Content Publisher, do not have to compete for the same resources as the core portal processes.

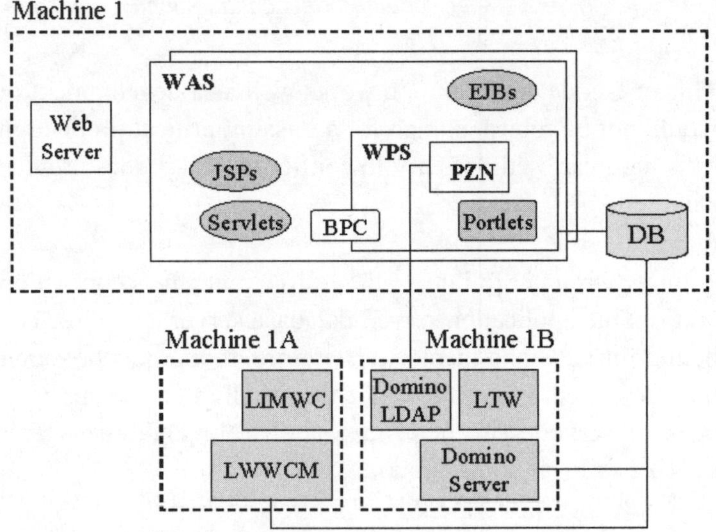

Figure 2.8: WebSphere Portal configuration on a one-node variant.

This is the "one-node variant" configuration, which is not to be mistaken for highly available or high performance configuration. The machine (or machines) hosting the Domino components simply denote parts of the portal topology that reside on a different machine. The database, denoted as DB, comprises the WebSphere Portal server database (WPS DB), the WebSphere Member Management database (WMMDB), Personalization (PZN)-related databases (FDBKDB and LMDB), and the Document Manager DB (JCRDB).

Two-Node Configuration

When properly designed, the two-node configuration really means separating out the back-end database server (tier 3), to run on a physically separate machine. Since Portal Server has to use an LDAP server for security purposes, the database server could co-host the LDAP server too, as shown in Figure 2.9. In large production environments, as stated before, we recommend running the LDAP Server on its own separate node.

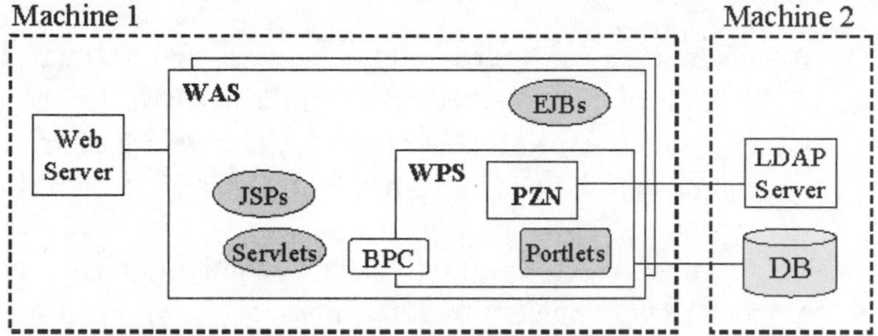

Figure 2.9: WebSphere Portal configuration on two nodes.

This is a better configuration because all database-related activity is confined to one or more machines in tier 3. Tiers 1 and 2, made up of the Web server, the application server, and the portal server, all exist on one machine. When any LDAP access is needed, or when back-end database access is required, the network hops from node 1 to node 2. Otherwise, simple servlet processing and the presentation of the JSPs are all taken care of on the "local" node.

Separating the database server from the application and portal servers represents a recommended best practice for the following reasons:

- Separating WebSphere Application Server and WebSphere Portal Server from the database server helps performance under heavy loads. Otherwise, full utilization of computing resources could become an issue; as resources get scarce, a degradation of performance might occur.
- With the database server separated, those components of tier 2 that are related mainly to the application server can use their cloning facility. WebSphere Application Server could be vertically or horizontally cloned without affecting the database server. This helps improve performance and assists with failover.
- Usually, database servers are already configured in a highly available (HA) manner, so putting Portal Server on the same machine would represent a single point of failure. Thus, separating the application server and the portal server from the database server maintains the HA architecture.

- High availability of the database server goes hand in hand with backup and restore. Enterprises usually have good backup and restore procedures in place for their back-end data. Housing the portal server's application data on the database server ensures that the portal data is always backed up.

- Database servers are generally optimized and well tuned. Again, housing WebSphere Portal server's data on the database server helps portal performance. Additionally, if a site makes extensive use of Personalization, that would require the use of a shared database.

We are suggesting a "two-node variant" configuration, separating the Domino components onto one or more machines, as shown in Figure 2.10. Separating the components to run on different machines also makes performance tuning a lot easier. If the enterprise site makes heavy use of the Web Content Management component, we suggest running LWWCM with Domino Server and Domino LDAP server on one machine and running the Lotus Team Workplace and Lotus Instant Messaging and Web Conferencing servers on different machines.

> **Note:** In a production scenario, it is recommended that the two products—Lotus Team Workplace (LTW) and Lotus Instant Messaging and Web Conferencing (LIMWC)—not be co-located on the same physical server because of resource contention issues.

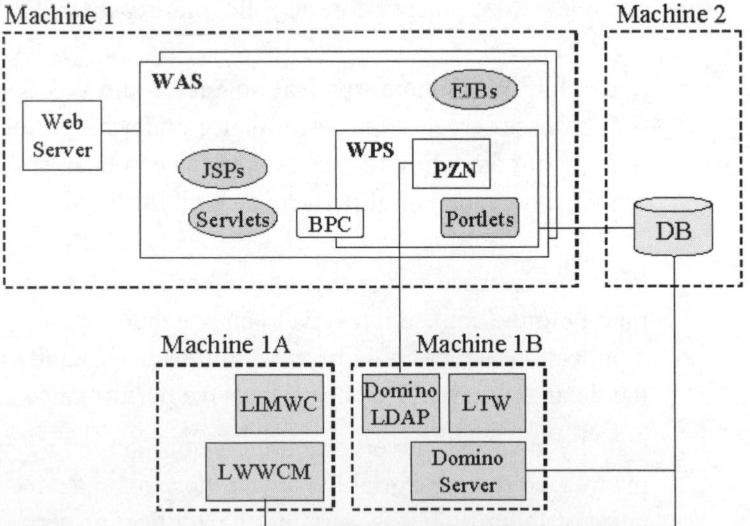

Figure 2.10: WebSphere Portal configuration on a two-node variant.

Tip: Although we do not discuss performance and capacity planning in this book, the database server and LDAP server need their own capacity planning, based on projected loads throughout the cluster and from other applications using the database and LDAP as well.

Three-Node Configuration

Three-node configuration is the classic three-tier setup that was introduced with the advent of application servers. In this scenario, tier 1 (the presentation tier), tier 2 (the business and application logic tier), and tier 3 (the back-end data store) are all running on separate machines, as shown in Figure 2.11.

This separation is possible because of the WebSphere V5.x HTTP plug-in. The HTTP plug-in behaves very much like a reverse proxy, but it is really using the HTTP transport to communicate between the Web server and the application server. The plug-in may also perform static content caching for certain HTTP servers, such as IBM HTTP Server, on certain platforms. The HTTP plug-in supports the clustering of and workload management (WLM) on application servers. During heavy loads, the Web server can send requests to multiple application-server machines. The HTTP plug-in provides for both vertical and horizontal scaling of the WebSphere environment.

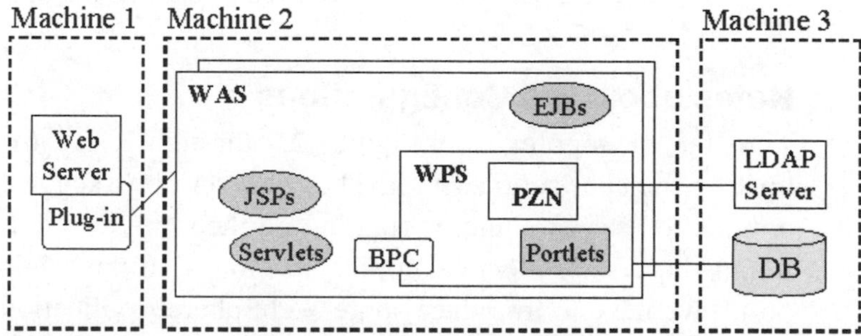

Figure 2.11: WebSphere Portal configuration on three nodes.

The HTTP plug-in also supports data encryption between the HTTP server and the application server, using HTTPS or HTTP over SSL. This makes the HTTP plug-in suitable for environments with two firewalls, such as a demilitarized zone (DMZ), where all network communication must be encrypted. Splitting the HTTP server is useful for sites serving static content from the HTTP server, as opposed to the

WebSphere Portal server doing that. The separation is also useful for sites performing Secure Sockets Layer (SSL) encryption/decryption at the HTTP server, because any form of encryption adds to the burden of the Central Processing Unit (CPU).

If you use the Domino Server, we suggest a "three-node variant" configuration, separating the Domino components as shown in Figure 2.12.

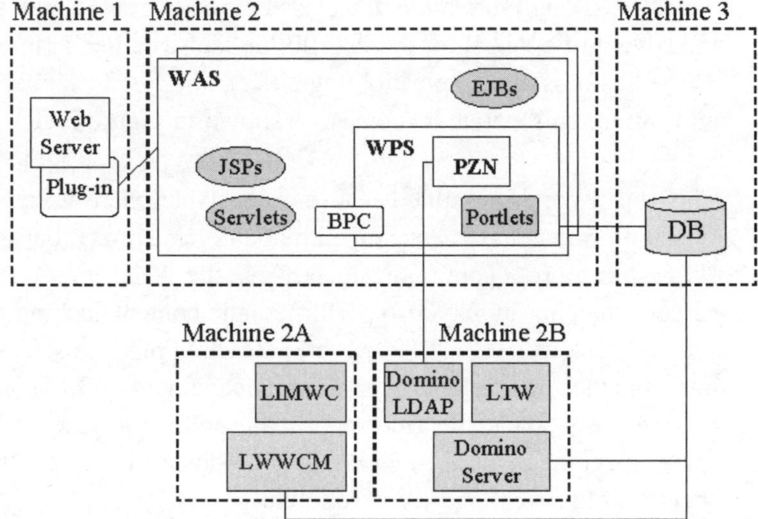

Figure 2.12: WebSphere Portal configuration on a three-node variant.

Notes about the Configurations

Thus far, the topologies in Figures 2.7 through 2.12 show the middle tier hosting the application server. The "shadow" box suggests that more than one application server could be running on the same machine. In fact, the additional servers are identical copies, or clones, of the original server. At this point, we have to introduce some WebSphere Application Server V5 concepts involving the WebSphere Application Server Network Deployment (ND) product. With ND, you can run multiple WAS instances and manage them together as a single *cell*.

One *deployment manager* process runs for the cell, which provides a central point of administrative control for all WAS instances. A cell's deployment manager communicates with all related node agents to propagate and synchronize configuration information across the cell.

A *cluster* is a set of WAS instances within a cell that has the same applications deployed on them. A WAS instance that is a member of a cluster is sometimes referred to as a *clone.* When creating a cluster, one of the options is to create a *Replication Domain*. This option is used for memory-to-memory replication for sharing persistent session data across servers and for enabling dynamic caching of servlets and JSPs. This method of providing session data failover is new in WebSphere Application Server V5.

A *replicator* is a WebSphere Application Server run-time component that handles the transfer of internal WebSphere Application Server data. Replicators operate within a running application server process. You must define replicators, as needed, as part of the cluster management.

WebSphere Portal Implications

WebSphere Portal uses replicators for dynamic caching and memory-to-memory session replication. Enabling replication for dynamic caching in a WebSphere Portal cluster environment is absolutely necessary to maintain data integrity between various WebSphere Portal nodes in the cluster. Replication also helps improve performance by generating data once and then replicating it to other servers in the cluster. Therefore, a replication domain with at least one replicator entry needs to exist for WebSphere Portal.

Vertical cloning refers to situations in which the clones all run on the same machine. *Horizontal cloning*, on the other hand, refers to situations in which clones are created to run on another machine. WebSphere Application Server supports both forms of cloning. It follows, therefore, that Portal Server also can be cloned.

Cloning works well with the three-node configuration (when tier 1, tier 2, and tier 3 are all running on separate machines). For example, if you were to introduce one vertical clone of the application server into Figure 2.12, the new layout would look similar to that in Figure 2.13.

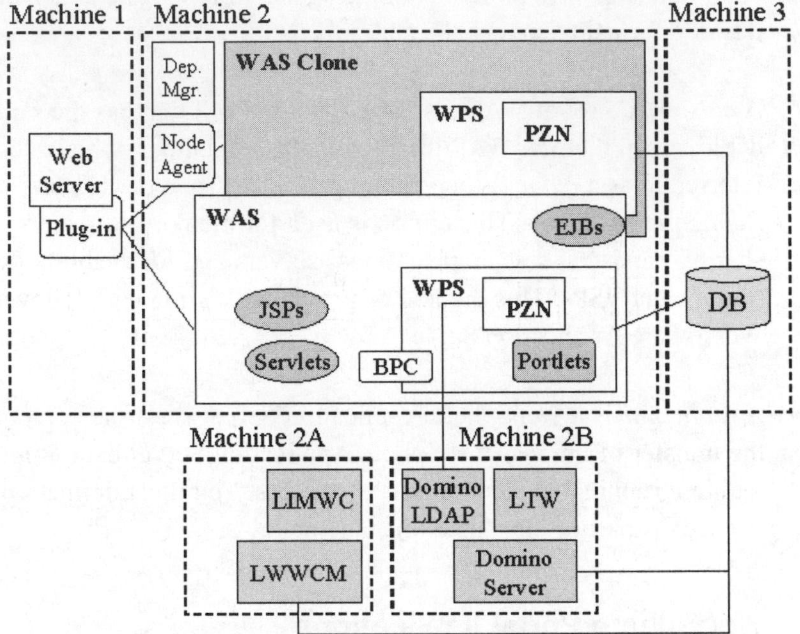

Figure 2.13: WebSphere Portal configuration on a three-node variant, with vertical cloning.

Note: In production environments, WebSphere Portal server requires global security to be set in WebSphere Application Server. That forces you to place common JAR files in a shared directory when you implement cloning.

Vertical cloning provides application failover within thc same physical machine. If you have a very powerful multiway processor, vertical cloning allows you to make maximum use of the computing resources of the machine. Also, if you are memory constrained, it allows you to open multiple JVMs to take advantage of system memory. However, use this approach only if you have the CPU capacity to support multiple clones.

Horizontal cloning, that is, running the application server clone on a separate machine, would make the layout look something like that in Figure 2.14. Cloning, as such, mainly involves components in tier 2—the application server layer. (Figure 2.13 shows Domino Server, whereas Figure 2.14 shows LDAP Server as it relates to any of the common ones like Tivoli Directory Server or SunOne

Directory Server or Novell eDirectory Server. It is not our intent to confuse the reader, but to show you configurations using different software components.)

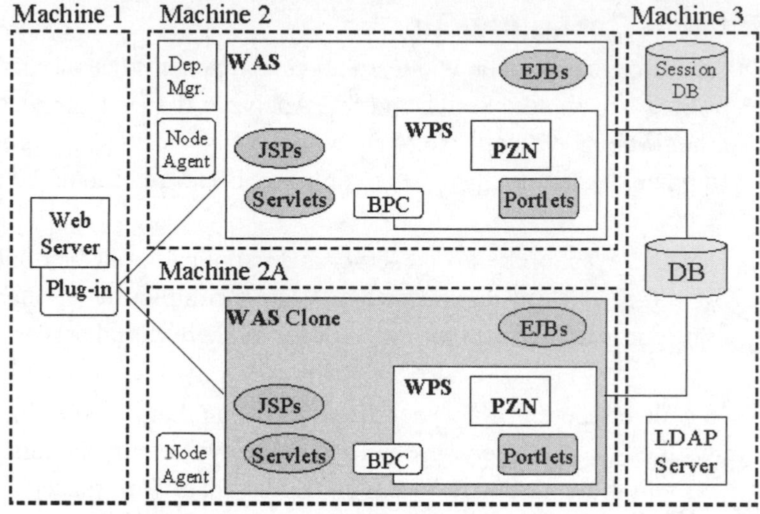

Figure 2.14: WebSphere Portal configuration with horizontal cloning.

Horizontal cloning provides not only application failover, but also hardware failover. The only requirement is that the application (in this case, Portal Server) must be distributed across multiple machines.

Tip: Vertical and horizontal cloning within the same configuration is also possible. However, it is beyond the scope of this book.

Figures 2.13 and 2.14 show Personalization components in both clones of a clustered environment. We want to point out that WebSphere Portal provides two property files that you can modify to customize the Personalization feature. These files are not managed by the WebSphere Application Server deployment manager. This means that if you make any changes to these files on a node in the cluster, those changes are not transferred to other nodes when you perform a synchronization of the cluster members. Instead you must manually copy the following properties files to each node in the cluster:

- <WPS_HOME>/shared/app/config/services/PersonalizationService.properties
- <WPS_HOME>/shared/app/config/services/FeedbackService.properties

On the topic of clustering, please refer to the excellent documentation that is available in the WebSphere Portal online help facility.

Other Configurations

Later in this book, you will learn about components that are part of WebSphere Portal Extend edition, like Search and Site Analyzer. If an enterprise is running these and other WebSphere Portal software components, what is an appropriate configuration? In other words, which software components can and should be co-located?

Because WebSphere Portal server is an application in WebSphere Application Server, the technical nuances that affect a complex WebSphere Application Server configuration are relevant even for WebSphere Portal server.

In a WebSphere Portal Extend configuration that includes Extended Search Server and the Site Analyzer there will be at least four extra servers. Our intent is not to sell you more hardware by having Lotus Team Workplace (LTW), Lotus Instant Messaging and Web Conferencing (LIMWC), and Lotus Workplace Web Content Management (LWWCM) on three different machines with Domino servers. It is to drive home the point that most of these software packages can be isolated and run as "independent" components. Some software components like Lotus Team Workplace and Lotus Instant Messaging and Web Conferencing, *must* be on different machines because those products compete for similar resources and resource conflicts could occur. You also have the option of co-hosting software packages and even running them on different operating systems (OSs) within the same configuration.

Installing and configuring a complex configuration that has multiple WebSphere Portal clones on multiple nodes along with Web Content Manager and all the Lotus components plus Site Analyzer, requires a lot of planning and takes time to set up. More important, it also requires careful management from the perspective of keeping things synchronized and within the confines of enterprise security.

Some companies prefer to separate intranet users from internet users by having dedicated servers that serve up totally independent content. Other companies have common content, and they maintain the separation via users, groups, and virtual hosts. The latter scenario is becoming more common with enterprises, especially given the ability to create virtual portals, which is covered in one of the later chapters.

Process Portals

All the topology diagrams thus far depicted a box named BPC that seems to span both WebSphere Application Server and WebSphere Portal Server. This is the Business Process Choreographer component that is part of WebSphere Business Integration Server Foundation (WBISF) V5.1. WBISF is one of the new components in WebSphere Portal V5.1. The intent was to indicate that the Business Process Container (BPC) can be configured either on *WebSphere_Portal* server or on the default *server1* of WebSphere Application Server, which would be our recommendation.

No drastic changes are necessary in the topologies, because WBISF is an integral part of WebSphere Application Server and requires it to run. The recommendation is to configure the Business Process Container on a server other than on *WebSphere_Portal* so that the portal server is not overloaded. With that said, Figure 2.15 shows how the one-node configuration would look. It is important to note that Personalization (PZN) and WebSphere Global Security play an important role in Process Portals.

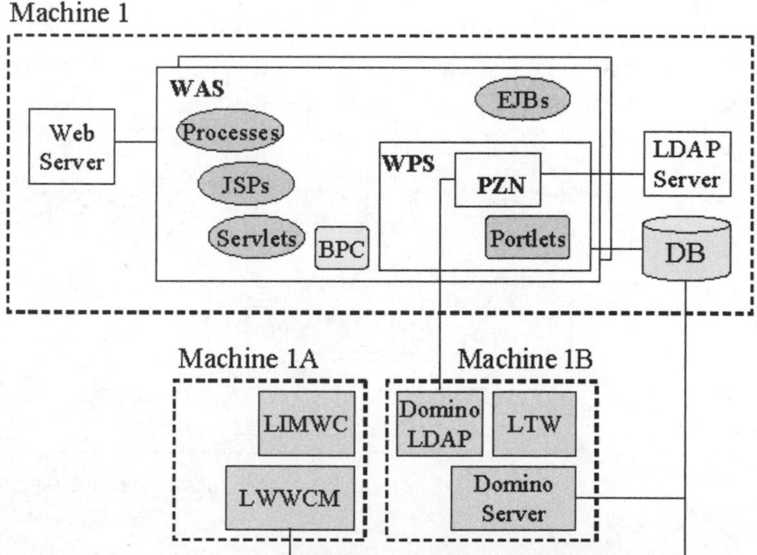

Figure 2.15: A Process Portal configuration in a one-node variant topology.

So what is a process portal? It is a corporate portal that is designed to present the right tasks to the right people at the appropriate time through a consistent and easy-to-use personalized interface. It benefits enterprises that have business processes.

Business processes can be noninterruptible or interruptible. Typically, *interruptible processes* are long processes that might require human intervention, such as a loan approval process or a parts ordering process or vacation approval. Processes like these that have human tasks can be presented via a portal. Thus, a process portal makes use of the underlying process workflow, along with the personalization engine and overall security infrastructure, to present the appropriate task to the user when he is signed into the portal. Process portals are discussed in Chapter 8.

In designing a topology for a process portal, the architect might like to maintain a separation of the different layers, especially the presentation layer and the process layer. An example topology is shown in Figure 2.16. Such a design also allows you to tune the portal machine (Machine 2) in a way different from the process machine (Machine 3).

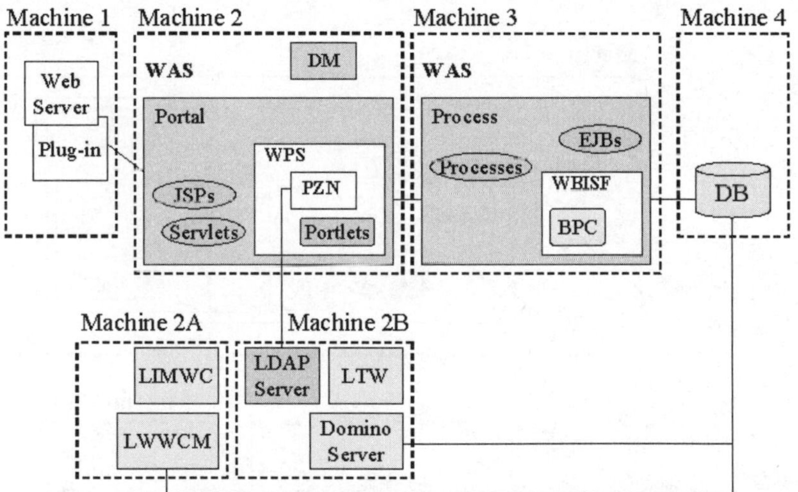

Figure 2.16: A process portal configuration that maintains separation of layers.

Another subtle change appears in Figure 2.16, wherein we replaced Domino LDAP with a generic LDAP Server. That was to indicate the fact that Domino Server can work with other LDAP Servers like IBM Tivoli Directory Server (TDS).

Separating the middle tier in such a way would also help in product upgrades. It is conceivable that the business processes are meant only for employees—that is, the process portal might be surfaced in an intranet portal, whereas the portal machine could be serving up content meant for both, intranet and Internet portals. As enterprises become more knowledgeable and familiar with process portals, we are quite sure that architects will find better ways to design them.

Door Closings

No matter which topology you choose, avoid last-minute surprises by configuring your test or staging system to look exactly like your proposed production system. For example, even if everything works fine on a single-node configuration, when some of the software components are configured to run on different machines, you have to make sure things are deployed properly and that inter-machine communications are not a bottleneck.

With the newest kind of portal, Process Portals, a few more components are introduced into the configuration, but they still follow the MVC paradigm, and the topologies do not drastically change.

Chapter 3
Installing the Portal

This chapter leads you through the process of planning your WebSphere Portal installation. It takes you step-by-step through the installation and configuration procedure.

WebSphere Portal can be installed in a number of different configurations. Pick a certain topology or architecture, and then decide how to install the various pieces that are required. This chapter covers portal installation on the Windows, Solaris, Linux, and AIX platforms, broadly organized into the following sections:

- Planning the installation
- Pre-installation
- WebSphere Portal installation
- Post-installation

The chapter ends with a section on uninstalling WebSphere Portal, followed by a summary.

Most of the installation scenarios in this chapter assume that you already have Web Sphere Application Server installed. The only exception is the Windows 2000 scenario, where the assumption is that nothing has been installed other than the OS. That scenario walks you through the entire installation process of all the software components.

Planning the Installation

Prior to starting the installation, use the installation worksheet found in Appendix A to gather information about your installation. Consider the following questions, since they will determine certain tasks to be performed during the installation:

- Are you installing the Enable edition or the Extend edition of WebSphere Portal?
- Do you want to use the quick, standard, or advanced installation?
- Will this be a typical or developmental installation?
- Will all the software pieces be installed on a single machine, or will they be split up?
- What type of security infrastructure will be involved?

Your organization's Information Technology (IT) architects or portal architects will weigh in on some of these questions.

Installation Options

WebSphere Portal's installation executable is found on the Setup CD. The most common and easy method of installation is using the *graphical* mode of installation. It is an easy-to-use installation wizard that asks a few straightforward questions and then invokes the installation process. All responses are stored in a response file. The product comes with a default response file that you can customize and use to perform a nongraphical installation. Using a response file to kick off a "silent" install is another way to install WebSphere Portal. Yet another way of installing is called the *console* method, which is interactive like the graphical method but without the graphics. No matter which method is employed, only a few parameters must be set, and you can get a base installation of WebSphere Portal ready in no time. The exception is archive installs, which is quickly explained below.

Archive Installs

In this release, a new method of installing WebSphere Application Server (WAS) and WebSphere Portal is named *archive install*. Archive install is used for the first fresh install of WebSphere Application Server and WebSphere Portal on a system.

If there is an existing WAS installation on the machine archive install cannot be used. The advantage to archive installs is that the install takes a fraction of the time that a traditional install normally takes.

To implement archive installs, pre-built WAS and WebSphere Portal systems are archived ("zipped") for each supported platform. The time consuming configuration steps that occur during install are done when the images are built. At install time, the files are extracted from the archive, and the system is then configured based on the platform and user input parameters.

Note: The only two platforms where archive installs are not supported are Z/OS and OS/400.

You will notice Archive Install CDs in the product suite. Look for the software CDs that have Archive Install in their labels. See Table 3.1.

Table 3.1: Archive Install CDs in WebSphere Portal Product Suite

CD	Portal Component
4-1	WebSphere Application Server Archive Install for Windows
4-2	WebSphere Application Server Archive Install for Linux (Intel)
4-3	WebSphere Application Server Archive Install for AIX
4-4	WebSphere Application Server Archive Install for Solaris
4-5	WebSphere Application Server Archive Install for HP-UX
4-6	WebSphere Application Server Archive Install for Linux (s390)
4-7	WebSphere Application Server Archive Install for Linux (PowerPC)
5-1	WebSphere Portal Archive (Disc 1 of 3)
5-2	WebSphere Portal Archive (Disc 2 of 3)
5-3	WebSphere Portal Archive (Disc 3 of 3)

Suffice to say that these archive images can be installed by specifying the –W parameter. For example:

```
-W archiveMediaPanel1.cdPath="<PATH_TO_CD4-1>".
```

Look for a full explanation of all these parameters under the installation topic in the product InfoCenter. This installation method is recommended for people starting out with WebSphere Portal and for demonstration and even development environments.

High-Level Steps

Seven high-level steps are common to all platforms and every installation configuration except archive installs

Step 1: Install Web Server

WebSphere Portal supports various Web servers; we use the IBM HTTP Server V1.3.26 (IHS). Before installing IBM HTTP Server, you should create some users and groups, following these steps:

1. Create a Windows 2000 user who is locally defined (not a member of a Windows domain) and a member of the Administrators group. You can create local users and assign group memberships by clicking the following:

   Control Panel → Administrative Tools → Computer Management → System Tools → Local Users and Groups

2. Assign the following rights to this user:

   - Act as part of the operating system
   - Log on as a service

   You can assign user rights via the User Rights Assignment screen. You get there via the Start menu:

   Start → Settings → Control Panel → Administrative Tools → Local Security Policy → Local Policies → User Rights Assignment

---

Note: We suggest creating a user named wpsadmin. The rest of this chapter and most of the book will use wpsadmin, unless specified otherwise.

Step 2: Check IP Ports

Make sure that no other existing services on the server use the following IP ports:

- 80 (standard HTTP port)
- 389 (LDAP port)
- 8008 (IBM HTTP Server Administration port)
- 8080 (WebSphere Portal port)
- 9091 (WebSphere Administrative Console port)

You can run the netstat command to find out which ports are used:

```
C:\> netstat -an
```

Step 3: Install Database Server

WebSphere Portal uses a database to store portal object information and user information. It supports common relational database products, such as IBM DB2, Oracle, Informix, and MS SQL Server. If you do not have or do not want to use an external database, WebSphere Portal comes with a built-in Java-based database called Cloudscape.

Actually, no matter what database you decide to use, Cloudscape is always used as the default database during installation. You then have to export the configuration from Cloudscape and import it into the "production" database, as explained in the post-installation steps in this chapter.

The database can be local or remote to the portal server. If the database is remote, WebSphere Portal uses JDBC to connect to the database via a Type 3 or Type 4 JDBC driver. If you use Cloudscape, it ends up residing on the same machine where portal server is installed.

Note: Cloudscape cannot be used in a clustered environment and does not support vertical cloning. It does not support Custom User Registry (CUR) for authentication.

Step 4: Install Directory Server

Any LDAP server could be used as the Directory Server. WebSphere Portal explicitly supports IBM Tivoli Directory Server (previously known as SecureWay or IBM Directory Server), Domino LDAP Server, SunOne Directory Server (previously known as iPlanet), Novell's eDirectory, and Microsoft Active Directory. We use the IBM Tivoli Directory Server V5.2 for illustrative purposes.

Step 5: Install WebSphere Application Server

WebSphere Application Server is the only application server that WebSphere Portal server can run on. Table 3.2 maps the application server versions with WebSphere Portal. You can use the installation manager of WebSphere Application Server or WebSphere Portal's Install Wizard to install WebSphere Application Server.

Table 3.2: WebSphere Application Server versions

WebSphere Portal	WebSphere Application Server	WebSphere Application Server e-Fixes
WP V4.1.2	WAS V4.0.2	PQ65395, PQ66355, WAS_CM_4.0.x_cumulative_eFix
WP V4.1.4	WAS V4.0.4	PQ55941, PQ56615, PQ57814, PQ58289, PQ58678, PQ58795, PQ59932, PQ69787, PQ61935
WP V5.0	WAS V5.0	PQ73644_fix-temp, PQ76567, PQ72597-eflx, PQ77008, PQ77142, WAS_CM_08-12-2003_5.0.0_cumulative_Fix, WAS_Plugin_07-01-2003_5.0.X_cumulative_Fix, WAS_Security_07-07-2003_JSSE_cumulative_Fix, WAS_Dynacache_05-08-2003_5.0.1_cumulative_fix
WP V5.0.2	WAS V5.0.2	PQ73644_fix-temp, PQ76567, PQ72597-efix, PQ77008, PQ77142, WAS_CM_08-12-2003_5.0.X_cumulative_Fix, WAS_Plugin_07-01-2003_5.0.X_cumulative_Fix, WAS_Security_07-07-2003_JSSE_cumulative_Fix, WAS_Dynacache_05-08-2003_5.0.1_cumulative_fix
WP V5.1	WAS V5.1.1	
WP V5.1.1	WAS V5.1.1	

Step 6: Install WebSphere Application Server e-Fixes

Some e-Fixes are required by WebSphere Application Server so that WebSphere Portal can work. Look at Table 3.2 for the required e-fixes. For the latest e-fix list, consult the product release notes. You can either apply the e-fixes manually or let the Install Wizard apply them for you.

Step 7: Install WebSphere Portal Enable Edition

Use the WebSphere Portal Install Wizard found on the setup CD of WebSphere Portal product to initiate the installation process.

Pre-Installation

This section deals only with the software pre-installation items. Make sure that the database server, directory server, Web server, and WebSphere Application Server are properly configured and running.

If the default application in WebSphere Application Server is running, and you are using default ports, you can test if the server is properly configured by bringing up the Snoop Servlet. In a Web browser, enter the following URL:

```
http://<HOST_NAME>/snoop
```

You should see something similar to Figure 3.1.

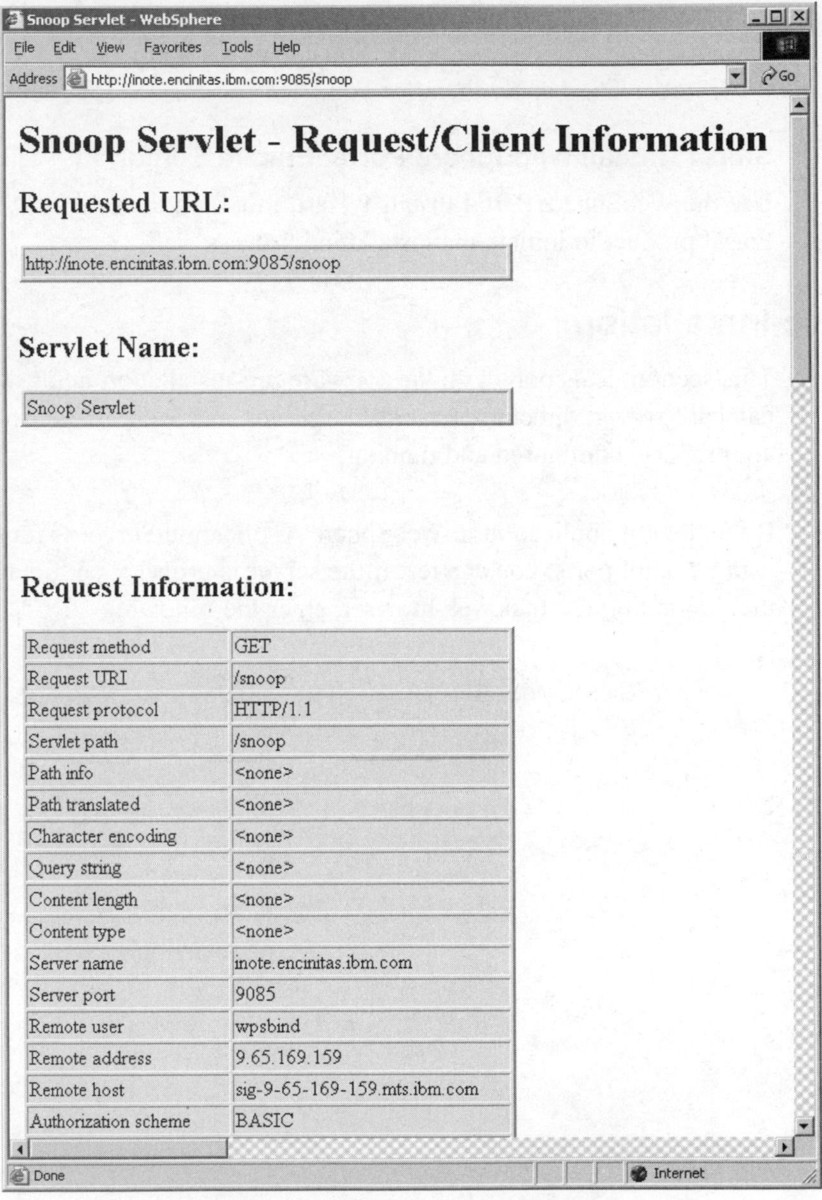

Figure 3.1: The output of Snoop Servlet.

From the installation directory, make a copy of the PortalUsers.ldif file. Modify it to match your domain, and then import it into the LDAP server. This will create two users, wpsadmin and wpsbind. Both of these users are in the wpsadmins group. This is explained in detail later in the chapter.

To conserve resources, stop the default server in WebSphere Application Server. Close the WebSphere Administrative Console, if it is open. You are now ready to start the WebSphere Portal installation.

Installing on Windows Platform

Before installing any of the WebSphere software components, make sure you have the correct level of the operating system. WebSphere Portal will run on Windows XP, Windows 2003, and Windows 2000 Workstation or Server. Windows 2000 Server or Professional with Service Pack 3 or higher and 128-bit encryption works best.

Installation Steps

1. Log in as a user with administrative authority on the computer, for example, **Administrator**. Insert the Setup CD from the WebSphere Portal product set. From the top level directory invoke **install** batch file (install.bat) either by double-clicking on it or via a command window.

Tip: We recommend copying all the CD images to a directory on the Windows machine. If the CD image subfolders are named CD1, CD1-1, CD2, etc. the installation wizard will automatically grab the CD images as required.

---

2. The installer starts off by copying relevant files into a temporary directory. If your system does not have the proper level of Java, the installer will install IBM JVM.

3. Select the language that you want the installation wizard to use. See Figure 3.2.

Figure 3.2: Language selection screen of the installer.

WebSphere Portal gives you a choice of English, French, German, Greek, Hungarian, Italian, Japanese, Korean, Polish, Portuguese, Portuguese (Brazil), Russian, Simplified Chinese, Spanish, Traditional Chinese, and Turkish. Click **OK**.

4. On the Welcome screen, as seen in Figure 3.3, you have the option to Launch and view the InfoCenter. In most cases you will click **Next**.

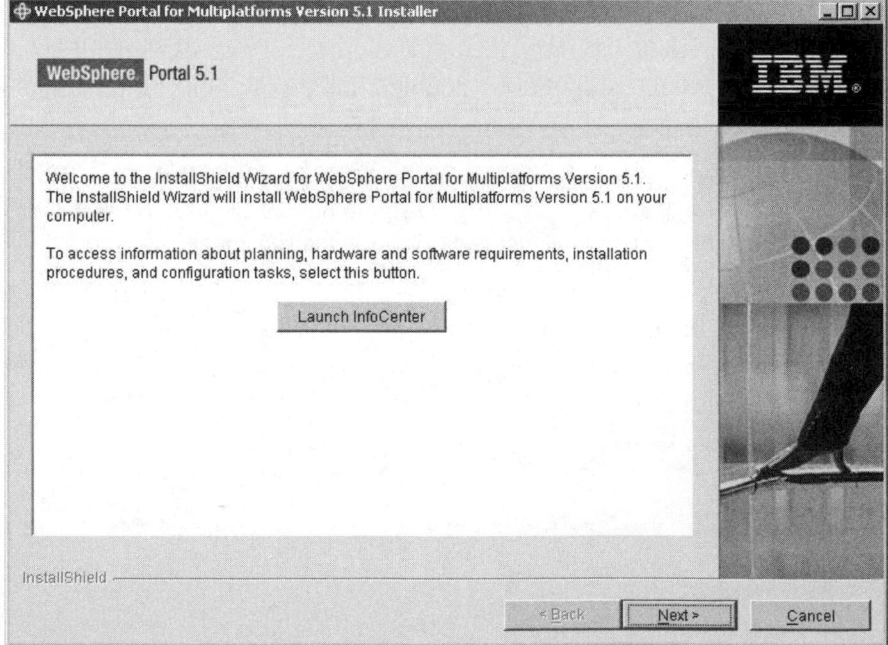

Figure 3.3: Installation wizard Welcome Screen.

5. **Accept** the Software License agreement and click **Next**. The German version of the Software License Agreement screen is shown in Figure 3.4.

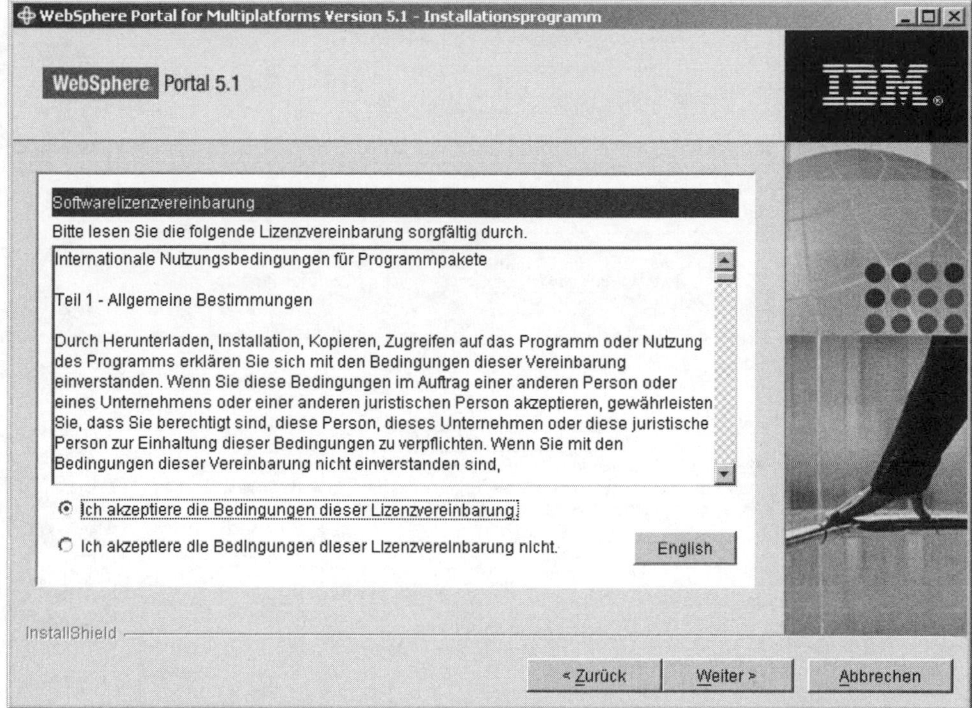

Figure 3.4: Software License Agreement screen in German.

6. You are presented with three installation options—Full, Custom, Test Environment. In this version, Full and Custom have a meaning different from that of previous versions.

   - *Full*—Uses the default settings and installs everything needed for WebSphere Portal, including WebSphere Application Server and IBM HTTP Server.
   - *Custom*—Use this option to install WebSphere Portal on an existing instance of WebSphere Application Server.
   - *Test Environment*—Installs a subset of WebSphere Portal as a WebSphere Portal Test Environment into IBM Rational Application Developer (IRAD) and products that extend IRAD.

Since this is a brand new installation, choose **Full**, as shown in Figure 3.5, and click **Next**.

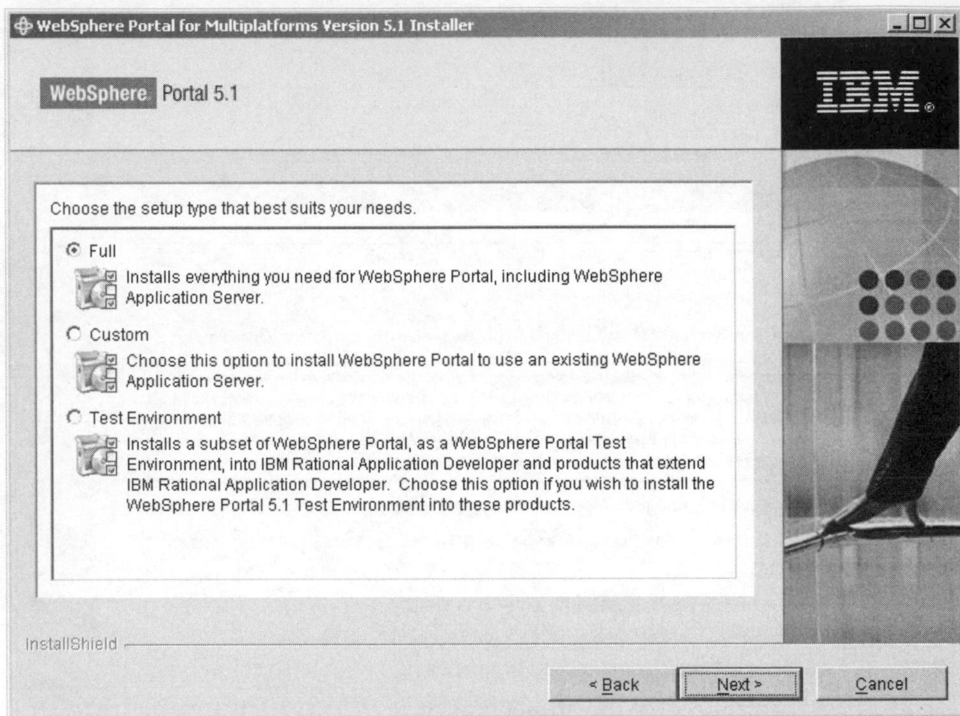

Figure 3.5: Screen to choose the type of WebSphere Portal setup.

Although we prefer installing all the software components individually, in this example, all components will run on the same machine. It not only makes sense to let the installation wizard install and configure all the required components, but it also makes things extremely simple.

7. If the machine you are installing on already has a previous installation of WebSphere Application Server, you will see the screen shown in Figure 3.6. It explains the co-existence scenario. Click **Next**.

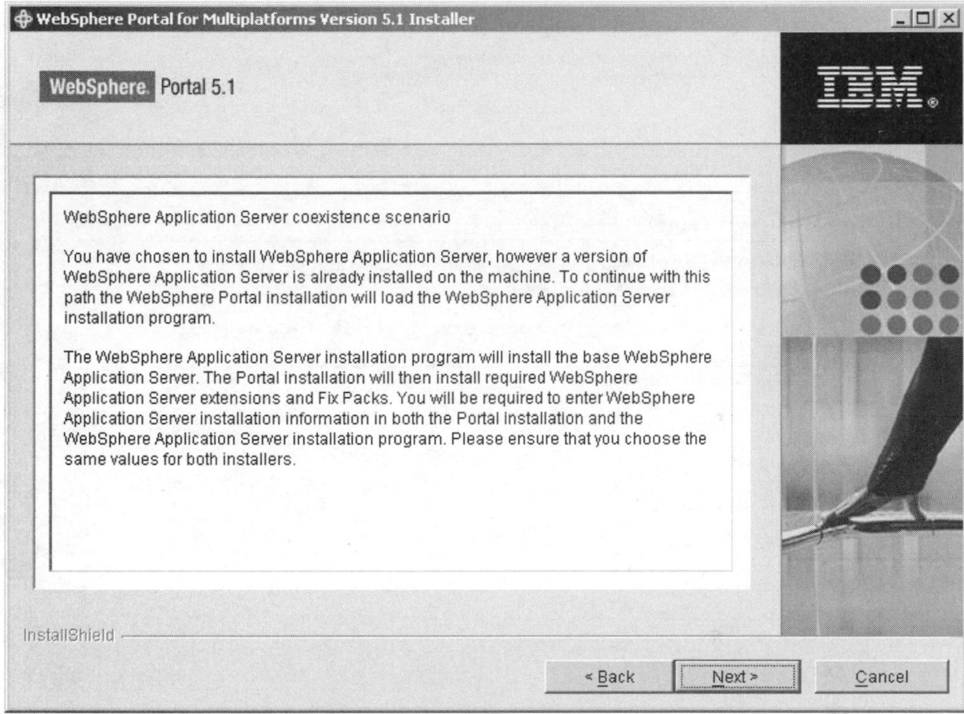

Figure 3.6: WebSphere Application Server co-existence screen.

8. By default, WebSphere Application Server gets installed in C:\Program Files\WebSphere\AppServer folder, as seen in Figure 3.7. Specify the full path where you want WebSphere Application Server to be installed. We chose C:\WebSphere\AppServer51. Click **Next**.

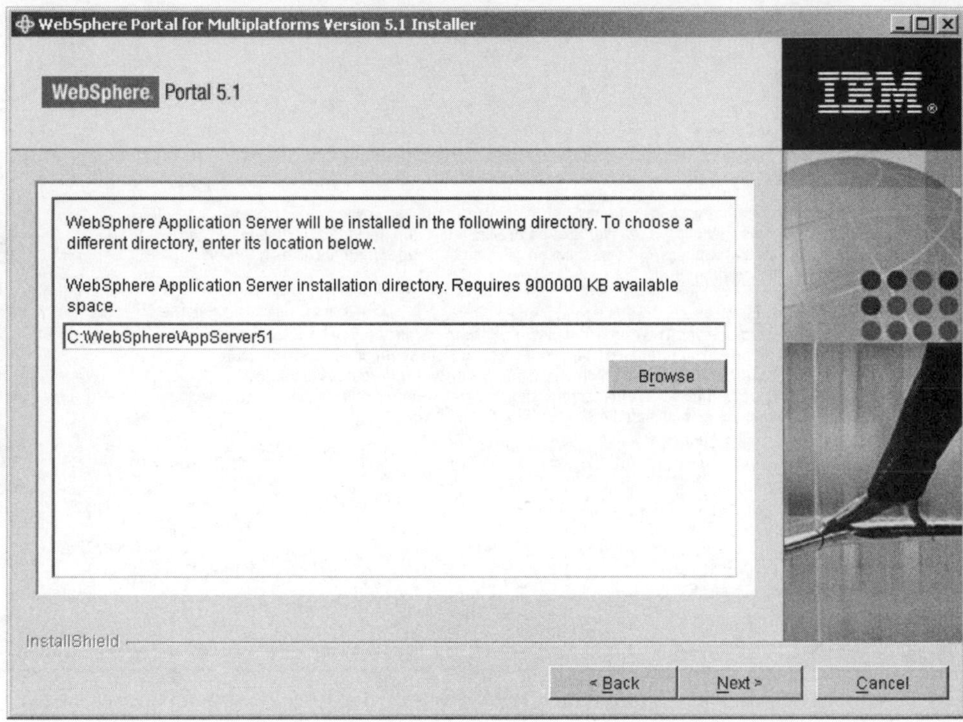

Figure 3.7: WebSphere Application Server installation directory.

9. Also by default, WebSphere Portal server gets installed in C:\Program Files\WebSphere\PortalServer. Specify where you want it installed. We chose C:\WebSphere\PortalServer. See Figure 3.8. Click **Next**.

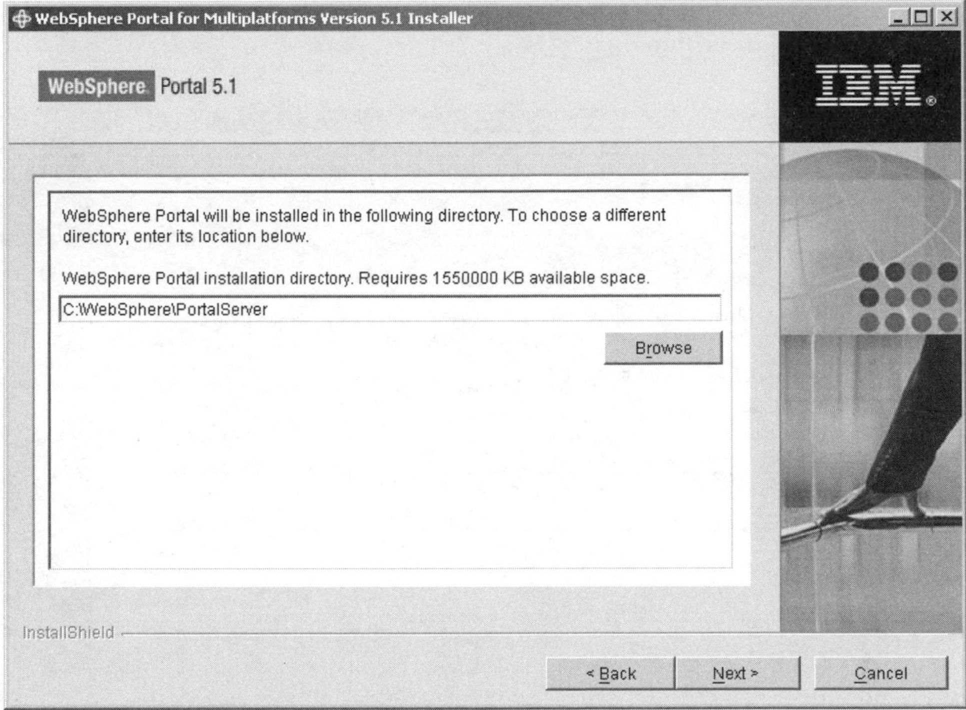

Figure 3.8: WebSphere Portal server installation directory.

10. You have the option to run WebSphere Application Server and WebSphere Portal server as a Windows service. If you select a server, remember to enter the System User ID and password, and then click **Next**. Even though Figure 3.9 shows that both servers were selected, we chose not to run them as Windows services, because we wanted to start and stop the servers at our discretion.

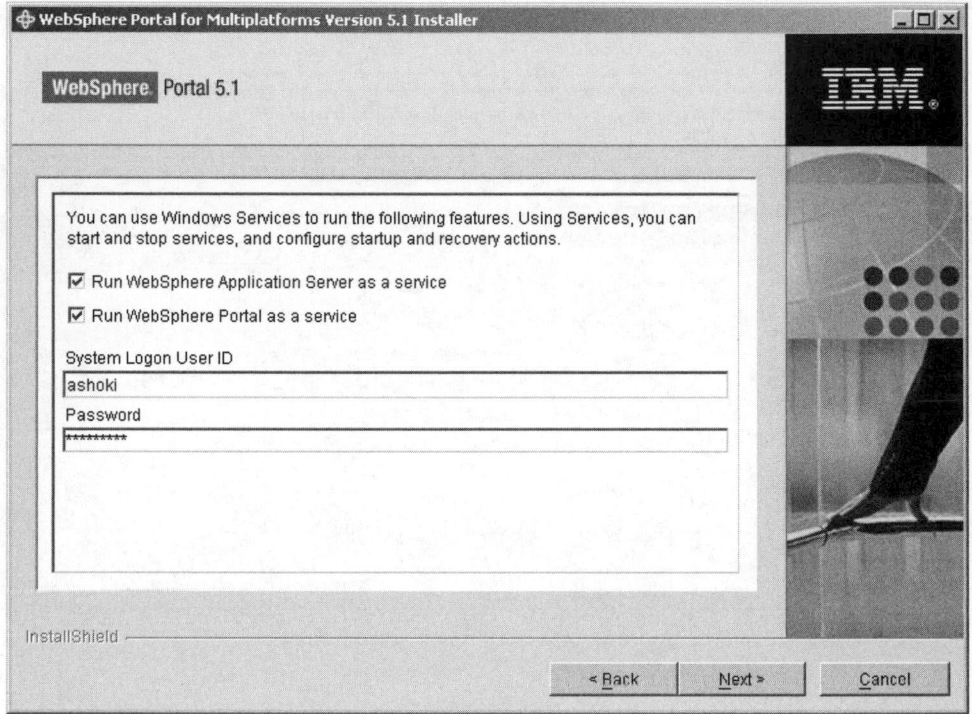

Figure 3.9: Screen to choose servers that could be run as a Windows service.

11. The installation wizard will now ask for the portal administrator user ID and password. The default user ID and password is wpsadmin. See Figure 3.10. Enter the information and click **Next**.

Note: The LDAP Data Interchange Format (LDIF) file that comes with the product has wpsadmin as the default portal administrator and password. If you are new to WebSphere Portal, our recommendation is to use the default user id and password, namely wpsadmin, during installation. These can be changed later in a production scenario.

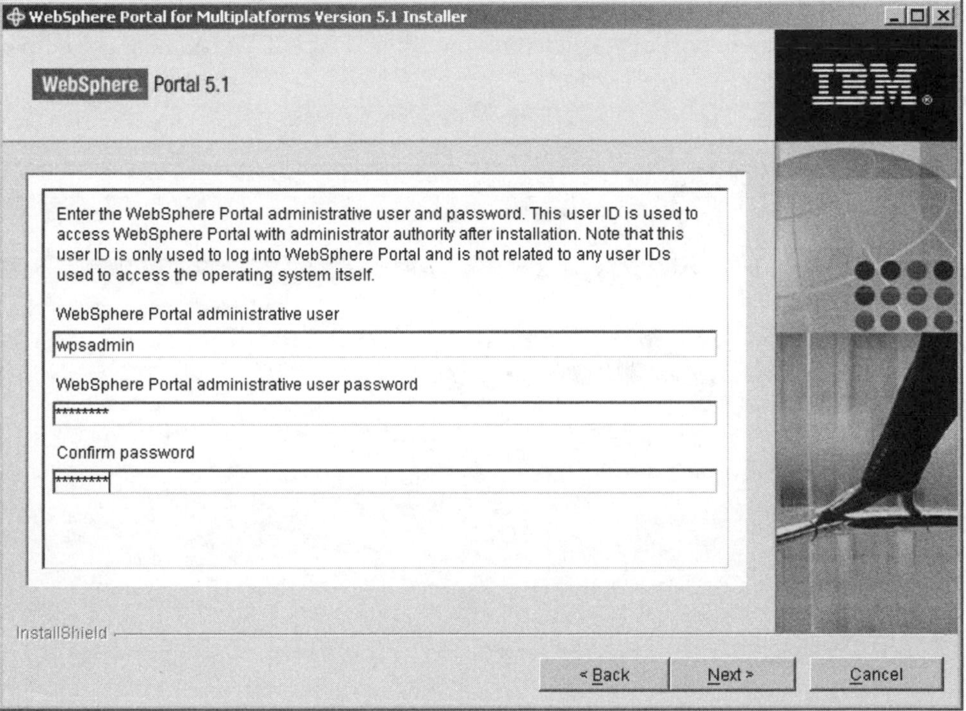

Figure 3.10: Portal administrative user ID and password.

12. On the confirmation screen, click **Next**.

Verifying the Installation

At this point, WebSphere Portal is installed on the system. Two URIs were configured, /portal and /myportal. If the default port of 9081 was not changed during the installation process, you can verify that the URIs work as designed:

1. Bring up the base WebSphere Portal page by entering the following URL in a Web browser:

```
http://<HOST_NAME>:9080/wps/portal
```

The default "Welcome" page shown in Figure 3.11 should be displayed, with two out-of-box portlets—Welcome portlet and About WebSphere Portal portlet.

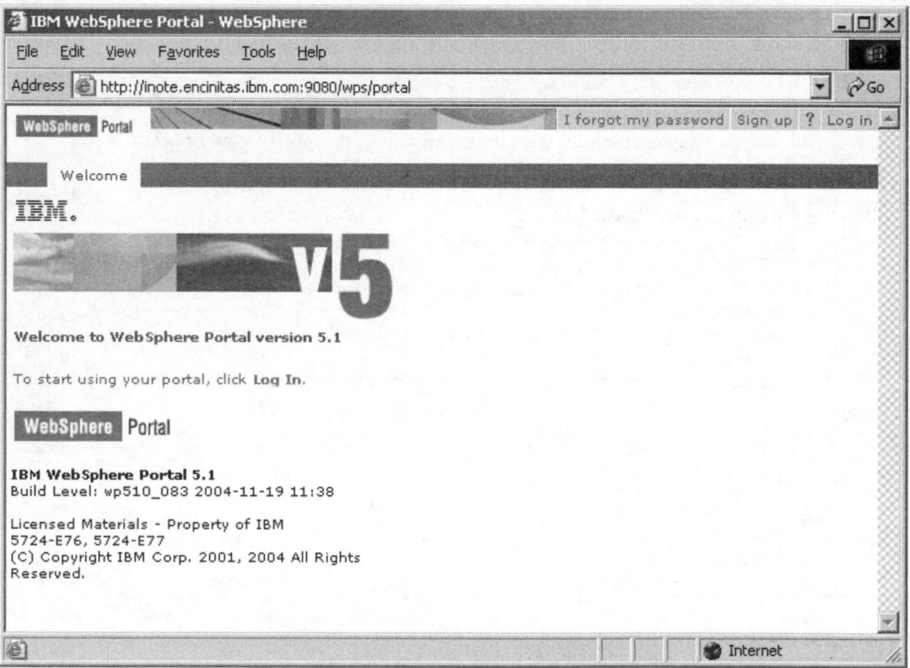

Figure 3.11: The unauthenticated WebSphere Portal screen.

2. To verify that a user can log into the portal, click the **Log in** link on the far right of the portal menu, or enter the following URL:

```
http://<HOST_NAME>:9080/wps/myportal
```

3. A challenge screen will be displayed, as shown in Figure 3.12. In the User ID and Password fields, enter **wpsadmin**. Click **Log in** or press the **Enter** key.

Figure 3.12: WebSphere Portal challenge screen.

4. If the user is successfully authenticated, you will see the page for authenticated users. Since we entered wpsadmin as the user, we see the default page for the portal administrator (Figure 3.13).

Note: The Administration option in the portal menu differentiates a portal administrator from other authenticated portal users.

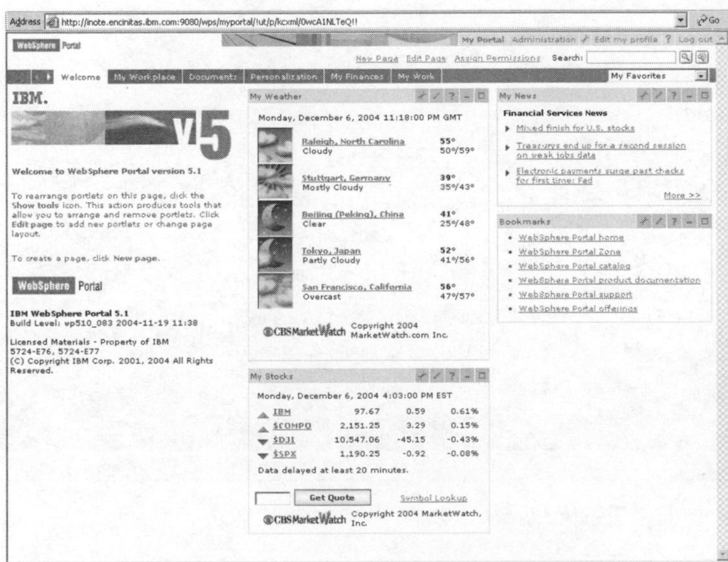

Figure 3.13: The authenticated WebSphere Portal screen.

You have now completed all the steps required to get WebSphere Portal installed on a Windows platform, and you have verified that the portal is up and operational.

Configuring a HTTP Server

Have you wondered why port 9080 has to be used in the portal URL? It is because WebSphere Application Server's built-in HTTP server is being used, and it listens on port 9080. How can we use the default port 80 for the WebSphere Portal URI? It is simple. We edit the wpconfig.properties file and run the WPSconfig utility.

Assume that IBM HTTP Server has been successfully installed and listening on port 80. That can be verified by entering the fully qualified host name in Web browser URL. You should see a screen similar to that in Figure 3.14.

Figure 3.14: IBM HTTP Server Welcome screen.

WebSphere Portal is configured to use an external HTTP server with the help of the WPSconfig utility found in <WPS_HOME>/config directory. As noted before, the WPSconfig utility uses wpconfig.properties as its input. That properties file is also found in <WPS_HOME>/config directory.

Make the two necessary edits to wpconfig.properties. Change the WpsHostName from localhost to the fully qualified host name and change the WpsHostPort number to 80, as shown in the listing.

```
# WpsHostName: The name of the WebSphere Portal host

# For example:
http://<WpsHostName>:<WpsHostPort>/<WpsContextRoot>/<WpsDefaultHome>

# For example "localhost" in the URL: http://localhost:80/wps/portal

###WpsHostName=localhost

WpsHostName=inote.encinitas.ibm.com


# WpsHostPort: The port used by WebSphere Portal

# For example:
http://<WpsHostName>:<WpsHostPort>/<WpsContextRoot>/<WpsDefaultHome>

# For example "80" in the URL: http://localhost:80/wps/portal

###WpsHostPort=9080

WpsHostPort=80
```

Ensure that WebSphere_Portal has been stopped. In a command window, change the directory to <WPS_PORTAL>/config. Then invoke the **httpserver-config** task:

```
C:\cd <WPS_HOME>\config

C:\WebSphere\PortalServer\config> WPSconfig httpserver-config
```

Look for the BUILD SUCCESSFUL message.

Verify HTTP Server configuration

Make sure the WebSphere_Portal application server is running. In a Web browser, enter the base portal URL: http://<HOST_NAME>/wps/portal. If the unauthenticated portal page is displayed, as shown in Figure 3.11, then we know that WebSphere Portal server can be accessed via IBM HTTP Server.

Tip: If the portal page does not show up, update the Web Server Plug-in via the WebSphere Administrative Console and restart the Web server, in this case the IBM HTTP Server.

WebSphere Portal Extend Edition

The prerequisites for WebSphere Portal Extend edition are the same as those for Enable edition. All the same software components used in installing Enable are used in Extend, except for the LDAP Server. One of the key features in Extend is Collaborative Services, which only works in conjunction with Domino LDAP Server.

Domino LDAP Server comes bundled with the Lotus Domino Application Server, commonly known as the Domino Server. The next several pages step through the installation and configuration of Domino Server and some of its subcomponents.

No single installation wizard will install WebSphere Portal Extend edition. Each of the components has its own setup or installation executable that has to be run separately. And this suits us fine, because we have always preferred taking the "component" view of things: If anything goes wrong, that specific component can be uninstalled and reinstalled without affecting the overall configuration. The final configuration step is performed by running one or more WPSConfig tasks.

Install Domino Server

On the Windows platform load CD #12-1 and go to **/server** folder. Invoke **setup.exe** to launch the installation wizard for Domino Server.

1. Click **Next** of the Welcome screen.

2. **Accept** the License agreement.

3. Enter a name and company name.

4. Choose the destination folders for the Server and the Data folder.

5. Select **Domino Enterprise Server** for the type of Setup, as shown in Figure 3.15. Click the **Customize** button.

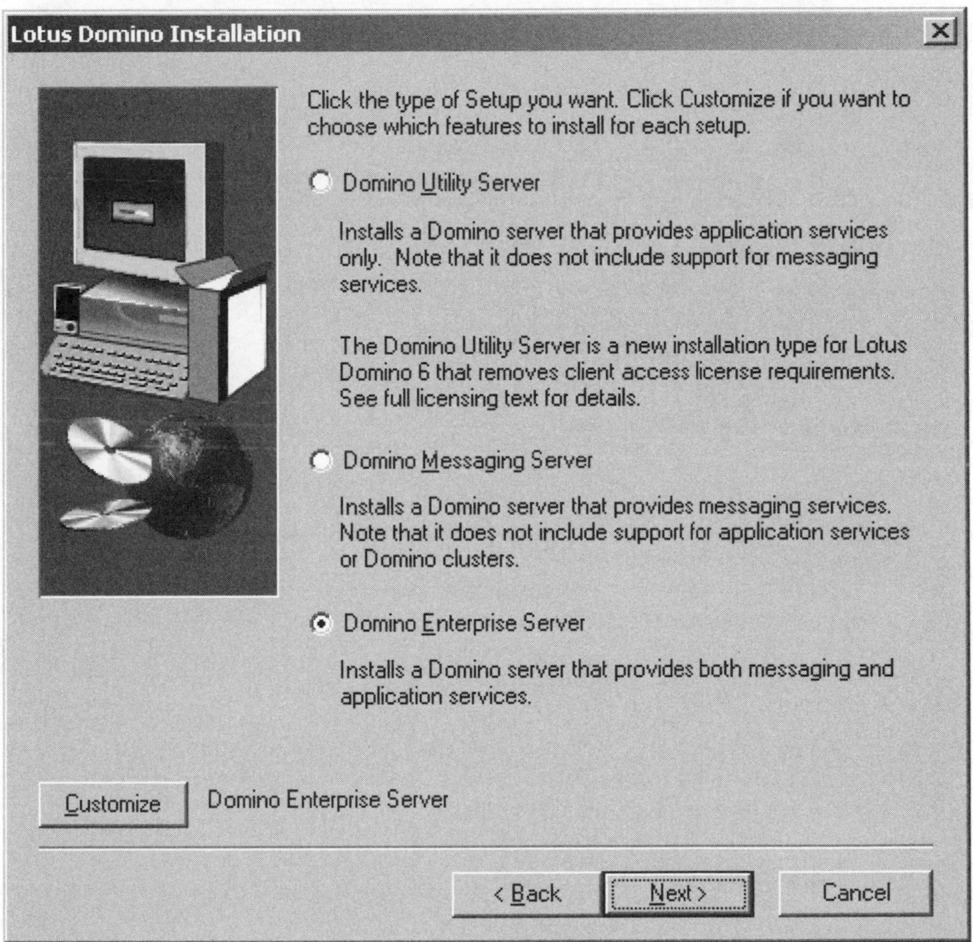

Figure 3.15: Choosing the type of Domino Server setup.

6. On the component selection screen, uncheck Notes Performance Monitor, as shown in Figure 3.16. Then click **Next**.

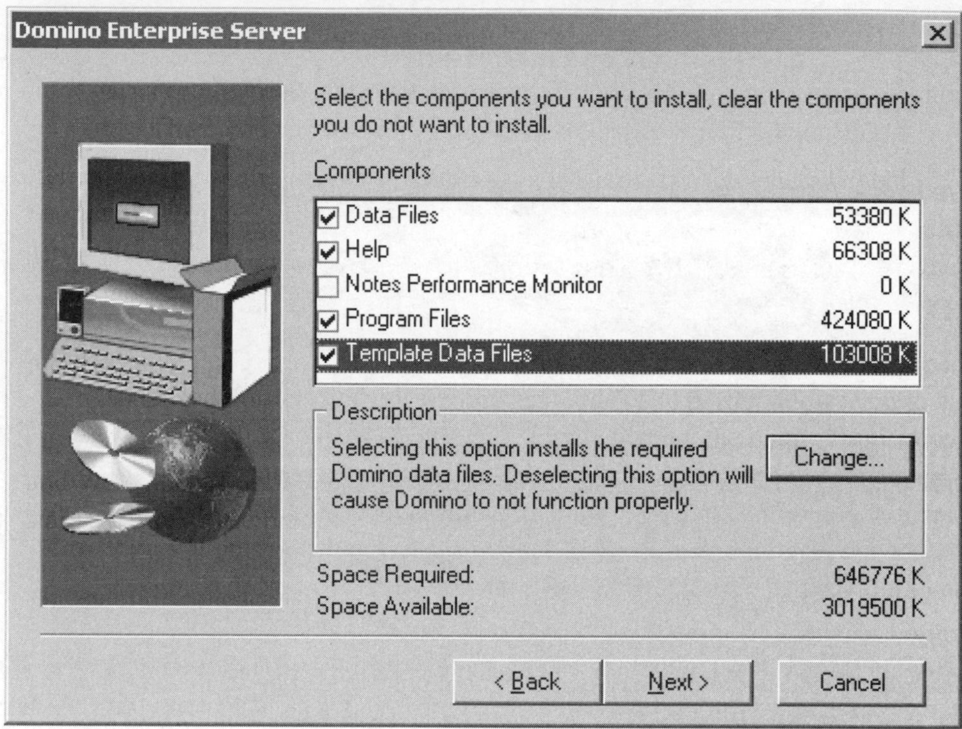

Figure 3.16: Selecting the required Domino components.

7. Choose a Program Folder.

8. Then click **Next** again to start the installation process.

9. Upon successful installation of Domino Server, click **Finish**.

Configure Domino Server

Follow these steps to configure Domino Server:

1. Use the Start menu to bring up the Domino Configuration UI:

   Start → Programs → Lotus Applications → Lotus Domino Server

You will have the option to start the server as a Windows service. See Figure 3.17. Choose the option that suits your environment and click **OK**. That will kick off the Domino Server setup wizard.

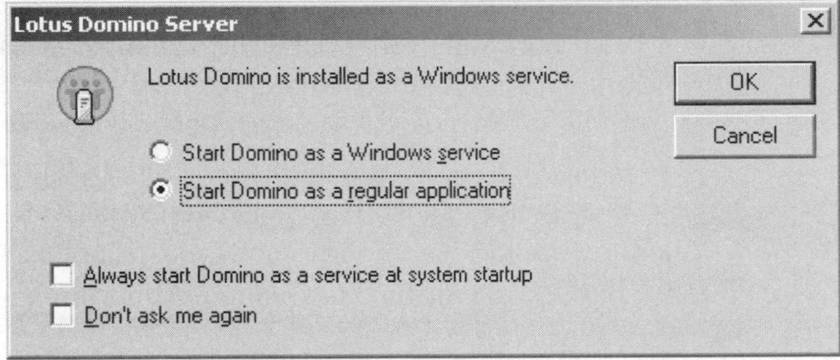

Figure 3.17: Selecting startup option for the Domino server.

Tip: To start the Domino Server on the Unix platform, go to a console window, switch to a Domino user (for example, su – notes1), and then invoke the command /opt/lotus/bin/server.sh.

---

2. Assuming this is the first Domino Server on the system, select **Set up the first server**, as shown in Figure 3.18. Click **Next**.

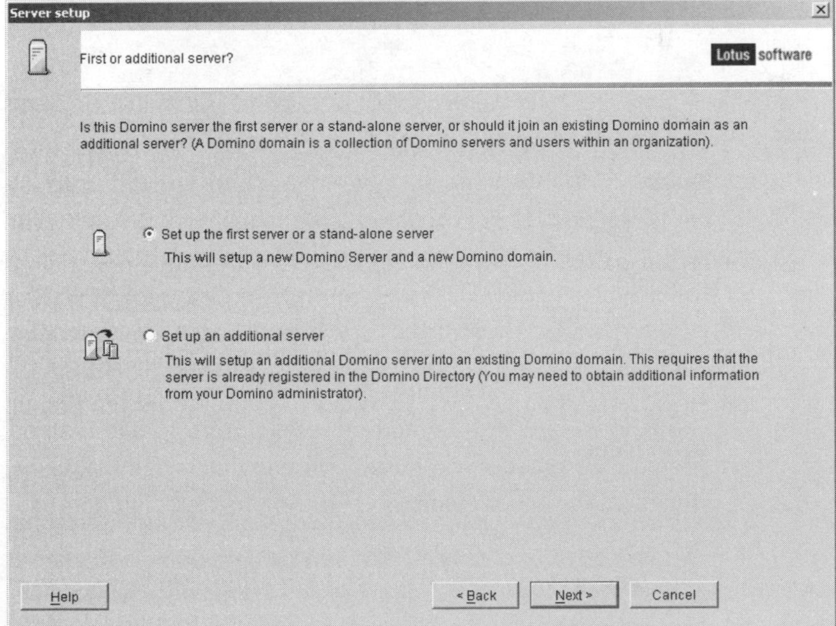

Figure 3.18: Specifying the Domino Server as the first server.

3. If you have an existing server ID file, use it. Otherwise, specify the server name. Our recommendation is to use the computer's host name. Giving it a descriptive title is optional. Click **Next**.

4. If you have an existing certifier ID file, use it. Otherwise, enter an Organization name, and then enter a password. See Figure 3.19. Click **Next**.

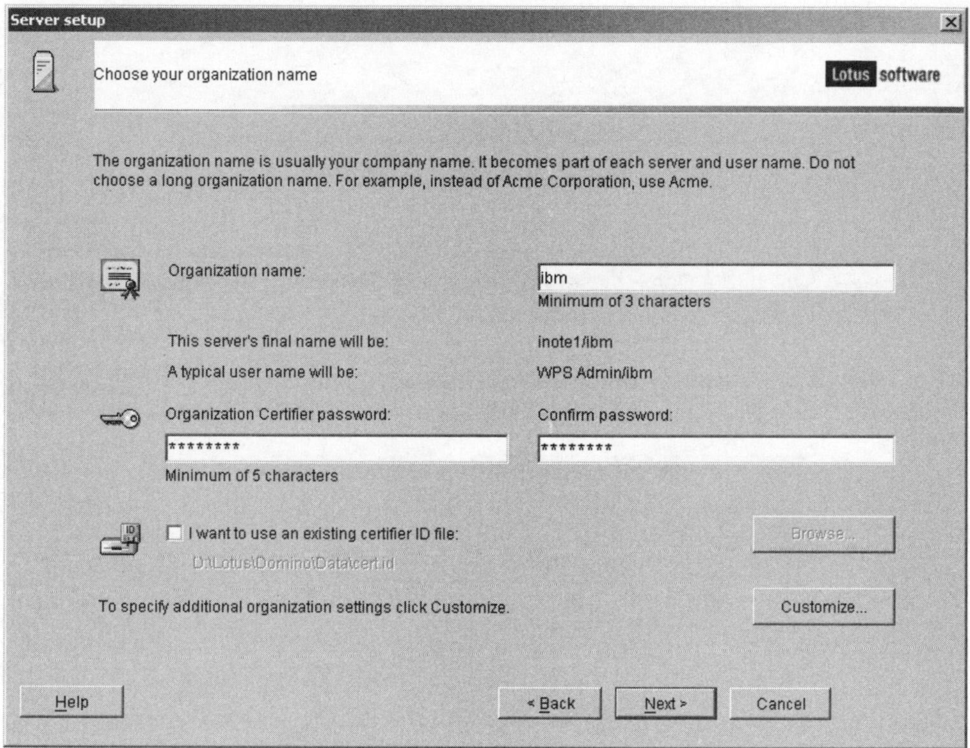

Figure 3.19: Choosing the organization name.

5. Choose a Domino domain name; this is usually the same as the organization name.

6. The wizard will display an administrator id. Change it or accept it, then enter the password. Also choose to save a local copy of the ID file, as shown in Figure 3.20.

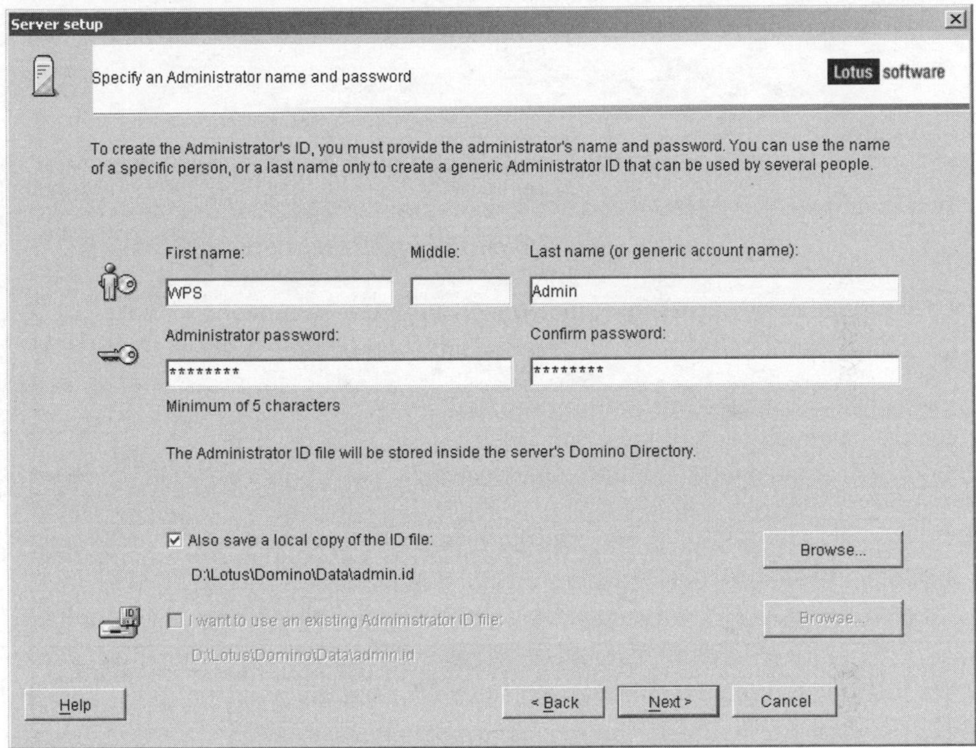

Figure 3.20: Specify the administrator ID and password.

7. On the screen to select the Internet services, choose those you want, but make sure LDAP services is selected, as seen in Figure 3.21.

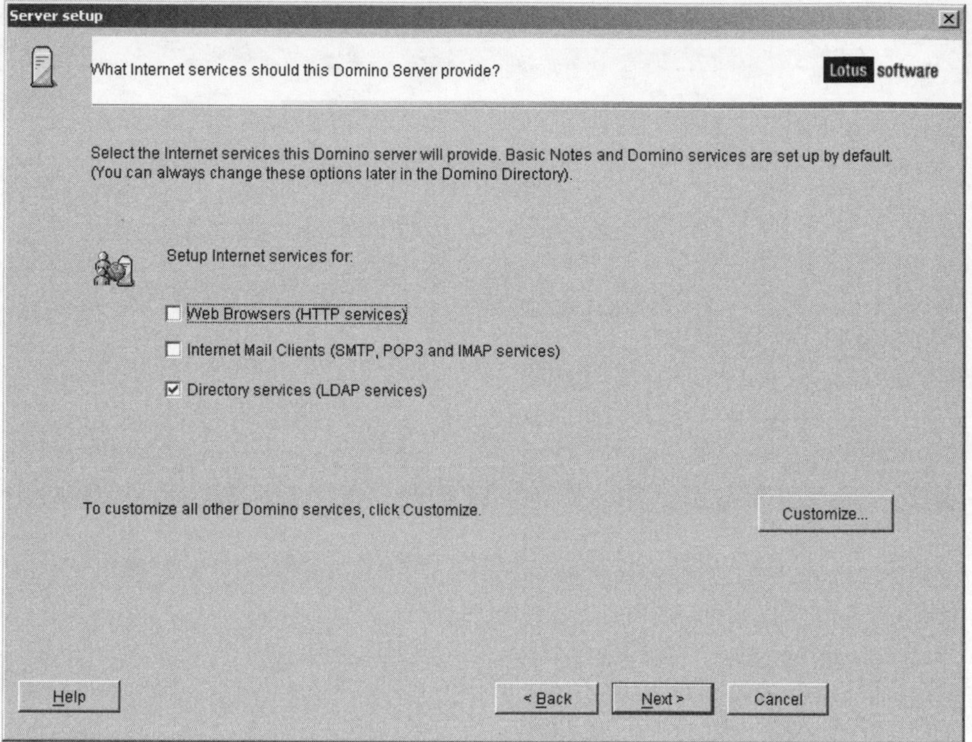

Figure 3.21: Specify the administrator ID and password.

8. The setup wizard then picks up the network settings.

9. Choose the security settings, but make sure the box to **Add LocalDomainAdmins group to all databases and templates** is selected. In our test environment, we allowed Anonymous access.

10. Review the options in the confirmation screen. Click **Setup** to finish the process.

11. Assuming the setup is successful, on the "Congratulations" screen, click **Finish**.

Install Domino Administrator

Follow these steps to install Domino Administrator:

1. Lotus Notes, Designer, and Administrative Clients for Windows are on CD #12-6. Invoke **setup.exe** from the root folder.

2. Click **Next** on the Welcome screen. Then enter the User Name and Organization.

3. Specify the folders where Notes and Notes\Data should be installed.

4. Select the program features to install. Make sure **Domino Administrator** is chosen, as shown in Figure 3.22.

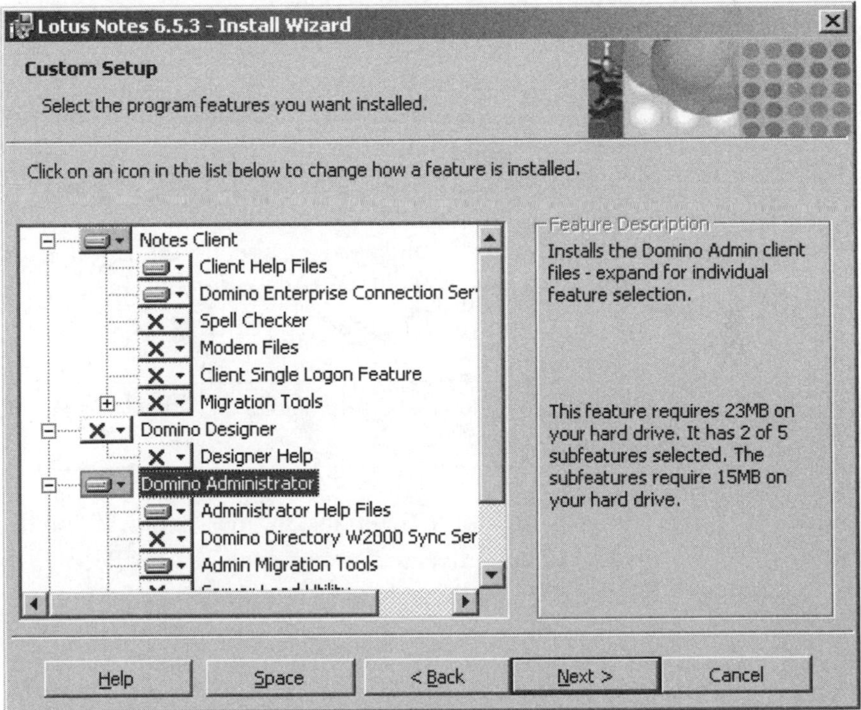

Figure 3.22: Specify the administrator ID and password.

5. Click **Install** to begin the installation. After the components have been successfully installed, click **Finish**.

Configure Domino Administrator

Follow these steps to configure Domino Administrator:

1. Relaunch the Domino Server from the Start menu. Look for the *Database Server started* message. Since we installed the Domino LDAP server too, we also see the message *LDAP Server: Started.*

2. Bring up the Domino Administrator via the Start menu:

   Start → Programs → Lotus Applications → Lotus Domino Administrator

3. This first time, the setup UI will guide you through the configuration. Enter your name and the Domino Server. Select **I want to connect to a Domino server**. Our test Domino server was inote1/encinitas.ibm.com. Even though we used WPS Admin as the user, we recommend using a user name, such as Domino Admin.

4. Select **Set up a connection to a local area network (LAN)** on the following screen.

5. In the Network settings screen, specify the Domino server name, choose TCP/IP for the protocol, and enter the fully qualified name of the Domino server, as shown in Figure 3.23. Click **Next**.

Tip: It is recommended that the domain of the Domain Server match the WebSphere Portal Domain.

---

6. You may choose to Setup instant messaging. If you do, that feature will be available in portlets that are provisioned for People Awareness. We chose to connect Manually and via a Direct connection.

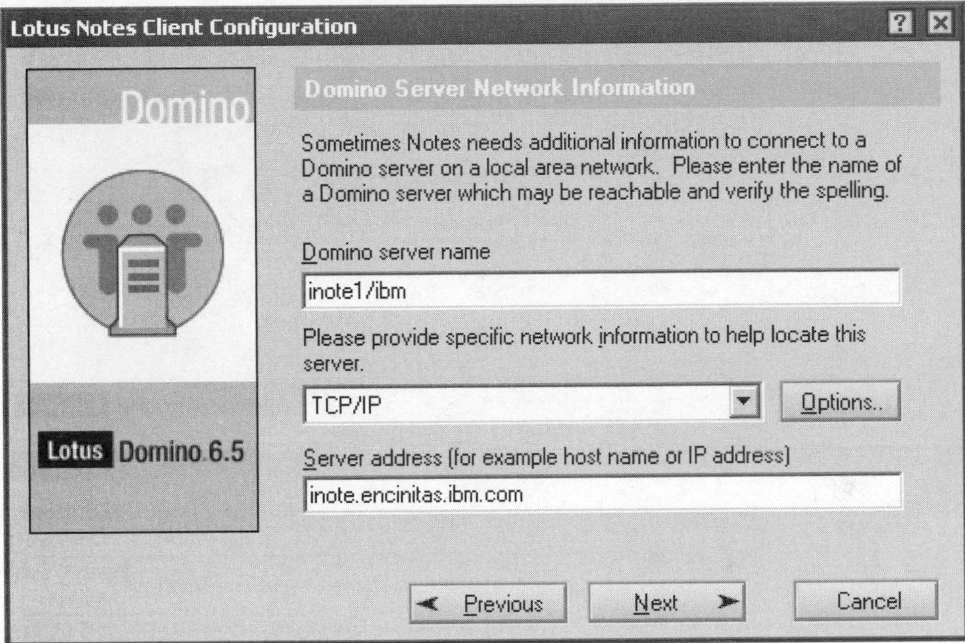

Figure 3.23: Screen showing the network settings during Notes Client configuration.

7. Finally, on the Additional Services screen, make sure Directory server (LDAP) is checked to connect via the LAN. Do not choose Internet Proxy servers. Click **Next**.
8. We specified Internet Directory and entered the fully qualified host name for the LDAP server.

Add WPS Users/Group

The Domino Server is now installed and partly configured, and the Domino Notes Client is configured. You now need to configure Domino LDAP Server. Continue to work within the Domino Administrator GUI, following these steps:

1. Click the server icon (on the left side of the screen, below the Favorites folder). Make sure you point to the Domino server (inote1/ibm), not to Local, as shown in Figure 3.24. (You could also achieve this by clicking **File → Open Server**, choosing your server, and clicking **OK**.)

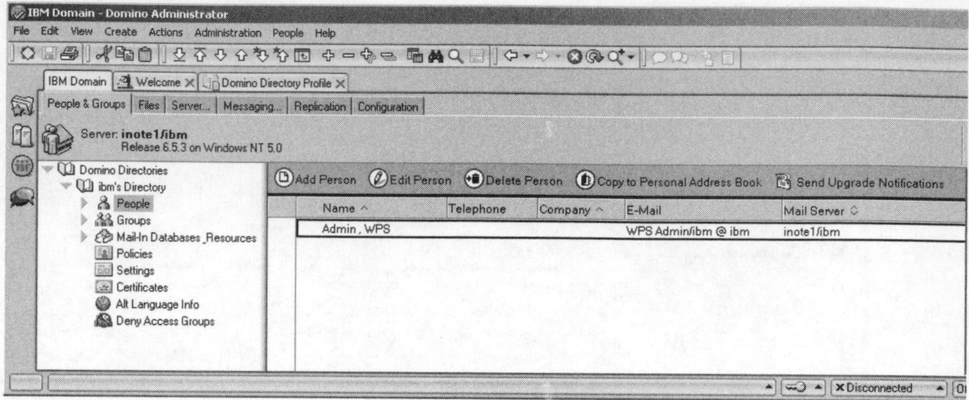

Figure 3.24: The Domino Server People screen.

2. In the People & Groups tab, with the administrator name displayed, you will be asked to certify by choosing a Certifier.

3. In the Choose a Certifier screen, make sure the server is pointing to your Domino server. Select **Supply certifier ID and password** and click the **Certifier ID** button.

4. Browse for ID files, select **Lotus\Domino\data\cert.id**, and click **Open**. A challenge screen will pop up. Enter the certifier password that was set up during installation and click **OK**.

5. On the right side of the screen, select **Tools → People → Register** to register the default WebSphere Portal users wpsadmin and wpsbind.

6. The screen to register a new user will be displayed. Check the **Advanced** box. Click the **Password Options** button.

7. In the Password Options window that pops up, set the Password Quality Scale in the middle as shown in Figure 3.25. Check the **Set internet password** box. Then click **OK**.

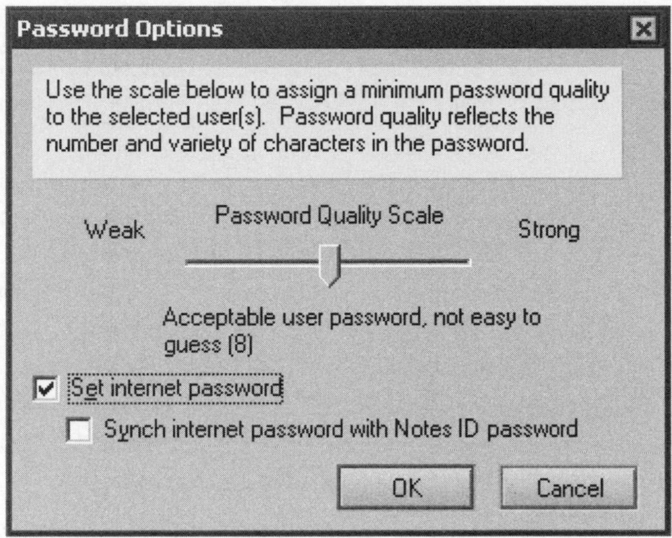

Figure 3.25: Password Options screen.

8. With the password options set, enter the people information:

   8.1. Enter **wpsadmin** for the last name, short name, and password of the first user. Click the green check mark. The screen is shown in Figure 3.26.

   8.2. Enter **wpsbind** for the last name, short name, and password of the second user. Click the green check mark again.

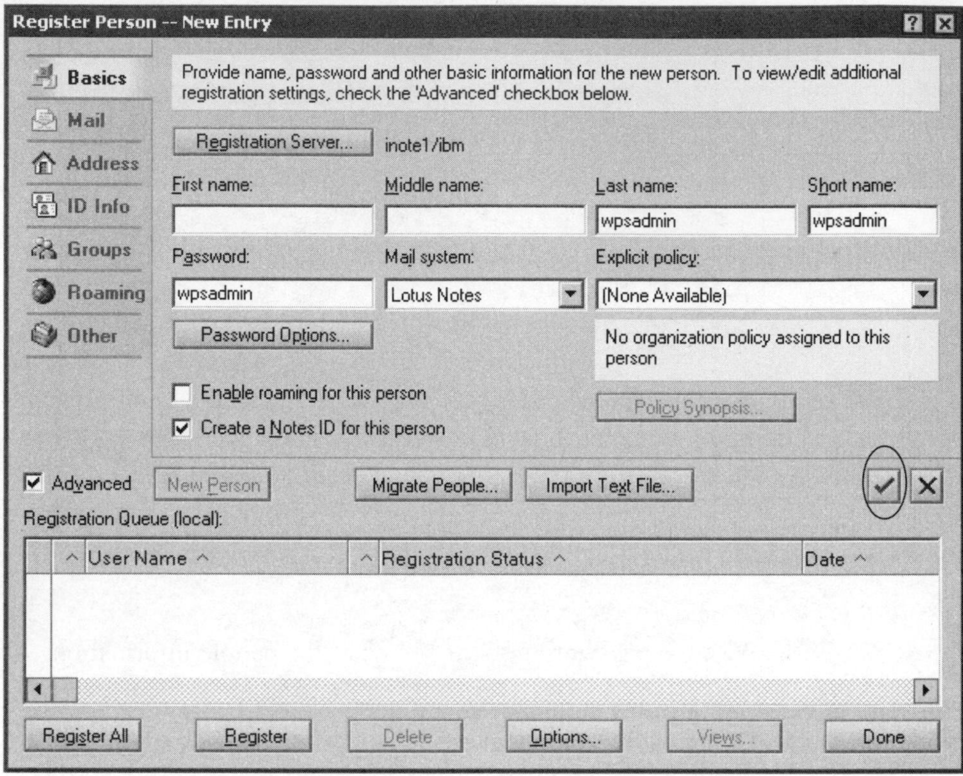

Figure 3.26: Registering a new person.

9. The registration queue should list two persons with the statuses showing *Ready for registration*. Click **Register All** button. Click **OK** on the success message, and then click **Done**.

10. Back on the Administration screen, press **F9** to refresh the view. You should see two new people—wpsadmin and wpsbind—along with Domino Administrator.

11. Select **Groups** in the left navigation bar, and then click **Add Group**. The Group screen is shown in Figure 3.27.

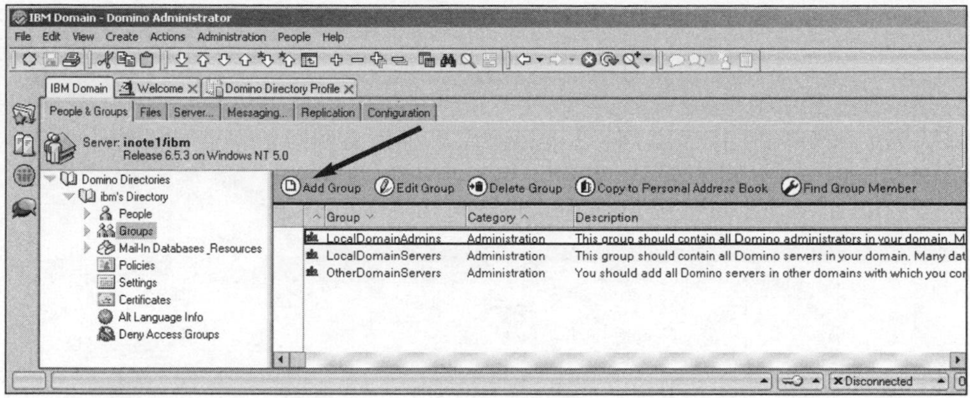

Figure 3.27: The Domino server Groups screen

12. Type **wpsadmins** in the Group name field, as shown in Figure 3.26. Choose **Multi-purpose** for the Group type. Click the **Members** down arrow to pop up a Names window. Make sure your server's Address Book is displayed.

    12.1. Select **wpsadmin** and click **Add**.

    12.2. Select **wpsbind** and click **Add**.

    12.3. Click **OK**.

13. You will return to the Group screen. Click **Save and Close**. The group wpsadmins should show in the list, as seen in Figure 3.28.

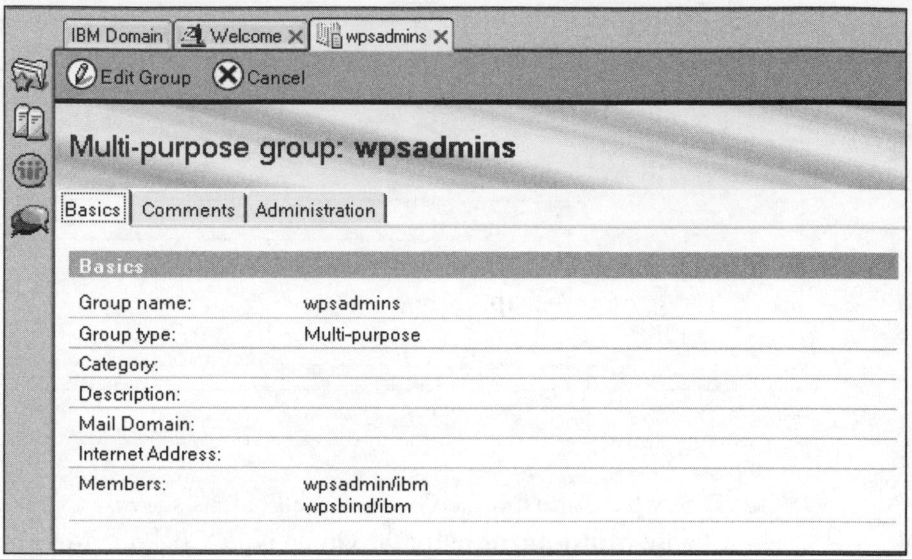

Figure 3.28: Newly created group with its members.

Quick Verification

In a Web browser, enter the following URLs:

```
ldap://<HOST_NAME>/cn=wpsadmins

ldap://<HOST_NAME>/cn=wpsadmin,<DOMAIN>

ldap://<HOST_NAME>/cn=wpsbind,<DOMAIN>
```

Details of the newly created users and group should be displayed in a pop-up window.

Update the Access Control List (ACL) in Domino Server's Names Database

You will continue to work within the Domino Administrator GUI. Follow these steps:

1. In the Administration view, click the **Files** tab. In the Filename column, highlight **names.nsf**. Right-click it, select **Access Control**, and choose **Manage...**

2. In the Access Control List window choose to **Show All** People and Groups. If wpsadmins group and users, wpsadmin, and wpsbind are not listed, make sure to add them. Then assign permissions to each user and group:

2.1. Select **wpsadmin.** The user type should be **Person**, and the Access should be **Manager**. Check **Delete documents**. Select the following four roles: **GroupCreator**, **GroupModifier**, **UserCreator**, and **UserModifier**. Click **Add**. See Figure 3.29.

2.2. Repeat step 2.1 for the user wpsbind.

2.3. Repeat step 2.1 for the group wpsadmins, but set the user type to **Person Group**.

2.4. Click **OK**.

One other step finishes up the configuration of Domino LDAP Server and Domino HTTP Server. Before starting that, you may want to restart Domino Server. That is easily done by entering **restart server** in the server's output window.

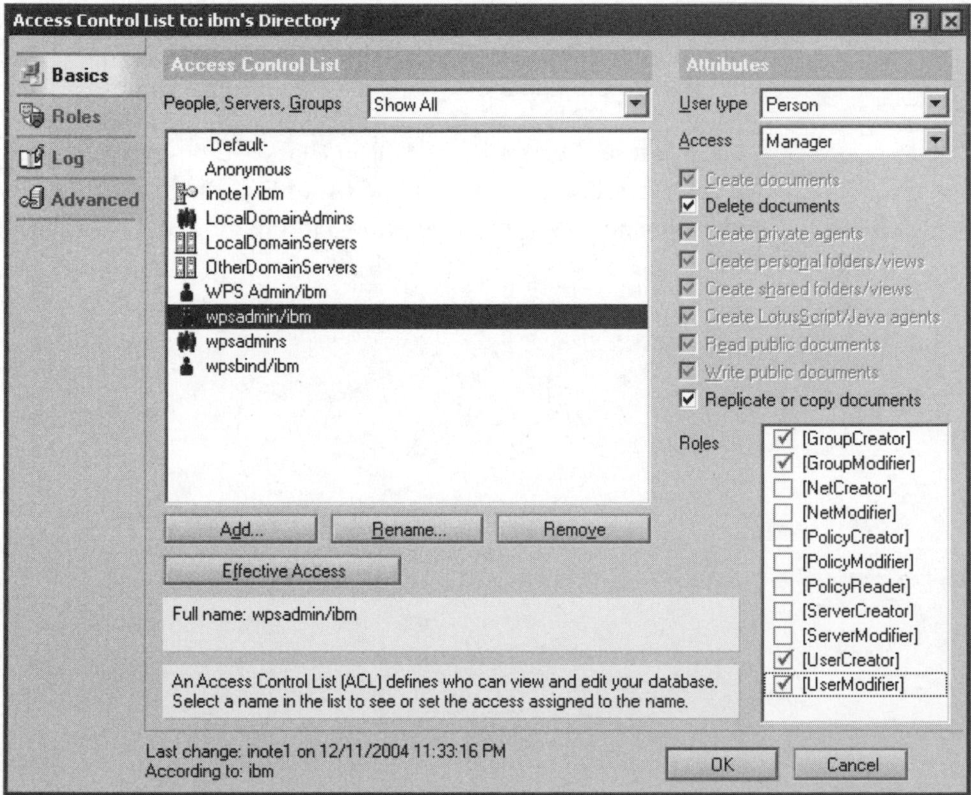

Figure 3.29: The Access Control List screen.

Configure Domino LDAP to Enable Write Access

Continuing to work within the Domino Administrator GUI, follow these steps:

1. In the Administration view, select the **Configuration** tab.

2. Expand **Server** in the left navigation bar, and select **Configurations**. Only one entry with a server name of "*- [All Servers]" should be highlighted. Click **Edit Configuration**.

3. In the Basics tab, check the **Yes** box to Use these settings as the default settings for all servers.

4. In the LDAP tab, click **Edit**, scroll down and check **Yes** to "Allow LDAP users write access." This setting ensures that portal users can use the self-care and self-registration features of WebSphere Portal.

    4.1. Click the button **Select Attribute Types** next to the link entitled Choose fields that anonymous users can query via LDAP. This will pop up the LDAP Attribute Type Selection window.

5. Select **dominoPerson** in the Object Classes drop-down list. Click the **Display Attributes** button. In the list of Selectable Attribute Types, choose **MailFile** and **MailServer**, as shown in Figure 3.30. Then click the **Add** button.

6. Select **dominoServer** in the Object Classes drop-down list, and click **Display Attributes** again (Figure 3.30). In the Fields list, select **HTTP_Hostname**, and click the **Add** button.

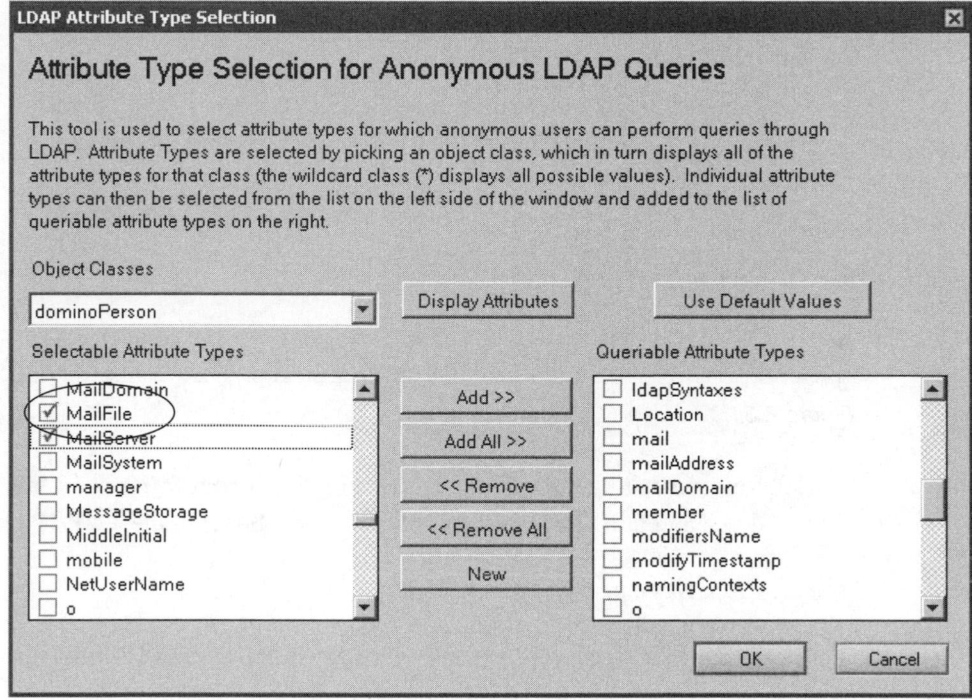

Figure 3.30: Choosing LDAP attributes.

7. Click **OK**. Then click **Save and Close**.

8. In the navigation bar under **Server**, select **Current Server Document**. Click **Edit Server**.

9. In the Internet Protocols tab, select the **HTTP** child-tab. After the fully qualified hostname, add a colon and type a port number other than 80, for example, 8080. Chances are, WebSphere is using port 80, hence Domino Server should listen on a different port.

   9.1. Select **Yes** to **Allow HTTP clients to browse databases**.

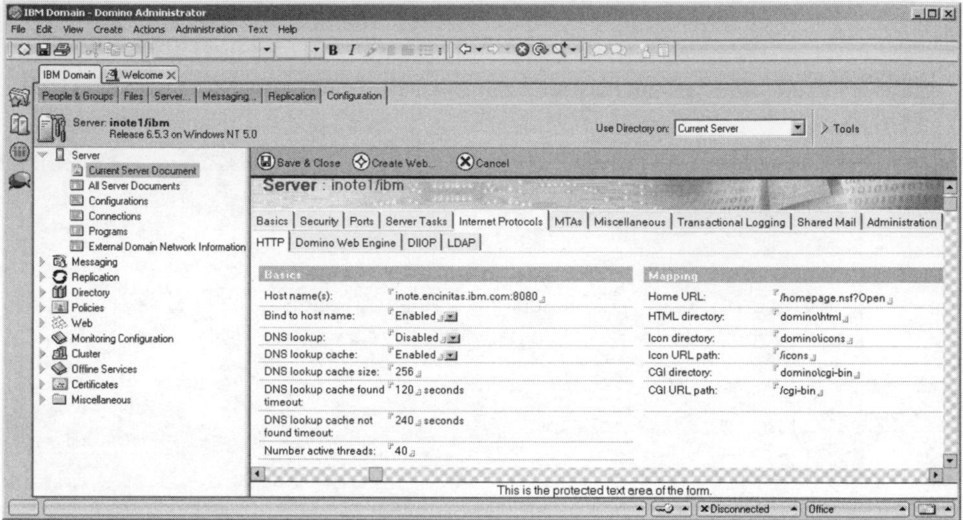

Figure 3.31: Choosing LDAP attributes.

10. Remember to go to the **Ports** tab and the **Internet Ports** child-tab. Scroll down and add **8080** (or whatever port you chose) to the **TCP/IP port number**.

11. Click **Save** and **Close**.

12. Domino Server is fully configured. **Exit** the Domino Administrator.

13. Restart Domino Server for all the changes to take effect.

Quick Verification

In a Web browser, enter the following URL:

```
http://<HOST_NAME>
```

You should see the IBM HTTP Server page. In the same Web browser, enter one of the following:

```
http://<HOST_NAME>:8080

http://<HOST_NAME.DOMAIN>:8080
```

You should see the Domino home page.

Configuring WebSphere Portal Extend Edition

Now that Domino Server and Domino LDAP are ready, the portal server can be configured to make use of Collaborative features which are part of the Extend edition of WebSphere Portal. This is done via the WPSconfig utility found in <WPS_HOME>/config directory. The WPSconfig utility uses wpconfig.properties as its input. That properties file is also found in <WPS_HOME>/config directory. The default wpconfig.properties file is listed in Appendix B.

Tip: You could use the security_domino.properties helper file to configure Domino LDAP server. The helper files are found in <WPS_HOME>/config/helpers directory. In any case, make a backup copy of the configuration file before modifying it.

(For more information, see the section on Configuring LDAP Server later in this chapter.) Follow the same six-step process to configure WebSphere Portal with Domino LDAP server. Table 3.3 lists the parameters that must be changed in the wpsconfig.properties file before validating and configuring with Domino LDAP server.

Table 3.3: Parameters in wpconfig.properties Relating to Lotus Domino Server

Parameter	Value
WasUserid	cn=wpsbind,o=ibm
WasPassword	Wpsbind
PortalAdminId	cn=wpsadmin,o=ibm
PortalAdminIdShort	Wpsadmin
PortalAdminPwd	Wpsadmin
PortalAdminGroupId	cn=wpsadmins
PortalAdminGroupIdShort	Wpsadmins
WpsContentAdministrators	cn=wpsContentAdministrators
WpsContentAdministratorsShort	wpsContentAdministrators
WpsDocReviewer	cn=wpsDocReviewer
WpsDocReviewersShort	wpsDocReviewer

Table 3.3: Parameters in wpconfig.properties Relating to Lotus Domino Server (continued)

Parameter	Value
DbUser	db2admin
DbPassword	db2admin
LookAside	False
LDAPHostName	<FULLY_QUALIFIED_HOST_NAME>
LDAPPort	389
LDAPAdminUid	Domino Admin
LDAPAdminPwd	Password
LDAPServerType	DOMINO502
LDAPBindID	cn=wpsbind,o=ibm
LDAPBindPassword	Wpsbind
WmmSystemId	cn=wpsbind,o=ibm
WmmSystemIdPassword	Wpsbind
LDAPSuffix	<none>
LdapUserPrefix	Cn
LDAPUserSuffix	o=ibm
LdapGroupPrefix	Cn
LDAPGroupSuffix	<none>
LDAPUserObjectClass	dominoPerson
LDAPGroupObjectClass	dominoGroup
LDAPGroupMember	Member
LDAPUserFilter	(&(|(cn=%v)(uid=%v))
LDAPGroupFilter	(&(cn=%v)(objectclass=dominoGroup))
LDAPsslEnabled	False

To enable Single-Sign On (SSO) between WebSphere Portal and Domino Server, four more parameters must be set in wpconfig.properties. Their default values are shown in parenthesis—LTPAPassword (password), SSOEnabled (true), SSORequiresSSL (false), SSODomainName (PORTAL_DOMAIN_NAME).

After running the WPSConfig tasks, assuming that you see a BUILD SUCCESSFUL message, WebSphere Portal should be fully configured with Domino Server. You can test it by entering the following URL:

```
http://<HOST_NAME>/wps/portal.
```

The familiar "Welcome" portal page seen in Figure 3.11 should be displayed.

Installing on Solaris

The following section steps through the installation of WebSphere Portal Enable Edition on the Solaris platform. Our test Solaris machine is consun71 in the encinitas.ibm.com domain. It is running SunOS 5.8, which equates to Solaris 2.8.

Solaris Prerequisites

Follow these steps to prepare for installation:

1. Log in as **root** and start a terminal session.

2. Disable access control for X-Windows display via the **xhost** command:

   ```
   # xhost +
   ```

3. Make sure that the DISPLAY environment variable is set by going to a command window and exporting the DISPLAY. If the installer has trouble starting in the graphical mode, you will see the following message: *The installer is unable to run in graphical mode. Try running the installer with the –console or –silent flag.*

   ```
   # export DISPLAY=lab-sun-021:0.0
   ```

4. WebSphere Portal server V5.1, like WebSphere Application Server V5.1, requires Java 1.4. If you do not already have that on the system, load the WebSphere Portal product CD #1.

5. Go to the /sunjava3/jdk folder on the CD and install the Java SDK (the JDK) via the **pkgadd** command:

```
# cd /cdrom/wpo4.1-1/sunjava3/jdk

# pkgadd -d . SUNWj3rt
```

   By default, the JDK gets installed in the /usr/j2se folder.

6. Check the version of Java on the system by typing **java –fullversion** in a command window. Typically, the version of Java that comes with this version of WebSphere Portal is 1.4.2_03-b02. The recommendation is to use the Sun JDK.

As noted in the WebSphere Portal product InfoCenter, several Solaris kernel values are typically too small for the messaging requirements of this version. The recommended values shown in Table 3.4 are to be treated as a starting point for WebSphere Portal. If other applications make use of messaging, the values will probably be higher. The current kernel values are set in the /etc/system file and can be viewed by running the command sysdef –i.

Table 3.4: Solaris System Kernel Settings

Parameter	Minimum Value
shmsys: shminfo_shmmax	4294967295
shmsys: shminfo_shmseg	1024
shmsys: shminfo_shmmni	1024
semsys: seminfo_semaem	16384
semsys: seminfo_semmni	1024
semsys: seminfo_semmap	1026
semsys: seminfo_semmns	16384

Table 3.4: Solaris System Kernel Settings (continued)

Parameter	Minimum Value
semsys: seminfo_semmsl	100
semsys: seminfo_semmnu	2048
semsys: seminfo_semume	256
msgsys: msginfo_msgmap	1026
msgsys: msginfo_msgmax	65535
rlim_fd_cur	1024

Installing WebSphere Portal on Solaris

Once all the prerequisites are met, installing WebSphere Portal on a Solaris machine is no different than installing it on the Windows platform. Having a multiplatform installation wizard is wonderful because the installation process and screens look the same on all platforms. Rather than repeat the same installation steps, we present some notes that you should be aware of when installing WebSphere Portal on Solaris.

Installation Notes

- Remember to create groups mqm and mqbrkrs on the machine where WebSphere Portal will be installed. And the user account that will be used to do the installation should belong to both these groups. In our case, user root was a member of mqm and mqbrkrs.

- If you use the standard graphical install wizard, we recommend copying all the CD images to a disk on the Solaris machine.

- If you are installing off physical CDs, do not change to the mounted /cdrom directory because that might hinder the unmounting and mounting of CDs.

- If you choose a co-existence scenario, remember to Modify ports for coexistence. The installation wizard will increment most of the default ports by 1 and display the set of new ports. Make sure these ports are not being used by any other process.

- In a production environment, remember not to install the various samples that come with the product. Figure 3.32 shows the various features and samples that can be installed.

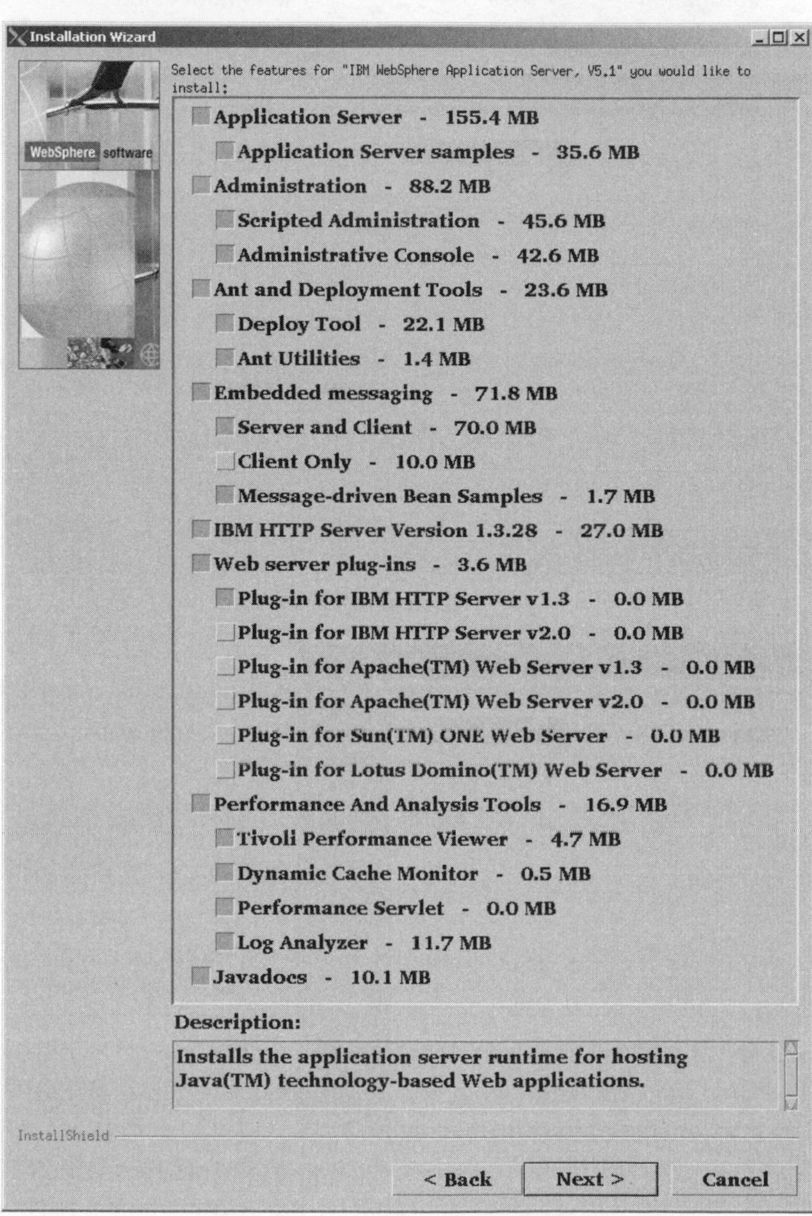

Figure 3.32: IBM WebSphere Application Server feature selection screen.

- Some of the log files that are created during installation:

  The output from the installation process is logged in <WAS_HOME>/logs/WAS.WBISF.install.log.

  The installer starts the process of installing WebSphere Portal capturing its log in /tmp/wpsinstalllog.txt.

  When the portlets are getting installed, the log is captured in <WPS_HOME>/wpinstalllog.txt.

  WebSphere Personalization installation details are written to /tmp/pzninstall.log.

- One way to verify if WebSphere Application server processes are running is to use the ps command and check for Java processes. In a command window, invoke the command **ps –aef | grep –i java**. See Figure 3.33. If you see WebSphere-related Java processes, then you know one or more WebSphere servers are running.

- To start the Domino Server on Solaris, go to a console window, switch to a Domino user (for example, su – notes1), then invoke the command **/opt/lotus/bin/server.sh**

xterm

```
# ps -aef | grep -i java
    root   716   698  0 11:31:06 pts/4     2:39 /opt/WebSphere/AppServer/java/jre
/bin/../bin/sparc/native_threads/java -server
    root   687   682  0 11:27:25 pts/4     0:07 /opt/WebSphere/AppServer/java/bin
/../bin/sparc/native_threads/java -classpath /
    root   698   687  0 11:27:28 pts/4     1:30 /opt/WebSphere/AppServer/java/jre
/bin/../bin/sparc/native_threads/java -Xmx128m
    root  1133  1130  0 18:46:32 pts/7     0:00 grep -i java
# 
```

Figure 3.33: Java processes indicating that WebSphere Application Server is running.

1. If WebSphere Application Server is not running, go to <WAS_HOME>/bin directory and invoke **startupServer.sh server1**.

   1.1. Wait for all the processes to come up; this may take a few minutes. If you look inside the StdOut.log, found in the <WAS_HOME>/logs directory, you should see the message *Server open for e-business*.

1.2. Make sure the DISPLAY variable is set correctly. From the <WAS_HOME>/bin directory, invoke **adminclient.sh**.

1.3. In a Web browser, enter the following URL to see the details of the snoop servlet:

```
http://<HOST_NAME>/servlet/snoop
```

Once WebSphere Portal is running, bring up a Web browser and enter the following URL:

```
http://<HOST_NAME>/wps/portal
```

You should see the same Welcome portal page seen in Figure 3.11.

Installing on Linux

Earlier in this chapter, we mentioned that two types of WebSphere Portal installations are possible: typical and development. This section discusses the steps to install the development version of WebSphere Portal Enable edition on a single machine running Red Hat Linux V7.3.

Before installing any of the WebSphere software components, make sure you have the proper level of the Operating System (OS). Please refer to the product release notes, which can be found at the following URL: www.ibm.com/software/info1/websphere/solutions/offerings/portallibrary.jsp.

Currently, the minimum supported levels of Linux are RedHat V7.2 or higher and Suse V7.2 or higher.

Linux OS Prerequisites

On Linux, WebSphere-related software requires certain prerequisite packages. They are:

- *libncurses.so.4*—Your system might have libncurses.so.5 instead of libncurses.so.4. You can attempt to download the required package from ftp://ftp.redhat.com/. Alternatively, as root, set up a symbolic link as follows:

```
ln -sf  /usr/lib/libncurses.so libncurses.so.4
```

- */bin/ksh*—In the Linux world, ksh does not get installed by default. You have to install pdksh (Public Domain Korn Shell) manually. That package is normally on CD #3 of the Linux OS. Alternatively, download it from www.cs.mun.ca/~michael/pdksh. Then, as **root**, set up a symbolic link as follows:

```
ln -sf  /usr/local/bin/ksh /bin/ksh
```

To install a package on Linux, use the following:

```
rpm -U -nodeps <package_name>_<version>.i386.rpm
```

It is also recommended that you create a user called wpsadmin. The root user can do that with the help of the useradd command.

Note: Most of the WebSphere-related software gets installed in the /opt directory. Ensure that it has at least 500 MB of disk space.

Installing WebSphere Portal Enable Edition—Test Environment

Once all the prerequisites are met, installing WebSphere Portal on a Linux machine is no different from installing it on any other platform, especially a Unix-based OS. We talked about the beauty of having a multiplatform installation wizard wherein the installation process and screens look the same on all platforms. In this section, we talk about installing a Test Environment using the graphical install method.

Our Linux test machine was running the KDE desktop interface. Rather than work with mounted CDs, we copied all the software to the Linux machine and, while logged in as user root, we invoked install.sh from the setup CD.

Tip: To mount the CD on Linux, right-click on the cdrom icon on the desktop, and select **mount**. The default mount is /mnt/cdrom.

---

1. As user root, invoke the install script. If you are using a remote terminal, make sure the DISPLAY is set.

```
[root@enclinux /]# /setupCD/install.sh
```

2. After the Welcome screen and the License agreement screen, the install wizard will warn you about not having any WebSphere process running. Then the setup type screen is displayed. Select **Test Environment**, as shown in Figure 3.34.

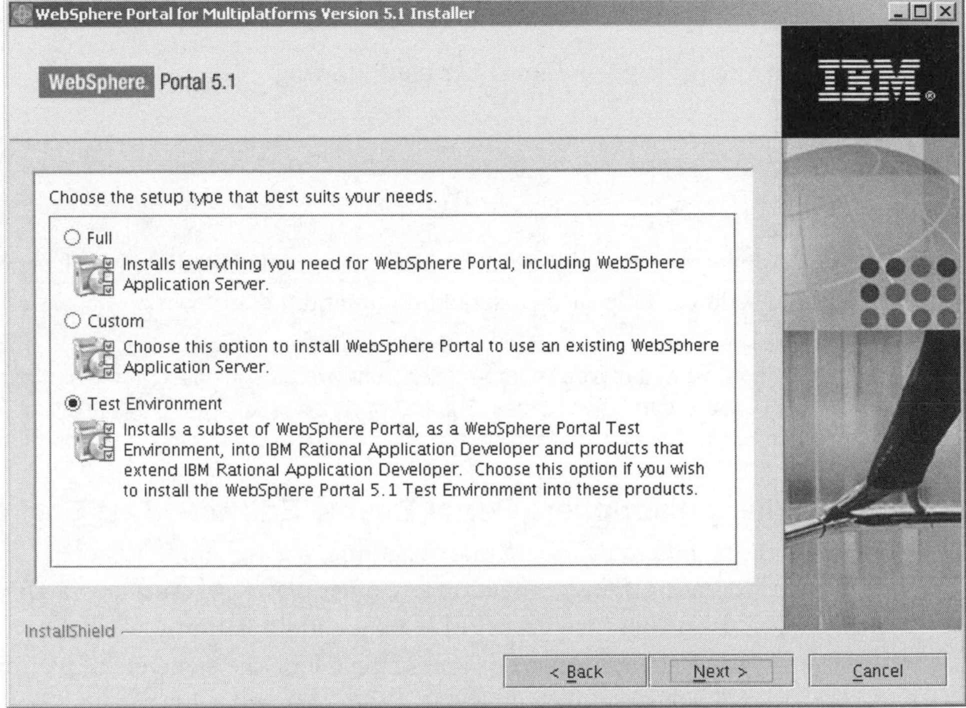

Figure 3.34: Choosing the type of setup for WebSphere Portal.

3. By default, WebSphere Application Server gets installed in /opt/Portal51UTE/AppServer, as seen in Figure 3.35. Note the amount of space required to accommodate this Test Environment.

4. Consequently, WebSphere Portal Server gets installed in /opt/Portal51UTE/PortalServer.

Note: Embedding messaging gets installed in /opt/mqm.

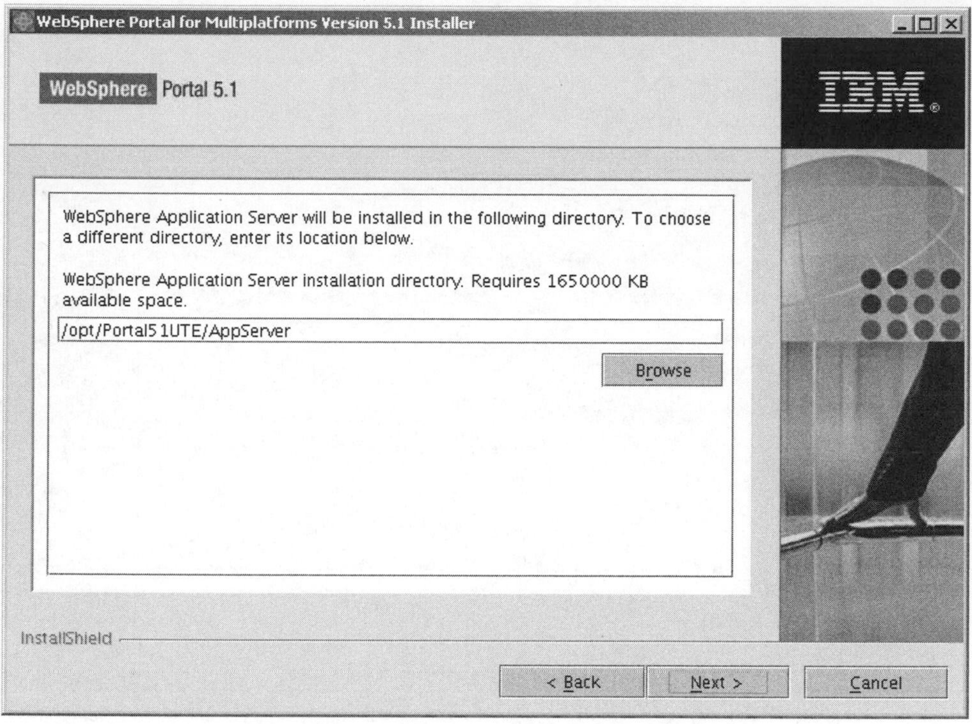

Figure 3.35: WebSphere Application Server installation directory.

5. Enter the portal administrator information and, after a couple of the usual installation screens, the process gets underway.

A subset of WebSphere Portal features gets installed that, used along with Rational Application Developer V6.0 IDE, constitute the development environment. In this scenario, you do not have the option to install component by component. The wizard installs all three major components, as seen in Figure 3.36. You don't even have the option of installing portal server on an existing instance of WebSphere Application Server. Thus, when you run the WebSphere Portal uninstaller, all the components get uninstalled.

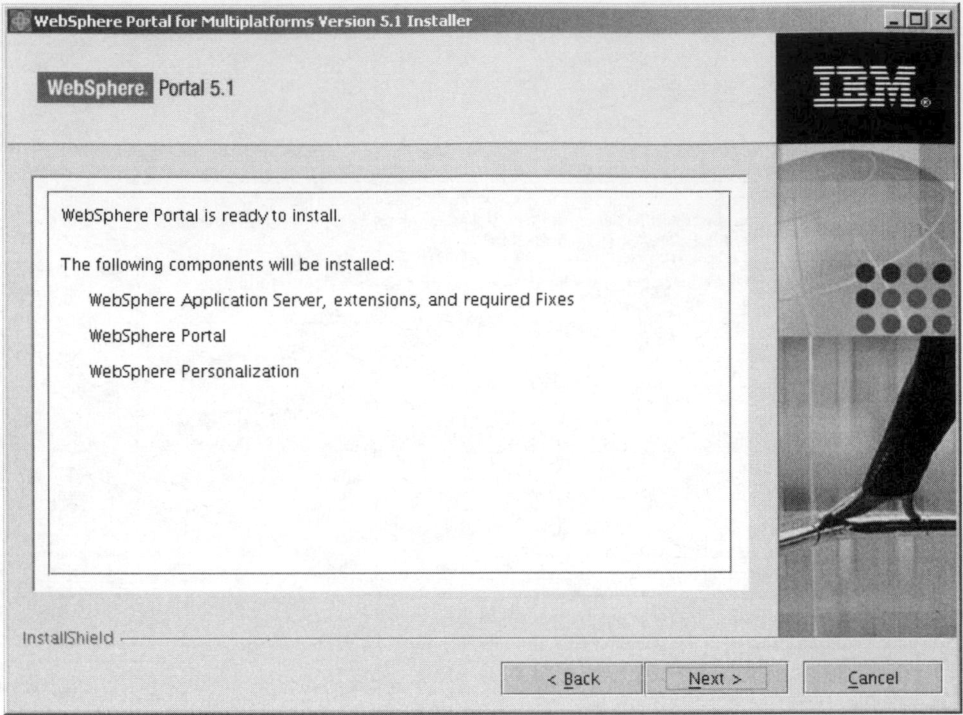

Figure 3.36: Components that get installed in WebSphere Portal Test Environment.

Installation Notes

For a typical installation that uses an LDAP Server, you would first have to remove all LDAP packages installed by default on Linux before starting the WebSphere Portal Setup Manager.

Use the rpm –qa | grep –i ldap command to find other LDAP servers. The LDAP servers you might find are:

- nss_ldap-172-2
- openldap-devel-2.0.21-1
- php-ldap-4.0.6-12
- openldap-2.0.21-1
- openldap-clients-2.0.21-1

Use the rpm –e <PACKAGE_NAME> command to erase or uninstall packages.

Installing on AIX

Installing WebSphere Portal on an AIX machine is not very different from installing on Solaris or Linux. As a matter of fact, once you have met the prerequisites, it is as easy as setting up WebSphere Portal on a Windows machine. The sequence of steps is the same as discussed in the other sections of this chapter, so rather than repeat the standard installation instructions, we detail the scenario of using an existing instance of WebSphere Application Server.

Hardware and Software Prerequisites

WebSphere Portal server V5.1 has the following hardware requirements:

- 1,200 MB disk space (minimum) for WebSphere Portal server including Cloudscape
- 1,700 MB disk space (minimum) for WebSphere Application Server including extensions and fixes
- 100 MB disk space (minimum) for IBM HTTP Server

For further details on requirements, refer to the individual product documentation available at the following web sites:

- For DB2, http://www.ibm.com/software/data/db2/udb/support.html
- For WebSphere Application Server, http://www.ibm.com/software/webservers/appserv/doc/latest/prereq.html
- For WebSphere Portal, http://www.ibm.com/software/webservers/portal/

Checking AIX OS Prerequisites

Before installing any of the WebSphere software components, make sure you have the proper level of the OS. For WebSphere Portal V5.1, the minimum recommended level of AIX 5.1 is maintenance Release 04.

- AIX 5L V5.3 (32 bit)
- AIX 5L V5.2 (32 bit) + ML01 + APAR IY44183
- AIX 5L V5.1 (32 bit) + ML04

Determine whether the server has the required maintenance release installed by issuing the following command:

```
instfix -i | grep ML
```

You should see output similar to this:

```
All filesets for 5.1.0.0_AIX_ML were found.

All filesets for 5100-01_AIX_ML were found.

All filesets for 5100-02_AIX_ML were found.

All filesets for 5100-03_AIX_ML were found.

All filesets for 5100-04_AIX_ML were found.

All filesets for 5100-05_AIX_ML were found.

All filesets for 5100-06_AIX_ML were found.
```

If no output is generated, you must upgrade AIX to the required maintenance release before continuing. For details on how to perform such an upgrade, please refer to the AIX product documentation.

Tip: AIX maintenance releases can be obtained from ftp://ftp.software.ibm.com/aix/fixes/51.

Additional File Sets That Might Be Required

The following AIX file sets are required to install or run DB2 in languages other than English:

- X11.fnt.ucs.ttf (AIX Windows Unicode True Type Fonts)
- XlC.rte 5.0.2.x

For Asian languages, the following file sets are also required:

- X11.fnt.ucs.ttf_CN (for zh_CN or Zh_CN)
- X11.fnt.ucs.ttf_KR (for ko_KR)
- X11.fnt.ucs.ttf_TW (for zh_TW or Zh_TW)

You can download file sets from http://techsupport.services.ibm.com/server/fixes.

Disabling Port 9090 on AIX system

AIX V5.2 and higher ships with a Web-based system manager utility called wsm-server that is used to control the server processes. This server utility runs on port 9090 by default. When installing WebSphere Portal V5.1, which also installs and uses WebSphere Business Integration Server Foundation V5.1, the wsmserver port 9090 must be disabled. The steps to disable port 9090 are as follows:

1. Make sure you are logged in as user "root".
2. Edit /etc/services file. Comment out the following line by placing the # character in front of it, then save it.

```
#wsmserver            9090/tcp
```

3. Edit /etc/inted.conf file. Comment out the following line, then save it.

```
#wsmserver  stream  tcp  nowait  root  /usr/websm/bin/wsmserver
    -start
```

4. Restart inetd process to pick up the configuration changes by invoking the following command:

```
Kill -HUP  'ps -ef  |  grep inetd  |  awk  '{print $2}''.
```

Installing WebSphere Portal

Make sure that the DISPLAY environment variable is set, and then change directory to where the CD images have been downloaded, specifically the cdSetup directory.

Tip: We recommend copying all the CD images to a disk on the AIX machine.

If you are using physical CDs, make sure you are logged in as user root. From the root directory, invoke the install script by typing in the full path name to install.sh:

```
# /mnt/wp51/cdSetup/install.sh
```

Tip: Do not change to the mounted cdrom directory and invoke the install script from there because that might prevent unmounting and mounting of CDs.

5. The installation wizard starts off and does a dependency check of the system. For a standard installation, follow the installation steps as detailed in the Solaris section of this chapter.

6. If after choosing the **Custom** setup, as we recommend, you want to use an existing instance of WebSphere Application Server (as shown in Figure 3.37), continue to follow the steps as detailed below.

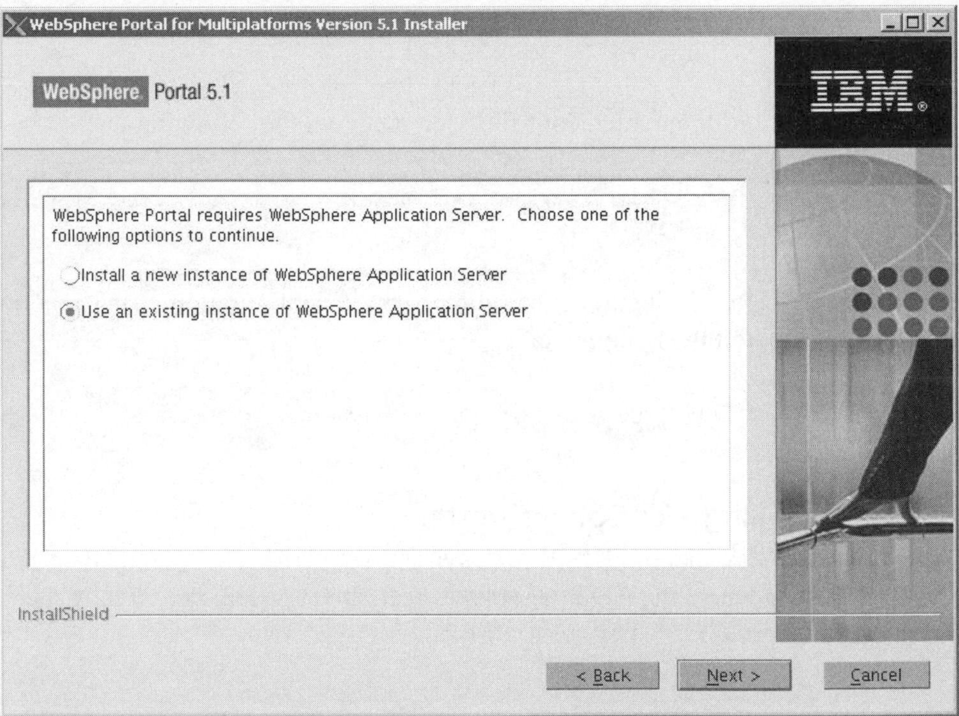

Figure 3.37: Choosing the option of using an existing instance of WebSphere Application Server.

7. The installer will attempt to locate existing instances of WebSphere Application Server, as shown in Figure 3.38. If it does not find any, use the **Browse** button to find and then specify the location of your existing WebSphere Application Server. Click **Next**.

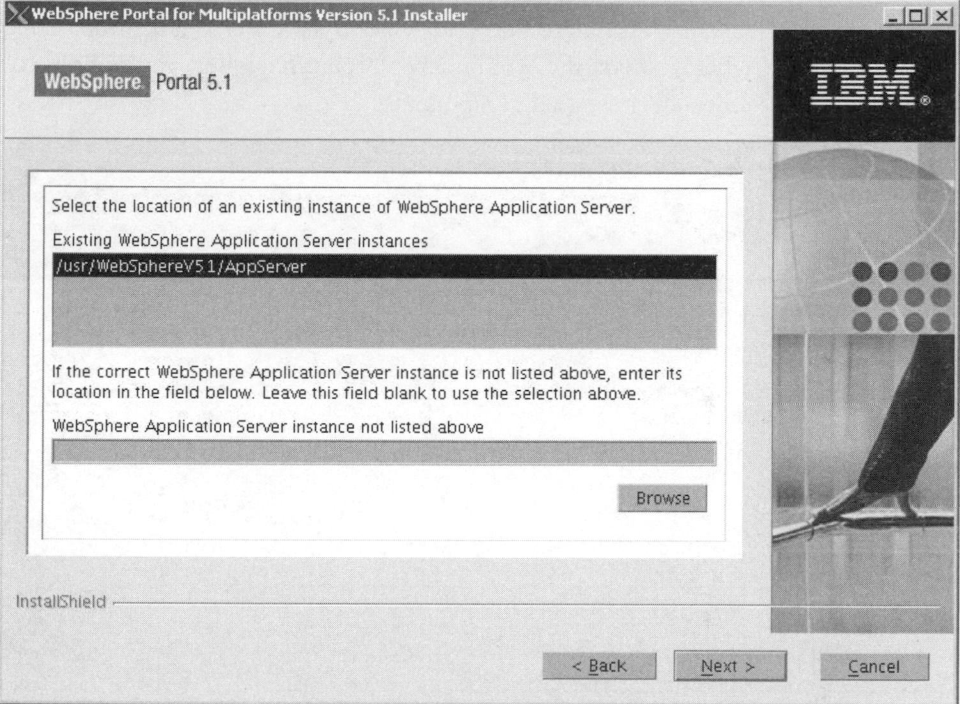

Figure 3.38: Specifying the existing instance of WebSphere Application Server.

8. Assuming that the specified WebSphere Application Server meets all the requirements, you can continue on with the installation of WebSphere Portal V5.1. If not, you might see a message as seen in Figure 3.39.

Figure 3.39: Error message indicating a non-compliant instance of WebSphere Application Server.

9. The installer asks for the installation directory for WebSphere Portal server. Specify the location where you want the software to be installed.

10. You will be asked for the WebSphere Portal administrator user ID and password. We recommend using wpsadmin. This can always be changed later.

11. On the confirmation screen, click **Next**. But notice the difference in Figure 3.40. compared to a standard installation. The installer will only install WebSphere Portal and WebSphere Personalization. Consequently, when you run the WebSphere Portal uninstaller, you only have the option to uninstall these two components.

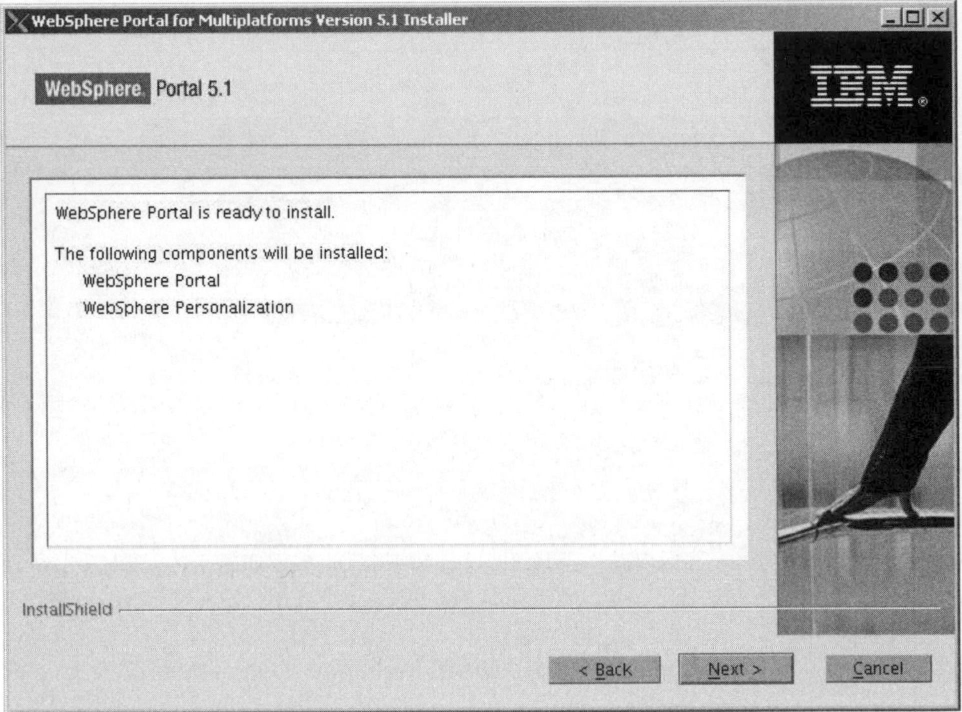

Figure 3.40: Confirming the WebSphere Portal components to be installed.

12. When the installation is completed, click **Finish** on the final screen.

Post-Installation Steps

No mandatory post-installation steps are required. However, we recommend doing the following:

1. To conserve resources, remember to stop the Default Server named *server1* via the WebSphere Application Server Administrative Console.

2. Verify that you can log into the portal by going to the URL http://<HOST_NAME>/wps/myportal. Log in as the portal administrator, using wpsadmin as the user ID and password.

3. Run the backupConfig command found in <WAS_HOME>/bin directory to get a snapshot of the WebSphere system. It is a simple utility that backs up the node configuration to a file. We prefer to use the nostop option, so that the servers are not stopped while the configuration is saved.

4. Execute the following in a command window:

```
backupConfig -nostop
```

   This will generate a zip file with a unique timestamp, as seen in Figure 3.41.

```
Select Command Prompt

C:\WebSphere5\AppServer\bin>backupConfig -nostop
ADMU0116I: Tool information is being logged in file
           C:\WebSphere5\AppServer\logs\backupConfig.log
ADMU5001I: Backing up config directory C:\WebSphere5\AppServer\config to file
           C:\WebSphere5\AppServer\bin\WebSphereConfig_2004-07-24.zip
ADMU5002I: 1,179 files successfully backed up
```

Figure 3.41: Output from executing the backupConfig command.

Database Configuration

Remember, WebSphere Portal gets installed with the Cloudscape database by default. If you want to use another, more robust, relational database, you have to manually transfer the information. This is done via the WPSconfig utility found in <WPS_HOME>/config directory. The WPSconfig utility uses wpconfig.properties as its input. That properties file is also found in <WPS_HOME>/config directory. The default wpconfig.properties file is listed in Appendix B.

Tip: Use the helper files to import database information from Cloudscape to other more commonly used relational databases. Make a backup copy of the configuration file before modifying it.

WebSphere Portal provides helper properties files that can be used to transfer database information from Cloudscape to other databases or to configure LDAP servers. These files, see Figure 3.42, are found in <WPS_HOME>/config/helpers directory.

helpers

Select an item to view its description.

See also:
My Documents
My Network Places
My Computer

Name	Size
bpeconfig.properties	13 KB
config_http.properties	3 KB
security_active_directory.properties	11 KB
security_disable.properties	3 KB
security_domino.properties	11 KB
security_ibm_dir_server.properties	11 KB
security_nds.properties	11 KB
security_novell.properties	10 KB
security_sun_one.properties	11 KB
transfer_db2.properties	8 KB
transfer_db2_zos.properties	9 KB
transfer_oracle.properties	8 KB
transfer_sqlserver.properties	8 KB

Figure 3.42: Helper property files provided by WebSphere Portal.

Transferring the information from one database to another involves four steps. In this case, we are transferring a new installation configuration which is contained in Cloudscape to DB2 which is the default setting in wpconfig.properties. Make sure you are in the <WPS_HOME>/config directory.

1. First, the databases have to be created in DB2. That can be done manually, or the following four tasks would have to be run:

```
WPSconfig action-create-database

WPSconfig action-create-local-database-jcr

WPSconfig action-create-pzn-databases-db2
```

2. Validate the database connection to the various WebSphere Portal related tables as shown. This is an optional step.

```
WPSconfig validate-database-connection-wps

WPSconfig validate-database-connection-pzn

WPSconfig validate-database-connection-fdbk
```

3. Modify the parameters in the helper properties file to suit your new database and run WPSconfig again, this time to import the contents of the helper file into wpconfig.properties. Our command looked like this:

```
WPSconfig DparentProperties="C:/WebSphere/PortalServer/config
/helpers/transfer_db2.properties" -DsaveParentProperties=true
```

4. Export the current configuration from Cloudscape by executing the database-transfer task.

```
WPSconfig database-transfer
```

Look for BUILD SUCCESSFUL message.

LDAP Configuration

The installation process of WebSphere Portal does not deal with security. Enabling WebSphere security and configuring a LDAP Server is part of the post-installation steps. Albeit an optional step, it is recommended in production portal environments. WebSphere Portal supports all the common LDAP servers, specifically:

- IBM Tivoli Directory Server (used to be known as IBM Directory Server)
- Domino Directory
- Sun ONE Directory Server (formerly known as iPlanet Directory)
- Windows Active Directory
- Novell eDirectory (part of Novell Directory Services or NDS)

Tivoli Directory Server Installation Steps

Installation of IBM Tivoli Directory Server V5.2, henceforth referred to as TDS, is presented in this section because it comes with the WebSphere Portal product. For the Windows platform, TDS is found on CD8-1.

1. Invoke **setup.exe** from the ismp folder of the TDS CD.

2. Select the language, which is English by default, and click **OK** to kick off the installation wizard.

3. Click **Next** on the Welcome Screen. Accept the License agreement and click **Next**.

4. The installation wizard will identify software components that are already installed on the system, such as Global Security Kit (GSKit) and/or DB2, as shown in Figure 3.43. Click **Next**.

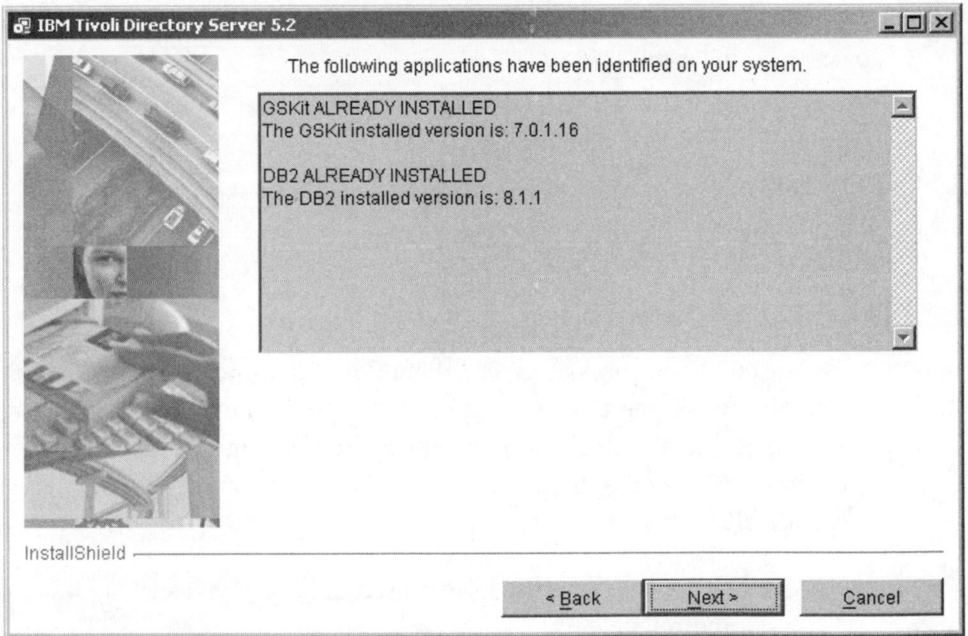

Figure 3.43: TDS installation wizard identifying applications already installed.

5. Enter the full directory path where you want TDS to be installed.

6. Choose English, or whatever language you prefer, for TDS.

7. The features selection screen is important. De-select the option to install IBM WebSphere Application Server–Express 5.0.2 because WebSphere Application Server should already be installed as part of the WebSphere Portal installation. See Figure 3.44.

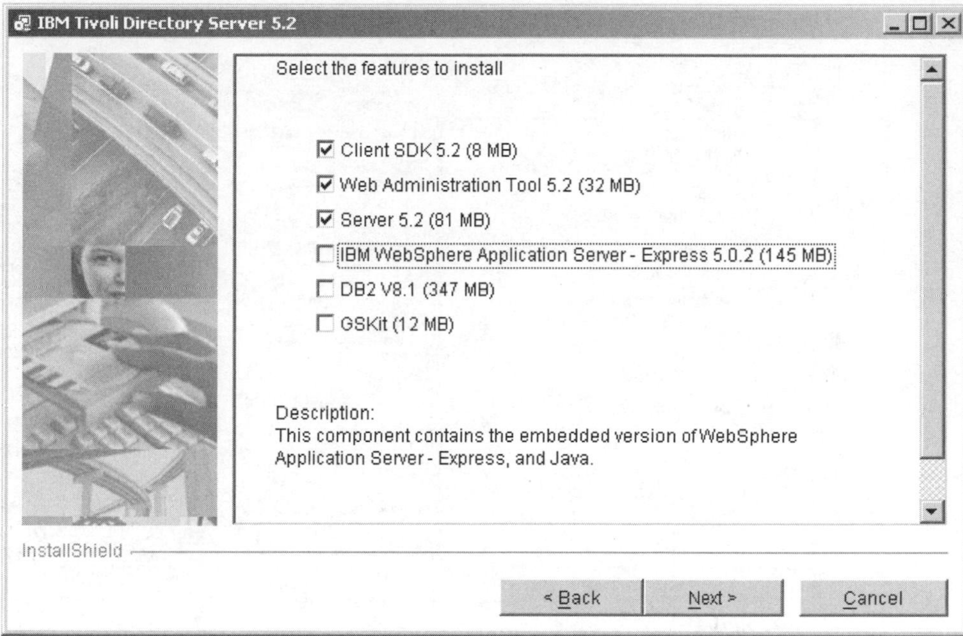

Figure 3.44: Choosing features during TDS installation.

8. Click **Next** a couple of times and then finally on the confirmation screen. When the installation is **Finish**ed, the Windows system has to be restarted.

9. On the Windows platform, upon a system reboot, the Directory Server Configuration Tool (ldapxcfg) is automatically kicked off. This tool is used to set the administrator password, configure the database, and import and export LDIF data.

   You can also invoke the Directory Configuration Tool via the Start Menu:

   Start → Programs → IBM Tivoli Directory Server 5.2 → Directory Configuration

   On Unix platforms, bring up the configuration tool by invoking ldapxcfg.sh.

10. The first task is to set the Administrator DN (Distinguished Name) and password. From the task list choose **Administration DN/password**. It is common to choose cn=root as the DN. Enter and confirm a password, as shown in Figure 3.45. Click **OK**.

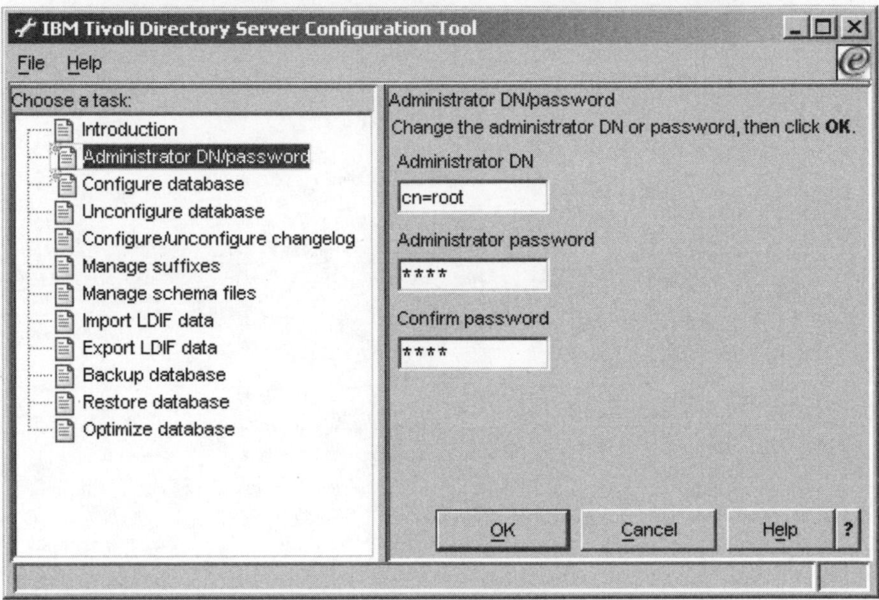

Figure 3.45: Setting the Administrator DN and password.

11. Click **OK** again in the successfully updated message window.

12. You then have to **Configure a database**. Since this is a brand new installation, choose **Create a new database**.

13. Specify the User ID and Password of the user who is allowed to configure a database in DB2.

14. Then specify a **Database name** (such as ldapdb) and choose to **Create a universal DB2 database** supporting UTF-8 and UCS-2.

15. Specify the location of the database. Remember, this database will grow as the number of portal users increases. On the confirmation screen (shown in Figure 3.46), click **Finish**. Look for the *IBM Tivoli Directory Server Configuration complete* message. Click **Close**.

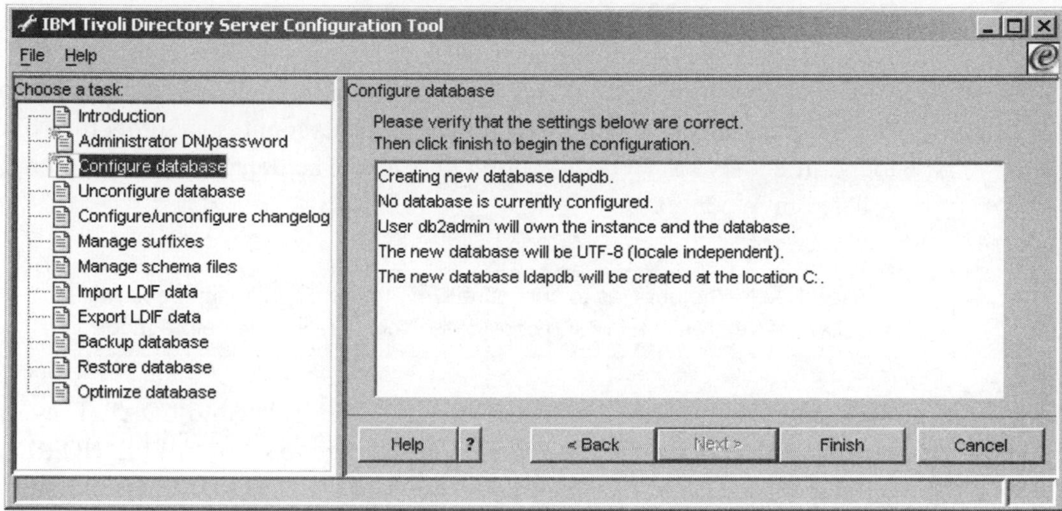

Figure 3.46: Settings for a new database.

16. The next task is to create a suffix that matches the WebSphere Portal Domain. Select **Manage suffixes** from the task list.

17. Enter the suffix, click on **Add**. In our test environment, we added dc=Encinitas,dc=ibm,dc=com. The new suffix gets added to the list of Current suffix DNs. Do not forget to click **OK** to save the new suffix.

18. The final task is to import a LDIF file. Remember to modify the supplied PortalUsers.ldif file to match the newly created suffix. In the Directory Configuration Tool, select **Import LDIF data**. Specify the location of the ldif file, choose **Standard import**. Scroll down and click **Import**.

19. Verify that six entries were successfully added. Click **Clear results** and then **Close** the screen.

20. Start the Tivoli Directory Server by either going to the Services Panel or invoking the **ibmslapd** executable found in the <TDS_HOME>/bin directory

---

Tip: After the Windows system is restarted, the IBM Tivoli Directory Admin Daemon V5.2 is automatically started. Remember to start the IBM Tivoli Directory Server V5.2 process manually.

Configuring LDAP Server

WebSphere Portal is configured to use a LDAP server with the help of the WPSconfig utility found in <WPS_HOME>/config directory. As noted before, the WPSconfig utility uses wpconfig.properties as its input. That properties file is also found in the <WPS_HOME>/config directory. The default wpconfig.properties file is listed in Appendix B.

Tip: Use the helper files to configure WebSphere Portal to interface with a LDAP server. Make a backup copy of the configuration file before modifying it.

WebSphere Portal provides helper properties files related to LDAP. They start with the name security, as seen in Figure 3.42, and are found in <WPS_HOME>/config/helpers directory. Two security helper files are used to turn on and turn off global security in WebSphere Application Server.

Configuring WebSphere Portal with a LDAP server is a six-step process. In this example, we enable security in WebSphere Portal using the Tivoli Directory Server on the Windows platform. Before you begin, make sure the application server, server1, is running and that the application server, WebSphere_Portal is stopped. Also ensure that you are in the <WPS_HOME>/config directory.

1. Modify the parameters in the helper properties file to suit your LDAP server and run WPSconfig to import the contents of the helper file into wpconfig.properties. Our command looked like this:

```
WPSconfig DparentProperties="C:/WebSphere/PortalServer/config/
helpers/security_ibm_dir_server.properties" -DsaveParent
Properties=true
```

2. Validate connection to the LDAP server by running the validate-ldap task:

```
WPSconfig validate-ldap
```

   If all goes well, you should see the BUILD SUCCESSFUL message

3. If WebSphere Application Server security is enabled, run the following task to enable portal server security:

```
WPSconfig secure-portal-ldap
```

4. If WebSphere Application Server security is not enabled, run the following task to enable WebSphere global security:

```
WPSconfig enable-security-ldap
```

In the case of a brand new installation, because security is not yet enabled anywhere, you will use the enable-secuirty-ldap option. In either case, you should see the BUILD SUCCESSFUL message. If the build fails, fix the erroneous attribute in wpconfig.properties and rerun the WPSconfig command.

5. Stop and restart application server - server1. Because security is now configured in WebSphere Application Server, when you stop any server, you will be challenged. The easiest thing is to invoke the command line option as shown:

```
<WAS_HOME>/bin/stopServer server1 -user wpsbind -password wpsbind
```

6. Similarly, stop and start *WebSphere_Portal*.

Verify Security Is Working

If you bring up the WebSphere Administrative Console as usual, the URL gets redirected to https://<HOST_NAME>:9044/admin/logon.jsp, and you will be challenged for a user ID and password. Enter wpsbind for both user ID and password. If you are validated, then security is correctly set up in WebSphere Application Server.

As always, access the portal login page through the following URL: http://<HOST_NAME>/wps/myportal. Enter wpsadmin for both user ID and password. If you are validated, then security is properly set up in WebSphere Portal to use a LDAP server, in this case IBM Tivoli Directory Server.

Tip: Remember to create a backup of the files wpconfig.properties and <WAS_HOME>/config/cells/<NODE_NAME>/security.xml.

Other Ways of Installing WebSphere Portal

Installing Using the Console Interface

The WebSphere Portal installation program provides a console interface, which let you perform an interactive installation from a command prompt without the need for a graphics terminal. To launch the installation program in a console mode, enter the following in a command window:

```
install -console
```

The initial screen is shown in Figure 3.47. At any time during the install process, enter 3 to Cancel.

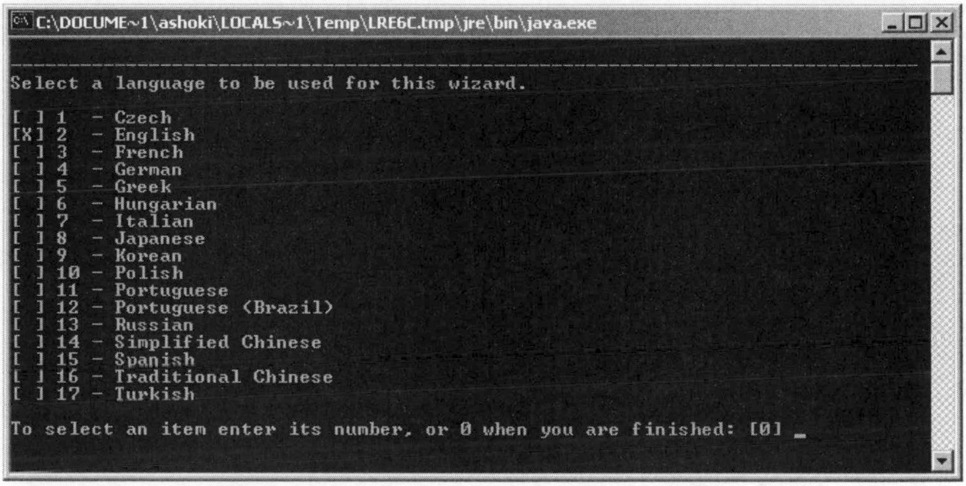

```
C:\DOCUME~1\ashoki\LOCALS~1\Temp\LRE6C.tmp\jre\bin\java.exe

Select a language to be used for this wizard.

[ ] 1  - Czech
[X] 2  - English
[ ] 3  - French
[ ] 4  - German
[ ] 5  - Greek
[ ] 6  - Hungarian
[ ] 7  - Italian
[ ] 8  - Japanese
[ ] 9  - Korean
[ ] 10 - Polish
[ ] 11 - Portuguese
[ ] 12 - Portuguese (Brazil)
[ ] 13 - Russian
[ ] 14 - Simplified Chinese
[ ] 15 - Spanish
[ ] 16 - Traditional Chinese
[ ] 17 - Turkish

To select an item enter its number, or 0 when you are finished: [0] _
```

Figure 3.47: Choosing features during a console mode installation.

Tip: Copy the contents of the setup CD to the hard drive on Unix systems and invoke install.sh from a relative path. For example, go to the /tmp directory and invoke /cdSetup/install.sh –console.

Installing Using a Response File

In environments where WebSphere Portal needs to be configured, the graphical method of installation is not recommended. The recommendation is to create a response file that has already worked on one system and duplicate that file on other hardware. The WebSphere Portal installation program comes with a default response file (installresponse.txt) that is found on the root directory of the Setup CD.

When you run the installation program on a system, the responses are gathered and automatically stored in <WPS_HOME>/log/responselog.txt. Copy that response file to the system where you want to install WebSphere Portal again, and invoke the install command as such:

```
install -option <PATH_TO_RESPONSE_FILE>
```

Make sure you modify certain parameters, such as the machine's hostname. Quite a few parameters can be specified in the response file or directly on the command line. Please refer to the product InfoCenter for all the details.

Uninstalling WebSphere Portal

Before you start uninstalling WebSphere Portal, consider the following options:

- Do you want to save any of the installed portlets?
- Do you want to save any of the themes or skins you have created?
- Will you be reinstalling?
- Do you want to disable global security within WebSphere Application Server?

Note: WebSphere Application Server and the WebSphere_Portal application should be running before starting the uninstallation process. If the WebSphere Administrative Console is open, close it.

It is possible to uninstall WebSphere Portal in more than one way. The easiest way is to run the uninstall script found in the <WPS_HOME>/uninstall directory. Or, on Windows systems, you can use the Add/Remove Software option in the Control Panel and, on Unix systems, you can use the Package Remove command (pkgrm).

1. Go to the uninstall folder of the WebSphere Portal installation directory and execute the uninstall script.

On Windows systems, you invoke uninstall.bat:

```
C:\<WPS_HOME>\uninstall> uninstall
```

On Unix systems, make sure the DISPLAY environment variable is set before running the uninstall.sh scrip

```
# <WPS_HOME>/uninstall.sh
```

2. Choose the language that is to be used by the uninstaller; click **OK**.
3. On the Welcome screen, click **Next**.
4. If you had installed WebSphere Portal and WebSphere Application Server via the install wizard, you will be presented with the option to install only WebSphere Portal or WebSphere Portal and WebSphere Application Server, as shown in Figure 3.48. Select the option and click **Next**.

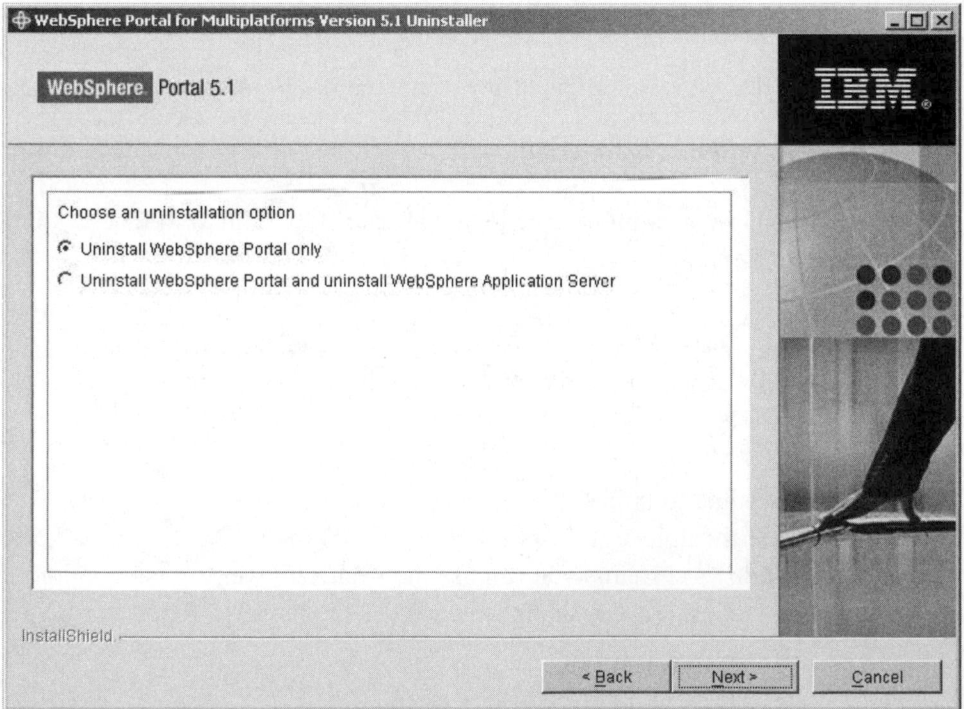

Figure 3.48: Screen showing the uninstallation options.

If you had installed WebSphere Portal on an existing instance of WebSphere Application Server, you will only have the option to uninstall WebSphere Portal.

5. Verify the options on the confirmation screen, as seen in Figure 3.49, and then click **Next**.

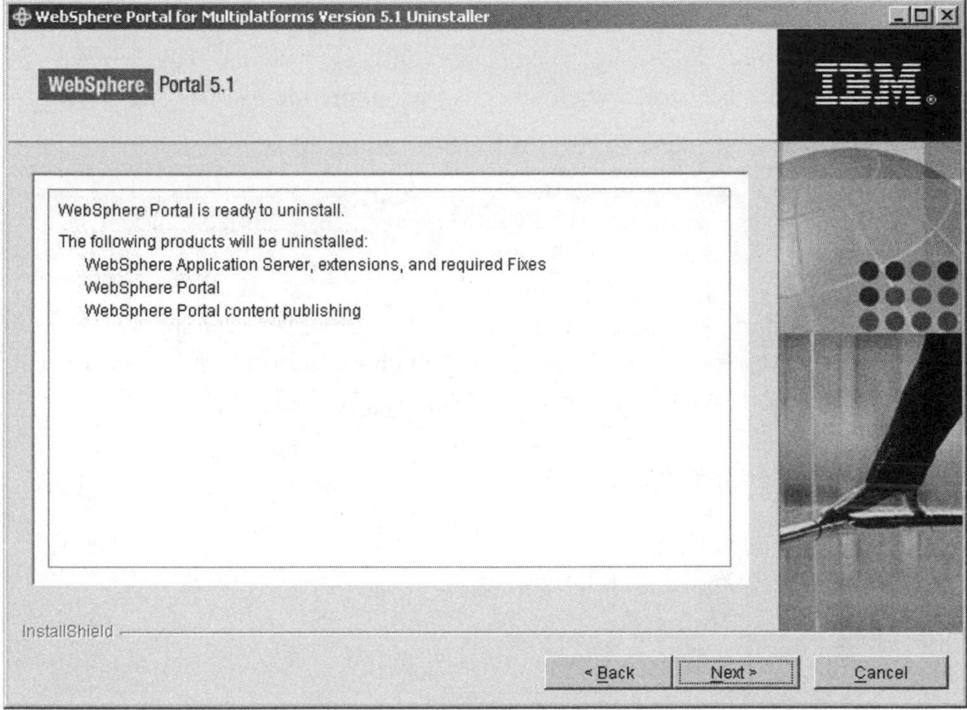

Figure 3.49: Screen showing the software components that will be uninstalled.

6. When the uninstallation process is complete, click **Finish**.

Tip: Regardless of how you uninstall Portal server, we recommend bringing up the WebSphere Administrative Console and making sure that all Portal Server–related components have been removed. If not, stop them and remove them manually.

Starting/Stopping WebSphere Portal Server

The most convenient way to start or stop WebSphere Portal server is via the WebSphere Administrative Console. In non-GUI environments, you could also use the command line commands, startServer and stopServer, that are found in <WAS_HOME>/bin directory. The syntax for those commands is:

```
startServer server1 or WebSphere_Portal

stopServer server1 or WebSphere_Portal
```

Remember to use the .sh extension on Unix systems. If WebSphere Global Security is enabled, then you have to supply the user ID and password to stop the server thus:

```
stopServer WebSphere_Portal -user wpsbind -password wpsbind
```

On Windows, you can use the Start Menu to start WebSphere Application Server and WebSphere Portal Server. If you chose to install them as services, then you can start and stop those processes from the Services panel.

The startup sequence is:

- Database Server
- External Web Server
- LDAP Server
- WebSphere Application Servcr
- WebSphere Portal Server

Door Closings

This chapter covers several possible installation configurations. As you have seen, the multiplatform installation wizard is a very versatile tool for installation, and it can be run any number of times on all platforms. The base Portal Server configuration can be installed using it. For advanced configurations, you have to use the installation wizards of the individual software components.

A lot more installation scenarios are explained in the WebSphere Portal Product InfoCenter, not to mention the fact that it can be also be installed on HP/UX and z/OS platforms.

Chapter 4

Customizing the Portal

If you have completed the steps in the previous chapters, WebSphere Portal is installed, and you can see the default welcome portal page with the portlets. Rather boring, you say? We agree. After all, the very essence of having a portal server is customizing and personalizing the Web site so that users feel welcome. Generally, as a first step, customers want to give the portal a pleasing and consistent corporate look. In WebSphere Portal terminology, this is called *customizing the portal*, and it is the subject of this chapter. The next step is usually providing a personal experience for each portal user or allowing an individual user to give it a radical look. That is called *personalizing the portal*, and that is explained in the next chapter.

Default Portal Look

WebSphere Portal 5.1 builds on the concept of *pages* and pages having nested pages. The user's access rights determine which pages get displayed. Each page can contain one or more pages, and only users who have adequate rights can see those pages. Pages can contain column containers, row containers, and portlets. You can populate row or column containers with portlets or other containers.

When you enter the following URL in a Web browser, the "Welcome" page shown in Figure 4.1 should appear:

```
http://<HOST_NAME>:9080/wps/portal
```

The default portal page displays a top-level Portal Menu bar with a question mark icon denoting the Help Menu and three links: *I forgot my password, Sign up*, and *Log in*. Then there is the Place Bar, with the *Welcome* label.

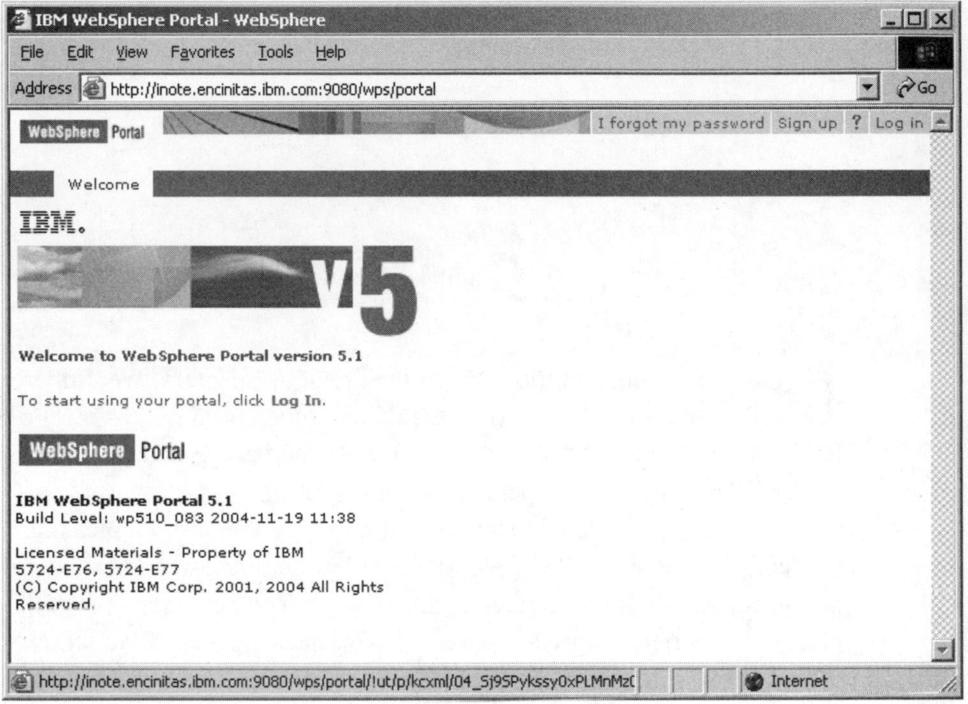

Figure 4.1: The default WebSphere Portal "Welcome" page.

The Welcome Page displays two portlets: the Welcome portlet, and the About WebSphere Portal portlet that shows the portal server version. It is not obvious, but these portlets are arranged in rows and columns on that page.

Table 4.1 lists the general portal icons and what they stand for. Icons can be modified, added, or removed. Almost everything that you see out-of-the-box is customizable.

Table 4.1: Portal Icons on the Welcome Page

Icon	Functionality
🔧	Show Tools
?	Help
▶	Next tab
◀	Previous tab
🔍	Search
🔍	Search Results

"Forgot Password" Feature

If a registered user has forgotten her password, clicking the "I forgot my password" link brings up the page shown in Figure 4.2. This page is a placeholder for a mechanism to retrieve a password. The actual retrieval mechanism might be a telephone call to the portal administrator or an e-mail notification to the support person.

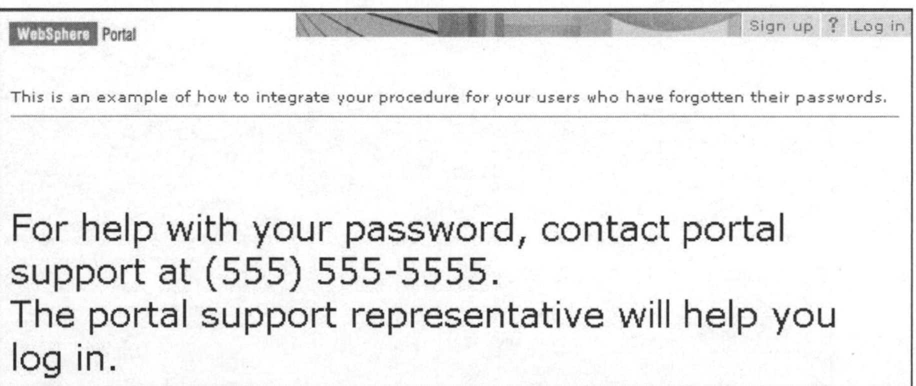

Figure 4.2: Placeholder screen for the "Forgot Password" functionality.

WebSphere Portal does not mandate what should be done about such features as forgotten passwords. Instead, it offers customization opportunities based on an organization's procedures. Some people see this as a weakness, but it is actually one of the strengths of the product—customization to the nth degree.

Self-Registration Feature

If available, new users can click on the Sign up link and register themselves with the portal. In some situations, this icon could be disabled and not shown. For example, some organizations prefer to control who signs up for their portals. Others might use intranet portals, wherein all employees are automatically given access to a portal, so there is no need to sign up. Where available, this portal feature works as follows:

1. The sign-up form shown in Figure 4.3 is presented when the user clicks the Sign up link. The fields displayed in this form are normally mapped to the fields in an LDAP directory server. Typically; the inetOrgPerson Schema in the LDAP directory is used. Some companies might choose to use other LDAP Schemas, such as ePerson or any other variation.

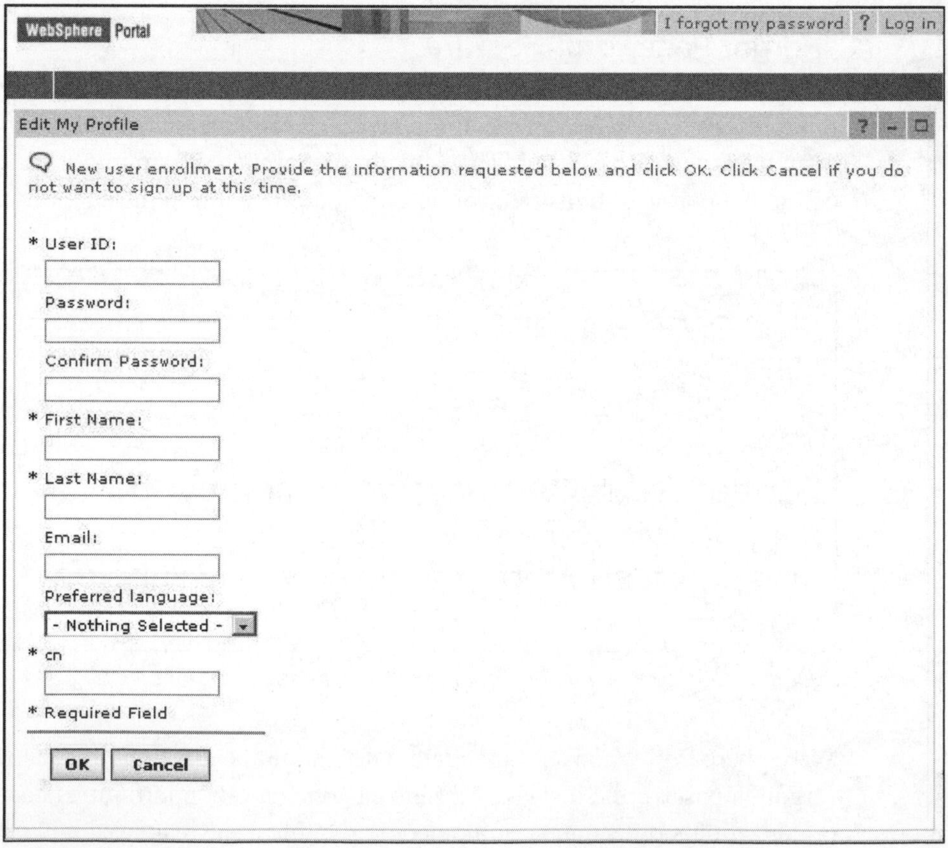

WebSphere Portal
I forgot my password ? Log in
Edit My Profile
New user enrollment. Provide the information requested below and click OK. Click Cancel if you do not want to sign up at this time.
* User ID:
Password:
Confirm Password:
* First Name:
* Last Name:
Email:
Preferred language:
- Nothing Selected -
* cn
* Required Field
OK Cancel

Figure 4.3: The new user sign-up screen.

2. Of the roughly 120 fields in the inetOrgPerson Schema, the most common seven fields are used by default. These fields can be replaced, labeled differently, removed, or added to. An asterisk indicates a required field that must have a value.

3. The user can create his own user ID, specify a password, and enter a first name and last name.

4. The password must be at least five characters long.

5. If no language is selected, you get the default language of your Web browser. Look at the language resolution rules listed below. WebSphere Portal offers language support for Arabic, Brazilian Portuguese, Czech, Danish, Dutch, English, Finnish, French, German, Greek, Hebrew, Hungarian, Italian, Japanese, Korean, Norwegian, Polish, Portuguese, Romanian, Russian, Simplified Chinese, Spanish, Swedish, Thai, Traditional Chinese, Turkish, and Ukrainian.

6. After you enter values in all the fields, click **OK**. If the registration is successful, you will get the congratulatory message shown in Figure 4.4.

7. All field values, except the user ID, can be changed after a successful registration. That is done by clicking on the Edit my profile link, which is visible after the user logs in.

Language Resolution Rules from the Product InfoCenter

1. If the user has logged in, the portal displays in the preferred language selected by the user.

2. If no preferred user language can be found, the portal looks for the language defined in the user's browser. If the portal supports that language, it displays the content in that language. If the browser has more than one language defined, the portal uses the first language in the list to display the content.

3. If no browser language can be found, for example if the browser used does not send a language, the portal resorts to its own default language.

4. If the user has a portlet that does not support the language that was determined by the previous steps, that portlet is shown in its own default language.

Help Feature

The Help icon (the question mark) on the menu bar brings up the online documentation. This documentation is well-organized and very informative. This is not to be confused with the product documentation, more commonly referred to as the InfoCenter. A third level of help also is available, the portlet-specific help discussed later in this chapter.

You can view the portal online help by clicking the question-mark icon on the portal menu bar. You should see the online help displayed in a new browser window. Figure 4.4 shows the online help in the Greek language, thus giving a whole new meaning to *help*!

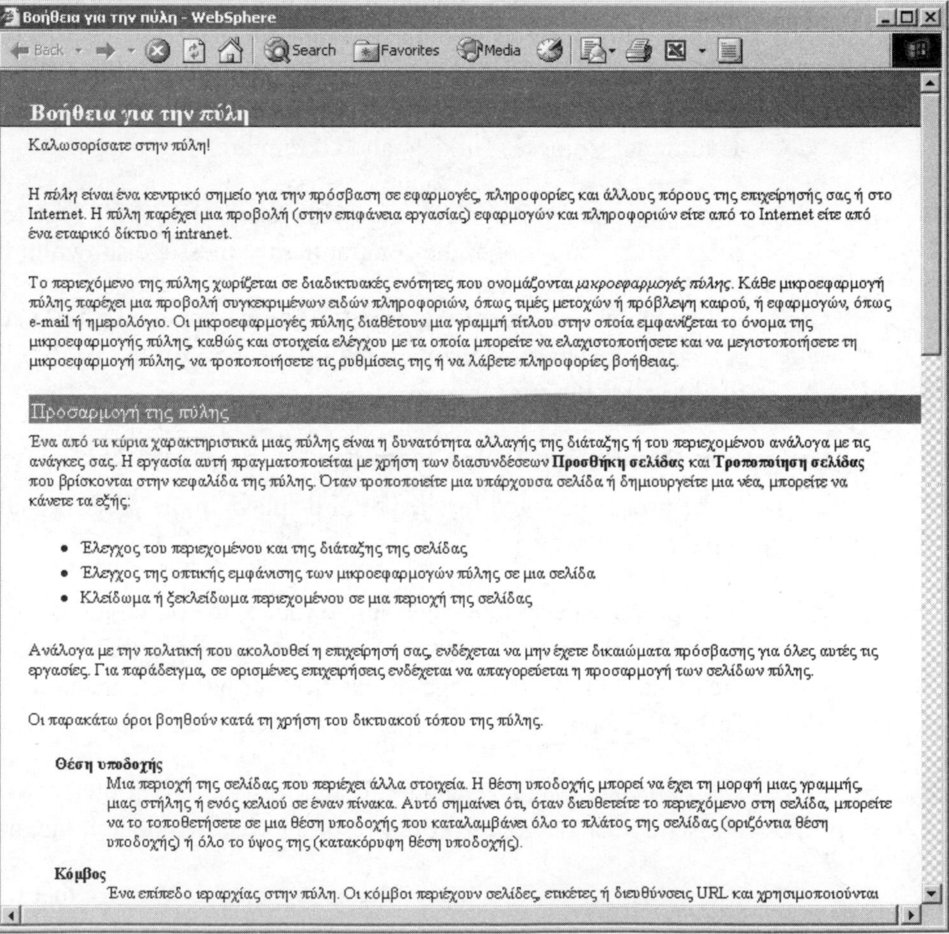

Figure 4.4: WebSphere Portal online help in Greek.

Login Feature

On the base portal page, click **Log in**, on the far right link to get to the portal login page. Another way of getting to the login screen is by entering the following URL in a browser:

```
http://<HOST_NAME>:9080/wps/myportal
```

Registered users can use their User ID and Password to log in to the portal. Figure 4.5 shows the portal administrator logging into the portal.

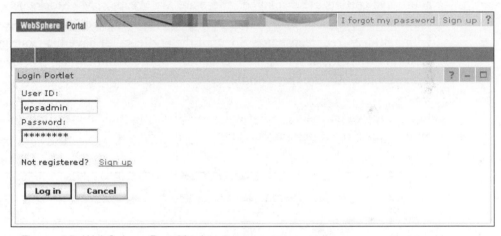

Figure 4.5: WebSphere Portal login screen.

In a brand new WebSphere Portal installation, two system users are created: wpsadmin and wpsbind. Their default passwords are also wpsadmin and wpsbind, respectively. During the installation process, you can create different default system users and passwords. These can be changed later. By default, the portal ID of wpsadmin is configured with an administrative role. The wpsbind ID, on the other hand, is used when binding with the LDAP server, as in the case of logging into the WebSphere Administrative Console.

Tip: In production environments, you should change the passwords for the two default users, wpsadmin and wpsbind.

Log On and Off as the Portal Administrator

On the login page, enter **wpsadmin** for the user ID and password, as shown in Figure 4.5. Then, press **Enter** or click the **Log In** button.

Out-of-the-box, the only indication you have that the portal administrator has logged in is the Administration link in the portal menu bar and the Assign Permissions link in the navigation bar, as shown in Figure 4.6.

In addition to the two portlets—Welcome and About WebSphere Portal—four additional portlets are displayed. These are My Weather, My Stocks, My News, and Bookmarks. The Weather, News, and Stocks content feeds come with a 30-day free license use. Some of the portlets will have the Configure icon (the wrench), denoting the fact that the portal administrator has the authority to configure these portlets.

In the following sections, we use the My Stocks portlet and the Reminder portlet to explain functions surrounding portlets.

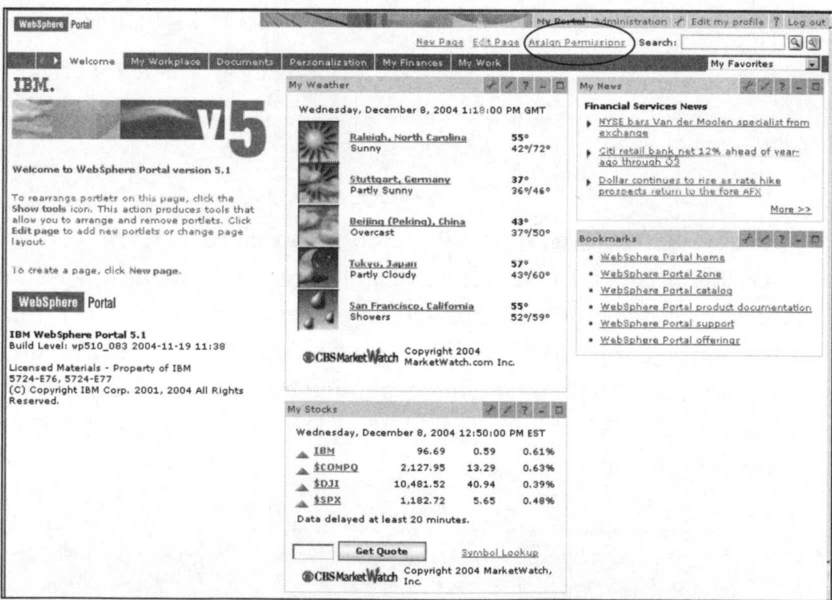

Figure 4.6: WebSphere Portal's "Welcome" page for the portal administrator.

An administrator has all access rights within the portal. You can delegate some or all administrator privileges to other users. Users who have been given administrative rights will also see those links. Any user who has administrative privileges can, within certain limits, also modify the content within the portlets.

The Administrative functions are covered in various sections in the book. A snapshot of all available functionality, from managing Pages to managing Virtual Portals, is shown in Figure 4.7.

Figure 4.7: Snapshot of available administrative functions in WebSphere Portal.

If you click the Log out link, the currently logged in portal user will be logged off, and that session will be properly terminated. You end up back at the default Welcome page.

If no activity occurs in your session, it will time out and automatically log you off. By default, the session timeout value is 1,800 seconds and is set in WebSphere Application Server. As with everything else in WebSphere Portal, that value can be changed.

To log back in, do not use the browser's Back button. Enter your user ID and password and click **Log in**.

Default Portlets

As mentioned, all unauthenticated users see the Welcome page in Figure 4.1, whereas the page in Figure 4.6 is what the portal administrator sees. Portlets can be moved and minimized, and their content can be changed. These changes can be done programmatically or by way of the portal UI.

If you notice, portlets have certain icons surrounding them. The icons related with portlets are listed in Table 4.2.

Table 4.2: Portlet-Related Icons

Icon	Functionality
☐	Maximize
‒	Minimize
?	Help
☐	Configure
✎	Edit
◀	Move back to previous state
🗗	Restore
	Functionality Available when Show tools Is Clicked
🗑	Delete
▼	Move portlet down
◀	Move portlet to the left
▶	Move portlet to the right
▲	Move portlet up

Tip: If you hover over an icon, its function is displayed.

To see how the icons work, follow these steps while logged into the portal as an administrator:

1. In the Welcome page, click the **Maximize** icon of the My Stocks portlet. The portlet will fill the whole page, as shown in Figure 4.8. This functionality is useful when you are working exclusively within a portlet for an extended time and would rather have a "magnified" view of it.

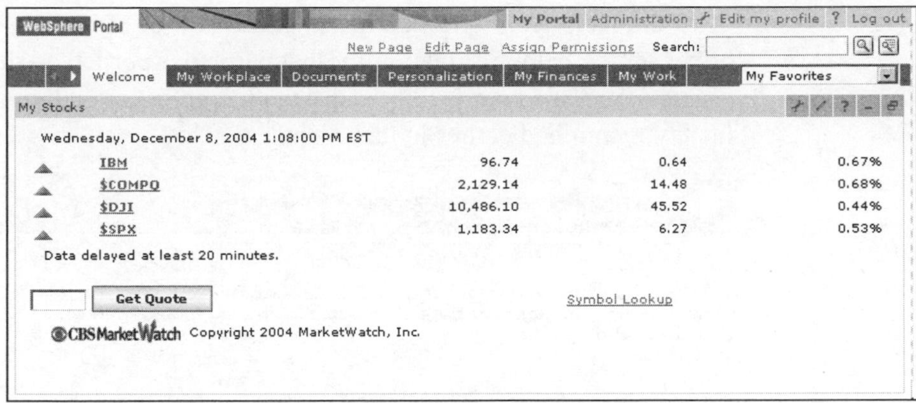

Figure 4.8: Maximized view of My Stocks portlet.

2. To go back to the original view, click the **Restore** icon.

3. Click the **Minimize** icon of the My Stocks portlet to shrink that portlet down to just its title bar, as shown in Figure 4.9. This is useful in scenarios when you want to work on certain portlet applications and do not want to be bothered by others. This is one of the salient features of portlets and portals.

Figure 4.9: WebSphere Portal's "Welcome" page with My Stocks portlet minimized.

4. Click the **Help** icon (question mark) in the skin of My Stocks portlet. This brings up the help information for that particular portlet, as shown in Figure 4.10. This help facility is different from the overall portal help facility mentioned earlier in this chapter.

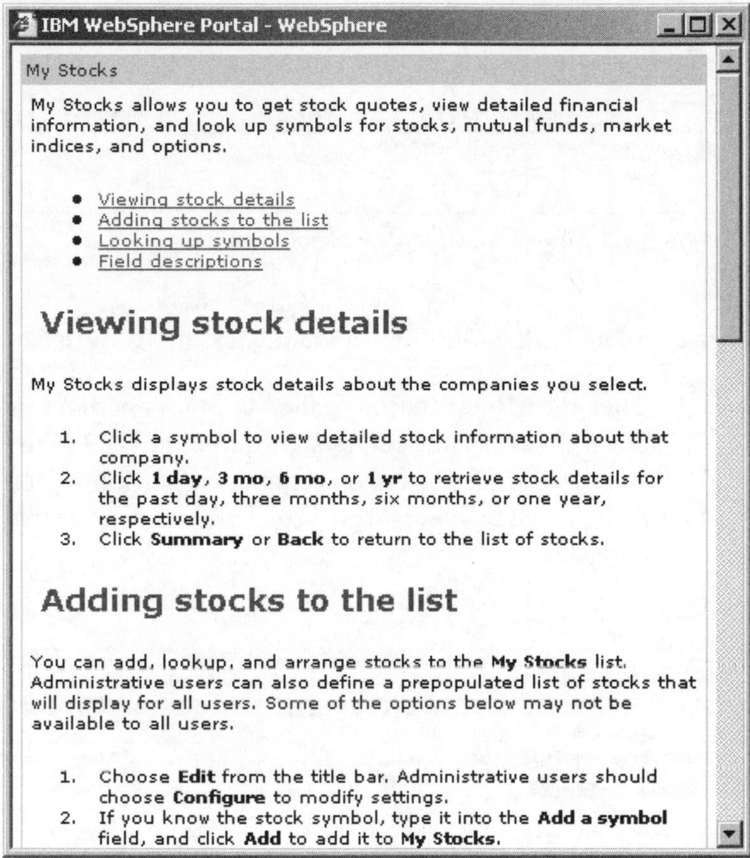

Figure 4.10: Context-sensitive help for My Stocks portlet.

5. Close the portlet Help Window. Restore the portlet back to its original size by clicking the **Restore** icon.

6. Click the **Edit** icon (pencil) in My Stocks portlet to get the portlet's edit screen, as shown in Figure 4.11. Here, you can customize certain attributes of the portlet.

Note: The portlet edit feature is available only in certain portlets, and only to users who are given the proper access rights by the portal administrator. Notice that the About WebSphere Portal portlet does not have an edit icon because it is simply displaying static text. A portal user can customize nothing there.

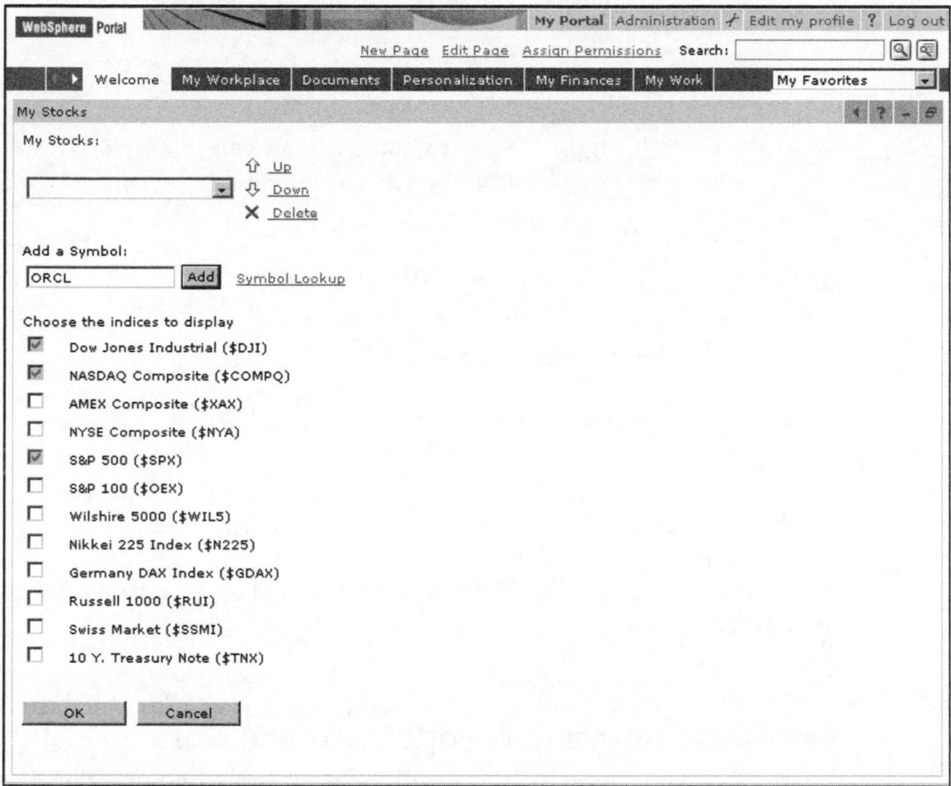

Figure 4.11: Editing the My Stocks portlet.

7. On the edit screen of My Stocks portlet, type in **ORCL** in the Add a Symbol field and click **Add**.

8. You could add more stock symbols if you wish. When done, click **OK**. The My Stocks portlet should now be displaying another stock symbol, as shown in Figure 4.12.

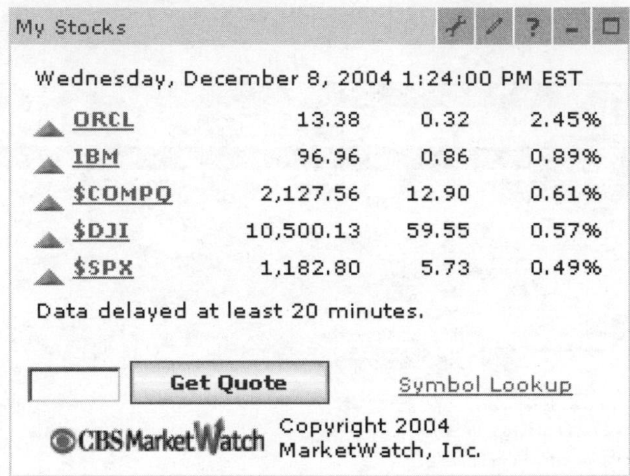

Figure 4.12: A modified My Stocks portlet.

9. Click **Log out** to log off as the portal administrator.

Beware: If the portal administrator makes a change to a portlet, everybody who logs into the portal and who has the right to view that portlet, will see that change.

Self-Registering a New Portal User and More

What kind of privileges do regular users have? Let's find out. The easiest way to do that is by registering a new user, as follows:

1. Click the **Sign up** link.

2. You will be asked to provide information about the new portal user. Fill in the fields as shown in Figure 4.13, and click **OK**.

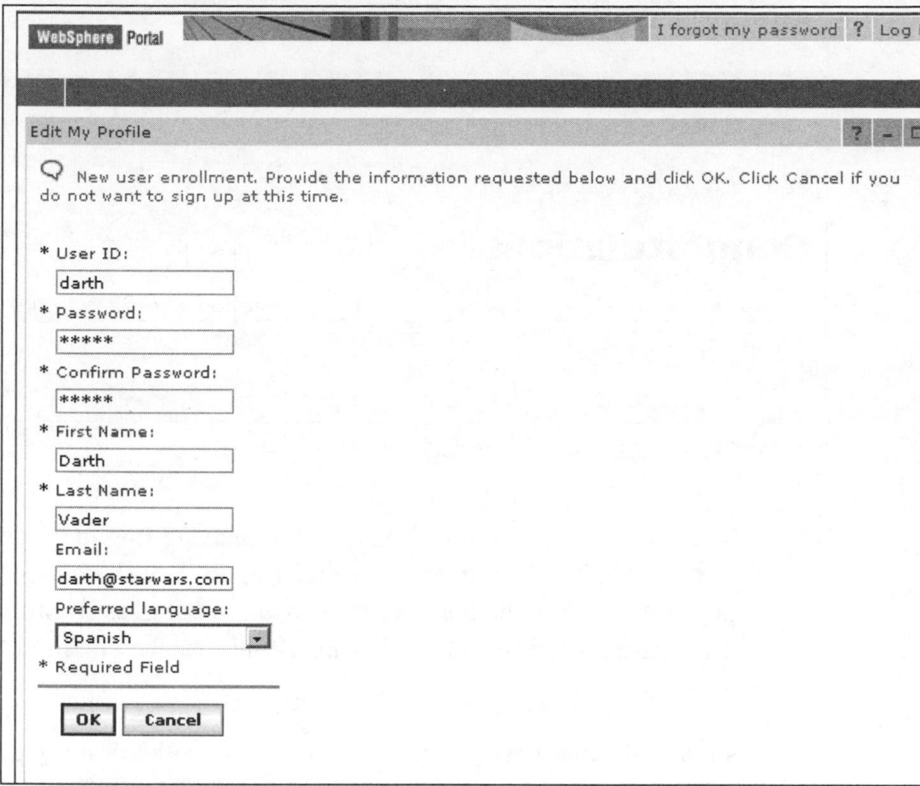

Figure 4.13: Registering a new portal user.

3. If the registration is successful, you will get the congratulatory message shown in Figure 4.14. If a problem occurs with any of the entered values, you will see a message *EJPAT0005E: User creation failed.* A link will be presented to View Details.

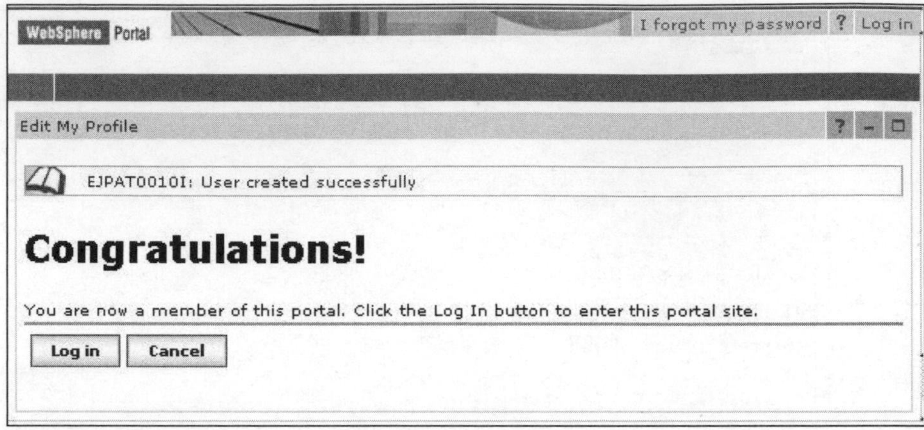

Figure 4.14: New user successfully registered.

4. To test if you can log in as the new user, click the **Log in** button. Enter darth as the user ID and password, and click **Log in**. You should see the Welcome page with most of the portal-related text in Spanish, as shown in Figure 4.15. The user darth was created indicating Spanish as the preferred language.

As stated earlier, all field values except the user ID can be changed after a successful registration. The user ID is changed by clicking on the Edit my profile link, which is visible only after the user logs in.

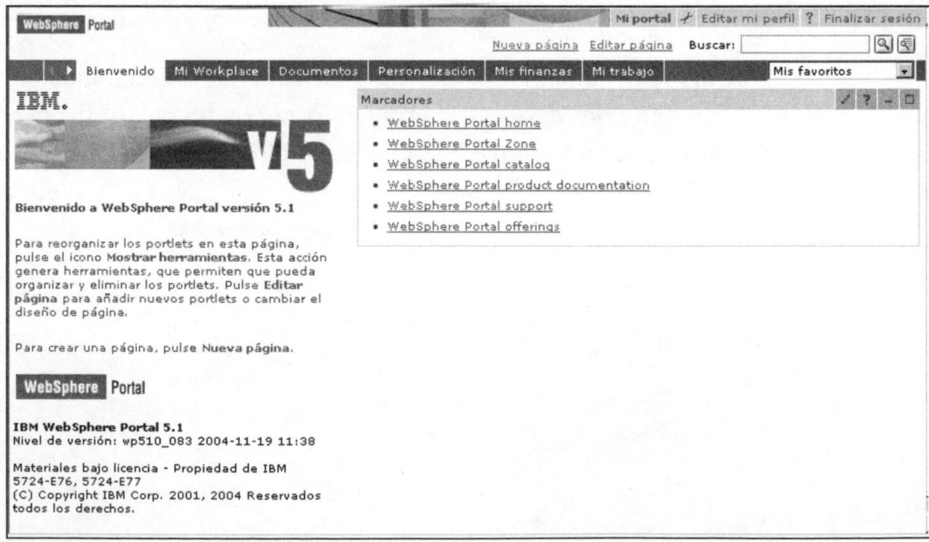

Figure 4.15: A new user's "Welcome" page in Spanish.

5. Log out as user darth by clicking on the link that reads **Finalizar sesión**.

When you log off, the default Welcome page is redisplayed in English. The language customization done for user darth is only visible to that user. Other authenticated users and unauthenticated users still see what the portal administrator has set.

How does an ordinary user get such access rights? Can these and other privileges be changed for one or more users? These and other security-related questions are answered in Chapter 7.

Layout

Web designers and graphic artists spend hours designing the layouts of Web pages. Organizations like to present a consistent layout across the enterprise, so that users get comfortable visiting their Web sites and know what to expect. In most cases, an enterprise's Web layout includes a masthead, a navigation bar on the left, a main area in the middle, and a menu bar above the main area. In WebSphere Portal, these areas fit on a page and are laid out in terms of row containers, column containers, and portlets, as shown in Figure 4.17.

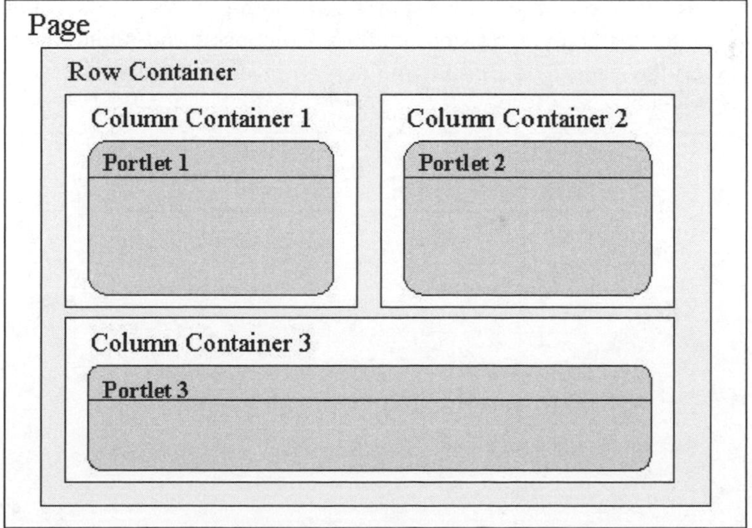

Figure 4.17: Sample page layout in WebSphere Portal.

An unauthenticated user cannot see or modify the page layout. The portal administrator and registered users can change the layout of pages. Let's see how that can be done:

6. Log in as user darth.

7. Before going any further, change the preferred language attribute to English by clicking the Edit Profile link (in Spanish, the **Editar mi perfil**). From the **Idioma preferido** (Preferred Language) drop-down, choose **Ingles** (English), and then click **Aceptar** (OK). The portal page should now display everything in English.

8. Click the **Edit Page** link on the Welcome page. You should see four labels: Content, Appearance, Locks, and Wires. By default, you will see the Edit Layout page, as shown in Figure 4.18.

9. Notice the different layout options you have when creating or editing a page. During page creation, you can choose any one of the options. The default is a two-column page, which is the format used for the Welcome page. The icons that you will see in the layout screen are listed in Table 4.3.

Note: You can actually choose to have more than three columns. After the page is created, portlets are chosen and added to the containers on the page. The Edit Layout screen gives users control over the page layout.

Table 4.3: Icons in the Edit Layout Screen

Icon	Functionality
	One-column layout. It is easy to switch from this to any other layout.
	Two-column layout. This is the default.
	Three-column layout.
	T layout.
	Reverse T layout.
	II layout.
	Edit Portlet.
	Delete Portlet.
	Move Portlet Down.
	Move Portlet Left.
	Move Portlet Right.
	Move Portlet Up.

10. As shown in Figure 4.18, the Welcome page is laid out in three columns, with all three portlets in the first column. Click the **Right Arrow** icon in the About WebSphere Portal portlet to move it to the middle column.

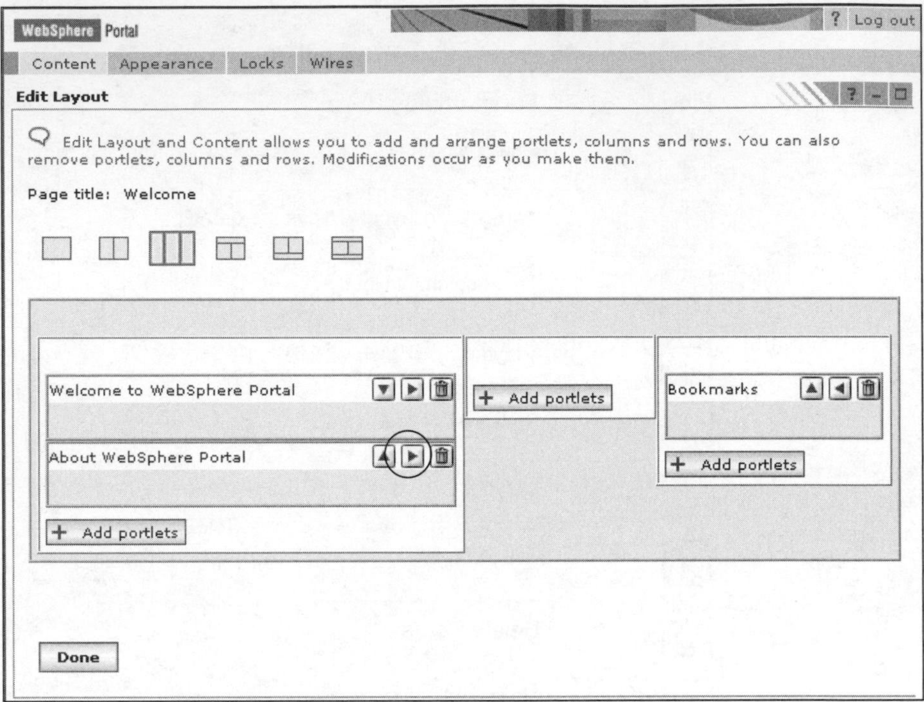

Figure 4.18: The Edit Layout and Content screen.

11. After the portlet has moved to the middle column, click **Done** to return to the page.

12. My Page, under the Welcome tab, now has a different look, as seen in Figure 4.19.

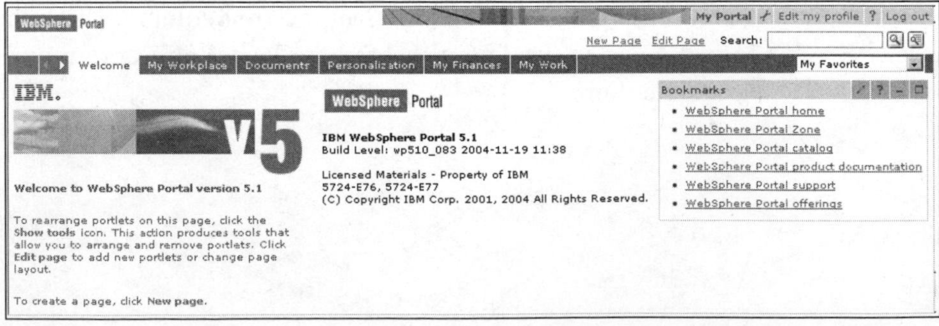

Figure 4.19: The Welcome page after a portlet was moved to the middle column.

13. To verify that this user's customization does not affect everyone else's view, **Log out** as user darth. The unauthenticated default Welcome page should still display, as in Figure 4.1.

Themes and Skins

Each label has a *theme* associated with it, and each theme has a set of *skins* associated with it. A theme determines the global appearance of all pages in the portal, to ensure visual consistency. Themes affect the navigational structure, banner, colors and fonts, available portlet skins, and other visual elements of a page. A theme consists of resources such as JSP files, cascading style sheets, and images. You normally have a default portal theme.

A skin defines the border around a portlet, thus determining the look of the portlet. It affects only portlets. You can select a skin for each portlet, if the theme has skins associated with it. A skin typically consists of a set of JSP files. A theme must have a default skin specified. That default skin is used for all pages in a page, unless otherwise specified by the user.

Skins are installed independently from themes, but a skin is normally associated with a theme. Themes and skins can be made available for one or more markups.

Note: A default theme is not required for the portal, but a default skin is mandatory.

The themes that are provided with WebSphere Portal V5.1 are shown in Table 4.5. The WebSphere theme is the default.

Table 4.5: Portal Themes in WebSphere Portal Enable Edition

Name	Theme Look-and-Feel
WebSphere	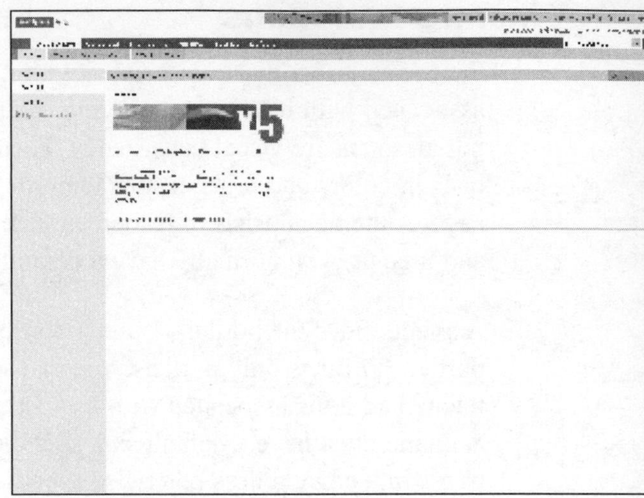
Science	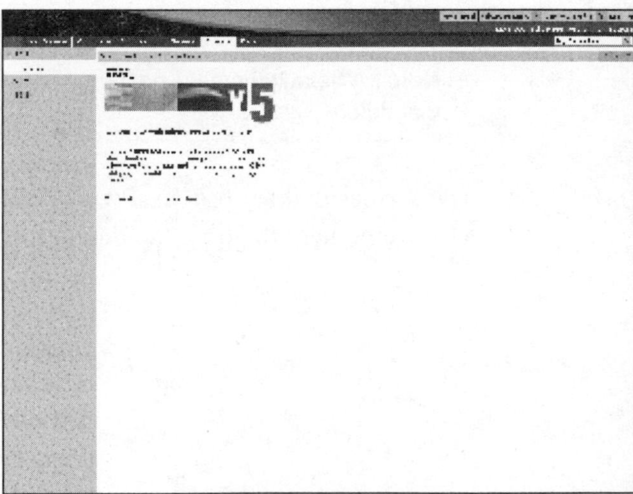

Table 4.5: Portal Themes in WebSphere Portal Enable Edition (continued)

Name	Theme Look-and-Feel
Finance	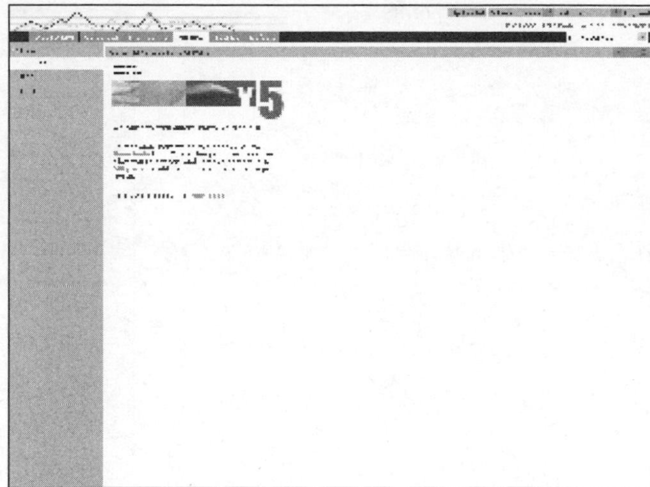
Engineering	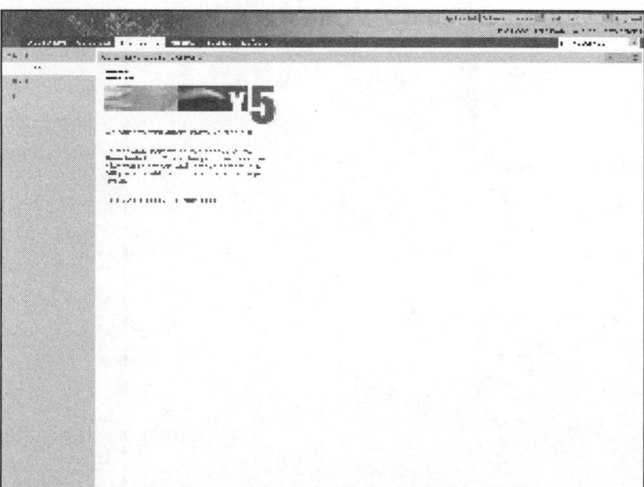

Table 4.5: Portal Themes in WebSphere Portal Enable Edition (continued)

Name	Theme Look-and-Feel
Corporate	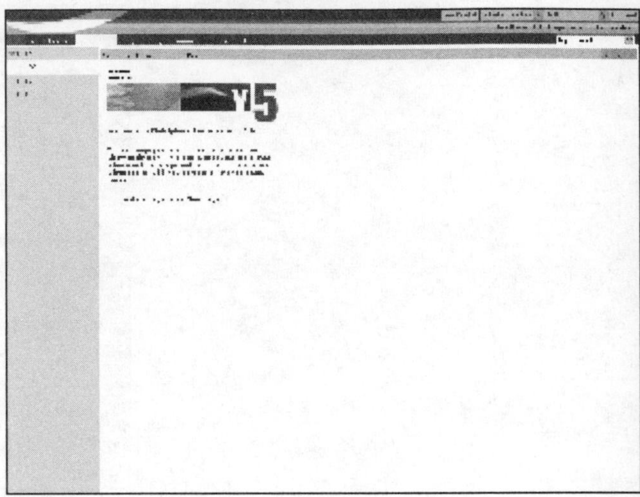
AdminLeftNavigation	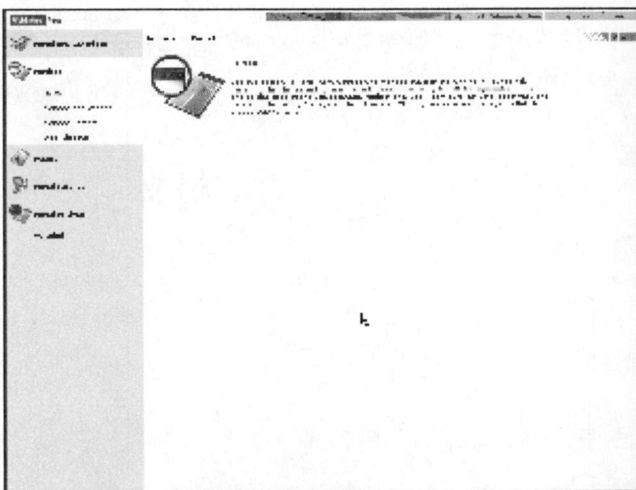

Table 4.5: Portal Themes in WebSphere Portal Enable Edition (continued)

Name	Theme Look-and-Feel
Admin	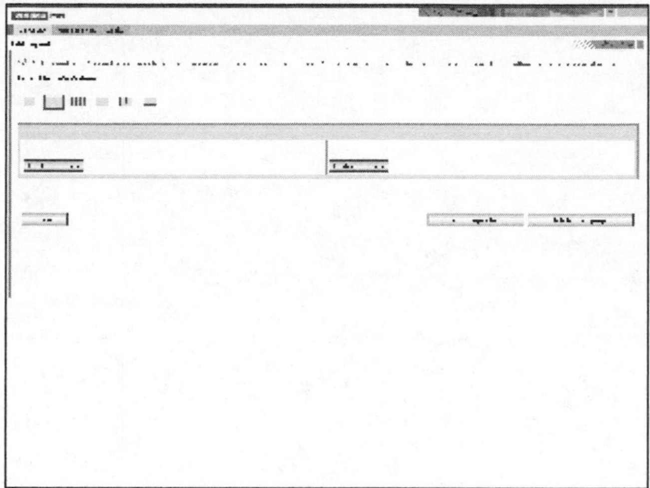

> **Note**: The Admin theme and the AdminLeftNavigation themes, with their associated NoSkin skin (shown in Table 4.6), are intended for administrative portlets. They should not be applied to other labels, pages, or portlets within the portal site.

Skins use a theme's name to select graphics that match the theme's colors. While WebSphere Portal provides all markups with skins, only HTML is provided with multiple skins. The skins that come with WebSphere Portal V5.1 are shown in Table 4.6.

Table 4.6: Portlet Skins Available in WebSphere Portal

Name	Appearance
Album	
Clear	
Corner	

Table 4.6: Portlet Skins Available in WebSphere Portal (continued)

Name	Appearance
Diamonds	
Echo	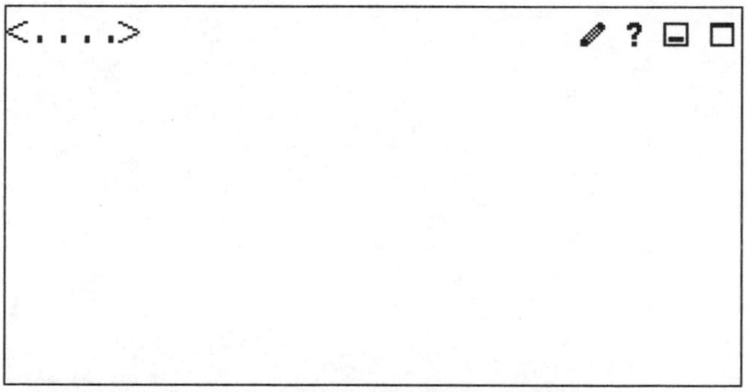
Fade	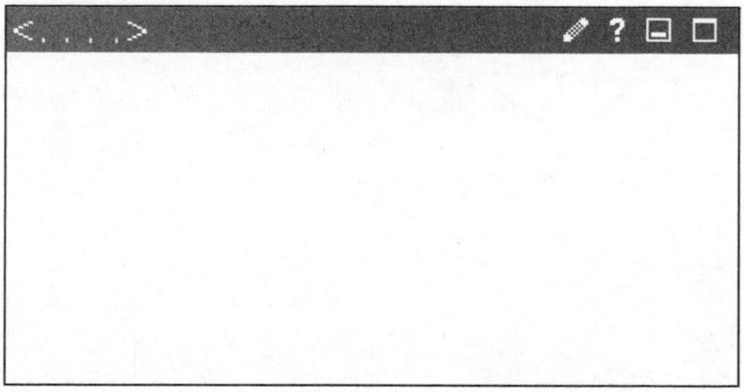

Table 4.6: Portlet Skins Available in WebSphere Portal (continued)

Name	Appearance
Hint	
NoBorder	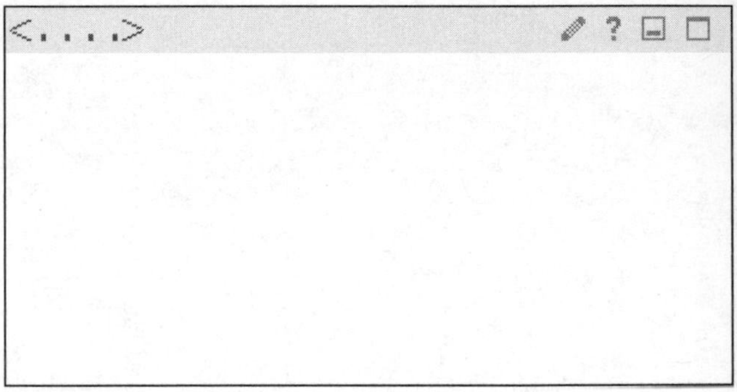
NoSkin	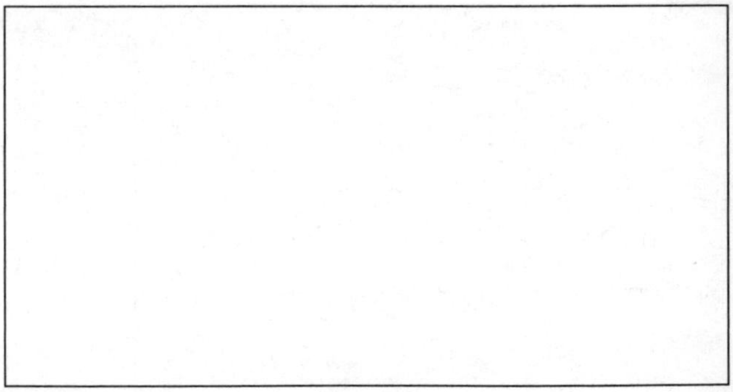

Table 4.6: Portlet Skins Available in WebSphere Portal (continued)

Name	Appearance
Outline	
Pinstripe	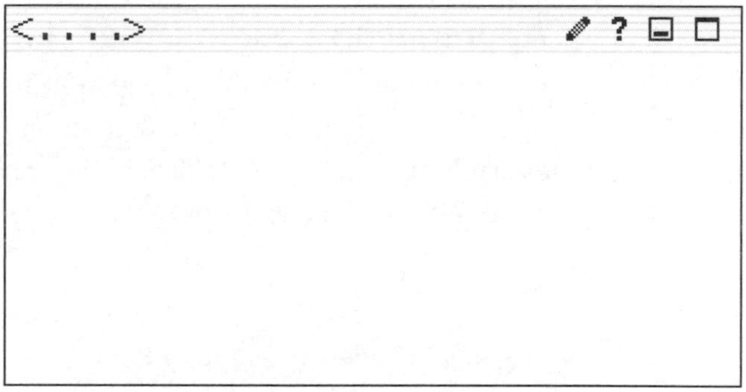
Shadow	

Table 4.6: Portlet Skins Available in WebSphere Portal (continued)

Name	Appearance
Wave	

Aggregation Search Order

Once you choose the theme and skin for your portal, that layout is used to aggregate the content of the defined applications, arrange the output, and integrate everything into complete pages. WebSphere Portal provides fully dynamic aggregation of pages from *page descriptors* held in the portal database.

Table 4.7: Order of Directory Search

In the /themes Folder

1. /*<locale_country>*
2. /*<locale>*
3. /*<client>*
4. /*<theme name>*
5. /*<markup>*

In the /skins Folder

1. /*<locale_country>*
2. /*<locale>*
3. /*<client>*
4. /*<skin name>*
5. /*<markup>*

Page components are rendered using JSPs, images, style sheets, and other resources. These resourccs are located in the file system in a path-naming convention that WebSphere Portal uses to locate the correct resources for the client. During aggregation, the portal server searches for themes and skins starting with the most specific subdirectory and moving up to the more general, higher-level directory. The directories associated with themes and skins are listed in Table 4.7.

For example, suppose a request for the file "Control.jsp" comes from a client using Internet Explorer 5 (ie5) with the locale set to en_US and the skin set to Pinstripe. WebSphere Portal's aggregator will search in the following order starting at level 1.

Note that all directory levels might not exist in a WebSphere Portal installation. If the file is required, it should exist in the base directory of /skins or /themes:

[skins directory]/[markup]/[skin name]/[client]/[locale]

1. /skins/html/Pinstripe/ie5/en_US/Control.jsp
2. /skins/html/Pinstripe/ie5/en/Control.jsp
3. /skins/html/Pinstripe/ie5/Control.jsp
4. /skins/html/Pinstripe/en_US/Control.jsp
5. /skins/html/Pinstripe/en/Control.jsp
6. /skins/html/Pinstripe/Control.jsp
7. /skins/html/ie5/en_US/Control.jsp
8. /skins/html/ie5/en/Control.jsp
9. /skins/html/ie5/Control.jsp
10. /skins/html/en_US/Control.jsp
11. /skins/html/en/Control.jsp
12. /skins/html/Control.jsp
13. /skins/Control.jsp

Creating a New Look

Now that you have seen the default look of WebSphere Portal and know what makes up the portal's look-and-feel, it is time to design your own new portal look. Creating a new look involves defining a new theme and the associated skin or skins. The following pages walk through the steps of creating a new theme and one new skin. We chose to show the creation of a new skin first because if a skin exists, it is easy to make it part of a theme.

New Skin

To define a new portlet skin, start by creating a subdirectory under <WAS_HOME>/installedApps/<NODE>/wps.ear/wps.war/skins/<MARKUP_LANGUAGE>/. That subdirectory name should match the skin name. Then, you create the supporting resources within that directory

---

Tip: Rather than start from scratch, we recommend copying the contents of an existing skin from the html folder, like Wave or Pinstripe, and renaming it.

Here are the steps to quickly create a new portlet skin called ourSkin:

1. Create a directory using the new theme name, <WAS_HOME>/installed Apps/<NODE>/wps.ear/wps.war/skins/html/ourSkin.
2. Copy all files and subdirectories from the Wave skin directory into the new ourSkin directory.
3. Change the graphics in the .jpg file. In this case, modify pinstripe.jpg. If you change the name of this file to match the skin name, remember to modify Control.jsp.
4. Optionally, create a preview graphic that shows up when that particular skin is pre-viewed:

    4.1 Create a screen shot of the skin.

    4.2 Reduce the screen shot to fit in the preview box. The recommended size is 307 by 159 pixels.

    4.3 Name the image preview.gif and copy it to the <WAS_HOME>/installedApps/<NODE>/wps.ear/wps.war/skins/html/ourSkin directory overwriting the old preview.gif.

These are the steps to add the new skin in WebSphere Portal:

1. Log into WebSphere Portal as the portal administrator. Click the **Administration** link.
2. Traverse down to **Portal User Interface → Themes and Skins**, as shown in Figure 4.20.

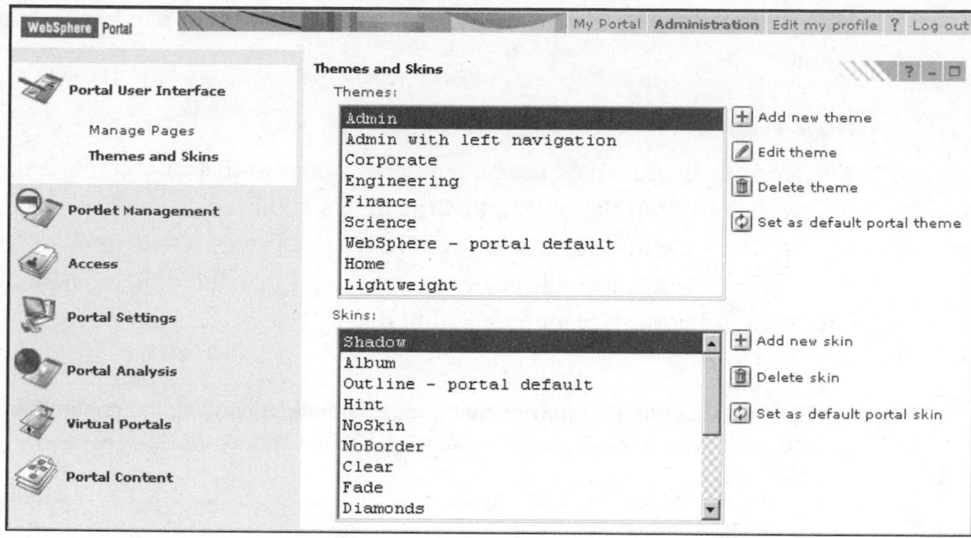

Figure 4.20: Screen to Add new skin and theme.

3. In the Skins section, click **Add new skin**. Enter ourSkin for both the Skin name and the Skin directory name. These names are case-sensitive.Click **OK**.

4. The new skin named ourSkin should be successfully added, as indicated in the screen shown in Figure 4.21.

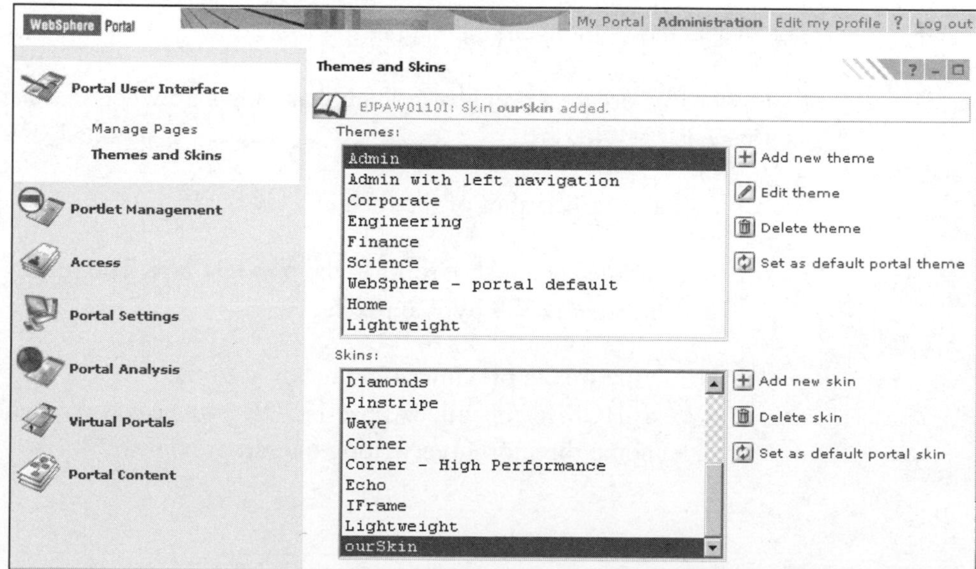

Figure 4.21: A new skin added to the list of skins in WebSphere Portal.

Now that new skin can be used on any existing portlet or can be made part of any theme.

New Theme

The steps to create a new theme are very similar to that of creating a new skin. To define a new portal theme, start by creating a subdirectory under <WAS_HOME>/installedApps/<NODE>/wps.ear/wps.war/themes/<MARKUP_LANGUAGE>/. The subdirectory name should match the theme name. Then, you create the supporting resources within that directory.

Tip: Rather than start from scratch, we recommend copying the contents of an existing theme from the html folder, such as Engineering or Science, and renaming it.

Here are the steps to quickly create a new theme called ourTheme:

1. Create a directory using the new theme name, <WAS_HOME>/installed Apps/wps.ear/wps.war/themes/html/ourTheme.

2. Copy all files and subdirectories from the Science Theme directory into the new ourTheme directory.

3. Change the graphics in the banner.jpg file.

4. Optionally, create a preview graphic that shows up when that particular theme is pre-viewed:

   4.1 Create a screen shot of the theme.

   4.2 Reduce the screen shot to fit in the preview box. The recommended size is 300 by 226 pixels.

   4.3 Name the image preview.gif and copy it to the <WAS_HOME>/installedApps/<NODE>/wps.ear/wps.war/themes/html /ourTheme directory overwriting the old preview.gif.

These are the steps to add the new theme in WebSphere Portal:

1. Log into WebSphere Portal as the portal administrator. Click the **Administration** link.

2. Traverse down to **Portal User Interface → Themes and Skins**, as shown in Figure 4.20.

3. In the Themes section, click **Add new theme**. Enter ourTheme for both the Theme name and the Theme directory name. These names are case-sensitive.

4. From the All skins list choose the skins you want for this new theme. Notice that ourSkin is also listed, and we chose that for this new theme, as seen in Figure 4.22. Click **OK**.

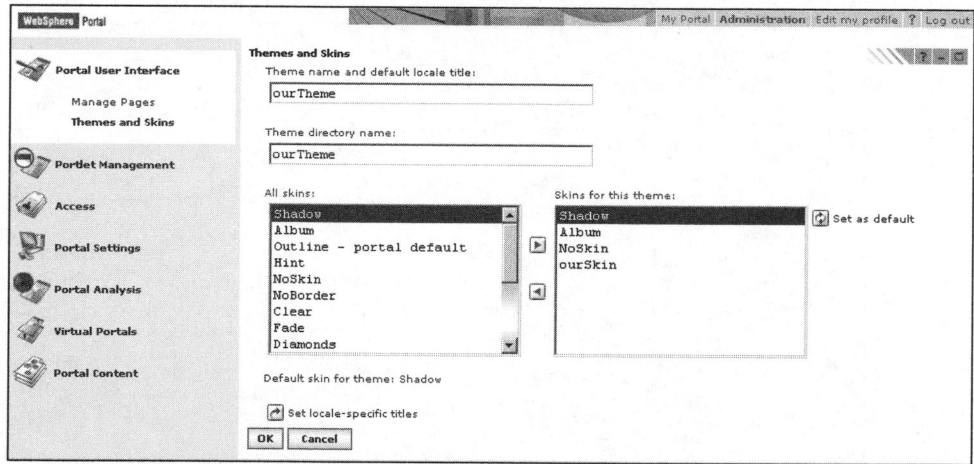

Figure 4.22: Adding a new Theme.

5. The new theme named ourTheme should be successfully added, and you will be returned to the Themes and Skins screen. The new theme, ourTheme, and the new skin, ourSkin, should appear in the respective lists.

You might have noticed that a skin called NoSkin also exists. Nothing dirty about this. Take a look at the Welcome portlet. It has no decoration around it, because it is using the NoSkin skin. Such portlets are useful to display a company's message or a legal notice because users cannot minimize or delete this portlet very easily.

Deploying the New Look

Using the resources created earlier in this chapter and those that come with the product, you can produce a customized portal by following these steps:

1. Log into the portal as the portal administrator.
2. Click the **Administration** link. Under Portal User Interface traverse down to Manage Pages.
3. In the main window from the list of titles, click **My Portal** link.
4. Create a new page by clicking **New Page** button. That screen is shown in Figure 4.23.

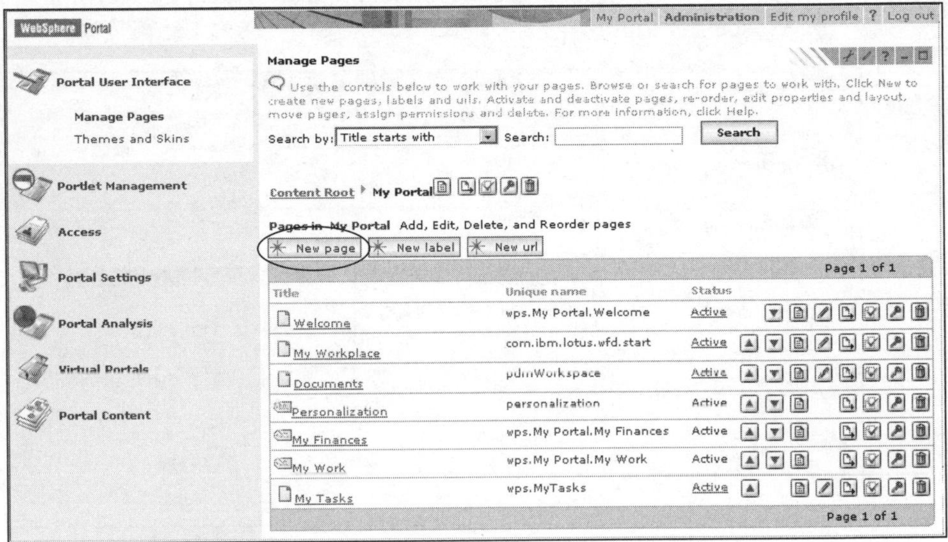

Figure 4.23: Creating a new portal page.

5. Name the page ourPage, choose the newly created, ourTheme, from the Theme drop down list. Click **OK**. Notice that quite a few options are available while creating a new page, but we chose the default of a two-column layout and a page supporting HTML markup. See Figure 4.24.
6. You should see the following message: *EJPAS0010I: ourPage has been created successfully*. Click **OK**.

WebSphere Portal

? Log out

Page Properties

New page: My Portal

Use the controls below to work with your pages to specify your page properties. Expand Options to choose page properties, page type, page layout, or page cache options.

Title:

ourPage

Theme:

ourTheme

☐ I want to make this page my private page

⊟ **Page Properties**

☑ This page can be added to a user's My favorites list.

☐ Other pages can share the contents of this page.

⊟ **Type of Page**

◉ A content page with these properties:

This page supports (at least one must be selected):

☑ HTML ☐ cHTML ☐ WML

⊟ **Page Cache Options**

Set the cache options for the page, the lesser value of cache expiry seconds between the page and the portlets used on the page will determine the actual cache expiry seconds.

Cache Scope

◉ Non-shared cache for a single user

○ Shared cache across users

Cache Expiration

◉ Cache always expires

○ Cache never expires

○ Cache expires after this many seconds 0

Cache Access Control

☐ Ignore access control in caches

OK **Cancel**

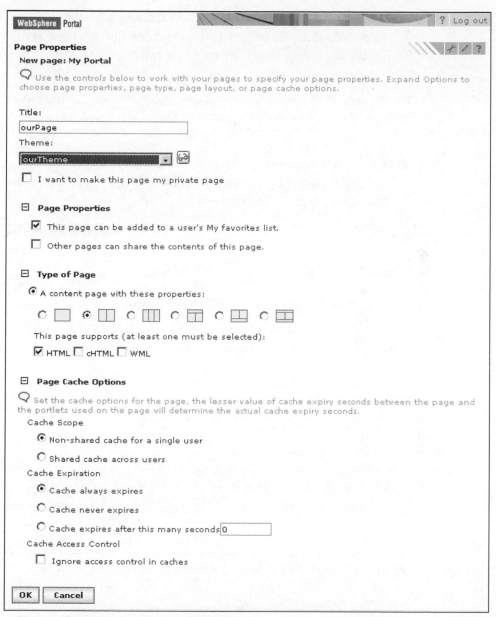

Figure 4.24: The new page properties screen.

7. Return to My Portal.

8. Use the arrow to pan to the right and click on **ourPage** tab. You will see the page with the newly created theme, ourTheme, but with no content.

9. Let's add a portlet or two to see how the new skin works. Click the **Edit Page** link. Because we went with the default two-column layout, you should see a Row container with two column containers.

Tip: There is no limit to the number of rows or columns you can have. We recommend you start with a two-column or one-column layout.

---

10. Click the **Add portlets** button in the left column container. Search for the Reminder portlet by entering **Reminder** in the search string and clicking on the **Search** button. See Figure 4.25.

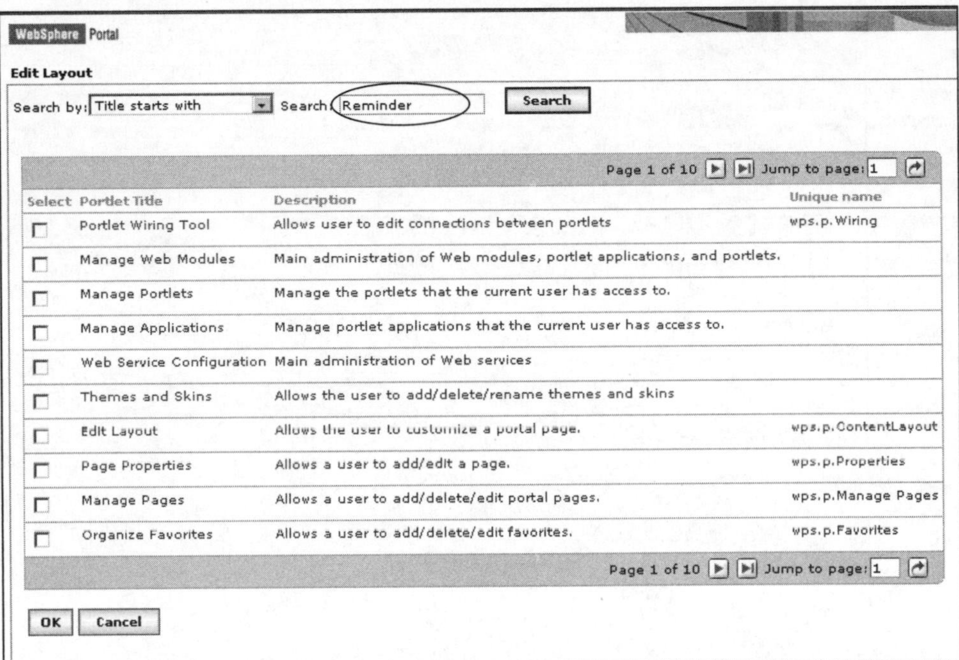

Figure 4.25: Searching for the Reminder portlet to add to a portal page.

11. When the Reminder portlet is returned, check the Select box on the left and click **OK**. You should see the message: *EJPAE0115I: New portlets are added successfully*. The Reminder portlet will be added to the left container.

12. Similarly, add the Banner Ad portlet to the right column. The Edit Layout page should look like that shown in Figure 4.26.

Tip: There is no limit to the number of portlets you can have on a page. We recommend having six to eight portlets on a page, depending on the nature of the users of the page, the design of the user's workflow, and the amount of content contained in the portlets.

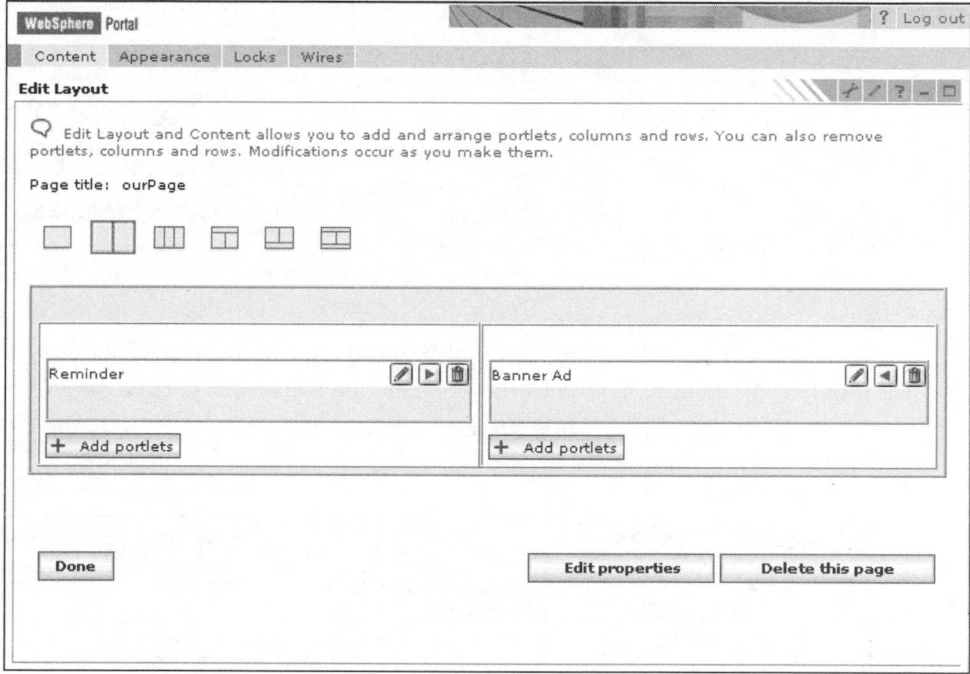

Figure 4.26: Edit Layout screen of ourPage.

13. You may edit the Reminder portlet by clicking on the **Edit** icon (the icon that looks like a pencil). Add some text as the reminder message. After editing the portlet, click **Done**.

14. On the Edit Layout page, click the **Appearance** tab. The Appearance portlet shows which skin each portlet is using. If unchanged, they will all use the theme's default skin.

15. For the Reminder portlet, choose the newly created, ourSkin, from the drop-down menu, as shown in Figure 4.27. The following message—*EJPAC0100I: Skin updated on portlet Reminder*—is displayed. Leave the Banner Ad portlet with the Theme default skin, which is the Shadow skin.

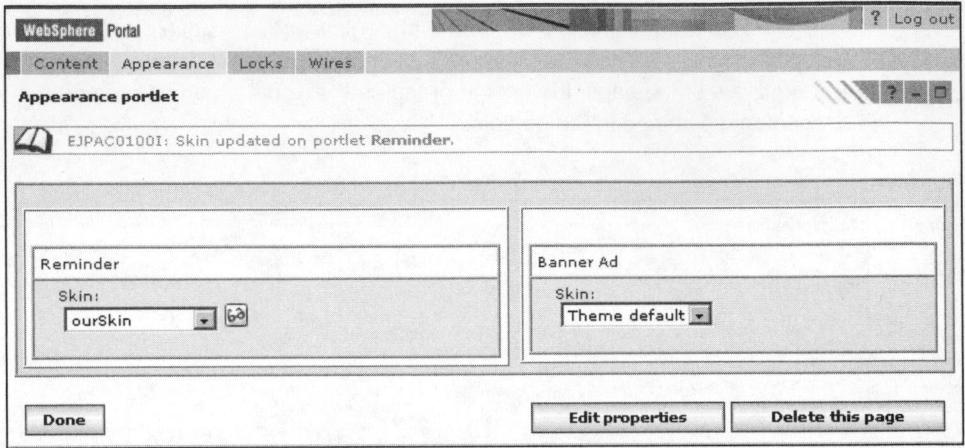

Figure 4.27: The portal page-layout screen in WebSphere Portal.

16. Click **Done**. You should now see the portal page with the new theme and two portlets. One of the portlets, the Reminder portlet, should be displaying the new skin, while the Banner Ad portlet shows up with the default theme skin. See Figure 4.28.

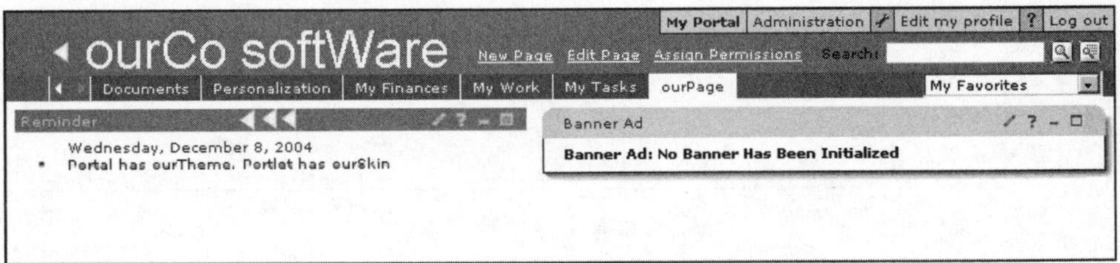

Figure 4.28: A new portal page with a new portal theme displaying a portlet with a new skin.

An exercise left to the reader is to change the name of the page from ourPage to ourCo.

Hint: Under Manage Pages, select ourPage and click the icon to Edit Page Properties.

To see the beauty of what you just did, log off as user wpsadmin and log back in as user darth. You will not see ourPage, because the person who creates the page has manage access and gets to decide who can view and/or manage the page. Since nobody else was given access to the newly created place and page, only users with administrative rights can see the ourPage page.

Notes on Creating New Themes and New Pages

We just saw that one of the quickest ways to display a page in the default theme is to create a new label at the My Portal level. But, if you create a new page at the context root level, you may find that the page does not show up anywhere. That is because the top-level navigation is actually embedded in the theme's tool bar—that is, in ToolBarInclude.jsp. This is what you do to get the new page link to display:

1. Add the link thus:

   Administration → Manage Pages → context root → ourLabel

2. Define a custom name:

   Administration → Portal Settings → Custom Unique Name

   Search on your link, edit, and add a unique name, for example wps.ourLabel.

   You do this because you set up the link to the page by this name.

3. Modify ToolbarInclude.jsp to add your new link. This file is found in <WAS_HOME>/installedApps/<NODE_NAME>/wps.ear/wps.war/themes/html/<THEME_NAME>. Here's some sample code.

```
<%– ourLabel Portal button –%>

<wps:if loggedIn="yes" portletSolo="no">
   <wps:urlGeneration contentNode="wps.ourLabel"
      portletWindowState="Normal">
   <td class="wpsToolBar" nowrap>
   <a class="wpsToolBarLink" href='<%
      wpsURL.write(out); %>'>our Label</a>
   </td>
   </wps:urlGeneration>

</wps:if>


<%– My Portal button –%>
<wps:if loggedIn="yes" portletSolo="no">
```

```
            <wps:urlGeneration contentNode="wps.My Portal"
              portletWindowState="Normal">
                <td class="wpsToolBar" valign="middle"
                  align="<%=bidiAlignRight%>" nowrap>
                <a href="<% wpsURL.write(out); %>"
                  class="wpsToolBarLink"><wps:text
                    key="link.my.portal" bundle="nls.engine"/></a>
                </td>
            </wps:urlGeneration>
        </wps:if>
```

Notice that the My Portal button section also was modified to make the new link active. The contentNode defines the destination link/page when the new link is clicked.

Note: The new ourLabel link will not show up within other themes, such as the Admin theme. The other theme's ToolbarInclude.jsp has to be modified as well to see the new link.

Here are some notes on creating and using new themes:

1. Do not use the WebSphere theme to create a new portal theme. Use either the Science theme or the Engineering theme as the starting point.

2. To ensure that everything about your new theme is picked up, restart your WebSphere Portal server. This behavior can be altered by modifying an attribute in <WAS_HOME>/config/cells/<NODE_NAME>/applications/wps.ear/deployments/wps/wps.war/WEB-INF/ibm-web-ext.xmi. Set reloadingEnabled to True. Then restart Portal server.

Tip: A performance impact accrues when running with reloadingEnabled set to True. Only use this setting during Theme development and testing; then reset it back to False. It is recommended that you do not set this value to True in a production environment.

Notes on Layout of the Portal Page

Before customizing your portal site, remember that underlying structure of the portal is determined by the portal JSPs. The portal page is composed of JSPs for *screens*, *themes*, and *skins* that are typically created by the Web designer of the portal. These JSPs reside in the corresponding /screens, /themes, /skins directories under <WAS_ROOT>/installedApps/<HOST>/wps.ear/wps.war. Within this location, subdirectories for markup, locale, and client types are used to support *portal aggregation.*

The starting place for building the portal page is Default.jsp in the /themes directory. The screen and skin are called by the corresponding <wps:screenRender/> and <wps:pageRender/> tags from the engine tag library. See Figure 4.29.

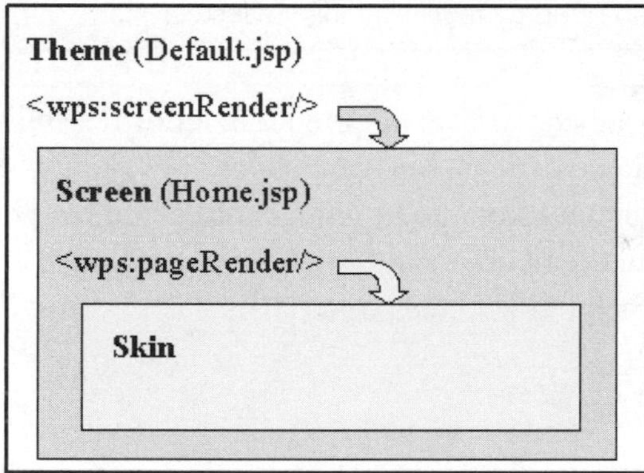

Figure 4.29: Portal page layout.

Enhancing the New Look

Now that you have the portal successfully displaying the new theme, you can modify the colors, banner, and various graphical elements to create your own personal, much more customized branding. If you browse through the newly created ourTheme directory, you will see all the language folders and essentially the following kinds of files:

- JavaServer Pages (JSPs)—Default.jsp, Banner.jsp, and ToolBarInclude.jsp are used to create the portal branding and determine how the screen layout looks. These are simple JSP files, and you can customize them to obtain the look you want.

- Images—Banner.jpg is the background image used by the portal. Depending on the theme you copied from to create your new theme, you might see another file called swish.jpg, which helps when viewing the banner graphics in a maximized view. You can either create new images with the same names or create completely new image files and modify the JSPs in the right places to point to your new images.

- Cascading style sheets (CSS)—Styles.css is the default cascading style sheet (CSS) used by the portal and portlets. HelpStyles.css is used for online portlet help. You can definitely customize the style definitions.

Note: Make sure you do not delete any style sheets or remove any style classes. Most of the colors of the title bars of the portlets or the separators can be manipulated by modifying this Styles.css file.

Although the above files do provide a lot of flexibility in editing and creating the portal and portlet branding, care should be taken when modifying these files because certain errors in the JSPs could cause the portal to not appear. Test and debug your theme in a tool like WebSphere Studio Site Developer (WSSD) before actually applying it to the portal.

Door Closings

As far as themes, skins, and layouts are concerned, the possibilities are endless within WebSphere Portal. To determine the theme and skin for the display of portal contents, WebSphere Portal server looks for resources using a bottom-up approach through the component directory structure.

As you have seen, a wide range of options is available to create labels and pages, and whoever creates a new page controls access to it. Therefore, plan carefully to determine what users can do with their portal pages before giving them access rights. This is covered in more detail during the discussion of portal security in Chapter 7.

Chapter 5
Personalizing the Portal

This chapter focuses on the personalization component of WebSphere Portal. WebSphere Personalization supports both a business rules approach and a collaborative filtering approach. This chapter, however, focuses primarily on the business rules approach, because this approach lends itself to common personalization requirements.

Overview of WebSphere Personalization

Personalization (PZN) is about targeting Web content and applications to specific users, based on certain information that is gathered and stored about them. This information is analyzed, and the user is presented with content that might be interesting to him. Personalization techniques can be used by a portal site to customize news feeds, provide specialized advice, target email and advertising, and promote products.

The Personalization authoring interface is targeted to business users, not application developers. The intent is to enable these business people to personalize content with little or no assistance from developers. As WebSphere Personalization matures, this is becoming easier. The personalization tooling dynamically provides some of the personalization artifacts that previously required application developers to build.

The Rule Editor, however, is the most important component in enabling business users. It is based on a point-and-click interface that minimizes the amount of typing the business user must do, and therefore minimizes opportunities for making mistakes. The rule language consists of easy-to-read logic statements that make it easy for business users to understand what a rule is doing. The editor helps you build complex rules in the interface by inserting ANDs where necessary to combine these logic statements (which you can change from AND to OR), and it prompts you for the location of parentheses to ensure the rule is logically correct.

Any personalization solution involves three components:

- *User profile*—Information about the users of the site, including user attributes.
- *Content model*—Attributes about the content, such as product descriptions and articles.
- *Matching technology*—A technique that matches users to the right content. This could include filtering, rules, recommendation engines, or a combination of all three.

New in This Release

The new release of WebSphere Portal V5. brings many significant changes to the Personalization component. Many of the changes have occurred in the Personalization interface, and these changes have made personalization much easier to use and administer. A push is also underway to reduce administrator and business user dependence on application developers and application developer–targeted tools. Some of the new features of Personalization are:

- A brand-new user interface
    - The interface has its own tab, independent from any other component in the portal. This helps emphasize the fact that WebSphere Personalization can be used not only with WebSphere Portal's Web Content Management product, but with third-party content management products, databases, and file based content.
    - The previously separate interface for configuring the WebSphere Personalization runtime is now completely integrated with the Author-time interface.

- The UI is implemented as two portlets (described later in this chapter). The Navigator Portlet allows you to browse, move, copy, and delete personalization objects. When you create new objects, or edit existing ones, the Editor Portlet is activated.

- Personalization now uses the DB2 Content Manager Runtime edition to store both authoring and runtime personalization artifacts. These artifacts had been stored in various places in database tables and on the file system. This repository is based on Java Specification Request 170 (JSR170), which defines a standard Java Content Repository, (JCR). This JSR was not finalized in time for this release, so the implementation was based on the proposal under review at the time. More information on JSR 170 can be found at http://www.jcp.org/en/jsr/deail?id=170. The many benefits of storing artifacts in a common repository include:

  - WebSphere Personalization identifies unique types in the repository through introspection and automatically creates a resource for each unique type it finds.

  - Dynamic content spots are available. Personalization, as well as any other component that uses the rule architecture can register a dynamic content spot and later invoke it. This eliminates the dependence on using the content spot wizards, which again reduces the dependence on application developers.

  - Moving personalized artifacts to remote systems becomes much easier to do. In this release, a Publish servlet is installed as part of the Personalization runtime. When you publish from the Personalization UI, the data is sent to the servlet on the remote system via HTTP, where it is placed in the DB2 Content Manager Runtime Edition repository. You can configure a publish server to use HTTPS if that is required. Content spots that are created outside of the Personalization UI, as well as resources for content outside of the repository, must be moved to the remote system by hand.

    This setup makes it easy to replicate personalization artifacts to a remote system. This is critical if, for example, you want your code to be identical on your Production and User Acceptance Test (UAT) systems when you move from UAT to Production.

  - All the major content management vendors are participating in the creation of JSR170. Once the specification is completed, a long-term goal is to make it possible to personalize content stored in other vendor repositories that comply with the specification.
  - Portal Document Manager stores all of its documents in the repository. Thus, you can use personalization to display PDM documents.
  - Web Content Management (WCM) content is not currently stored in the repository. WCM development is working on a short-term solution that will allow you to personalize WCM content as if it was stored in the repository. The long-term solution is to base WCM on the repository

- A new Personalized List portlet is provided that allows you to create personalized portlets without writing any code. The portlet allows you to simply show all resources of a specified type, display the output from a content spot, or execute a specified rule. You can have a details page generated for you or provide your own custom JSP page. You can configure a number of things about how the details page is displayed, including how the content is categorized. You can further customize the details page by providing your own Cascading Style Sheets.
- Personalization is becoming more a core portal function usable by any portal application or other portal components such as PDM, WCM, and LWP. The user interface is implemented as portlets with reusable rule editors.

Types of Personalization

The personalization of Web content is classified into different types based on how it is done. Enterprises can decide which is the best method based on their content and user base. The three types of personalization are described below:

- *User profile-based*—Also called *simple filtering*, this displays content based on predefined groups or user profiles. For example, when a user registers on a portal site, the user is automatically assigned to a group based on registration information. The portal might display news based on the group, or ask the user to select the news feeds she would be interested in seeing. (This can be accomplished using business rules, but it may be overkill.)
- *Rules-based*—In rules-based personalization, business users define rules based on a user's needs and preferences or based on business requirements.

- *Collaborative filtering*—This displays information based on a combination of individual user preferences and/or behaviors. These preferences and behaviors are used to find similar or like-minded users. Collaborative filtering technology uses advanced statistical modeling to extract trends about usage patterns of the visitors to a Web site.

WebSphere Personalization provides support for all three types of personalization. Tooling support allows developers to develop Web pages that are targeted to users' interests and allows users to select content suited to their unique needs. WebSphere Personalization also provides easy-to-use Web-based tools to assist business users in creating rules to determine the content displayed to a site visitor.

You can use business rules, collaborative filtering, or both on a given portlet or web page. Business rules work well when the relationships and dependencies between content are well defined. A downside to business rules is that you must modify or create new rules every time you wish to change how you personalize the content. Collaborative filtering, on the other hand, will discover relationships and dependencies on its own, thereby changing what content is displayed without you having to modify anything. One hurdle faced in using collaborative filtering is that it requires lots of data to make good recommendations. It also works best if there are lots of content and users.

Personalization Components

The rules-based personalization solution consists of an authoring server and a runtime server. The runtime environment is automatically installed when you install the authoring server. The authoring environment requires WebSphere Portal. You can also install the runtime separately; it doesn't require WebSphere Portal. It only requires WebSphere Application Server. Therefore, you can still develop personalized non-Portal Web sites. Before we describe the various components in detail, Figure 5.1 gives a glimpse inside the Personalization Server.

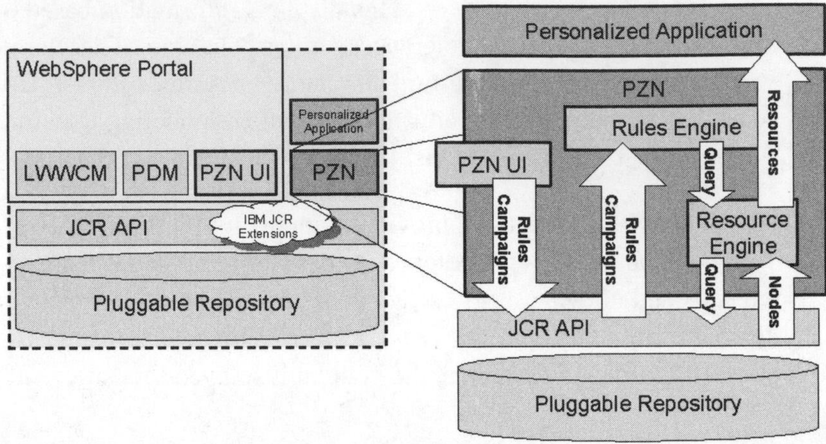

Figure 5.1: Inside the Personalization Server.

Authoring Environment Components

The authoring environment consists of the following two elements:

- *Personalization wizards*—Wizards are available through WebSphere Studio Application Developer (WSAD) and Rational Application Developer (RAD). These wizards assist in implementing the personalization-interface APIs if your user and content data is in a relational database, in an LDAP directory, or in IBM Content Manager. If this data is in any other place, you will have to implement the APIs yourself, but WSAD or RAD provide the complete environment to develop the necessary classes. They also provide wizards to create *content spots*, which are placeholders for content. A content spot gets populated when a rule mapped to that spot is executed.

- *Personalization browser*—The Personalization browser is also referred to as the Personalization UI. It is a browser-based, easy-to-use tool for the business user to manage rules and campaigns. It is implemented as the following two portlets:

    - The Personalization Navigator portlet gives you the ability to work with all your personalization artifacts. This portlet is essentially a JCR repository browser and provides a number of standard views. You can view all objects in the repository, all Personalization objects, all Rules, all Campaigns, all Rule Mappings, and all Resource Collections. In addition to browsing objects, you manage these objects here as well. Other actions that you can initiate from this portlet include:

  - Import and register resource collections
  - Create (author), delete, move, and edit rules, campaigns, content spots, application objects such as a shopping cart, and publish servers
  - Map rules to content spots
  - Export all or part of the Workspace
  - Work with versioning control
  - Publish the personalization artifacts to a remote system

- The Personalization Editor portlet is just what its name implies. Whenever you create or edit a new personalization object, this portlet is activated and expanded. Here, you edit all your personalization objects.

- The Personalized List portlet allows users to build simple personalized portlets without having to build a custom portlet. You use this portlet by making a copy and then simply configuring your new portlet to display a list of resource instances. You can also provide a custom detail JSP to provide a detailed view.

Runtime Environment Components

The primary components of the runtime deal with the three "R"s — Resources, Rules, and Recommendations:

- *Resource engine*—The resource engine receives queries from the Rules engine, resolves them, executes them, and returns content to the Rules engine. The resource engine provides the services that enable customers to define users, content, and application objects to WebSphere Personalization.

- *Rules engine*—Rules-based personalization involves tailoring a Web page for each user based on his profile and a set of business rules. A rule maps a user to the target content. The Rules engine executes all personalization rules and invokes the Resource engine to request content.

- *Recommendation engine*—This is provided by the Likeminds Personalization Engine, which processes recommendation rules. Likeminds uses collaborative filtering technology to select the right content based either on user preferences or on behavior it has tracked.

- *Logging framework*—This is used to record information about Web site usage for use by the Recommendation engine.

At a high level, the runtime processing starts when a client requests a Web page, which is a JSP with an embedded rule. The JSP compiler of WebSphere Application Server invokes the rule-wrapper Java bean that calls the API of the Rules engine. That interface actually executes the rule.

Rule processing involves accessing the resources defined to the resource engine and retrieving user and content data from the data store (the *customer data store*). Queries to the customer data store are handled by user-provided implementations of the personalization APIs for accessing resources.

Personalization Artifacts

Some of the main concepts and artifacts used in WebSphere Personalization are described in the following sections.

Resources

Users and content are defined by resource classes that you can build using wizards or by writing custom code. Think of resources as a set of adapters that enable the Resource engine to use the customer's existing user and content information by calling a standard interface. This is achieved by requiring all resources to implement three Java interfaces.

The wizards will generate resources for JDBC compliant databases, LDAP repositories, and IBM CM. (RAD V6 does not generate IBM CM resources.) To override the user ID, password, or data source entered in the resource wizards' use the file

<WPS Home>\shared\app\config\PersonalizationResourceCollections.properties.

Every personalized application or portlet has one user resource and a content resource for each type of content that is personalized. Personalization provides a resource for content stored in the DB2 Content Manager runtime edition Java content repository implementation. Portal also provides a built-in content resource for Portal Documents and a built-in user resource for the Portal User. Use these resources to quickly start personalizing the Portal.

To create a custom resource, you must implement the following three interfaces:

- com.ibm.websphere.personalization.resources.Resource
- com.ibm.websphere.personalization.resources.ResourceDomain3
- com.ibm.websphere.personalization.resources.ResourceManager3

Generally, a good approach to creating a custom resource is to use the wizards to generate a standard resource and then modify the methods you require for your resource.

- The Resource interface maps your User and Content models to the actual data in your repository. Five methods must be implemented, but in many cases these can have an empty implementation (with the exception of the getId() method that returns the primary key for the resource). You must also implement a getter and setter method for each fixed property in the resource. So, if a balance property exists in the resource, you must code a setBalance() and getBalance() method.

- The ResourceDomain3 interface is the workhorse that selects or queries resources based on the resources fixed properties. Three methods must be implemented:

  - findById() returns a single resource instance based on its primary key.

  - findResourcesByQuery() returns all resource instances that meet the specified query.

  - findResourcesByProperty() returns all resources having the specified value for the property.

- The ResourceManager3 interface is used to dynamically add, delete, and update Resource instances. This is also the interface you use for update rules. It contains four required methods.

Content Spots

For every different type of personalized content you plan on displaying on a page, you must define a content spot. Content spots are implemented as Java beans and are also referred to as *rule trigger beans*. At runtime, when code in the JSP references the content spot, the bean calls the Rule engine to execute the rule mapped to the content spot. This Rule engine gets the personalized content from the Resource engine and passes it back to the bean.

Conceptually, it can be useful to think of content spots as areas on a page reserved for personalized content. You can map any rule to the content spot that returns the correct type of content.

Rules

Rules are the business logic defining how personalization works on a Web site. You can use four types of rules to personalize your Web site:

- Profilers divide site visitors into categories (such as gold, silver, and bronze) based on their attributes stored in the data store. Profilers can also categorize based on other conditions, like the current date and time, the type of browser being used, data collected through implicit and explicit profiling, session attributes, and request attributes and parameters.

  An example of a profiler rule is shown in Figure 5.2. In this example, the profile UserClearance is set to Confidential if the Role attribute of the user is either Manager or Executive. Otherwise, the user is treated as a Regular employee.

UserClearance is
Confidential when
current Personnel.ROLE is equal to Manager or
current Personnel.ROLE is equal to Executive
Otherwise Regular

Figure 5.2: Example of a profiler rule.

- Actions determine what data will be selected or updated. Actions can also sort the returned results. Three different types of action rules exist:

- *Select* action rules retrieve content from a data store. These are the most commonly used business rules.
- *Update* action rules are used to update content in the user profile.
- *E-mail* action rules are used to send an e-mail message. The recipient lists, subject line, and the sender can be explicitly entered or retrieved from resource attributes. The e-mail body is a separate file, which means it can also be personalized.

Figure 5.3 shows an example of an action rule that selects content marked as Confidential.

Select Content
whose News.CONFIDENTIAL is equal to Y

Figure 5.3: Example of an action rule.

- *Bindings* combine actions and profilers. In a binding rule, one or more profilers are combined with action rules to form a complete rule. Basically, a binding says "If a visitor is classified as some classification, do some action." An example is shown in Figure 5.4, where GetNewsByClearance says that if the user's classification is Confidential (classified as such because the user is either an executive or a manager), then do the GetConfidentialNews action. It also implies that the GetSiteNews rule is always executed.

When UserClearance is
Confidential
do GetConfidentialNews
Always
GetSiteNews
order as is
show all items

Figure 5.4: Example of a binding rule.

- *Recommendations* are used to personalize content using the LikeMinds recommendation engine. The recommendation engine requires that data be recorded in the LikeMinds database via the logging bean APIs included with Personalization. Different methods are used to recommend content:

- Site navigation by user. This method uses the LikeMinds ClickStream engine.
- Explicitly expressed user preferences. This uses the LikeMinds Preference engine.
- Market basket analysis—based on association with content returned from a rule. This method uses the LikeMinds Item Affinity engine.

Campaigns

Campaigns are used by WebSphere Personalization to group a set of Rule Mappings to achieve specific personalization behavior. You can think of a campaign as a way to provide special content or information to a set of targeted users during a specific period.

All default Rule Mappings are visible in the Normal View. These mappings are always active. You create a campaign with a start date, an end date, a priority, and a split value. You then add existing rule mappings to the campaign for each content spot that you wish to personalize during this campaign. When multiple campaigns are active, the rule mappings from the campaign with the highest priority are used. If more than one campaign with the same priority is mapped to the same spot, then Personalization randomly picks one of the mappings based on their split value.

E-mail Promotions

E-mail promotions used to be called e-mail campaigns in prior releases. From a business perspective, they are very much like the campaigns we just described because they also target content to users at a specific point in time. The two major differences are that the content is e-mail and that the use of the campaign is not initiated by a site visitor, but by a time-based, potentially recurring event. This difference in how e-mail promotions are activated also functionally differentiates them from e-mail rules mapped to content spots.

To create an e-mail promotion, you must first create an e-mail action rule. Note that the recipient list in the rule will not be used by the e-mail promotion. Next, you create a rule event. A rule event requires a rule that returns a list of recipients from the user resource collection. You must also specify a rule to execute for each user returned from the resource collection. The last required setting is the Start Date, which is the date and time the event should be processed. A repeat checkbox is provided if you want to make the promotion recurring.

Note: The rule that is executed for each user doesn't have to be an e-mail rule, although sending e-mails is the most common thing that rule events are used for. You can also run update rules and binding rules combining updates and e-mails in a rule event.

WebSphere Personalization Development Process

A number of steps are involved in the process for developing a personalized portlet. These steps primarily involve working with Personalization Server, but may also require some administrative tasks with WebSphere Application Server and WebSphere Portal Server.

Step 1: Identify Your Business Requirements

First and foremost, you need to identify the reasons and goals for developing your personalized Web site. What kinds of users are you targeting? What is the content you want to personalize, and what attributes of the content do you need to choose to match the right content to each user? The most important goal of a personalized Web site is to match the right content with the right user, delivering content that is of personal interest to the site visitor. Here are some examples of goals that lend themselves to a personalized solution:

- Develop a personalized site for premium customers
- Recommend products to targeted customers based on their purchasing ability
- Provide content to a company's employees, such as benefits, internal news, and competitive information
- Display special messages and give access to restricted applications that the site visitor is authorized to access
- Provide purchasing suggestions based on the previous purchases of site visitors, or for cross-sell and up-sell purposes
- Provide information and applications based on the role and interests of each employee on a company's self-service intranet
- Target documents or content relevant to the user's current activity

Step 2: Develop Your User and Content Models

Personalization is about matching users with content fitted to their needs. The information you have about your users is your *user model*, and the information you have about your content is your *content model*.

Deciding on the user model is critical to any personalized solution. What kind of information do you know about your site users, and is it sufficient to provide the type of personalized experience you are planning? The extent to which personalization can be achieved depends largely on the amount of information available about the site visitor. This information, whether in a relational database or an LDAP directory, should be accessible to the personalization runtime. Also, in consultation with business managers, you must decide how to group or classify the site's visitors based on their interests.

The content model consists of all the content that you can display to site visitors, as well as information about that content that you can use to decide when to display it. The key to delivering personalized content is *metadata*, which is information about the content. The metadata could consist of attributes about the content, such as title, category, and authorization level. Generally, not everything on the Web site needs personalization, so you also have to decide which content should be personalized.

Step 3: Develop a Matching Strategy Approach

This step goes hand-in-hand with step 2. As part of designing your portlet, portal, or Web site, you need to decide how you want to match content with site visitors. In general, we find that business rules are the matching strategy used for most personalized applications. You can also use both business rules and collaborative filtering in the same application or portlet, or even on the same page.

Step 4: Create User and Content Resources

The next step is to implement the user and content resources. As we mentioned earlier, Personalization resources are Java classes that represent users and content stored in an external data store. At a minimum, any personalization solution should have at least one user resource. Generally you need a content resource for each different type of content you want to personalize. You should also keep in mind that a built-in content resource for Portal Documents and a built-in user resource for the Portal User is available.

Step 5: Design the Page Layout

The next step is to meet with business managers and graphic designers to decide how the site should look. There are several different approaches for designing the site. If you are starting from scratch, most likely the graphic designers will lay out the desired look and feel and provide you with the HTML layouts. Taking an existing static site that you want to personalize is another common approach. In either case, the HTML pages will need to be changed to JSPs so that you can personalize them and add dynamic content.

A useful approach to designing the personalized portions of your pages is to take screen shots of the static pages and print them out so that you can write on them. For each page, draw and label a box for each area of the page that you want to contain personalized content. Then for each box, identify the source of the content. You must also ensure that the metadata or attributes associated with the content allow you to deliver the right content to the current user.

Step 6: Add Content Spots to Your JSPs

Once resources have been defined, content spots can be created and placed on the JSP pages. As mentioned earlier, a content spot is a section of a Web page where a rule will be invoked to get personalized content. You can define as many content spots as you want on a page. Rules are later mapped to these content spots in the Personalization UI.

Step 7: Write Scriptlet Code to Display Personalized Content

The next step is to write the JSP scriptlet code to display the personalized content returned for each content spot on the page. For each content spot, it is a matter of getting the desired data from the content spot Java bean and formatting it for display on the page. Although this is something that you can write by hand, an easier way to generate the scriptlet code is to use the page designer of WSAD.

In the version 5 releases of WSAD, the support for dynamic tables and dynamic elements has been removed. Fortunately, the old editor that contains this support, Page Designer Classic, is still shipped with the product.

To install and configure Page Designer Classic in WSAD V5.X:

1. Make sure that WSAD is not running.
2. From a Command Window, go to the bin directory where you installed WSAD (e.g., C:\WSAD\bin), and execute pdclassic.exe.

3. When you start WSAD, a Configuration Changes dialog box opens, as shown in Figure 5.5. In the Detected changes area, make sure the Page Designer Classic check box is selected and click Finish.

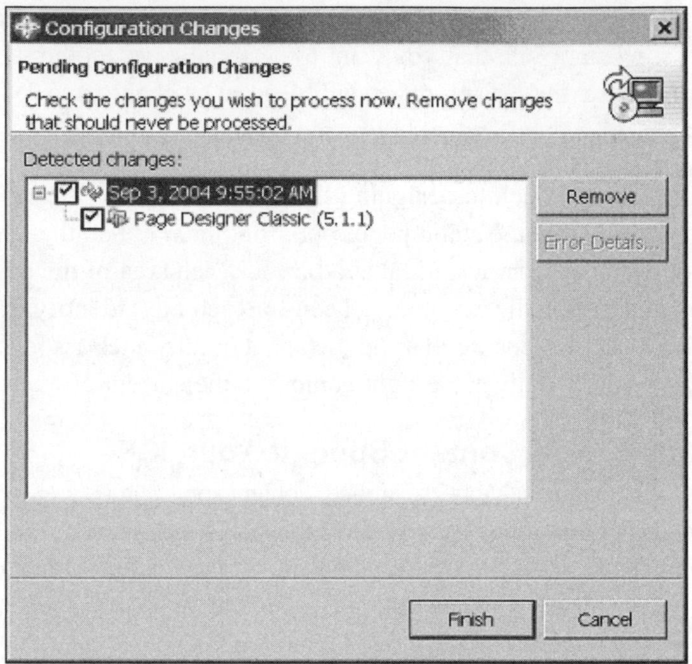

Figure 5.5: Configuration Changes Dialog.

4. When the Install/Update dialog box shown in Figure 5.6 opens, click **Yes** to restart WSAD.

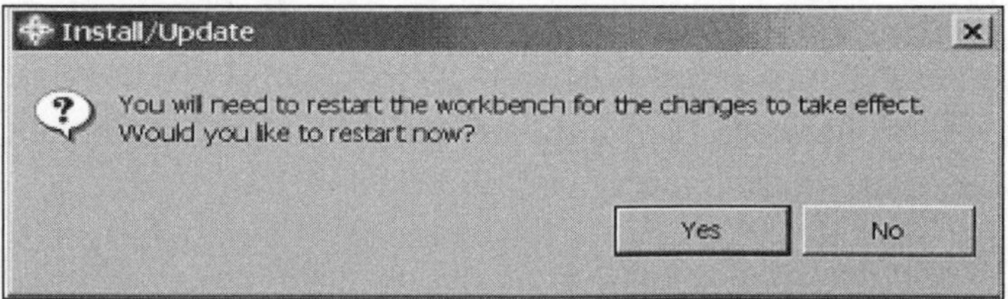

Figure 5.6: Workbench restart prompt.

You now have Page Designer Classic installed. You can select any JSP or HTML file, right-click it, and then select **Open With → Page Designer Classic**.

Step 8: Identify the Current User to the Personalization Runtime

If you don't know who is the current user of your Web site, it is extremely difficult to provide them with a personalized experience! So, it is important that you don't miss this step. What you need to do depends on how you are running Portal. The personalization runtime obtains the current users' user ID from one of three places (listed below). It is in a different format depending on where it is obtained. The Personalization runtime uses this user ID as the primary key when it tries to find the current user in the User Resource Repository. Therefore, it must be correctly mapped or translated into the format used in the User Resource. Personalization looks for the user ID in these places:

- If you are running Portal with security enabled, the user ID is obtained from the WebSphere Application Servers' security context. This id contains additional information, such as the users' DN and the application server information. For example, if IBM Tivoli Directory Server is the LDAP being used for security, the name will be of the format: user:blueagave.raleigh.ibm. com:389/uid=user1,cn=users, dc=raleigh,dc=ibm,dc=com.

- If you are running Portal without security enabled, the Personalization runtime looks for the request attribute pzn.userName, and uses its value if it is set. In the previous example, the user ID is user1, so you should set pzn.userName to user1.

- If security is not enabled and pzn.userName is not set, the runtime uses the Portal user ID. This name will look like uid=user1,o=default organization.

So, in the first and third cases, you must strip out all of the extra information so that the Personalization runtime can get a match for the user ID. The recommended practice is to write a translator class and register it with the WebSphere Personalization runtime. You must implement the translateAuthID method of the AuthIDTranslator interface. This method simply strips out the extra characters that are included in the user ID and then returns the name in the format used for the user ID in the user resource. The built-in Portal User resource does this translation for you.

The final step is to register the AuthIDTranslator class with the user resource in the Personalization user interface. Note that this translator will be invoked regardless of where the Personalization runtime gets the user ID, so it should be able to handle all three formats as input.

Step 9: Import Resources and Register Translator

It is time to develop business rules, but first you must import any resources created outside the Personalization workspace. We highly recommend that you create a new folder for each personalization project you create in the workspace. This will allow you to view only the objects from the project you are working on in the browser. Also, using folders as a project structure makes it easy to publish each project individually. (Publish supports publishing either the entire workspace or a selected item or folder.)

Now that your user resource is available in the Personalization UI, it is a good time to register the translator class by editing the user resource and updating the value of the translator attribute to the class you provide.

Step 10: Develop Business Rules Defining What Each Visitor Sees

After all the resources are created and then imported to the Personalization UI, it is time to author the business rules. These are typically written by business users who understand the business goals of the Web site, the users who visit the Web site, and the content that is used to personalize the Web site.

As you will see later in the chapter, when we build our sample personalization portlet, the Personalization Editor portlet is based on a very easy-to-understand, point-and-click interface. This makes it possible for business users to create complex rules without writing any code.

Step 11: Map the Rules to the Content Spots

Once the rules have been created in step 10, they can be associated with the content spots defined in step 6. One of the beauties of WebSphere Personalization is that you change the content a user sees by mapping a different rule to a content spot. The new mapping becomes active immediately on the local system and on any remote system you publish it to.

By using campaigns, more than one rule can be mapped to a single content spot. In these cases, the rule mappings are ordered based on their priorities and then executed in order until one of the rules returns content.

Step 12: Publish the Personalization Artifacts

Earlier in this chapter, we mentioned that WebSphere Personalization no longer has an independent administrative or authoring database. Personalization uses the DB2 Content Manager Runtime edition for storing rules, campaigns, dynamic content spots, and other objects for both authoring and runtime. The only personalization artifacts that don't reside in this common database are the class files for the resources and content spots. These class files reside in either your application or in a shared library. If you are working on the local system, there is no need to publish anything, since the artifacts are already in the repository.

One of the big benefits of storing all the artifacts in a common repository is that it is very simple to publish the artifacts to any remote system that has the WebSphere Personalization runtime installed. You simply create a publish server using the New menu in the Personalization Navigator. The key parameter is the publish servlet URL on the remote system. You can specify that you want to delete remote objects that have been deleted from the local system. The only things you must move by hand are the resources and content spots, which optimally will be stored in a shared library that makes them easy to find and move.

Menu options are provided to either publish the entire workspace, Publish Workplace, or a single item or subfolder, Publish Selected. Either way, you can specify a user ID and password if required by the remote system.

Step 13: Deploy and Test the Pages

Once you have mapped a rule to each of your content spots, it is time to deploy your pages and see if you get the results you expect. Since this is a Portal book, this means deploying your portlet. You can modify your rules or map different rules to your content spots and simply refresh the browser window to view the results.

Developing a Simple Portlet Using Rules-Based Personalization

This section follows the thirteen steps described in the previous sections to create a personalized portlet that simulates a simple banking news application. The model consists of two simple tables: Customer is the user-model data store and Customernews is the content-model store. Visitors to the site are profiled based on the balance in their bank accounts (which is part of the user model) as follows:

- *Basic* if account balance <= \$100
- *Advantage* if account balance >\$100 and <= \$1,000
- *Preferred* if account balance >\$1,000 and <=\$10,000
- *Premium* if account balance >\$10,000

Action rules are defined for each profile, as shown in Table 5.1.

Table 5.1: Action Rules for the Sample Portlet

Method	Action Rule
GetCurrentUser	This action rule gets information about the current user.
GetBasicNews	This action rules gets content classified as Basic, targeted for customers whose balance is less than or equal to \$100.
GetAdvantageNews	This action rule gets content classified as Advantage, targeted for customers whose balance is between \$100 and \$1,000.
GetPreferredNews	This action rule gets content classified as Preferred, targeted for customers who have a balance between \$1,000 and \$10,000.
GetPremiumNews	This action rule gets content classified as Premium, targeted for customers who have a balance over \$10,000.

Create a JDBC Driver and Data Source

In previous versions of WebSphere Personalization, if the runtime couldn't find a data source defined for a Personalization Resource it would create one under the covers "for you." Unfortunately, data sources created that way never showed up in the WebSphere Administration Console and could be problematic. (They could never be modified or deleted.) This is no longer the case is this release. You *must* create a data source for all your resources. Make a note of the JNDI name, as you will want to use it when you create your Personalization Resources.

Create a Portlet Application Project in WSAD

With the goals of the project finalized and our data sources defined, it is time to create the actual portlet. The rest of this chapter focuses on building this personalized portlet. Start by creating a portlet project in WebSphere Studio Application Developer (WSAD):

1. Start WebSphere Studio Application Developer by clicking **Start → Programs → IBM WebSphere Studio Application Developer → IBM WebSphere Studio Application Developer**.

2. Open the Portlet Perspective in WSAD.

3. Create a new portlet application project by clicking **File → New → Portlet application project**.

4. Enter the project name and check the **Configure advanced options** checkbox, as shown in Figure 5.7, and click **Next**.

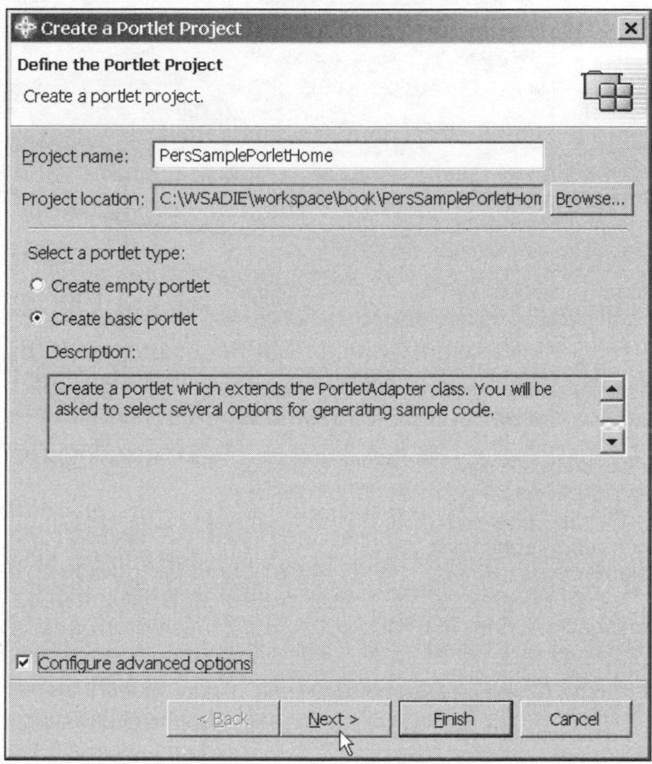

Figure 5.7: Defining the portlet project.

5. Set the name of the project and the Context root as shown in Figure 5.8, and then click **Next**.

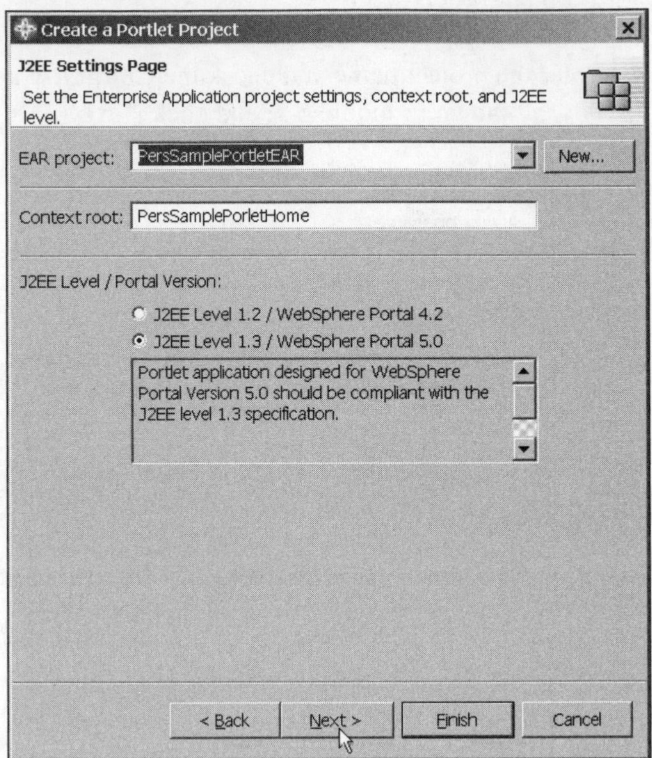

Figure 5.8: Naming the project and setting the context root.

6. Set the portlet title and click **Next**, as shown in Figure 5.9.

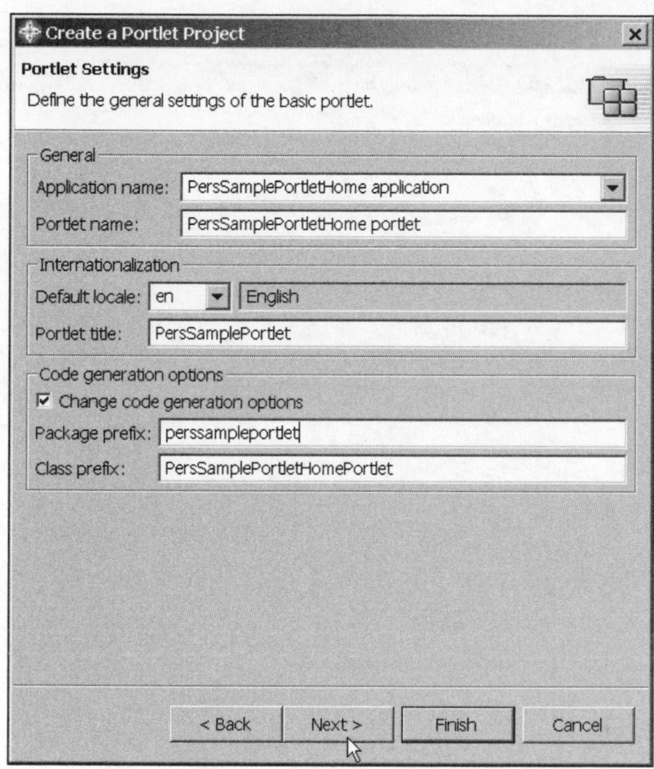

Figure 5.9: Filling in the Basic portlet parameters.

7. Finally unclick the **Add action listener** checkbox, as shown in Figure 5.10, and click **Finish**.

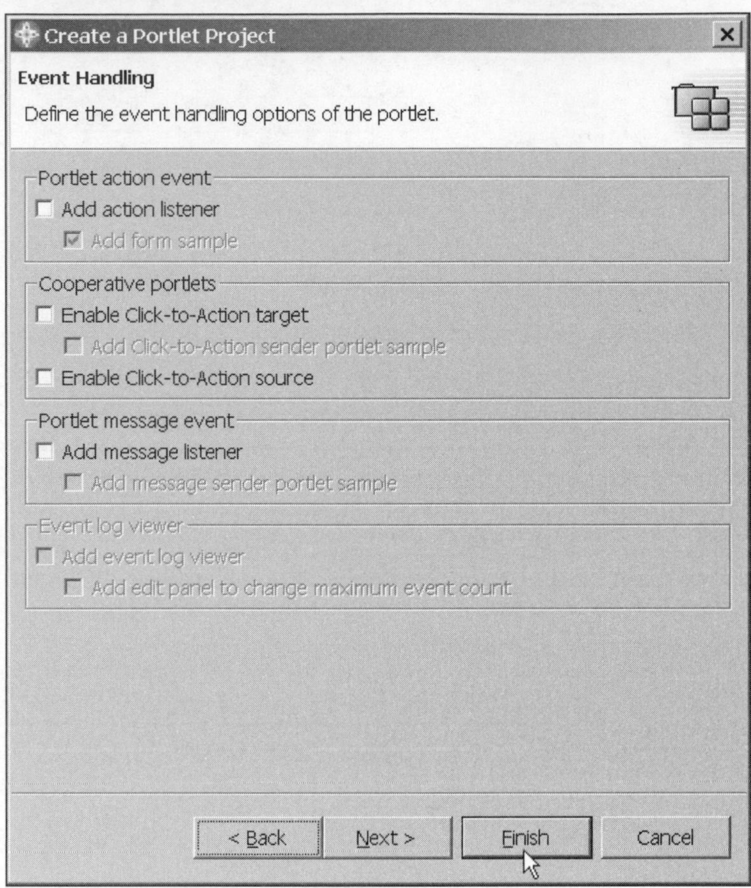

Figure 5.10: Finishing the project wizard.

8. In the Navigator, you should see two folders called PersSamplePortletEAR and PersSamplePortletHome, populated as shown in Figure 5.11. The portlet project is now created.

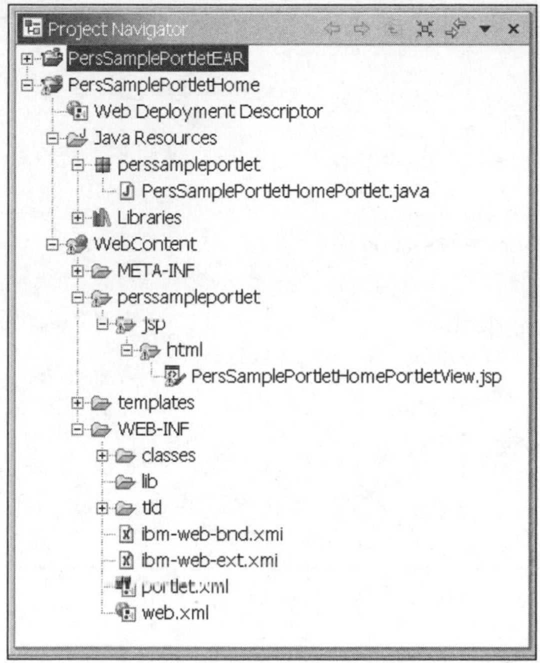

Figure 5.11: Portlet project file structure in WSAD.

Create Resources and Content Spots

Now you have to create the user and content resources corresponding to the Customer and Customernews tables. The previously separate User wizard and Content wizard have been combined into one User and Content Resource wizard. A check box on the first screen of the wizard determines if a user or content resource is created.

Note that the wizards we will use with WSAD are not the most current versions. These older wizards contain settings that made sense in previous versions of Personalization but are no longer used or needed. The most current wizards come with RAD V6. The main reason we are using WSAD is to leverage the use of Page Designer Classic. Once you see what the generated code looks like, you can move to RAD V6 and use all the most current tooling to write your own JSP code to display the personalized content.

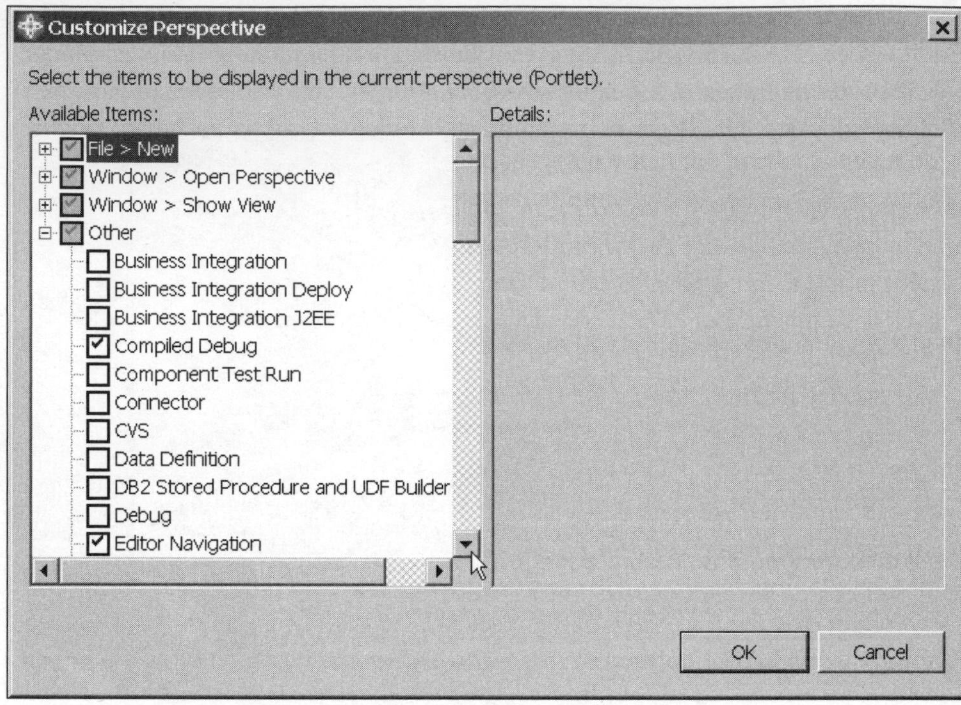

Figure 5.12: Adding the Personalization wizards 1.

Tip: If you do not see the User and Content, and Content Spot wizards in the WSAD toolbar, you can add them manually. Click **Window → Customize** Perspective. You will see the screen shown in Figure 5.12. Expand **Other** and make sure the WebSphere portal content publishing wizards check box is selected as shown in Figure 5.13. Click **OK.** This adds the wizards to the WSAD toolbar.

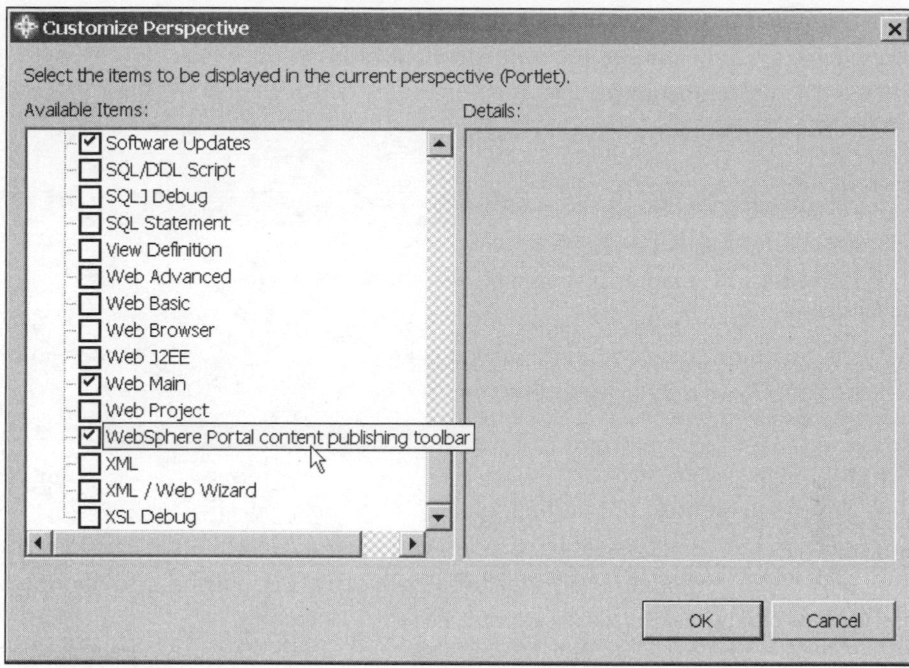

Figure 5.13: Adding the Personalization wizards 2.

1. Select the PersSamplePortletHome project and then click on **Create a WPCP resource**, as shown in Figure 5.14.

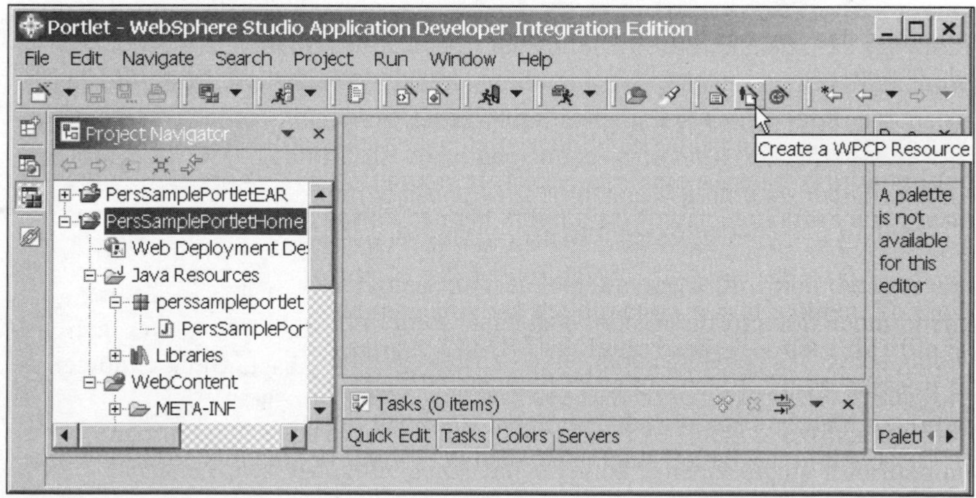

Figure 5.14: Starting the Resource wizard.

2. The Specify Protocol and Data Model screen shown in Figure 5.15 is where you specify that you want to create a User resource. This is also where you would select LDAP if you were using LDAP for Portal security. Click **Next**.

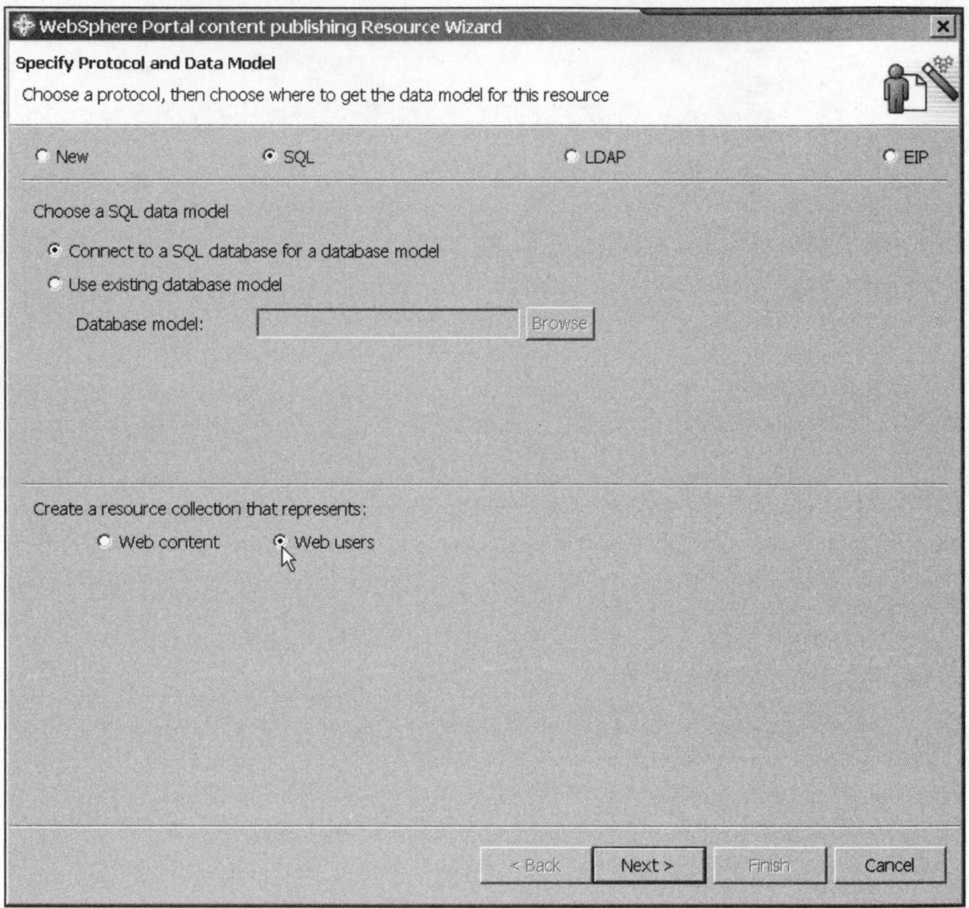

Figure 5.15: Selecting the type of resource to create.

3. Fill out the Database Connection screen as shown in Figure 5.16. Specify a valid user ID and password for the database. Click **Connect to Database**.

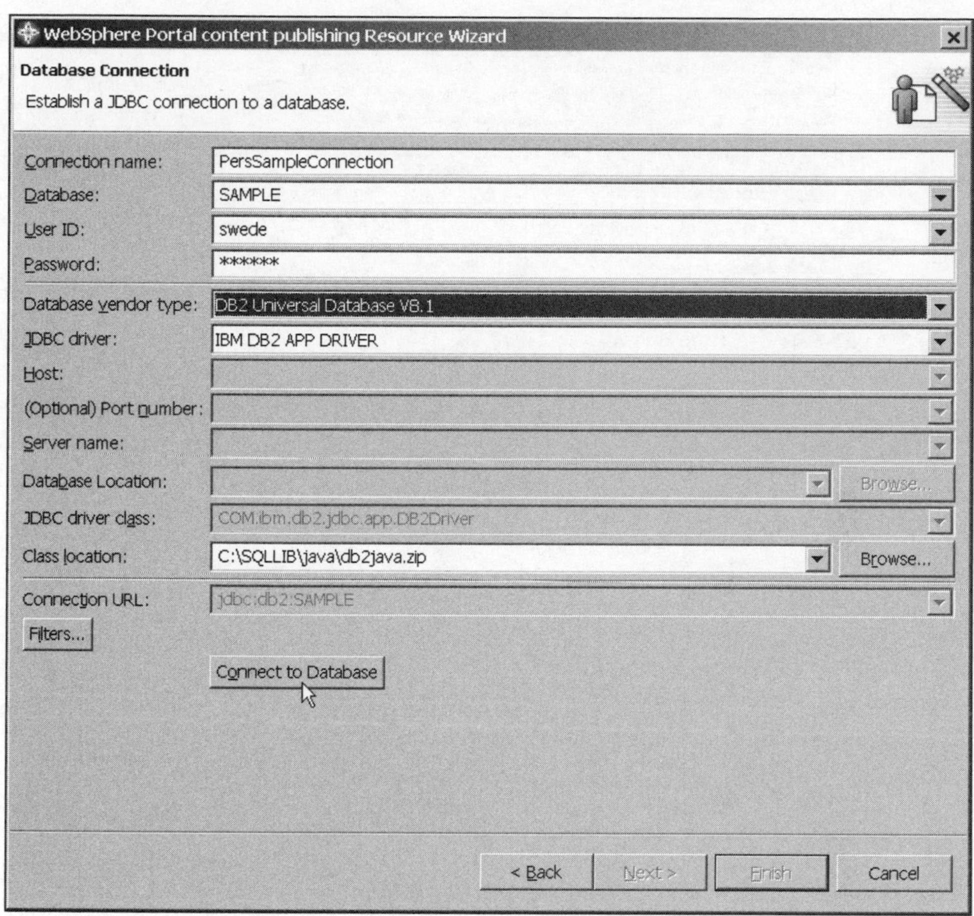

Figure 5.16: Connection to the database.

4. This brings you to the Tables tab of the Construct a Web Content Resource window. Select the **Tables** tab. Select the **CUSTOMER** table from the Available Tables list, as shown in Figure 5.17, and add it to the Selected Tables list. This will be your primary table for the user resource.

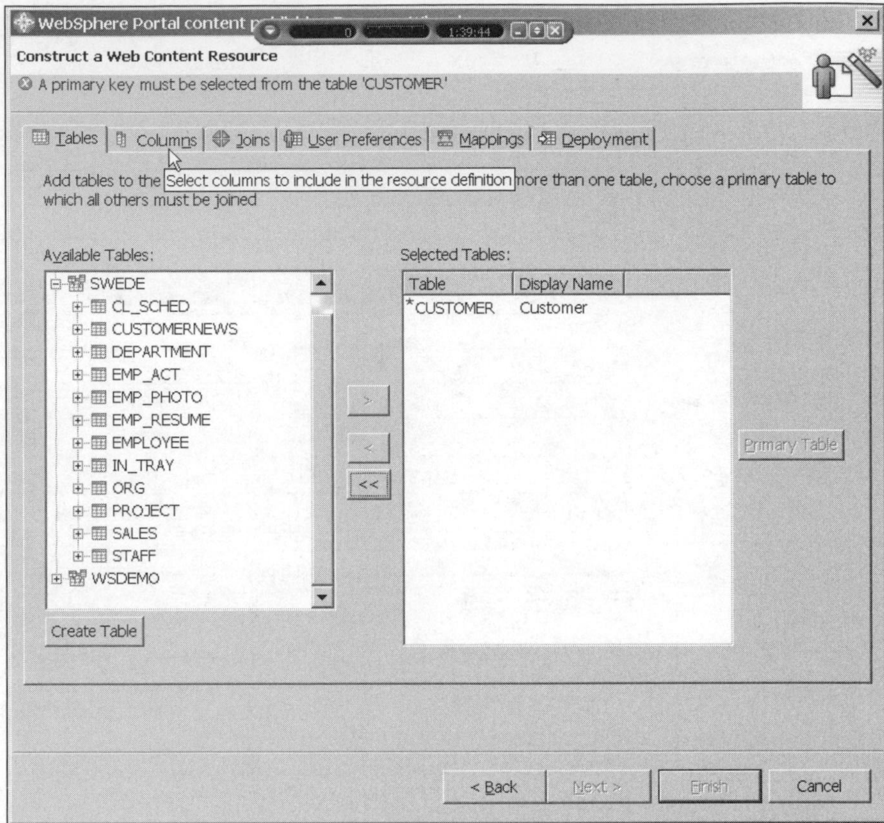

Figure 5.17: Choose the CUSTOMER table as the primary user resource.

5. Double-click on the Customer table in the right pane to edit its values. Ensure that the Enable runtime metadata check box is deselected, as show in Figure 5.18, and click **OK**. If you skip this step, you may run into problems later on!

Figure 5.18: Disabling runtime metadata.

6. Select the Columns tab and click the >> button to select all the columns in the table. You only need to select the primary key and any columns that you want to use to profile your users. In this case, the table is small so you can just select all the columns.

7. Select the Deployment tab and make sure the correct user ID and password are specified. Here, you must also ensure that the DataSource you specify matches the JNDI name of the data source you created in the first step of this exercise. Refer to Figure 5.19.

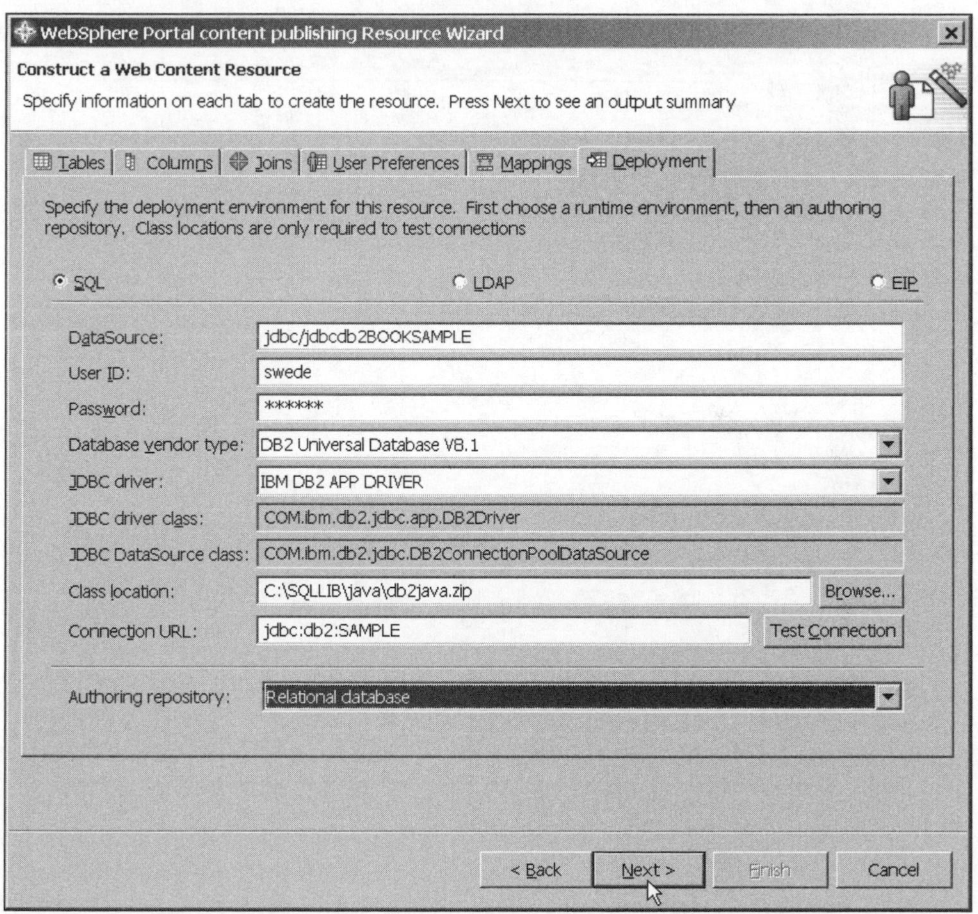

Figure 5.19: Setting the Deployment environment parameters.

8. Click **Next** and notice the files that will be created by the wizard, as shown in Figure 5.20. You can modify the generated file names if you desire. Ensure that the Include schema names in the generated Resource Runtime Manager check box is deselected. Here, you should specify that you want a Content Spot be generated for this resource. This saves you the trouble of running the Content Spot wizard. Click the **Finish** button.

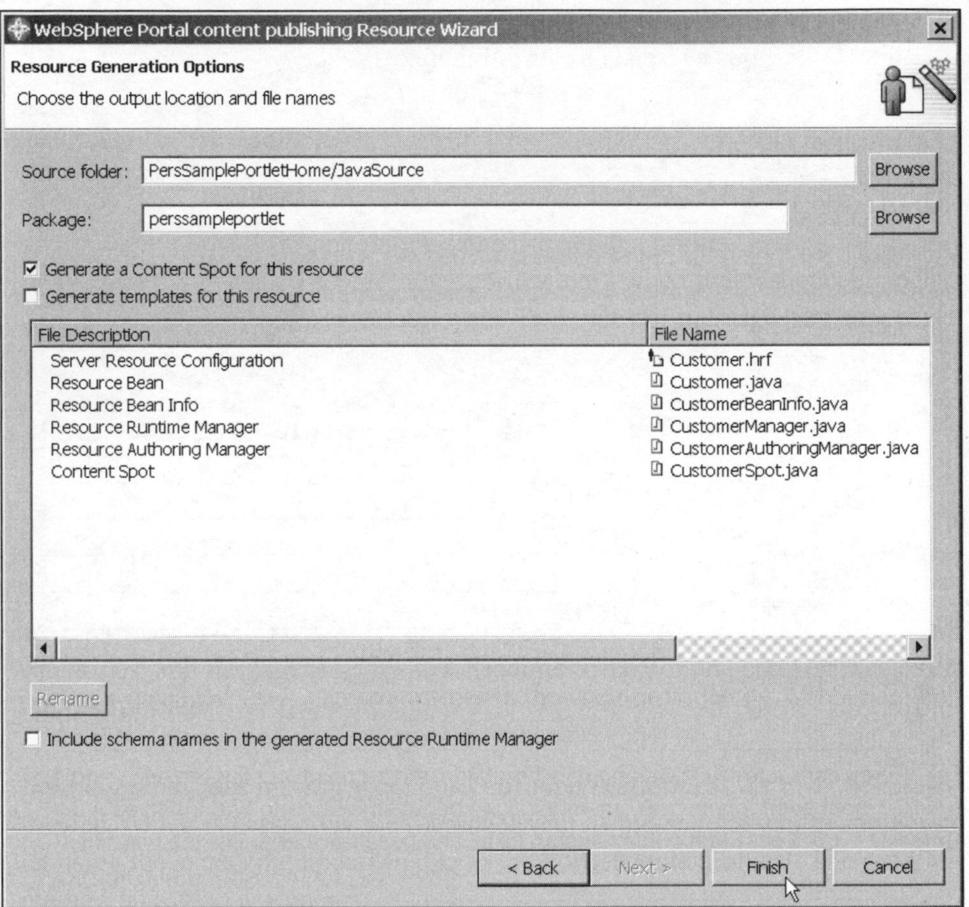

Figure 5.20: Files that will be created for the user resource.

Figure 5.21 highlights the files that the wizard generates. Notice that the Java files are compiled and placed in the appropriate place in the project. If you need to make changes to the resource, you can do so by double-clicking **Customer.hrf**, and stepping through the wizard.

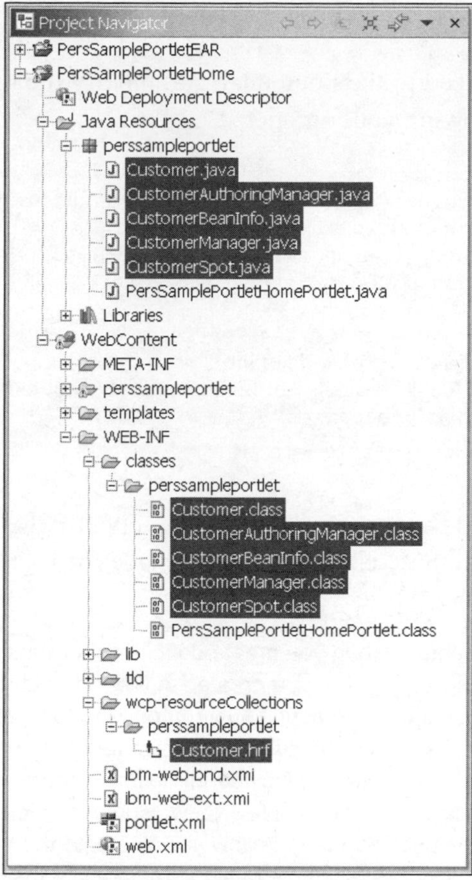

Figure 5.21: File structure in WSAD.

9. Repeat steps 2 through 7 to create the content resource files. When you have to choose a database table, select **CUSTOMERNEWS**.

Add the Content Spot and Code to the JSP

To add the content spots to the JSP file and write the associated code, follow these steps:

1. In WSAD, go to the /WebContent/perssampleportlet/jsp/html folder. Open **PersSamplePortletHomePortletView.jsp** with Page Designer Classic.

2. Go to the Design tab. Erase the existing lines in the JSP. Drag the **CustomerSpot.class** and **CustomernewsSpot.class** files and drop them onto the JSP.

3. Click **OK** to accept the default values for the bean.

4. Proceed to the Source tab and modify the useBean tag as shown in the following code snippet:

```
<jsp:useBean class="perssampleportlet.CustomerSpot"
  id="customerSpot">
<% customerSpot.setRequest(request); %>
</jsp:useBean

<jsp:useBean class="perssampleportlet.CustomernewsSpot"
  id="customernewsSpot">
<% customernewsSpot.setRequest(request);%>
</jsp:useBean>
```

The changes shown are required for every JSP that will talk to the personalization runtime, and these changes must be made for every content spot on the page.

Tip: By default, when you create definitions for these content spots in the Personalization UI, they are created in the root folder of the browser, which is named Workspace. Because it is a good idea to keep the content spots in the same folder structure as your project, we recommend that you change the display name of the bean to include the folder hierarchy you want the content spot to reside in. For example, you would specify id="/PersSample/customer Spot" in the useBean tag to allow you to create the content spot definition in the Workspace/PersSample directory along with the rest of your project.

---

5. Back in the Design tab type in **ACME Incorporated**. It is a good idea to have some static content such as this in the JSP page, so that you can verify the portlet is being displayed. (If your personalized content isn't returned the page is completely blank.)

6. Press **Enter** several times to create some white space, and then add a table, which will be populated by the rule. Go to the Design tab in the JSP editor. From the menu, choose **Insert→Table**. Select two rows and one column. Click **OK**.

7. Double-click the table to bring up its attributes window, as shown in Figure 5.22. This step specifies which resources are to be used to populate the table. Select the **Dynamic** tab, and then follow these steps:

7a. Check the **Loop** box.

7b. Specify **1** for the Start row and **1** for the End row.

7c. Click the **Browse** button to bring up the Bean Property Selection dialog.

7d. Select **customerSpot.ruleContent[]** and click **OK**.

7e. Click **OK** on the Attributes dialog to dismiss it.

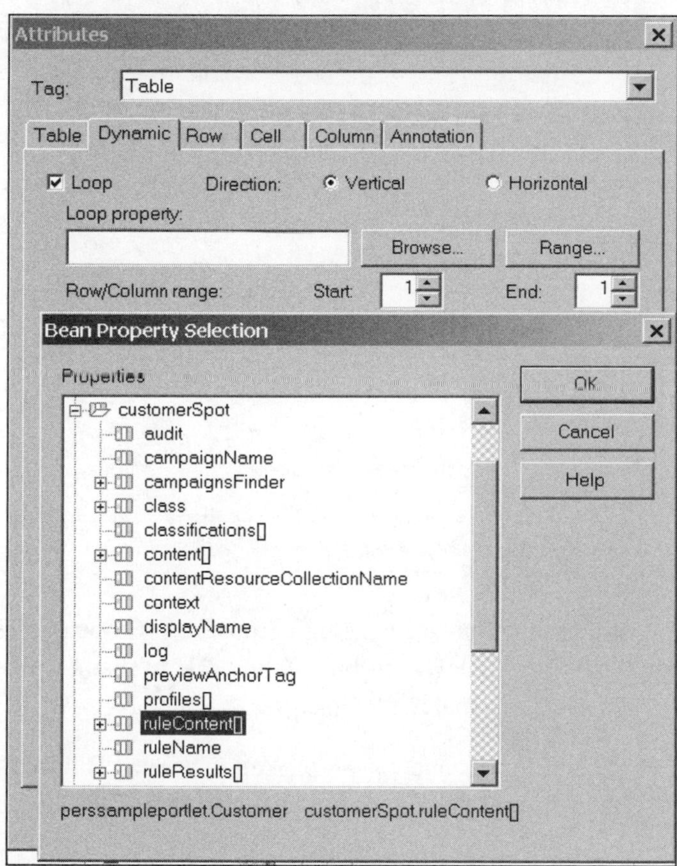

Figure 5.22: Setting the properties for the table.

8. Next, specify the attributes that will be used to populate the table, as follows:

8a. In the first row, type **You are logged in as:**. Click to the right side of the text.

8b. From the menu, select **Insert → Dynamic Elements → Property Display**. The screen that will be displayed is shown in Figure 5.23.

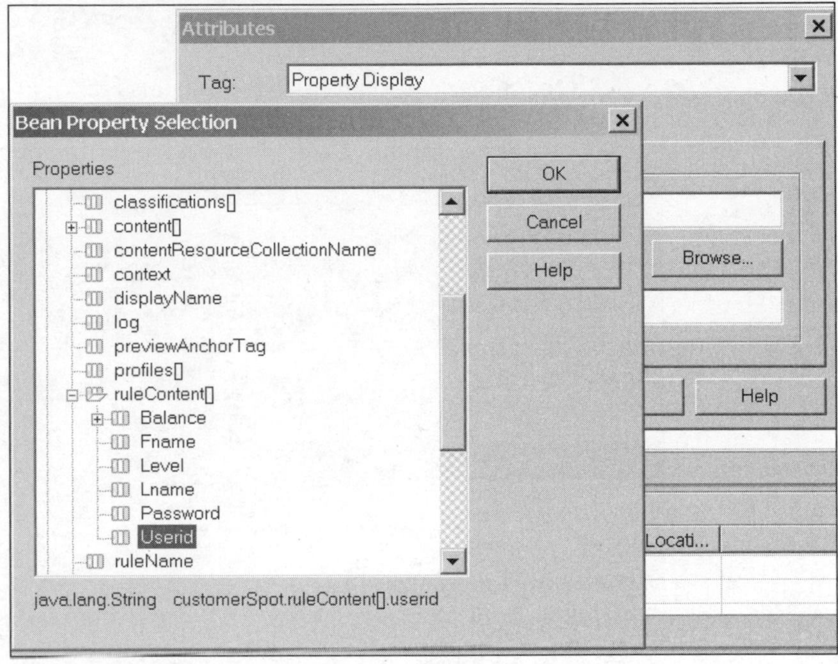

Figure 5.23: Specifying attributes.

8c. Click **Browse** to bring up the Bean Property Selection screen. Select the **USERID** attribute. Click **OK** to dismiss this screen, and again for the Attributes screen..

8d. In the second row, type **Your account Balance is:**. Repeat steps 8b and 8c, and this time select the attribute **BALANCE**.

9. Complete PersSamplePortletHomePortletView.jsp by adding a second table to the page:

9a. Choose two rows and one column. Again set the dynamic loop property on this table.

9b. The start and end row should be 2.

9c. Set the loop property to customernewsSpot.ruleContent.

10. Specify the attributes that will be used to populate this second table:

    10a. In the first row of the table, type **Here is your personalized news**

    10b. In the second row, you will insert the content. To do this again, click in the second row, and select **Insert → Dynamic Elements → Property Display**.

    10c. From the Bean Property Selection screen, choose the content attribute. Click **OK** to dismiss the screen.

11. You are done adding content to the JSP, so save PersSamplePortletHome PortletView.jsp.

Export the WAR File

To export the WAR file from WSAD, follow these steps:

1. Back in WSAD, right-click the **PersSamplePortletHome** folder and select **Export...**

2. The Export window is displayed. Select **War file** and click **Next**.

3. Choose the location to which you want to export the WAR file, as shown in Figure 5.24, and click **Finish**.

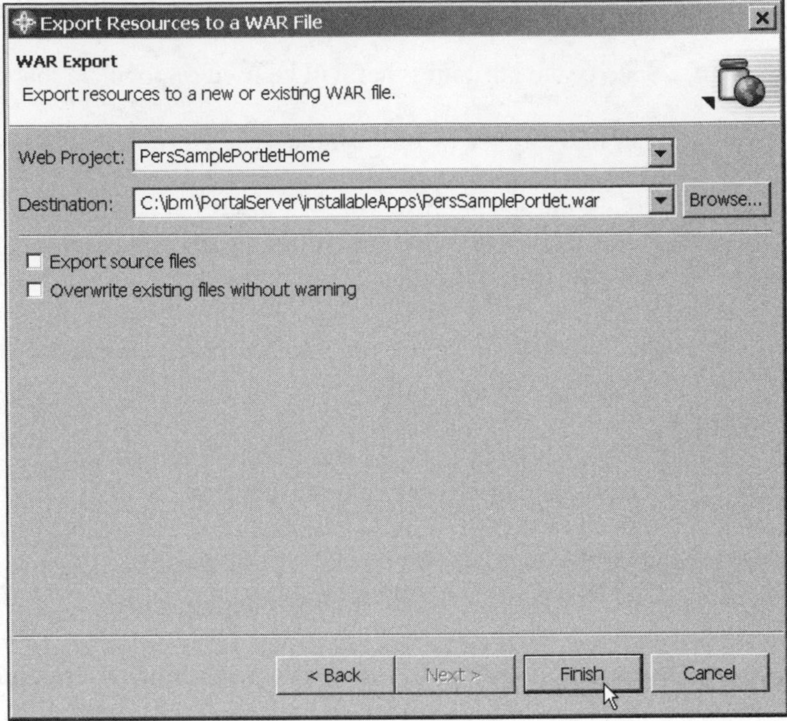

Figure 5.24: WAR file export screen.

Deploy the Portlet into WebSphere Portal

The last step in working with the portlet is to deploy it into WebSphere Portal by installing the WAR file and then placing the portlet on a page. This is easily done by logging in as the Portal Administrator. Under Administration, go to the **Portlet Management → Web Modules** page and install the portlet by pointing to the exported WAR file and clicking **Next**, as shown in Figure 5.25.

Figure 5.25: Installing the PersSamplePortletHome portlet.

On the second screen, as shown in Figure 5.26, simply click **Finish** to install the portlet.

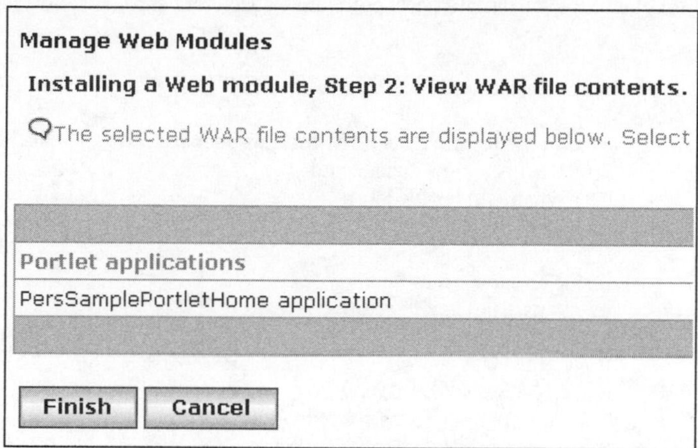

Figure 5.26: Installing the PersSamplePortleHome portlet.

Note: Remember to add all authenticated users to the User role for the portlet.

Finally, add the portlet to a page. That completes the task of deploying the Personalization Sample Portlet into WebSphere Portal.

Create an AuthIDTranslator Class

In this sample, we don't have security turned on, so we don't have to use a translator class, but it is a recommended practice to use one. In this way, you only have to write the code once, and it is used by any portlet that uses the user resource it is registered to. Figure 5.27 shows an implementation that maps a Portal user ID to the simple id. This code also works for the format returned by IBM Tivoli Directory Server.

```
package com.ibm.poc.pzn;

import com.ibm.websphere.personalization.security.*;
public class UserInfo implements com.ibm.websphere.personalization.security.AuthIDTranslator
{

  public String translateAuthID (String name) {

          System.out.println("The name that has been passed is : " + name);
          String delim = new String ("uid=");
          int x = name.indexOf(delim);

          // find comma
          String comma = new String (",");
          int y = name.indexOf(comma,x);

          // get uid
          if ((x >= 0) && (y>=0))
                    name = name.substring(x+4,y);
          System.out.println(" **** New name:  " + name);
          return name;

  }
}
```

Figure 5.27: The AuthIDTranslator class.

Place the Resources in a Shared Library

The resources and content spots you created in WSAD must be placed in the classpath so that they are available to the Personalization portlets. The best way to do this is to put them into a shared library and associate the shared library with the Personalization Workspace EAR.

Import the Resources into the Workspace

This is the last step before you can start creating business rules. The xml definitions of the resources you created must be imported into the workspace. These definitions are used to create an object in the workspace that represents the resources. The actual resources are not imported. This is also a good time to set the translator class for the user resource.

1. Create a new folder under the Workspace folder in the Personalization Navigator by selecting the Workspace folder and then click **New → Folder**. Name the folder PersSample. This will be used to hold all of the personalization files for this sample.

2. Select this new folder and click **Import**, as shown in Figure 5.28.

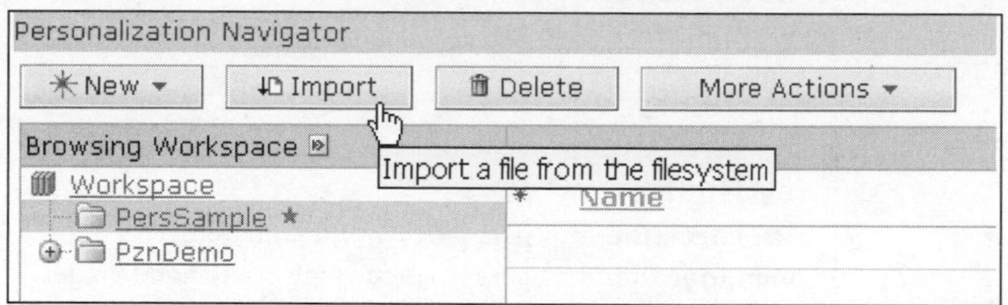

Figure 5.28: Importing a resource.

3. Click **Browse**, and browse to the Customer.hrf file in the Portal Servers InstalledApps directory. Select Customer.hrf and click **Import**.

4. Do steps 2 and 3 again, this time importing Customernews.hrf. You should now see both collections, as shown in Figure 5.29:

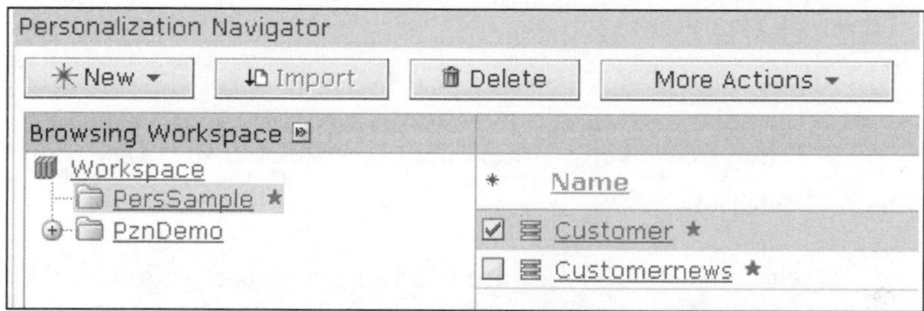

Figure 5.29: The new resources in the browser.

5. Double-click on the Customer resource, or select it and then click **Edit** in the Personalization Editor. Refer to Figure 5.30 to add the Translator class to the Resource.

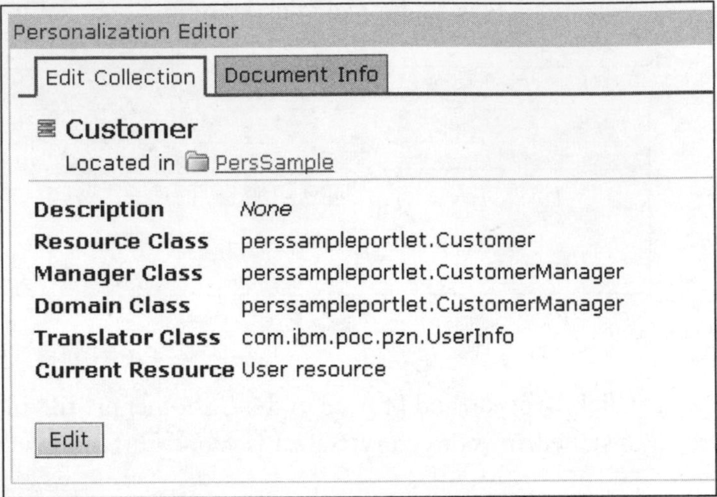

Figure 5.30: Adding the translator to the user resource.

Create the Rules

The following types of rules will be created:

- The UserLevel profiler rule classifies the user based on the balance in her account.
- Several *action rules* are used to get information about the current user and fetch news articles based on the suitable level.
- A *binding rule* ties the classifier and action rules.

Create the UserLevel Profiler Rule

Back in the Personalization UI, perform the following steps:

1. Select the PersSample folder and click **New → Rule** to activate the Personalization Rule Editor.
2. Create the new rule as follows, using Figure 5.31 for guidance:

   2a. Name the profiler UserLevel.

   2b. Make sure Profiler is selected from the Rule Type list box.

2c. Click **Profile** in the rule body, and name this profile Basic.

2d. Click **Resource.Attribute** and select **current Customer** for the Resource and **Balance** for the Attribute.

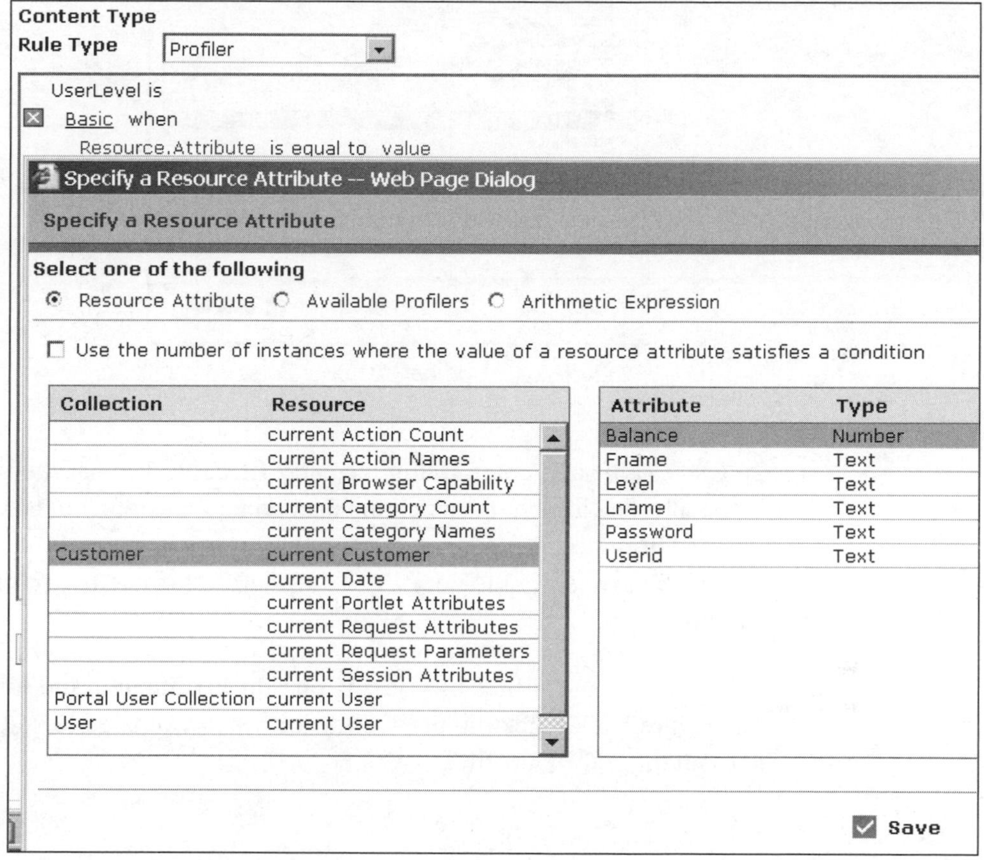

Figure 5.31: Creating the profiler rule.

2e. Click **is equal to** and change it to **is less than or equal to**. See Figure 5.32 to see all the different options you have for comparing numbers.

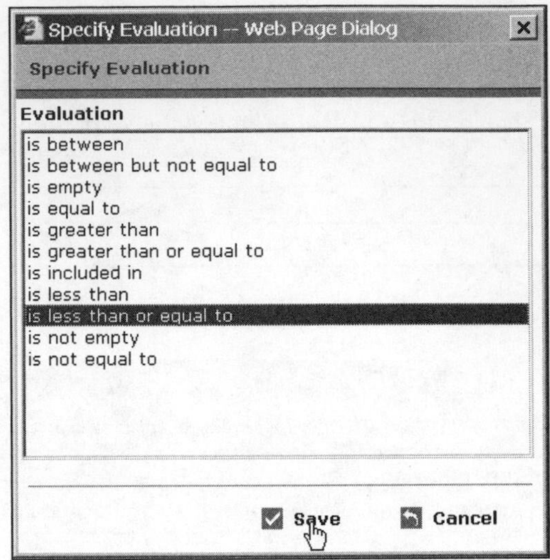

Figure 5.32: Comparison operators.

2f. Click **value** and enter **100** in the entry field. Notice that the value must be of type Number to match the data type of Customer.balance and that, in addition to entering a numeric value, you click one of the other radio buttons to specify the number as a resource attribute or arithmetic expression.

3. Continue adding profiles by clicking on **add Profile** until the rule looks like Figure 5.33. Click on **add Condition** when you need to add more than one condition for a profile.

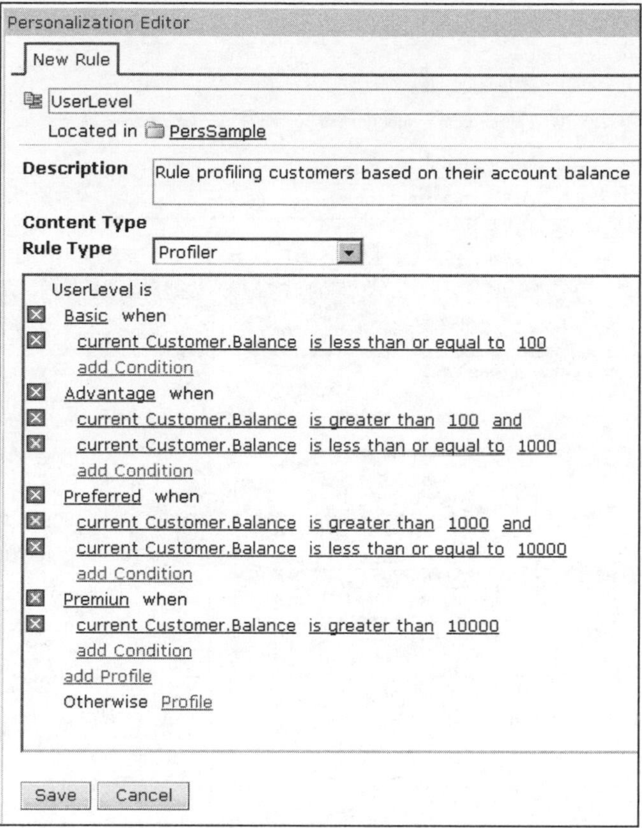

Figure 5.33: UserLevel profiler rule.

Create the GetCurrentUser Action Rule

Create a second new rule and follow these steps:

1. Name the rule GetCurrentUser.
2. Make sure Select Content is selected from the Rule Type list box.
3. Select **Resource attribute**, then choose Resource: current Customer and Attribute: **Userid**, as shown in Figure 5.34.

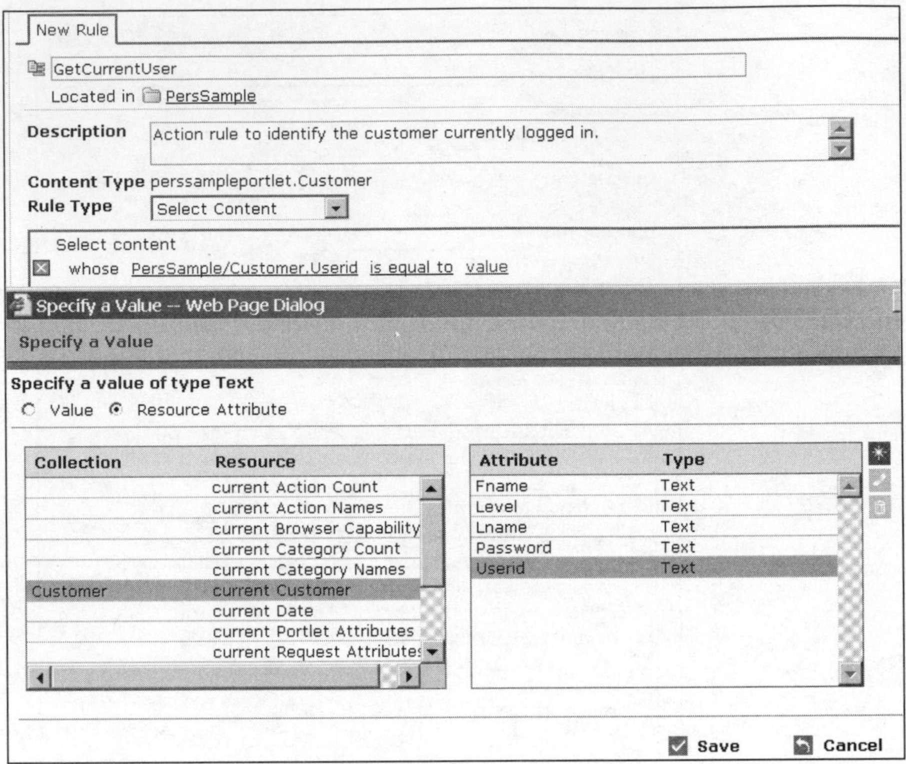

Figure 5.34: Composing an action rule.

4. Save the value. Notice that it changes from Customer.Userid to current Customer.Userid, as shown in Figure 5.35:

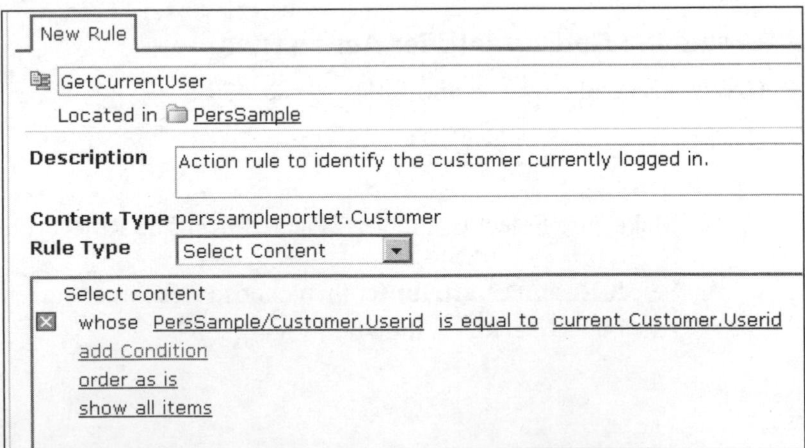

Figure 5.35: The completed GetCurrentUser action rule.

Create the GetBasicNews Action Rule

Follow these steps to create the second, more traditional, action rule:

1. Create the GetBasicNews action rule as shown in Figure 5.36.

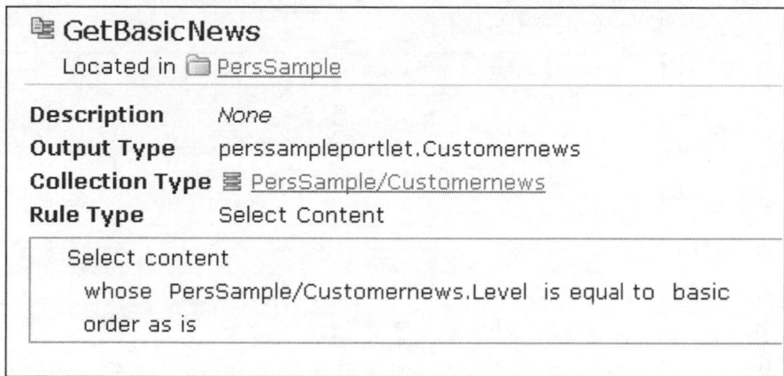

Figure 5.36: The completed GetBasicNews action rule.

Create the Remaining Action Rules

Create the remaining four rules following the same pattern as the GetBasicNews rule. The details of the remaining rules are provided in Table 5.2.

Table 5.2: Remaining Action Rules for the Sample Portlet

Rule Name	Rule
GetAdvantageNews	Select content whose Customernews.LEVEL is equal to advantage.
GetPreferredNews	Select content whose Customernews.LEVEL is equal to preferred.
GetPremiumNews	Select content whose Customernews.LEVEL is equal to premium.
GetRequiredNews	Select content whose Customernews.LEVEL is equal to all.

Create the GetCustomerNews Binding Rule

Now, create a binding rule to combine the profiler rule with the action rules:

1. Name the rule GetCustomerNews.

2. Click **Profiler** to list available profilers. Select the **UserLevel** profiler, as shown in Figure 5.37.

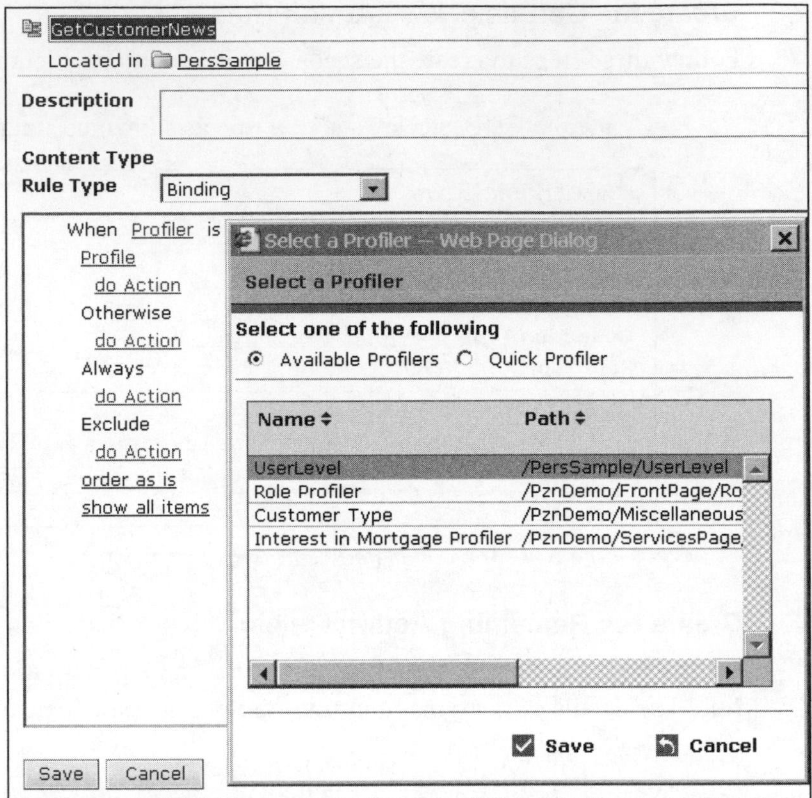

Figure 5.37: Composing the GetCustomerNews binding rule.

3. Click **Save**.

4. Click **Profile**. You are presented with a list of profiles that have been defined by the profiler, as shown in Figure 5.38.

5. Choose **Basic**. Click **Save**.

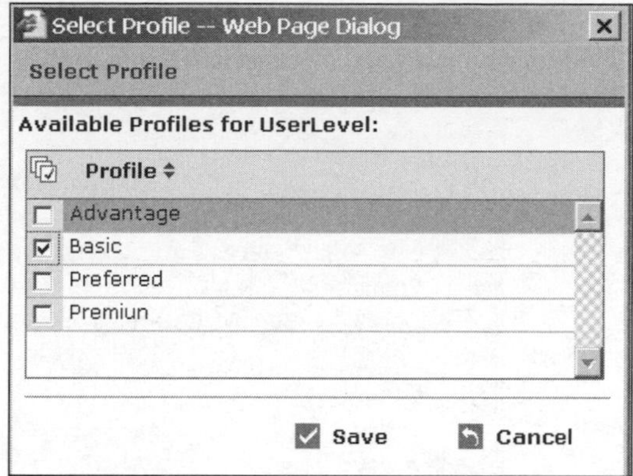

Figure 5.38: A list of available profiles.

6. Click **do Action**. You are presented with a list of action rules that have been defined.

7. Select the most applicable action. In Figure 5.39, GetBasicNews is selected. Notice that you are not limited to actions, but can also nest profiler rules in a binding rule.

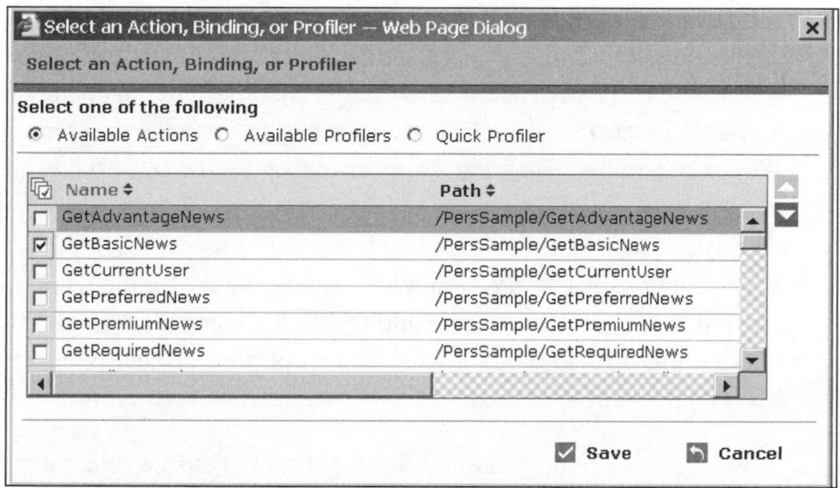

Figure 5.39: A list of available action rules.

8. Complete the GetCustomerNews binding rule as shown in Figure 5.40.

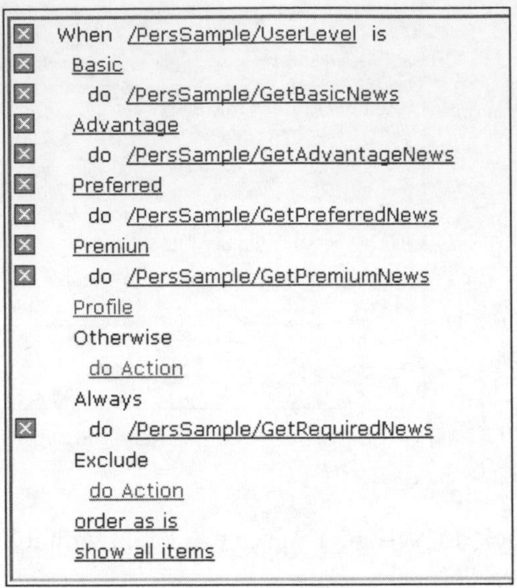

Figure 5.40: The completed binding rule.

Associate Rules with Content Spots

The next step is to take the rules that were just created and assign them to content spots. You must also create definitions in the workspace for all the content spots you create outside the workspace, such as those created using the RAD and WSAD wizards. Unless you included the folder hierarchy in the display name of the content spot in the JSP, these content spot definitions *must* be created in the Workspace folder. They must also have exactly the same name as the original content spot.

If you had specified "/PersSample/CustomerSpot" for the display name when you created the content spot you could create the content spot definition in the PersSample directory along with the rest of your project. We recommend that you keep the content spot definitions with the rest of your project.

1. In the Personalization UI select the Workspace folder and click **New → Content Spot**. Refer to Figure 5.41 to fill in the values for CustomerSpot. You can save time by setting the rule mapping right here, since the rules are all created. Only rules that return the type specified for the Output Type are listed in the Default Mapping list box.

Personalization Editor	
New Content Spot	
CustomerSpot	
Located in PersSample	
Description	
Output Type	Customer This resource class is used by the resource collection "/PersSample/Customer".
Default Mapping	/PersSample/GetCurrentUser
Save Cancel	

Figure 5.41: Creating a new content spot.

2. Create the CustomernewsSpot content spot, and map the GetCustomerNews binding rule to it.

Test the Portlet

Now, you get to test the portlet. Follow these steps:

1. Create three users via the Portal Self Registration menu. For testing purposes, make the user IDs and passwords user1, user2, and user3.

2. Log in to the portal as user1. Go to the page where you added the portlet. You should see a result similar to Figure 5.42.

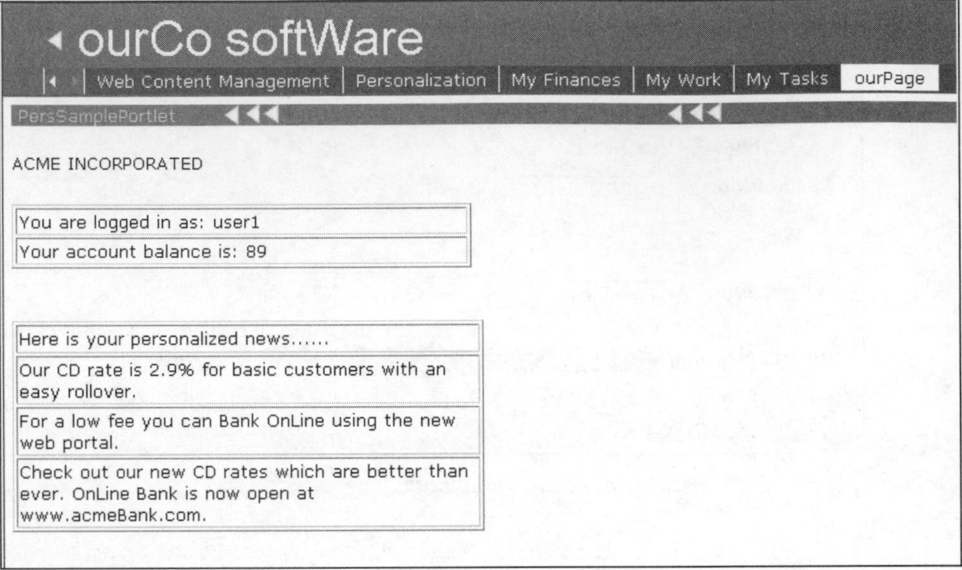

Figure 5.42: View of the portlet for user1.

3. Log off as user1.

4. Log in to the portal as user2. You should see the screen shown in Figure 5.43. Notice that user2 has a balance of $1002, and so has been classified as a preferred customer. User2 sees news relevant to preferred customers.

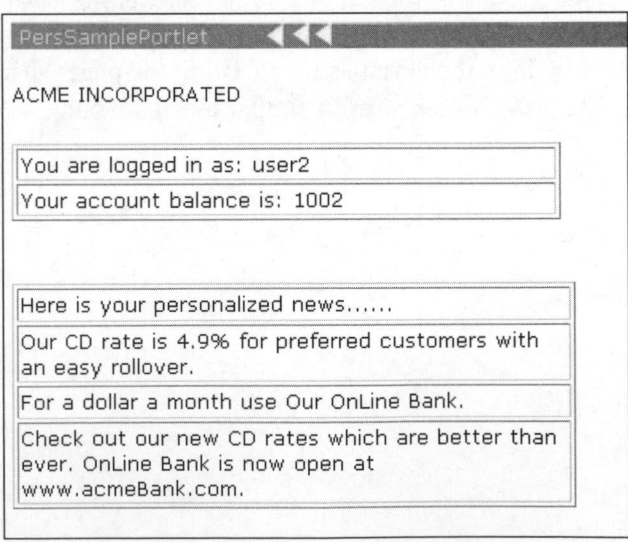

Figure 5.43: Personalized news for user2.

5. Log off as user2.

6. Last, log in to the portal as user3. Can you tell how user3 is profiled, and do you see news unique to that class of users? Hint: check the CD rate.

That concludes the exercise of creating, deploying, and testing a personalized portlet.

Miscellaneous Topics

WebSphere Personalization is a very mature, robust component that provides lots of functionality. In this section, we give you an overview of some of the more interesting features and touch upon its performance aspects.

Content Spot Exits

Content Spot exits allow you to modify the standard content spot processing. To code an exit, you simply need to implement the RuleExit interface.

Prior to executing the default rule, the aboutToExecuteRule() callback method is invoked allowing you to:

- Access request and session information
- Get the names of the campaign and rule to be executed
- Set information in the personalization context, such as the user, which may could change what content is returned
- Change which rule is executed or bypass rule execution completely

After the rule executes, the getFilteredResults() callback method is called to allow you to modify the result set. You can add, remove, or modify items from the results.

This function should be used with care. This is not something that business users should normally code, although they certainly need to understand what one of these exits does, because it affects the processing of the business rules a user writes. Note that instances of the same content spot exit class are used for all content spots.

Using Personalization Programmatically

You can access all types of WebSphere Personalization rules from within a Java application. You simply create the content spot bean, set the request object on it, set the rule on the bean, and then trigger the rule. This is interesting because normally personalization processing occurs when the JSP page is being built for display. This capability allows you to do personalization processing before the page is built, thus allowing you to use business rules to decide what page to display for example. It allows you to personalize the user experience in nonstandard ways limited only by your imagination.

You can also access resource collections directly without using business rules. All you need to know is the name of the resource collection. There may be times when you don't want the overhead of the Rules engine, though as we pointed out in the performance section, typically rules aren't the source of performance problems.

Debugging

As with most problems in WebSphere, the first thing you should do when you experience problems is look in the Application Server logs where you are running Personalization. This often provides the answer to your problem or clues to help you know what to look at.

If you don't see any problems in the log, or if you need more information to figure out what is going on, you can turn on additional personalization tracing. For personalization problems, the following two specifications will provide extensive information about what is going on in the guts of Personalization. The first specification is for the runtime trace, the second is for the authoring trace.

- com.ibm.websphere.personalization.*=all=enabled
- com.ibm.dm.pzn.ui.*=all=enabled

If you are using WebSphere Portal, tracing is enable through Portal trace services. To specify and enable tracing in WebSphere Portal, go to **Administration → Portal Analysis→Enable Tracing**. You can also edit <WPS_Home>/shared/app/config/log.properties. If you are running Personalization outside Portal as a standalone runtime server, use WebSphere Application Server's dynamic tracing facility to turn on tracing for the application server.

Performance

Typically, performance problems associated with personalization are attributed to the database repository. Some of the things you can look at in the databases used as data stores for personalization resources include:

- Make sure the databases are tuned
- Try not to join more than three tables in a resource
- Whenever possible, use inner joins instead of outer joins; ensure that making this change still provides the desired results, because inner and outer joins are functionally different
- Double click on all tables in each resource and make sure that the use run-time metadata checkbox is unchecked
- Rule complexity in and of itself doesn't typically lead to performance problems; you do need to understand though, that each select action in a rule results in a separate query

WebSphere Personalization also caches result sets returned from resources. Caching is controlled by the

<WPS Home>\shared\app\config\services\PersonalizationService.properties file.

You can turn caching on or off globally for all resource collections. You can also control caching for each individual collection separately. Finally, you can set caching globally and then override the setting for individual collections.

The options you have are to enable/disable caching, set the cache timeout, set the cache priority, and most important, you can set the maximum size result set that you wish cached. By default, caching is globally enabled, the timeout is 300, the priority is 1, and the maximum size set cached is 25. The file has examples for setting individual resource collections.

Another thing to check when experiencing performance problems is the application server logs to see if any exceptions are being thrown. You may find that you have other errors and exceptions that are causing or contributing to degraded performance.

Personalization Samples

Two personalization samples are shipped with WebSphere Portal. One sample demonstrates rules-based personalization, while the other is a collaborative filtering sample.

The YourCo Rules-Based Sample

This sample is not documented in the Info Center. You can find the sample in the <WPS Home>\pzn\V5.1\sample directory.

A readme.html file in the documentation directory tells you how to install this sample. We strongly recommend that the first thing you do when you are starting with WebSphere Personalization is to install and explore this sample. The source is also included, so this is an excellent learning vehicle.

The readme.html file documents the users who are defined for the sample. If you log into Portal with one of these user IDs, the sample will look and work great but you won't be able to view anything in the Navigator portlet, because the sample users don't have the authorization to use the portlet. Instead, I recommend that you log in as wpsadmin or some other administrative ID. The sample won't display any personalized content, but a user information portlet on the first page lets you switch to any of the users defined by the sample. Now, you can play with the sample, yet still go back and look at the rules that are generating the content.

The Movie Critic Collaborative Filtering Sample

This sample is well documented in the Info Center. If you think that collaborative filtering might be part of your solution, or you don't understand this capability well enough to know if it applies, you should explore this example.

Door Closings

One of the key aspects of creating a portal is providing users the ability to personalize a Web site. All portal visitors should feel that they are visiting a portal site created just for them, with the content they are interested in. The personalization component of WebSphere Portal makes it easy to do just that—give the user experience a personal touch.

Chapter 6
Portal Building Blocks

From a user's perspective, a portlet is a window on a portal page that provides a specific service or piece of information. For example, there are calendar portlets and a portlets that let users access their e-mail. From an application-development perspective, portlets are pluggable modules that are designed to run inside a portlet container or a portal server.

The *portlet container* provides the runtime environment in which portlets are instantiated, used, and destroyed. The *portal runtime* provides the infrastructure to access user-profile information, participate in window and action events, communicate with other portlets, access remote content, look up credentials, and store persistent data. WebSphere Portal comes with the Portlet API (Application Programming Interface) to provide this support. The Portlet API, presented in this chapter, is the first step toward developing a standard API.

WebSphere Portal also supports the new Portlet API, as specified by JSR 168. This specification passed through the Java community process recently and has been adopted by other portal server vendors too. IBM provided a reference implementation for the JSR in WP V5.0.2.1, and it is fully supported in this WP V5.1. The two major sections of this chapter accommodate discussion of both the APIs. We discuss the IBM Portlet API first, and then the JSR 168 API.

The IBM Portlet API

Portlet Concepts

A portlet is created using the Portlet API. Once created and packaged as an application, the portlet has a lifecycle within the portlet container. The portlet operates in certain modes and is displayed in a certain state on the portal page. These concepts are explained in the next few sections.

Portlet and Servlet API

The abstract portlet class is the central abstraction of the Portlet API. It extends HttpServlet from the Servlet API. Therefore, portlets are special kinds of servlets that can run inside a portal server. Unlike servlets, however, portlets cannot send redirects or errors to browsers, forward requests, or write arbitrary markup to the output stream.

Portlets are administered more dynamically than servlets—for example, portlets can be updated without having to restart the portal server. Typical administration operations on portlets include:

- Portal applications consisting of several portlets can be installed or removed using the portal administrative interface.
- An administrator can change the settings of a portlet. For example, the portal administrator can change the configuration parameters for a portlet and point it to different values.
- Portlets can be created and deleted dynamically by administration portlets. A good example of this would be the Clipping portlet, which creates a new portlet instance whenever an administrator creates a new clipping.

The portlet container uses the J2EE architecture implementation provided by WebSphere Application Server. Hence, portlets are packaged in WAR files (Web Archive) files as are J2EE Web applications, and they are deployed like servlets. Just like a servlet, a portlet is defined to the application server using the Web application deployment descriptor (web.xml). This file defines the portlet's class file, the servlet mapping, and the read-only initialization parameters. A more extensive description of the deployment descriptor follows later in this chapter.

Portlet Lifecycle

Theportlet lifecycle is similar to the servlet lifecycle. They both follow the same creation, deployment, usage, and deletion steps. Figure 6.1 shows the lifecycle of a portlet as it is created, placed on a page, and accessed by users.

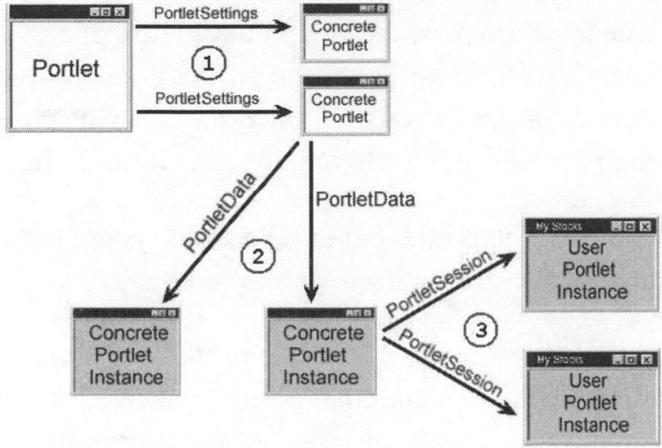

Figure 6.1: Lifecycle of a portlet, from the WebSphere Portal InfoCenter.

In step 1 of Figure 6.1, a new portlet is either deployed or installed by the portal administrator. This operation results in the creation of a *concrete* portlet, which is a portlet parameterized by a single PortletSettings object. Each portlet can have many concrete portlets. PortletSettings objects are read/write accessible and can be persisted. These objects contain configuration parameters, which are defined in the portlet deployment descriptor.

The use of concrete portlets allows many instances of a portlet to run with different configurations, without creating extra portlet class instances. During the lifecycle of a single portlet, many concrete portlets can be created and destroyed. No object explicitly represents the concrete portlet. The same concrete portlet can be shared across many users.

Step 2 of Figure 6.1 shows placing a portlet on a page. This results in the creation of a concrete portlet instance, which is a concrete portlet parameterized by a single PortletData object. A PortletData object can be used to persist information for a portlet that has been added to a page. For example, a user can edit a stock-quotes portlet and save a list of stock symbols to be tracked. An example of this is shown later in this chapter.

In step 3 of Figure 6.1, the scope of the PortletData depends on the scope of the page that contains the concrete portlet:

- If the portal administrator puts a concrete portlet on a group page, then the PortletData object contains data stored for the group of users. This holds true for a group of users who have View access to the page. However, if users have Edit access to the portlet on a group page, then a new concrete portlet instance is created for each user who edits the portlet. In this case, the PortletData object contains data for each user who edits the portlet.

- If a concrete portlet is put on a user's page, the PortletData contains data for that user.

When a user logs into the portal, the portal server creates a PortletSession for each of the user's portlets. A concrete portlet instance parameterized by a PortletSession is known as a *user portlet instance*. Many user portlet instances can exist per concrete portlet instance.

Portlet Application

A portlet application is a logical group of related portlets that share the same context. The context contains all resources, like images, property files, and classes. All portlets must be packaged as part of a portlet application.

A portlet application parameterized with a single PortletApplicationSettings object is called a *concrete portlet application*. Many concrete portlet applications may exist for each portlet application. A concrete portlet application contains at least one concrete portlet from the portlet application.

Portlet Modes

Portlet modes allow a portlet to display a different user interface, depending on the task required. The Portlet API essentially supports modes: View, Help, Edit, and Configure. Table 6.1 lists the functionality of each mode.

Table 6.1: Portlet Mode Functions

Portlet Mode	Functionality
View	When a user initially loads a portlet on the portal page, it is displayed in View mode. This is the default mode of a portlet.
Help	The portlet provides online help for users to obtain more information, when Help mode is supported by the portlet.
Edit	When supported by the portlet, Edit mode provides a page for users to custom-ize the portlet for their own needs. For example, a mail portlet can provide a page for users to specify the location of their mail servers, usernames, and passwords.
Configure	When supported, Configure mode provides a page for portal administrators to configure a portlet for a user or a group of users.

Portlet States

Portlet states allow a user to change how the portlet is displayed within the portal. This behavior is similar to how any Windows application is manipulated. Portlet states are maintained in the PortletWindow.States object with a Boolean value. The Portlet API supports three states in a portlet: Normal, Maximized, and Minimized. These are described in Table 6.2.

Table 6.2: Portlet States

Portlet State	Definition
Normal	When a portlet initially gets constructed on the page, it shows up in this state. It shows up along with the other portlets.
Maximized	When a portlet is maximized, it takes up the entire body of the portal, hiding all other portlets on that page.
Minimized	When a portlet is minimized, only the portlet's title bar is displayed on the page.

Solo State

Starting with WPS 5.0, there is support for a new state called the Solo State. In Solo State the portlet takes over the entire screen by hiding any portal theme elements like banner page, navigation, or tool bar. Also, no facility exists in the portlet deployment descriptor to declare a portlet's support for solo state. A portlet can enter solo state in the following two ways:

- From outside a portlet, using the <wps:URLGeneration portletWindowState="solo"/> tag
- From inside a portlet, using the <portletAPI:createURI state="solo"/> tag or the createURI(PortletWindow.State SOLO) method

A portlet cannot enter solo state unless a user has logged in. It is up to the developer of the portlet to decide which elements are to be hidden. A portlet can exit out of solo state by using the createReturnURI() method to return to the normal portal interface.

Portlet Development

Now that you know about portlet concepts, it is time to delve into portlet development. At a high level, portlet development can be divided into the following three tasks:

1. Program a portlet
2. Build the portlet
3. Test the portlet

You will learn about building and testing a portlet first, and then get into the details of portlet programming.

Building a Portlet

This section discusses the steps required to create a simple portlet that displays "Hello World" when rendered. For this example, we assume that a Java file called HelloWorldPortlet.java has already been written. The steps to creating the portlet WAR file are listed here:

1. Set up the portlet development environment.
2. Compile the Java code.
3. Create the deployment descriptors.
4. Set up the directory structure for the WAR file.
5. Package the portlet into a WAR file.

Step 1: Set Up the Portlet Development Environment

To develop portlets, you must set up the development environment, which will make the task of writing, testing, and debugging portlets easier. At a minimum, we recommend the following tools:

- WebSphere Application Server and all its prerequisites.
- An integrated development environment (IDE) for Java development, such as WebSphere Studio Application Developer (WSAD). You can develop portlets using your own favorite editor, but WSAD has a portlet development toolkit, which makes the task of writing portlets much easier. The Portal toolkit also lets you set up a Portal environment inside WSAD, which you can use to test and debug your portlets. Plus, you can also use the built-in remote debugging capability of WSAD to debug portlets at runtime.
- WebSphere Portal server, if you are not using the built-in Portal test environment.
- A HTML editor that handles Java Server Page (JSP) files, such as WSAD. WSAD provides a semi-WYSIWYG editor that assists in the development of Web pages.

Note: If you are not using WSAD for development, make sure your system's PATH variable is set up to use the JDK that is shipped with WebSphere Application Server.

Step 2: Compile the Java Code

For now, assume you have written the portlet code. (You will see the details on writing the actual code in subsequent sections.) Here are the steps to create the portlet WAR file and test it by deploying it to the portal:

1. Copy the code in Figure 6.2 and save it in a file called HelloWorldPortlet.java.

```
import java.io.*;

import org.apache.jetspeed.portlet.*;
import org.apache.jetspeed.portlets.*;
import com.ibm.wps.portlets.*;

public class HelloWorldPortlet extends PortletAdapter {

  public void init( PortletConfig portletConfig ) throws
    UnavailableException {
    super.init( portletConfig );
  }

  public void doView( PortletRequest request, PortletResponse response )
    throws PortletException, IOException {
    PrintWriter writer = response.getWriter();
```

Figure 6.2: Source code for HelloWorldPortlet (part 1 of 2).

```
    writer.println( "Hello World! This is sample output text for the
      doView() method." );
  }
/*
  public void doHelp( PortletRequest request, PortletResponse response )
   throws PortletException, IOException {
   PrintWriter writer = response.getWriter();
   writer.print( "Hello! This is sample output text for the doHelp() method." );
  }
*/

/*
  public void doEdit( PortletRequest request, PortletResponse response )
    throws PortletException, IOException {
    PrintWriter writer = response.getWriter();
    writer.print( "Hello! This is sample output text for the doEdit()
      method." );
  }
*/


/*
  public void doConfigure( PortletRequest request, PortletResponse
    response ) throws PortletException, IOException {
    PrintWriter writer = response.getWriter();
    writer.print( "Hello! This is sample output text for the
      doConfigure() method." );
  }
*/

}
```

Figure 6.2: Source code for HelloWorldPortlet (part 2 of 2).

2. Notice that the HelloWorldPortlet code simply prints out a "Hello World" message to the portlet window in the browser.

3. To set up for code compilation, all the relevant JAR files must be in the CLASSPATH environment variable. At a minimum, the following files should always be in your CLASSPATH:

   - <WAS_HOME>/lib/app/portlet-api.jar
   - <WAS_HOME>/lib/app/wps.jar
   - <WAS_HOME>/lib/app/wpsportlets.jar

4. Now the code can be compiled using the *javac* command. Once the CLASSPATH has been set, the portlet can be compiled using the following command:

```
javac -classpath %CLASSPATH% HelloWorldPortlet
```

5. You now need to package these files as a WAR file. The WAR file typically contains Java class files, source files, descriptors, and other resource files (like images required by the portlet). The HelloWorld Portlet example has no special resource files. Descriptors are required in all WAR files. This example has two descriptors: Deployment Descriptor and Portlet Descriptor. Both are XML-based files.

Tip: An IDE like WebSphere Studio Application Developer (WSAD) creates all the files needed for packaging a portlet.

Step 3: Create the Deployment Descriptors

As mentioned, the WAR file contains two deployment descriptors, web.xml and portlet.xml, containing the information necessary for the portal server to install and configure the portlet.

In the web.xml Deployment Descriptor, each portlet is defined as a servlet within the Web application, including the portlet class and any initialization parameters. A sample web.xml file for the HelloWorldPortlet is displayed in Figure 6.3. If you have seen a Web application Deployment Descriptor before, this web.xml file for the HelloWorldPortlet should look familiar. Notice that the servlet class name is the name of the Portlet class file.

```
<?xml version="1.0" encoding="UTF-8"?>
<!DOCTYPE web-app PUBLIC "-//Sun Microsystems, Inc.//DTD Web Application
2.2//EN" "http://java.sun.com/j2ee/dtds/web-app_2_2.dtd">
<web-app id="WebApp">
        <display-name>HelloWorldPortlet</display-name>
        <servlet id="Servlet_1">◄──────────── (1)
                <servlet-name>HelloWorldPortlet</servlet-name>
                <display-name>HelloWorldPortlet</display-name>
                <servlet-class>HelloWorldPortlet</servlet-class>
        </servlet>
        <servlet-mapping>
                <servlet-name>HelloWorldPortlet</servlet-name>
                <url-pattern>/HelloWorldPortlet/*</url-pattern>
        </servlet-mapping>
        <welcome-file-list>
                <welcome-file>index.html</welcome-file>
                <welcome-file>index.htm</welcome-file>
                <welcome-file>index.jsp</welcome-file>
        </welcome-file-list>
</web-app>
```

Figure 6.3: Web.xml file for HelloWorldPortlet.

The Portlet Descriptor, portlet.xml, contains information about the portlet. This file defines the portal server characteristics of the portlet application. This includes portlet application names, portlet titles, and other portlet configuration data. Figure 6.4 shows HelloWorldPortlet's portlet.xml.

If you use WSAD for portlet development, its portlet development wizards will generate the web.xml and portlet.xml files for you. This saves you the effort of creating these files by hand and worrying about coming up with unique uid attributes.

```
<?xml version="1.0" encoding="UTF-8"?>
<!DOCTYPE portlet-app-def PUBLIC "-//IBM//DTD Portlet Application 1.1//EN" "portlet_1.1.dtd">
<portlet-app-def>
   <portlet-app uid="DCE:14058390-523c-1201-0000-005d33a24140:1" major-version="1" minor-version="0">
      <portlet-app-name>HelloWorldPortlet application</portlet-app-name>
         <portlet id="Portlet_1" href="WEB-INF/web.xml#Servlet_1" major-version="1" minor-version="0">
            <portlet-name>HelloWorldPortlet portlet</portlet-name>
            <cache>
               <expires>0</expires>
               <shared>NO</shared>
            </cache>
            <allows>
               <maximized/>
               <minimized/>
            </allows>
            <supports>
               <markup name="html">
                  <view/>
               </markup>
            </supports>
         </portlet>
   </portlet-app>
   <concrete-portlet-app uid="DCE:14058390-523c-1201-0000-005d33a24140:1.1">
      <portlet-app-name>Concrete HelloWorldPortlet application</portlet-app-name>
      <concrete-portlet href="#Portlet_1">
            <portlet-name>Concrete HelloWorldPortlet portlet</portlet-name>
            <default-locale>en</default-locale>
            <language locale="en">
               <title>Concrete HelloWorldPortlet portlet</title>
               <title-short></title-short>
                <description></description>
                <keywords></keywords>
            </language>
      </concrete-portlet>
   </concrete-portlet-app>
</portlet-app-def>
```

Figure 6.4: Portlet.xml file for HelloWorldPortlet.

The **<portlet-app-def>** field is the top-level element that contains information about the portlet application. This required element should include exactly one <portlet-app> element and one or more <concrete-portlet-app> elements.

The <portlet-app> Section

The required <portlet-app> element contains information about the portlet application. The uid attribute for each portlet must be unique within the application. Table 6.3 lists the elements of <portlet-app>.

Table 6.3: Fields of <portlet-app>

Field	Required?	Sub-element of	Definition
<portlet-app-name>	Yes	<portlet-app>	There should be exactly one of these, indicating the name of the portlet application. In Figure 6.4, the name is "HelloWorldPortlet application."
<portlet>	Yes	<portlet-app>	This contains elements that describe a portlet belonging to a portlet application. Both of Its attributes, *id* and *href*, are required. The *id* must be unique within the portlet application. The *href* points to the identifier of the servlet in the web.xml field. In Figure 6.4, this value ("WEB-INF/web.xml#Servlet_1") points to the <servlet id="Servlet_1"> field in web.xml file (Figure 6.3).
<portlet-name>	Yes	<portlet>	This signifies the name by which the portal runtime knows about the portlet. However, this is not the name that shows up on the portal page.
<cache>	No	<portlet>	This element signifies how the portal handles caching its output.
<expires>	Yes, if <cache> specified	<cache>	This indicates the number of seconds after which the portlet will be refreshed. The following are its possible values: • -1 means that the portlet is always cached; its content will never be refreshed. • 0 means the portlet's output will always be re-freshed. This is the default if no <cache> is specified. • Any value over zero is the number of seconds the portlet output is cached. Once the time limit is met, a subsequent request to the portlet will cause it to refresh its output.

Table 6.3: Fields of <portlet-app> (continued)

Field	Required?	Sub-element of	Definition
<shared>	Yes, if <cache> specified	<cache>	Takes a value of "yes" or "no," indicating whether the portlet's output is cached and shared with all users, or each individual user.
<allows>	No	<portlet>	This element indicates the different states a portlet will support. For any portlet, there can be at most one <allows> element.
<maxi-mized>	No	<allows>	Specifying this indicates whether the portlet can be maximized. In maximized state, the portlet takes over the entire portal page and replaces all other portlets on the page. When specified, the maximize button is placed on the portlet's title bar.
<mini-mized>	No	<allows>	This element indicates whether the portlet can be minimized. In minimized state, only the title bar of the portlet is shown. When specified, the minimize button is placed on the portlet's title bar.
<supports>	Yes	<portlet>	This generally indicates the different modes and types of markups that are supported by the portlet. Every portlet must support the View mode and also should support at least one Markup type.
<markup>	Yes	<supports>	Valid names are "html," "wml," or "chtml." A given portlet can support all the different types of markups. If multiple markups are supported, they should be specified separately.
<view/>	Yes	<markup>	This indicates that the portlet supports View mode. Every portlet must support this mode.
<edit/>	No	<markup>	If Edit mode is supported by the portlet, then methods must be supplied that let users customize the portlet. If Edit mode is supported, a small pencil icon appears on the portlet's title bar.
<help/>	No	<markup>	If help is supported, the portlet must supply the output that will display the help information in the portlet window when a user clicks the help icon.
<config-ure/>	No	<markup>	This indicates that the Configure mode is supported. This mode lets an administrator specify special attributes at a group level.

The <concrete-portlet-app> Section

The <concrete-portlet-app> tag contains information about the concrete portlet application. At least one of these must exist in the portlet.xml file. Table 6.4 explains some of the elements in this section.

Table 6.4: Fields of <concrete-portlet-app>

Field	Required?	Sub-element of	Definition
<portlet-app-name>	Yes	<concrete-portlet-app>	This tag indicates the name of the portlet application.
<concrete-portlet>	Yes	<concrete-portlet-app>	There should be at least one <concrete-portlet> element per each <concrete-portlet-app>. Its *href* attribute points to the identifier of the portlet.
<portlet-name>	Yes	<concrete-portlet>	This element indicates the name of the portlet. However, this is not what is displayed on the portal page.
<default-locale>	Yes	<concrete-portlet>	This indicates the locale that will be used if the default locale cannot be determined.
<language locale>	Yes	<concrete-portlet>	There should be one language element defined for each language that the portlet supports. WebSphere Portal, at present, supports all group-1 countries, so this element can have the following values: • en for English • de for German • fr for French • es for Spanish • ja for Japanese • ko for Korean • zh for Simplified Chinese • zh_TW for Traditional Chinese • pt for Brazilian Portuguese • it for Italian • iw for Hebrew • cs for Czechoslovakian • tr for Turkish • pl for Polish
<title>	Yes, for each <language> element	<language>	This should be translated into the locale. It appears as the title on the title bar of the portlet, on the portal page.
<title-short>	No	<language>	This indicates a translated short title.

Table 6.4: Fields of <concrete-portlet-app> (continued)

Field	Required?	Sub-element of	Definition
<description>	No	<language>	This generally provides a translated description of the portlet.
<keywords>	No	<language>	Any translated keywords could be specified here.
<config-param>	No	<concrete-portlet-app>	This element generally consists of <param-name> and <param-value> elements that the portlet accepts as input parameters. A portlet can accept any number of configuration parameters. The administrator can change these values when configuring the concrete portlet. A portlet can access these values through the PortletSettings object.

Step 4: Set Up the Directory Structure for the WAR File

A portlet WAR file format contains the Java classes and resources needed for a single portlet application. The resource files contain images, JSP files, and the property files containing any translated text. Before you create the WAR file for your portlet, you must arrange the class and resource files in the proper directory structure. A portlet application consists of the structured hierarchy of directories shown in Table 6.5.

Table 6.5: Portlet WAR File Directory Structure

Directory	Directory Contents
/	This is the root directory of the portlet, which is the document root for serving any unprotected files.
/images	This directory contains all the images that are needed by the portlet. It can be called anything; it doesn't necessarily have to be "images." This directory is generally unprotected and can have any number of nested directories.
/WEB-INF	This is the directory where the two portlet descriptors, web.xml and portlet.xml, reside. Anything under the WEB-INF directory is generally protected and cannot be accessed directly by the client.
/WEB-INF/lib	This is the location where any JARs should be stored.

Table 6.5: Portlet WAR File Directory Structure (continued)

Directory	Directory Contents
/WEB-INF/classes	This is the location where any class files should be stored. This is also the place where any locale-specific property files could be stored.
/META-INF	The manifest of the WAR file, manifest.inf, is stored in this directory. Also, if Java 2 security is used, the was.policy file is present here. During deployment the runtime copies this file to appname.ear/META-INF directory.

The directory structure of your HelloWorldPortlet should look similar to Figure 6.5.

Step 5: Package the Portlet into a WAR File

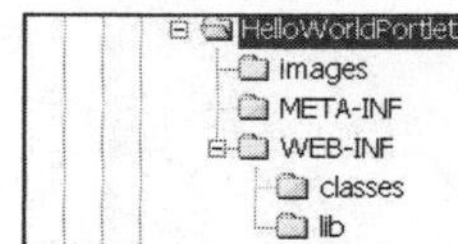

Figure 6.5: Directory structure of HelloWorld Portlet.

Now that the code is compiled, the descriptors are done, and the directory structure is laid out, it's time to create the WAR file. Use the JAR utility provided with the JDK shipped with WebSphere application Server (or any JDK). The directories that should be part of the WAR file include the WEB-INF directory and any directories that contain images, JSPs, or resource directories. The command is as follows:

```
jar -cf HelloWorldPortlet.war WEB-INF images
```

Testing the Portlet

Most of the work was done during the portlet's build process. To test the portlet, it first must be installed in WebSphere Portal server and then deployed onto a portal page.

Installing the Portlet

Now that the WAR file has been created, it's time to install it into WebSphere Portal:

1. Log in to the portal as the Portal Administrator (wpsadmin).

2. Click on **Administration,** and in the left navigation pane traverse down to **Web Modules → Portlet Management**. Click the **Install** button, as shown

in Figure 6.6. This should bring you to the Manage Web Modules screen, where you install the portlet.

3. Click **Browse**; look for and select **HelloWorldPortlet.war**, then click **Next**.

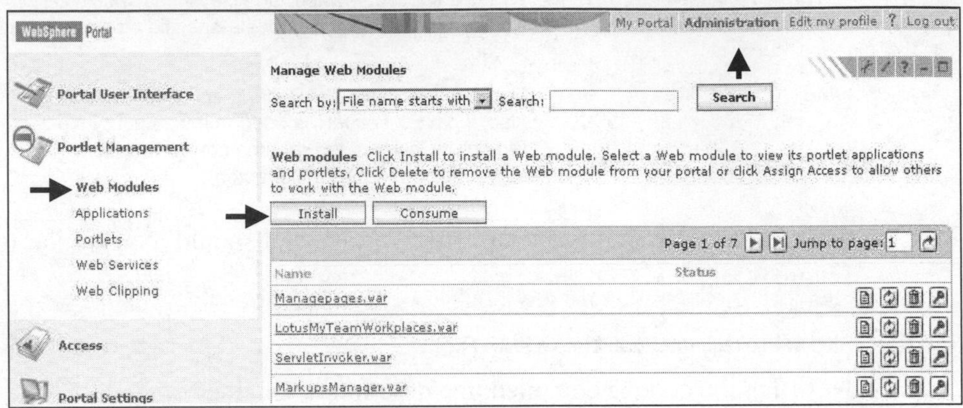

Figure 6.6: Portlet installation screen.

4. After the WAR file has been introspected, the Install Web Module screen should show up, indicating that the HelloWorld portlet will be installed. Click Finish. You should be returned to the Local Install screen with the message Web module was successfully installed.

If the portlet installs successfully, it has already passed half the test.

Deploying the Portlet

The final task is to place the portlet on a portal page:

1. Assuming you are still logged in as the Portal Administrator (wpsadmin), select the page on which you would like to place the portlet and click **Edit Page**.

2. Add the portlet to a container.

3. Now, when you bring up the page, you should see the HelloWorld portlet, as shown in Figure 6.7.

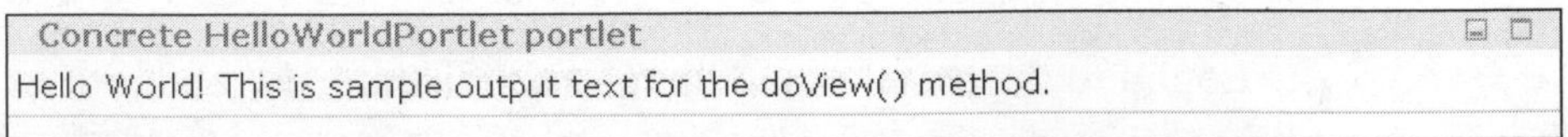

Figure 6.7: The deployed HelloWorld portlet.

Congratulations! You have created and deployed the first portlet.

Programming a Portlet

Now that you have seen how to build, deploy, and test a portlet, the following sections cover what it takes to code a portlet—or rather, the aspects of portlet programming. You'll look at the methods invoked in the portlet's lifecycle, examine the core objects, and learn about Portlet Events.

> **Note:** All portlets extend the Portlet class by extending one of its subclasses, which provide the necessary helper methods.

Portlet Lifecycle

Earlier in the chapter, we mentioned the portlet lifecycle. Now, we present the method calls that get invoked in the lifecycle. The Portlet container calls the following methods of the abstract portlet:

- *init()*—This method is called when the portal is initialized. The portal creates exactly one instance of the portlet, which is shared among all the users of the portal, just as a servlet is shared among all users of the application server.
- *initConcrete()*—This method is called after the portlet has been constructed. The concrete portlet is initialized using the PortletSettings object, just before the portlet is accessed for the first time. The PortletSettings object consists of any parameters that have been defined as part of the deployment descriptor for the portlet.
- *service()*—The portal calls this method when the portlet is required to render its content using the request/response pair. The markup will be different, depending on the mode of the portlet and the requesting client device type. The service method will call one of the following methods, depending on the mode:
  - *doView()—This method is called when the portlet must render content for the View mode.*
  - *doEdit()—This method is called when the portlet must render content in Edit mode.*
  - *doHelp()—This method is called when the portlet must render content in Help mode.*
  - *doConfigure()—This method is called when the portlet must render content in Configure mode.*

Methods only need to be implemented for the modes that the portlet supports. For example, if a portlet supports only the View mode, only the doView method must be implemented.

- *destroyConcrete()*—This method is called when the portlet is taken out of service. This could happen when an administrator deletes a concrete portlet instance during runtime of the portal server. This method gives the portlet a chance to clean up any resources that are being held.

- *destroy()*—This method is called when the portal is terminating and portlets are taken out of service. Finally, the portlet is garbage-collected.

Helper Classes

Portlets should not extend the abstract Portlet class directly, but rather extend Portlet-Adapter or any other helper class that in turn extends Portlet. By extending one of these classes, you avoid having your portlet change due to changes in the abstract Portlet class. Moreover, it saves you the work of having to implement all the methods of the Portlet interface, even if your portlet does not need to use them all. By using the Portlet-Adapter class, you only have to overwrite the methods you really need.

In its service() method, the PortletAdapter class invokes methods corresponding to the portlet mode. Portlets that extend this class can overwrite the doView(), doEdit(), and doHelp() methods without having to test the mode or write a specific service() method. Additionally, the PortletAdapter enables a portlet to store variables with the concrete portlet. Concrete portlet variables differ from Java instance variables because they are bound to the portlet class or non-concrete portlet. PortletAdapater provides the methods setVariable(), getVariable(), and removeVariable(), used to work with concrete portlet variables.

Core Objects

In the HelloWorldPortlet sample, you saw three important core objects:

- PortletRequest
- PortletResponse
- PortletSession

HelloWorldPortlet extended PortalAdapter, and the doView() method took two parameters, PortletRequest and PortletResponse. Let's go a little bit deeper and learn about these core objects, since they are used in most portlets.

PortletAdapter

The PortletAdapter class provides a default implementation of the AbstractPortlet class. In fact, it is not recommended to extend the AbstractPortlet class directly, because the AbstractPortlet class can be changed. It is better for a portlet to be derived from the PortletAdapter or any other derived class. That way, any changes made to the AbstractPortlet class will not break the portlet implementation. Also, only the methods that need to be implemented have to be overwritten.

Also the PorletAdapter class invokes the required methods corresponding to the mode in the service method. So portlets extending the PortletAdapter class just have to overwrite the doView(), doHelp(), doEdit() methods without having to test the mode of a portlet or a write a specific service() method.

PortletRequest

The PortletRequest encapsulates the request sent by the client to the server. This object is passed to the portlet through the login(), beginPage(), endPage(), and service() methods. It is a subclass of the HttpServletRequest. Some of the objects that can be accessed through PortletRequest are:

- *Attributes*—the name/value pairs associated with the request. These are valid only for the scope of the request. The portlet can get, set, and remove attributes during one request.

- *Parameters*—the name/value pairs sent by the client as part of the URI query string as part of a request. These parameters are most often posted from a form. The portlet can get, but not set, parameters from a request.

- The *Client interface* represents the client device with which the user connects to the portal. It defines methods to obtain information about clients, such as browsers running on PCs, WAP phones, PDAs, and voice gateways. In the upcoming example, you will see how to write a portlet to support multiple markups based on the client type. The Client is extracted from the PortletRequest using the getClient() method. The following information can be obtained from the Client:

  - *User agent*—Through the getUserAgent() method, the portlet can get the exact string sent by the client to identify itself to the portal.
  - *Markup*—Through the getMarkupName() method, the portlet can get the string that indicates the markup type supported by the client, such as WML.
  - *Mime type*—Through the getMimeType() method, the portlet can get the preferred mime-type that this client device supports.
  - *Capabilities*—Portal also has a capabilities abstraction class called Capability. This object contains detailed information about what the client can support, such as what level of markup is supported (for example, WML 1.1 versus WML 1.2). It also describes more specific capabilities, like what specific type of function is supported (for example, JavaScript versus no JavaScript).

- *PortletData* contains information about the concrete portlet instance. Also, it is through the data that the portlet has access to the personalized data. The portlet has write access to the personalization data only when it is in Edit mode. This is specific to a given user. You will see an example of this later in the chapter.

- The *PortletSession* object represents user-specific, transient data for more than one request. Together with the portlet, the session makes up the concrete portlet instance.

- The *PortletSettings* object represents the configuration of a concrete portlet that is saved to a persistent store. The configuration holds information about the portlet that is valid per concrete portlet for all users, and it is maintained by the administrator. The portlet can therefore only read the dynamic configuration. The portlet has write access to the dynamic configuration data only when it is in Configure mode. These parameters could also be specified in the portlet.xml file.

- *Mode* provides the current or previous mode of the portlet. A portlet can have four modes: View, Edit, Help, and Configure. The default service method of the Portlet-Adapter calls the corresponding doView(), doEdit(), doHelp, or doConfigure() methods based on the mode of the portlet. The code snippet in Figure 6.8 shows how the default service method calls the individual methods.

```
Public void service (PortletRequest request, PortletResponse response)
                              throws PortletException, IOException
{
        //Get the mode of the portlet
        PortletMode mode = request.getMode();
        if (mode == Portlet.Mode.VIEW)
                doView(request,response);
        else if (mode == Portlet.Mode.EDIT)
                doEdit(request,response);
        else if (mode == Portlet.Mode.HELP)
                doHelp(request,response);
        else if (mode == Portlet.Mode.CONFIGURE)
                doConfigure(request,response);
}
```

Figure 6.8: Code showing the logic for different modes.

- The *PortletWindow* object represents the state of the current portlet. This object can be used to determine if the portlet is currently in the maximized, minimized, or normal state.

- The *ModeModifier* object can be used to set the portlet to its current, previous, or requested mode in an action before the portlet is rendered. For example, if the portlet is in Edit mode, the ModeModifier object can perform an action and then return the portlet back to Edit mode for further user inputs.

PortletResponse

The PortletResponse object encapsulates information that is sent back to the client from the server. PortletResponse is generally passed via the beginPage(), endPage(), and service() methods. It is used by the portlet to send content back to the browser. It is a subclass of the HttpServletResponse object that provides methods to create portlet URIs. You will see these methods in example 2, later in this chapter.

There are three methods for creating the PortletURI:

- *public PortletURI createURI()*—creates a portlet URI pointing to the current portlet mode. The returned URI can be further extended by adding portlet-specific parameters and by attaching an action. You will see how to attach an action to the URI in example 4, later in this chapter.

- *public PortletURI createURI(PortletWindow.State state)*—creates a portlet URI pointing to the current portlet mode and given portlet window state. The returned URI can be further extended by adding portlet-specific parameters and by attaching an action. A portlet can use this method to enter into Solo state.

- *public PortletURI createReturnURI()*—creates a portlet URI pointing at the referrer of the portlet. This is normally the previous screen or URL shown in the browser. The returned URI can be further extended by adding portlet-specific parameters and/or by attaching an action. This method is very useful to return from the Edit mode. This method could also be used to exit out of Solo state.

PortletRequest also provides a method for mapping every variable or name used in the output stream into the portlet's namespace. This ensures that no conflicts occur with similar names on the page.

PortletSession

The third object that makes up the core portal objects is PortletSession. PortletSession holds user-specific data for the concrete portlet instance of a portlet. PortletSession is useful only for saving any transient data. For anything that needs to be saved to a data store, use PortletData instead.

PortletSession is a subclass of the HttpSession, so all the rules that apply for storing anything in HttpSession apply here, too. Anything that is stored in PortletSession should be serializable, especially in a cloned environment, where the session is serialized to a shared database.

The PortletSession object is not available on the default page, or on any page that does not require a user to log in. However, a documented way of getting a session on the anonymous page exists, but it should be avoided if possible. The PortletSession is created for each portlet on a page during login. To get a PortletSession, the getSession() method available from the PortletRequest must be used. It will return an existing session, or create one if nothing is available.

Portlet Events

Portlet events contain information about an event to which a portlet might need to respond. For example, clicking a link or a button will generate an action event. To know about this event, the portlet needs to have an *event listener* implemented within the portlet class. Table 6.6 shows the primary events supported by the portlet API.

Table 6.6: Primary Portlet Events

Portlet Event	Definition
Action event	This event is generated when a HTTP request is received by the portlet container associated with the action, i.e., a button or a link has been clicked.
Message event	This event is generated when another portlet within the portlet application sends a message. You will see this functionality in example 6, later in this chapter.
Window event	This event is triggered when a user changes the state of the portlet window.

The portlet container is responsible for delivering these events to the respective event listeners before generating the new content that the event requires. Once content generation starts, events cannot be delivered. Hence, messages cannot be sent from inside the beginPage(), service(), and endPage() methods. The resulting events are discarded by the container.

The event listener is implemented in the portlet class itself. The listener can access the PortletRequest from the event and respond using the PortletRequest or PortletSession attributes.

Action Events

An action event is sent to the portlet by the portlet container when a HTTP request is received that is associated with PortletAction. To receive action events, the portlet must implement the ActionListener interface. Generally, an action is linked with HTTP references or buttons in HTML forms. The ActionEvent is triggered when the link or button is clicked. The associated Action is then carried back to the portlet, which can follow different processing paths based on the user's actions. There are two types of Actions:

- *Simple Portlet Action String*—Actions created as simple actions can be executed multiple times, enabling a user's Back button to work. Links created with simple portlet actions are represented in the URL rather than in the session. Therefore, portlets with simple actions can be placed on an anonymous page where no session exists. Simple portlet actions are associated with action events using the getActionString() method. An example of this is shown later in this chapter, in example 2. The concept of simple actions has been supported only since WebSpghere Portal Server 4.2.

It also must have an object with the type PortletAction. The PortletAction is linked to a URI that references the action. This is done using the PortletURI class and its addAction() method, which can then be used to get the associated ActionEvent and the PortletRequest.

- *PortletAction*—The PortletAction object has been deprecated in V5.0. Although it is still being supported, its use is discouraged. The recommended method for supporting action events is by using the simple portlet action string.

Message Events

Message events can be sent from one portlet window to another. Messages can be sent to any one portlet or all portlets, as long as they are all be members of the same portlet application and on the same page as the portlet sending the message. A MessageEvent can be sent to other portlets only when the portlet container is going through its event-processing cycle. Two types of messages are supported by WebSphere Portal:

- *Single-addressed messages* are sent to a specific portlet by specifying the portlet name in the send() method.
- *Broadcast messages* are sent to all portlets on the page.

Message events are useful when a portlet needs to reflect information that is changing in another portlet. For example, one portlet might show a list of news categories, and the other might show headlines based on the category clicked in the first portlet.

For portlets to pass messages, an object of type PortletMessage must be implemented, which is passed via the MessageEvent. A message is sent to another portlet using the send() method available in the PortletContext object. The send() method takes two arguments:

- *portletName* is the name of the portlet that receives this request. To send the message to a specific portlet, specify the name of the portlet as it is defined by the <portlet-name> tag in the portlet Deployment Descriptor. By specifying null in place of the portlet name, the message will be sent to all the portlets in a page that belong to the same portlet application.

- *message* is the message to be sent. The message must be a PortletMessage object or any subclass that implements that interface. In Figure 6.8, the message is instantiated in a DefaultPortletMessage object containing the category string from the action that was performed.

The portlet receiving the message must implement the MessageListener interface and an object with the type PortletMessage. Later in this chapter, example 4 demonstrates a very simple way of doing intraportlet communication.

Window Events

The portlet container sends a WindowEvent whenever a user clicks one of the control buttons on the portlet title bar, such as minimize, maximize, or restore. A WindowEvent can display more information when the user maximizes the portlet than would be shown in its normal state. To receive window events, the WindowListener interface must be implemented at the portlet class.

The IBM Portlet API provides a WindowAdapter class that implements empty methods of the WindowListener. By extending WindowAdapter, the portlet developer needs to implement only those callback methods that are needed by the portlet. Without the WindowAdapter, you must implement all callback methods, even if the method is empty.

You can use WindowListeners to set a new timestamp and then return the time-stamp in the getLastModified method. This method enables the portlet developer to inform the container when the current cache entry for the portlet should be invalidated and its content refreshed. This is one way of refreshing the portlet cache. The portlet cache holds the complete output of the portlet. As a result, the portal server does not call the portlet's service() or doView() methods when the user changes the portlet state.

Basically, in the portlet Deployment Descriptor, the WindowListener and supported portlet states are registered and caching is enabled. Next, the WindowListener sets the timestamp to the LAST_MODIFIED attribute of the portlet's session. Finally, the portlet's getLastModified() method returns the timestamp when the request is made. Thus, the PortletWindowListener would extend WindowAdapter. In it would be methods like WindowMaximized and WindowRestored, which would setLastModified events.

Configuration Objects

Four objects can primarily store and retrieve configuration data:

- PortletConfig
- PortletSettings
- PortletApplicationSettings
- PortletData

PortletConfig

PortletConfig provides a nonconcrete portlet with its initialization configuration. This configuration contains information about the portlet class and is valid for every concrete portlet instance that is derived from this portlet.

The portlet's initial configuration information is read from the associated servlet Deployment Descriptor in the Web Deployment Descriptor file. This information is generally set by the developer, is read-only, and cannot be changed. These parameters are generally defined in the web.xml using the <init-param> tag.

PortletConfig is passed to the portlet by the init() method of the abstract portlet. Portlet-specific initialization parameters are accessed using the getInitParameters() method. These parameters are generally name/value pairs. They are available for the duration of the nonconcrete portlet instance.

PortletSettings

The PortletSettings object provides a concrete portlet with its dynamic configuration. This information is valid for all concrete instances of the concrete portlet. The PortletSettings Object can be accessed using the getPortletSettings() method available with the PortletRequest.

The concrete portlet's configuration is read from the portlet Deployment Descriptor. These parameters are generally set in the portlet.xml file and can be accessed using the getAttribute() method available in PortletSettings. They can be changed by an administrator when the portal server is running. These attributes are read-only and can only be written by the portlet in Configure mode. They are saved as name/value pairs in the portlet Deployment Descriptor and are defined using the <config-param> tag. The use of PortletSettings is demonstrated later in this chapter, in example 5.

PortletApplicationSettings

The PortletApplicationSettings object provides the concrete portlet application with its dynamic configuration. This configuration holds information about the portlet application that is shared across all portlets included in the application.

A concrete portlet application's configuration is initially read from the portlet's Deployment Descriptor. This configuration is read-only and can be written to only when the portlet is in Configure mode.

PortletApplicationSettings can be accessed using the getApplicationSettings() method, available from the PortletSettings object. These attributes are stored as name/value pairs in the Deployment Descriptor. These attributes can be get, set, and removed by any portlet in the portlet application. Any changes to the attributes can be committed using the store() method.

PortletData

User-specific data that is specified in Edit mode can be persisted. This portlet data can be saved, retrieved, or deleted using the PortletData object. Data can be stored to PortletData only in Edit mode, and it is specific to the user. PortletData holds data for the concrete portlet instance.

One concrete portlet instance is present for each occurrence of a portlet on a page. This page can be owned either by a single user or by a group of users. PortletData contains user-specific data on a user page and group-specific data on a group page.

Attributes stored in PortletData are stored as name/value pairs. The portlet can get, set, and remove any attributes. These values can be committed and persisted using the store() method. PortletData can be modified only in Edit mode. Thus, any portlet that depends on a user to customize the portlet by going into Edit mode should not be placed on the anonymous user's page.

Examples

Using the portlet API, we will now demonstrate the following examples:

- Example 1—How to add functionality to remember the URI of a portlet.
- Example 2—Use of ActionEvents.
- Example 3—Portlet-to-portlet communication.

- Example 4—How to use PortletConfig.
- Example 5—Demonstration of use of PortletSettings.
- Example 6—Usage of PortletData.

Example 1—Adding Functionality to Remember the URI of a Portlet

This example is another version of the HelloWorldPortlet that shows how data from a form is passed as a parameter to the calling portlet. When the portlet loads, the user is presented with a form on which to enter his or her name. When the user clicks the Submit button, the portlet says "Hello <Name of the user>."

Prior to displaying the portlet, control first passes to the doView() method. The portlet initially saves the URI of the portlet. The PortletURI object is created using the createURI() method, shown as ① in Figure 6.9.

```
private String getURL(PortletResponse response) {
   PortletURI uri = response.createURI(); ← (1)
   return uri.toString();
}
```

Figure 6.9: Showing how PortletURI is created.

Next, the portlet checks for the name stored as part of the PortletRequest. If it is null, then the PortletURI object created in the previous step is saved in a bean (see ① in Figure 6.10) and forwarded to view.jsp, which has a form for the user to enter a name.

```
public void doView(PortletRequest request, PortletResponse response) throws PortletException, IOException {
   String name = "";
   // Make a bean
   HelloWorld3PortletBean bean = new HelloWorld3PortletBean();
   // Save name in bean
   bean.setPortletName("HelloWorld3 portlet");
   bean.setReturnURI(getURL(response)); ← (1)
   name = request.getParameter("lName");
   if (name == null) name = "";
   if (name.length() == 0) {
      request.setAttribute("HelloWorld3PortletBean", bean);
      getPortletConfig().getContext().include("/jsp/View.jsp", request, response);
   }
   else {
      bean.setName(name);
      // Save bean in request
      request.setAttribute("HelloWorld3PortletBean", bean);
      // Invoke the JSP to render
      getPortletConfig().getContext().include("/jsp/View.jsp", request, response);
   }
}
```

Figure 6.10: Code listing of doView().

Figure 6.11 is the code that makes up View.jsp. Notice the use of the URI saved in the bean for the Action tag (indicated by ① in Figure 6.11).

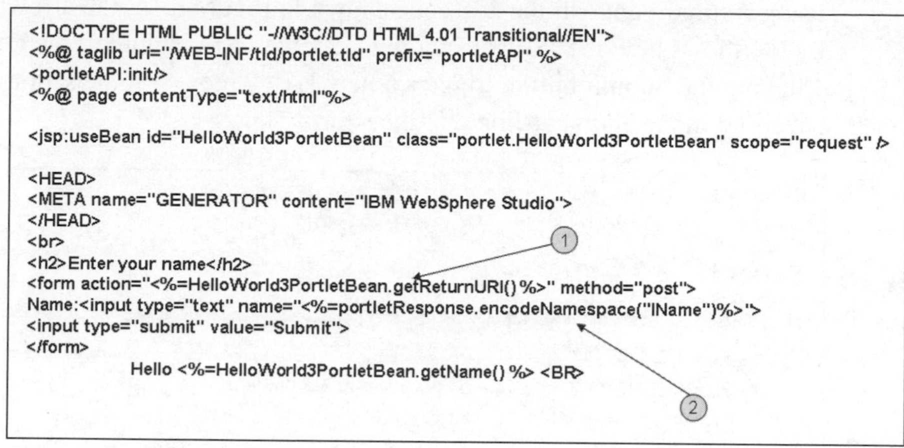

```
<!DOCTYPE HTML PUBLIC "-//W3C//DTD HTML 4.01 Transitional//EN">
<%@ taglib uri="/WEB-INF/tld/portlet.tld" prefix="portletAPI" %>
<portletAPI:init/>
<%@ page contentType="text/html"%>

<jsp:useBean id="HelloWorld3PortletBean" class="portlet.HelloWorld3PortletBean" scope="request" />

<HEAD>
<META name="GENERATOR" content="IBM WebSphere Studio">
</HEAD>
<br>
<h2>Enter your name</h2>
<form action="<%=HelloWorld3PortletBean.getReturnURI() %>" method="post">
Name:<input type="text" name="<%=portletResponse.encodeNamespace("lName")%>">
<input type="submit" value="Submit">
</form>
        Hello <%=HelloWorld3PortletBean.getName() %> <BR>
```


Figure 6.11: Code snippet of View.jsp.

Notice that the variable name is bound into the portlet's namespace using the method encodeNamespace(). This method ensures that any attributes passed to the portlet's output do not clash with similar names in other portlets. It also binds the value passed into the portlet's unique namespace. Figures 6.12 and 6.13 show how the portlet looks before and after a user has interacted.

HelloWorld3Portlet

Enter your name

Name: [ ] Submit

Hello

Figure 6.12: HelloWorldPortlet before entering a name.

HelloWorld3Portlet

Enter your name

Name: [ ] Submit

Hello Vishy Gadepalli

Figure 6.13: HelloWorldPortlet after entering a name and clicking Submit.

Example 2—Using Action Events

This example creates another version of the HelloWorldPortlet, but in this case using ActionEvents. In the JSP code shown in Figure 6.14, the arrow identified by ① shows how the JSP is using the URI, which is including the PortletAction. Clicking the Submit button triggers a new HTTP request to be sent to the URL specified in the action attribute of the <form> tag.

```
<!DOCTYPE HTML PUBLIC "-//W3C//DTD HTML 4.01 Transitional//EN">
<%@ taglib uri="/WEB-INF/tld/portlet.tld" prefix="portletAPI" %>
<portletAPI:init/>
<%@ page contentType="text/html"%>

<jsp:useBean id="HelloWorld4PortletBean" class="portlet.HelloWorld4PortletBean" scope="request" />

<HEAD>
<META name="GENERATOR" content="IBM WebSphere Studio">
</HEAD>
<br>
<h2>Enter your name</h2>
<form action="<%=HelloWorld4PortletBean.getReturnURI() %>" method="post">   <-- 1
Name:<input type="text" name="<%=portletResponse.encodeNamespace("lName")%>">
<input type="submit" value="Submit">
</form>
        Hello <%=HelloWorld4PortletBean.getName() %> <BR>
```

Figure 6.14: How the URI of the portlet is passed to the action attribute.

To see how the URL for the action is constructed, look at the code in Figure 6.15. First, the createURI() method creates a URI object. Next, the addAction() method associates the action with the URI.

```
private String getSubmitURL(PortletResponse response) {
      PortletURI sendURI = response.createURI(); <-- ①
      sendURI.addAction("submit"); <-- ②

      return sendURI.toString();
}
```

Figure 6.15: How the action object is created.

After the user clicks the Submit button on the JSP, the control returns to the portlet's actionPerformed() method, shown as ① in Figure 6.16. The PortletRequest object is accessed from the ActionEvent using the event.getRequest() method (the ② in the figure). Once the PortletRequest object is available, any parameters sent as part of the request can be accessed using the getParameter() method (the ③ in the figure).

```
public void actionPerformed(ActionEvent event) {   ←── ①
    PortletRequest request = event.getRequest();   ←── ②

    request.getSession().setAttribute("lName", request.getParameter("lName"));
}                                                        ↑
                                                         ③
```

Figure 6.16: The actionPerformed() method.

Example 3—Implementing Portlet-to-Portlet Communication

This example uses two portlets—a sender and a receiver. The sender portlet displays a list of categories. Based on what was clicked, the receiver portlet displays the name of the category that was clicked in the sender.

The sender portlet is NewsCategory, shown in Figure 6.17. As you can see, this portlet implements the ActionListener interface (labeled ① in the figure) and has the actionPerformed() method (labeled ②). In the actionPerformed() method, a DefaultPortletMessage object (labeled ③) is created using the string that is needed to pass to the receiver portlet. Finally, the message is sent to the receiving portlet using the send() method (labeled ④).

```
public class NewsCategory extends PortletAdapter implements ActionListener {   ←── ①
  public void init(PortletConfig portletConfig) throws UnavailableException {
    super.init(portletConfig);
  }

  public void doView(PortletRequest request, PortletResponse response) throws PortletException, IOException {
    PortletURI sendURI = response.createURI();
    sendURI.addAction("send");
    request.setAttribute("actionURI", sendURI.toString());
    // Invoke the JSP to render
    getPortletConfig().getContext().include("/jsp/CategoryView.jsp", request, response);
  }

  public void actionPerformed(ActionEvent event) {   ←── ②
    PortletRequest request = event.getRequest();
    String category = request.getParameter("category");
    String portletName = request.getParameter("portletName");
    if ( category != null && category.trim().length() > 0 ) {
      DefaultPortletMessage message = new DefaultPortletMessage(category);   ←── ③
      try {
        getPortletConfig().getContext().send(portletName, message);   ←── ④
        // to send message to all portlets on the page
        //getPortletConfig().getContext().send(null, message);
      } catch ( AccessDeniedException ade ) {
        System.out.println("Could not send Message to "+portletName);
      }
    }
  }
}
```

Figure 6.17: NewsCategory, the message sender.

The send() method takes two arguments:

- *portletName* is the portlet that receives this request. In Figure 6.17, the message is sent to NewsDetail. To send the message to a specific portlet, specify the name of the portlet as it is defined by the <portlet-name> tag in the portlet Deployment Descriptor. By specifying null in place of the portlet name, the message will be sent to all the portlets in the page that belong to the same portlet application.
- *message* is the message to be sent, which must be a PortletMessage object or any subclass that implements that interface. In Figure 6.17, the message is instantiated in a DefaultPortletMessage object containing the category string from the action that was performed.

Now let's take a look at the receiver portlet, NewsDetail.java, shown in Figure 6.18. This portlet implements the MessageListener interface (labeled ① in the figure) and has a messageReceived() method (labeled ②). The message is retrieved using the getMessage() method (labeled ③). It is then set as an attribute into the session, where the portlet can retrieve it.

```
import com.ibm.wps.portlets.*;
import org.apache.jetspeed.portlet.event.MessageListener;
import org.apache.jetspeed.portlet.event.MessageEvent;
import java.io.*;
import java.net.*;
import java.util.*;
import javax.servlet.ServletConfig;
import org.apache.jetspeed.portlet.*;
public class NewsDetail extends PortletAdapter implements MessageListener{   ← ①
  public static final String CATEGORY_KEY = "category";
  public void init(PortletConfig portletConfig) throws UnavailableException {
    super.init(portletConfig);
  }
  public void doView(PortletRequest request, PortletResponse response) throws PortletException, IOException {
            PrintWriter writer = response.getWriter();
    String category = (String)request.getSession().getAttribute(CATEGORY_KEY);
    if ( category == null ) category = "";

    request.setAttribute("category", category);
    // Invoke the JSP to render
    getPortletConfig().getContext().include("/jsp/DetailView.jsp", request, response);
  }

  public void messageReceived(MessageEvent event) {   ← ②
    DefaultPortletMessage message = (DefaultPortletMessage) event.getMessage();   ← ③
    PortletRequest request = event.getRequest();
    request.getSession().setAttribute(CATEGORY_KEY, message.getMessage());
  }

}
```

Figure 6.18: NewsDetail, the message receiver.

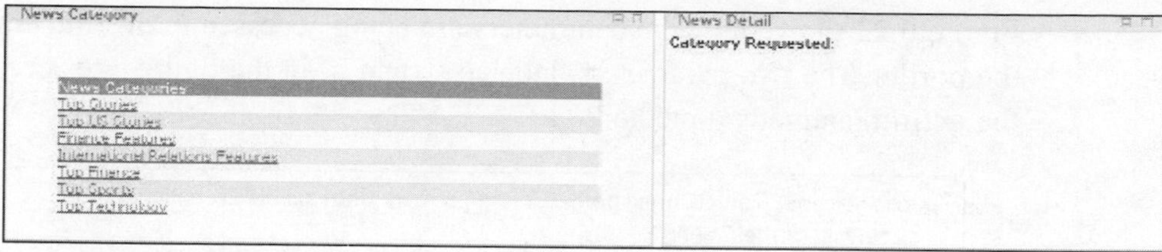

Figure 6.19: NewsCategory and NewsDetail portlets before message is passed between them.

The resulting portlets are shown in Figure 6.19 as they would appear to the user. Clicking on TopUSStories in NewsCategory portlet causes TopUSStories to be displayed in the NewsDetail portlet, as shown in Figure 6.20.

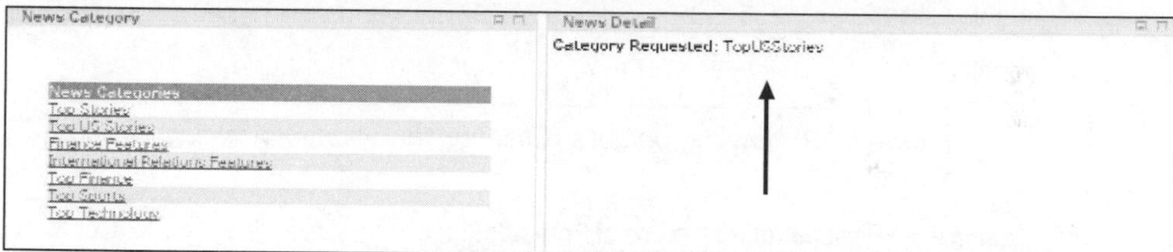

Figure 6.20: NewsCategory and NewsDetail portlets after a message is passed.

Example 4—How to Use *PortletConfig*

Figure 6.21 shows what the parameters look like in the web.xml file. In the sections labeled ① and ②, two parameters are being defined: content.url and stylesheet.url.

```
<?xml version="1.0" encoding="UTF-8"?>
<!DOCTYPE web-app PUBLIC "-//Sun Microsystems, Inc.//DTD Web Application 2.2//EN" "http://java.sun.com/j2ee/dtds/web-app_2_2.dtd">
<web-app id="WebApp">
        <display-name>WPSSampleXSL</display-name>
        <context-param>                                        ①
                <param-name>content.url</param-name>
                <param-value>/WEB-INF/xml/greeting.xml</param-value>
        </context-param>
        <context-param>                                        ②
                <param-name>stylesheet.url</param-name>
                <param-value>/WEB-INF/xsl/html/greeting.xsl</param-value>
        </context-param>
        <servlet id="Servlet_1">
                <servlet-name>WPSSampleXSLPortlet</servlet-name>
                <display-name>WPSSampleXSLPortlet</display-name>
                <servlet-class>WPSSampleXSLPortlet</servlet-class>
        </servlet>
        <servlet-mapping>
                <servlet-name>WPSSampleXSLPortlet</servlet-name>
                <url-pattern>/WPSSampleXSLPortlet/*</url-pattern>
        </servlet-mapping>
        <welcome-file-list>
                <welcome-file>index.html</welcome-file>
                <welcome-file>index.htm</welcome-file>
                <welcome-file>index.jsp</welcome-file>
        </welcome-file-list>
</web-app>
```

Figure 6.21: Web.xml file showing how parameters could be specified.

Figure 6.22 shows how the parameters are being accessed in the init() method of the portlet. The two parameters, labeled ① and ② in the figure, are accessed using the getInitParameter() method.

```
public void init( PortletConfig portletConfig ) throws UnavailableException {
   super.init( portletConfig );
   contentURL = portletConfig.getInitParameter("content.url");      ← (1)
   stylesheetURL = portletConfig.getInitParameter("stylesheet.url"); ← (2)
   if(getPortletLog().isInfoEnabled())
   {
      getPortletLog().info("contentURL: " + contentURL);
      getPortletLog().info("stylesheetURL: " + stylesheetURL);
   }
   if(contentURL == null || stylesheetURL == null)
      throw new UnavailableException("Not all properties defined in portlet config");
   else
      return;
}
```

Figure 6.22: How the portlet's initial configuration information is read.

Example 5—Demonstrating the Use of PortletSettings

Figure 6.23 shows how the configuration parameters are defined in the <concrete-portlet> block of the portlet.xml file. As you can see, one parameter is specified for the concrete portlet instance called FileLocation.

```
<concrete-portlet-app uid="DCE:725e32e0-c058-1201-0000-0513c4000a3c:1.1">
            <portlet-app-name>TextViewer application</portlet-app-name>
            <concrete-portlet href="#Portlet_1">
                  <portlet-name>TextViewer portlet</portlet-name>
                  <default-locale>en</default-locale>
                  <language locale="en">
                        <title>TextViewer portlet</title>
                        <title-short></title-short>
                        <description></description>
                        <keywords></keywords>
                  </language>

                  <config-param> ← (1)
                     <param-name>FileLocation</param-name>
                     <param-value>E:\\WPSDescription.txt</param-value>
                  </config-param>
            </concrete-portlet>
</concrete-portlet-app>
```

Figure 6.23: Portlet.xml snippet showing configuration parameters for the portlet.

The PortletSettings object can be accessed with the getPortletSettings() method, available from PortletRequest. This can be used to access the portlet-specific configuration parameters using the getAttribute() method. The sample code in Figure 6.24 shows how the parameters defined in the portlet Deployment Descriptor are accessed in the portlet. The result, as it would appear in the browser window, is shown in Figure 6.25

```
public void doView(PortletRequest request, PortletResponse response) throws PortletException, IOException {
   PortletSettings ps = request.getPortletSettings();     (1)
   String txtFileName = ps.getAttribute("FileLocation");   (2)
   // Make a bean
   TextViewerBean bean = new TextViewerBean();
   // Save name in bean
   bean.setPortletName("TextViewer portlet");
   // Save bean in request
   request.setAttribute("TextViewerBean", bean);
   PrintWriter writer = (PrintWriter) response.getWriter();
   writeFileContents(txtFileName, writer);
}
```

Figure 6.24: How PortletSettings is used.

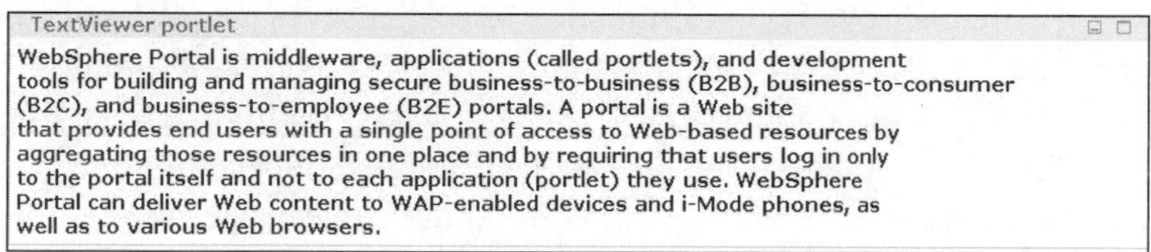

TextViewer portlet
WebSphere Portal is middleware, applications (called portlets), and development
tools for building and managing secure business-to-business (B2B), business-to-consumer
(B2C), and business-to-employee (B2E) portals. A portal is a Web site
that provides end users with a single point of access to Web-based resources by
aggregating those resources in one place and by requiring that users log in only
to the portal itself and not to each application (portlet) they use. WebSphere
Portal can deliver Web content to WAP-enabled devices and i-Mode phones, as
well as to various Web browsers.

Figure 6.25: TextViewerPortlet displaying the contents of WPSDescription.txt via the PortletSettings object.

Example 6—Demonstrating the Use of PortletData

This example displays how PortletData is used. In this portlet, the user edits the greeting in the Edit mode of the portlet and saves it to persistent storage using the PortletData object. The doView() method accesses the PortletData object to obtain the string to display. If the user has not specified a string in Edit mode, the default string is displayed. This string is stored in the HelloWorld5Portlet bean and is accessed in the View.jsp.

Figure 6.26 shows how PortletData is used in the View mode of a portlet to get to the persistent store. As you can see in the line labeled ①, the PortletData object is accessed from the PortletRequest object by using the method getData(). Once the PortletData object is available, you can get to anything stored in the PortletData object by using the getAttribute() method (labeled ②).

```
public void doView(PortletRequest request, PortletResponse response) throws PortletException, IOException {
    // Make a bean
    HelloWorld5PortletBean bean = new HelloWorld5PortletBean();
    PortletSession session = request.getPortletSession();
    PortletContext context = getPortletConfig().getContext();
    PortletData portData = request.getData(); ←—— ①
    String userName = (String)portData.getAttribute("userName"); ←—— ②
    if ((userName == null) || (userName.equals(""))) {
            userName = defaultString;
    }
    // Save userName in bean
    bean.setUserName(userName);
    // Save name in bean
    bean.setPortletName("HelloWorld5 portlet");
    // Save bean in request
    request.setAttribute("HelloWorld5PortletBean", bean);
    // Invoke the JSP to render
    getPortletConfig().getContext().include("/jsp/View.jsp", request, response);
}
```

Figure 6.26: How information saved in PortletData is extracted.

The code snippet in Figure 6.27 shows how information can be stored in the PortletData object. In Edit mode, the portlet saves the URI and passes it to the edit.jsp. Once the Submit button is clicked in the JSP, the control goes to the actionPerformed() method. The PortletData object is extracted from the PortletRequest by using the getData() method (labeled ① in the figure). The name that the user entered is extracted from the request and saved in the PortletData object using the setAttribute() method (labeled ②) and the store() method (labeled ③). The store() method causes the user information to be saved to persistent storage, so that it is available the next time doView() is called.

```
public void actionPerformed(ActionEvent event) {
    DefaultPortletAction action = (DefaultPortletAction) event.getAction();
    if (action != null) {
       if (action.getName().equals("save") ) {
          PortletRequest request = event.getRequest();
          PortletData portData = request.getData(); ←—— ①
          String userName = request.getParameter("lName");
          try {
             // Save the name specified by the user
             if (userName != null) {
                portData.setAttribute("userName", userName); ←—— ②
                portData.store(); ←—— ③
             }
          }
          catch (Exception e) {
             System.err.println("Could'nt write the usesrdata to persistent store");
          }
       }
    }
} // actionPerformed()
```

Figure 6.27: Code showing how a value is stored in PortletData.

Figure 6.28 shows the portlet before it was edited. Figure 6.29 shows the portlet in Edit mode.

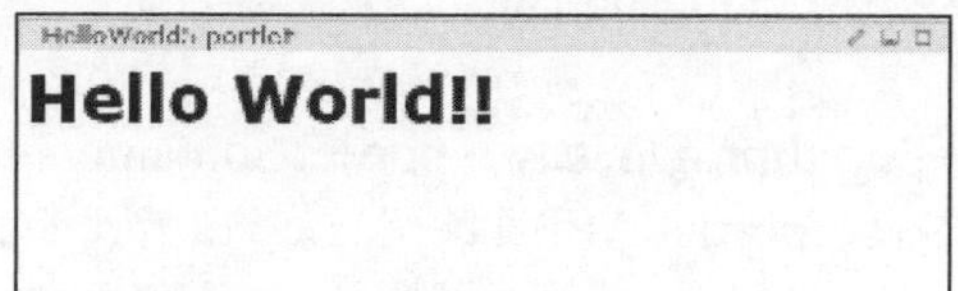

Figure 6.28: The default view of the HelloWorld5 portlet.

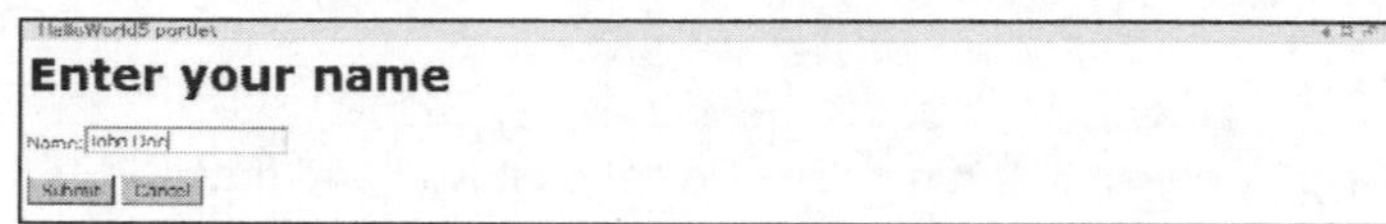

Figure 6.29: The HelloWorld5 portlet in Edit mode.

And Figure 6.30 shows the portlet after something is specified in Edit mode.

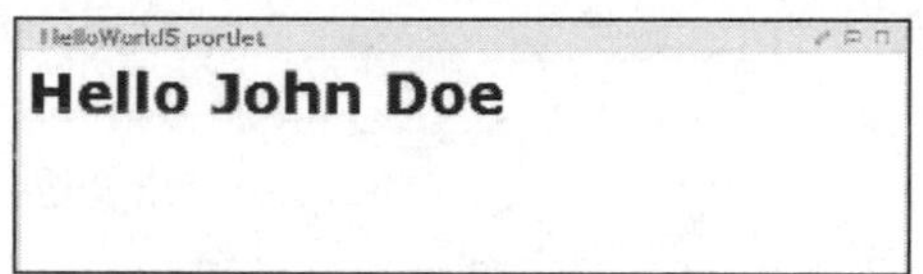

Figure 6.30: HelloWorld5 fetching the name from the PortletData object.

That wraps up the discussion of the IBM portlet API. While there are a lot more richer capabilities available in the IBM portlet API, the hope is that this section gave you enough information to get started in writing portlets.

The JSR 168 Portlet API

In this section, we take a more detailed look at the JSR 168 Portlet API. It was available as a technical preview in WebSphere Portal V5.0.1, and it has been officially supported starting with WebSphere Portal V5.0.2.1. Because the JSR 168 specification has just been released, it does not provide all of the functionality that is available in the proprietary IBM API. However, the API is a good first step in coming up with a standard that will allow portlet providers to build portlets that can be used with different portal server products. In this section, we look at some of the details of the JSR 168 API and see how it differs from the IBM proprietary API. For more information about the portlet specification, see http://jcp.org/jsr/detail/168.jsp.

WebSphere Portal provides two portlet containers to support the IBM Portlet API and the JSR 168 portlet API. There is no difference in the way portlets from either API are deployed. However, a difference does exist in the functionality that they support, and that is discussed in this section. The basic concepts of a portlet in both the IBM Portlet API and JSR are the same; in this section, we concentrate on the differences.

Tip: Portlets that run in IBM Portlet container and the JSR 168 container can reside on the same portal page.

Portlet and Servlet API

While the IBM portlet API extends the servlet API and many of the main interfaces, JSR 168 API does not extend the servlet API, but shares many of the same characteristics. JSR 168 takes advantage of much of the functionality provided by the servlet specification, such as deployment, classloading, Web applications, Web application lifecycle management, session management, and request dispatching. JSR 168 portlets can call servlets and package them in the same portlet application. Portlets, servlets, and JSPs within the same portlet application share the same classloader, application context, and session.

Portlet Representation

Unlike the IBM portlet API, no concept of a concrete portlet application or concrete portlet is present in the JSR 168 specification. The number of configuration layers is opaque to the programming model; the portlet configuration is contained within a single PortletPreferences object that aggregates these configuration layers. Figure 6.31 shows the logical representation of a portlet.

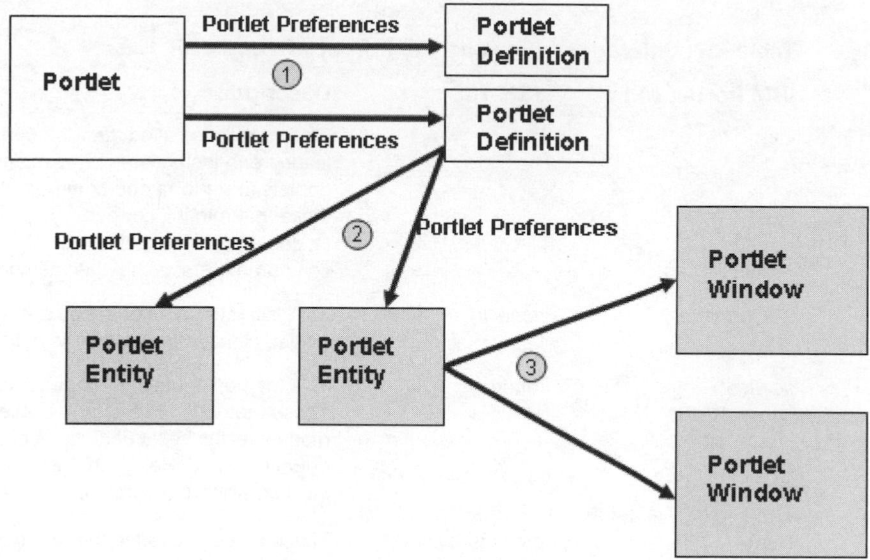

Figure 6.31: Lifecycle of a portlet, from the WebSphere Portal InfoCenter.

The portlet preferences are defined in the portlet.xml file. If these are marked as read only in the portlet.xml, only the administrator can change these ① through the configure mode of a portlet or through the admin portlets. Preferences, which are not marked read-only ② can be customized by the user in Edit mode. The parameterized view of a portlet for an individual user interaction is called a *portlet window* in JSR 168 terminology. The specification adds *render parameters* as a new way to hold an interaction state for a portlet window. A portal page can contain more than one portlet window for a single portlet, with each portlet window associated with unique portlet mode, state, and render parameters ③.

Portlet Life Cycle

The basic portlet life cycle in both the IBM Portlet API and JSR 168 is the same.

- *init*—Initialize the portlet and put the portlet into service
- *handle requests*—Processes different kinds of action and renders requests
- *destroy*—Puts portlet out of service

However, a slight difference exists in the actual methods, as explained in Table 6.7.

Table 6.7: Differences between the Portlet API and JSR 168

IBM Portlet API	JSR 168	Description
init()	init()	This method is called after the portlet has been loaded and instantiated. This method is used by portlets to perform one-time operations, especially those that might incur performance costs. The portlet can access its configuration, including initialization parameters, within this method.
initConcrete()	none	JSR 168 does not have the concept of a concrete portlet. Hence, this method is not needed.
service()	render()	This method is used to render output to the client. These methods are typically applied using the mode-specific implementations of doView(), doEdit(), and doHelp(). In JSR 168, this method is invoked when the portal receives a render request.
None	processAction()	This method is used in the JSR168 portlet to process any received parameters, update state, and perform any other necessary action processing. In the IBM Portlet API, this part is generally done by implementing the ActionListener interface and implementing the actionPerformed() method.
destroyConcrete()	none	Because no concept of a concrete portlet exists in the JSR 168 API, this method is not applicable.
destroy()	destroy()	This method is called when the portal is terminating and portlets are taken out of service. Finally, the portlet is garbage-collected.

Request Handling

Just like servlets, portlets use the Request/Response paradigm to interact with clients. Unlike servlets, however, where all the request/response handling is done in the servlet methods, portlets are rendered in two phases. In the case of the IBM portlet API, request processing is done in the actionPerformed() method and the render phase is done in the service() method. Both the methods take the same PortletRequest and PortletResponse objects as arguments.

In the case of the JSR 168 API, action request handling is done in the processAction() method. The main difference in this case is the PortletRequest and PortletResponse objects are different from those available in the service() method. During the action, the portlet can set the render parameters or session attributes that are available in the render call, but request attributes are not transferred between the action and render phase.

Portlet Window States

Both portlet APIs support three portlet window states: normal, minimized, and maximized. The IBM portlet API supports an additional solo state. There is no solo state in JSR 168. The JSR API has the concept of *custom window states*. At deployment time, the portal can map custom portlet window states from the portlet descriptor to its own custom window states, or it can ignore them. At runtime, portlets use PortalContext.getSupportedWindowStates() to retrieve the modes supported by the portal and adapt accordingly. WebSphere Portal does not support custom window states for JSR 168.

Portlet URLs

Portlet URLs allow a portlet to create a URL to itself. It is used when a user clicks on a link or action that causes the portlet to call itself. In the case of the IBM portlet API, this is accomplished using the PortletResponse.createURI() method.

In the case of JSR 168, portlet URLs are created using the RenderResponse.createRenderURL(), which creates a URL that triggers the render() method of the portlet. RenderResponse.createActionURL() creates a URL that triggers the processAction() method of the portlet before the render() method.

HTML form processing must be done using an action URL. Render and action parameters are separate for JSR portlets; parameters set on an action URL are not available to the render() method unless they are passed explicitly using ActionResponse.setRenderParameter().

URLs to Portlet Resources

In a portlet, resources cannot be invoked using relative URLs. For URLs pointing to these resources to work, they must be encoded using the encodeURL() method of the portlet response. Resources include any file in the portlet application that is referenced or invoked from the portlet or one of its JSPs, including:

- Images
- Applets
- Multimedia
- JSPs
- Servlets

In the IBM portlet API, the path to the resource is specified using the encodeURL method of the PortletResponse object. For example:

```
<%= portletResponse.encodeURL("/images/test.jpg") %>.
```

In the JSR 168 API, you also have to add the context path of the portlet from the request, as in:

```
<%= portletResponse.encodeURL(renderRequest.getContextPath() +
"/images/test1.jpg") %>
```

Invoking JSPs

In the IBM portlet API, JSPs are invoked from the portlet class using the PortletContext.include() method. In the JSR 168 API, JSPs are invoked using the include() method on the PortletRequestDispatcher object. The PortletRequest Dispatcher object is reached by calling either the getRequestDispatcher() or the getNamedDispatcher() method available with the PortletContext object.

Render Parameters

These parameters are attached to the render request, and they stay the same for every render request until a new action occurs. This allows the storing of navigational state in the render parameters instead of the session. The portlet should put all state information it needs to redisplay itself correctly into render parameters. This makes it easier to save bookmarks and provides better support for the use of the browser's Back button.

When the portlet is the target of an action, render parameters are reset. In the action, the portlet can set new render parameters to represent the new navigational state after the action is completed. The developer can use render URLs to set render parameters directly, without having to go through an action. Because render parameters may be bookmarked, portlets should be prepared to handle invalid parameters. Such parameter values should be handled gracefully and should not lead to exceptions. From the JSP, the portlet can set render parameters using the <portlet:renderURL/> tag. This feature of saving the navigational state of the portlet is only available in the JSR 168 portlet API.

Deployment Descriptors

The IBM portlet API and the JSR both support the concept of one portlet class instance for each portlet configuration in the Web deployment descriptor and one or more portlets defined in a portlet application in a WAR file. Similarly the portlet deployment descriptor (portlet.xml) describes the portlet application and the portlets, whereas the Web deployment descriptor (web.xml) defines the associated Web application.

Some differences are present in the deployment descriptors of the JSR API-based portlets. Because, according to the JSR, a portlet is no longer considered a servlet, the portlet deployment descriptor no longer contains a reference to a servlet in the Web deployment descriptor. The JSR spec requires that all portlets and portlet-related settings must be defined in the portlet deployment descriptor, portlet.xml file, and any Web resources that are not portlet-related must be defined in the web.xml descriptor file. The following must be defined in the Web deployment descriptor or web.xml file.

- Portlet application description using the <description> tag
- Portlet application name using the <display-name> tag
- Portlet application security role mapping using the <security-role> tag

Figure 6.32 shows an example of a web.xml file.

```
<?xml version="1.0" encoding="UTF-8"?>
<!DOCTYPE web-app PUBLIC "-//Sun Microsystems, Inc.//DTD Web
Application 2.3//EN" "http://java.sun.com/dtd/web-app_2_3.dtd">
<web-app id="WebApp_ID">
  <display-name>HelloWorldPortlet</display-name>
  <description>Hello World Portlet</description>

  <welcome-file-list>
   <welcome-file>index.html</welcome-file>
   <welcome-file>index.htm</welcome-file>
   <welcome-file>index.jsp</welcome-file>
  </welcome-file-list>
  <taglib id="PortletTLD">
   <taglib-uri>http://java.sun.com/portlet</taglib-uri>
   <taglib-location>/WEB-INF/tld/std-portlet.tld</taglib-location>
  </taglib>
</web-app>
```

Figure 6.32: Web deployment descriptor for a JSR portlet.

```
<?xml version="1.0" encoding="UTF-8"?>
<portlet-app xmlns="http://java.sun.com/xml/ns/portlet/portlet-
  app_1_0.xsd" version="1.0"
xmlns:xsi="http://www.w3.org/2001/XMLSchema-instance"
xsi:schemaLocation="http://java.sun.com/xml/ns/portlet/portlet-
  app_1_0.xsd http://java.sun.com/xml/ns/portlet/portlet-app_1_0.xsd"
id="helloworldportlet.HelloWorldPortletPortlet.5484484b00">
  <portlet>
   <portlet-name>HelloWorldPortlet</portlet-name>
   <display-name>HelloWorldPortlet portlet</display-name>
   <display-name xml:lang="en">HelloWorldPortlet portlet</
     display-name>
   <portlet-class>helloworldportlet.HelloWorldPortletPortlet</
     portlet-class>
   <init-param>
     <name>wps.markup</name>
     <value>html</value>
   </init-param>
   <expiration-cache>0</expiration-cache>
   <supports>
     <mime-type>text/html</mime-type>
     <portlet-mode>view</portlet-mode>
   </supports>
   <supported-locale>en</supported-locale>
   <resource-bundle>helloworldportlet.nl.HelloWorldPortletPortlet
     Resource</resource-bundle>
   <portlet-info>
     <title>HelloWorldPortlet portlet</title>
   </portlet-info>
  </portlet>
</portlet-app>
```

Figure 6.33: Example of portlet deployment descriptor of JSR portlet.

Figure 6.33 shows an example of the portlet deployment descriptor or portlet.xml file. As you can see, the portlet class name no longer contains a reference to the Web deployment descriptor or web.xml file. Also, because no concept of a concrete portlet exists in the JSR, no section of either concrete portlet application or concrete portlet is present. The spec requires that the following types of configuration and deployment information be contained in the portlet deployment descriptor:

- Portlet application definition
- Portlet definition

To uniquely identify a portlet application, a unique identifier is added to the <portlet-app> definition element, as shown by ① in Figure 6.33. The modes of a portlet—maximized, minimized—which were defined using the <allows> tag in the IBM API are not required here. They are supported by default by the JSR. Any custom states, however, will have to be defined.

Limitations of JSR 168 API

JSR 168 based portlets have the following limitations:

- *Portlet URL security*—The setSecure() method of the PortletURL interface is not supported. The portlet URL will always be the same security level of the current request. According the portlet spec, the setSecure() method of the PortletURL interface allows a portlet to indicate if the portlet URL must be a secure URL or not (i.e. HTTPS or HTTP).
- *Programmatic security*—The isUserInRole() method of the portlet request is not supported and always returns false. Any <security-role-ref/> elements in the portlet deployment descriptor are ignored. The getUserPrincipal() method of the portlet request always returns null if application server security is not enabled. However, the getRemoteUser() method of the portlet request always returns a unique value for each user, even with security disabled, so that it can be used for personalization purposes, such as storing user-specific preferences. Therefore, the code fragment request.getRemoteUser() != null can be used to check if a user has logged in. The return value with disabled security might not be a human-readable string, and it will be different from the value returned when security is enabled.
- *Invalidation-based caching*—As a result of an action, a portlet can actively invalidate the cache using the invalidate method on the portlet request. This allows for more fine-grained cache control because the portlet can determine, on the result of this action, whether to invalidate the cache content for only the current portlet mode and markup or for all of the portlet's modes and markups. In JSR 168, an action invalidates all cached markup.

Examples

This section demonstrates the use of the JSR 168 portlet API through examples. We develop the same examples that were done using the IBM Portlet API. Because JSR 168 API does not support portlet-to-portlet communication, Example 3 from the IBM Portlet API (Portlet-to-Portlet Communication) is omitted.

Example 1—Adding Functionality to Remember Portlet's URI

This is another version of the HelloWorldPortlet that shows how data from a form is passed as a parameter to the calling portlet. When the portlet loads, the user is presented with a form on which to enter his name. When the user clicks the Submit button, the portlet says "Hello <Name of the user>."

Prior to displaying the portlet, control first passes to the doView() method. The portlet initially saves the URI of the portlet. The PortletURI object is created using the createURI() method, shown as ① in Figure 6.32.

```
private String getURL(RenderResponse response) {
    PortletURL uri = response.createRenderURL(); ← 1
    return uri.toString();
}
```

Figure 6.34: Showing how PortletURI is created.

In the IBM portlet API, this is done using the createReturnURI() method. In JSR, this is accomplished by calling the createRenderURL() method, which calls the renderAction() method of the portlet.

Next, the portlet checks for the name stored as part of the PortletRequest. If it is null, then the PortletURL object created in the previous step is saved in a bean (see ① in Figure 6.34) and forwarded to view.jsp, which has a form for the user to enter a name.

```
public void doView(RenderRequest request, RenderResponse response) throws
PortletException, IOException {
    // Set the MIME type for the render response
    response.setContentType(request.getResponseContentType());
    // Make a bean
    HelloWorld3JSRBean bean = new HelloWorld3JSRBean();
    bean.setRenderURI(getURL(response)); ← 1

    String name = "";
    name = request.getParameter("lName");
    if (name == null) name = "";
    if (name.length() > 0) {
        bean.setName(name);
    }
    request.setAttribute("HelloWorld3JSRBean", bean);
    // Invoke the JSP to render
    PortletRequestDispatcher rd =
    getPortletContext().getRequestDispatcher(getJspFilePath(request, VIEW_JSP));
    rd.include(request.response); ← 2
}
```

Figure 6.35: Code listing of doView().

Also notice how the JSP is called. In the IBM Portlet API, we used the PortletContext.forward() method. In the JSR 168 API, JSPs are invoked using the include() method on the PortletRequestDispatcher object as shown by ② in Figure 6.35.

Figure 6.36 shows the code for View.jsp. Notice the use of the URI saved in the bean for the Action tag (indicated by ① in Figure 6.34).

```
<%@ page session="false" contentType="text/html" import="java.util.*,javax.portlet.*,helloworld3jsr.*" %>
<%@taglib uri="http://java.sun.com/portlet" prefix="portlet" %>
<jsp:useBean id="HelloWorld3JSRBean" class="helloworld3jsr.HelloWorld3JSRBean" scope="request" />
<portlet:defineObjects/>

<HEAD>
<META name="GENERATOR" content="IBM WebSphere Studio">
</HEAD>
<br>
<h2>Enter your name</h2>
<form action="<%=HelloWorld3JSRBean.getRenderURI() %>" method="post">

Name:<input type="text" name="lName">
<input type="submit" value="Submit">
</form>
Hello <%=HelloWorld3JSRBean.getName() %> <BR>
```

Figure 6.36: Code snippet of View.jsp.

Figures 6.37 and 6.38 show how the portlet looks before and after a user has interacted.

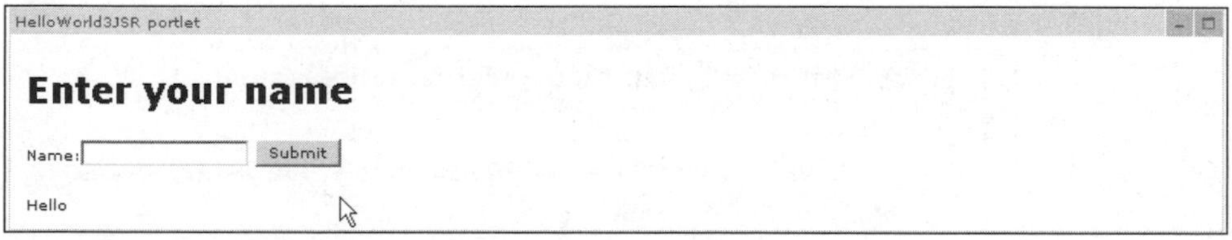

HelloWorld3JSR portlet

Enter your name

Name: Submit

Hello

Figure 6.37: HelloWorldPortlet before entering a name.

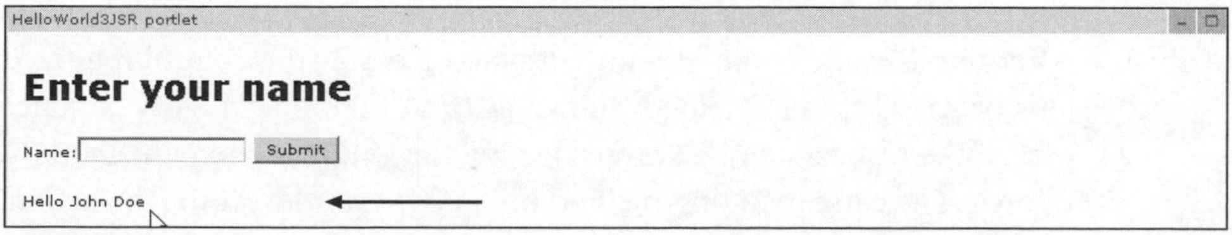

HelloWorld3JSR portlet

Enter your name

Name: Submit

Hello John Doe

Figure 6.38: HelloWorldPortlet after entering a name and clicking Submit.

Example 2—Using Action Events

This example creates another version of the HelloWorldPortlet, but in this case using ActionEvents. In the JSP code in the Figure 6.39, the arrow identified by ① shows how the JSP uses the URI, which is invoking the Action. Clicking the Submit button triggers a new HTTP request to be sent to the URL specified in the action attribute of the <form> tag.

```
<%@ page session="false" contentType="text/html" import="java.util.*,javax.portlet.*,helloworld4jsr.*" %>
<%@taglib uri="http://java.sun.com/portlet" prefix="portlet" %>
<portlet:defineObjects/>

<%
HelloWorld4JSRPortletSessionBean sessionBean =
    (HelloWorld4JSRPortletSessionBean)renderRequest.getPortletSession().getAttribute(HelloWorld4JSRPort
    let.SESSION_BEAN);
%>

<h2>Enter your name</h2>
<form action="<%=sessionBean.getSubmitURI() %>" method="post">  ①
Name:<input type="text" name="<%=HelloWorld4JSRPortlet.FORM_TEXT%>">
<input name="<%=HelloWorld4JSRPortlet.FORM_SUBMIT%>" type="submit" value="Submit">
</form>

Hello <%=sessionBean.getFormText() %> <BR>
```

Figure 6.39: How the URI of the portlet is passed to the action attribute.

To see how the URL for the action is constructed, look at the code in Figure 6.40. The method createActionURL() on the RenderResponse object creates a URL that triggers the processAction() method of the portlet before the render() method ①.

```
private String getSubmitURL(RenderResponse response)
{
    PortletURL actionURL = response.createActionURL();  ①
    return actionURL.toString();
}
```

Figure 6.40: How the action object is created.

After the user clicks the Submit button on the JSP, the control returns to the portlet's processAction() method, shown as ① in Figure 6.41. Any parameters sent as part of the request can be accessed using the getParameter() method (② in the figure). The corresponding method in the IBM portlet APi is the actionPerformed() method.

```
public void processAction(ActionRequest request, ActionResponse response) throws PortletException,
java.io.IOException {
    if( request.getParameter(FORM_SUBMIT) != null ) {
        HelloWorld4JSRPortletSessionBean sessionBean = getSessionBean(request);
        if( sessionBean != null )
            sessionBean.setFormText(request.getParameter(FORM_TEXT));
    }
}
```

Figure 6.41: The processAction() method.

Example 3—How to Use PortletPreferences

In the IBM Portlet API, customization and personalization data are stored using different objects: the PortletSettings for customization data and PortletData for personalization data. Both allow only String values to be stored.

In the JSR 168, customization and personalization data are stored using one object, the PortletPreferences. If the same setting is defined on both levels, the user level takes precedence. This has the advantage in those cases where this behavior is needed in the portlet, the programmer does not need to check in two objects to see if this setting is set. The drawback is that the policy user-overwrites-customization-settings cannot be changed.

Figure 6.42 shows how the configuration parameters are defined in the <concrete-portlet> block of the portlet.xml file. As you can see, one parameter is specified for the concrete portlet instance called FileLocation.

```
<concrete-portlet-app uid="DCE:725e32e0-c058-1201-0000-0513c4000a3c:1.1">
        <portlet-app-name>TextViewer application</portlet-app-name>
        <concrete-portlet href="#Portlet_1">
                <portlet-name>TextViewer portlet</portlet-name>
                <default-locale>en</default-locale>
                <language locale="en">
                        <title>TextViewer portlet</title>
                        <title-short></title-short>
                        <description></description>
                        <keywords></keywords>
                </language>

                <config-param>
                   <param-name>FileLocation</param-name>
                   <param-value>E:\\WPSDescription.txt</param-value>
                </config-param>
        </concrete-portlet>
</concrete-portlet-app>
```

Figure 6.42: The portlet.xml file showing configuration parameters for the portlet.

In JSR 168, user settings are stored, set, and retrieved using the PortletPreferences object, which represents name/value pairs in <preference/> elements of the portlet deployment descriptor. Preferences can be marked read-only, in which case they can only be modified by someone with administrative privileges, typically using a configure mode. Otherwise, the portlets can be modified in any portlet mode.

Figure 6.43 shows how the PortletPreferences are defined in the portlet.xml file. In the example, the preference FileLocation, identified by ① can be changed in the edit mode of the portlet. In the same example, the value of Locale can be changed only in the configure mode of the portlet, because it is marked as read-only, as identified by ②.

```
<portlet-preferences>
    <preference>
        <name>FileLocation</name>
        <value>C:\WPSDescription.txt</value>   ← (1)
    </preference>
    <preference>
        <name>Locale</name>
        <value>en_US</value>
        <read-only>true</read-only>   ← (2)
    </preference>
</portlet-preferences>
```

Figure 6.43: How the portlet's initial configuration information is read.

Figure 6.44 shows an example of how the preferences defined in the portlet.xml are accessed. The PortletPreference object is accessed using the getPrefernces() method of the request object, as shown by ①. Once the PortletPrefernce object is available, values saved can be accessed using the getValue() method, as shown by ②.

```
PortletPreferences preferences = renderRequest.getPreferences();   ← (1)
if( preferences!=null ) {
   String value = (String)preferences.getValue(HelloWorld5JSRPortlet.EDIT_KEY,"");
                                      ↑
                                     (2)
```

Figure 6.44: Example showing how the preferences are accessed.

Figure 6.45 shows an example of how preferences could be saved after being modified by the user in either the Edit or Configure mode. First, the

PortletPrefernce object is accessed using the getPrefernces() method of the RenderRequest object, as shown by ①. Next, any value modified by the user is saved using the setValue() method, as shown in ②. Finally, the PortletPrefernces are saved to the persistent data store using the store() method available with the PortletPreferences object ③ so that the new value is available, the next time the portlet is called.

```
public void processAction(ActionRequest request, ActionResponse response) throws PortletException,
     java.io.IOException {
          if( request.getParameter(FORM_SUBMIT) != null ) {
               // Set form text in the session bean
               HelloWorld5JSRPortletSessionBean sessionBean = getSessionBean(request);
               if( sessionBean != null )
               sessionBean.setFormText(request.getParameter(FORM_TEXT));
          }
          if( request.getParameter(EDIT_SUBMIT) != null ) {
               PortletPreferences prefs = request.getPreferences(); <-- (1)
               try {
                    prefs.setValue(EDIT_KEY,request.getParameter(EDIT_TEXT)); <-- (2)
                    prefs.store(); <-- (3)
               }
               catch( ReadOnlyException roe ) {
               }
               catch( ValidatorException ve ) {
               }
          }
     }
}
```

Figure 6.45: Example showing the manipulation if PortletPrefernces object.

Door Closings

The subject of portlet programming alone could fill a book. Although the JSR 168 API is a good start, we are certain that more features will be added. The JSR 168 API is a quite robust set of interfaces, but its key importance is that portlet server vendors have settled on a standard set of APIs; that bodes well for customers, portlet developers, and the user community at large. For more information on portlet programming, see *Programming Portlets* by Ron Lynn, Joey Bernal, and Peter Blinstrubas (2005; MC Press www.mc-store.com).

We recommend checking the IBM portlet catalog periodically to find out the latest portlet releases. You can find the portlet catalog at the following URL:

http://www.ibm.com/software/webservers/portal/portlet/catalog.

Chapter 7

Portal Gatekeeper

In previous chapters, references were passed to security in WebSphere Portal by way of registration, privileges, user IDs, and passwords. For example, Chapter 3 discussed how to use IBM Tivoli Directory Server as the LDAP server, and Chapter 4 talked about authenticated and unauthenticated users.

It is time to look "behind the security gates." How and where is security set up? Who controls the access control lists (ACLs)? How often do users have to sign in? How do you use Secure Certificates and integrate with third-party authentication products? This chapter answers those and other security-related questions with actual examples.

Users and Groups

WebSphere Portal offers a centralized point of access control over portal resources (which can be augmented with a security manager external to the product, such as Tivoli Access Manager or Netegrity Site Minder). It also offers a centralized point of administration for users and groups if a customer does not already have an administration tool for its user registry. These tools allow a customer to better define portal users and manage users' access rights.

WebSphere Portal uses WebSphere Member Manager (WMM; previously known as WebSphere Member Services) to manage profile data for users and groups. It keeps track of the overall attributes and the values of those attributes for individual users and groups. WMM federates an external user registry (such as an LDAP server) with an internally managed database to produce the overall user profile. The default database that is created during installation is named WMM—the WebSphere Member Manager. If a user chooses to share the WebSphere Portal Server (WPS) database and the WMM database, then only the WPS database will be created.

WMM allows users to be assigned to access groups, which are simply groups of users in the user registry. (In LDAP, these might be instances of the groupOfUniqueNames or accessGroup object classes.) These user groups are used by WPS to grant specific permissions for access-control purposes. WMM itself does not assign any roles (in the J2EE sense of the word) to its members and does not deal with authorization.

The following features are associated with WebSphere Member Manager:

- *Profile Management*—The portal administrator manages user profiles and data using the Manage Users portlet.
- *User Repository*—This collection of profile data for users, groups, and organizational entities can be configured for storage in a database or a directory server.
- *Group Membership*—The group memberships of users in WebSphere Portal Server can be used when making access-control decisions.

Member Types

A *registered user* is a type of member. Upon registering with the portal, a user becomes a registered user with a user ID and password that is stored in the user registry.

Member Groups

A member group is an arbitrary collection of members, which typically consists of users. These users, for example, could be grouped together to represent certain assigned roles. Although J2EE roles are not supported in WebSphere Portal, user groups can sometimes approximate that function.

Note: If installed with IBM Tivoli Directory, WMM creates a dummy member entry in a group when the group is created. The value is specified in the grpDummyMember attribute in wmm.xml. This dummy member entry is necessary, because Tivoli Directory supports the X.500 definition of a group as requiring at least one member.

Required Groups and Users

A minimum of one group and one user is required for WebSphere Portal. Depending on the directory server you use, you could use existing user accounts, or you can create new user accounts to use with WebSphere Portal.

The required group is wpsadmins or an equivalent. The portal administrative user must be a member of this group in the directory. If content management functions are configured, it is recommended that the following groups should also be configured in LDAP:

- wpsContentAdministrators
- wpsDocReviewer

These groups should also be created in the LDAP, with the same authority as granted to the wpsadmins group.

User Repository

The user repository refers to the data store that holds the member profile data. Either a database or a directory server is used as the repository. When an LDAP directory is used, the profile data is first stored in it using standard object classes. Then, based on the configuration, profile data that is a superset of the LDAP classes may be stored in a database.

WebSphere Member Manager must access the user's authentication and registry group information from the Authentication Component, which is usually an LDAP server or a database. WMM does not support a local operating system (OS) as the authentication registry. The authentication registry is specified in the WebSphere Portal Server during installation and is recorded in <WPS_HOME>/wmm/wmm.xml. This file can be manually edited to modify the initial configuration settings. The default wmm.xml file is shown in Figure 7.1.

Warning: Do not edit the wmm.xml file. Internal database contents that are based on the installation of WebSphere Portal will be incorrect if a user registry with different structure is substituted for the original registry.

```
<?xml version="1.0" encoding="UTF-8"?>
<wmm name="member manager"
                  description="member manager"
                  defaultRealmName="portal"
                  horizontalPartitioning="false"
                  lookAside="false"
                  configurationFile="wmmAttributes.xml"

uniqueIdGeneratorClassName="com.ibm.ws.wmm.uniqueid.WMMUniqueMember
  IdentifierGenerator"
                  maximumSearchResults="200"
                  searchTimeOut="120000"
                  maximumSearchResultsForSortingAndPaging="500"
                  maximumTotalSearchResultsForSortingAndPaging="1000"
                  pagingMemberObject="true"
                  timeToRemovePagedCacheEntry="900"
                  userSecurityNameAttribute="uid"
                  passwordAttribute="userPassword">

    <supportedMemberTypes>

        <supportedMemberType name="Person"
                  rdnAttrTypes="uid"
                  defaultParentMember="o=Default Organization"
                  defaultProfileRepository="DB1"/>

        <supportedMemberType name="Group"
                  rdnAttrTypes="cn"
                  defaultParentMember="o=Default Organization"
                  defaultProfileRepository="DB1"/>

        <supportedMemberType name="Organization"
                  rdnAttrTypes="o"
                  defaultParentMember="o=Default Organization"
                  defaultProfileRepository="DB1"/>

        <supportedMemberType name="OrganizationalUnit"
                  rdnAttrTypes="ou"
                  defaultParentMember="o=Default Organization"
                  defaultProfileRepository="DB1"/>

    </supportedMemberTypes>
```

Figure 7.1: The wmm.xml file listing found in <WPS_HOME>/wmm folder (part 1 of 3).

```
    <repositories>

          <!--
*****************************************************************************
                databaseType      dataAccessManagerClassName

*****************************************************************************
               db2           com.ibm.ws.wmm.db.dao.db2.WMMDB2Dao
               oracle        com.ibm.ws.wmm.db.dao.oracle.WMMOracleDao
               cloudscape
com.ibm.ws.wmm.db.dao.cloudscape.WMMCloudscapeDao
                sqlserver
com.ibm.ws.wmm.db.dao.sqlserver.WMMSQLServerDao
                informix
com.ibm.ws.wmm.db.dao.informix.WMMInformixDao

*****************************************************************************
          -->

    <databaseRepository name="wmmDB"
            UUID="DB1"
            supportTransactions="true"
            wmmGenerateExtId="true"
            adapterClassName="com.ibm.ws.wmm.db.DatabaseRepository"
            supportDynamicAttributes="true"
            supportGetPersonByAccountName="false"
            profileRepositoryForGroups="DB1"
            dataSourceName="jdbc/wmmDS"
            databaseType="cloudscape"

dataAccessManagerClassName="com.ibm.ws.wmm.db.dao.cloudscape.
WMMCloudscapeDao"
            saltLength="12"
            dbEncryptionKey="rZ15ws0ely9yHk3zCs3sTMv/ho8fY17s">

       <readMemberType>
           <memberType name="Person"/> <memberType name="Group"/>
<memberType name="Organization"/> <memberType name="OrganizationalUnit"/>
       </readMemberType>
       <createMemberType>
           <memberType name="Person"/> <memberType name="Group"/>
<memberType name="Organization"/> <memberType name="OrganizationalUnit"/>
       </createMemberType>
       <updateMemberType>
           <memberType name="Person"/> <memberType name="Group"/>
<memberType name="Organization"/> <memberType name="OrganizationalUnit"/>
       </updateMemberType>
```

Figure 7.1: The wmm.xml file listing found in <WPS_HOME>/wmm folder (part 2 of 3).

```
        <deleteMemberType>
            <memberType name="Person"/> <memberType name="Group"/>
<memberType name="Organization"/> <memberType name="OrganizationalUnit"/>
        </deleteMemberType>
        <renameMemberType>
            <memberType name="Person"/> <memberType name="Group"/>
<memberType name="Organization"/> <memberType name="OrganizationalUnit"/>
        </renameMemberType>
        <moveMemberType>
            <memberType name="Person"/> <memberType name="Group"/>
<memberType name="Organization"/> <memberType name="OrganizationalUnit"/>
        </moveMemberType>

        <nodeMaps>
            <nodeMap node="o=Default Organization"
            pluginNode="o=Default Organization"/>
        </nodeMaps>
      </databaseRepository>

   </repositories>

</wmm>
```

Figure 7.1: The wmm.xml file listing found in <WPS_HOME>/wmm folder (part 3 of 3).

Nested Groups

Two groups are nested if one of the groups contains the other group as a member. WebSphere Portal supports nested groups to enable a simple inheritance of access control. Permissions for nested groups are treated as cumulative.

There is more than just the wmm.xml file. In WebSphere Portal V5.1, the XML files related to WMM can be found in <WPS_HOME>/wmm. Figure 7.2 shows the file listing of that particular directory.

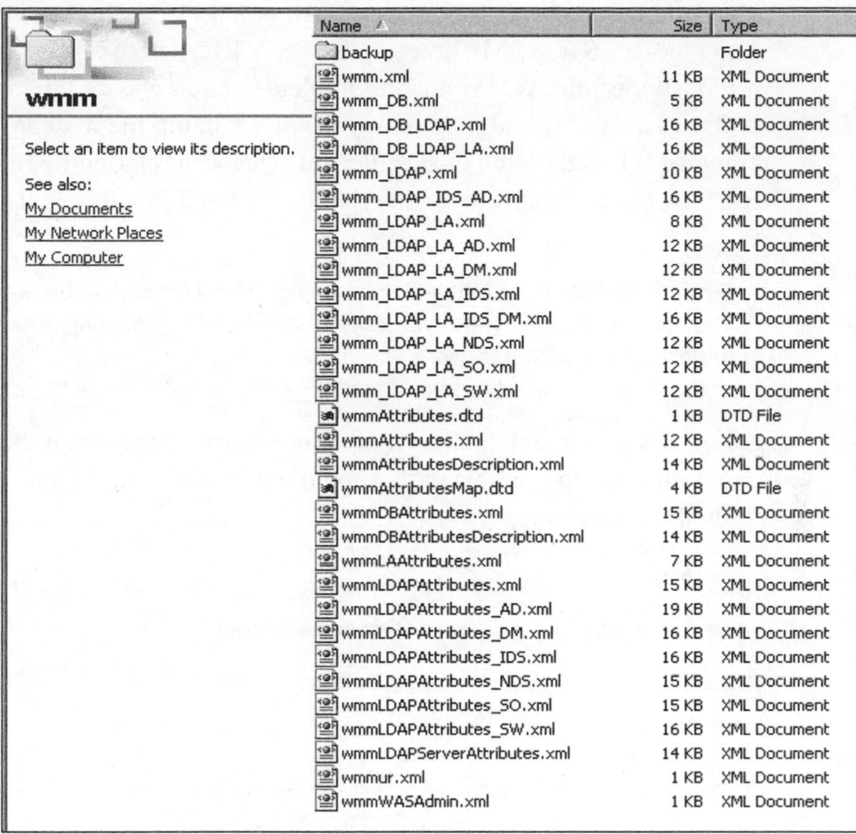

Figure 7.2: The <WPS_HOME>/wmm directory listing.

Configuring WebSphere Member Manager

Configuration parameters for WMM are generated during WebSphere Portal installation. Those parameters, plus the configuration of LDAP Directory (or any other data source), is contained in <WPS_HOME>/wmm/wmm.xml. The WebSphere Portal user repository consists of one of three data sources:

- LDAP only
- Database only, which might be accessible only through a Custom Registry
- A database (look-aside repository) and a LDAP directory server

If LDAP is used, the mapping of profile attributes to LDAP object classes and attributes is defined in wmmLDAPServerAttributes.xml, which is instantiated from various templates that are vendor-specific - <WPS_HOME>/wmm/wmm LDAPAttributes_XXX.xml, where XXX can be AD (Active Directory),

DM (Domino), IDS (IBM Directory Server V5.1) , NDS (Novell eDirectory), SO (Sun One), or SW (IBM Directory Server V4.1). These XML files specify names of repositories, the WMM adapter implementation classes, and mapping between attributes in WMM and the repositories. By default, the mapping of the LDAP directory is based on the inetOrgPerson schema supported by most LDAP directories. The LDAP password is encrypted and stored in wmm.xml.

Tip: Passwords stored in the WMM-related XML files should be encrypted. You can use the wmm_encrypt utility in <WPS_HOME>/config/work/wmm/bin to encrypt an ASCII password.

Table 7.1 shows the default attributes as defined in the wmm.xml file. Entries that are not documented in this table should not be changed without consulting IBM product technical support.

Table 7.1: Attributes Affecting Member Manager

Attribute	Default Values
wmm name	member manager
description	member manager
defaultRealmName	portal
horizontalPartitioning	false
lookAside	false
configurationFile	<*WPS_HOME*>/wmm/wmmAttributes.xml
uniqueIdGeneratorClassName	com.ibm.ws.wmm.uniqueid.WMMUniqueMemberIdentifierGenerator
maximumSearchResults	200
searchTimeOut	120000
maximumSearchResultsForSorting-AndPaging	500

Table 7.1: Attributes Affecting Member Manager (continued)

Attribute	Default Values
maximumTotalSearchResultsFor-SortingAndPaging	1000
pagingMemberObject	true
timeToRemovePagedCacheEntry	900
userSecurityNameAttribute	uid
passwordAttribute	userPassword
supportedMemberType name	Person Group Organization OrganizationalUnit
rdnAttrTypes	uid cn o ou
defaultParentMember	o=Default Organization
defaultProfileRepository	DB1
databaseRepository name	wmmDB
UUID	DB1
supportTransactions	true
wmmGenerateExtId	true
adapterClassName	Com.ibm.ws.wmm.db.DatabaseRepository
supportDynamicAttribute	true
supportGetPersonByAccountName	false
profileRepositoryForGroups	DB1
dataSourceName	jdbc/wmmDS
databaseType	cloudscape
dataAccessManagerClassName	com.ibm.ws.wmm.db.dao.cloudscape.WMMCloudscapeDao

Table 7.1: Attributes Affecting Member Manager (continued)

Attribute	Default Values
saltLength	12
dbEncryptionKey	<encrypted key>
memberType name	Person Group Organization OrganizationalUnit
nodeMap node	o=Default Organization
pluginNode	o=Default Organization

A sample attributeMap.xml file is shown in Figure 7.2. This is from a standard WebSphere Portal installation on a Windows 2000 machine using IBM Directory Server.

```
<?xml version="1.0"?>
<!DOCTYPE attributeMap SYSTEM "attributeMap.dtd">
<attributeMap>
    <entry entryName="User">
        <pluginAttributeMap>
            <map>
                <objectAttribute attrName="uid"/>
                <pluginAttribute name="uid" readOnly="false"/>
            </map>
            <!-- ACTIVED_SETTINGS
            <map>
                <objectAttribute attrName="userAccountControl"/>
               <pluginAttribute name="userAccountControl" readOnly="false"/>
            </map>
                  ACTIVED_SETTINGS -->
            <map>
                <objectAttribute attrName="cn"/>
                <pluginAttribute name="cn" readOnly="false"/>
            </map>
            <map>
                <objectAttribute attrName="logonPassword"/>
                <pluginAttribute name="userPassword" readOnly="false"/>
            </map>
            <map>
                <objectAttribute attrName="sn"/>
                <pluginAttribute name="sn" readOnly="false"/>
            </map>
            <map>
```

Figure 7.3: Sample attributeMap.xml file (part 1 of 3).

```
            <objectAttribute attrName="givenName"/>
            <pluginAttribute name="givenName" readOnly="false"/>
         </map>
         <map>
            <objectAttribute attrName="preferredLanguage"/>
            <pluginAttribute name="preferredLanguage" readOnly="false"/>
         </map>
         <map>
            <objectAttribute attrName="phone1"/>
            <pluginAttribute name="homePhone" readOnly="false"/>
         </map>
         <map>
            <objectAttribute attrName="zipCode"/>
            <pluginAttribute name="postalCode" readOnly="false"/>
         </map>
         <map>
            <objectAttribute attrName="mail"/>
            <pluginAttribute name="mail" readOnly="false"/>
         </map>
         <map>
            <objectAttribute attrName="address1" size="50"/>
            <objectAttribute attrName="address2" size="50"/>
            <objectAttribute attrName="address3" size="50"/>
            <objectSeparator attrSeparator="/"/>
            <pluginAttribute name="postalAddress" readOnly="false"/>
         </map>
      </pluginAttributeMap>
   </entry>
   <entry entryName="Organization">
      <pluginAttributeMap>
      </pluginAttributeMap>
   </entry>
   <entry entryName="OrganizationalUnit">
      <pluginAttributeMap>
      </pluginAttributeMap>
   </entry>
  <entry entryName="Group">
      <pluginAttributeMap>
         <map>
            <objectAttribute attrName="uniqueMemberIdentifier"/>
            <pluginAttribute name="uniqueMember" readOnly="false"/>
         </map>
           <map>
            <objectAttribute attrName="description"/>
            <pluginAttribute name="description" readOnly="false"/>
         </map>
         <map>
            <objectAttribute attrName="cn"/>
            <pluginAttribute name="cn" readOnly="false"/>
         </map>
         <!-- ACTIVED_SETTINGS
         <map>
            <objectAttribute attrName="cn"/>
            <pluginAttribute name="samAccountName" readOnly="false"/>
```

Figure 7.3: Sample attributeMap.xml file (part 2 of 3).

```
            </map>
                 ACTIVED_SETTINGS -->
        </pluginAttributeMap>
    </entry>
</attributeMap>
```

Figure 7.3: Sample attributeMap.xml file (part 3 of 3).

WMM provides a set of services to act upon and manage profiles such as create, read, update, delete, and search for members. A facility to manage groups is also present in the profile repository. When using LDAP, not all attributes might get stored in LDAP. A lookaside profile repository can be used, and WMM provides an adapter (com.ibm.ws.wmm.db.DataBaseFederationAdapter) to interact with it. This combination of LDAP plus a lookaside database is needed to support Member Manager.

Note: Using a lookaside database can slow down performance. If you plan to use a lookaside database, set it up before configuring security.

WebSphere Member Manager New Security Provisions

WebSphere Portal V5.1 has the same security provisions as it did in previous versions. Figure 7.4 shows the software components that are involved when security is enabled in WebSphere Portal and only a single registry is used. That single registry could be a LDAP directory or the WMM DB or a Custom User Registry (CUR). WebSphere Application Server provides the necessary classes to implement security using a particular registry.

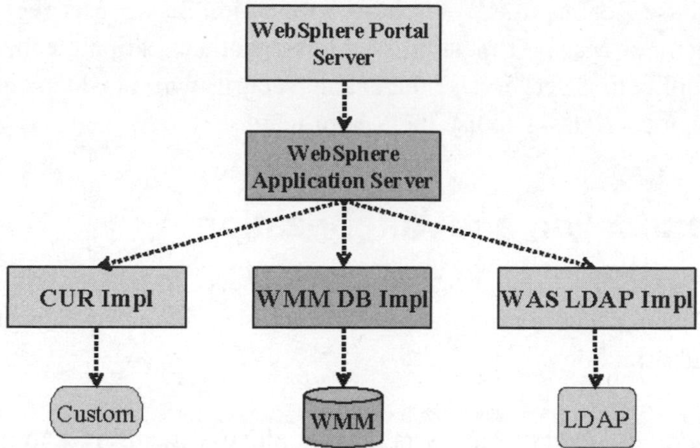

Figure 7.4: WebSphere Security when only one registry is used.

Support for multiple registries will be available in the next point release of WebSphere Portal. These can be multiple registries of the same kind, like multiple LDAP directories, or they could be a heterogeneous environment that includes a LDAP directory and a WMM database or a CUR. The new WebSphere Member Manager User Registry (WMMUR) can be used in conjunction with Realms, when configuring Virtual Portals. A realm is actually a subset of the WMM namespace. Figure 7.5 shows how security is provisioned for multiple registries using WMMUR.

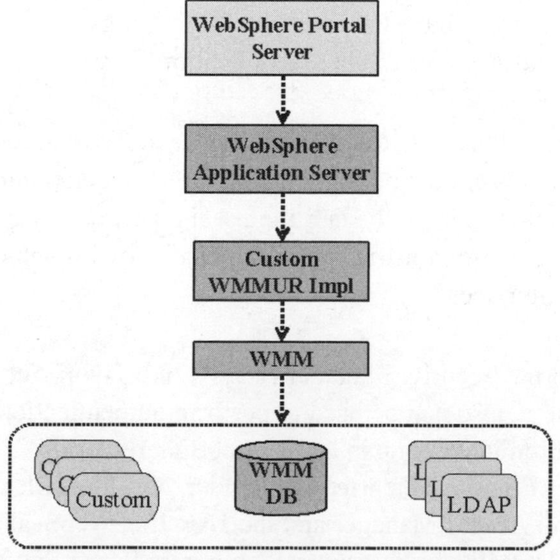

Figure 7.5: WebSphere Security with WMMUR.

To use Realms, the WebSphere Application Server user registry provided by Member Manager must be used as the authentication mechanism in WebSphere Application Server. Use the enable-security-wmmur-ldap and enable-security-wmmur-db tasks to use the Realm feature.

Authentication and Authorization

In WebSphere Portal Server, security is used to control access to portal resources, such as pages and portlets. As always, security has two facets: authentication and authorization.

Authentication means users have to identify themselves to gain access to the system—in this case WebSphere Portal. Users can either identify themselves immediately upon entering the system, or they could be challenged when they try to access a protected resource. This is just a matter of company policy and philosophy. Some organizations' intranets make you identify yourself up front, and then give you access to everything after that. Other organizations, to promote "friendly" Internet portal sites, give free access to most information, but challenge unauthenticated users if they try to access sensitive information.

Authorization indicates the rights a user has within the system. And we will see later, authorization equates to access control. Being authenticated does not necessarily mean you have the authority to do things. Authorization in WebSphere Portal is independent of WebSphere Application Server.

WebSphere Portal relies on WebSphere Application Server for authentication. WebSphere Application Server performs authentication by either using a directory server that is accessible via a Lightweight Directory Protocol (LDAP), or alternatively, it can use non-LDAP user registries by implementing Custom User Registry (CUR) interfaces.

An External Security Manager (ESM), like Tivoli Access Manager's WebSEAL component, also can be used to perform authentication. This is done using Trust Association Interceptors (TAIs). WebSphere Portal V5.1 supports Tivoli Access Manager (TAM), Netegrity SiteMinder, and RSA ClearTrust. It includes the TAI for Tivoli Access Manager and the JAR file, WebSealTAIwas5.jar, can be found in <WAS_HOME>/lib directory. WebSphere Portal Server typically does its own authorization, but it can also integrate with an ESM to control access to portal resources by externalizing the roles and using Access Control Lists (ACLs) to control role membership.

Setting Up Portal Security

You can use WebSphere Portal without other security products. Actually, the standard installation does not use WebSphere Application Server or a third-party authentication proxy to verify proof of identity. The standard installation does not activate WebSphere Application Server Global Security, nor does it protect the Web application at /wps/myportal. This scenario relies on WebSphere Portal Server to authenticate, using WPS DB. The Portal Server saves user information and preferences in WPS DB. When a user logs in, his identity is verified against what is stored in that database. This configuration assumes a one-machine setup in a development or demonstration environment only.

If you remember, during the installation process in Chapter 3, after the standard installation was completed, a WPSConfig task was run to enable security using a LDAP server as the directory. That in turn enabled Global Security in WebSphere Application Server. In such a configuration, Application Server security is activated, and the /wps/myportal URL is protected within Application Server, with a setting of All Authenticated Users and a challenge mechanism of Custom Form-based Challenge. These settings cause Application Server to redirect any unauthenticated user requests to the login form, where the user can enter an identity and password to access the Portal Server.

During a Typical installation, you are given the choice to use an LDAP server. The Application Server acts as the challenge mechanism for Portal Server, and a database registry holds user account information. You can choose to configure WebSphere Portal in one of three ways:

- *LDAP+DB*—You expect WebSphere Application Server and WebSphere Member Manager to both be talking to the same LDAP server. Member Manager augments LDAP with a database to fill out the user profile.
- *DB-Only*—WebSphere Portal provides a Custom Registry to allow WebSphere Application Server to talk to the Member Services database, which is used as the sole source of the user information (and Member Services can talk to its own database, natively).

- *Custom*—The customer must provide a WebSphere Application Server Custom Registry as well as a Member Manager plug-in (also known as a *Member Repository implementation*) to allow WebSphere Application Server, WebSphere Portal server, and WebSphere Member Manager to talk to the custom user registry.

When users log in, WebSphere Application Server does the authentication, and WebSphere Member Management accesses the directory for additional information to build the user profile that WebSphere Application Server does not fetch. If the user is not found in the authentication registry, authentication fails. The flow is shown in Figure 7.6.

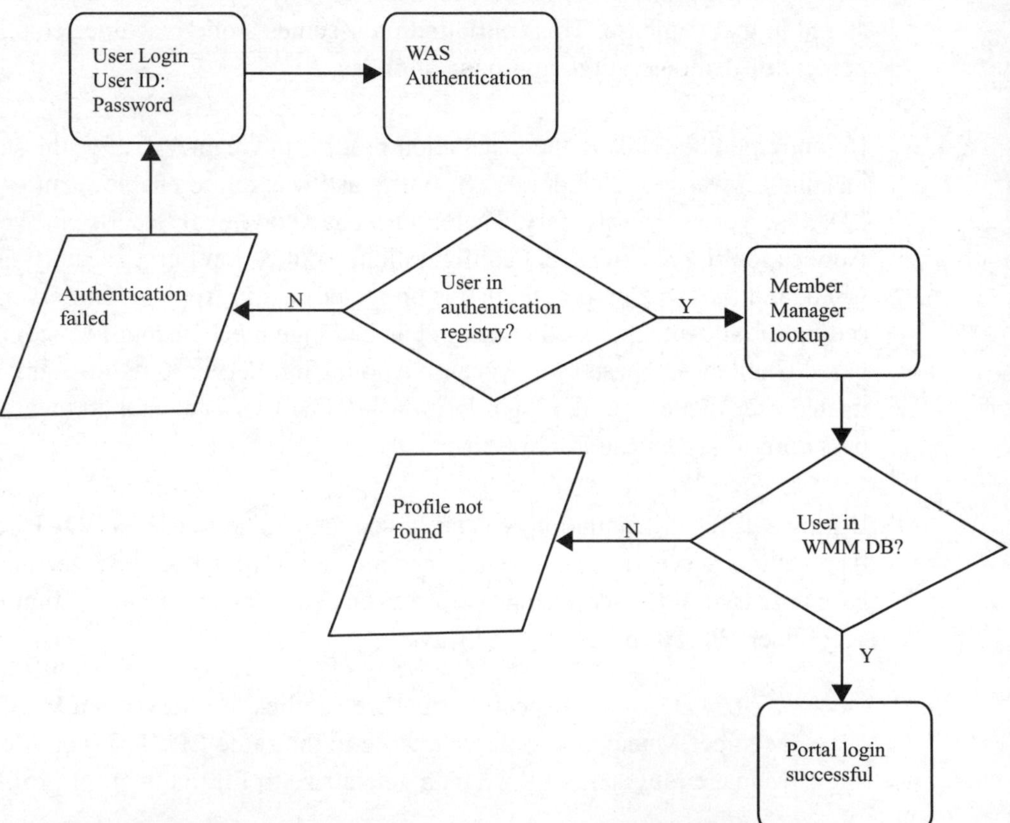

Figure 7.6: The authentication process flow when a user logs in to the portal.

If the user is found in the authentication registry, but not in the member database, then you do not yet have a profile extension built up for that user, and one is then constructed. The user lookup, with the proper password, must succeed for the user to successfully log in to the portal. This is a production-ready, out-of-the-box environment that does not require a lot of manual configuration to implement.

Organizations that already have a user registry in LDAP prefer to use the LDAP configuration. The supported directories are IBM Tivoli Directory Server, Netscape iPlanet Directory Server, Domino LDAP Directory, Novell eDirectory, and Microsoft Active Directory.

About Passwords and Timeouts

When a user is logged into the portal, the session is active and the password is valid as long as the user is making use of the portal. If there is no activity for a long period, the user's session is automatically closed, and you might see the screen Figure 7.6. This session idle timeout is controlled by the timeout parameter in WebSphere Administrative Console.

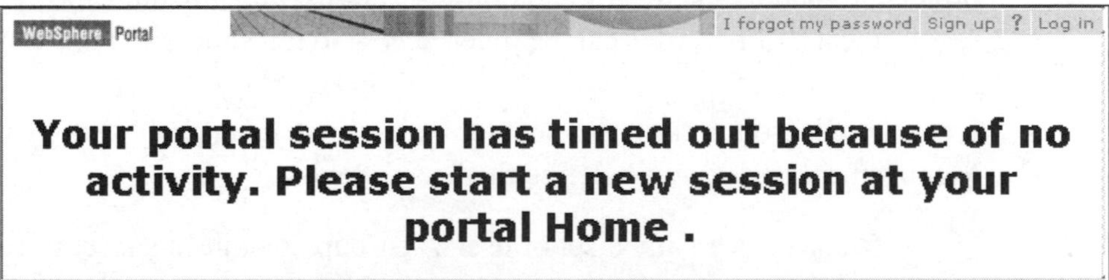

Figure 7.6: Screen showing a timed out portal session.

There is also an absolute authentication timeout (the LTPA Token timeout) that WebSphere Application Server security manages. This is not subject to activity—it is not kept alive by activity nor timed out by inactivity. It is independent of the session idle timeout. Once this timeout expires, the user is asked to re-authenticate by WAS Security. WebSphere Portal has no control over this. Authentication proxies and Trust Association Interceptors can overrule this behavior by asserting an identity to WAS again.

Independent of both of those timeout parameters is the security credential cache. The WebSphere Portal configuration tasks that enable WebSphere security automatically set the Security Cache Timeout to a value specified in the wpconfig.properties file found in <WPS_HOME>/config directory. The parameter is called **cacheTimeout,** and the default value is 600 seconds. Old passwords are stored in cache for that amount of time.

Access Control

In WebSphere Portal, authorization is called *access control*. Like everything else, a couple of portlets let you configure access to portal resources by granting permissions to users and groups, based on roles. These portlets, if so desired, can also pass control of resources to and from external security mechanisms.

Note: A user with administrative authority can deploy portlets, so make sure such a user is also in the WebSphere Application Server Administrative Role. You can do this by adding that user to the administrative group or by putting the user in the Administrative Role under Security Center in the WebSphere Application Server Administrative Console.

Access control is performed at group level and at user level. Application Server protects servlets and Enterprise Java Beans (EJBs), but WebSphere Portal server protects resources like pages and portlets. Successful authentication is the only requirement before a user can be given access to a resource.

Even though groups and roles seem to be used interchangeably, an Identity Management purist would define them as follows:

- *Group*— is a named set of users. A group contains a subset of the users provisioned to a particular resource, and it can give access rights to a part of the resource. In an access control relationship, group is usually the principal. In a portal semantic, any roles/permissions/rights granted to a group, are inherited by members of that group.

- *Role*—is a named set of permissions, where permissions are tuples of {action,resource}. A description of a particular type of user that must be provisioned to one or more resources. In the portal semantic, when a role is granted to a principal (either a user or group), then all permissions contained in that role are granted to that principal.

In the access control relationship permission-to-role mappings define the role, and principal-to-role mappings (for both user principals and group principals) define what rights a user has within the system.

Resources

WebSphere Portal resources are organized in a hierarchy and thus propagate their access control configuration to all of their child resources. Resource instances are specific resources, such as a single portlet or a page that belong to a resource type, namely Portlet resource type and Page resource type. A unique resource type is called Virtual Resources; this resource type protects sensitive operations in a portal and is the parent resource for all resource instances. This is illustrated in Figure 7.7, in which the blank squares indicate resource instances and the labeled rectangles indicate virtual resources.

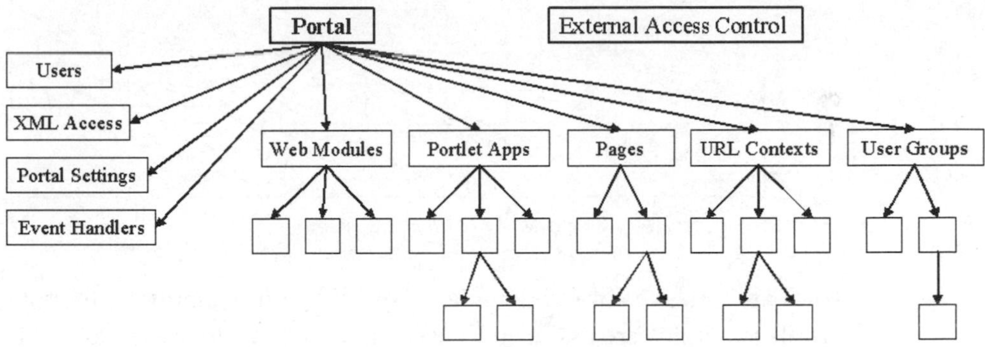

Figure 7.7: WebSphere Portal Resource hierarchy illustration.

It is more efficient to assign roles on virtual resources and resource instances, because when you administer them, the child resources inherit roles from their parent by default. Assigning roles to specific resource instances, however, offers more granular access control.

Roles

WebSphere Portal access control is based on roles. A role combines a set of permissions with a specific WebSphere Portal resource, and this set of permissions is called a *role type*.

Note: Make sure you always have at least one user with the Administrator@Portal role. If no user has this role, the portal will be inoperable.

Seven roles types or templates are defined in WebSphere Portal, and they are organized in a hierarchy, as shown in Figure 7.8. Each role type contains all permissions that are contained in the role types directly beneath it in the hierarchy.

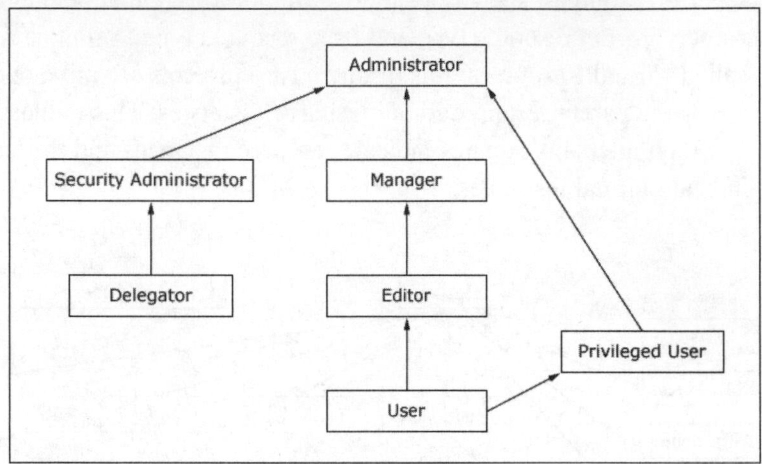

Figure 7.8: WebSphere Portal Role Types .

Roles are instances of role templates that are built by applying the role template to a resource. Roles are assigned to users and groups that are contained in the user registry. Roles can be assigned in any of three ways:

- Explicitly assigned by someone with the necessary authorization, such as the portal administrator.
- Implicitly assigned through group membership. If a group has a role, all members of the group automatically acquire the role. Nested groups (groups that are members of another group) inherit role assignments from their parent groups.
- Inherited through a role assignment on a parent resource. Roles on a resource automatically apply to all children of that resource by default.

Resource Permissions Portlet

This portlet allows you to control role assignment propagation or inheritance. It is also used to assign roles explicitly to specific users and groups, create or delete roles on externalized resources and page resources under the control of an ESM, or bring externalized resources back under the control of WebSphere Portal.

The Resource Permissions portlet can be accessed in three ways. Make sure you are logged into the portal as the portal administrator.

1. Click the **Administration link → Access → Resource Permissions.**

2. Click the **Assign permissions** link in the portal banner.

3. Click the **Set Permission** icon in the Manage Pages portlet. The end result is shown in Figure 7.9.

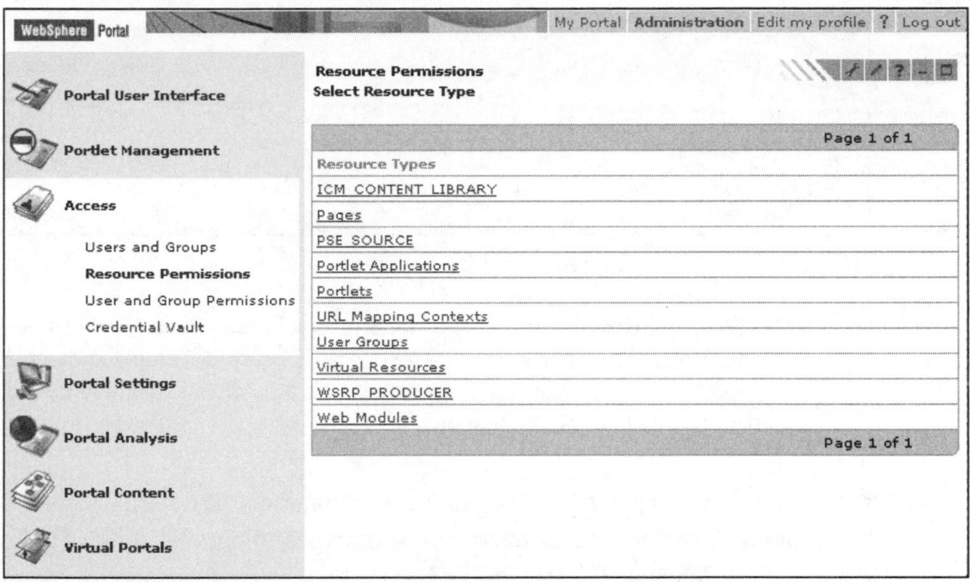

Figure 7.9: Resource Permissions portlet.

User and Group Permissions Portlet

This portlet allows you to view and modify the roles that users and groups have on WebSphere Portal resources. The portlet indicates whether a role is explicitly assigned, implicitly acquired through group membership, or inherited through the resource hierarchy.

To get to the User and Group Permissions portlet, make sure you are logged into the portal as the portal administrator. Click **Administration link → Access → User and Group Permissions**, as shown in Figure 7.10.

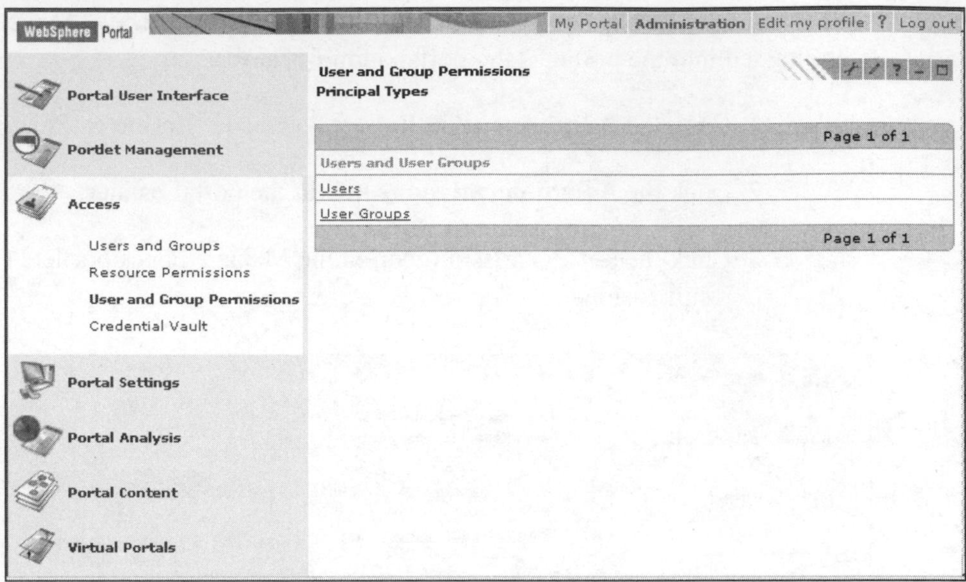

Figure 7.10: User and Group Permissions portlet.

Note: When you externalize the roles for a resource, any access control inheritance from internally controlled parent resources is severed. The recommendation is to explicitly assign at least one user or group to the Administrator role before externalizing any roles on the resource using the Resource Permissions portlet.

The Action Control List (ACL) portlet is the interface to control access rights to portal resources. Five permission levels can be assigned to portal resources to limit access: View, Edit, Manage, Create, and Delegate. View is the lowest in the hierarchy. A None category also exists, in which no permissions have been assigned.

Permission Controls

Table 7.2 summarizes the permission controls for the resources. Here are some common rules of thumb for assigning permissions:

- Permissions are cumulative, so if you have Edit permission, you inherit View permission. Similarly, having Manage permission automatically gets you View and Edit permissions.
- A user with Manage permission for a resource can also delete the resource.
- When creating a new resource, the creator automatically gets Manage and Delegate permission for that resource.

Table 7.2: Resources and Permissions

Resource	Permission	Control Description
Portlet Application	View	Gives the right to view the portlet application. Users and groups still need proper permissions to access the portlets in that application.
	Edit	N/A (not applicable)
	Manage	Gives the right to edit portlet application settings that apply to all users and groups who have permissions to view the portlet application, activate/deactivate, and delete the portlet application.
	Create	Gives the right to install a new portlet application or copy an existing one in the portal. The creator still needs to delegate appropriate permissions to other users and groups.
Portlet	View	Gives the right to view the portlet. Users must have View permission for the page containing that portlet in order to see the portlet.
	Edit	Gives an individual user the right to edit the portlet settings.
	Manage	Gives the right to edit portlet settings to users or groups who have permission to view and delete the portlet.
	Create	Gives the right to create a new portlet or copy an existing portlet. The creator still needs to delegate appropriate permissions to other users and groups.
Page	View	Gives the right to view the page. Users must have View permission for the page in order to see the page.
	Edit	Gives the right to create new components, add portlets, and edit page settings. If the user has only Edit permission to the page, a new page is created and assigned to the user, and any modifications only apply to that user.
	Manage	Gives the right to add portlets, edit page settings, or delete the page. Users with appropriate permissions will be able to see those changes.
	Create	Gives the right to create a new page or copy an existing page. The page creator automatically gets Manage and Delegate access to that page. To assign permissions to other users or groups, the creator still needs Delegate authority for the other users or groups.
User	View	N/A
	Edit	N/A

Table 7.2: Resources and Permissions (continued)

Resource	Permission	Control Description
	Manage	Gives the right to change a user's profile data and remove an existing user. By default, users have Manage and Delegate access over themselves as individual users.
	Create	Gives the right to create a new user. The creator automatically gets Manage and Delegate permission for the new user.
User Group	View	N/A
	Edit	N/A
	Manage	Gives the right to rename a user group, add and remove group members, and remove the group. This does not include the right to remove a user completely.
	Create	Gives the right to create a new user group. The creator automatically gets Manage and Delegate access for that user group.
Resource Collection	View	Gives the right to view the resource collection.
	Edit	Gives the right to add new resources to the collection.
	Manage	Gives the right to edit the resource settings that apply to all users and groups having View permission to the resource collection. A user with Manage authority inherits Edit and View permissions and can also delete the resource collection.
	Create	Gives the right to install a new resource collection or copy an existing one. The creator of the collection automatically gets Manage and Delegate authority. To assign permissions to other users or groups, the creator still needs Delegate authority for the other users or groups.
Portal	View	N/A
	Edit	N/A
	Manage	Gives the right to create any new permission for the portal; to execute an XML configuration request using the portal configuration service; and to get, update, and remove portal services settings.
	Create	N/A

Table 7.2: Resources and Permissions (continued)

Resource	Permission	Control Description
External ACL	View	N/A
	Edit	N/A
	Manage	Gives the right to declare whether an access control decision is made based on an internal or external access control system. A user with Manage authority has the option of moving resources to and from an external control in the ACL portlet.
	Create	N/A
All other resources	View	Gives the right to view the resource.
	Edit	Gives the right to edit the resource settings that apply only to that user.
	Manage	Gives the right to edit the resource settings that apply to all users and groups having view permission to that resource. A user with Manage authority inherits Edit and View permissions and can also delete the resource.
	Create	Gives the right to install a new resource or copy an existing one. The resource's creator automatically gets Manage and Delegate authority. To assign permissions to other users or groups, the creator still needs Delegate authority for the other users or groups.

Delegate Permission

Delegate permission is rather special. It is required by an administrator. A user with Delegate permission for any portal resource can grant other users those permissions. Users may only grant permissions of the same level or lower than the permissions they themselves have for that resource. If a user has Edit and Delegate permission, then that user can only grant Edit or View permission to another user or group.

Also, an administrator can only give a user permission for a resource if the administrator has Delegate permission over a group of which that user is a member. This is how WebSphere Portal subdivides the user population as well as the resource domain for delegated administration.

Initial Settings

During Portal Server installation, initial access rights are assigned for the portal administrator and some user groups. As stated in Chapter 3, the default portal administrator is wpsadmin in the user group wpsadmins.

When the database is initialized, permission for the portal administrator and administrator group is set to Manage Portal and Delegate authority on all configured portal resources. (Manage permission on Portal gives administrators the right to give themselves full control over the portal, but they don't necessarily start out with full control over the portal—a subtle but important distinction.) View access is set for all authenticated users. Anonymous users have View access to any resource on the Welcome page.

Tip: If you choose to customize your LDAP settings and want to substitute another user for wpsadmin, that user must have a password and exist in LDAP prior to installation. The same holds true for the wpsadmins group.

Access-Control Scenario

The following sections examine some of the practical aspects of security settings within WebSphere Portal. Most of the functions demonstrated here are to be performed while logged in as the Portal Administrator (wpsadmin).

Scenario

A company, ourCo, has three departments, ourHR (human resources), ourIT (information technology), and ourAC (accounting). All employees of the company are in the ourCo group. People working in each of the departments are also members of their respective groups—ourHR group, ourIT group, ourAC group—each with its own portal site managed by the departmental portal administrator (HRadmin, ITadmin, or ACadmin). Also, the ITadmin has Manage privileges over the HR and accounting portals.

1. Start by logging in to the portal as user wpsadmin. Click the **Administration** link.

2. Create User Groups and subgroups:

   2a. Traverse down to **Access Users and Groups**.

2b. Click the **New group** button (see Figure 7.11).

2c. On the next screen, in the ID field, enter **ourHR**. Click **OK**.

2d. You should see a message *EJPAL0110I: User group created successfully!*

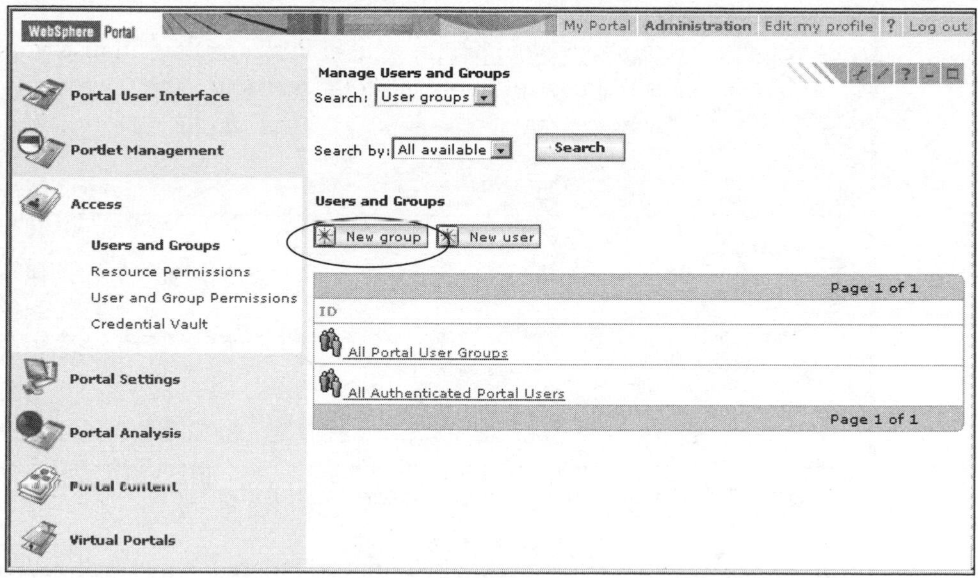

Figure 7.11: The New group button on Manage Users and Groups screen.

2e. Similarly, create the ourIT, ourAC, and ourCo groups.

2f. When completed, click **All Portal User Groups**. The screen should look like that in Figure 7.12.

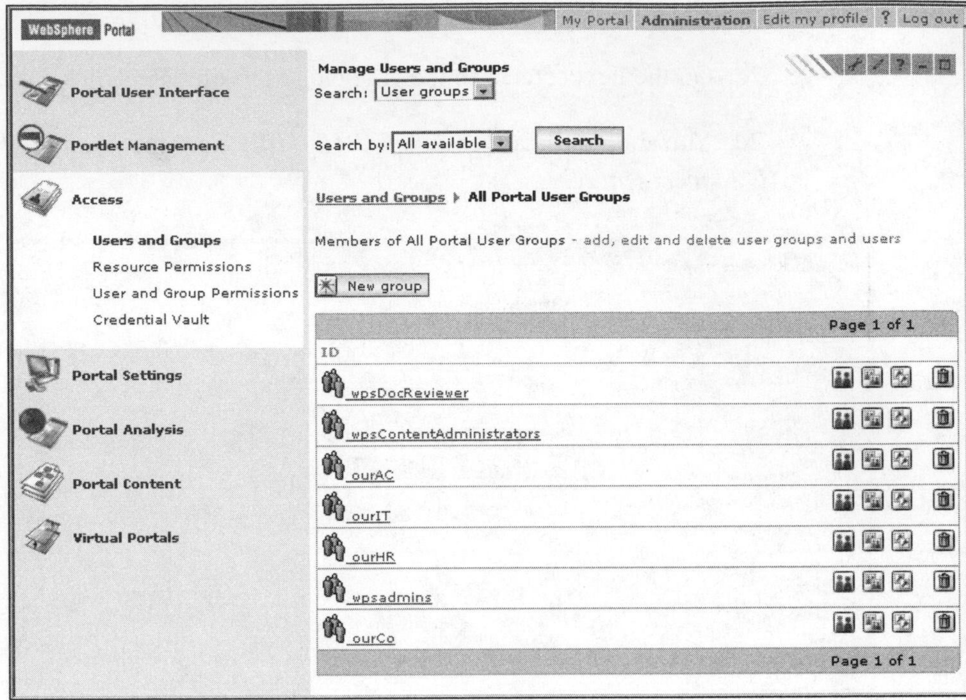

Figure 7.12: Screen showing the newly created four user groups.

2g. On the same screen, click **ourCo**. Ignore the message *EJPAL1010W: Sorry, no user or user group was found!*

2h. Click the **Add member** button.

2i. With the Search field pointing to User groups and Search on All available, click the **Search** button.

2j. All User groups will be returned except ourCo. Check the box in front of ourAC and click **OK**. See Figure 7.13.

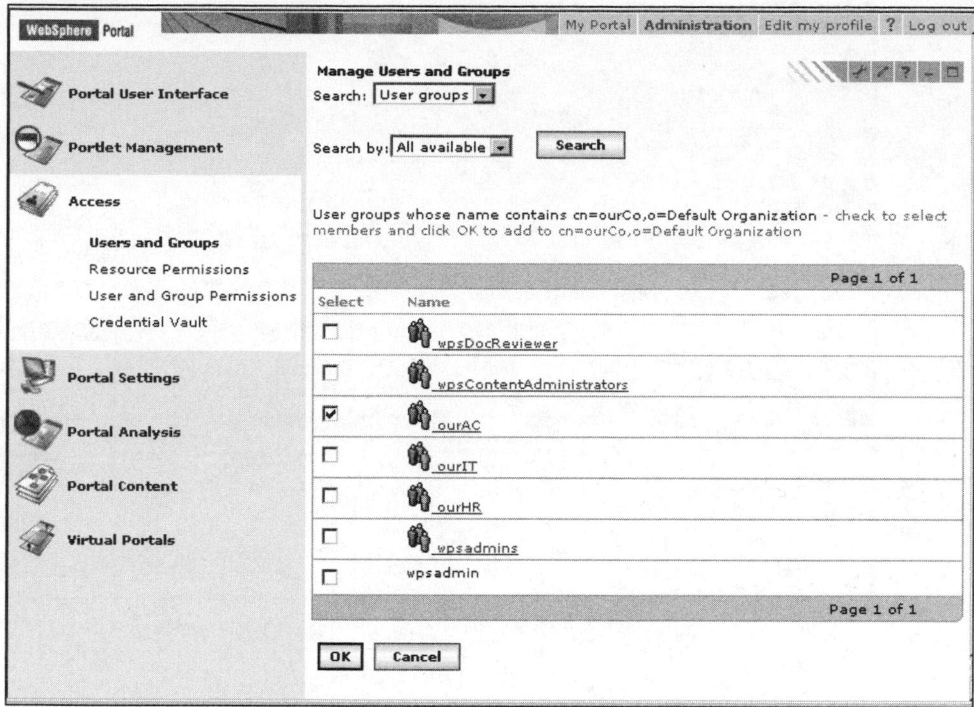

Figure 7.13: Selecting a member to add to a user group.

2k. On the next screen, you should see the message *EJPAL0140I: User or user group has been successfully added to the selected group*. And ourCo should have one member in it, namely ourAC.

2l. Similarly, add ourHR group to ourCo. When completed, ourCo should contain two groups, as shown in Figure 7.14.

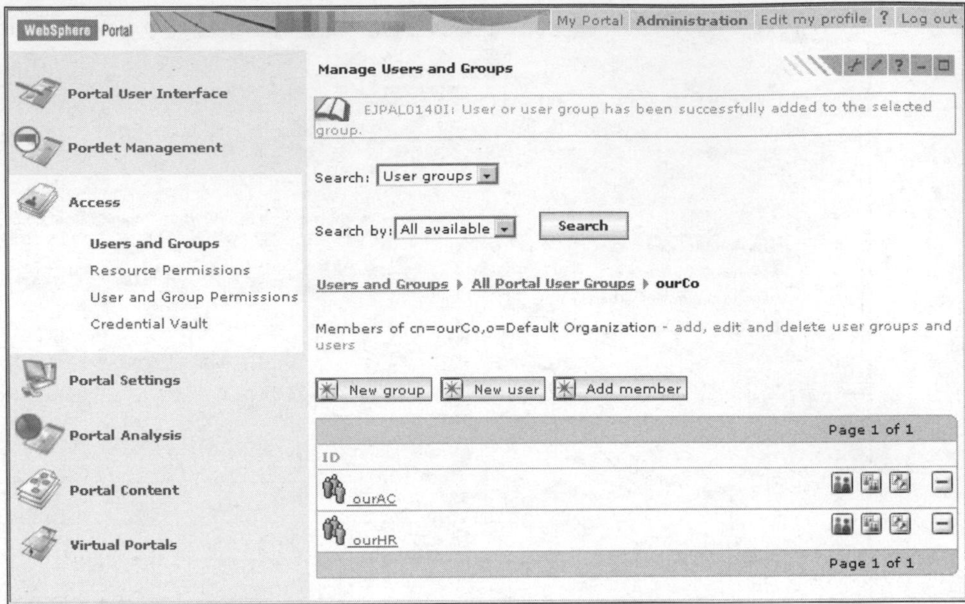

Figure 7.14: Now, ourAC and ourHR are members of ourCo user group.

3. Create administrators for the group portals and the members:

   3a. From the Administrative link, select **Access → Users and Groups**.

   3b. Click the **New user** button. (See Figure 7.11.)

   3c. On the next user information screen, enter the values for user ACadmin, as shown in Figure 7.15. Click **OK**.

   3d. Assuming there was no previous user id of acadmin, you should see a message *EJPAL0100I: User created successfully!*

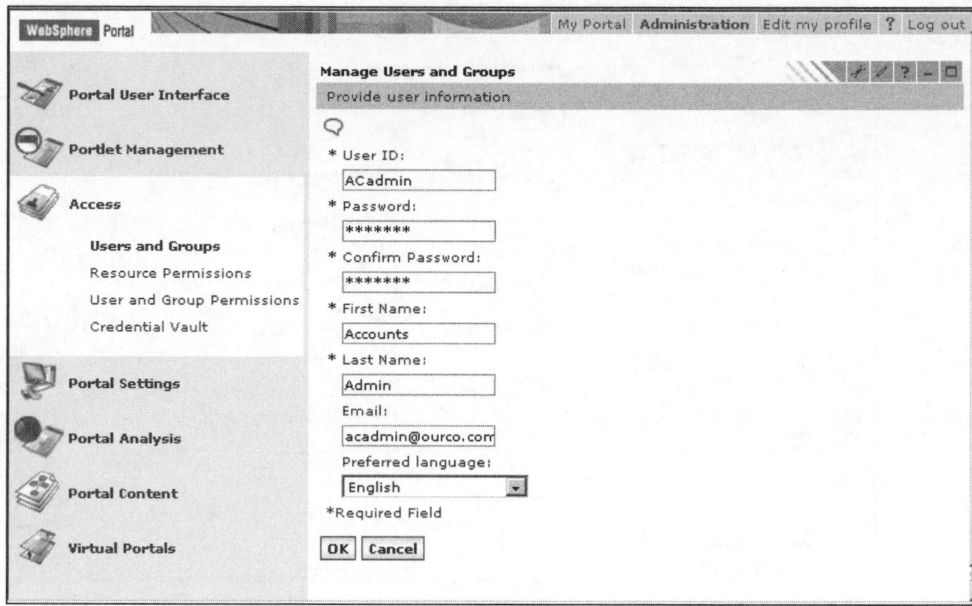

Figure 7.15: New User Information screen.

3e. Similarly, create users ITadmin and HRadmin. Also create a normal user called CoUser. Use the information in Table 7.3.

Table 7.3: New User Information

User ID	ITadmin	HRadmin	CoUser
Password	ITadmin	HRadmin	CoUser
First Name	IT	HR	Co
Last Name	Admin	Admin	User
Email	itadmin@ourco.com	hradmin@ourco.com	couser@ourco.com
Preferred Language	English (or your preference)	English (or your preference)	English (or your preference)

3f. When completed, click the **All Authenticated Portal Users** link. The screen should look like that in Figure 7.16.

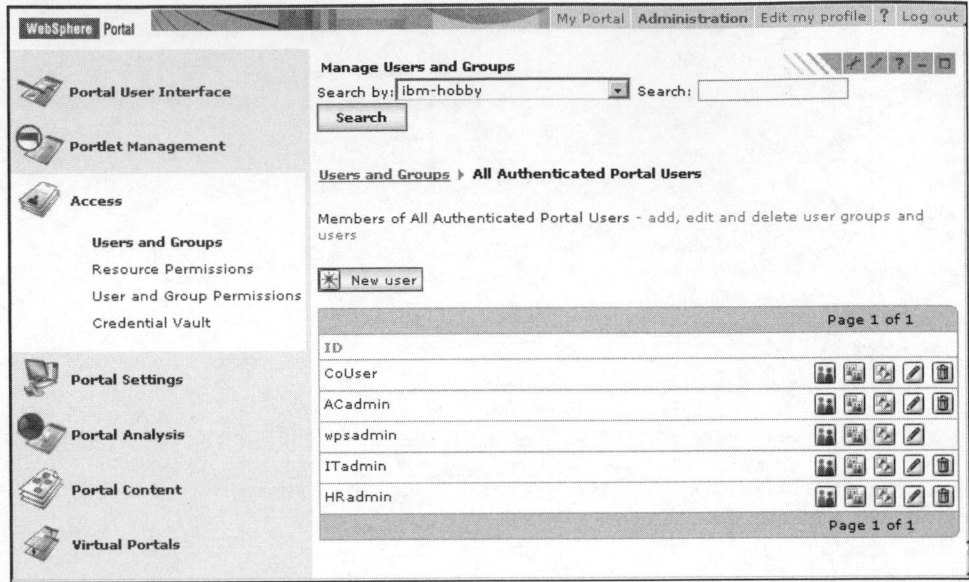

Figure 7.16: Newly created users.

3g. Return to **Users and Groups**; click **All Portal User Groups**. Now choose the group into which you want to add members, as before.

3h. Click **ourAC**. Then click the **Add member** button.

3i. Check the box in front of ACadmin and click **OK**. ACadmin is now a member of user group ourAC.

3j. In a similar manner, make ITadmin and ACadmin members of ourIT. Make HRadmin a member of ourHR. Additionally, make ITadmin a member of ourCo. You have made users who will act as administrators of their respective groups, and ITadmin will also be the company administrator.

3k. To round things off, make the portal user CoUser a member of ourCo.

4. In Chapter 4, you saw how to create a page and add portlets to a page via the Manage Pages option. Using that knowledge, create a new label called ourCo under My Portal. Create three pages under this label—ourAC, ourHR, ourIT. You may also create a subpage in each of three pages. And

you might want to give ourCo a new theme. You will use those pages and subpages to assign permission inheritance, as shown in Figure 7.17.

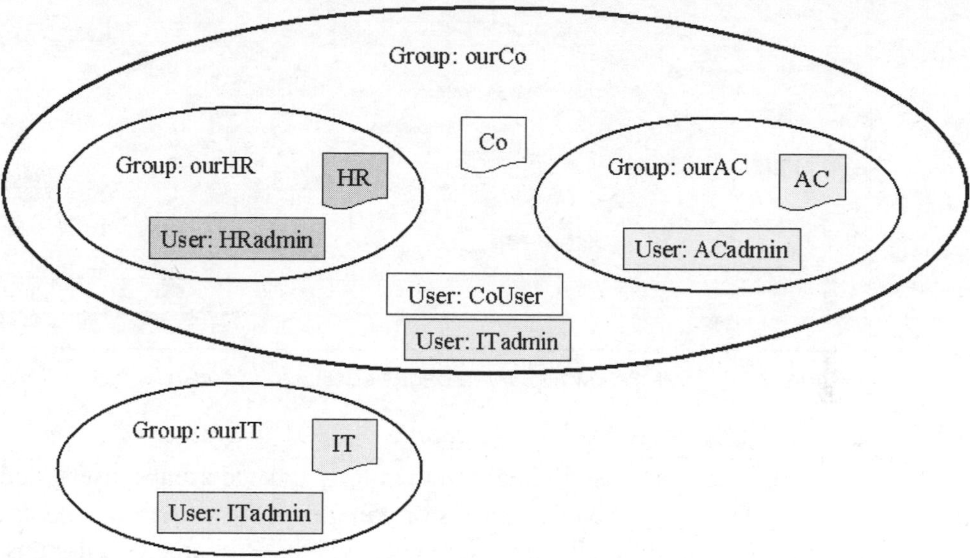

Figure 7.17: User and group permission inheritance.

After you create the new label and pages, the Manage Pages screen should look something like that shown in Figure 7.18.

Tip: Sometimes the following Content Root ▸ My Portal ▸ ourCo is referred to as *bread crumbs*.

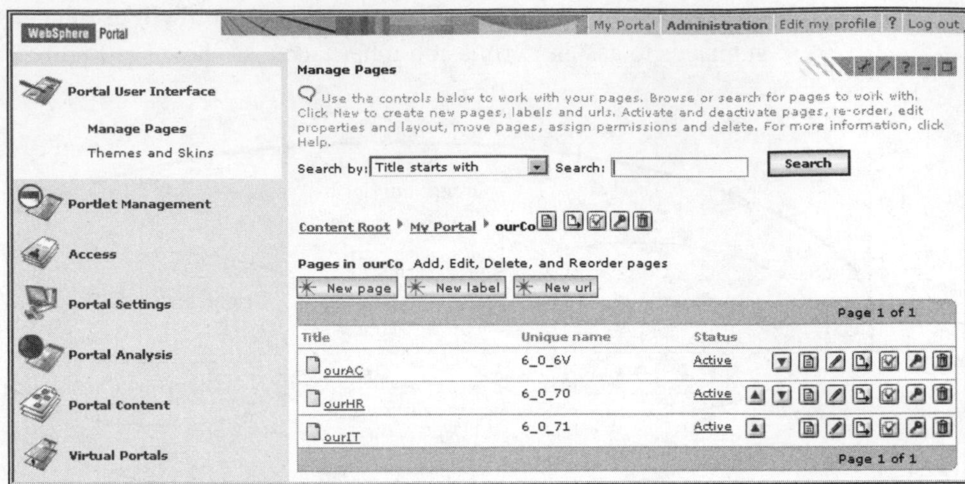

Figure 7.18: Screen shows the three pages contained in ourCo label.

5. Assign access privileges to the newly created groups, users, and pages. There are a couple of ways of doing this. We will use the Assign Permissions link and assign users via the Resource Permissions portlet.

5a. Make sure you are logged in as the portal administrator (wpsadmin). Click the **ourCo** label to see the three pages—ourAC, ourHR, ourIT.

5b. Select **ourAC** page, then click the **Assign Permissions** link.

5c. On the Resource Permissions screen, in the Allow Inheritance column, uncheck that option for Privileged User and User.

5d. Click **Apply** and then **OK** on the confirmation screen. You should see a message *EJPAO4023I: Propagation/Inheritance modified successfully.*

5e. Click the **Edit Role** icon for Privileged User.

5f. Click the **Add** button. Then search for All available User Groups. From the returned results list, select **ourAC**. Click **OK**. See Figure 7.19.

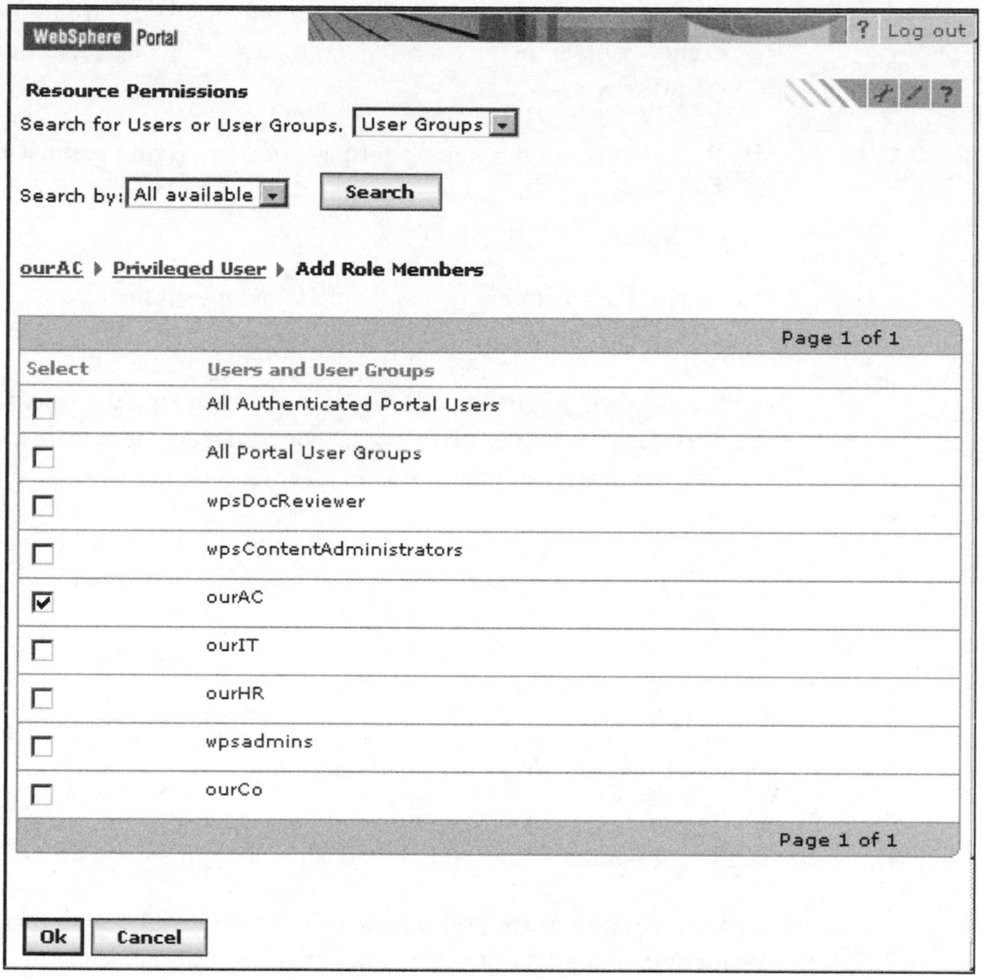

WebSphere Portal ? Log out

Resource Permissions

Search for Users or User Groups. User Groups

Search by: All available Search

ourAC ▸ Privileged User ▸ **Add Role Members**

Page 1 of 1

Select	Users and User Groups
☐	All Authenticated Portal Users
☐	All Portal User Groups
☐	wpsDocReviewer
☐	wpsContentAdministrators
☑	ourAC
☐	ourIT
☐	ourHR
☐	wpsadmins
☐	ourCo

Page 1 of 1

Ok Cancel

Figure 7.19: Searching and giving resource permissions to a User Group.

5g. You should see a message *EJPAO4003I: Members successfully added to the role*. Click **Done**.

5h. You will be returned to ourAC portal page. Log out as wpsadmin.

5i. Log back in as ACadmin. Click **ourCo**, and you should see all the three pages. Log out as ACadmin.

5j. Log back in as ITadmin. Click **ourCo**, and you will see only two of the three pages. The ourAC page is not seen because inheritance to all privileged users was taken away, and only the User Group ourAC was explicitly given permission. So, all members belonging to ourAC will see that page.

5k. Repeat steps 5a through 5g for page ourHR, giving permission to User Group ourHR. Repeat those same steps for the page ourIT, but give permission to User Group ourCo.

5l. A quick test is to log out as the portal administrator and log in as HRadmin. You will see that user HRadmin can only see ourHR page.

5m. Log out and log back in as ITadmin. Even though the User Group ourIT was not specifically given access to ourIT page, it is visible because ITadmin was also part of ourCo User Group.

5n. Log out and log back in as CoUser. Again, you should be able to see ourIT page under ourCo label, because CoUser was explicitly made part of ourCo User Group.

Note: You could choose to give a user or User Group permissions to View or Edit a page, but not a particular portlet that appears on that page. In that case, the page would be visible, but not the portlet.

The following important points were demonstrated by this scenario:

- Access permissions for portal resources can be given to portal User Groups. Similarly, portal users can be given explicit permissions.
- If a user is a member of a User Group, that user inherits all the group's permissions.
- Similarly, if a group is a member of another User Group, the member group inherits all the parent group's permissions.
- If a user belongs to more than one User Group, that user inherits the highest permission for each particular resource.
- If a group belongs to other User Groups, that group inherits the highest permission from the parent groups.

Using External Security Managers

As we have mentioned before, it is possible to integrate WebSphere Portal with an External Security Manager (ESM). This integration can be for authentication and coarse-grained URL access control only (essentially single sign-on with the ESM as a front-end security service and protection of the /wps/myportal URL stub) or for both authentication and fine-grained authorization/access control.

To accomplish ESM integration for authentication only, all that is required is a Trust Association Interceptor (TAI) for WebSphere Application Server that works with the specific front-end security service. TAI is a WebSphere Application Server interface/function, not a Portal function. Because Portal uses the end user identity set by WAS when processing a request, if WebSphere Application Server is configured with a TAI that asserts an end user identity, then no further authentication is required by WebSphere Portal. Later in the chapter, further discussion presents Trust Association Interceptors, and a flow is shown in Figure 7.27. TAIs exist for many popular security products. WebSphere Portal no longer supplies any TAI modules, but IBM provides a TAI for integrating Tivoli Access Manager with WebSphere Application Server, There are vendor-supplied TAIs for integrating with third-party security products like Netegrity's SiteMinder and RSA's Entrust. Any TAI that works in WebSphere Application Server will work with WebSphere Portal.

Accomplishing ESM integration for fine-grained access control is a bit more complex. In this integration, Portal roles are placed under the membership control of the ESM. Thus, entries are written into the protected object space of the ESM, which correspond to Portal roles on a resource that is "externalized." Then the ESM mechanisms are used to determine who has membership in those Portal roles. The actual definition of the roles (the permissions that make up the roles, including the Portal resources to which those roles apply) are still stored only in the WebSphere Portal database. But the ESM is consulted by WebSphere Portal to determine the "principal-to-role mapping," that is, the users (or groups) that have the permissions embodied in those roles.

The two specific instances of ESM supported for externalizing fine-grained authorization are IBM's Tivoli Access Manager and Netegrity SiteMinder. The specific versions supported are documented in the supporting software matrix for Portal. The Portal SPI that is used to integrate with these ESMs is not public, and IBM has only implemented this interface for these two specific ESMs. Thus, no other security vendor products are currently supported by IBM for Portal external access control (it would be possible to arrange the necessary DOUs to disclose this interface to a third party who wished to implement for another vendor, but keep in mind this interface is subject to change and will evolve in the direction of the JSR115 "JACC" model).

When Portal externalizes a Portal role to an ESM, an entry corresponding to the Portal role is written into the object space of the ESM. The actual resource name may be part of the role name, but the entry in the ESM space is a Portal role, not a portal resource, as in previous releases. Then the ESM mechanism, such as an ACL, is used to determine membership in the role—thus, only a single permission bit is ever used, not multiple permissions corresponding to portal access rights, as in previous releases.

Directory Server Support

Out of the box, WebSphere Portal V5.1 supports these commonly used directory servers:

- *Tivoli Directory Server*–One of the most common LDAP servers; useful in getting WebSphere Portal running.
- *Lotus Domino Application Server*–Used with Extend edition when you want to work with WebSphere Content Manager and Lotus Collaborative Components.
- *SunOne Directory Server*–Another common LDAP server that is popular on Solaris platforms.
- *Microsoft Active Directory*–Used in a Windows environment only.
- *Novell eDirectory Server*–Another common LDAP server that is used on Windows and Unix environments.

Installing WebSphere Portal with the Typical option gives you the choice to use an LDAP server. The other options are to use a database or a Custom User Registry (CUR). The settings for LDAP and other authentication registries are enumerated in Table 7.4. If enterprises are already using an LDAP directory server, it makes a lot of sense to incorporate that server into the portal configuration, and this is easily done. We recommend, however, running the portal server and the LDAP server on separate machines.

Table 7.4: Settings for Supported Authentication Registries

Portal Configuration	Authentication Registry	Description
LDAP	LDAP	When the authentication registry is a directory server, the user ID and passwords are created and stored in the registry. The profile information is split between LDAP and a database, based on XML files that configure Member Services.
DATABASE only	Custom Registry	Using a custom registry for the Portal Server database makes that registry part of the Member subsystem, and the profile information gets stored in the same database. The user ID and passwords are created, stored, and updated in the database registry. If you are manually configuring WAS security, you must select Custom User Registry as the authentication registry for Application Server, and supply the class name com.ibm.wps.puma.WMSCustomRegistry. If you allow Portal Server's installation manager to configure WAS security, select DATABASE for Member Services configuration to properly configure Application Server.
OTHER (non-LDAP, non-database)	User-supplied Custom User Registry	Member Services will not create or update any user entry in the authentication registry if the registry is an unrecognized database. WAS security should be manually configured with the installed Custom User Registry. In this case, Portal Server cannot be configured for global security. During Portal Server installation, you have to choose OTHER during Member Services configuration. Profile information is stored in the database as well as the custom registry.

LDAP Configurations

The LDAP server, also known as the directory server, should be installed and configured before attempting WebSphere Portal installation. Configuration consists of creating a *suffix* (i.e., an LDAP container), under which users reside. Installation also creates two administrative users, wpsadmin and wpsbind, as mentioned in Chapter 4. Both of these users belong to wpsadmins group.

The suffix is usually created manually via the directory server's client. To facilitate creating the initial users, a sample LDAP Data Interchange Format (ldif) file is supplied on the Setup CD. The file is named PortalUsers.ldif. The schema in this file must be modified to suit the domain settings of your site and then imported into the LDAP directory. Figure 7.20 lists the default PortalUsers.ldif file.

```
version: 1

# NOTE: you must edit this file before importing it and replace all
# occurrences of the default suffix "dc=yourco,dc=com" with the suffix
# that your LDAP server is configured for.

dn: dc=yourco,dc=com
objectclass: domain
objectclass: top
# Add lines according to this scheme that correspond to your suffix
dc: yourco,dc=com
dc: yourco

dn: cn=users,dc=yourco,dc=com
objectclass: container
objectclass: top
cn: users

dn: cn=groups,dc=yourco,dc=com
objectclass: top
objectclass: container
cn: groups

dn: uid=wpsadmin,cn=users,dc=yourco,dc=com
objectclass: organizationalPerson
objectclass: person
objectclass: top
objectclass: inetOrgPerson
uid: wpsadmin
userpassword: wpsadmin
sn: admin
givenName: wps
cn: wps admin


dn: uid=wpsbind,cn=users,dc=yourco,dc=com
objectclass: top
objectclass: person
objectclass: organizationalPerson
objectclass: inetOrgPerson
uid: wpsbind
userpassword: wpsbind
sn: bind
givenName: wps
cn: wps bind

dn: cn=wpsadmins,cn=groups,dc=yourco,dc=com
objectclass: groupOfUniqueNames
objectclass: top
uniquemember: uid=wpsadmin,cn=users,dc=yourco,dc=com
cn: wpsadmins
```

Figure 7.20: Default PortalUsers.ldif.

LDAP Settings

During installation, default LDAP values are presented based on the type of directory server being used. These should be modified to suit your site's domain settings. Table 7.5 shows some of the general settings.

Table 7.5: Directory Server Settings Used by WebSphere Portal

Settings	SecureWay	Domino	SunOne	Active Directory
User DN format	uid=username, cn=users,dc=yourco,dc=com	CN=ShortName,O=dominoDomain	uid=username,ou=People,dc=yourco, dc=com	cn=username, cn=users,dc=yourco, dc=com
Group DN format	cn=groupname, cn=groups,dc=yourco,dc=com	CN=groupname	cn=groupname,ou=Groups,dc=yourco, dc=com	cn=groupname, cn=users,dc=yourco, dc=com
User DN prefix	uid	CN	uid	cn
User DN suffix	cn=users	O=dominoDomain	ou=People,dc=yourco,dc=com	cn=users
Group DN prefix	cn	CN	cn	cn
Group DN suffix	cn=groups	Leave blank	ou=Groups,dc=yourco,dc=com	cn=users
Administrator group DN	cn=wpsadmins, cn=groups,dc=yourco,dc=com	CN=wpsadmins	cn=wpsadmins,ou=Groups,dc=yourco, dc=com	cn=wpsadmins, cn=users,dc=yourco, dc=com
Portal administrator DN	uid=wpsadmin, cn=users,dc=yourco,dc=com	CN=wpsadmin,O=dominoDomain	uid=wpsadmin, ou=People,dc=yourco,dc=com	cn=wpsadmin, cn=users,dc=yourco, dc=com
Portal user ID	uid=wpsbind, cn=users.dc=yourco,dc=com	CN=wpsbind,O=dominoDomain	uid=wpsbind, ou=People, dc=yourco,dc=com	cn=wpsbind,cn=users, dc=yourco,dc=com

---

Note: When using Active Directory on a Windows 2000 server running Domino Server, make sure that you specify a port other than 389 for the Domino LDAP Server. Active Directory grabs hold of port 389 and will try to authenticate all requests using that same port.

Single Sign-on

One of the biggest requirements that portal customers have of their portal sites is Single Sign-on (SSO). The requirement, in its simplest form, is that once a user logs in to the portal site, she should not be challenged again when accessing other applications via that portal.

Implementing SSO is obviously more easily said than done. In some cases, the issues really are beyond what the portal can address, involving legal issues, back-end systems that have been working fine over the years with their own authentication mechanisms, and users having multiple user IDs across different applications in the enterprise. However, this section discusses how SSO can be implemented in WebSphere Portal, and where it is already being used.

SSO in Portal Server has two levels. First, the Credential Vault Service encapsulates the functionality of SSO for the portlet developer in an object provided by the Service. The second level is a bit more flexible, but requires portlet developers to directly utilize the SSO functions of WebSphere Portal server and manage their own connections and authentication to back-end applications. The SSO functions of WebSphere Portal server utilize the authentication subset of the Java Authentication and Authorization Service (JAAS).

SSO and JAAS

The underlying application server implements the JAAS architecture. JAAS provides a way to authenticate subjects and provides fine-grained access control. JAAS is part of the standard Java security model; it provides application independence from underlying authentication and authorization mechanisms. JAAS performs login and logout operations using a modular service provider interface. Credentials that are established through the portal server JAAS login modules include user and group distinguished names, user ID and password, and single sign-on tokens like Lightweight Third Party Authentication (LTPA). In a distributed J2EE environment, portlets can use the JAAS Application Programming Interface (API) to access JAAS-enabled back-end applications

- The single sign-on functions of WebSphere Portal use a subset of JAAS. The used subset is the authentication portion; WebSphere Portal does not support true JAAS authorization.

- WebSphere Portal Server builds a JAAS subject for each logged-on user, consisting of *principals* and *credentials*. A *principal* is a piece of data like a user ID or user DN, which can identify the subject. A *credential* is a piece of data like a password or a CORBA (Common Object Request Broker

Architecture) credential, which can authenticate a subject. The subject carries around the principals and credentials that can be used by the portlet directly or via the credential service.

SSO Using LTPA Tokens

Resources protected by WebSphere Portal use CORBA API credentials and an encrypted LTPA cookie to authenticate users. If you choose to use a third-party authentication server, Application Server typically uses a TAI (Trust Association Interceptor) to trust the external authentication proxy and set up its security context. The exception is if the third-party authentication proxy or server has been configured to provide native Application Server identity tokens, such as an LTPA token.

Although LTPA tokens offer better security than TAIs, currently, only Policy Director WebSEAL can use LTPA tokens. For that reason, in this chapter our focus on authentication is to show the usage of TAIs.

SSO Using the Credential Vault

Portlets need to provide some form of authentication to access back-end systems that require their own authentication. These back-end applications could be remote or legacy applications. To provide Single Sign-On (SSO), portlets must be able to store and retrieve user credentials associated with a particular application and use those credentials to log in on behalf of the user.

WebSphere Portal offers a nice feature called the *Credential Vault*, where users and administrators can safely store credentials for authentication. Portlets and portal users can use the appropriate Credential Vault portlet service to manage multiple identities.

The Credential Vault is organized as follows:

- The portal administrator can partition the vault into several *vault segments*. Vault segments are created and configured only by portal administrators.
- A vault segment contains one or more *vault slots*. Vault slots are the "folders" where portlets store and retrieve a user's credentials. Each slot can hold one credential.
- A vault slot is linked to a resource in a *vault implementation*, where users' credentials are actually stored. The resource within the vault implementation

corresponds to an application or back-end system that requires its own authentication.

Figure 7.21 provides a pictorial representation of the organization of the Credential Vault.

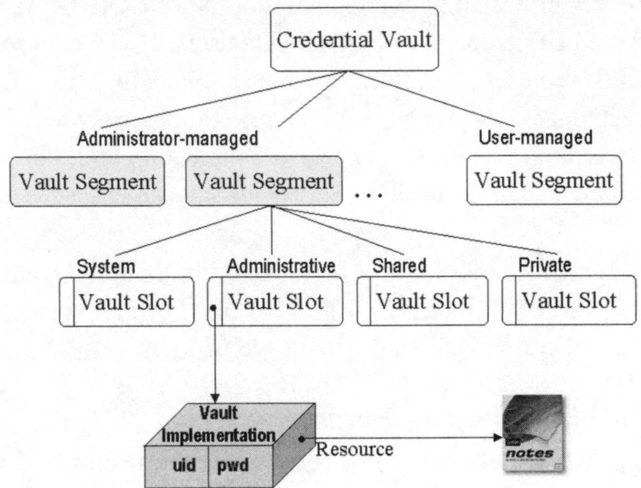

Figure 7.21: Credential Vault organization.

Vault Segment

A vault segment can be either administrator-managed or user-managed. On behalf of a portal user, portlets can set and retrieve credentials in both types of vault segments, but portlets can create vault slots only in user-managed segments. Typically, only one-user managed vault segment resides in the vault provided by WebSphere Portal.

Note: The default vault comes preconfigured with one administrator-managed vault segment and one user-managed vault segment. You cannot have more than one user-managed vault segment. The default vault uses Base 64 encoding to encode stored passwords.

WebSphere Portal provides one simple database vault implementation for mappings to the secrets of other enterprise applications. Two types of vault segments can be created:

- The administrator-managed vault allows users to update mappings, but users may not add new applications to this vault. Users cannot create slots in this vault. An example of an administrator-managed vault is the Lotus Notes database.

- The user-managed vault allows users to add application definitions under the user vault and store a mapping there. A personal mailbox is an example of this type of vault.

To use another vault implementation, you need your own vault adapter to work with WebSphere Portal. In addition to the vault adapter, you must configure the portal server to use the new vault. Newly plugged-in vaults can only be managed by an administrator.

Here are the high-level steps to implement your own vault:

1. Edit the <WPS_HOME>/shared/app/config/services/VaultServices.properties configuration file to specify Vault Adapter Implementation. See the default file in Figure 7.22.

2. After the vault has been plugged in, restart the portal.

3. Add a segment to your vault using the Credential Vault portlet.

```
# Licensed Materials - Property of IBM, 5724-E76, (C) Copyright IBM
Corp. 2004 - All Rights reserved.

# Vault Service Configuration File
# IBM WebSphere Portal Server, Release 4.1, 2002
#
# This configuration file is used to specify Vault Adapter
Implementations.
# For each implementation, a unique string type and class name must be
# specified.  Optionally, a configuration file, managing resources, and
read
# only flags may be specified.

# Comma delimited list of Vault Adapter Implementation Types
types=default

# For each Vault Adapter Implementation Type, the following properties
may be
# defined.  In order to differentiate each type's settings, the keys are
in
# the following format:
#
#     <type>.<key>
```

Figure 7.22: Sample VaultServices.properties file (part 1 of 2).

```
#
# The keys are:
#     vaultadapter:  Required - Vault Adapter Implementation Class
Name, minus
#                        the .class extension
#     config:  Optional - Path of a configuration file your adapter may
need
#     manageresources:  Specifies if the VaultAdapter should create and
delete
#                 resources.  Note, the adapter must have internal support
#                       to manage resources if this property is set to
true.  If
#                       omitted, this property will be set to false
#     readonly:  Specifies if the underlying vault for this adapter
should be
#                 considered readonly.  If true, the manageresources
property is
#                 ignored.  If omitted, the property will be set to
false

default.vaultadapter=com.ibm.wps.services.credentialvault.DefaultVault
default.config=defaultvault
default.manageresources=true
default.readonly=false
systemcred.dn=uid=wpsadmin,o=default organization

# Distinguished Name of the user that System Credentials will be stored
under.
```

Figure 7.22: Sample VaultServices.properties file (part 2 of 2).

Vault Slot

The Credential Vault provided by WebSphere Portal distinguishes four different types of vault slots:

- A *system slot* stores system credentials in a way that the actual secret is shared among all users and portlets.
- An *administrative slot* allows each user to store a secret for an administrator-defined resource, like Lotus Notes.
- A *shared slot* stores user credentials that are shared among the user's portlets.
- A *portlet private slot* stores user credentials that are not shared among portlets.

Credential Object

Credentials are set and retrieved as credential objects. This is done by way of the Credential Vault portlet service, which is part of the following Java package:

```
com.ibm.wps.portletservice.credentialvault.credentials.Credential
```

All credential types that are available within the portal are registered in a credential type registry. WebSphere Portal classifies these objects as *passive* and *active* credential objects.

Passive credential objects are containers that hold the credential's secret. Portlets using passive credentials need to extract the secret out of the credential and communicate with the back-end application to perform authentication. WebSphere Portal supplies the following passive credential objects:

- *SimplePassive* stores secrets as serialized Java objects. This is intended for future use only, because the vault service does not support binary large object (BLOB) secrets.
- *UserPasswordPassive* stores secrets as userid/password pairs.
- *JaasSubjectPassive* stores secrets as javax.security.auth.Subject objects. This is intended for future use because the vault service does not support this type of secret.

Active credential objects hide the credential's secret from the portlet. There is no way of extracting the secret out of the credential. In return, active credential objects offer business methods that take care of authentication. This allows portlets to trigger authentication to remote servers using standard mechanisms, such as basic authentication, HTTP form-based authentication, or POP3 authentication, without even knowing the credential secrets.

With active credential objects, the portal does the authentication on behalf of the portlets with already authenticated connections. From a security perspective, the portlets never touch the credential secrets. Hence, there is no risk a portlet will ever violate any security rules. This is the preferred way of using credential objects.

WebSphere Portal supplies the following active credential objects:

- HttpBasicAuth stores userid/password pairs and supports HTTP basic authentication.
- HttpFormBasedAuth stores userid/password pairs and supports HTTP form-based authentication.
- JavaMail stores userid/password pairs and leverages the authentication functionality of the javax.mail API.
- LtpaToken authenticates with a back-end system that is within the same WebSphere SSO domain as WebSphere Portal.
- SiteMinderToken is used when SiteMinder is the authentication proxy for WebSphere Portal and is within the same SiteMinder SSO domain.
- WebSealToken is used when WebSEAL is the authentication proxy for WebSphere Portal and is within the same WebSEAL SSO domain.

In addition to the active and passive credential types listed here, additional credential objects can easily be registered in the credential type registry.

Configuring Tivoli Access Manager Vault Adapter

WebSphere Portal includes a vault adapter for Tivoli Access Manager (TAM). You can use the TAM plug-in with the Credential Vault service.

> **Note:** Users storing credentials in the Access Manager vault must be defined in TAM as Global Sign-On (GSO) users.

The following instructions assume that Tivoli Access Manager and WebSphere Portal are running on the same machine, in this case a Windows 2000 machine named iyengarnote.

1. Edit the <WPS_HOME>/shared/app/config/services/VaultService.properties file to modify the types property by adding accessmanager:

```
types=default, accessmanager
```

2. Add the following lines in the VaultService.properties file:

```
accessmanager.vaultadapter=com.ibm.wps.sso.vaultservice.AccessMa
  nagerVaultAdapter
accessmanager.config=services/accessmanagervault
accessmanager.manageresources=true
accessmanager.readonly=false
```

3. Create a file named <WPS_HOME>/shared/app/config/<accessmanager.config_value>, where <accessmanager.config_value> is the value for accessmanager.config from step 2.

4. Add the following lines, where pduser is TAM administrator and pdpw is the password.

```
pduser=sec_master
pdpw=<PASSWORD>
```

5. Remember, you can encrypt the password using the PropFilePasswordEncoder script in <WAS_HOME>/bin.

6. Make sure that the TAM utilities pdjrte and SrvSslCfg, have been run so that the Access Manager vault can access the GSO lockbox from within WebSphere Portal.

Credential Vault Creation

Use the Credential Vault portlet to add and manage a vault segment:

1. Start by logging in as the portal administrator (wpsadmin). In the Administration link, traverse to **Access → Credential Vault**. That brings up the Credential Vault screen, as shown in Figure 7.23.

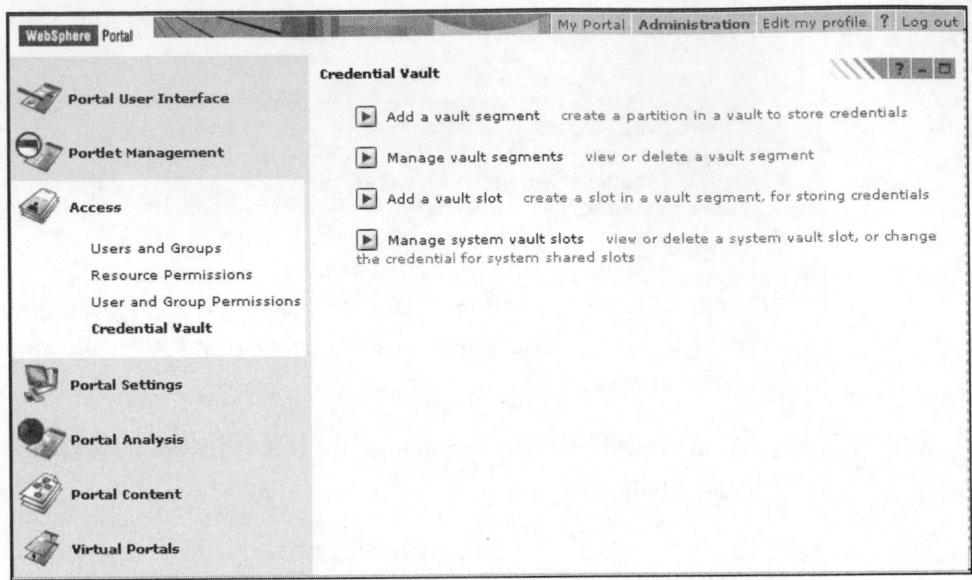

Figure 7.23: Credential Vault screen.

2. Choose **Add a vault segment**. The next screen shows four fields, as seen in Figure 7.24.

   2a. The only vault available is the default, which exists in the WebSphere Portal database. The number in parentheses indicates the number of administrator-managed segments defined for this vault.

   2b. The comma-separated list of names shows the resources located in the vault.

   2c. You must give the vault segment a name.

   2d. Optionally, you can enter a description of the vault segment.

3. Enter **ourVault Segment** as the name for the vault segment and optionally enter a brief description, as shown in Figure 7.24.

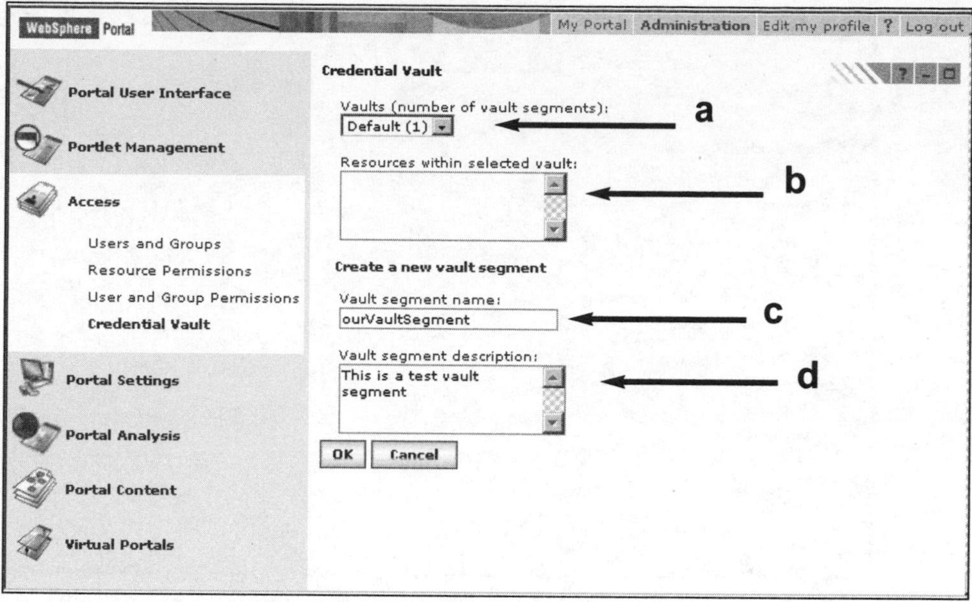

Figure 7.24: Creating a new vault segment.

4. Click **OK**. You should see a message *EJPAZ0008I: The vault segment was created successfully.*

5. Go back to the Add a vault segment screen; the number of segments in the Default vault should be 2. Click **Cancel**.

6. Click **Manage vault segments**. You should see the newly created segment, as shown in Figure 7.25. From this screen, you can also delete vault segments.

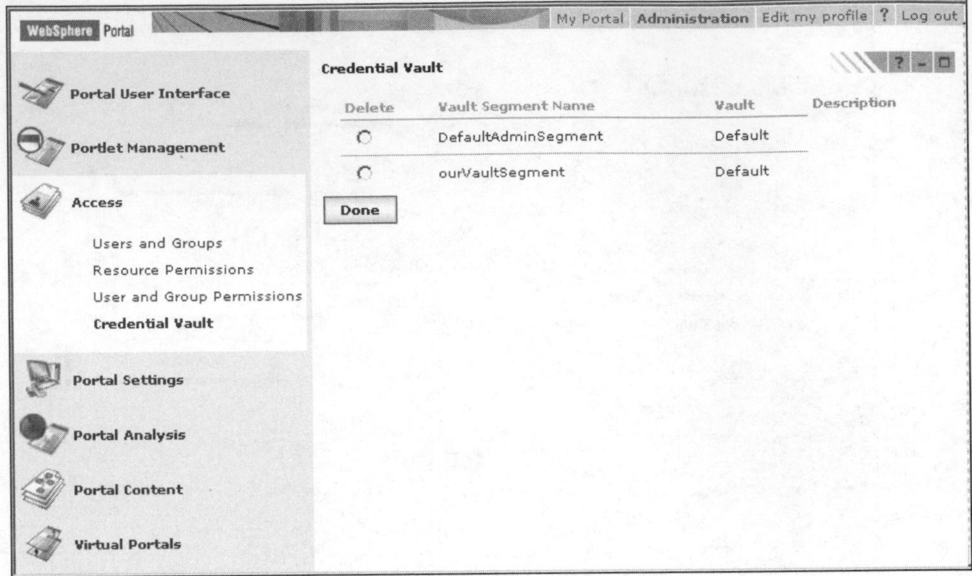

Figure 7.25: Screen to manage vault segments.

7. Click **Done** to return to the initial screen.
8. Click **Add a vault slot.** Refer to Figure 7.26 to fill out this screen:

   8a. The only vault available is Default.

   8b. Enter the name of the vault slot, **ourVault Slot**.

   8c. Choose the vault segment created in the previous steps.

   8d. Create a new vault resource, or choose an existing one. In this example, choose **new** and give it the name **ourVaultResource**.

   8e. Check the **Vault slot is shared** box so that all users share the user ID and password. By checking this box, you create a system credential slot and provide the user ID and password to all users. If you do not check the box, the user ID and password fields are not enabled, and credentials are not shared with other users.

   8f. Optionally, enter a description of the vault slot being created.

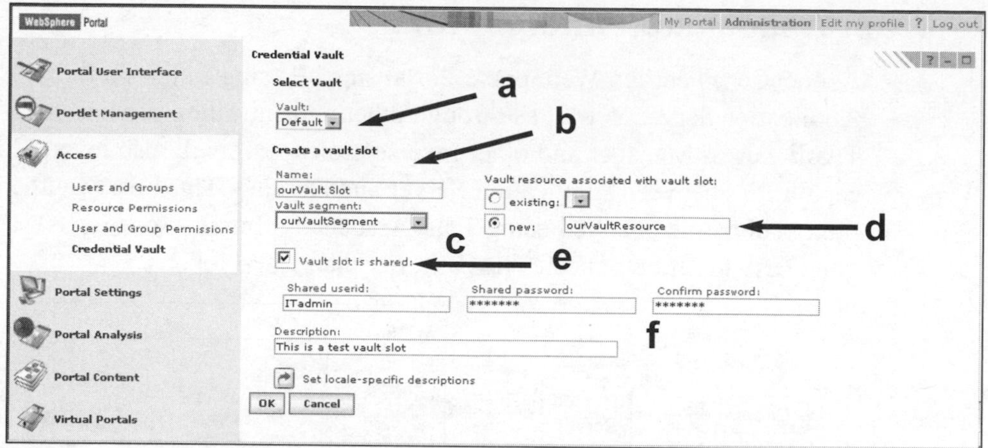

Figure 7.26: The screen for adding vault slot details.

9. Click **OK**. You should see the message *EJPAZ0014I: The vault slot was created successfully.*

10. Back at the screen for selecting a security-vault management task, click **Manage system vault slots**. You should see the newly created vault slot.

11. Click **Done**. You now have a vault slot in which you can store and retrieve credentials. Passing it to back-end applications enables single sign-on.

Portlets can use the Credential Vault portlet service object to obtain the credentials by calling its getCredential() method. With the returned credential, you have two options:

- Take a *passive* credential—Get the password or key by calling credential.getUserSecret() method and pass it in the application-specific call. Portlets using passive credentials extract the secret and do all the authentication communication with the back-end application.

- Use an *active* credential—Log into the back-end system and call the authenticate method credential.getAuthenicatedConnection(). Portlets cannot extract the secret out of the credential, because active credential objects hide the secrets. Additional methods perform the authentication.

Trust Association Interceptors

As mentioned earlier, WebSphere Portal supports single sign-on through the Application Server as well as through other authentication proxies, such as IBM Tivoli Access Manager and other reverse proxy servers. It also leverages the SSO capabilities between Application Server and Domino. Third-party authentication proxy support is obtained using Trust Association Interceptors (TAIs), which are quite easy to set up but offer less security than LTPA tokens.

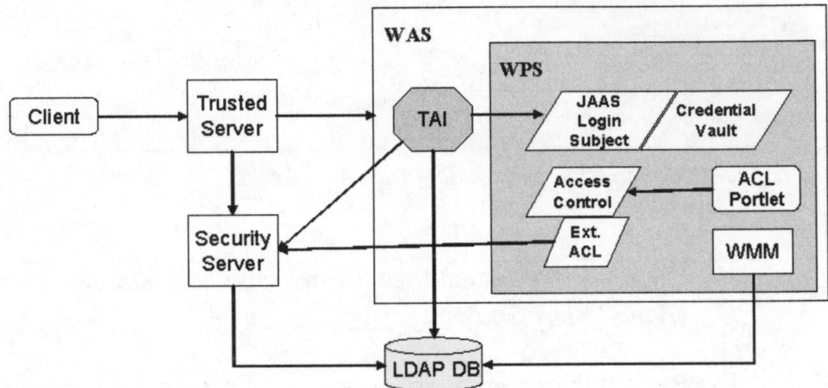

Figure 7.27: Trust Association flow.

When a third-party authentication provider, such as Tivoli Access Manager WebSEAL, is configured, that authentication provider determines the challenge mechanism and how it does its authentication. Whenever a request attempts to access a secured resource, WebSphere Application Server invokes the TAI, which validates that the request comes from a legitimate third-party authentication proxy and returns the user's authenticated identity to WebSphere Application Server. Figure 7.27 depicts the trust association flow. The TAI normally returns a distinguished name (DN) or a short name. WebSphere Application Server performs a registry lookup to verify the DN or convert the short name to a distinguished name before searching for group memberships for that user. If the registry lookup fails, WebSphere Application Server refuses to trust the user. If the registry lookup succeeds, WebSphere Application Server generates an LTPA token for the user and stores it as a cookie for subsequent authentication during the user's session.

Configuring Tivoli Access Manager TAI

If you use Tivoli Access Manager (TAM) to perform authorization for the portal, you must also use Tivoli Access Manager to perform authentication for the portal.

Using Tivoli Access Manager to perform only authorization is not supported. Configuring WebSphere Portal to work with TAM really involves creating and working with WebSEAL *junctions*.

The junctions between WebSEAL and WebSphere Application Server and WebSphere Portal can be configured to be encrypted or not. If you choose not to use client-side certificates to identify the WebSEAL server, or if you choose not to use an SSL junction, you can identify the WebSEAL server to the TAI using a Basic Authentication (BA) header. In this case, a password is placed into the Basic Authentication header and also configured into the TAI. This represents a "shared secret" that only the TAI and the WebSEAL server know. Configuration of a TAM TAI is a two-step process:

1. Enable trust association in WebSphere Administrative Console.
2. Set up the TAI that is going to receive HTTP requests from the trusted proxy server.

Note: Security based on a LDAP server should already be configured in WebSphere Portal.

Here are the detailed configuration steps for a non-SSL junction:

1. The presumption here is that WebSphere Portal is already installed and configured to work with a database server and a LDAP Directory, meaning that security is enabled in the portal.

2. Tivoli Access Manager (TAM) is also installed along with WebSEAL server. The recommendation is to run the TAM/WebSEAL server on a system separate from WebSphere Portal.

3. Make sure WebSphere Administrative Server (server1) and WebSphere Portal server is stopped.

4. One of the underlying requirements of the TAI is the creation of a trusted user account, in TAM's user registry, which WebSphere Application Server can use. This will be the ID and password that WebSEAL uses to identify itself to WebSphere Application Server. The recommendation is *not* to use

sec_master or wpsadmin as that trusted user account. Create the trusted user account in TAM via the Web Portal Manager or via the pdadmin command and make that account valid:

```
pdadmin> user create <webseal_userid> <webseal_userid_DN>
<first_name> <sur_name> <password>
pdadmin> user modify <webseal_userid> account-valid yes
```

5. Edit wpconfig.properties, found in <WPS_HOME>/config. Look for the TAM section and modify the appropriate properties. These are shown in Table 7.6.

Table 7.6: Attributes in wpconfig.properties

Attribute	Default Value	Description
Affecting Tivoli Access Manager		
PDAdminId	sec_master	TAM administrative ID
PDAdminPw	<password>	Password for TAM administrative user
PDPermPath	<WAS_HOME>/java/jre/PdPe rm.properties	Location of TAM AMJRTE properties file
PDServerName	amwps5	Unique application name of new Tivoli server in TAM Policy Server
SvrSslCfgPort	7223	Configuration port for the application
SvrSslCfgMode	remote	Configuration mode of SvrSslCfg command
TamHost	<TAM_Policy_Server_host-name>	TAM Policy Server used when running PDJrteCfg
PDPolicyServerList	<TAM_Policy_Server_host-name>:7135:1	Hostname, port, and priority combinations for TAM Policy server when running SvrSslCfg
PDAuthzServerList	<TAM_Authorization_Server_hostname>:7136:1	Hostname, port, and priority combinations for TAM Authorization server
PDKeyPath	<WAS_HOME>/java/jre/lib/se curity/pdperm.ks	Encryption keys used for SSL communica-tion between AMJRTE and TAM

6. Save wpconfig.properties file and validate the pdadmin connection. From <WPS_HOME>/config directory, run the WPSconfig task:

```
WPSconfig validate-pdadmin-connection -DpdAdminPw=<password>
```

7. If the validation task succeeds, edit the wpconfig.properties file again. This time, look for the WebSEAL section and modify the appropriate properties. These are shown in Table 7.7.

Table 7.7: Attributes in wpconfig.properties

Attribute	Default Value	Description
Affecting WebSEAL		
JunctionType	tcp	Acceptable values are tcp and ssl
JunctionPoint	/wpsv5	Junction point to WebSphere Portal instance
WebSealInstance	instance-webseald-<HOST_NAME>.com	WebSEAL instance to create the junction
TAICreds	iv-user,iv-creds	Headers inserted by WebSEAL that the TAI uses to identify requests
Affecting WebSEAL TAI		
WebSealHost		WebSEAL TAI's hostnames parameter (optional)
WebSealPort		WebSEAL TAI's ports parameter (optional)
WebSealUser	wpsadmin	For TCP junction, reverse proxy identity
BaUserName	Wpsadmin	For SSL junction only
BaPassword	Wpsadmin	For SSL junction only

8. Save the wpconfig.properties file and run the enable-tam-tai task. From <WPS_HOME>/config directory, invoke WPSconfig:

```
WPSconfig enable-tam-tai -DSmAdminPw=<password>
-DBaPassword=<password>
```

If the enable-tam-tai task succeeds, then configuration to needed at the WebSphere Application Server side.

9. Bring up the WebSphere Administrative Console. When you are challenged (because global security is enabled for Portal Server), enter **wpsbind** for both the user identity and the user password.

   9a. In the navigation bar of the Administrative Console, traverse down to **Security → Authentication Mechanisms → LTPA.** Under Additional Properties, click **Trust Association**.

   9b. Check the box for **Trust Association Enabled** in the LTPA settings group, as shown in Figure 7.28.

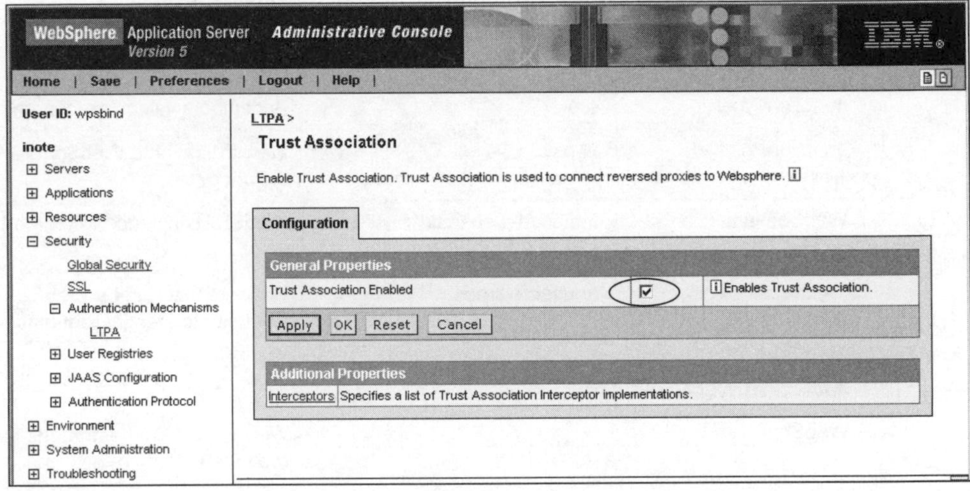

Figure 7.28: Enabling Trust Association in the WebSphere Administrative Console.

   9c. Click **OK**. Click **Save** and **Save** again to apply the changes to the master configuration.

   9d. Again click **Security → Authentication Mechanisms → LTPA**. Under Additional Properties, click **Interceptors**.

   9e. From the list of Interceptor Class names click **com.ibm.ws.security.web.WebSealTrustAssociationInterceptor**. Optionally, under its Additional Properties, click Custom Properties and add any name/value pair of properties.

   9f. Make sure you save the Master Configuration.

   9g. Logout and restart the WebSphere Administrative Server to ensure that the changes take effect.

10. Test to see if it works. To test access through WebSEAL, enter the following URL in a Web browser:

```
https://<HOST_NAME>:443/servlet/snoop
```

The TAM challenge shown in Figure 7.29 should pop up. Enter **wpsadmin** for both the user name and the password, and click **OK**. The snoop servlet details should be displayed.

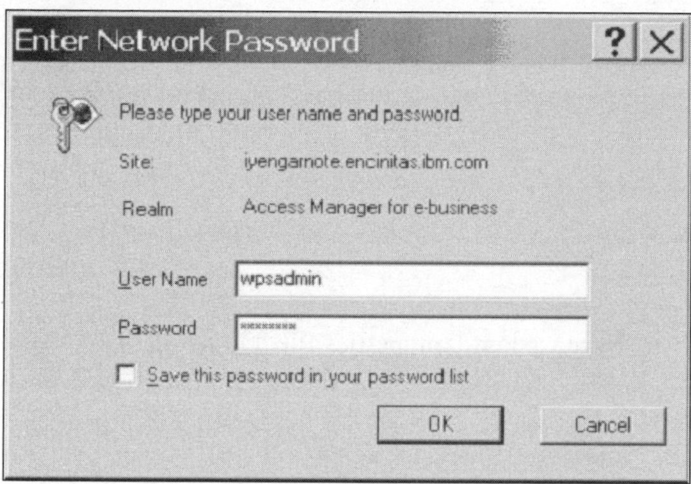

Figure 7.29: Tivoli Access Manager's challenge screen.

Configuring Netegrity SiteMinder TAI

WebSphere Portal includes TAI configuration settings for Netegrity SiteMinder. It works with the Netegrity SiteMinder Web agent, which is installed in the HTTP server that directs requests to WebSphere Application Server. Like TAM, configuring WebSphere Application Server and WebSphere Portal to work with Netegrity SiteMinder TAI is a two-step process:

1. Enable trust association in the WebSphere Application Server Administrative Console via the Security Center screen, as shown in Figure 7.26.
2. Set the Netegrity SiteMinder (SM) related parameters in wpconfig.properties and configure them by running the WPSconfig task, as described in the earlier section on TAM TAI. Although Table 7.8 shows a number of parameters, it is essential to set only one attribute or parameter, namely SMConfigFile.

Table 7.8: Attributes in wpconfig.properties

Attribute	Default Value	Description
Affecting Netegrity Siteminder		
SMConfigFile	<SM_HOME>/smwastai/conf/WebAgent.conf	Location of SiteMinder TAI WebAgent.conf file
SMDomain	WebSphere Portal v5	SiteMinder Domain name
SMScheme	Basic	SiteMinder Authentication scheme
SMAgentPw	<password>	Password for SM agent
SMUserDir	<SM_UserDirectory_Object>	SM User Directory object referencing the LDAP server
SMFailover	False	True or false
SMServers	<SM_Policy_Server_host-name>	SM Policy Server host name

3. Save wpconfig.properties file and run the enable-sm-tai task. From <WPS_HOME>/config directory, invoke WPSconfig:

```
WPSconfig enable-sm-tai
```

Door Closings

Security is a vast topic that means different things to different people. It can involve an all-encompassing directive across the enterprise or a simple login portlet on one's portal page. Every portal Request for Proposal (RFP) or Proof of Concept (POC) invariably has a line item entitled "security and single sign-on." It is one of the main yardsticks of a portal product. WebSphere Portal truly comes out on top when measured by how it handles security.

For starters, we recommend implementing an intranet portal with basic LDAP security turned on. Thereafter, organizations should look at their enterprise-wide security policies, make sure consistency exists across the enterprise, and then integrate those policies into the portal. At that point, external customers and business partners can be operating safely on the same portal.

Chapter 8
Portal and Beyond

This chapter discusses the Search, Site Analytics, Process Portals, and WebSphere Portal Application Integrator (WPAI); components that make the WebSphere Portal one of the premier portal servers in the market. The Search component comes in three variations. Site analytics is provided by WebSphere Site Analyzer, which can actually provide metrics at the portlet level. Process Portals are one of the most useful applications of portals in a process-centric environment. The discussion about WPAI is tempered, because it is based on WebSphere Portal V5.0.x. It is undergoing some changes, and the update will be available as a V5.1 point release in the near future.

Tip: Tivoli Web Site Analyzer and IBM Lotus Extended Search use the same default port number. If installed on the same server you must change the port number used by IBM Lotus Extended Search and regenerate the Web server plug-in in WebSphere Application Server before Tivoli Web Site Analyzer can run. The other possibility is to install IBM Lotus Extended Search first and then install Tivoli Web Site Analyzer, that way nonconflicting ports are assigned.

Search

Three search technologies are available to integrate with WebSphere Portal V5.1. They are:

- Portal Search Engine (PSE), used to search web, and Portal content
- IBM Lotus Extended Search (ES), included with WebSphere Portal Extend Edition and includes a federated search and meta-search engine
- WebSphere Information Integrator OmniFind Edition, an enterprise search product that is sold separately but that can be integrated into WebSphere Portal

Figure 8.1 shows which search facility is available in which edition of the product. This section covers the Portal Search Engine and Extended Search. The IBM Enterprise Information Portal (EIP) product has been replaced with the new WebSphere Information Integrator OmniFind Edition. OmniFind, as it is commonly referred to, is a separate product that is available as an add-on component. Although an extensive discussion is beyond the scope of this book, this chapter briefly touches on the OmniFind search.

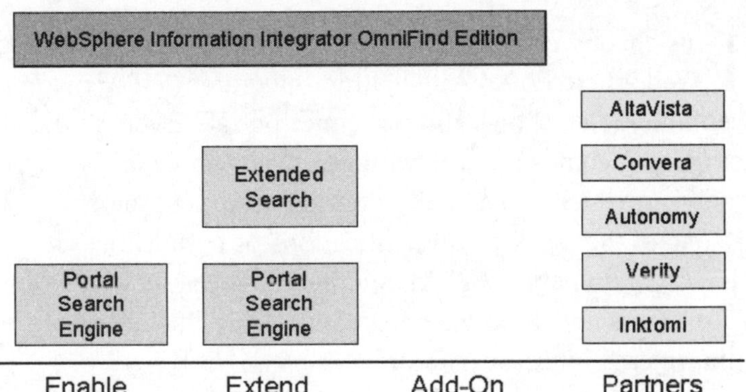

Figure 8.1: Search engines mapping in WebSphere Portal.

WebSphere Portal Search

The WebSphere Portal Search Engine, or PSE for short, is integrated into WebSphere Portal as three portlets—Search Administration portlet Taxonomy Manager, Search Administration portlet Collections Manager, and Document Search portlet for users. These portlets, except the Taxonomy Manager, get installed as part of the base WebSphere Portal installation. Table 8.1 shows the installation status of the available search portlets. Out of the box, you will also notice a search box in the default portal themes. Clicking on that Search button takes the user to a special Search Page that hosts the Search Center.

Table 8.1: Status of Portal Search Portlets

Portlet	Status
Administration portlets	
Manage Search Collections	Installed and deployed
Manage Search and Browse	Installed and deployed as part of Manage Search Collections
Pending Search Collection Items	Installed and deployed as part of Manage Search Collections
Taxonomy Manager	Not installed and not deployed
Taxonomy Viewer	Not installed and not deployed
User portlets	
Search and Browse	Installed, but not deployed
Search Center	Installed and deployed

You have to create a Search Collection of the source before you can initiate a search. The Search Administration portlet is used for administrative tasks. As an administrator you must:

- Define the content that you want to make available for search
- Define the properties of the full text index, which allows for fast and efficient searches

Create Collection

The simplest explanation of a collection is a set of files. You then index a collection by finding unique items in the data, with references pointing back to the data source. Indices help in speeding up searches. They can be stored locally or on a remote machine. By storing the index locally, you can perform searches offline, but you might not be able to view the documents returned by the search.

Creating a collection is simple. Users who have portal administration authority can do this. Assuming you are logged in as the portal administrator, follow these steps:

1. Click the **Administration** link.
2. Select **Portal Settings → Search Administration**.

3. You will see PortalCollection listed in the Search Collections list. We can work with that default name. On the right of that portlet, click **Edit Content Source** to edit the Content Sources in Collection pane.

4. Quite a few parameters appear on the configuration screen. We can modify a couple of them to demonstrate how things work:

   4a. For Crawl source type, select **Web site**.

   4b. Enter an URL of your choice. We use http://www.ibm.com.

   4c. Set the **Number of documents to collect** equal to 200. You could even control the collection based on time.

   4d. Click **Save**.

5. Back on the administration page, click **Start Collecting**. The Running Status will change to *Yes*. Depending on the number of documents you are collecting, this process takes a few minutes to complete. When it is done, the screen should look similar that in to Figure 8.2.

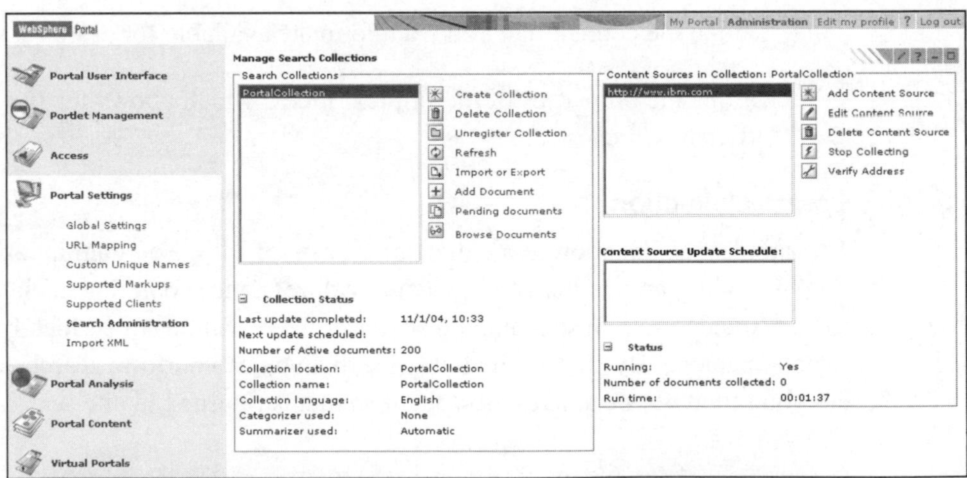

Figure 8.2: Manage Search Collections screen after a completed collection.

Note: If you run another collection task under the same name and location, the new documents will be appended to the existing collection.

Perform Search

At this point, all authenticated users in WebSphere Portal have access to the Search portlet in the navigation bar. Now that we have activated the default collection, the search functionality should work.

Enter a search string, for example iseries, and click the icon with the big magnifying glass, which is the **Search** icon. You should see results similar to that shown in Figure 8.3.

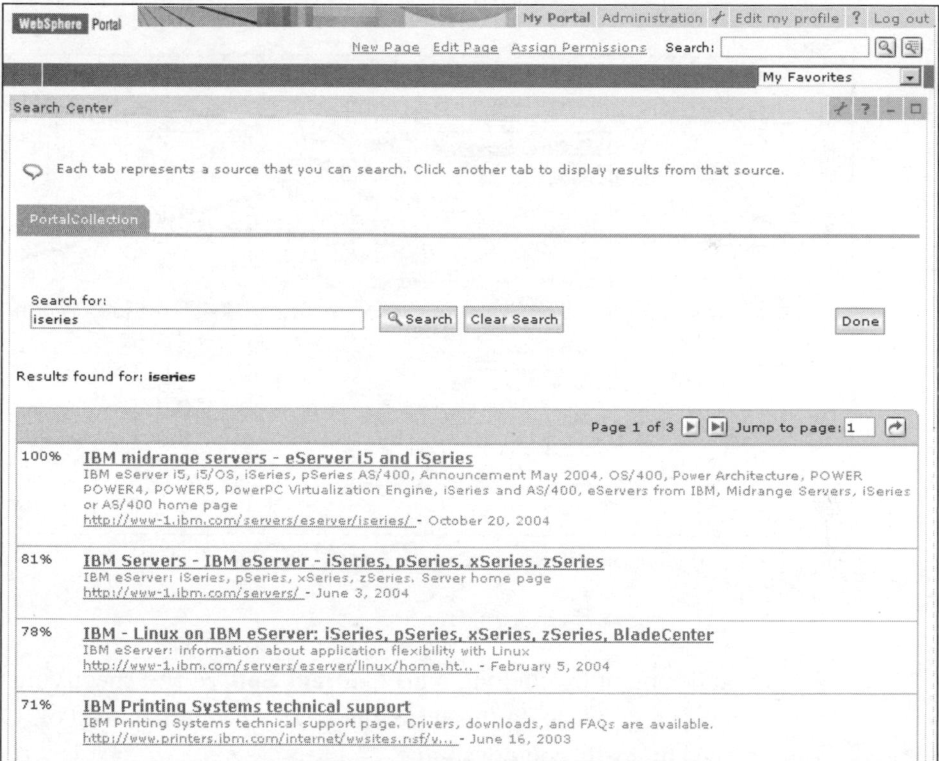

Figure 8.3: Search results as returned by the Search portlet.

If the string exists in a document, that document title will be returned as a link, as part of the Results set. By default, results are sorted by relevance. By editing the portlet, you could choose to have results sorted by date. Clicking any of the links in that screen should display that document in a separate browser window. If not, remember to right-mouse click and choose **Open in New Window**. Clicking **Done** returns you to the main portal page.

Notes on Collections

The default collection, named PortalCollection, is in a folder under <WAS_HOME>. If you create a new collection, you do not have to specify the full path for the location. The specified location will be placed under <WAS_HOME>.

After you create a new Collection in the Manage Search Collections portlet, the next step is to register the collection. Highlight the collection name in the list and click **Register Collection**. See Figure 8.4.

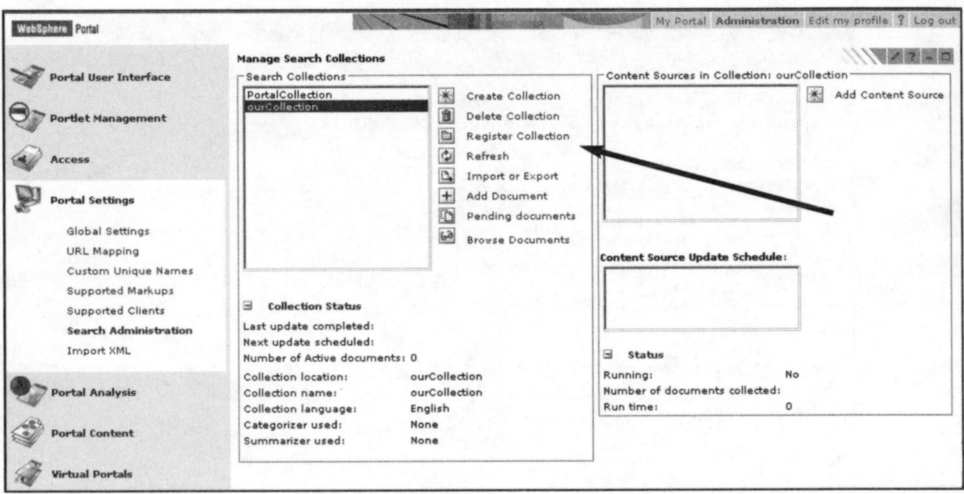

Figure 8.4: Screen showing the newly created collection.

We can add content by clicking **Add Content Source** and specifying the URL where the content exists. In this case, the new collection, named ourCollection, was mapped to as its content source.

Going back to the search portlet, enter **computer** in the search string and click the **Search** icon. You should see results similar to that shown in Figure 8.5. If the search string is found in both those collections, two sets of results will be returned.

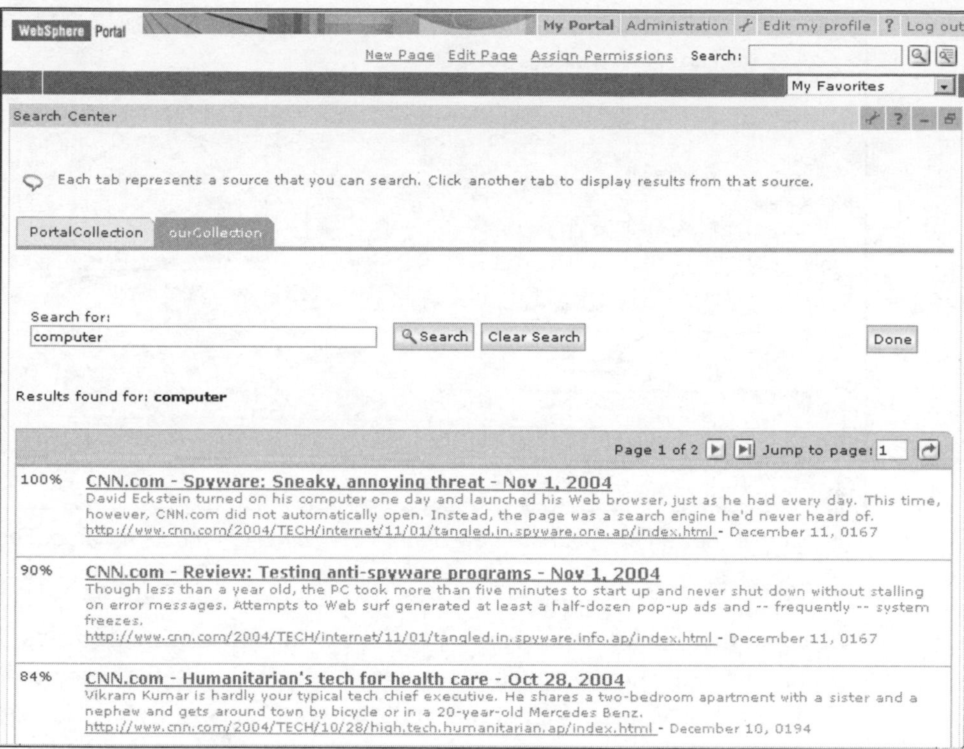

Figure 8.5: Search results returned by two collections.

Notes on Taxonomy

Creating a collection with User-Defined Categories enables the Category Tree menu item in the Manage Search Collections portlet, as shown in Figure 8.6. Typically, enterprises will already have a well laid out taxonomy with various categories defined because this is how they classify or file their intellectual capital. For example, a legal corporation would have categories like civil, corporate, criminal, immigration, and the like.

For example, we created a new collection called ourCC and specified User-Defined Categorizer plus an Automatic Summarizer. You can see those settings under the Collection Status in Figure 8.6.

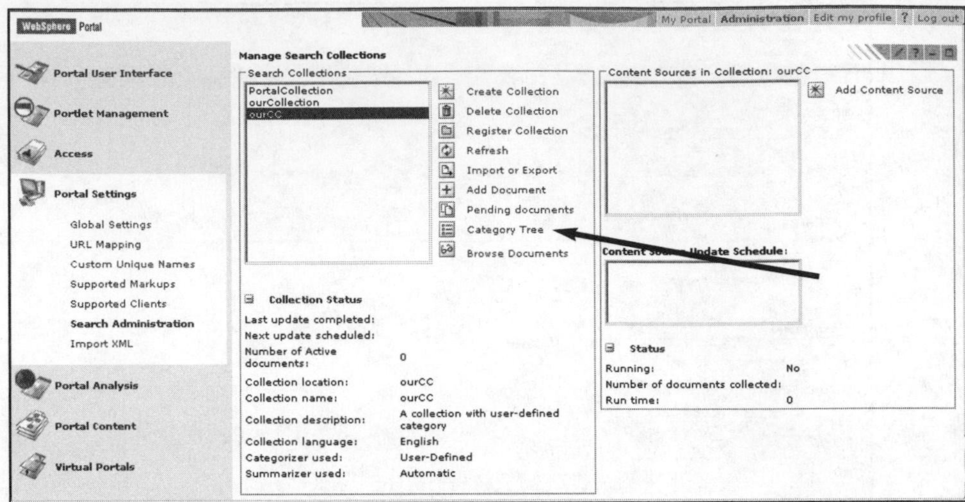

Figure 8.6: Search showing the new Search Collection with custom Categories.

You can then click the **Category Tree** option to define the categories. This takes you to a screen showing a Category Tree on the left with the name root. On the right, you see Manage Categories and Manage Category Rules. Change the name root to Legal. Then add new subcategories by entering a value in the Sub-category name field and clicking **Create**.

After you have the categories defined, click **Manage Rules** to specify how you determine the classification of a certain document. The rules we created for this sample Category Tree illustrate the steps; then we use all the rules to categorize the content. Figure 8.7 shows the screen after the first steps were completed.

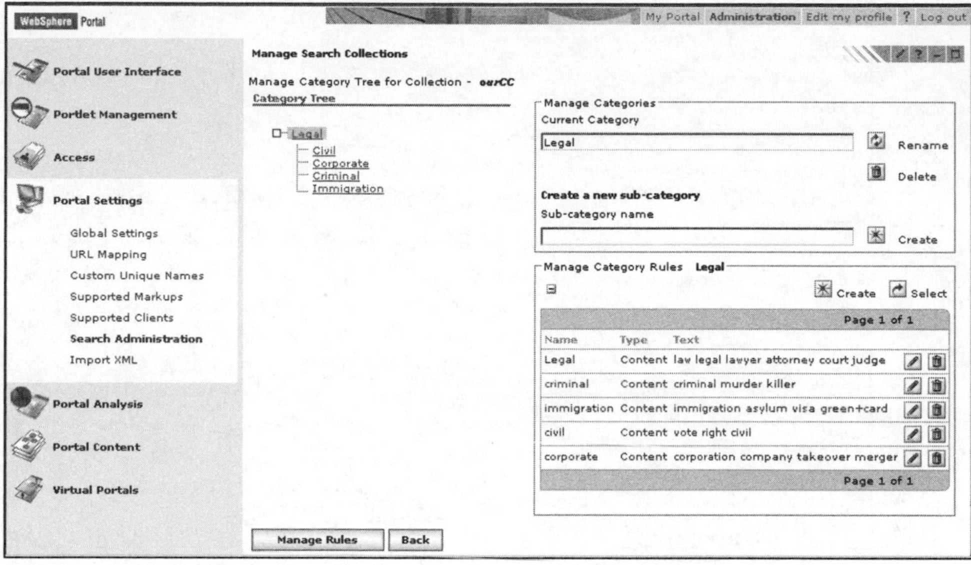

Figure 8.7: Category Tree with rules.

Click **Back** to return to the Manage Search Collections page. Click **Add Content Source**. Specify the URL (http://www.lawyers.com) and Start Collecting. Remember to register the new collection named ourCC by clicking **Register Collection**.

You can test this new collection by searching for a string like “green card” and looking at the Search Results under the Collection named ourCC in the Manage Search Collections portlet. The results will be sorted not only by relevance, but also categorized, as shown in Figure 8.8.

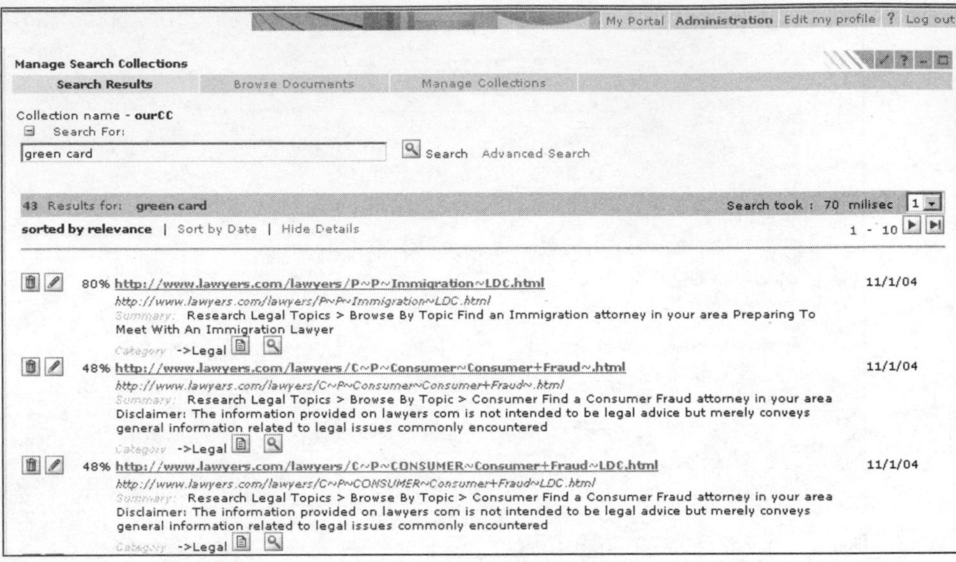

Figure 8.8: Categorized search results from a new Source Collection.

To edit or view taxonomy, remember to install the TaxonomyEditor.war application module that is found in <WPS_HOME>/installableApps. It contains two portlets—Taxonomy Manager and Taxonomy Viewer. After installing them, deploy them to a portal page and then use it to edit, manage, and delete taxonomies.

Note: Typically, a search result page is completed and readied for transmission in less than 0.5 seconds.

This is only one flavor of the most common features of WebSphere Portal Search. Take some time to investigate the advanced features by referring to the portlet online help and the WebSphere Portal product InfoCenter.

Notes on Security

Be aware of the user's access rights when deploying Search functionality in portal pages. The Crawler now supports basic HTTP authentication. Search collections are secured through Portal Access Control, and the search results are filtered based on user access rights for secured resources in the portal.

Actually, when it comes to search collections, security is enforced at two levelsCollection level and Document level. The Access Control Portlet manages security at the collection level, and the search results of portal pages are filtered during search time at the document level. All these inherent checks ensure that the users do not see collections or documents that they are not authorized to search or view.

Extended Search

The Extended Search (ES) server, also known as IBM Lotus Extended Search (ILES), although available as a stand-alone product is best bundled with WebSphere Portal Extend edition. ES, which runs as another application in WebSphere Application Server, is installed separately after WebSphere Portal is installed and configured.

WebSphere Portal V5.1 works with Extended Search V4.0 or higher. ES can be installed and configured on the following operating systems:

- Microsoft Windows NT version 4.0 with SP6
- Microsoft Windows 2000 Server or Advanced Server with SP2 and SP3
- IBM AIX version 5.1 or version 4.3.3 with fix level ML-4330-06
- Sun Solaris version 9 or version 8 or version 7 with MU4
- Red Hat Linux for Intel V7.3

For the latest product information, including updates, access the Extended Search Web site at *http://www.lotus.com/extendedsearch*. IBM Lotus Extended Search is really a federated search engine. It complements Portal Search Engine index and search features by extending its reach to search additional data sources.

At the heart of the ES system is the server, which is responsible for posting searches to the various data sources linked in the ES domain. The IBM Lotus Extended Search server consolidates information from the heterogeneous searches into a single homogeneous results list. Figure 8.9 shows the ES server's components, along with the various clients that make up an ES system.

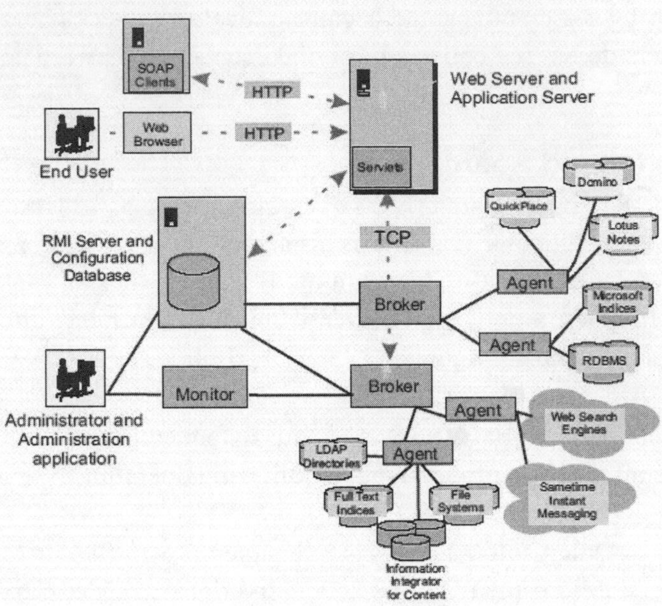

Figure 8.9: Extended Search, component view.

ES includes a Web crawler process that can traverse the links at given Web sites and download data to a file system of your choice. As with saved search results, the data can be stored in its native form or it can be wrapped in XML. Once stored, you can index the data and use it for data mining or knowledge management.

The default installation sets up a *remote method invocation (RMI)* server to handle database communications. To take advantage of the EJB environment, you must install WebSphere Application Server, Advanced Edition. ES is the base search service in WebSphere Portal Extend edition. It also provides a predefined Search portlet that enables users to search across a variety of data sources, including relational databases, Lotus Notes and Domino databases, popular Web search engines, and documents stored in local or remote file systems.

Note: The ES portlet is downloadable from the Portlet catalog.

The following pages cover ES server installation, configuration, and startup, as well as ES portlet deployment and usage.

ES Installation and Configuration

Before you start, make sure the computer has an IP address and that port 6001 is not being used. If port 6001 is in use, make note of an unused port that can be used. Then, follow these steps:

1. Make sure WebSphere Application Server is running.
2. Install the ES server software by invoking the setup.exe script on the product CD. (On our test Windows machine, this script was found in the \ldes\win folder.) Follow these steps to perform the installation:

   2a. Click **Next** on the Welcome screen.

   2b. Accept the license agreement and click **Next**.

   2c. Specify the directory where you want ES to be installed. On Windows, the default installation directory is C:\Program Files\IBM\Extended Search.

   2d. Choose the **Typical** Installation.

   2e. Make sure the machine details are correct on the following screen. You could use the short host name, but we recommend that you enter the fully qualified host name, as shown in Figure 8.10. Click **Next**.

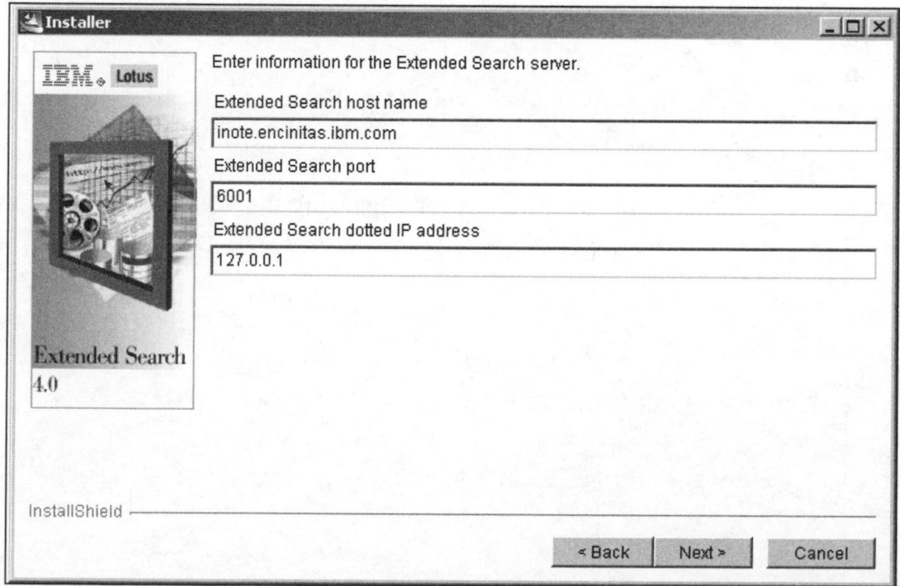

Figure 8.10: ES installation screen showing details of the host computer.

2f. Specify the application server in use. When using ES in the portal framework, you have to specify **WebSphere Application Server** (in this example, WebSphere V5.0 or higher). See Figure 8.11. Click **Next**.

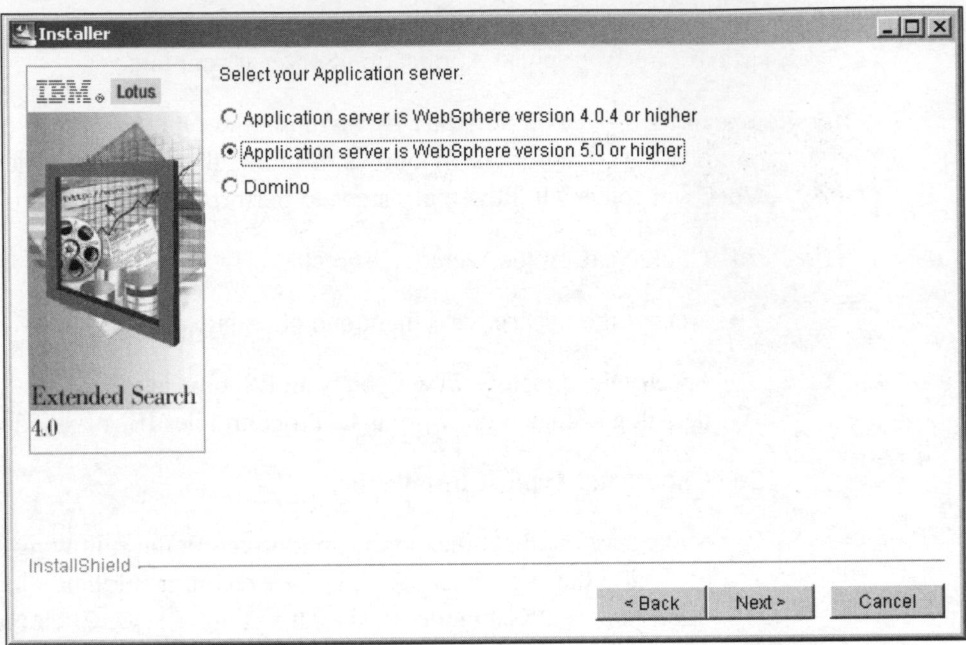

Figure 8.11: ES installation screen showing Application server selections.

2g. Specify the path where WebSphere Application Server is installed and click **Next**.

2h. Verify the information regarding the Web server and Application server (Figure 8.12).

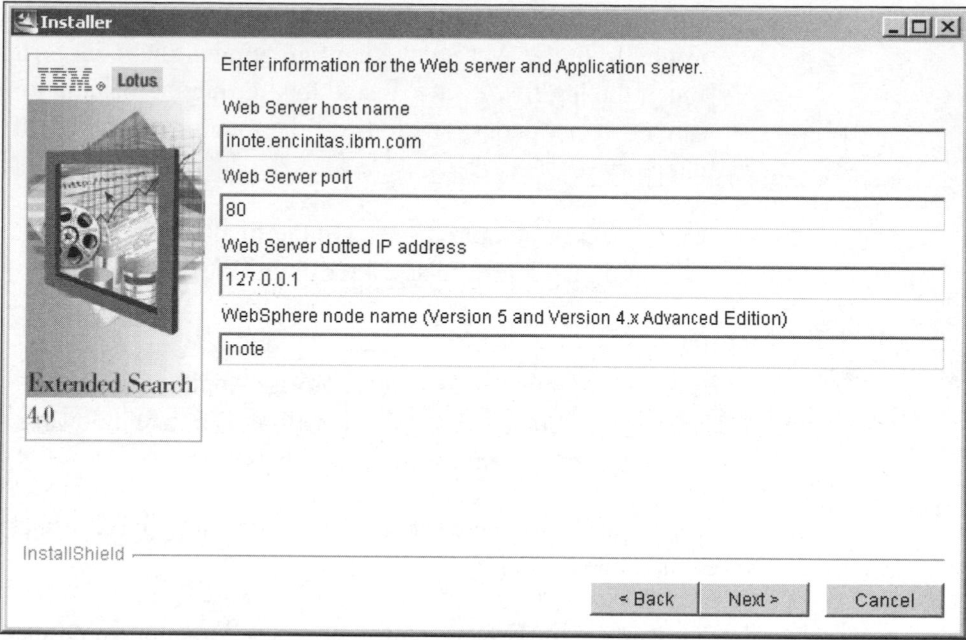

Figure 8.12: ES installation screen showing Web server and Application server details.

2i. If security is enabled in WebSphere Application Server, enter the WebSphere Administrator ID and password. We used wpsbind because we added that user ID as a WebSphere Administrator. The installation wizard sets up an Enterprise Application.

2j. The Configuration Database server name should be displayed on the next screen. If not, enter the fully qualified host name and click **Next**.

2k. You will be asked to choose between DB2 and Oracle. We used **DB2**. Make sure the SQLLIB path is entered. Click **Next**.

2l. Enter the database administrator ID and password on the following screen. (In our test scenario, we used db2admin). Enter the password again to confirm and click **Next**.

2m. The confirmation screen should be displayed. If everything looks all right, click **Next**. If not, go back and make the appropriate changes.

2n. The installer will set some environment variables and configure the database named IBMES. Click **Next** when required.

2o. Now, WebSphere Application Server is configured. Make sure the results from the WebSphere configuration are without errors. You can watch the log file, es_ws_install.log, during the installation to make sure no errors occur. The logs can be found in <ES_HOME>/log directory.

2p. Click **Next** three more times. On the final screen, choose to restart the system immediately or at a later time. Click **Finish**.

ES Startup

The ES installation program creates an Enterprise Application called *ExtendedSearchserver* and starts it. After installing ES on Windows system, you should reboot the system. Then, follow these steps:

1. Whichever backend database server you are using, DB2 or Oracle, make sure it is up and running.
2. Then start the LDAP server and finally the WebSphere Application Server.
3. Bring up WebSphere Application Server Administrative Console, go to **Applications → Enterprise Applications**, and make sure ExtendedSearch is running. See Figure 8.13.

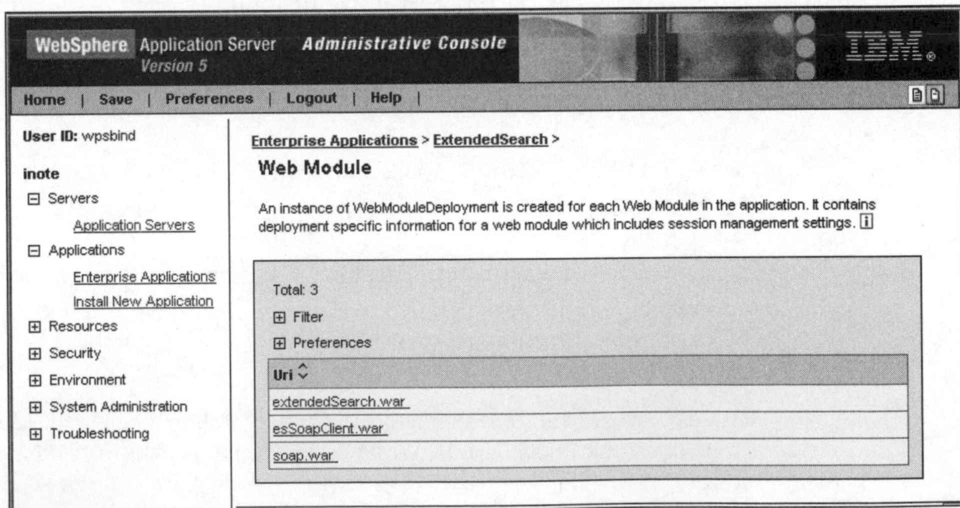

Figure 8.13: WebSphere Administrative Console showing the Extended Search application.

4. The Extended Search RMI Server comes up automatically on Windows, hence you should make sure the database server is running first. You can run the netstat –an command and look for 20000. The ES RMI Server listens on that port.

5. Bring up the ES server by selecting **Start → Programs → IBM Extended Search → Extended Search Server**. This actually kicks off a command window echoing the various startup commands, as shown in Figure 8.14. Notice it is listening on Port 6001.

```
Extended Search Server: inote.encinitas.ibm.com (6001)
IBM Lotus Extended Search V4.0, (c) Copyright IBM Corp. 1997, 2003

12/14/04 7:59:25 PM DBCSSI0005 Starting Communications.
12/14/04 7:59:25 PM DBCSSI0003 Communications has been started.
12/14/04 7:59:25 PM DBCSSI0004 Starting the Extended Search Server.
12/14/04 7:59:27 PM DBCSSI0014 The Inbound Monitor has been started.
12/14/04 7:59:28 PM DBCSSI0017 Server Task desCfg.exe (0) has been started.
12/14/04 7:59:29 PM DBCSSI0017 Server Task desXml.exe (0) has been started.
12/14/04 7:59:29 PM DBCSSI0017 Server Task desXml.exe (0) has been started.
12/14/04 7:59:29 PM DBCSSI0017 Server Task desSAR.exe (0) has been started.
12/14/04 7:59:29 PM DBCSSI0017 Server Task desSAR.exe (0) has been started.
12/14/04 7:59:29 PM DBCSSI0017 Server Task desSAR.exe (0) has been started.
12/14/04 7:59:29 PM DBCSSI0017 Server Task desLink.exe (0) has been started.
12/14/04 7:59:29 PM DBCSSI0017 Server Task desLink.exe (0) has been started.
12/14/04 7:59:29 PM DBCSSI0017 Server Task desLink.exe (0) has been started.
12/14/04 7:59:29 PM DBCSSI0017 Server Task desLink.exe (0) has been started.
12/14/04 7:59:29 PM DBCSSI0017 Server Task desLink.exe (0) has been started.
12/14/04 7:59:29 PM DBCSSI0017 Server Task desDiscover.exe (0) has been started.

12/14/04 7:59:30 PM DBCSSI0017 Server Task desCrawl.exe (0) has been started.
12/14/04 7:59:30 PM DBCSSI0006 Starting the Performance Monitor.
12/14/04 7:59:30 PM DBCSSI0015 Starting the Web definitions download.
> _
```

Figure 8.14: Command window displaying ES startup messages.

6. You can run the ES Verification program to make sure all the ES components are working properly. (**Start → Programs → IBM Extended Search → Extended Search Verification Program**). The verification program not only can verify the ES System but also Search & Document Retrieval.

7. Next, bring up the ES Administration Application via the Start Menu. (**Start → Programs → IBM Extended Search → Extended Search Administration**). This used to be an applet in the previous version. See Figure 8.15.

Tip: To update IBM Lotus Extended Search with Fix Pack 2, you should shut down the ES server, WebSphere Application Server, and the RMI server. Apply the Fix Pack, then restart the Windows system. ES will then be ready for use with WebSphere Portal V5.1.

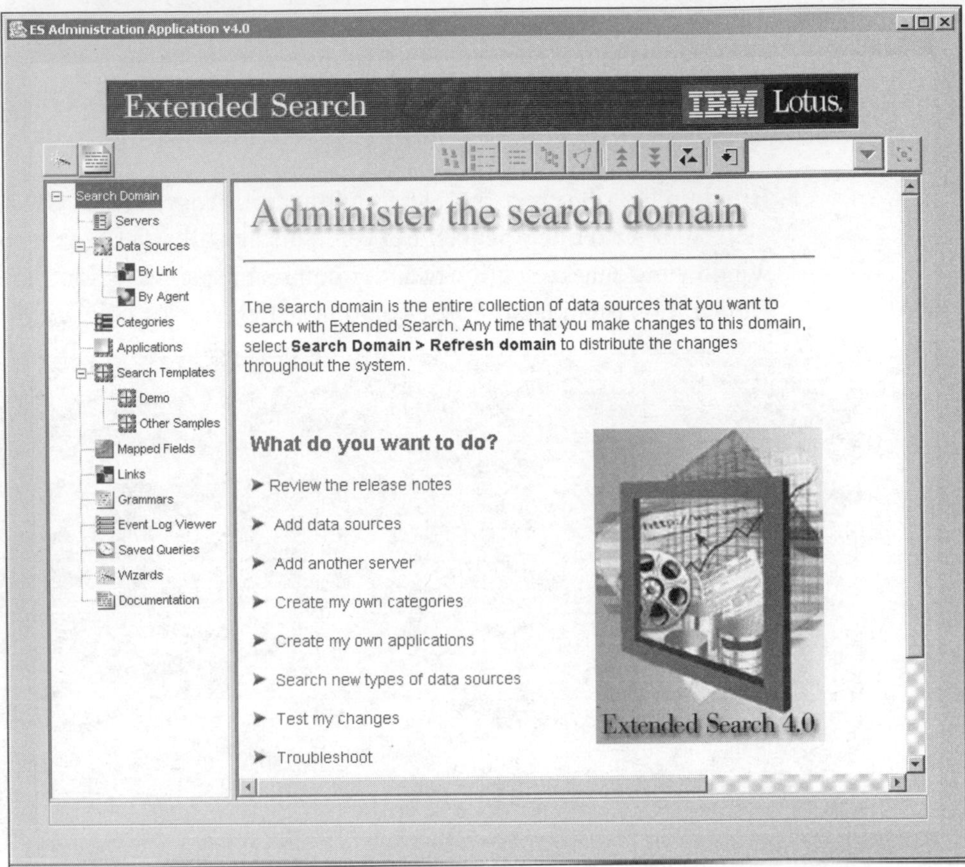

Figure 8.15: ES Administration Application.

ES Portlet Installation

The IBM Lotus Extended Search Portlets for IBM WebSphere Portal provide an interface to the search capabilities of a local or remote Extended Search server. Similarly to what you saw with the WebSphere Search portlet earlier in this chapter, you must deploy the Extended Search portlet. The difference is that, by default, the ES portlet is not installed. Actually, when you expand the downloaded portlet ZIP file from the portlet catalog, you get three WAR files corresponding to the three ES portlets: Simple, Enhanced, and Advanced.

- *Simple Extended Search*—Presents a simple interface that enables users to submit a query and view search results. The query uses search processing options predetermined by the portlet manager or by a user with edit privileges.

- *Enhanced Extended Search*—Has a more advanced interface that enables users to view the sources that will be searched and the options that will be used to process the query. The portlet manager and users with edit privileges have greater control over defining default settings for searches.

- *Advanced Extended Search*—A sample portlet that shows application developers many of the more advanced features of Extended Search, such as saving and scheduling queries, editing saved queries, saving search result documents to a file system, e-mailing search results, and submitting multiple queries at the same time. This portlet is provided for demonstration purposes only and is not supported.

Before you can install these portlets, you must do some setup. Along with thc portlet WAR files, other files are needed to deploy the ES SOAP services that are required by the portlets. Follow these steps:

1. Make sure ES V4.0.x is installed, configured for use with WebSphere Application Server, and working.

2. Make sure you are logged into the portal as the portal administrator.

3. For illustration purposes, create a page called ourSearch under ourCo page.

4. Go to **Administration → Portlet Management → Web Modules** and click the **Install** button to install the downloaded ES Portlets.

5. Browse for and install the three portlet WAR files one by one—esSimpleSearch.war, esEnhancedSearch.war, esAdvancedSearch.war.

ES Portlet Deployment and Usage

To deploy the ES portlets, start (as usual) by making sure you are logged in as the portal administrator. Edit the newly created ourSearch page and add the three portlets to that page. We added the Simple and Enhanced ES portlets. See Figure 8.16.

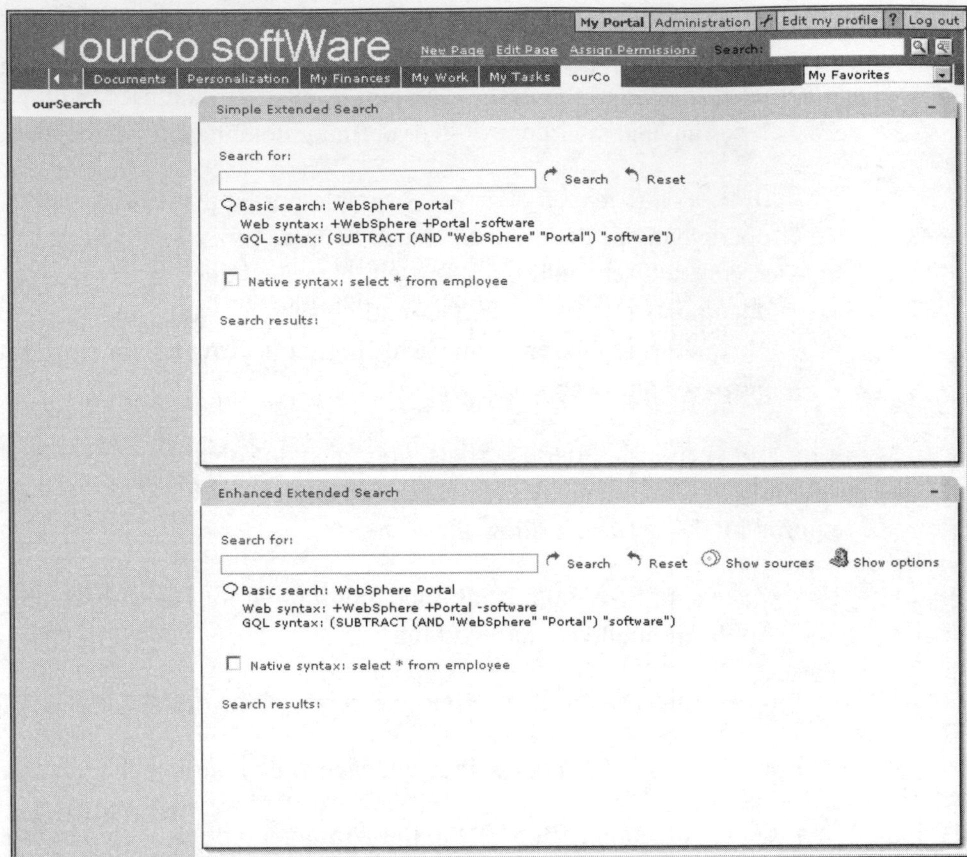

Figure 8.16: Portal page showing the Simple and Enhanced ES portlets.

The Simple and Enhanced ES portlets have a Configure icon (on the Advanced ES portlet, use the Edit icon). Click the Configure icon to configure these portlets as follows:

1. Assuming that you are still logged in as the portal administrator, click the **Configure** icon in the Simple Extended Search portlet. The configuration screen should be displayed.

2. Select **Change application name or server URL.**

   2a. Specify the name of the ES search application. In this example, we used Demo.

2b. Specify the HTTP address of the ES server you want to use to process search requests and the port it is listening on. We took the default of http://localhost:80/esSoap/servlet/rpcrouter, because the ES server was running on the same machine as the WebSphere Portal server.

2c. Click **OK**.

3. Back on the configuration screen, select **Configure default settings → Sources** to select the sources or categories of sources that will be searched by default.

4. Rather than search all sources, which is the default setting, we chose to search the ES documentation from the File System Sources, and Google from the list of Web Sources. Click **OK**.

5. Again on the configuration screen, select **Configure default settings → Options** to select the search processing options that will be applied by default. We accepted all the default settings.

6. Remember to increase the time-out value if you are searching more sources, or if you think the search will take time. Then, click **OK**.

7. Back on the configuration screen, make sure you click **Done**.

8. In the portlet, enter a string to search and click **Search**. The results will be returned in the bottom half of the portlet window.

Note: If you click Reset in the portlet, all the configurations settings are cleaned out for a new search.

The same functionality is available in the Enhanced and Advanced ES portlets, with some extra features, like the ability to build a query, save queries, or view search sources. Your enterprise must decide which Search portlet should be made available to portal users. The general setup steps for all the search portlets are described below.

1. In all portlets, change the search application name or ES server URL.

   1a. Specify the name of Extended Search search application you want to use.

1b. Specify the HTTP address of the Extended Search server you want to use to process search requests. If Extended Search and WebSphere Portal do not reside on the same server, or if the Extended Search server is not configured to be localhost at port 80 (the default setting), you must update the default value.

1c. In the Simple and Enhanced portlets, select the sources or categories of sources that will be searched by default.

1d. In the Simple and Enhanced portlets, select the default options that will be used to process search requests and return results.

1e. In the Enhanced portlet, specify the search constraints that will be used to prune the result set.

1f. In the Enhanced portlet, select the types of messages (critical, informational, and so on) that will be displayed during query processing.

1g. In the Advanced portlet, specify the number of queries that can be processed at the same time.

Notes on Extended Search

In Extended Search, there is no need to create or maintain a central index. ES translates each query into the native search language of the target data source and uses search and retrieval methods native to each data source. Additional support exists for file systems and LDAP directories, and for catalogs, indexes, and mail folders created with Microsoft Site Server, Microsoft Index Server, and Microsoft Exchange, and SharePoint Server.

With the ability to access data from a wide range of sources, security is an important element. ES enforces field usage restrictions, enabling you to control the fields in which a user can search or view results. Certain links can require a user ID when connecting to the data source, enabling you to restrict access to authorized users. User Exits allow for the additional validation of user IDs and the mapping of multiple IDs, in accordance with the policies of your organization.

More information about IBM Lotus Extended Search can be obtained from http://www.lotus.com/extendedsearch.

WebSphere Information Integrator OmniFind Edition

WebSphere Information Integrator OmniFind Edition, also referred to simply as "OmniFind," is a recent addition to the WebSphere product family. A separate product that is designed to provide Enterprise-level search capabilities to a variety of applications and environments, it complements WebSphere Portal particularly well. With OmniFind, you can extend WebSphere Portal's search capabilities into the native filesystem (Windows and UNIX), various content management systems, collaboration systems (IBM Lotus Notes and Microsoft Exchange), IBM DB2 and other relational data sources, web sites and newsgroups, as well as other, customizable sources.

OmniFind delivers high-quality search results from massive (20M documents/-collection) collections, with subsecond response time. Releases in the near future hold the promise of raising that limit to 100M documents per collection, also with subsecond response time. It also provides an extensive set of tools for customizing the processing of data that is indexed, including support for both rules-based and model-based categorization, and custom annotation through the Unstructured Information Management Architecture (UIMA) framework.

OmniFind has been developed to use IBM's Search and Indexing Application Programming Interface (SIAPI), making it very extensible and adaptable into nearly any kind of customer environment. Further, the fact that SIAPI is also implemented by Portal Search Engine, upgrading from Portal Search to OmniFind has been designed to be a simple process. OmniFind ships with sample portlet (shown in Figure 8.17) and stand-alone user interfaces, plus all the source code that is necessary for a customer to develop any kind of UI as necessary.

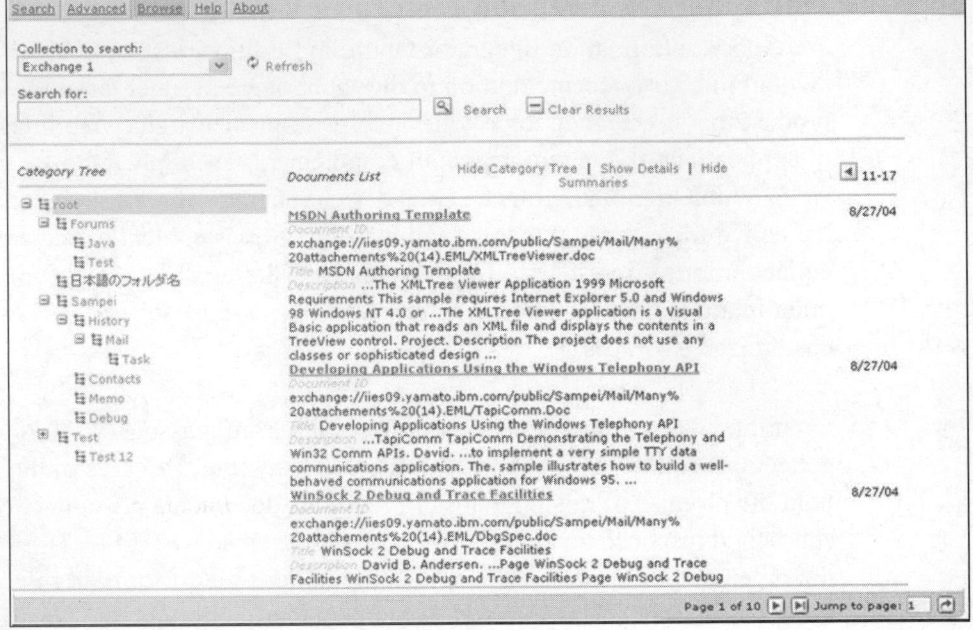

Figure 8.17: Portal page showing the OmniFind portlet.

With WebSphere Information Integrator for Content OmniFind Edition you can access more content or data sources, and it scales very well. It can leverage the taxonomy defined in the portal for navigation and classification and presents a common administrative look and feel. An easy-to-use migration wizard allows customer to move their PSE collection into the WebSphere Information Integrator for Content OmniFind Edition environment in four steps:

- From WebSphere Portal, export PSE settings to XML files
- Copy files to the OmniFind Edition index server
- Import settings using migration wizard
- Modify using OmniFind Edition's Administration Console.

Further information on OmniFind can be found at http://www-306.ibm.com/software/data/integration/search.html

Site Analytics

Portal site administrators want to know who is accessing their site, how site visitors are entering and exiting the site, how long they stay, and which pages get the most visits. Portlet developers are curious to find out if the portlets they developed have returned any error conditions, how much resource the portlets use, and how they perform. Business sponsors want to know how effective the latest online marketing or e-mail campaign was, whether people signed up for a newly advertised program, or how many referrals they got.

IBM Tivoli Site Analyzer gets you these metrics. It is a software component that comes with the Extend edition of WebSphere Portal, and it can be quite useful for monitoring and maintaining a portal site.

Site Analyzer Installation

We do not envision enterprises wanting to install Tivoli Site Analyzer (SA) the first time that they use WebSphere Portal Server. Our experience has been that, after the production portal site is up and running, organizations decide to obtain usage metrics on the site. Our recommendation is to install SA on a machine separate from the one running the core Portal Server, because you do not want the SA resources competing with portal resources. That is also the reason why the installation of SA is presented in this section, rather than in Chapter 3, on WebSphere Portal Server installation.

We assume that you have WebSphere Portal already working on a Windows platform, using DB2 as the database. If not, please refer to the appropriate section in Chapter 3 on installation. Site Analyzer software for all platforms is found on CD16 of the WebSphere Portal product set. It requires about 65MB of disk space.

Note: If you are using an Oracle database, you have to create a userid called saadmin, which will be used as the schema under which Site Analyzer's administrative tables will be stored.

---

1. In the case of Windows, invoke **setup.exe** from the WIN folder of the Tivoli Site Analyzer CD.

2. Click **Next** on the Welcome Screen and **Accept** the license.

3. On the next screen, make sure the correct instance of WebSphere Application Server is picked up. If not, enter the proper directory and click **Next**.

4. Assuming that wpsbind has been added as the Administrator for WebSphere, on the IBM WebSphere Security Screen, enter wpsbind as the user who has administrator access to WebSphere server. Enter saadmin as the administrative user for SA, as shown in Figure 8.18. Click **Next**.

Tip: In case wpsbind is not acceptable to the installation wizard, try the full DN for that user, as in: uid=wpsbind,cn=users,dc=encinitas,dc=ibm,dc=com.

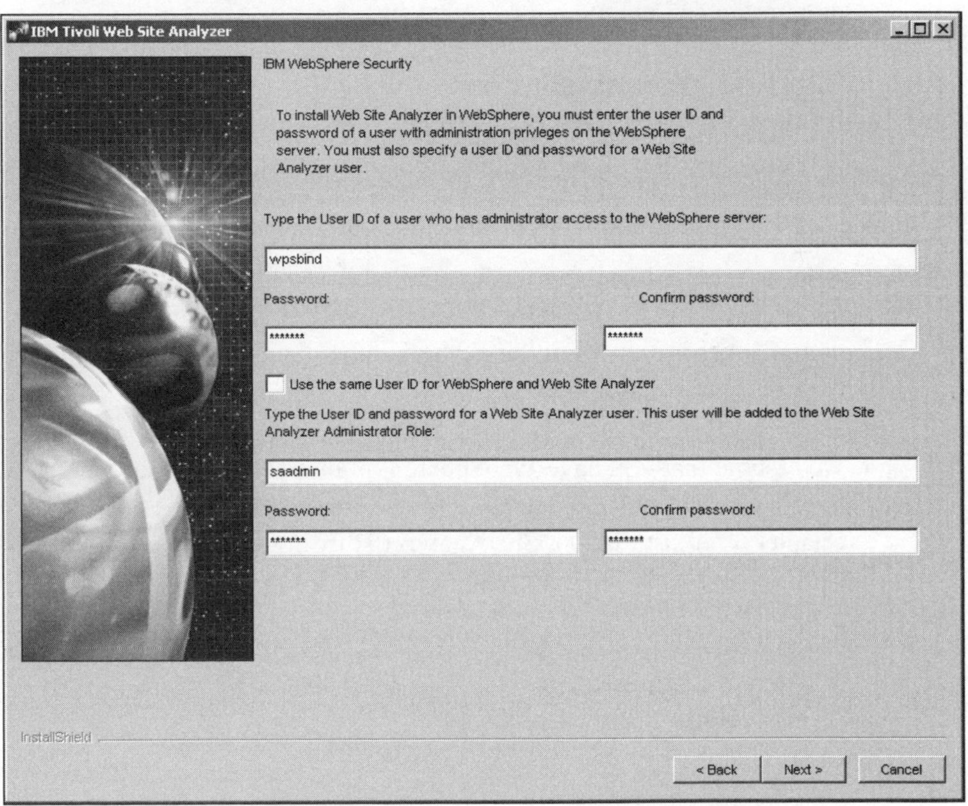

Figure 8.18: Administrative user IDs and passwords.

5. The installation wizard detects servers and asks whether a new server should be installed or if it should use an existing server. Choose to install a new server, as shown in Figure 8.19. We recommend naming the server Site_Analyzer because it is easier to use that name on a command line when starting and stopping the server. Click **Next**.

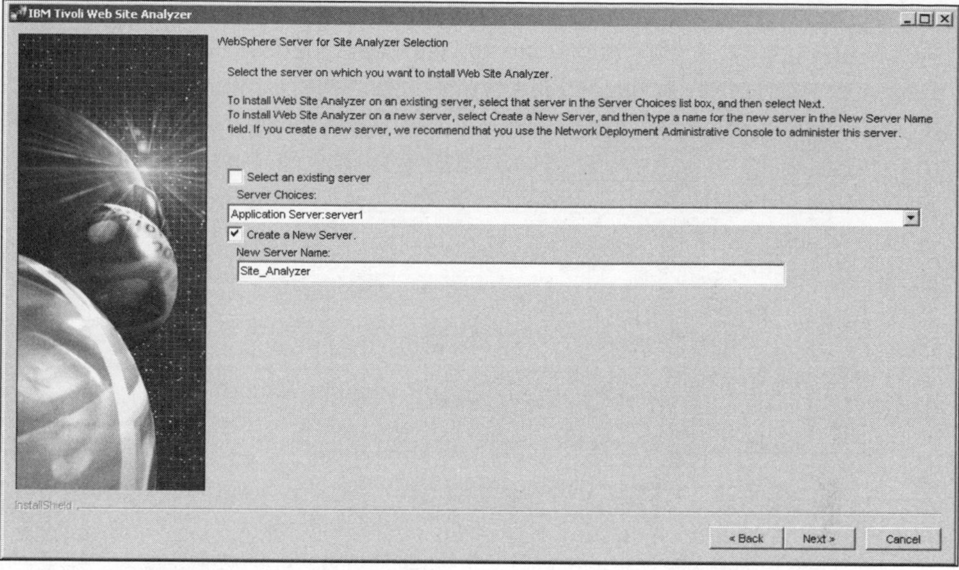

Figure 8.19: Server screen for Tivoli Site Analyzer.

6. We are using DB2; choose the option to **Create a new local database**. Click **Next**. We recommend that you use a separate database by creating a new one, rather than use an existing one, because once you start doing site analyses, this database can grow quite large.

7. On the database parameters screen, verify the path to the JDBC driver. Accept all the details of the administrative database, as shown in Figure 8.20. Just to be safe, clear the passwords for the database administrator and re-enter them. Click **Next**.

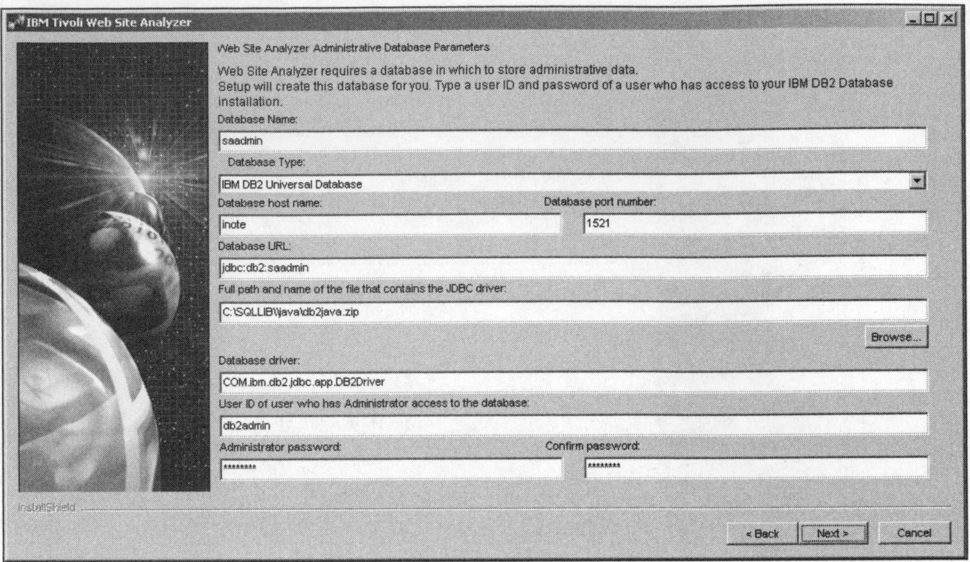

Figure 8.20: Site Analyzer administrative database details.

8. In the next screen choose to **Use the Web Site Analyzer Administrative database in which to store DNS and IP data**. Click **Next**. In a production environment, we recommend you store DNS and IP information in a separate database, which is normally named sadns.

9. The next screen asks about the project database. Again, choose **Use the Web Site Analyzer administrative database in which to store project data**. Click **Next**. In a production environment, we recommend you store project information in a separate database, which is normally named saprojct.

10. Accept the default temporary directory of <WAS_HOME>\temp.

11. Then accept the default installation directory of <WAS_HOME>\SA.

12. Click **Next** on the confirmation screen to kick off the installation process. After the installation is complete, and hopefully successful, click **Finish** on the final screen.

13. Bring up the WebSphere Administrative Console (**Start → Programs → IBM WebSphere → Application Server V4.0 AE → WebSphere Administrator's console**).

14. At the challenge screen, enter **wpsbind** for the user name and password. Click **OK**.

15. When WebSphere Application Server Console is displayed, expand the node by clicking on the plus sign. Expand the Application Servers folder. You should see the Site Analyzer server.

16. In a command window, go to <WAS_HOME>/bin and start the SA server, as shown in Figure 8.21. Look for the message *Server Site Analyzer open for e-business.*

```
C:\WebSphere\AppServer51\bin>startServer Site_Analyzer
ADMU0116I: Tool information is being logged in file
           C:\WebSphere\AppServer51\logs\Site_Analyzer\startServer.log
ADMU3100I: Reading configuration for server: Site_Analyzer
ADMU3200I: Server launched. Waiting for initialization status.
ADMU3000I: Server Site_Analyzer open for e-business; process id is 4528
```

Figure 8.21: Starting up Site Analyzer server.

17. If you expand the Enterprise Applications folder, you will see the Site_Analyzer_Application. Make sure it is running. You can log out from the WebSphere Administrative Console.

SA Usage

1. To test SA's installation, from the Start menu, bring up Site Analyzer (**Start → Programs → IBM WebSphere → Web Site Analyzer → Web Site Analyzer**). Alternatively, in a Web browser, enter the following URL (where <HOST_NAME> is the fully qualified machine name of the server where Site Analyzer is installed):

```
http://<HOST_NAME>:<port_number>/SiteAnalyzer/Admin/index.html
```

2. You will be challenged as shown in Figure 8.22. Assuming you set up the administration role for the Site Analyzer application properly, type **saadmin** for the user name and password, and click **OK**. The Tivoli Site Analyzer UI should be displayed.

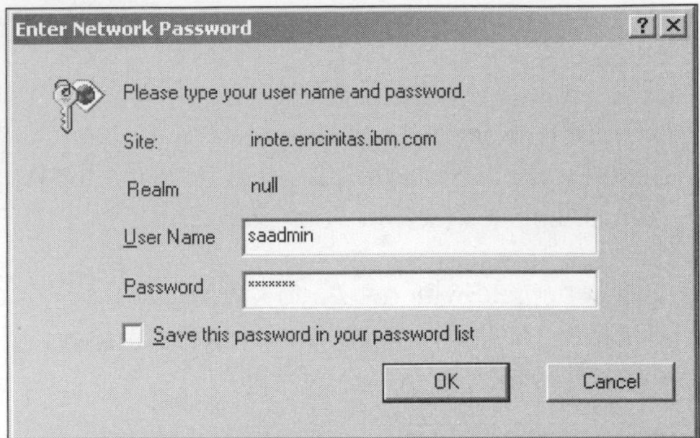

Figure 8.22: Challenge screen when bringing up the SA URL in a browser.

Site Analyzer comes with a sample application. First-time users of SA can follow the product documentation and work with this sample. The product InfoCenter is also excellent. It can be accessed at http://<WAS_HOME>\installedApps\Site_Analyzer_Application.ear\InfocenterWebapp.war\en\docframeset.html.

Create New Project

The first time you work with SA, a project wizard starts up. All work in SA is done within a framework of a project. Rather than canceling the project wizard, let's quickly create a test project. If you need to restart the SA administrative user interface, enter the URL http://<HOST_NAME>/SiteAnalyzer/Admin/index.html. Then, follow these steps:

1. The wizard states that it will help in the creation of a project and with the database location and connection setup. Click **Next**.

2. Name the test project ourCo, as shown in Figure 8.23. Click **Next**.

Note: Online help is available throughout the product, but in a subtle way. All names that are underlined are actually HTML links to online help. So, clicking on Project Name brings up the relevant information about that field.

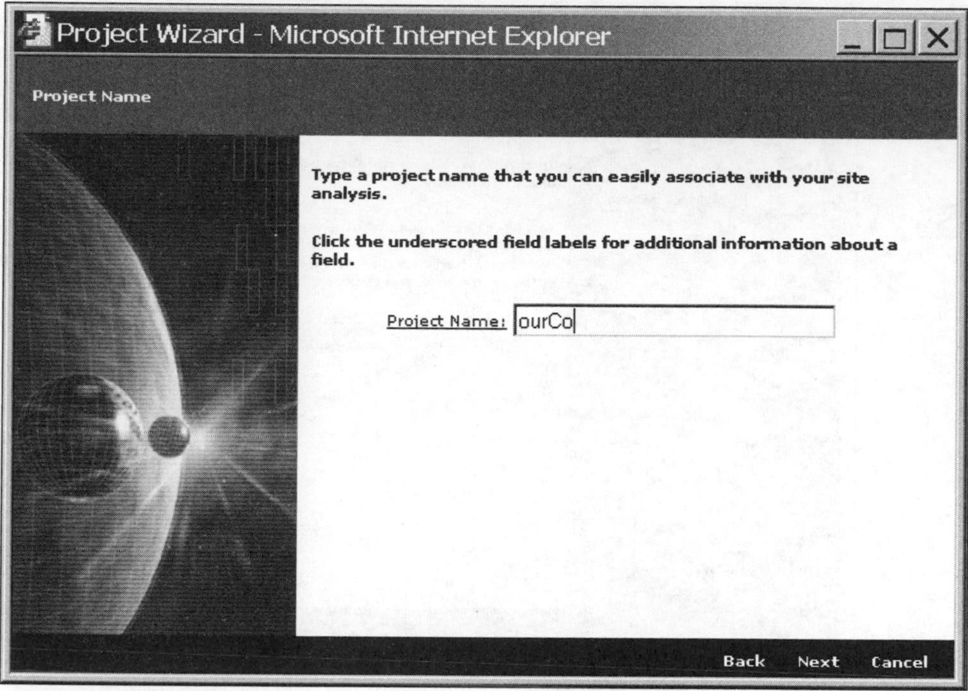

Figure 8.23: Entering a project name in the SA project wizard.

3. For the host name of the Web site, enter something like **www.ourco.com** and/or all the aliases that point to your Web site. After entering the name, click the plus sign (+) to get a result similar to Figure 8.24. After you are done entering all the host names, click **Next**. (To delete a name, highlight it and click the **X** icon.)

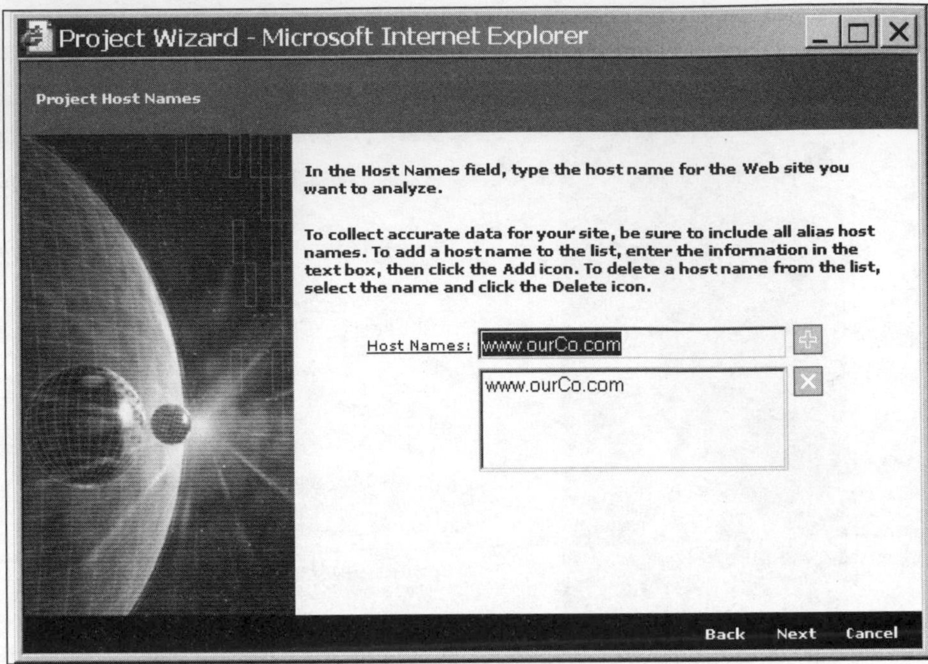

Figure 8.24: Entering project host names in the SA project wizard.

4. On the Database Information screen in Figure 8.25, the database URL and the JDBC driver should be filled in. Verify those values. Enter the user ID and password to connect to the database and click **Next**.

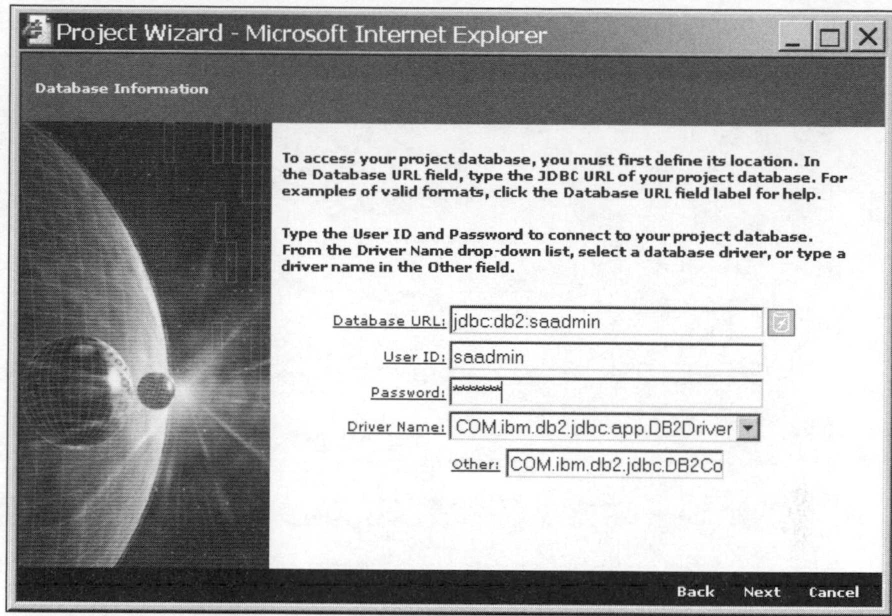

Figure 8.25: Entering database information in the SA project wizard.

5. Click **Finish** on the final screen. A project is created, and it will appear in the SA user interface, as shown in Figure 8.26. The project name, ourCo, is shown in the navigation bar on the left side.

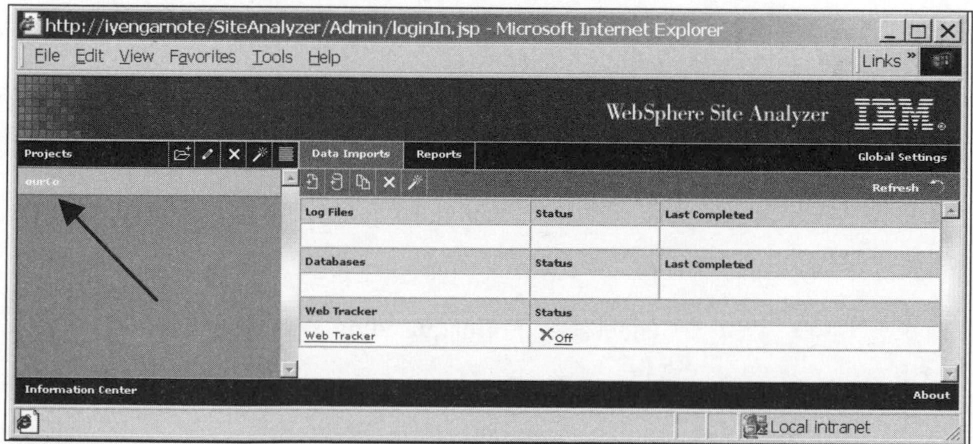

Figure 8.26: SA user interface showing the creation of a project by the wizard.

6. Click the **Reports** tab to see fields pertaining to various preconfigured reports that can be run any time, as shown in Figure 8.27.

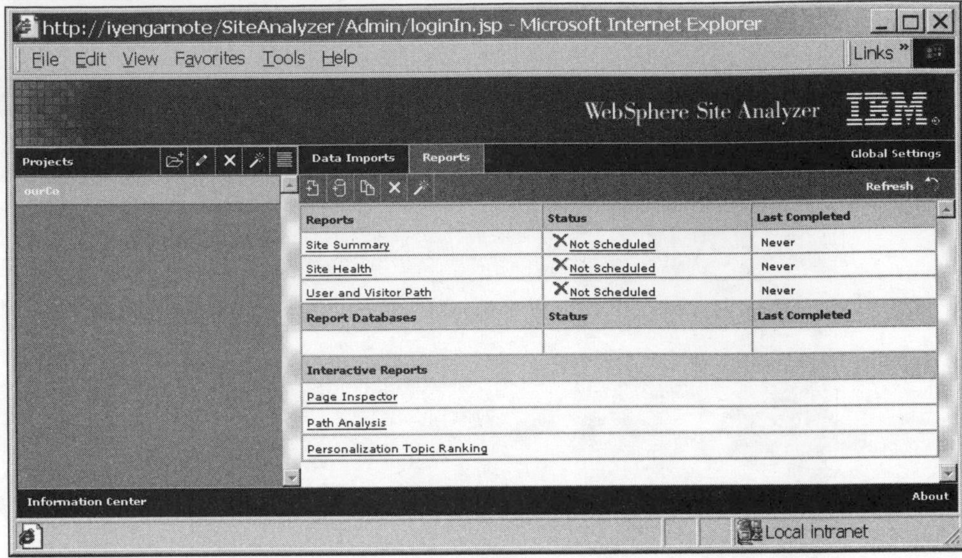

Figure 8.27: The Reports tab after the SA project wizard creates a project.

Notes on Log Files

WebSphere Site Analyzer works with log files generated by any of the following:

- HTTP Server
- FTP Server
- Supplemental Server
- Personalization Server
- Edge Server
- WebSphere Portal server

Further, SA supports the following log file syntaxes:

- NCSA Combined Log Format
- W3C Extended Log Format, used by Microsoft Internet Information Server 4.0 and 5.0.
- NCSA Common Log Format (access log)
- NCSA Separate Log Format (three log)

If you select AutoDetect, Site Analyzer will automatically identify the log file type, provided it is in one of the above formats.

Specify Log File

The project is created. Now you need to associate one or more log files with the project for subsequent analysis. This is done via the Log File wizard, as follows:

1. In the Site Analyzer GUI, click the left-most icon under Data Imports to add a log file.

2. You will be asked for log file information. Fill in the information, as shown in Figure 8.28. Then, click **Schedule Log File** in the left navigation bar.

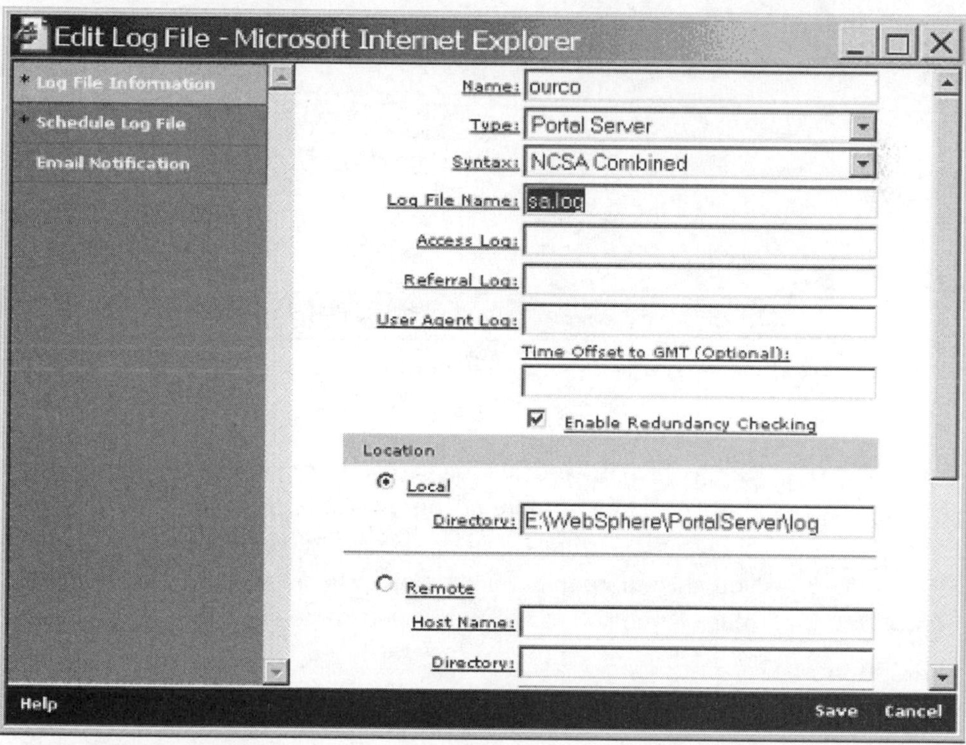

Figure 8.28: Log file information screen.

3. Specify when to run the analysis and how often to run it, as follows:

   3a. Choose a Start Time about five minutes from now.

   3b. Select **Never** as the End Date.

   3c. Select **Once** as the Frequency.

3d. Choose **Make Active** and **Run after Save**, as shown in Figure 8.29.

3e. Click **Save**, and the log file will be scheduled for analysis.

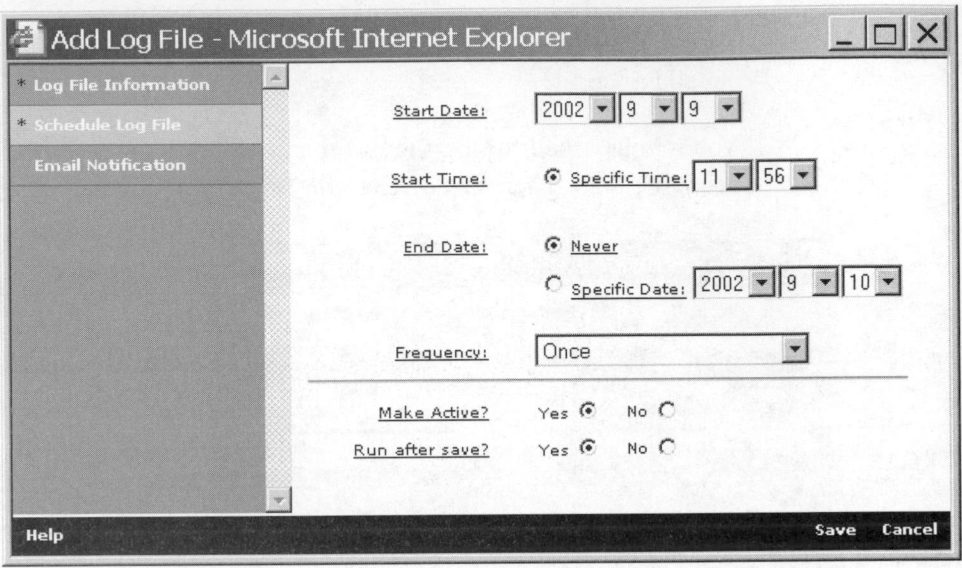

Figure 8.29: Scheduling a log file.

4. On the E-mail Notification screen in Figure 8.30, you can choose to send e-mails to one or more accounts. You can also choose to be notified if there are errors, warnings, and/or successes. Make the appropriate selections. If you have more than one person to be notified, remember to click on the plus (+) icon.

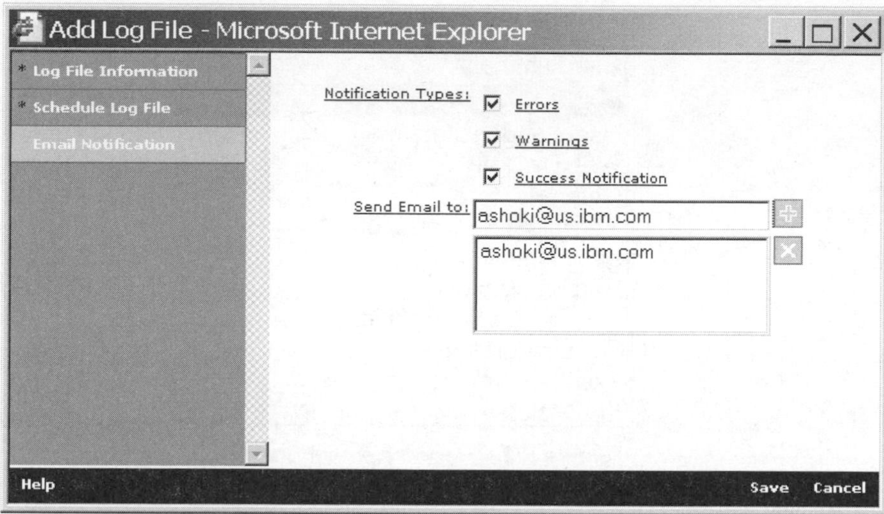

Figure 8.30: E-mail notification screen.

5. Click **Save**. The Site Analyzer GUI should display the status that a log analysis is scheduled, as shown in Figure 8.31.

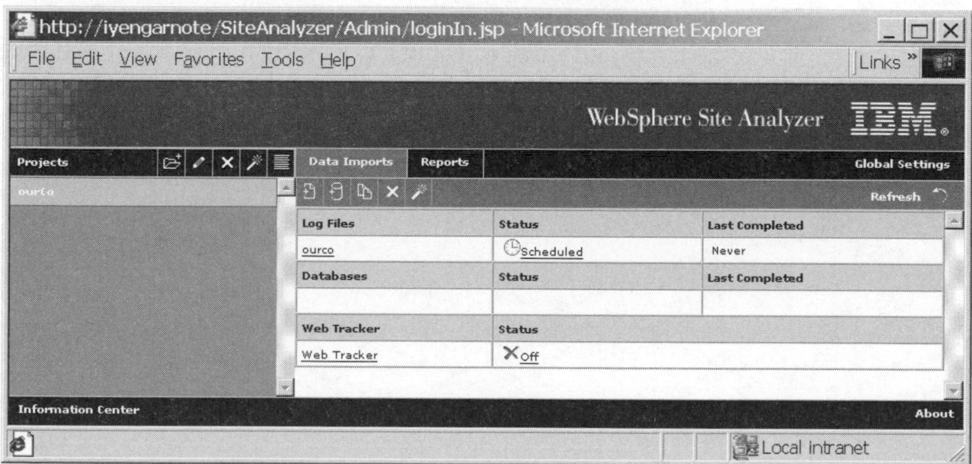

Figure 8.31: SA UI showing a log analysis scheduled.

Create a Report

A report is composed of at least one report element. Report elements retrieve data from a database and generate a data table and graph according to your specifications. Any report element that ships with SA can be used, or you can create your own via the Global Settings menu option. Report elements are grouped as shown in Figure 8.32.

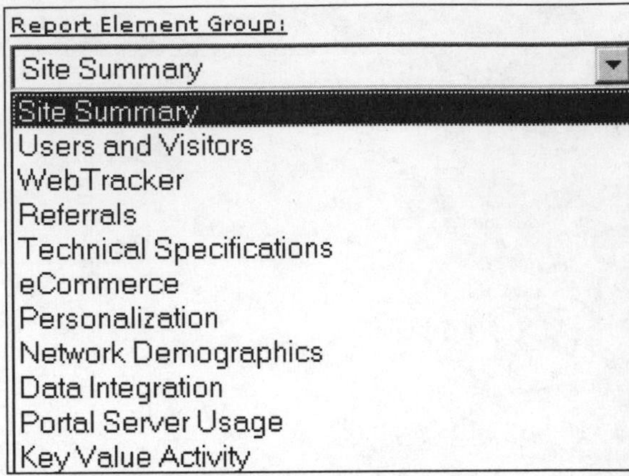

Figure 8.32: Report element groupings.

To create a report, follow these steps:

1. With the ourCo project is selected, click the **Reports** tab, and click the **Add Report** icon.

2. Name the report **ourCo Report 1**, as shown in Figure 8.33. Select the **ourCo** database and click the right arrow (=>). Specify the dates in the Absolute Range, choose your language, and select one or more glossary terms.

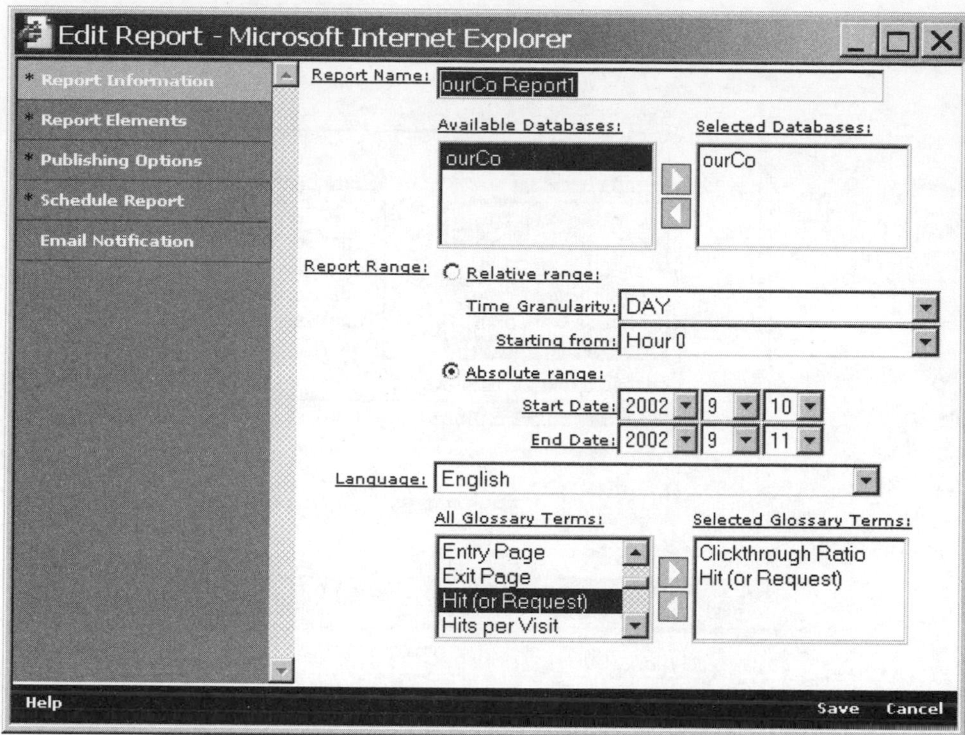

Figure 8.33: Report's information screen.

3. Click **Report Elements** in the left navigation bar, and click its plus sign. From the Portal Server Usage group, choose the top six report elements. Click the right arrow to populate the Selected Report Elements list, as shown in Figure 8.34. Click **Save**.

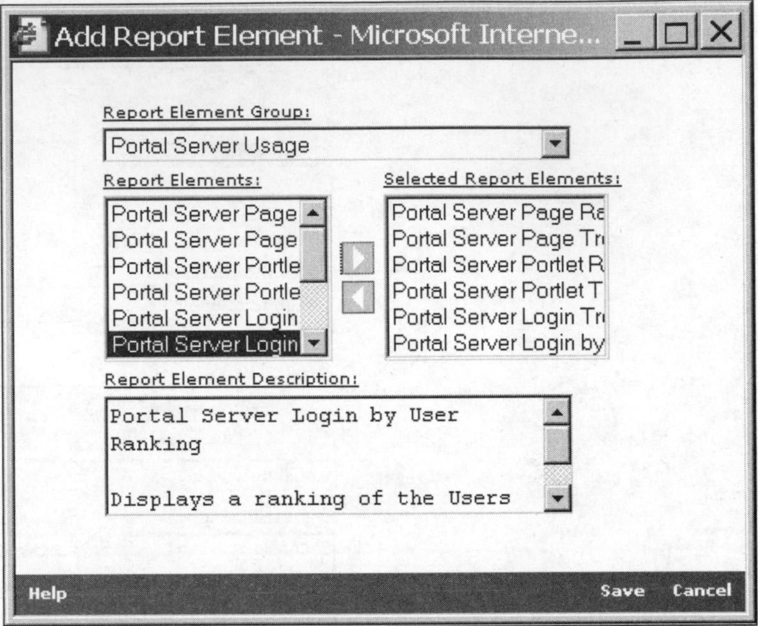

Figure 8.34: Adding report elements.

4. Click **Publishing Options** in the left navigation bar.

5. For test purposes, choose **File System Publish** and specify a **Local Directory** such as C:\ourCo. Notice you also have the options FTP Publish and e-mail Publish.

6. Click **Schedule Report** in the left navigation bar.

7. Complete the following steps to specify when and how often to run the analysis:

   7a. Keep the current date selected, which is the default.

   7b. Choose a Start Time about five minutes from now.

   7c. Set the End Date to **Never**.

   7d. Select **Once** as the frequency.

   7e. Choose **Make Active** and **Run after Save**, as shown in Figure 8.35.

   7f. Click **Save**, and the report will be scheduled to run.

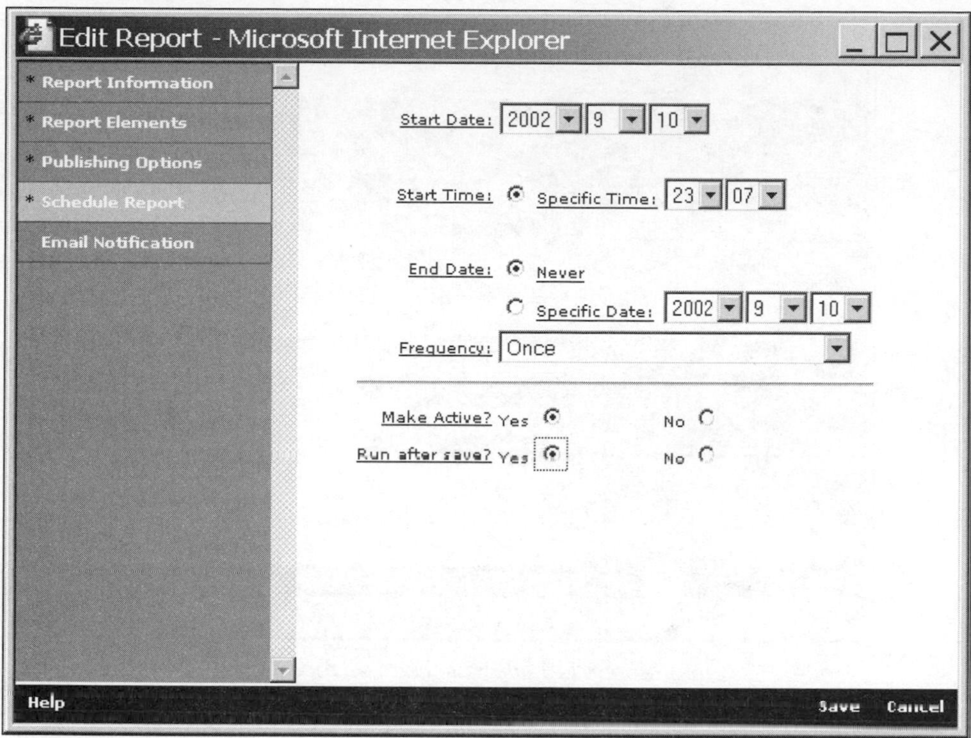

Figure 8.35: Scheduling a report.

8. Skip e-mail notification, and click **Save**.

The main UI should display a report named ourCo Report 1, scheduled to run in five minutes. If you click on the Scheduled link in the Status column, a pop-up will be displayed showing you the status of the run.

After the report is run at the scheduled time, the display should look like that shown in Figure 8.36. Notice ourCo Report1 says “complete.”

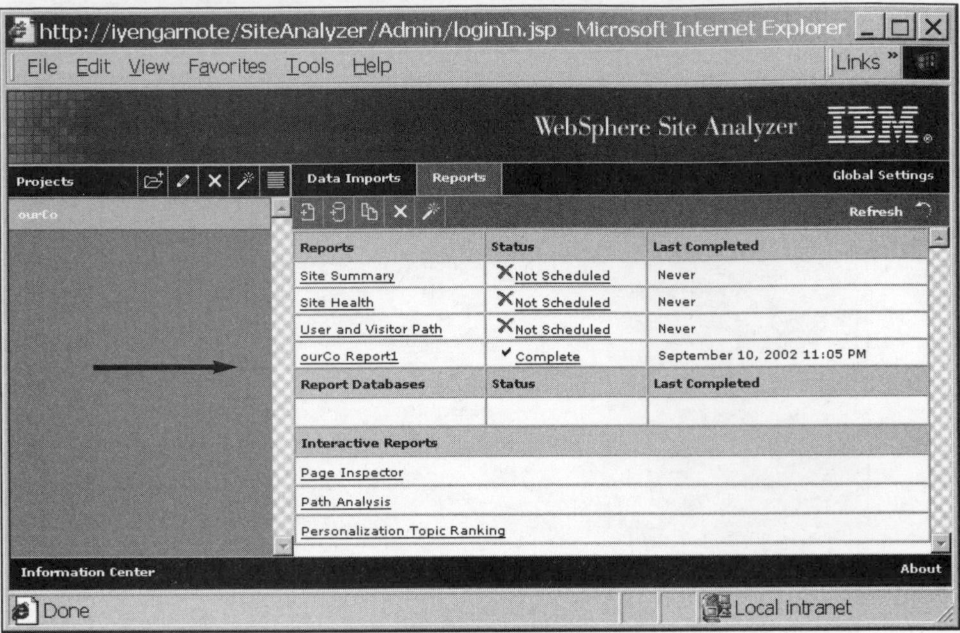

Figure 8.36: The Reports tab after a scheduled report was successfully run.

After the report is run, a folder will be created in the path you specified in step 5. As you move down in that path, you will see an index.html file, which you can bring up in a Web browser. The report might look similar to Figure 8.37.

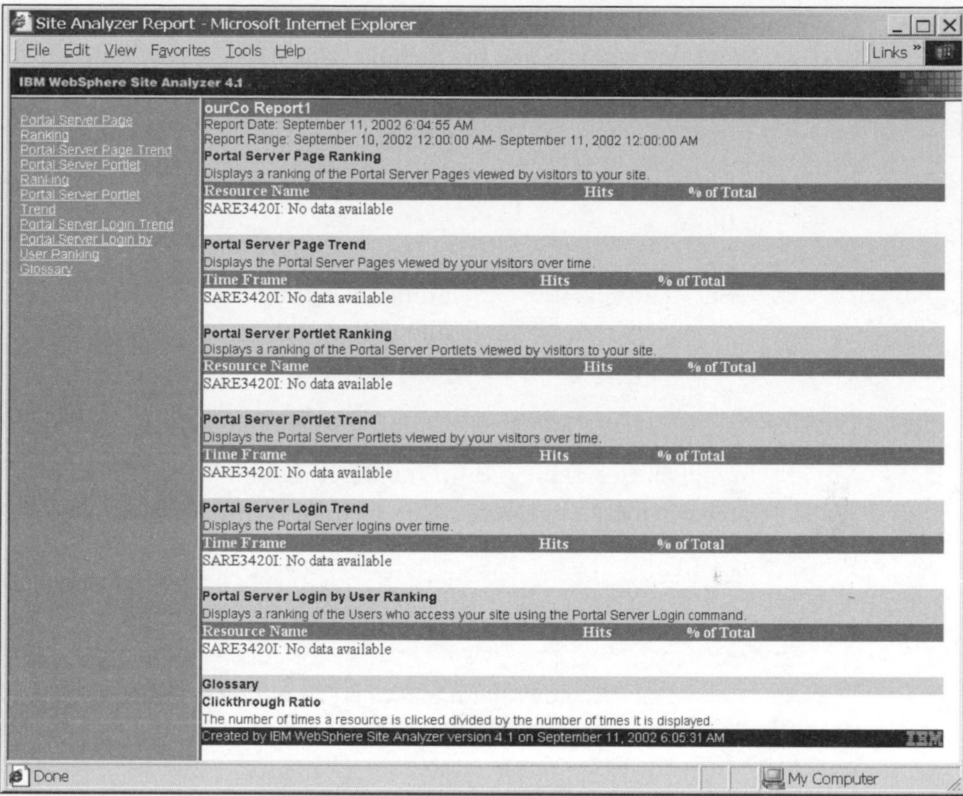

Figure 8.37: The report details.

You might notice that the report contains no data. So what happened? By default, WebSphere components do not generate log files that Site Analyzer can read. Hence, there was no data in any of the logs we specified. The next section shows how to enable WebSphere Portal server to log.

Enable Portal Server Logging

Site analysis logging is not enabled by default. To configure WebSphere Portal for site analysis logging, edit the SiteAnalyzerLogService.properties file found in <WPS_HOME>/shared/app/config/services folder. The following steps enable logging:

1. You have the option of setting the values for the three tokens: $APPSERVER_NAME, $CREATE_TIME, and $CLOSE_TIME.

2. Specify the value for the parameter SiteAnalyzerFileHandler.fileName. Or you can use the default value of log/sa.log.

3. Specify the value for the parameter SiteAnalyzerFileHandler.backupfile Name. Or you can use the default value of log/sa_$CREATE_TIME.log.

4. You may set the date format parameter SiteAnalyzerFileHandler.dateFormat.

5. Control the interval at which the log files are backed up by modifying the following:

   - SiteAnalyzerFileHandler.minutesPerLogFile
   - SiteAnalyzerFileHandler.hoursPerLogFile
   - SiteAnalyzerFileHandler.daysPerLogFile

6. Then activate the loggers by setting the parameters to true. Hint: Look for *islogging*. See Table 8.2 for the description of the loggers and the report elements that they affect.

Table 8.2: Loggers in Tivoli Site Analyzer

Logger name	Activity logged of HTTP requests that include the URLs	Report Element
SiteAnalyzer-SessionLogger	/Command/Login /Command/Logout	Login Trend User Ranking
SiteAnalyzerUser-ManagementLogger	/Command/UserManagement/CreateUser /Command/UserManagement/DeleteUser /Command/UserManagement/CreateGroup /Command/UserManagement/DeleteGroup	Summary Summary Trend
SiteAnalyzerPageLogger	/Page/* /Command/Customizer/CreatePage /Command/Customizer/EditPage /Command/Customizer/DeletePage	Page Ranking Page Trend Command Trend Page Edit Ranking Page Edit by User ranking
SiteAnalyzerPortlet-Logger	/Portlet/*	Portlet Ranking Portlet Trend
SiteAnalyzerPortletAction Logger	/PortletAction/*	
SiteAnalyzerErrorLogger	/Error/Portlet /Error/Page	

After the values are set and the file is saved, restart the WebSphere Portal application server to commit the changes. Upon re-start, check the <WPS_HOME>/log directory to make sure a log file named sa.log is being generated as you access the WebSphere Portal.

Tip: To disable logging, either comment out the activated loggers or set them to false and restart WebSphere Portal Server.

The Log File information can now be entered. In the Report tab of the Site Analyzer GUI, click **ourCo Report 1**. Specify sa.log (or sa*.log) as the log file name, and verify the directory where this log file is located, as shown in Figure 8.38.

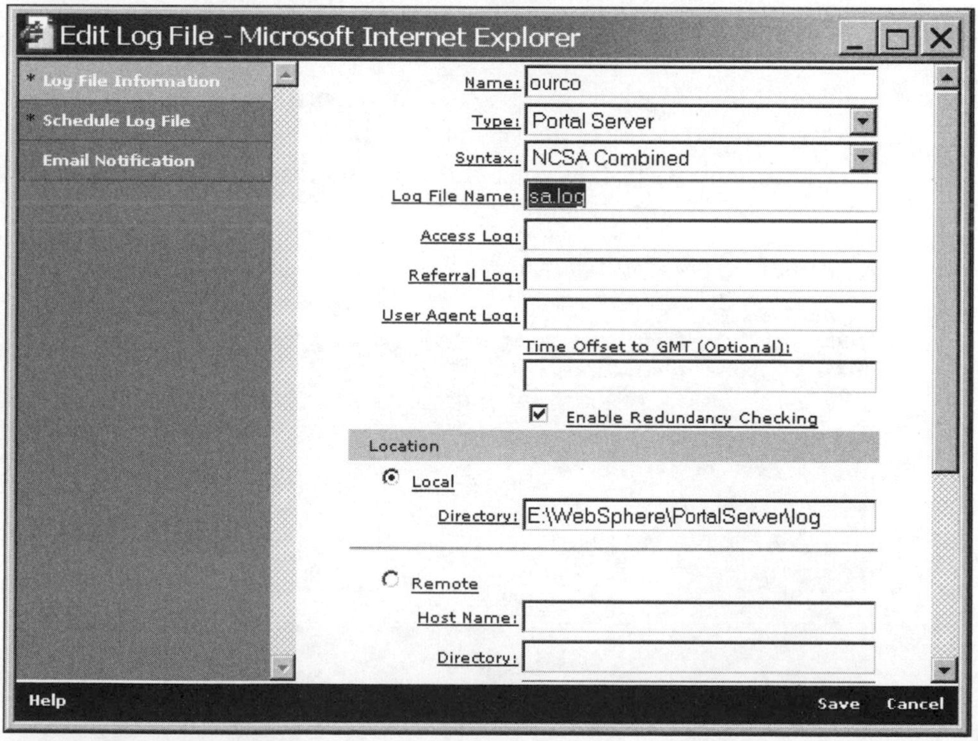

Edit Log File - Microsoft Internet Explorer

* Log File Information
* Schedule Log File
Email Notification

Name: ourco
Type: Portal Server
Syntax: NCSA Combined
Log File Name: sa.log
Access Log:
Referral Log:
User Agent Log:
Time Offset to GMT (Optional):
Enable Redundancy Checking
Location
Local
Directory: E:\WebSphere\PortalServer\log
Remote
Host Name:
Directory:

Help Save Cancel

Figure 8.38: Log file information.

Click **Schedule Log File** and schedule the log file to be analyzed upon saving, and then save and close the Edit Log File window. After the scheduled time, click the **Complete** link for that log file in the Site Analyzer's Data Imports tab. The Status window will be displayed. View it, and then close it.

Now, follow these steps to create a new report:

1. In the **Reports** tab of the Site Analyzer GUI, click **ourCo Report1**. The Edit Report window will appear. Keeping everything the same as in step 5 in the previous section, schedule the report to run, after specifying a time. Click **Save** to close the window.

2. After the scheduled time, you might have to click on the **Refresh** icon in the SA GUI. The status of ourCo Report1 should say "complete." Another report will be added to the folder that was created earlier.

3. Move down in C:\ourCo\ourCo_Report1\ourCo, or whatever path you specified. Go to the latest folder and bring up index.html in a browser. Figure 8.39 shows one of the report elements that we had chosen: the Portal Server portlet ranking.

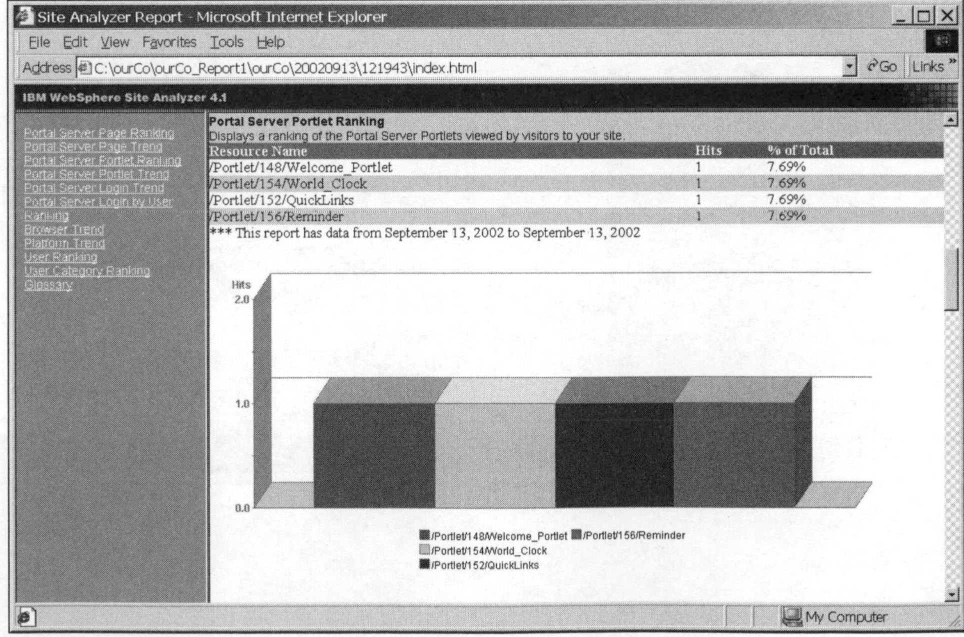

Figure 8.39: A generated report element.

This is just one illustration of a report generated by Site Analyzer; with Site Analyzer, the possibilities are endless.

Creating Custom Report Elements

If the report elements that come with the product are not sufficient, you have the capability to create custom report elements. It is a matter of enabling Site Analyzer to accept a custom report element and then creating a report that uses that report element.

The process for implementing a custom report element is as follows:

1. The Site Analyzer configuration file is found in <WAS_HOME>/SA/config and is called sa.config. Edit that file by setting SA Report Element (sare) tag customElementsAllowed property to true, as shown:

   ```
   sare.ReportMaster.customElementsAllowed=true
   ```

2. Create your own report.jsp and descriptor.jsp.

3. Use the SA Administration GUI to create a custom report element group. To do that, select **Global Settings**, select **Report Element Groups**, click the **Add** icon, and then specify a group name.

4. In Global Settings, select **Custom Report Elements**. Click the **Add** icon and specify your custom report element name, the group name, the description, and the names and locations of report.jsp and descriptor.jsp.

Note: You cannot put custom report elements in the default Site Analyzer groups; you must use a newly created group name.

The report.jsp file uses information in the descriptor.jsp file to format the report. It also creates the HTML and related files for the report, and it retrieves data for the report from a report database. At a minimum, you need to have the following Java code in a report.jsp file:

```
<%@ page import="com.ibm.sa.admin.reports.ReportConstants" %>
<%@ page import="com.ibm.sa.external.reports.ReportElementParameters" %>
<%
ReportElementParameters mReportElementParameters = null;
mReportElementParameters =
(ReportElementParameters)session.getValue(ReportConstants.cReportElement-
Parms);
mReportElementParameters.success = true; %>
```

The descriptor.jsp file contains information about the report, such as the number of rows, what to measure (such as hits or pages), the order in which to rank data (such as ascending or descending), and the output type (such as a table or chart).

For more information on writing the report.jsp and the descriptor.jsp, and on other customized features of Site Analyzer, refer to the product InfoCenter. On a Windows system, it is available via **Start → Programs → IBM WebSphere → Web Site Analyzer → InfoCenter**. On other systems, open the file <WAS_HOME>/installedApps/<NODE>/Site_Analyzer_Application.ear/InfocenterWebapp.war/en/docframeset.html.

Notes on Other Reports

You probably noticed Web Tracker on the Site Analyzer UI. Web Tracker is a data collection method in Site Analyzer that uses single-pixel technology to provide near real-time information about site usage. When Web Tracker is enabled, usage information is automatically sent directly from your user's browser to Site Analyzer for immediate processing. Web Tracker is just one of the many functions available in WebSphere Site Analyzer.

Some of the built-in reports include Site Summary, Site Health, User and Visitor Path, and Interactive Reports like Page Inspector, Path Analysis, and Personalization Topic Ranking. This short overview does not do justice to the versatility and power of Site Analyzer. We suggest you look at the InfoCenter to understand what can be done with Tivoli Site Analyzer to help make your portal site truly successful.

Process Portals

As mentioned in Chapter 2, process portals are a new concept that benefits process-centric organizations. WebSphere Portal provides the various pieces needed to put together a Process Portal. The main components of Process Portal are some special portlets, a business process container, a personalization engine, and an underlying workflow. Personalization was already covered in detail in Chapter 6. In this section, we discuss the configuration steps and the usage of the special portlet called My Tasks, which is available out-of-the-box.

During the WebSphere Portal installation process, WebSphere Business Integration Server Foundation (WBISF) is installed. In this section, we assume that the option to create sample Business Process Container on the application server, server1, was chosen. Furthermore, we assume that WebSphere Portal security has been enabled using a LDAP server. This is important, because tasks are displayed based on user credentials, and that requires that the user log into the portal.

Configuring WebSphere Application Server

1. Bring up the WebSphere Administrative Console and, in the navigation panel, traverse down to **Applications Enterprise Applications**. Both the BPE Container and BPEWebClient on server1 should be running. Figure 8.40 shows BPEContainer_inote_server1 and BPEWebClient_inote_server1.

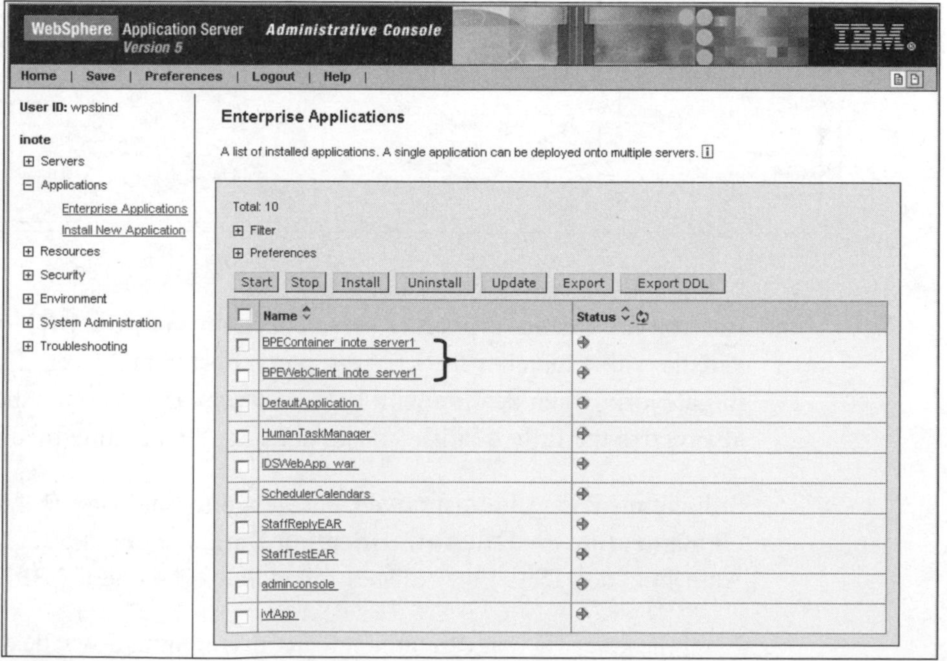

Figure 8.40: Enterprise Applications screen in WebSphere Administrative Console.

2. Still in the WAS Administrative Console, traverse down to **Resources → Staff Plug-in Provider**. You will see three or more plug-in providers already configured.

3. Click **LDAP Staff Plug-in Provider → Staff Plug-in Configuration → LDAP Staff Plug-in Configuration sample → Custom Properties**. Make sure that the Base DN Value matches the LDAP suffix that is being used by WebSphere Portal. If not, enter the suffix in the Value field, as shown in Figure 8.41 and click **OK**.

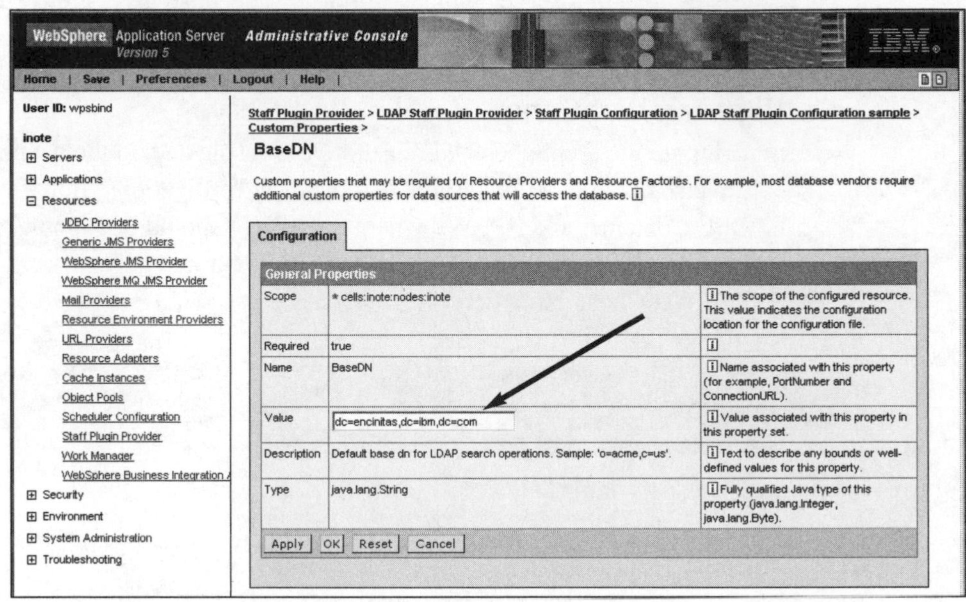

Figure 8.41: Custom Properties of a Staff Plug-in Provider.

4. Back on the custom properties screen click on **ProviderURL** and make sure the value matches the LDAP server's host name. Even if localhost might work, when dealing with LDAP servers, it is recommended that you always use the fully qualified host name. Save that value by clicking **OK**.

5. Still in the WAS Administrative Console, go to **Security → JAAS Configuration → J2C Authentication Data**. Among the J2C Authentication Data Entry aliases found, click the one for BPE.

6. Enter the User ID that can authenticate in WebSphere Application Server and WebSphere Portal and enter the corresponding password. Then click

OK. We use wpsbind because, by default, that user ID is set up to bind WAS against LDAP. See Figure 8.42.

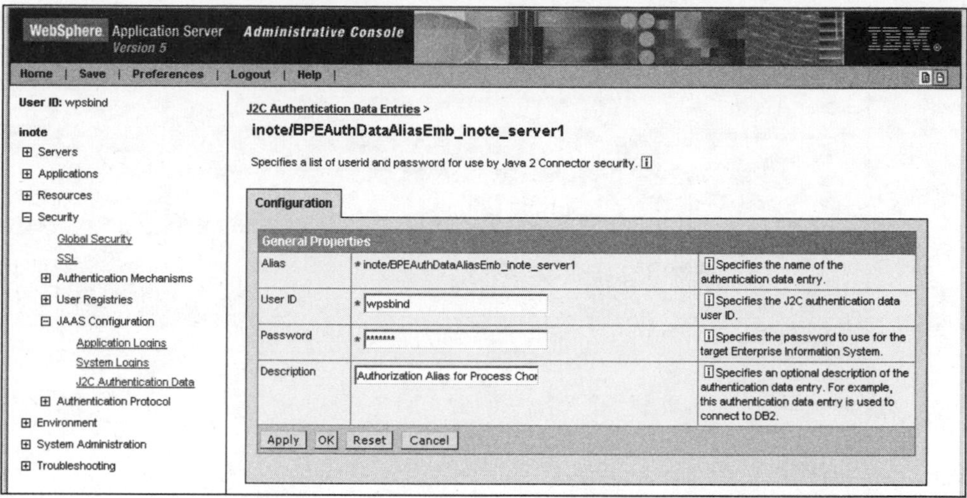

Figure 8.42: Custom Properties of a Staff Plug-in Provider.

7. Finally, for this demonstration, we installed two sample process applications and started them. Figure 8.40 shows them as StaffReplyEAR and StaffTestEAR.

Business Process Choreographer Client setup

1. In a web browser, bring up the BPE Web client by entering the following URL: http://<HOST_NAME>:9085/bpe/webclient. Log in using wpsbind as the User ID and Password. The user's My To Dos screen will be displayed.

2. In the navigation pane, click **My Templates**. Select one of the processes, StaffWithReply, and click **Start Instance**, as shown in Figure 8.43.

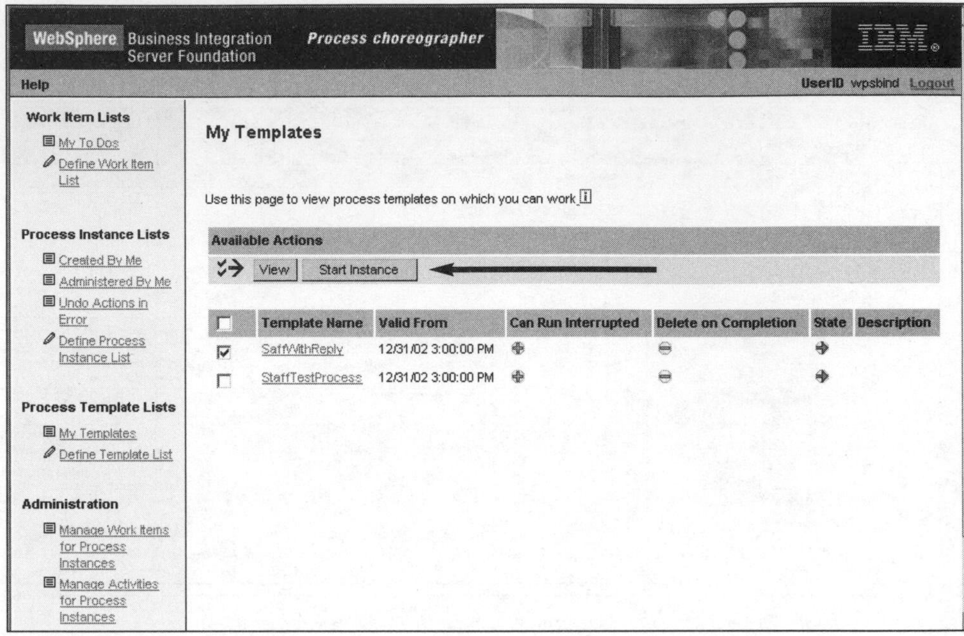

Figure 8.43: My Templates screen in the Process Choreographer Web Client.

3. The Process Input Message screen is displayed. Enter **SWR** for the Process Instance Name and any string for Process Input Message. Click **Start Instance** again to kick off the instance. See Figure 8.44. The screen will return to My To Dos, saying that "No work items available." The task should now be displayed in the Created By Me section.

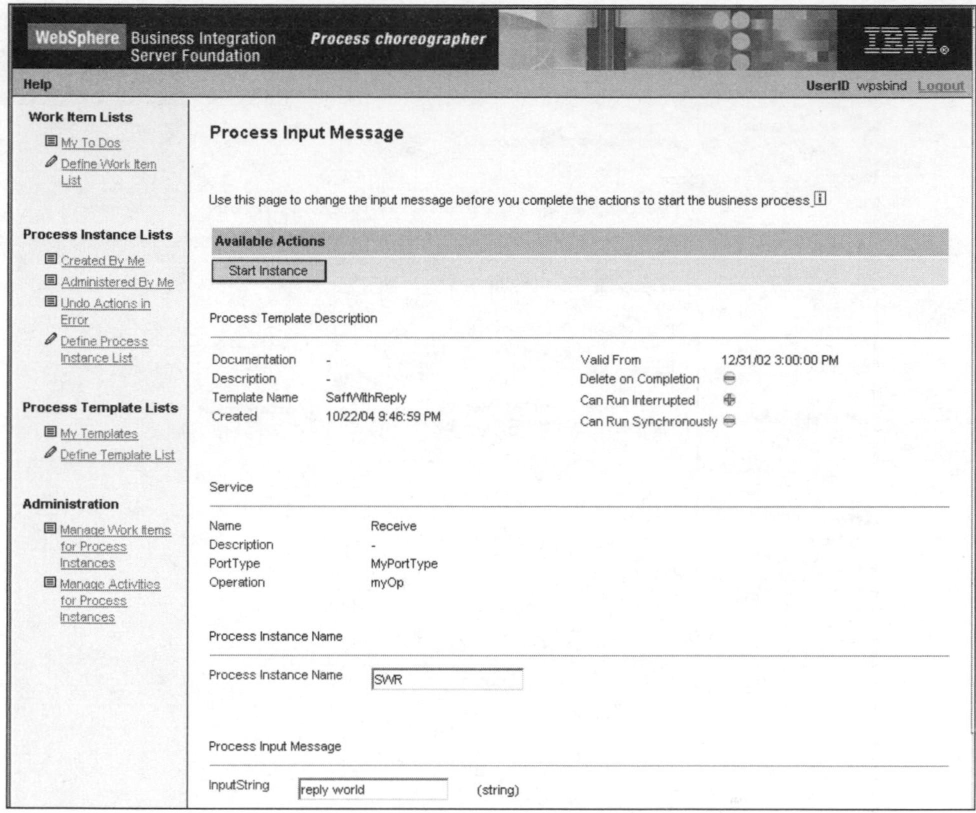

Figure 8.44: Process Input Message screen.

4. In the navigation pane, click **Created By Me**. The newly created process by wpsbind is displayed and the State should show as Running.

5. Log out as user wpsbind from the BPE Web Client.

6. Log back into the BPE Web Client using wpsadmin as the User ID and Password, and in the navigation pane, click **My Templates**.

7. Select the other process, StaffTest, and click **Start Instance**. In the Process Input Message screen, enter **STP** for the Process Instance Name and any string for Process Input Message, as shown in Figure 8.45. Click **Start Instance** again to kick off the instance.

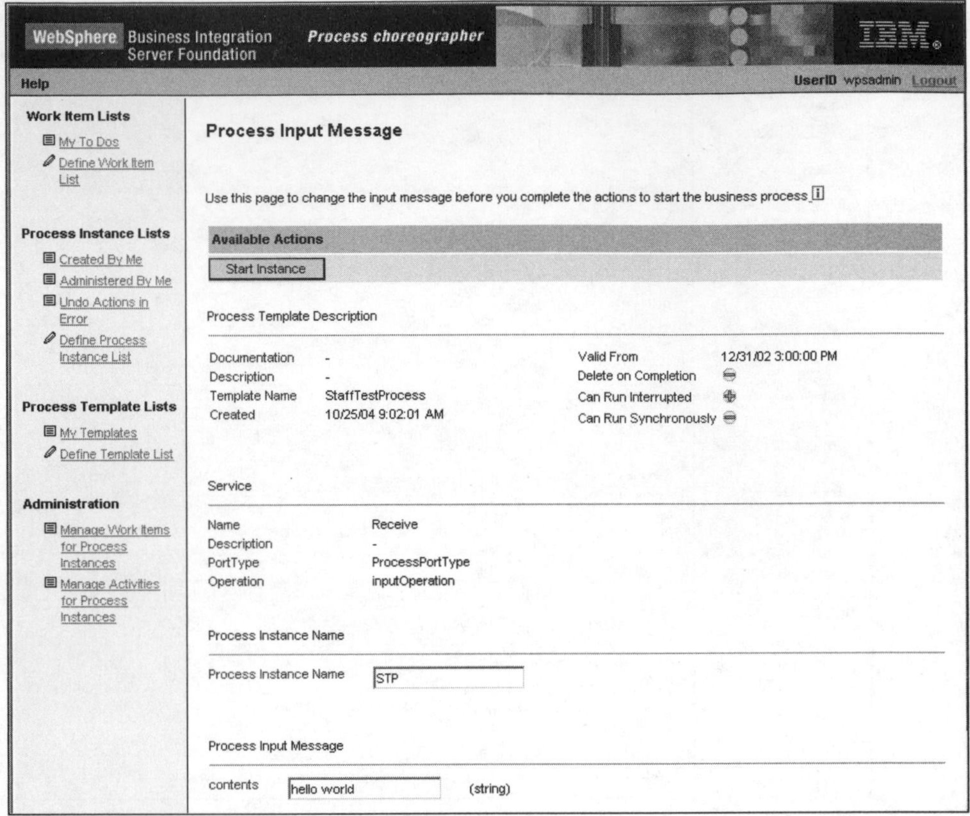

Figure 8.45: Process Input Message screen.

Now we have one process instance SWR started by wpsbind and another called STP started by wpsadmin. If you log back into the BPE Web Client as wpsbind, both those process instances are displayed under My To Dos.

WebSphere Portal Setup

1. In a Web browser, bring up the portal login page: http://<HOST_NAME>/wps/myportal. In the Login Portlet, enter **wpsbind** as the User ID and Password. Click **Log in**.

2. Click the right arrow (=>) on the Place Bar and select **My Tasks**. The My Tasks portlet should display the two created tasks, as shown in Figure 8.46.

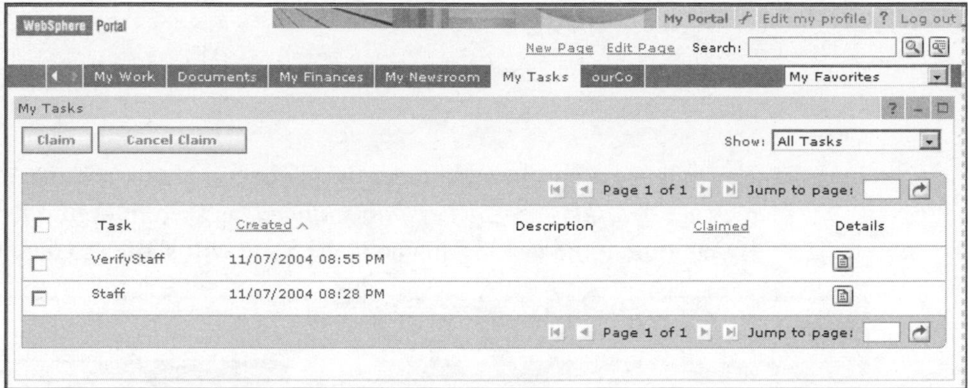

Figure 8.46: My Tasks portlet showing two tasks.

3. Log out as user wpsbind from the portal.

4. Log back into the portal using wpsadmin as the User ID and Password. Click the right arrow on the Label or Place Bar and select **My Tasks**. The My Tasks portlet will display only the one task, VerifyStaff, that was created by wpsadmin.

5. If you click on the **Details** icon, the portlet will display detailed information about that task. Notice it is in a state of "Not claimed," as seen in Figure 8.47. Click **Done** to return to the tasks screen.

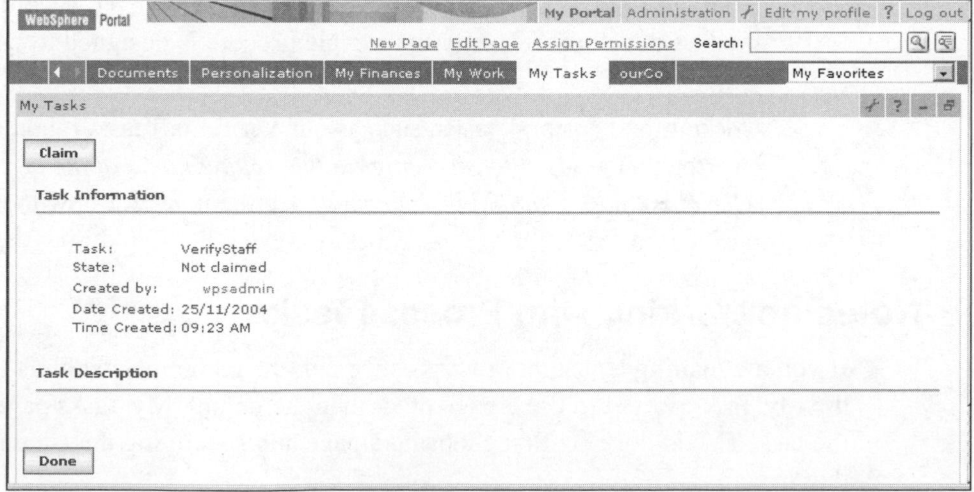

Figure 8.47: Details about the VerifyStaff task.

My Tasks Portlet Usage

1. Back at the tasks screen, check the box next to the VerifyStaff task and click **Claim**.

2. You will see a check mark under the Claimed column and the message *1 task(s) are successfully claimed,* as seen in Figure 8.48. If you look at the task details now, the State will show as Claimed.

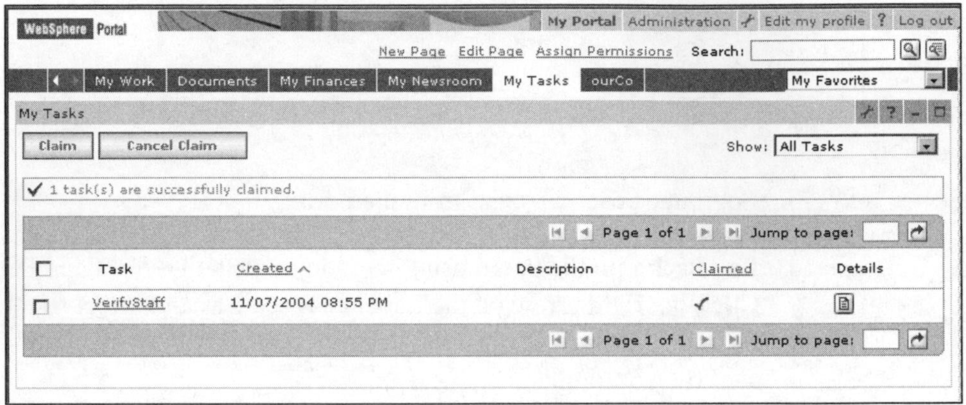

Figure 8.48: Claiming a task via the My Tasks portlet.

3. Click the task named **VerifyStaff**. You should be able to work with that specific task. By default, the My Tasks portlet is configured to display launched process tasks on the My Tasks page. However, according to product development, only the sample process is designed to work that way.

   Clicking on "custom" tasks, such as our VerifyStaff task, might display an error that reads *Please configure the unique name of the page under which task pages should be launched.* See the notes for how to proceed in these cases.

Notes on Working with Process Tasks

If you are running a custom process as we did, the recommendation is to configure the My Tasks portlet to use a page other than the default My Tasks page to launch the task. This is done by first choosing a page and specifying the Unique Name of that page.

The product InfoCenter enumerates the following steps to change the container for task pages:

1. Make sure the new task page container has been assigned a unique name. For this step, use the Custom Unique Names portlet under Portal Settings.

2. Invoke the following command specifying the unique name of the new container for value:

```
WPSconfig.{bat | sh} enable-page-as-task-page-container -
DPageUniqueName=value
```

3. Edit the My Tasks configuration and set the MyTasksPageUniqueName parameter to the unique name of the new task page container.

4. Invoke the following command specifying the unique name of the previous container for value:

```
WPSconfig.{bat | sh} disable-page-as-task-page-container -
DPageUniqueName=value
```

Some of the details are explained here. To obtain the Unique Name of a page, go to the portal Administration tasks. Click **Portal Settings → Custom Unique Names**. **Choose Pages** as the Resource Type.

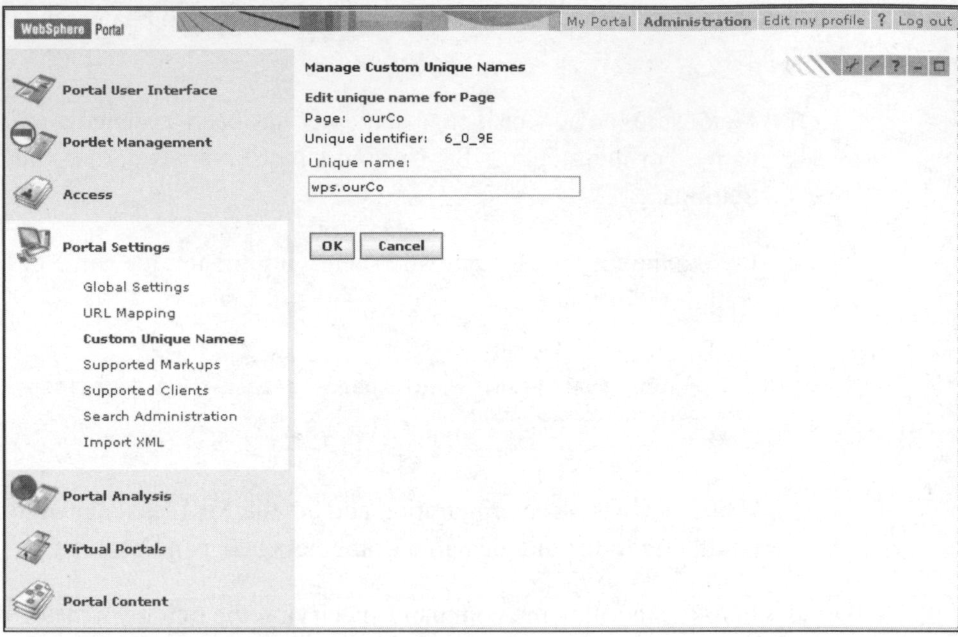

Figure 8.49: Giving a unique name to a portal page.

1. Search for the page you want. In this case, search for ourCo. If no Unique Name exists, click the Edit icon and give the page a unique name (such as wps.ourCo). Click **OK**. Remember the unique name. See Figure 8.49.

2. Go back to My Tasks page and the My Tasks portlet. If you click the **Configure** icon (the wrench) and enter the new Unique Name for a page, you may get an error that says *Transformation definition with the entered unique name does not exist*. A WPSconfig task has to be executed.

3. Go to <WPS_HOME>/config and, in a command window, run the following task:

```
WPSconfig enable-page-as-task-page-container
-DpageUniqueName=wps.ourCo
```

The MyTasks portlet should now accept the new Unique Name (wps.ourCo). Enter it and click **OK**. If that page is acceptable, you will be back on the tasks screen.

Note: If you change the task list page, modify the following attribute in ConfigService.properties file. It is located under <WPS_HOME>/shared/app/config/services:
processintegration.myTasksPageUniqueName = <unique_name_for_new_page>

4. Clicking on the task link in MyTasks portlet should now display the task in a separate window; the user is able to work on the task just as they would with WebSphere Business Integration Server custom clients or the Business Process Test Client.

Using this portlet along with custom-coded process-centric portlets and programmatically tying them to an alert or notification framework really shows that the portal is an ideal interface for the human component of business processes.

WPAI or APB

Commonly referred to as WPAI in the past, WebSphere Portal Application Integrator is now known as IBM Application Portlet Builder (APB) in V5.1. It enables users to create portlets without programming, with connectivity to back-end applications from relational databases to Enterprise Information Systems (EISs). Through the use of selected business object (BOs) in the back-end system, users can specify the data fields to be displayed in a portlet and, once it is created, it is made available for general use in the portal.

In this release of WebSphere Portal V5.1, APB refers to two portlet builders: the JDBC Portlet Builder and the Domino Portlet Builder. These are also referred to as the JDBC Business Object Builder and Portlet Builder for Domino. The JDBC Portlet Builder supports connection to Cloudscape and Oracle as a WebSphere data source. It does not support SQL Server and DB2 on OS/390. The Domino Portlet Builder works with Domino Server V5 and higher. The product Infocenter has a good explanation of APB.

Note: The Application Portlet Builders cannot be used as remote Web Services for Remote Portlets (WSRP).

By default, the Domino Builder and the JDBC Builder are already deployed during the WebSphere Portal installation process. Any authenticated user can access them by traversing down to the Developers Area page. For example, you access the JDBC Builder page thus: **My Portal → My Work → Developers Area → JDBC Builder**, as shown in Figure 8.50. The initial configuration screen is the same for all portlet builders.

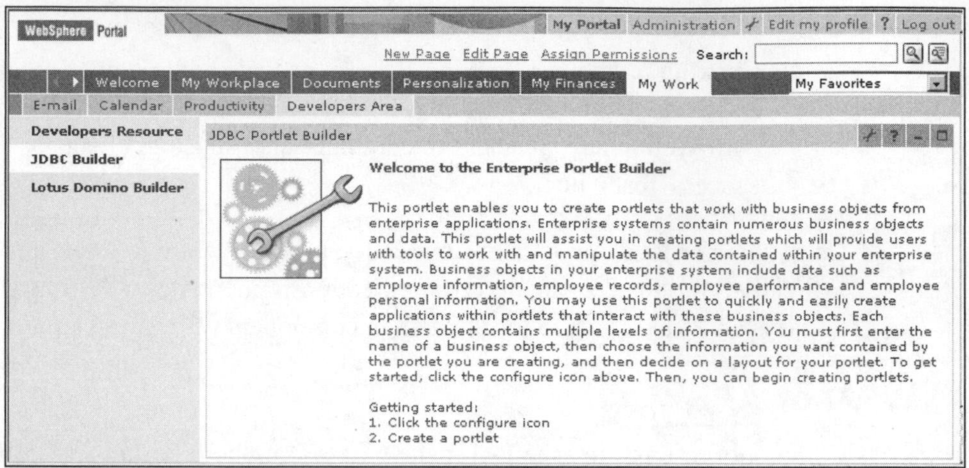

Figure 8.50: JDBC Portlet Builder initial screen.

The goal of these portlet builders is to enable even business users or power users to build a large number of portlets that access data and applications from major back-end systems. At a high level, the steps are:

- Power User creates a portlet instance
- Portal Administrator places new portlet on a page
- End user executes the portlet instance

All these portlets make use of J2EE Connector (J2C) technology to connect to the back-end systems. The portlets created are enabled for Click-to-Action (C2A), single sign-on (SSO), and people awareness. The builders have an intuitive user interface based on Java Server Faces (JSF) and use Service Data Objects (SDOs) for access. Since the portlets access the back-end systems using their native interface, these portlets perform well. The portlet builders come packaged in a WAR file that can be downloaded from the IBM WebSphere Portlet catalog. You install and configure the portlet, then use it to build the required back-end portlets.

Here, we briefly discuss the Siebel Portlet Builder that came with the older WebSphere Portal Application Integrator (WPAI) because we think the basic concepts will remain the same in the new portlet builders. With the previous version of WPAI, you could connect to DB2, Oracle, Informix, SQL Server, Cloudscape, Domino, SAP, Siebel, and PeopleSoft.

WPAI Configuration

You should install the WPAI Default Runtime Template Application first, and then install the WPAI Builder Application that contains the portlet builders. Before you can work with the portlet, some configuration steps must be done on the WebSphere Application Server side. A Resource Adapter Archive (RAR) file is associated with these back-end systems, and it gets installed in WebSphere Application Server.

Install the Resource Adapter

1. In the WebSphere Administrative Console, traverse to **Resources → Resource Adapters**. Then click the **Install RAR** button.

2. On the following screen, point to the Siebel RAR file, as shown in Figure 8.51. Then click **Next**.

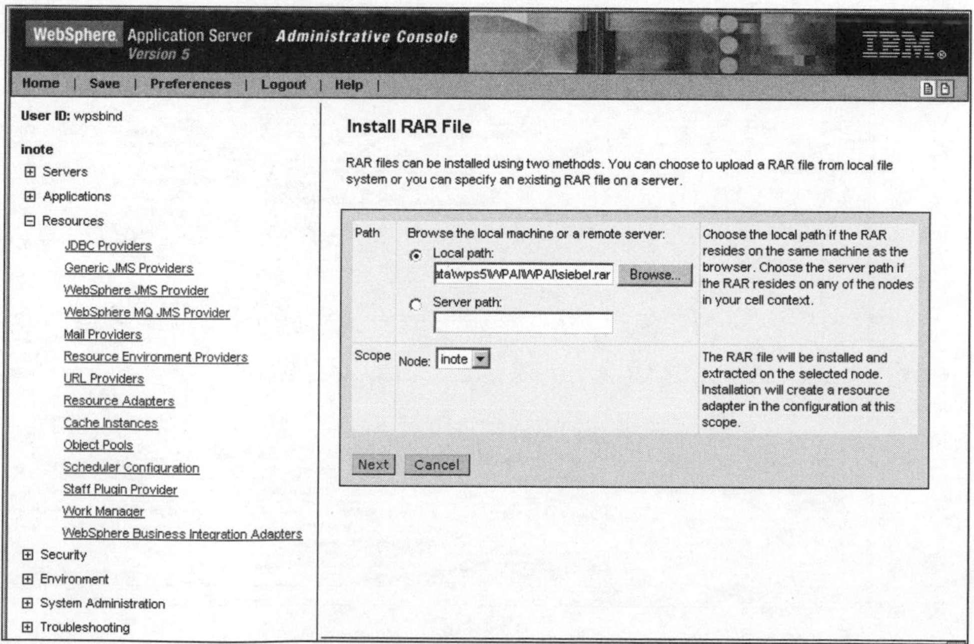

Figure 8.51: Screen to specify Siebel RAR file.

Create a J2C Adapter

3. Give it a descriptive name like Siebel J2C Adapter. Remember to leave the Archive Path blank. Specify the full path to the Siebel JAR files: SiebelJI.jar, SiebelJI_Common.jar, and SiebelJI_enu.jar. Click **OK** to create the adapter. See Figure 8.52.

4. Do not click **Save** yet. Click on the newly created **Siebel J2C Adapter** link.

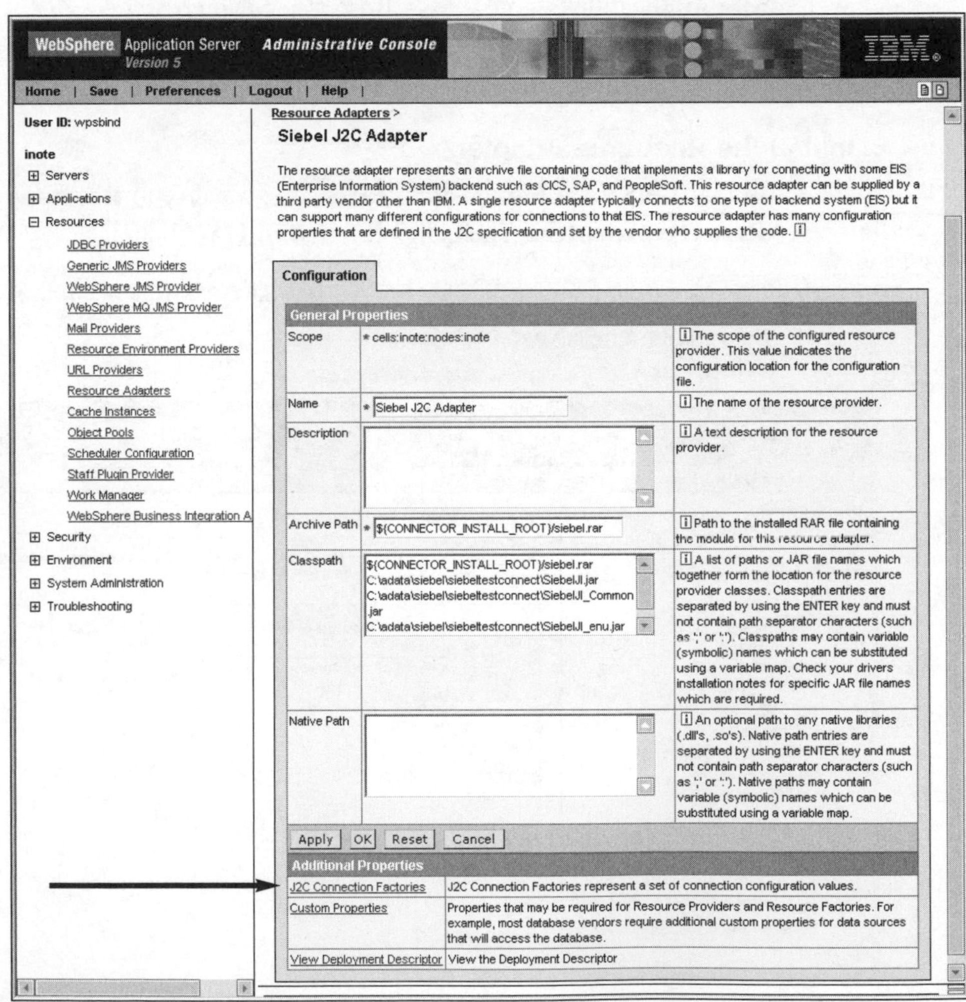

Figure 8.52: Siebel J2C Adapter configuration screen.

Create a Java Connection Factory

5. On the Siebel J2C Adapter screen, click **J2C Connection Factories**. A new connection factory must be created. On the J2C Connection Factories screen, click **New**.

6. Give the connection factory a name, such as Siebel_CF, and specify a JNDI name. This JNDI name is important because it is used later when configuring the portlet. A commonly used JNDI name is eis/siebel. Leave the other parameters with default values. Click **OK** to create the connection factory.

7. Click on the newly created **Siebel_CF** link. Scroll to the bottom of the next screen and click on **Custom Properties**. The back-end systems have their unique way of connecting to these properties, which is specified by a Connection String.

Specify Properties for the Java Connection Factory

8. One of the properties should be connectString. Click on it and, in the Value field, enter the appropriate connection string for the Siebel server that you will connect to. For example inote://inote/senterprise/SSEObjMgr_enu/inote. Click **OK**.

9. Click on **jarPath** and fill in the full path of the directory where the Siebel jar files can be found. Click **OK**. The screen should look like that in Figure 8.53.

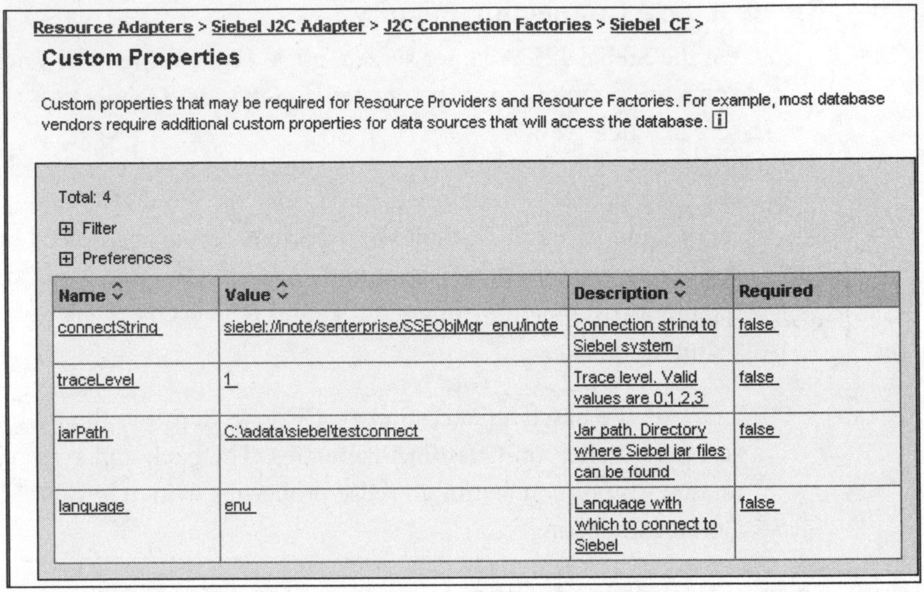

Resource Adapters > Siebel J2C Adapter > J2C Connection Factories > Siebel_CF >

Custom Properties

Custom properties that may be required for Resource Providers and Resource Factories. For example, most database vendors require additional custom properties for data sources that will access the database.

Total: 4

⊞ Filter

⊞ Preferences

Name	Value	Description	Required
connectString	siebel://inote/senterprise/SSEObjMgr_enu/inote	Connection string to Siebel system	false
traceLevel	1	Trace level. Valid values are 0,1,2,3	false
jarPath	C:\adata\siebel\testconnect	Jar path. Directory where Siebel jar files can be found	false
language	enu	Language with which to connect to Siebel	false

Figure 8.53: Custom properties of Siebel Connection Factory.

10. Click **Save**. Then click Save again in the window to save everything to the master configuration.

11. Finally copy the JAR file from <WAS_HOME>/installedConnectors /siebel.rar/siebeladapter.jar to <WAS_HOME>/lib.

12. For all the changes to take effect, restart server1 and then restart WebSphere_Portal server.

Configuring WebSphere Portal server

In this section, we take you through the steps of using the Siebel Builder to create a portlet that accesses a Siebel system.

1. Start by creating a Siebel Builder page. Traverse to **My Portal → My Work → Developers Area** and create a new page called Siebel Builder.

2. Edit the Siebel Builder page. Search for Siebel and add the Siebel Portlet Builder portlet to that page. Then click **Done**.

3. Back on the Siebel Builder page, you will see the configuration screen again. As the portlet instructions say, click the **Configure** icon (wrench).

On the following screen, enter the JNDI binding path, user ID, and password. See Figure 8.54. The JNDI path should be the same as that specified when creating the Siebel Java Connection Factory. Click **OK**.

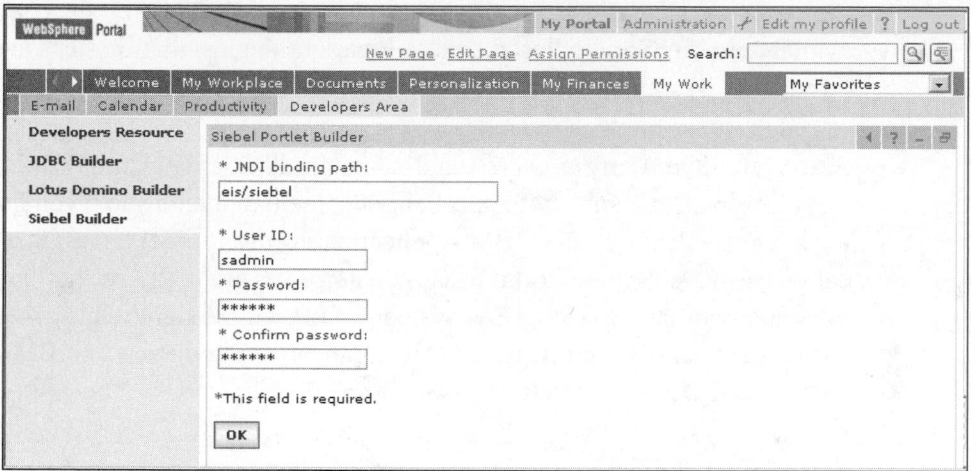

Figure 8.54: Siebel Portlet Builder configuration screen.

4. If the parameters are correct, and the portlet successfully connects to the back-end server, you will see the portlet morph into the new portlet creation screen.

From here, you can follow the screens to build the portlet by clicking on the **New portlet** button. At a high level, the final steps are:

- 4a. Build a Business Object (BO).
- 4b. Choose the Business component.
- 4c. Choose the fields pertaining to the BO that you want to work with.
- 4d. The builder will ask for details on the fields and what you want displayed in the portlet.
- 4e. Finally a portlet will be created that can be deployed.

The beauty of these portlet builders is that you do not have to do any programming, and you can use the builder to even enable click-to-action in the portlets. If the output fields need to be changed, you can also edit the portlet after it has been created.

Door Closings

Search, Site Analytics, Process Portals, and Application Portlet Builder are topics that could each warrant a separate chapter. Our intent here was to help you with the concepts, so that you know what can be accomplished with the components available in WebSphere Portal, and to highlight the installation steps and walk through some simple examples.

Search and Site Analyzer were stand-alone products at one point, hence each of those components come with excellent documentation and show you how to use the advanced features. The IBM Application Portlet Builder (APB) is a very critical piece in WebSphere Portal because enterprises are really seeing the need to integrate with their existing EAI systems. APB will be tightly integrated with IBM's next generation Integrated Development Environment, the IBM Rational Application Developer (RAD).

Process Portal is not really a component, but rather a new concept, and we are really excited about it—as are numerous companies that have processes (especially workflow processes) in place. It represents a truly practical use of portals. We think a lot more innovative features will be added to portal software, and you can bet that WebSphere Portal will be leading the way. Now we truly have gone beyond a simple portal.

Chapter 9
Portal Content and Collaboration

We all know "content is king." Now how do we contribute content to the portal? Is there a workflow process for portal users to follow? Can we use third-party content management tools to integrate with WebSphere Portal? This chapter talks about the Content Management (CM) component available in WebSphere Portal. Its full name is Lotus Workplace Web Content Management (LWWCM) but is more commonly referred to as Web Content Management or WCM. You will also learn about Collaborative Components, the true icing on the WebSphere Portal cake. By integrating the powerful collaborative features of the Lotus product set, WebSphere Portal offers users something unique—collaboration. This chapter shows you how collaboration is achieved and discusses its limitations. Usage is left to the reader's imagination.

Collaborative Components

A few of the features available through the Collaborative Components in WebSphere Portal include:

- Find out who is using the portal.
- Have a quick chat with suppliers or business partners while they are all accessing the enterprise portal, thereby decreasing e-mails.
- Having an e-meeting to discuss a press release before publishing it.

Collaborative Places

Collaborative places in WebSphere Portal are community areas in the portal where common pages and applications are organized. Members use these places to work together on common projects, communicating with each other to make effective decisions.

A collaborative place can be *personal* or *shared.* A personal place provides a private workspace where individual users can manage daily work needs. This includes portlets that access e-mail, a calendar portlet, portlets for corporate resources, and project database portlets tailored to that user. A shared place can be set up for teams working on a project, for enterprise-wide communities that need access to the same resources, or as a place to store and share information and have discussions. A shared place can be restricted to certain members of the community, or it can be made public.

Access to a collaborative place is controlled through a membership list. Members can be designated as *managers*, *designers*, or *participants* in the community. As the names suggest, managers can add new members to the community, designers can change the layout and content, and participants are only allowed to visit and use the workplace.

Collaborative Portlets

The collaborative portlets for Lotus Advanced Collaboration software are included in the WebSphere Portal offering. They have built-in features that allow portal users to take actions on documents or user names that appear in a portlet. Some of these portlets are enhanced versions of the portlets provided in WebSphere Portal Enable.

From within the portlet, a portal user can see if other users are online, then select from a menu of options to interact with those users. Based on the context of the portlet, users can take actions directly from the portlet, with or without launching the entire application. For example, Lotus Notes e-mail portlets make any e-mail author's name live, with online awareness and menu options, without altering the underlying e-mail application.

Collaborative portlets provide access to a variety of applications such as e-mail, discussion, team room, instant messaging, team collaboration, calendar, to-do list, and document management. Most of these portlets are part of the Collaboration Center. They roughly map to the following products: Lotus Notes/Domino, iNotes, Lotus Team Workplace (LTW), Lotus Instant Messaging and Web Conferencing (LIMWC), Domino Document Manager, and Directory Search. Table 9.1 lists the collaborative portlets, with a brief description.

Table 9.1: Collaborative Applications in WebSphere Portal

Application	Description
Lotus Instant Messaging Contact List	Displays the Lotus Instant Messaging list (formerly the Sametime Contact list).
Who is Here	Displays the Lotus Instant Message list of users signed on to the portal page (formerly the Sametime Who is Here).
People Finder	Quick search and Advanced search of people and their details is possible with this portlet.
Lotus My Team Workplaces	The old Lotus QuickPlace portlet allows users to find, work in, and request new Team Workplaces.
Lotus Web Conferencing	Allows users to find, attend, and schedule e-meetings as well as view meeting details.
Domino Web Access (iNotes)	Provides iFrame-based access to iNotes-enabled Domino servers and mail files. This includes access to the Welcome, Mail, Calendar, To-Do List, Contacts, and Notebook functions.
Notes and Domino	Displays users' mail, calendar, and to-do lists from their traditional Lotus Domino mail files. The "my" name indicates that these portlets auto-detect each user's mail file settings, and thus do not need to be configured individually for each user. The apps are Lotus Notes View, Lotus Notes Mail, My Lotus Notes Mail, My Lotus Notes Calendar, My Lotus Notes To Do, Lotus Notes Discussion, and Lotus Teamroom.
Domino Document Manager	Provides Domino-based document management (formerly Domino.Doc).
Directory Search	Allows searching and selection of names of people or groups.
Team Workplaces	Displays up to six different Lotus Team Workplaces in separate browser windows.
Inline Team Workplaces	Displays a Lotus Team Workplace (formerly QuickPlace) inside a portlet.
Search Center	Allows a full-text search of portal pages, document libraries, search collections, and any additional content sources specified by your administrator.

Table 9.1: Collaborative Applications in WebSphere Portal (continued)

Application	Description
Lotus Instant Messaging Connect	Launches Lotus Instant Messaging client software in a separate browser window.
Webpage Portlet	Displays any Web page inside an iFrame. This is not quite a "collaborative" technology, but it is included here, because it is based on iFrame technology.

In addition to the collaborative portlets that come with the product, other portlets for Lotus collaborative technologies can be downloaded from IBM's portlet catalog. The IBM WebSphere Portlet catalog can be accessed from http://www-3.ibm.com/software/webservers/portal/portlet/catalog. Most enterprises will have their collaborative needs well served by the Collaboration Center, which gets installed out-of-the-box. Collaborative portlets do not support caching in their current form. Caching was disabled, because Domino users are used to receiving dynamic information. If you are deploying the Domino portlets in a large enterprise, you might want to consider enabling caching on the portlets by adding the caching tag to the portlet.xml file within the portlet's Web application.

Collaboration Center

The Collaboration Center is a set of pages deployed during the installation of WebSphere Portal. These pages provide multiple customized instances of the following eight portlets:

- Domino Document Manager
- Domino Web Access (iNotes)
- Lotus Instant Messaging Contact List
- Lotus My Team Workplaces
- Lotus Web Conferencing
- Notes and Domino
- People Finder
- Who Is Here

The Collaboration Center is preconfigured to use Domino and WebSphere Portal Extend products and servers. However, it still requires additional set-up, which requires planning and additional configuration of all involved servers, collaborative software, and of the Collaboration Center itself. You get to the Collaboration Center by clicking on **My Workplace**. Figure 9.1 shows the Collaboration Center Welcome portlet.

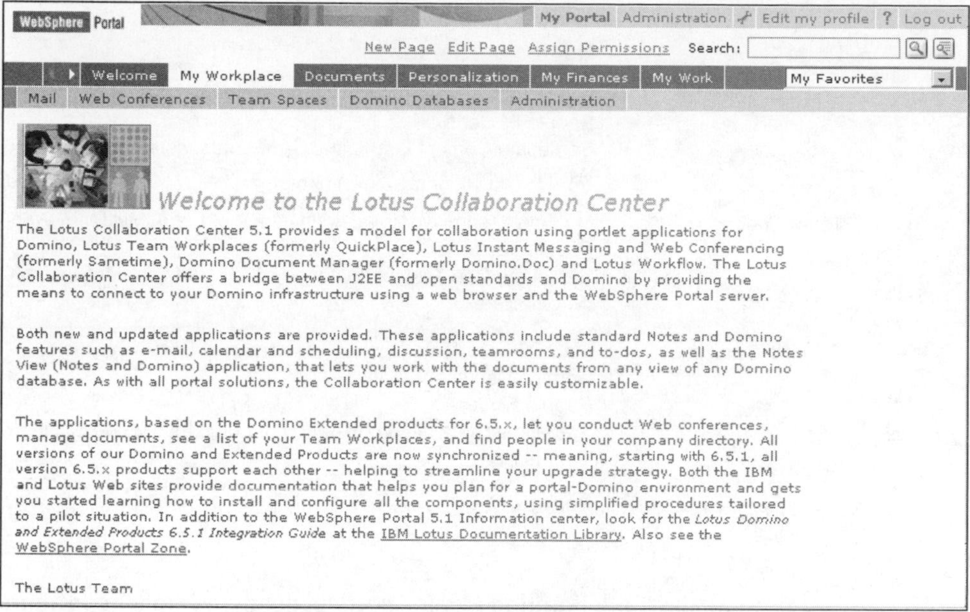

Figure 9.1: Lotus Collaboration Center Welcome page.

As the Welcome page says, the Lotus Collaboration Center offers a bridge between open standards like J2EE and Domino by providing the means to connect to the Domino infrastructure using a Web browser and the WebSphere Portal Server. Five subpages appear under My Workplace: Mail, Web Conferences, Team Spaces, Domino Databases, and Administration. A description of the content of each page is listed in Table 9.2.

Table 9.2: Collaboration Center Pages and Their Content

Page	Named portlet instances
Mail	Mail (contains instance of Domino Web Access) Calendar (contains instance of Domino Web Access) Address Book (contains instance of Domino Web Access) People Finder Sametime Contact List (instance of Lotus Instant Messaging Contact List)

Table 9.2: Collaboration Center Pages and Their Content (continued)

Page	Named portlet instances
Web Conferences	Lotus Web Conferencing People Finder Sametime Contact List (instance of Lotus Instant Messaging Contact List) Who Is Here
Team Spaces	My Lotus Team Workplaces (instance of Lotus My Team Workplaces) People Finder Sametime Contact List (instance of Lotus Instant Messaging Contact List) Who Is Here
Domino Databases	Lotus Notes View (instance of Notes and Domino portlet) Domino Document Manager People Finder Sametime Contact List (instance of Lotus Instant Messaging Contact List) Who Is Here
Administration	Bookmarks

To reiterate, the Collaboration Center portlets need additional configuration: Figure 9.2 shows the Web Conferences page; this particular portal instance was configured using DB2 and Tivoli Directory Server. Although the machine had an instance of Sametime server running, notice how the Sametime Contact List portlet and Who Is Here portlet indicate that the Sametime server has not been configured to work with the portal. And the Lotus Web Conferencing portlet has a message to set up the Lotus Instant Messaging and Web Conferencing (LIMWC) Server. But the People Finder portlet is functional. Notice that a search for wps returned the two portal users from LDAP server, wpsadmin and wpsbind.

Similarly, if you go to the Team Spaces page, you will notice that that the My Lotus Team Workplaces portlet has a message to set up the Lotus Team Workplace (LTW) Server.

Figure 9.2: Not fully configured Collaboration Center page.

Configuring Lotus Instant Messaging and Web Conferencing

Like most other configuration steps, configuring WebSphere Portal and Lotus Instant Messaging and Web Conferencing (LIMWC; formerly the Sametime server), involves running the WPSconfig utility found in the <WPS_HOME>/config directory. As noted before, the WPSconfig utility uses wpconfig.properties as its input. That properties file is also found in the <WPS_HOME>/config directory.

Tip: Make a backup copy of the wpconfig.properties file before modifying it.

Configuring WebSphere Portal with a LIMWC server takes a couple of steps. Before you begin, make sure the application server, server1, is running and that the application server, WebSphere_Portal is stopped. Also ensure that you are in the <WPS_HOME>/config directory.

1. Edit wpconfig.properties and modify only the four parameters shown in Table 9.3.

Table 9.3: Lotus Instant Messaging and Web Conferencing-Specific Properties

Property	Description	Value
LCC.Sametime.Enabled	Flag that determines if LIMWC is enabled	True
LCC.Sametime.Server	Fully qualified name of LIMWC server	my.server.com
LCC.Sametime.Protocol	Protocol used to connect to the LIMWC server	http
LCC.Sametime.Port	Port number the Sametime server is listening on	80

2. You could run the specific task to configure Lotus Collaborative Services to use Lotus Instant Messaging and Web Conferencing only as shown:

```
WPSconfig lcc-configure-sametime -DDBPassword=<password> -
DWmmDbPassword=<password>
```

Or you could change and save other Lotus Collaborative Services values in wpconfig.properties and then run the overall configuration task:

```
WPSconfig lcc-configure-all
```

Look for the *Build Successful* message.

3. At a command line, change to the <WAS_HOME>/bin directory and start the WebSphere_Portal.

Tip: The LIMWC installation might automatically create a Web SSO configuration document. If so, delete that document before proceeding with the rest of the configuration steps.

The next major step is to configure single sign-on (SSO) between WebSphere Portal and Lotus Instant Messaging and Web Conferencing. The high-level tasks are:

- Create the WebSphere LTPA key
- Import the WebSphere LTPA key into Domino
- Enable multiserver single sign-on authentication

Configuring Lotus Team Workplace

The steps to configure Lotus Team Workplace (LTW) Server are similar. The only differences are the four properties in wpsconfig.properties file and the task name when running the WPSconfig utility. The four parameters specific to LTW are shown in Table 9.4.

Table 9.4: Lotus Team Workplace-Specific Properties

Property	Description	Value
LCC.QuickPlace.Enabled	Flag that determines if LTW is enabled	true
LCC.QuickPlace.Server	Fully qualified name of LTW server	my.server.com
LCC.QuickPlace.Protocol	Protocol used to connect to the LTW server	http
LCC.QuickPlace.Port	Port number the QuickPlace server is listening on	80

You then run the specific task to configure Lotus Collaborative Services to use Lotus Team Workplace Server.

```
WPSconfig lcc-configure-quickplace -DDBPassword=<password> -
DWmmDbPassword=<password>
```

Again, the major step is to configure single sign-on (SSO) between WebSphere Portal and Lotus Team Workplace. The high-level tasks are:

- Create the WebSphere LTPA key
- Import the WebSphere LTPA key into Domino
- Enable multiserver single sign-on authentication
- Create the Domino Web Server Configuration database (domcfg.nsf)
- Update the Notes.ini file

What Are Collaborative Services?

Collaborative Services, formerly Collaborative Components, are more than just JavaBeans with a set of methods that expose collaboration functionality to portlet developers. These services include the API, the Javadoc, and the JSP samples that get installed when you install WebSphere Portal. The sample enterprise application (cs.ear) includes Java methods and JSP tags for creating custom portlets or extending the functionality of those existing portlets that include the advanced collaborative features of Domino and Extended products. The samples show how to access Lotus software products like Domino, QuickPlace, and Discovery Server and how to add online awareness and person menus to create people links. These interfaces are not a replacement of the existing APIs. They are useful for building custom portlets or adding functionality to portlets, such as menus or online awareness.

Steps to Deploy the Collaborative Services Enterprise Application

You can deploy the Collaborative Services samples available in the Enterprise Application (cs.ear) by following these high-level steps:

1. Ensure that SSO is enabled on the server where the collaborative services enterprise application (cs.ear) is installed—either on default server1or WebSphere_Portal.
2. Bring up the WebSphere Administrative Console (http://<HOST_NAME>:9091/admin).
3. Expand Applications in the navigation window and click **Install New Application**.
4. Browse and select the **cs.ear** file found at <WPS_HOME>/InstallableApps.
5. Click **Next** in the series of screens that follow. When you arrive at the screen that asks for a virtual host, select **default_host**.
6. Map the module to the default server1. Make sure it is available to All Authenticated users.
7. Click **Finish**. After the CS enterprise application is successfully installed, Save the Master Configuration.

8. Click on **Enterprise Applications** in the navigation window. Look for the name cs. Select it, and click the **Start** button to start the Enterprise Application. See Figure 9.3.

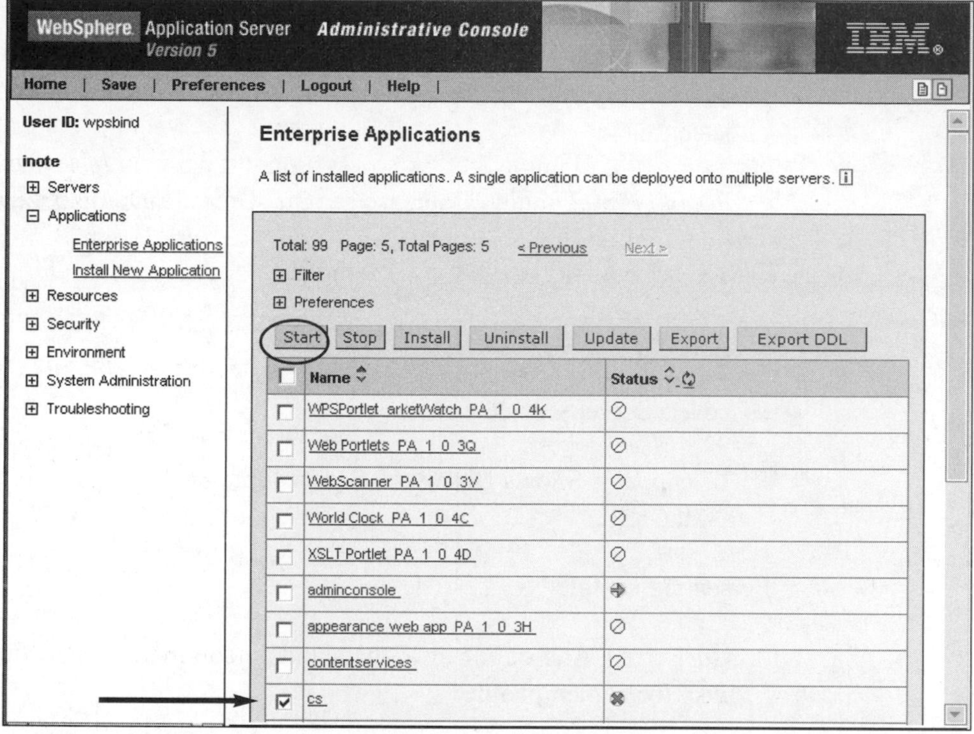

Figure 9.3: WebSphere Administrative Console to start cs enterprise application.

After the samples are deployed and configured as explained in the product Infocenter, you can launch them from a Web browser using the URL: http://<HOST_NAME>:9085/cs/index.jsp. See Figure 9.4.

Tip: Before the samples can be used, edit the CSEnvironment.properties file located in <WAS_HOME>/installApp/<NODE>/cs.ear/cs.war/config.

The following samples are provided:

- DominoService samples
  - *dbpicksamp.jsp*—Domino Directory sample: Selection lists for Servers, Databases, and View

  - *viewsamp.jsp*—Notes View sample: Add collaborative features to Notes database views, launch columns and people links
  - *calsamp.jsp*—Notes Calendar view sample: Add collaborative features to a Notes Calendar view
  - *dbdocsamp.jsp*–Notes Document sample: Add a document to a Notes database
  - *dbsamp.jsp*—Domino Database sample: Create a Domino database
- QPService (QuickPlace Service) sample
  - *qpsamp.jsp*—Create a QuickPlace
- DiscoveryServerService sample
  - *dssamp.jsp*—Shows Discovery Server functionality including profile and K-Map
- Person tag sample
  - *psamp.jsp*—Add online awareness and person menus to create people links for named people
- Menu tag sample
  - *msamp.jsp*
- Domino LDAP sample
  - *ldapsamp.jsp*

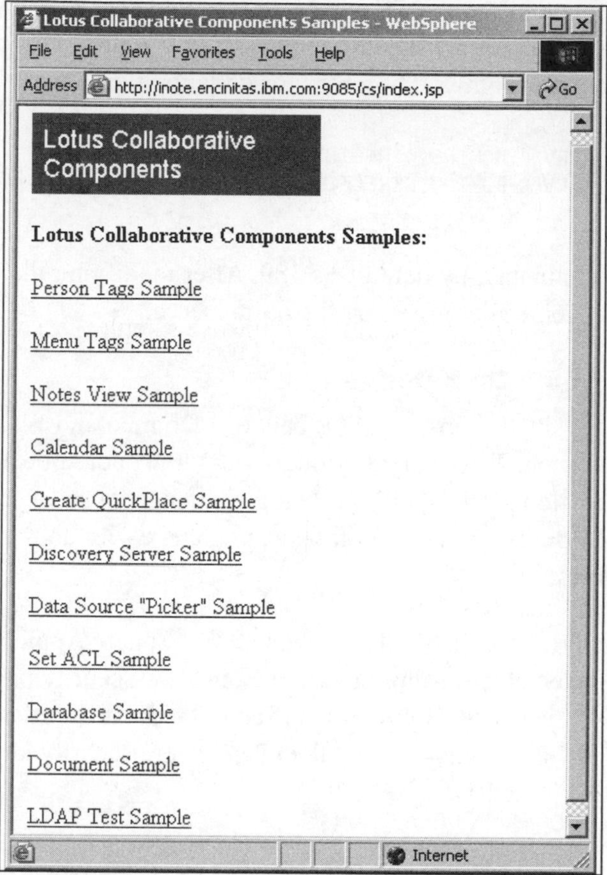

Figure 9.4: Collaborative Components Samples page.

Lotus Domino Integration

A Domino server is needed to make all features of the collaborative portlets and Collaborative Components available to portal users. The Domino Directory Server or the Domino LDAP Server is required to look up various user values and attributes, such as the mailfile. The Domino server is used as the data source, and the Domino Data Source servers must have HTTP, LDAP, and Domino IIOP enabled.

Portal Settings to Support Domino

You will configure WebSphere Portal to use the Domino Directory Server during the post-installation steps. One of the tasks is to modify certain parameters in the CSEnvironment.properties file. This collaborative services environment properties file is found in the <WAS_HOME>/installedApps/<NODE>/cs.ear/cs.war/config directory. The following entries pertain to Domino integration. They are required to enable the Domino Directory for collaboration:

```
CS_SERVER_DOMINO_DIRECTORY.enabled=true
CS_SERVER_DOMINO_DIRECTORY_1.hostname=inote.encinitas.ibm.com
```

The port number, by default, is 389. After modifying the CSEnvironment.properties file, remember to restart the portal server.

Single Sign-On Settings

Enabling single sign-on (SSO) between Domino and WebSphere Portal is key to collaboration. A user logging on to the portal should be able to use Domino-based collaboration portlets without being challenged a second time. Using Lightweight Third-Party Access (LTPA) tokens, you can easily do that. The high-level steps are as follows:

1. Create an IBM LTPA token in WebSphere Application Server via the WebSphere Administrative Console's Security pages. Figure 9.5 shows the screen for LTPA settings (**Security → Authentication Mechanisms → LTPA**), which is also the place where security keys can be generated and exported.

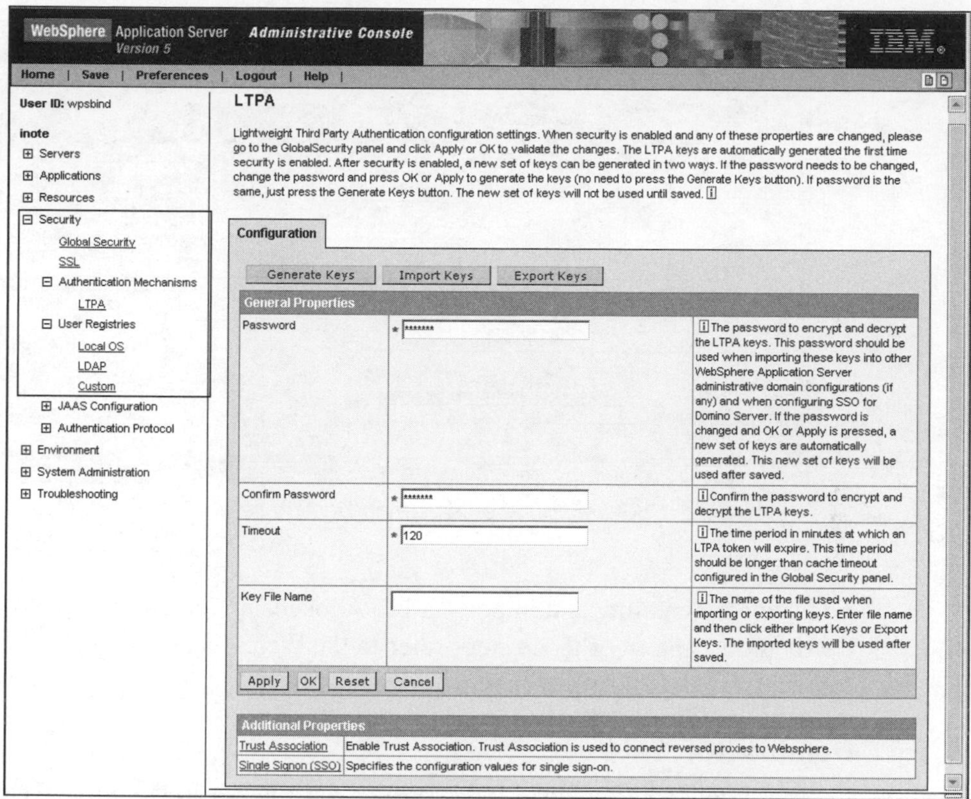

Figure 9.5: LTPA settings screen in WebSphere Administrative Console.

In the navigation pane under **Security → User Registries** a menu entitled LDAP is present. Here, you specify that Domino is the LDAP server of choice.

2. Import the LTPA token generated by WebSphere Application Server into Domino; this token is then used for all Domino servers within the Domino domain. The Domino server LTPA token screen is shown in Figure 9.6.

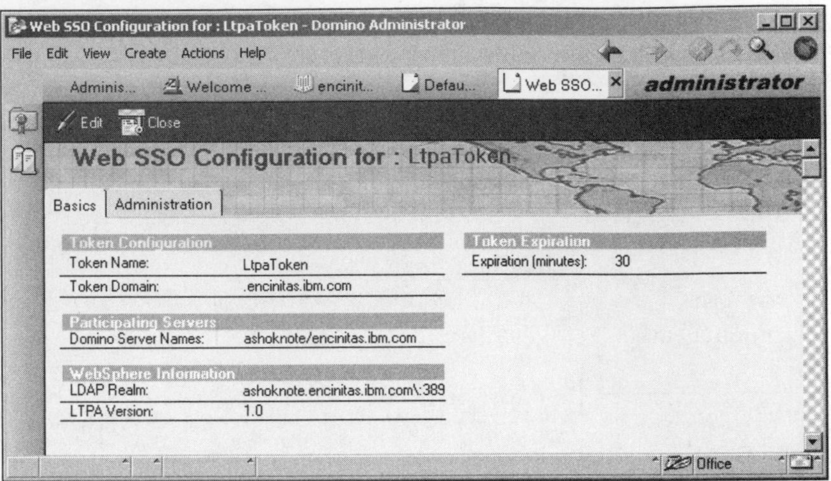

Figure 9.6: SSO configuration screen in Domino server.

The steps for creating and importing LTPA tokens are given in Chapter 3. For a detailed description of those steps refer to the WebSphere Portal product Infocenter.

Domino IIOP Settings

Internet Inter-Orb Protocol (IIOP) settings must be set in Domino, because some of the collaborative portlets and services use IIOP to access Domino server and get information from the database.

You can either load the IIOP task in your Domino Server Console or add it to the notes.ini file and restart the Domino server. If you are using IBM HTTP Server as the Web server in the WebSphere Portal environment, the collaborative portlets and components use the values in the diiop_ior.txt file to open IIOP sessions with the collaboration servers. So, you have to copy the diiop_ior.txt file from its original location at C:\lotus\Domino\Data\domino\html to the IBM HTTP Server \htdocs directory.

Note: If you are running more than one collaboration server in the portal environment, make sure the diiop_ior.txt file is the same across the Domino domain.

Adding People Awareness Tags to a Portlet

We just saw that people awareness in the form of online presence (names displayed as hyperlinks) in WebSphere Portal is supported by Lotus Collaborative Services. In some contexts, the Person menu is available; the Person menu is provided by the Person JSP tag. The Person Tag provides contextual collaboration functionality related to a named person. It generates the HTML that renders both the specific set of actions to display on the Person menu and the online presence state to display for that person, taking into account the Domino and Extended products and servers that are installed and enabled in the portal environment.

One way to add people awareness to a portlet is by including the following lines in your JSP, and then using the Person Tag:

```
..
<%@taglib uri="/WEB-INF/tld/people.tld" prefix="peopleservice" %>
<%@taglib uri="/WEB-INF/tld/menu.tld" prefix="menu" %>
..
```

This is an example of using the Person Tag:

```
..
<peopleservice:person value="CN=Darth Vader,dc=starwars,dc=com"
valuetype="LDAPDN" displayName="Darth Vader" />
..
```

Document Management

Another new component in WebSphere Portal V5.1 is the Document Manager. Document management tools enhance work productivity and streamline complicated document management processes by providing a centralized location for documents, as well as methods for tracking the changes generated by members of a work team. Files exist in a centralized location in a tree directory structure separate from client machines. Here, any authorized person can access them, thus allowing for the easy exchange of documents among team members. Depending on a user's access rights, she can read, edit, or delete files, as well as create and delete folders and special views. The Document Manager supports JSR 170 Content Repository. More information about JSR 170 can be found at http://www.jcp.org/en/jsr/detail?id=170.

In short,Document Manager is an ideal solution for diverse and widespread workgroups needing a single focal point to control document management and information development processes. You can access the Document Manager Portlet by clicking on **Documents** in the portal menu. Before you can use it, the portlet requires additional configuration steps. Click the Configure icon (wrench) to specify the settings, as shown in Figure 9.7.

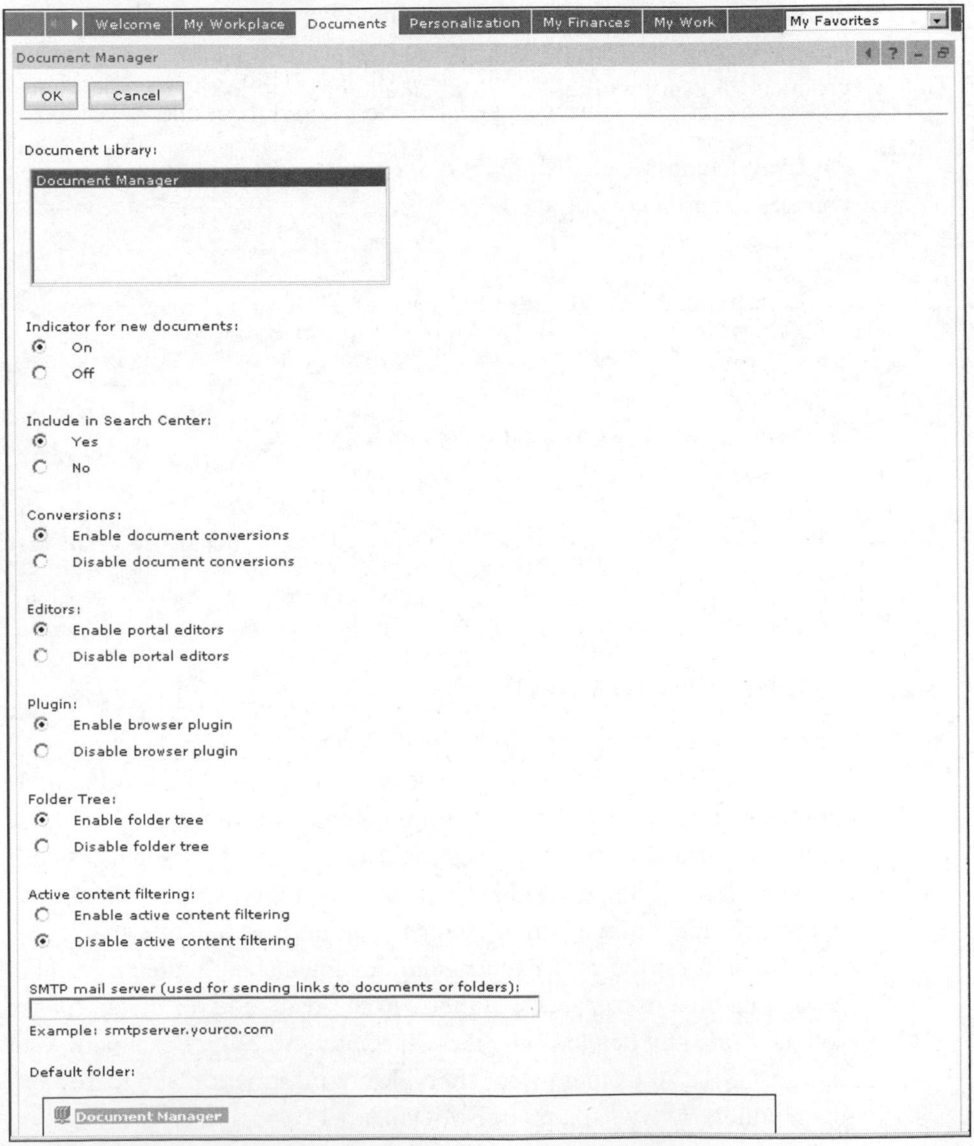

Figure 9.7: Document Manager portlet settings.

We will work with the default Document Library called Document Manager. By turning On the indicator for new documents, the portal will display New every time a document is added to the library. Accept the remaining default settings. Click **OK** to save the settings. If you click the Edit icon (pencil), you can set things like the number of documents to display per page, number of days to show the document as new, and the like. Do not make any changes to the defaults. Click **Cancel**.

The next step is to set up user access. User, Editor, Manager, and Administrator are the four roles that can be assigned to users. To assign access and roles from the Manage Document Libraries page, the user should meet one of the following criteria:

- Be a member of the Content Administrators group, which is set to wpsContentAdministrators user group by default

Or

- The user needs to possess the following authority or higher:
    - User authority on the Portal Content administrative page
    - User authority on the Manage Document Libraries portlet
    - Administrator authority on the ICM_CONTENT_REPOSITORY virtual resource
    - User authority on the Resource Permission page and the Resource Permission portlet
    - Delegator authority on the User and User Groups resources

You may want to set two other settings before using the Document Manager Portlet—the browser plug-in and the file type definitions. The Manage Document Libraries portlet provides a browser plug-in that allows users to import their local files into a document library. Also, the Document Manager Portlet provides a browser plug-in that allows users to work with documents in editing applications that are installed on their computers. The file type definitions enable Document Conversion Services for the Document Manager Portlet, which provides users the ability to open various file types in HTML format. Because we want to demonstrate how the portlet can be used, we did not configure these settings.

Document Manager Portlet Usage

In the Document Manager Portlet, click **Import File**. In the Import Document window (shown in Figure 9.8), give a title to the document, browse for the file, and select it. Optionally, give a description and choose the language. Then click **Publish**.

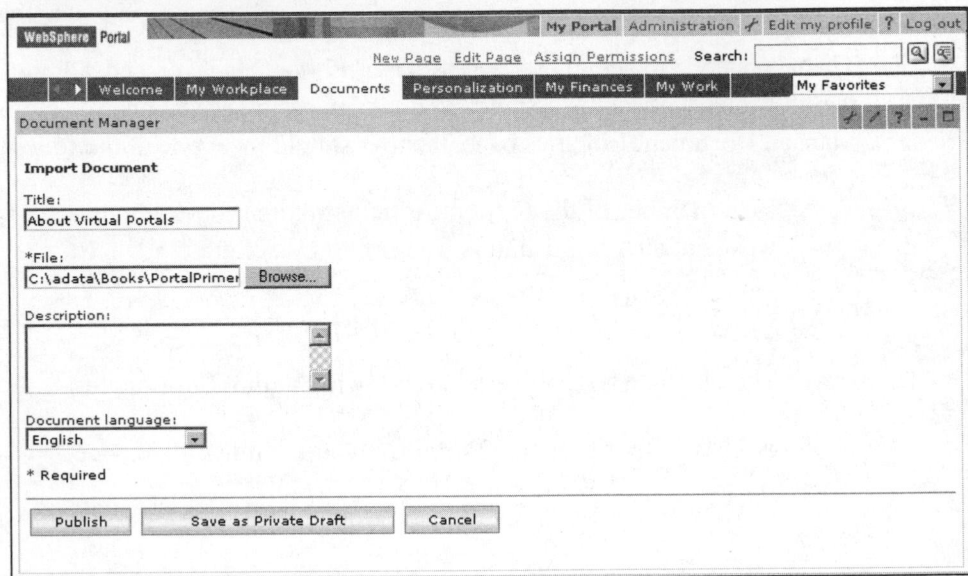

Figure 9.8: Importing a document.

After the document is successfully imported into the library, you will see the newly imported document carries the New! tag, along with the Author and the Date. See Figure 9.9.

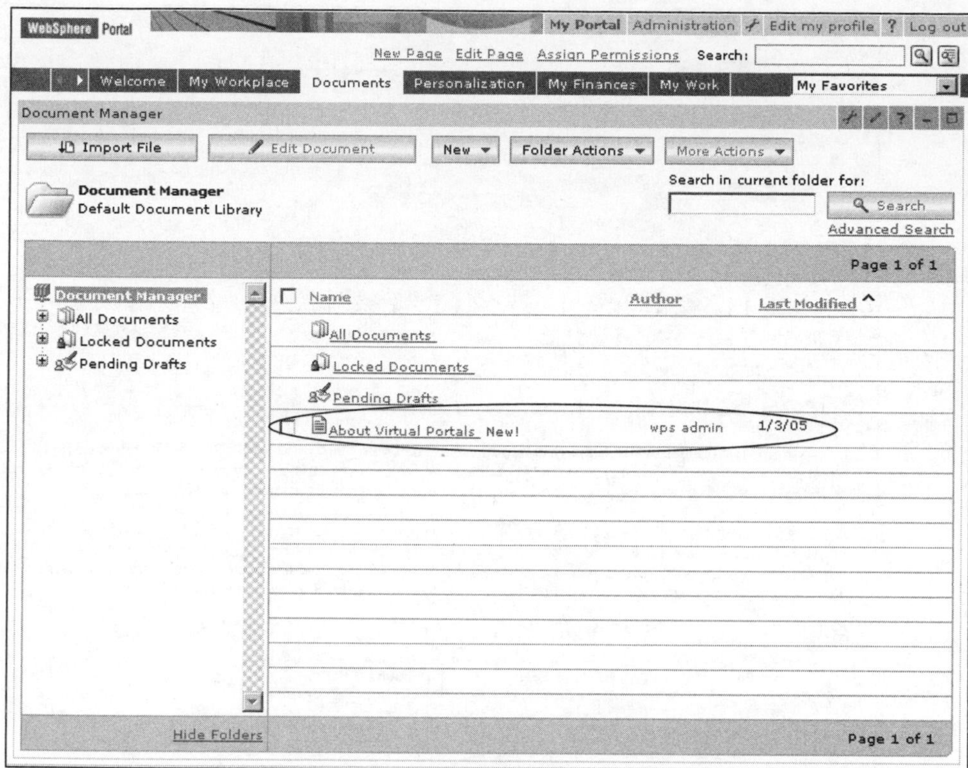

Figure 9.9: Document Manager portlet showing the newly imported document.

If you click the document's title, the document will be displayed within the portlet, along with a description of the document. At this point, you can replace the existing document, edit it, lock it, or perform other actions like copy, move, delete, convert, and the like, as shown in Figure 9.10.

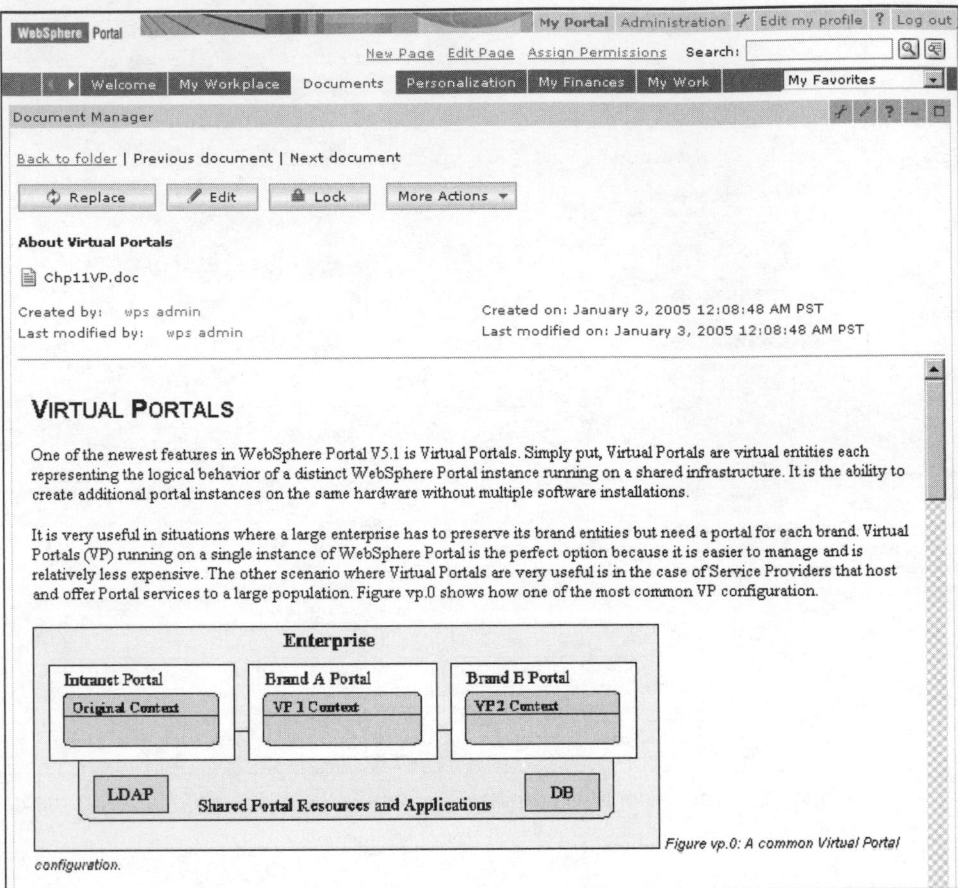

Figure 9.10: Document Manager portlet displaying contents of an imported document.

We demonstrated one of the simplest task of importing a document into a document library, but a lot more can be done using the Document Manager Portlet, such as searching folders in the library, setting up draft approvals using a workflow, and providing People awareness.

Web Content Management

Web Content Management is available in WebSphere Portal V5.1 through the Lotus Workplace Web Content Management (LWWCM) component. The current version of LWWCM is V5.1. The software is on CD3 and is installed during the WebSphere Portal installation process, along with the Personalization component. The installed folders can be found under <WPS_HOME>/wcm.

LWWCM provides a sophisticated content management system for Web sites that can be used by both nontechnical and technical users. It manages:

- The content and design of pages in a Web site
- The framework and navigation of a Web site
- The creation, editing, approval, and publication process of portal content

By default, LWWCM is installed using the Cloudscape database as the data repository. If you would like to use a different data repository, you will need to edit the Web Content Management section of wpconfig.properties file and then run the WPSconfig utility. LWWCM Application data and resources can be stored in the following databases:

- DB2 V8.1 FP6 or higher (Enterprise and Workgroup editions)
- Oracle V9.2.x
- IBM Content Manager V8.2 FP7 (IBM Information Integrator for Content V8.2 FP 3 must also be installed)
- Cloudscape V5.1.x
- SQL Server 2000 SP 3a or higher
- DB2 UDB for Z/OS 7.1

The parameters specific to LWWCM are shown in Table 9.5.

Table 9.5: Web Content Management-Specific Properties

Property	Description	Value
WcmEncoding	Flag that sets the default encoding for the site. Possible values are: UTF-8, Shift_JIS, EUC_KR, GB2312, and Big5	UTF-8
WcmMgrPersistence	CM for IBM Content Manager or JDBC for a database	JDBC
WcmResPersistence	CM for IBM Content Manager or JDBC for a database	JDBC
WcmTable	Optional parameter to name the database table that manages WCM items	AJPE

Table 9.5: Web Content Management-Specific Properties (continued)

Property	Description	Value
WcmResourceTable	Optional parameter to name the database table that manages WCM resources	AJPE_RESOURCES
WcmReadAhead	Number of items to read ahead	Do not change
WcmResourceMaxSize	Size in MB used to allocate space within a database for WCM resources	
WcmDbType	Type of database to use as a WCM repository. Possible values: db2, oracle, sqlserver, cloudscape, db2_zos	db2
WcmDbName	Database name for the WCM repository	WCMDB
WcmDbSchema	Schema name for the WCM repository	
WcmDbUser	User name that can connect to the database	db2admin
WcmDbPassword	Password of the user who can connect to the database	<password>
WcmAdminGroup-IdShort	WCM administrators group ID defined in WebSphere Portal	Wcmadmins
WcmDbUrl	The URL to the database used to store WCM data	db2:jdbc:db2:WCMDB
WcmFileSystemData-Location	Location of the file system data directory to transfer	
WcmDbDriver	JDBC provider class name	COM.ibm.db2.jdbc.app.Db2 Driver
WcmDbDriverDs	Data source of the class (z/OS only)	
WcmDsName	Data source to be used (z/OS only)	
WcmDbLibrary	Directory and name of the zip file containing the driver class	<SQLLIB>/java/db2java.zip
WcmDbNativeLibrary	Native DB2 library directory (z/OS only)	
WcmDbSqljProperties	Path name of the DB2 JDBC property file (z/OS only)	

Once the properties are modified and saved in wpconfig.properties, you can run the specific task to configure WCM. Make sure WebSphere_Portal has been stopped. Change to the <WPS_HOME>/config directory and run the task as shown.

```
WPSconfig config-wcm-repository
```

Look for a *Build successful* message. Just to be safe, you might want to remove any existing data repository first by running the remove-wcm-repository task:

```
WPSconfig remove-wcm-repository
```

LWWCM Portlets

Three portlets are shipped with WebSphere Portal related to LWWCM:

- *Authoring portlet*—The user interface for LWWCM used to create, edit, and manage all WCM items.
- *Local Rendering portlet*—Used to display WCM content within a portlet. This portlet is used with the same instance of WebSphere Portal that LWWCM is installed with.
- *Remote Rendering Portlet*—Used to display WCM content within a portlet located on a different WebSphere Portal server.

To install the Authoring and Local Rendering portlets. you must run the Authoring Portlet Configuration task using the WPSconfig utility as shown:

```
WPSconfig configure-wcm-authoring
```

As usual, make sure you get the *Build successful* message. Now, when you log into the portal, you should see a new portal menu item called Web Content Management. Clicking on that will display two subpages, Authoring and Content Preview. The default view of the Web Content Authoring portlet is shown in Figure 9.11.

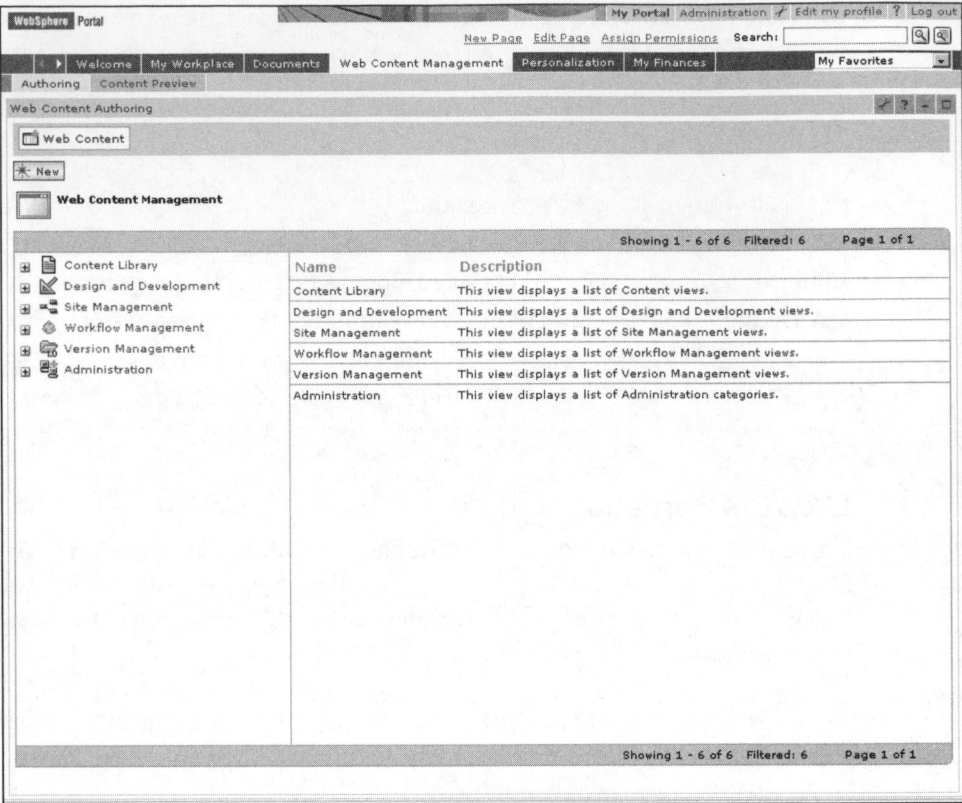

Figure 9.11: Default view of Web Content Management Authoring Portlet.

Tip: You could also bring up the Authoring page by going directly to the servlet URL: http:// <HOST_NAME>:9080/wps/myportal/wcmAuthoring.

Configuration and Architecture Notes

LWWCM uses a set of configuration files to customize the behavior of the various features. The following files are used to configure a WCM solution; these files are found in the <WPS_HOME>/wcm/config folder:

- *connect.cfg*—Used to configure different parameters relating to WCM application and Authoring Portlet.
- *aptrixjpe.properties*—Used to configure parameters relating to Authoring and Content Portlet.
- *aptrixsearch.properties*—Used to set parameters used by the Search Module.

Architecturally, LWWCM includes two distinct environments, Authoring and Delivery. In the Authoring environment content authors create, add, and update portal content. The Delivery environment covers the dissemination of content to portal users. This is the Basic Architecture. See the note about a clustered environment at the end of this chapter.

Sometimes, enterprises break this Basic Architecture into three environments by adding a Staging system. This third LWWCM server sits between the Authoring and Delivery environment, thus matching the various roles. A Staging server is mostly used to aggregate changes to a Web site over time and batch publish it to the Delivery server. A Staging server also is used to aggregate content from multiple Authoring servers before syndicating to a Delivery server. Content flows automatically from the Authoring to the Staging and Delivery systems.

The Authoring System is the source of change and is typically used only by the content authors. Content *authors* create content via the use of templates and resource components. Content *developers*, on the other hand, create Sites and Site Areas.

Tip: A WCM portlet can be accessed by anonymous users, if the portal server is configured to have anonymous sessions. This is done by setting the public.session=true in NavigatorService.properties file. This file is found in the <WPS_HOME>/shared/app/config/services folder.

Authoring Portlet Sample

The online help system contains excellent WCM examples. The one described here is a simple Site Creation Example. This example renders a simple Web page by creating and linking various WCM items. Broadly, the steps require you to create the following:

- A Simple Workflow
- A Site and Site Area
- A Presentation Template
- An Authoring Template
- A Content Item
- Components

The assumption here is that you are logged in as the portal administrator (wpsadmin) and wpsadmin is a member of the group, wcmadmins.

Create a Simple Workflow

1. Click on **Workflow Management** in the navigation pane of the Web Content Authoring Portlet.
2. Select **Workflow Stages** and click the **New** button.
3. Choose **Workflow Stage** from the drop-down list and click **OK**.
4. Enter a **Name** to identify the workflow. We called our sample workflow ourTest Stage.
5. In the Properties section, click **Select Actions** under Execute on Entering Stage and select **Publish**.
6. Accept all the other defaults and click **Save**. You should see a message *ourTest Stage was saved successfully*. See Figure 9.12.

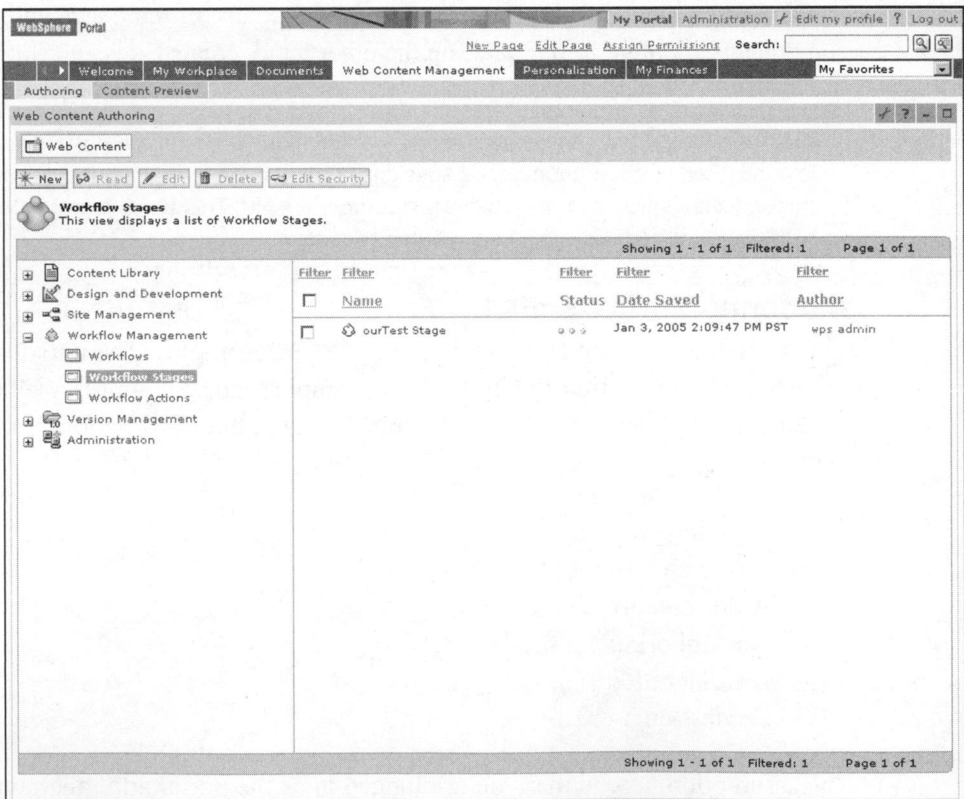

Figure 9.12: Screen showing a newly created Workflow Stage.

7. Select **Workflows** in the navigation pane and click the **New** button.

8. Make sure Workflow is selected. Click **OK**.

9. Two fields are required, Name and Workflow Stages. Name the workflow ourWorkflow and make sure you choose the stage (ourTest Stage) that was created in the previous step.

10. Click **OK**. Then click **Save and Close**. The newly created ourWorkflow should be displayed in the list of Workflows.

Create a Site

1. Click on **Site Management** in the navigation pane of the Web Content Authoring Portlet.

2. Select **Site Framework** and click the **New** button.

3. Make sure Site is selected. Click **OK**.

4. Enter a Name to identify the site. We called our sample site ourSite.

5. Then click **Save and Close**. The newly created ourSite should be displayed in the list of Sites.

6. It is not imperative to create a Site Area, but we recommend you do. Select **Site Areas by Title** in the navigation pane and click **New**.

7. Make sure Site Area is selected. Click **OK**.

8. Select the newly created ourSite. Keep the Link Order as Start and click **OK**.

9. Enter a Name to identify the Site Area. We called our sample site area ourSite Area. You should now have a Site Area (ourSite Area) with a Site (ourSite) as its parent, as seen in Figure 9.13.

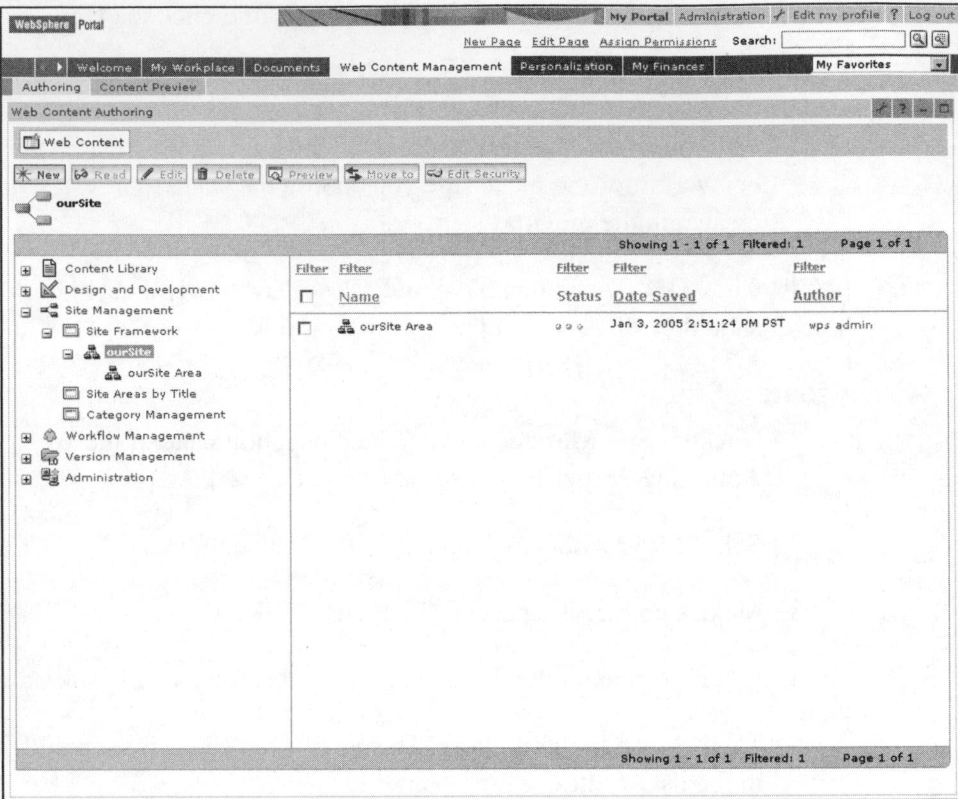

Figure 9.13: Screen showing newly created Site and Site Area.

Create a Presentation Template

1. Click on **Design and Development** in the navigation pane of the Web Content Authoring Portlet.

2. Select **Presentation Templates** and click the **New** button.

3. Make sure Presentation Template is selected. Click **OK**.

4. Enter a Name to identify the site. We called the site ourPTemplate.

5. Add the HTML code shown below. Figure 9.14. is the actual screenshot of the code box in the Web Content Authoring Portlet.

```
<html>
<head></head>
<body TEXT="Black" BGCOLOR="White" BACKGROUND="" LEFTMARGIN="0"
RIGHTMARGIN="0" TOPMARGIN="0" BOTTOMMARGIN="0">

<table width="100%" border="1">
<tr>
<td></td>
<td></td>
<td></td>
</tr>
</table>

</body>
</html>
```

Figure 9.14: HTML code added to the Presentation Template.

6. Then click **Save and Close**. You should see a message *ourPTemplate was saved successfully*.

7. The newly created ourPTemplate should be displayed in the list of Presentation Templates.

Note: Presentation Templates can only be viewed and tested after a Content Item has been created and associated with the Presentation Template you wish to view.

Create an Authoring Template

1. Click on **Design and Development** in the navigation pane of the Web Content Authoring Portlet.

2. Select **Authoring Templates** and click the **New** button.

3. Make sure Authoring Template is selected. Click **OK**.

4. Enter a Name to identify the site. We called this template ourATemplate.

5. Click the **Component Manager** button. Then Add a Text Component called ourBody (Figure 9.15). Click **OK**.

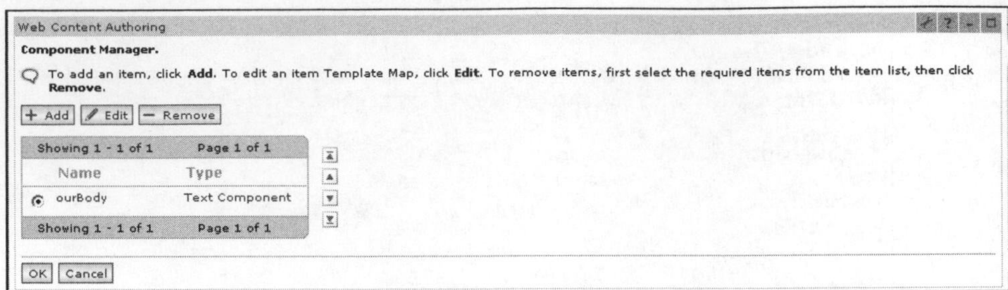

Figure 9.15: Adding a Text Component to the Authoring Template.

6. **Save and Close** the Authoring Template. You should see a message *ourATemplate was saved successfully*.

7. The newly created ourATemplate should be displayed in the list of Authoring Templates.

Create a Content Item

1. Click on **Content Library** in the navigation pane of the Web Content Authoring Portlet.

2. Select **Content By Title** and click the **New** button.

3. Make sure Content is selected. Click **OK**.

4. Make sure you select the Authoring Template that was created—ourATemplate. Select the Site that you created—ourSite. And select the Site Area—ourSite Area.

5. Accept the Link Order as Start. Click **OK**.

6. Two fields are required, Name and Workflow. We named this content item ourContent. Make sure you choose the workflow (ourWorkflow) that was created in a prior step.

7. Enter some text in the text component called ourBody. We entered the following: *This is our Content Item demonstrating WCM in WebSphere Portal V5.1.*

8. Then click **Save and Close**. You should see a message *ourContent was saved successfully*.

9. The newly created ourContent should be displayed in the list of Content by Title.

Create Components

1. In the Web Content Authoring portlet traverse down to **Site Management → Site Framework → ourSite.**

2. Select **ourSite Area** and click **Edit.**

3. In the Edit panel, click **Select Default Content**. Choose ourContent and click **OK**.

4. In the Edit panel, click **Edit Template Mapping**. Click **Add**. Associate a Presentation Template to an Authoring Template for this Site Area by selecting ourATemplate and ourPTemplate. Then click **OK.**

5. Click **OK** again on the Template Mapping screen.

6. The Edit panel should look similar to that shown in Figure 9.16. Click **Save and Close**.

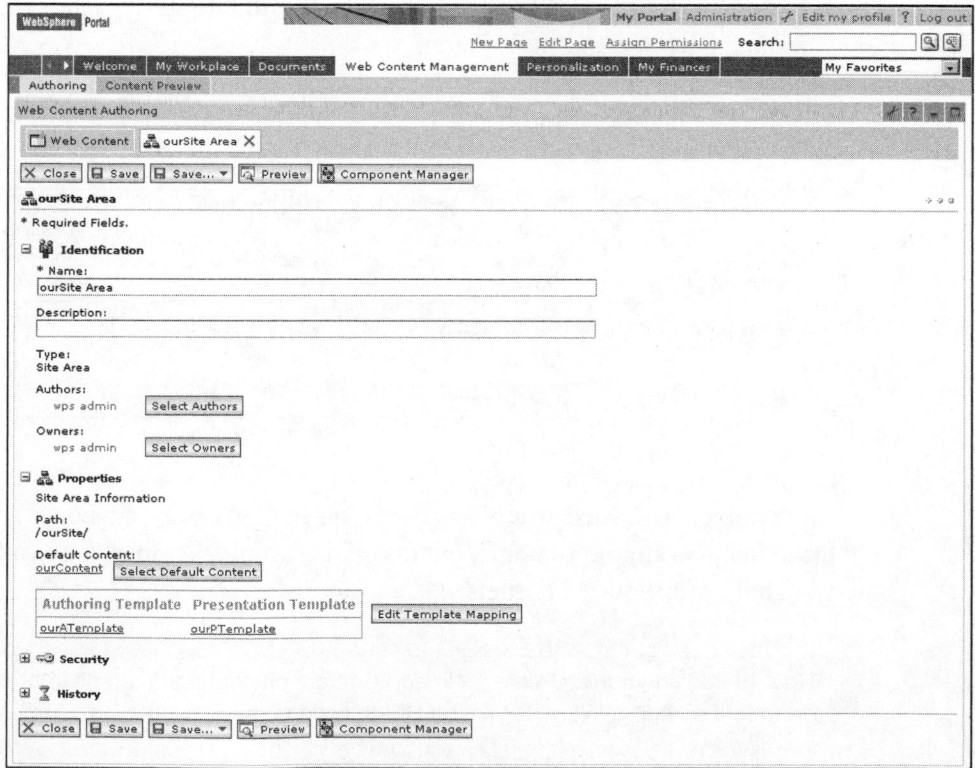

Figure 9.16: Site Area Edit screen.

7. Traverse down to **Design and Development → Presentation Templates**. Then select ourPTemplate and click the Edit button.

8. Enter the following Web Content Management Tag into one of the Table Cells of the Presentation Template HTML code. Using "current" as the context means that the content of this WCM Tag will change depending on which Content Item is currently being referenced:

```
<AptrixCmpnt type="Content" context="current" key="ourBody"/>
```

9. Click **Save and Close**.

Preview Web Page

1. In the Web Content Authoring portlet, traverse down to **Content Library → Content by Site Area → ourSite → ourSite Area**. Select our Content and click the **Preview** button.

2. If all the mappings are correct, you should see the Web page shown in Figure 9.17.

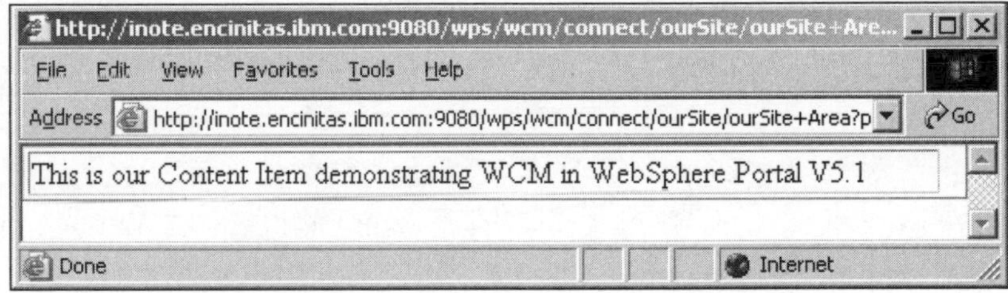

Figure 9.17: Content Preview screen.

Other components, such as a Navigator or an Image, can be added and previewed. This is just one simple example, but other interesting examples are available in the online help of LWWCM portlets.

Tip: To add an image: Create an Image Component first and map an image file to it, then add a WCM Tag to the HTML code in the Presentation Template, as shown:

```
<AptrixCmpnt type="ourImage" />
```

If you preview the Site Area, the Web page should look something like that shown in Figure 9.18.

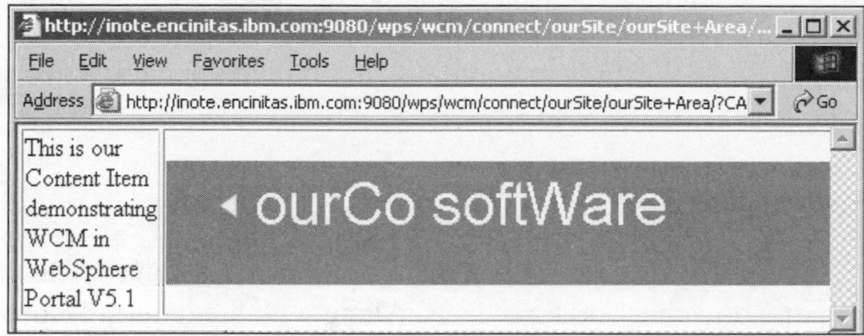

Figure 9.18: Content Preview screen showing the added Image component.

WCM Clustering Notes

Web Content Management applications cannot be clustered themselves, but they can be installed in a clustered environment. A Web Content Management application cannot be used as an "authoring application" in a clustered environment. It can only be used as a staging or delivery application. This means that although the Authoring Portlet is installed on Web Content Management staging and delivery applications in a clustered environment, you cannot use the Authoring Portlet to author content.

On staging and delivery applications, the Authoring portlet is only used to manage syndication and caching. Each Web Content Management application installed in a clustered environment must use a separate data repository. Syndication must be used to keep each Web Content Management application synchronized.

Tip: On the primary node, WCM is installed under <WPS_HOME>/wcm folder. On the secondary node, the WCM folder is usually <WPS_HOME>/wcm2.

If, at any stage, you remove a Web Content Management Application from a cluster, you will need to do the following:

- Edit the wpconfig.properties file that is located under the <WPS_HOME>/config folder and ensure that DbSafeMode=false.
- Edit the DeploymentService.properties file that is located under the <WPS_HOME>/shared/app/config/services folder and ensure that wps.appserver.name=WebSphere_Portal.

Refer to the WebSphere Portal product Infocenter for detailed steps about creating WCM clusters.

Door Closings

Content Management and Collaboration are two features that set WebSphere Portal apart from other portal products. Along with the built-in Document Manager, everything that portal users need by way of content creation, deployment, and management is well integrated within the product. Lotus Workplace Web Content Management is one of the components in WebSphere Portal and delivers end-to-end Web content management in the portal. Collaboration takes on a whole new meaning with products like Lotus Instant Messaging and Web Conferencing and Lotus Team Workplaces. As far as we know, no other portal product offers the kind of collaboration that WebSphere Portal does.

Chapter 10
Portal Crossings

How does one go about converting an existing Web client into a portlet? Or as some people have started to call it, How do you "portletize an application?" Although no silver bullet exists, this chapter shows you some ways of doing this without having to write code, and it points out the things to watch out for. We will take a look at a couple of quick ways of "portletizing" Web artifacts by using the Web Clipper and the Web Page portlet. Some of the common out-of-box portlets are discussed in this chapter, including the powerful cooperative portlets, commonly referred to as *click-to-action* (C2A) portlets.

You will also learn about virtual portals, one of the newest and probably the most anticipated features of WebSphere Portal V5.1. Finally, we talk about Web Services and discuss how Web Services for Remote Portlets (WSRP) is implemented in WebSphere Portal. The chapter closes with a brief discussion of multilingual portlets.

Out-of-Box Portlets

Table 10.1 lists all the portlet applications (WAR files) installed by default during WebSphere Portal Server installation. The number of portlets has drastically increased in this version of WebSphere Portal. This chapter concentrates on those that are well-suited to bringing existing Web artifacts up in a portal.

Table 10.1: Portlet Applications and the Contained Portlets

WAR File Name	Portlets Contained in the WAR File
Managepages.war	Manage Pages Organize Favorites
lwppeoplefinder.war	People Finder
pickerPortlet.war	Directory Search
ServletInvoker.war	ServletInvoker
MarkupsManager.war	Manage Markups
ImportXML.war	Import XML
LotusWebConferencing.war	Lotus Web Conferencing
appearance.war	Appearance portlet
JspServer.war	JSP Server
ClientsManager.war	Manage Clients
mylist.war	My To Dos
ManageVirtualPortals.war	Virtual Portal Manager
Tracing.war	Enable Tracing
pdm.war	Document Manager
Properties.war	Page Properties
QuickLinks.war	QuickLinks
WebPortlets.war	Web Clipping Editor WebPortlet HTML Template
newsgroup.war	Newsgroups
dominowebaccess.war	Domino Web Access
docviewer.war	Word Document Viewer Excel Document Viewer PDF Document Viewer Rich Text Document Viewer PowerPoint Document Viewer
UniqueNames.war	Manage Custom Unique Names
ManageLibraries.war	Manage Document Libraries
FileServer.war	FileServer
DeppWelcome.war	Domino Extended Products Welcome
reminder.war	Reminder

Table 10.1: Portlet Applications and the Contained Portlets (continued)

WAR File Name	Portlets Contained in the WAR File
worldclock.war	World Clock
ManageWebservices.war	Web Service Configuration
tpl.war	EIP Federated Search EIP Advanced Search
LotusMyTeamWorkplaces.war	My Lotus Team Workplaces
xslt.war	RSS Portlet
PortletManager.war	Manage Applications Manage Portlets Manage Web Modules
Blurb.war	Information Portlet Welcome to WebSphere Portal
urlmapping.war	URL mapping portlet
portletWiring.war	Portlet Wiring Tool
SametimeWhoIsHere.war	Who Is Here
selfcare.war	Edit My Profile
Bookmarks.war	Themes and Skins
ThemesAndSkinsManager.war	SQL
CPPCalendar.war	Calendar
sql.war	My Query Reports
CPPMail.war	Mail
BOBuilderPortlet.war	Portlet Builder for Domino JDBC Business Object Builder
contentlayout.war	Edit Layout
bannerad.war	Banner Ad
ManagePrincipals.war	Manage Users and Groups
csv.war	CSV File Viewer
DominoStruts.war	Domino Template Domino Data Form Viewer Domino Iframe Viewer
TasksPortlet.war	My Tasks
SametimeContactList.war	Sametime Contact List

Table 10.1: Portlet Applications and the Contained Portlets (continued)

WAR File Name	Portlets Contained in the WAR File
login.war	Login Portlet
ResourceView.war	User and Group Permissions Resource Permissions
Settings.war	Global Settings
Exchange3.war	Microsoft Exchange Contacts Microsoft Exchange Calendar Microsoft Exchange Mail Microsoft Exchange Tasks Microsoft Exchange Notes
SetPermissionsPortlets.war	Page Locks
pznruleportlet.war	Personalized List
SearchAdmin.war	ManageSeed List Pending Search Collection Items Manage Search and Browse Manage Search Collections
FrequentUsers.war	FrequentUsers
SpellCheckerService.war	Spell Checker Portlet
MarketWatch.war	My Weather My News My Vertical News My StocksCurrency Calculator CT Chart CT Stock Company Tracker CT Profile CT News Retirement Planner
SearchAndBrowse.war	Search and Browse
WelcomePortlet.war	About WebSphere Portal
BusinessObjectFrameStruts.war	Business Object Framework
CredentialAdministration.war	Credential Vault
Ilwwcm-localrendering-portlet.war	Web Content Viewer
pznauthorportlet.war	Personalization Navigator Personalization Editor
docPicker.war	Document Picker
notes2.war	Lotus Notes View

WebSphere Portal Server provides some out-of-box portlets that let you convert all or part of an existing Web page into a portlet. These portlets provide basic functionality, such as serving static HTML or JSP files, or providing the functionality to integrate a news feed (serving the news feed in RSS format).

FileServer Portlet

The FileServer portlet can display any static HTML file in the portlet window. By default, this portlet serves up the contents of a file called test.html, which is located in the /FileServerPortlet/html directory of the portlet's WAR file. To serve any other HTML file, you have to copy that file to the /FileServerPortlet/html directory and then modify the portlet's URL parameter to point to the new file.

The steps to change the portlet to serve any other HTML file instead of default test.html are as follows:

1. Copy the file (help-doc.html) to the FileServer portlet's HTML directory, the location of which is shown below:

   ```
   <WPS_HOME>/installedApps/FileServer_<portlet_id>.ear/FileServer.
   war/FileServerPortlet/html
   ```

   where <portlet_id> is a unique identifier created during the installation of the portlet.

2. Log in to the portal as the Portal Administrator (wpsadmin). Under Administration, navigate to **Portlet Management → Portlets**.

3. Search for and select **FileServer** from the list of portlets. Then click the **Configure** icon (wrench) to edit the parameters of the portlet.

4. Delete the ozld URL parameter by clicking the **Delete** icon. Add a new URL parameter to point to /FileServerPortlet/html/help-doc.html, as shown in Figure 10.1.

5. Click **OK**. You should see a message *EJPAQ3309I*: *Successfully saved changes to portlet FileServer.*

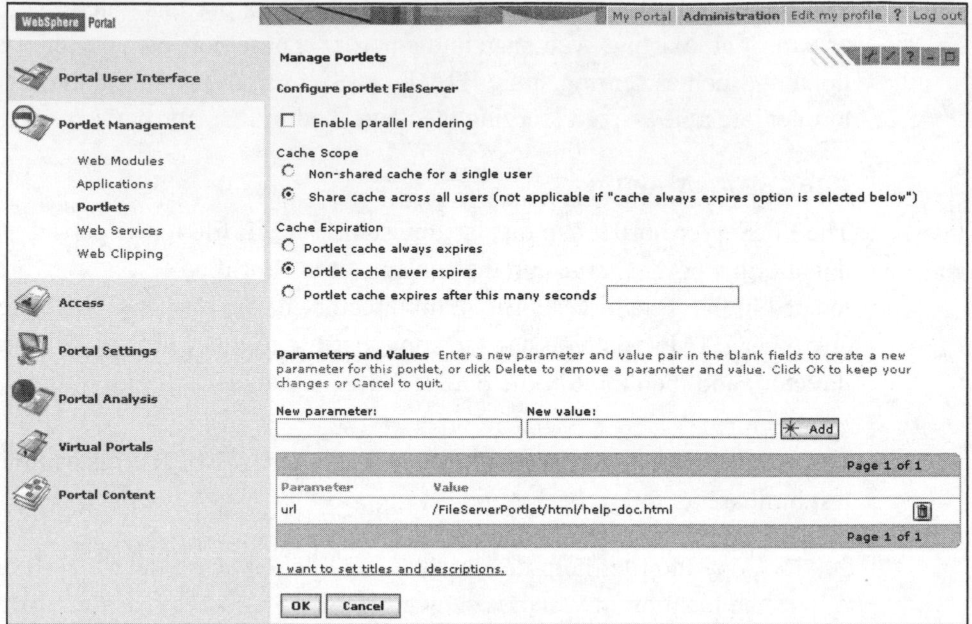

Figure 10.1: New URL parameter for FileServer portlet.

6.Load the portal page where you had placed the FileServer portlet. The portlet should now display the new HTML file, as shown in Figure 10.2.

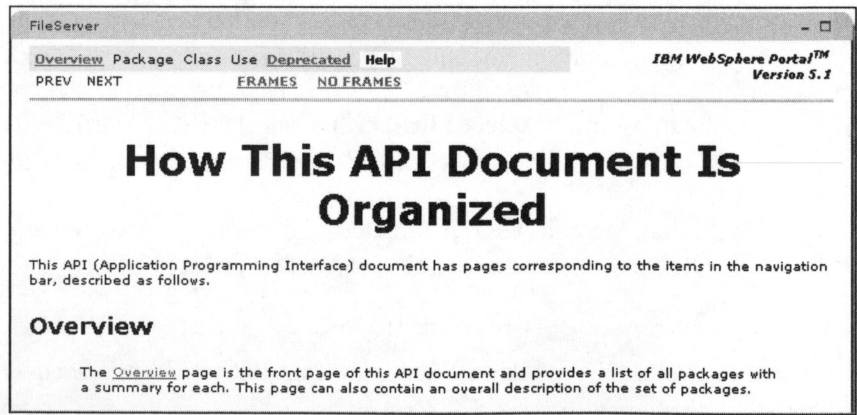

Figure 10.2: The FileServer portlet serving a new HTML file.

JSP Portlet

The JspServer portlet will display any Java Server Page (JSP) in the portlet window. By default, this portlet serves up the contents of a file called very_simple.jsp, which is located in the JSP directory of the portlet's WAR file.

This portlet works the same way as FileServer. To make the portlet serve another JSP, the steps are as follows:

1. Copy the JSP file (my_simple.jsp) to the JspServer portlet's JSP directory, the location of which is shown below:

```
<WPS_HOME>/installedApps/JSPServer_<portlet_id>.ear/JspServer.
war/jsp
```

where <portlet_id> is a unique identifier created during the installation of the portlet.

2. Log into the portal as the Portal Administrator (wpsadmin). Under Administration, navigate to **Portlet Management → Portlets**.

3. Search for and select **JspServer** from the list of portlets. Then click the **Configure** icon (wrench) to edit the parameters of the portlet.

4. Delete the old URL parameter by clicking the **Delete** icon. Add a new URL parameter to point to /JSP/my_simple.jsp.

5. Click **OK**. You should see a message *EJPAQ3309I*: *Successfully saved changes to JSP Server.*

6. Load the portal page where you had placed the JspServer portlet. The portlet should now display the new JSP file, as shown in Figure 10.2.

Next, change the URL parameter to point to the new JSP file, as follows:

7. Select **JspServer** from the list of portlets, and click **Modify Parameters**.

8. Modify the URL parameter to point to the new JSP file and click **Save**.

9. Display the page that has the JSPServer portlet deployed. You should see the portlet shown in Figure 10.3.

Figure 10.3: JspServer portlet showing new JSP file.

Here is the JSP code that produced the output in the portlet:

```
<%@ page import="org.apache.jetspeed.portlet.*" %>
<%@ page import="org.apache.jetspeed.portletcontainer.*" %>
<%@ page import="com.ibm.wps.portlets.*" %>

<%@ taglib uri="/WEB-INF/tld/portlet.tld" prefix="portletAPI" %>
<portletAPI:init/>

<html>
<body>
<B>You are logged in as <%=portletRequest.getUser(*).getUserID() %>
</B>

</body>
</html>
```

ServletInvoker Portlet

ServletInvoker invokes any servlet as a portlet. As with FileServer and JspPortlet, to invoke any servlet as a portlet, you have to change the URL parameter to point to the servlet. The steps for changing the URL for the ServletInvoker portlet are as follows:

1. Log into the portal as the Portal Administrator (wpsadmin). Under Administration, navigate to the **Portlet Management → Portlets**.
2. Search for and select **ServletInvoker** from the list of portlets. Click the **Configure** icon (wrench) to edit the parameters of the portlet.
3. Modify the URL parameter to point to a known servlet. In our case, we pointed to the snoop servlets running in the default server of WebSphere Application Server, as shown in Figure 10.4. Click **OK** to save the configuration. The following message is displayed: *EJPAQ3309I: Successfully saved changes to portlet ServletInvoker.*
4. Now deploy the portlet on a page, and the referenced servlet should be displayed inside of the portlet.

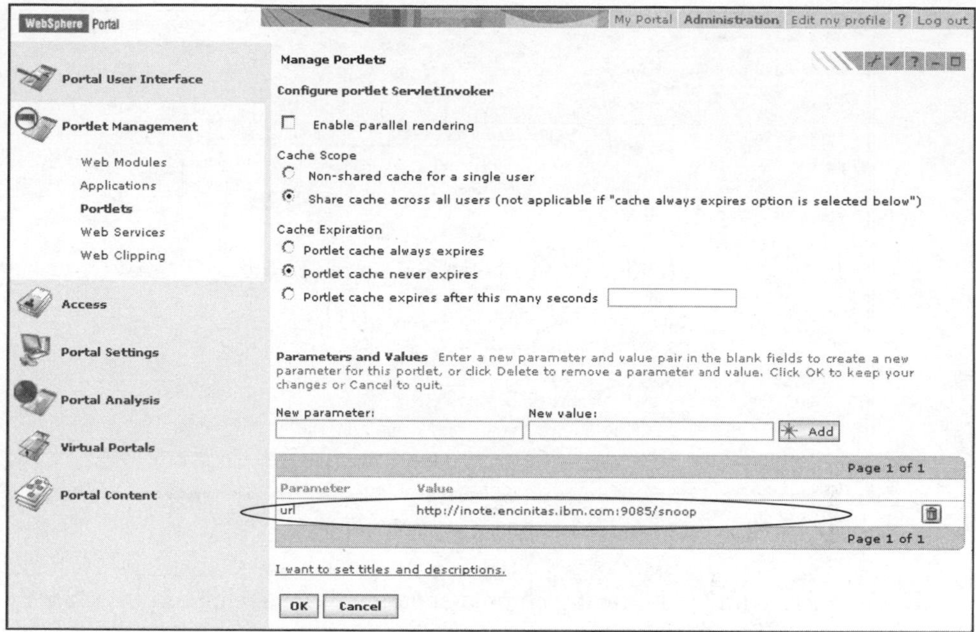

Figure 10.4: ServletInvoker portlet configuration screen.

FileServer, JspServer, and ServletInvoker are examples of portlets that easily "portletize" existing Web artifacts. This might not work for complicated JSPs or servlets, and it is not recommended in every scenario, but it is the first step in displaying existing JSPs, servlets, and HTML files in a portal framework.

CSV File Viewer Portlet

The CSV File Viewer portlet displays a file with data that uses a comma as the delimiter. Comma-separated values (CVS) is a simple ASCII file format for storing data in tabular form. Each line in a CSV file represents a row in a table. The values in each line, which are separated by commas, map to columns in the table. Here are the steps to configure the CSV File Viewer after it has been deployed:

1. Click the **Edit** button of the CSV File Viewer portlet by clicking the **Edit (the pencil icon)** icon.

2. Enter the URL of the CSV file, as shown in Figure 10.5.

3. Click **Save**.

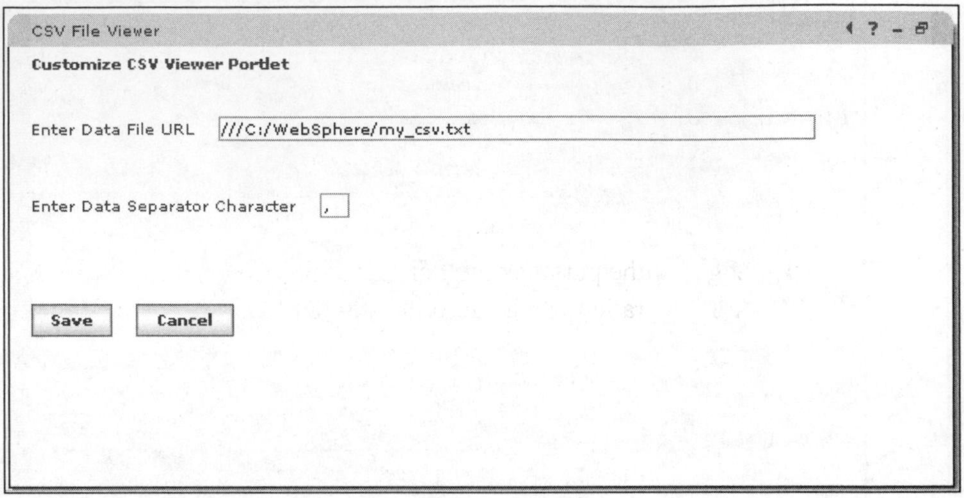

CSV File Viewer

Customize CSV Viewer Portlet

Enter Data File URL ///C:/WebSphere/my_csv.txt

Enter Data Separator Character ,

Save Cancel

Figure 10.5: CSV File Viewer portlet edit screen.

Using a file with the following comma-separated data as input to the CSV File Viewer portlet produces the results displayed in Figure 10.6:

```
userid,password,firstname,last name,balance,
user1,user1,user1,user1,89,
user2,user2,user2,user2,1002,
user3,user3,user3,user3,107,
user4,user4,user4,user4,55000
user5,user5,user5,user5,11101
user6,user6,user6,user6,9999
```

Note: By default, the comma is the data separator character. However, this is a configurable parameter in the portlet's edit screen. You could use any other separators, like a semicolon, a question mark, or even a space.

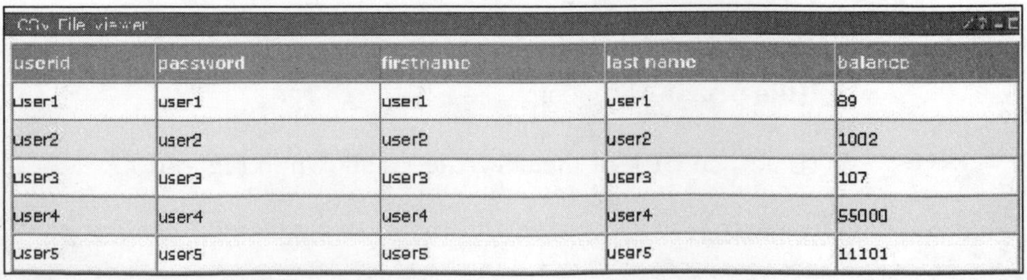

CSV File Viewer

userid	password	firstname	last name	balance
user1	user1	user1	user1	89
user2	user2	user2	user2	1002
user3	user3	user3	user3	107
user4	user4	user4	user4	55000
user5	user5	user5	user5	11101

Figure 10.6: CSV File Viewer portlet.

XSLT Portlet

The eXtensible Stylesheet Language Transformation (XSLT) portlet or the Rich Site Summary (RSS) portlet will display remote URLs that provide data using RSS. RSS is a lightweight XML format designed to syndicate headlines so that Web sites or applications can include them. Here are the steps to use the RSS portlet to display content:

1. Log into the portal as the Portal Administrator (wpsadmin). Under Administration, navigate to the **Portlet Management → Portlets**.

2. Click the **Configure** (wrench) icon.

3. Delete the old URL parameter by clicking the **Delete** icon. Add a new URL parameter to point that will return news in RSS format. The example in Figure 10.7 points to http://news.com.com/2547-1_3-0-5.xml, which returns news headlines from CNet.

4. The other parameter is a stylesheet. XML files provide the data; the presentation is specified in an XSL file. The RSS portlet comes with stylesheets for displaying the information as HTML or WML. Use the rss.xsl file for the Stylesheet parameter. (The name of the stylesheet parameter is stylesheet.html for HTML and stylesheet.pda in the case of markup for PDA)

5. Click **OK**. You should see a message that indicates that the changes have been successfully changed.

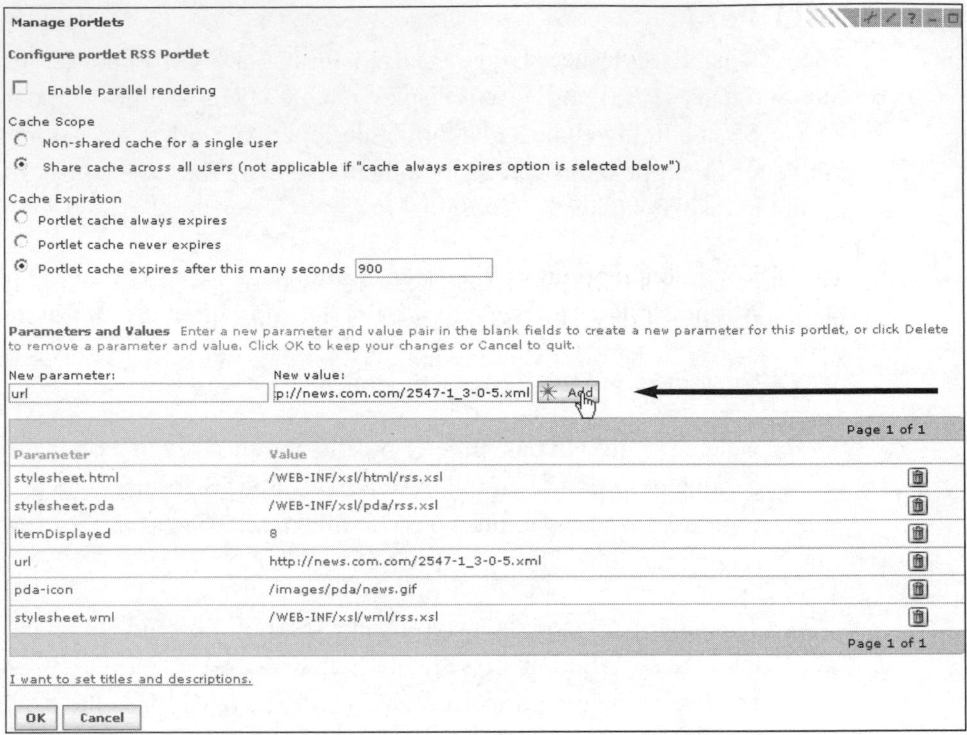

Figure 10.7: Modifying the URL parameter of the RSS portlet.

6. Bring up the page containing the RSS portlet. You should see the CNet news feed inside the portlet, as shown in Figure 10.8.

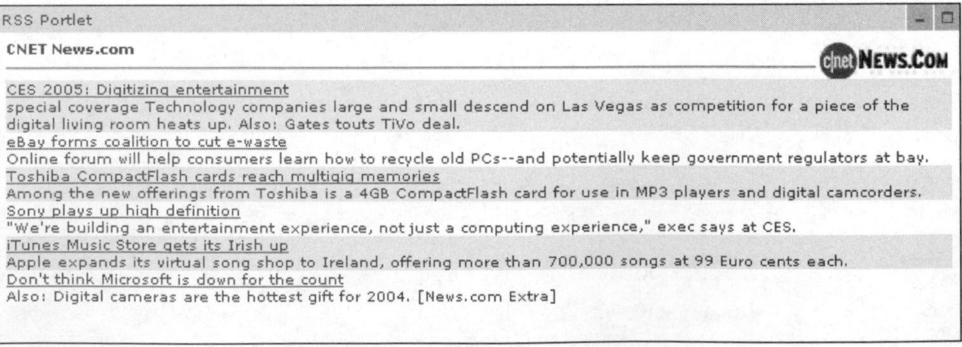

Figure 10.8: RSS portlet, displaying the headlines returned from the Moreover news feed.

If you have a URL that returns data in XML format, and you have a stylesheet for it, the RSS portlet can also be used to display this data. Just change the URL parameter in the portlet to point to any URL that will return data in XML format. Then, depending on what device you are supporting, change the stylesheet.wml or stylesheet.html parameter to point to the URL of the stylesheet. Using an XSL file allows you to change the presentation in the future without having to alter the data.

The three portlets (CSV, XSLT, or RSS) are examples of portlets that format incoming data. If data is to be retrieved from a database or exists in a delimited file, it can easily be presented via the CSV portlet. RSS or XSLT, on the other hand, deal with live data feeds. This is a quick way of getting up-to-date portal content into the site.

Note: Enterprises might have to pay a fee to receive some of the news feeds.

Webpage Portlet

The Webpage portlet enables you to add an existing Web application to a portlet. The Webpage portlet essentially uses an iFrame tag to serve up the URL being pointed to.

There are some disadvantages with iFrame. First, not all browsers support it. Second, there is no way of maintaining the state of the application you are hooking up with, which means that whenever the page gets refreshed or the portlet is minimized or maximized, the portlet goes back to the original screen. Still, this portlet is a good way to integrate existing Web applications into a portal in proof-of-concept situations.

Here are the steps to configure the Webpage portlet:

1. Add the Webpage portlet to a page.

2. Click the **Edit** icon (pencil) in the Webpage portlet title bar.

3. Enter a portlet title and URL, as shown in Figure 10.9. You may adjust the height and width of the portlet. Click **Save**. The contents of the referenced web site will be displayed within the portlet.

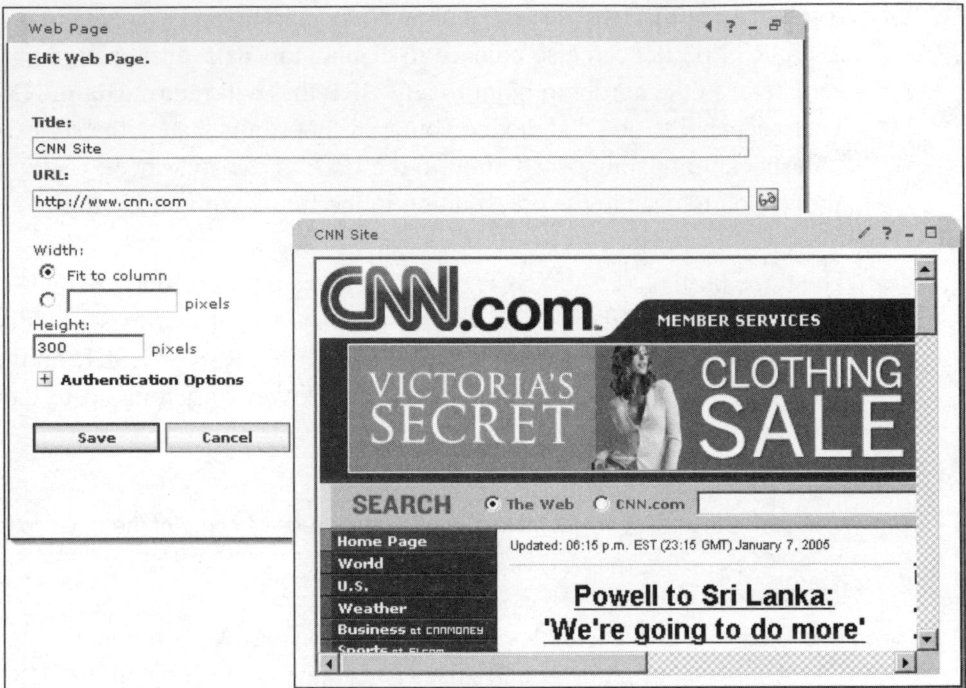

Figure 10.9: Configuring the Webpage portlet to display the CNN Web site.

Document Viewer Portlets

WebSphere Portal ships with a bunch of document viewer portlets. These portlets let you browse Word, Excel, PowerPoint, PDF, or RTF (Rich Text) files. These portlets can be configured to view the files either within the portlet or in another window as long as the browser has the necessary viewer plugins.

The following steps show how to configure the PDF Document Viewer portlet:

1. Select and add the Document Viewer portlet to a page.
2. Click the **Edit** icon (pencil) on the portlet window.
3. Enter a document's URL.
4. Specify whether you want to view the document within the portlet or in a new window. You may adjust the height and width of the portlet. Click **Save**. The referenced document will be displayed.

Figure 10.10 shows the PDF Document Viewer portlet configured to display a PDF file and the resulting view of the portlet.

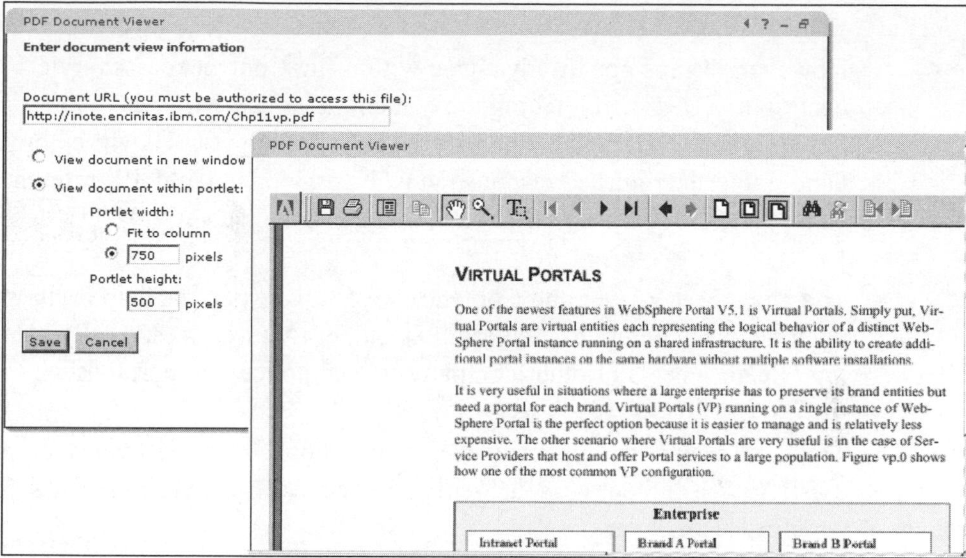

Figure 10.10: Document Viewer portlet displaying a PDF file.

ContentAccessServicePortlet

The Portlet API that comes with WebSphere Portal Server provides ContentAccessService as one of the supported services. It allows you to connect to any external URL from inside a portlet. The code sample below shows how ContentAccessService can be used to log into an external URL using the IBM API:

```
public void doView (RenderRequest request, RenderResponse response )
                        throws PortletException, IOException
{
        ContentAccessService cas = (ContentAccessService)
getPortletConfig().getContext().getService(org.apache.jetspeed.
portlet.service.ContentAccessService.class);
        cas.include ("http://www.yahoo.com", request, response );
}
```

In a JSR 168 compliant portlet, you will need to use JNDI to get a reference to the service.

The ContentAccessService portlet can be used to connect to JSPs or servlets inside an intranet. This service can also be SSL (HTTPS). The only input required is the URL, in HTTP form.

However, there is one disadvantage with using ContentAccessService. After connecting to a URL and fetching the content, it simply writes to the portlet's output. So, any links to any other files or images in the target URL will be broken. To handle this, the returned response must be parsed, and all URL references need to be rewritten so that they point back to the original server.

The Document Viewer and ContentAccessService portlets help bring existing documents or content to the portal. Document Viewer is especially useful in posting HR documents or other company-related notices for portal users.

The next section on Clipper Portlets, truly shows the easiest ways to "portletize" existing Web content without writing any code. These work in browsers that support HTML 4 tags.

Clipper Portlets

Clipping allows the administrator to "copy" content, images, tables, forms, table cells, and more from Web sites. The configuration and location for the clipped content is saved into a portlet that can be administrated like any other portlet.

The ClippingPortlets.war file contains the following portlets:

- Web Clipping
- Web Clipper HTML Template
- Web Clipper Multidevice Template

These portlets are automatically added during the installation process, as administration portlets. Because they are administration portlets, you have to be logged in as the portal administrator to work with them. Actually, a Web Clipping page exists under **Administration → Portlet Management → Web Clipping** where all the work is done, as shown in Figure 10.11. This is where you can add, edit, or delete clipped portlets. Initially, the list of portlets will be empty.

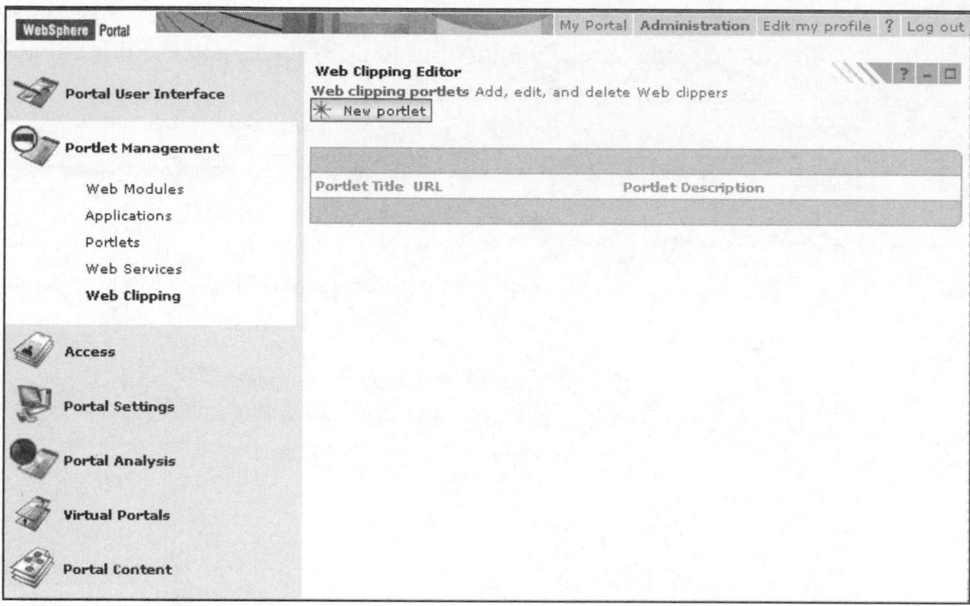

Figure 10.11: Web Clipping screen.

You can capture things that you want inside the "new" portlet in three ways:

- Visually select the components from a Web page
- Take all the contents from a URL
- Specify the contents between a start and end tag

The following examples use http://www.ibm.com as the source for clipped portlets.

Example 1: Visually Selecting HTML Components

To visually select the elements of a Web page that you want to clip, follow these steps:

1. On the Web Clipping page, click **Add**.

2. Enter a name for the portlet, in this case, myclip1, and give it a description. (A description is recommended, but not required.)

3. Specify the URL, http://www.ibm.com. This is the most important step.

4. By default, the connection timeout parameter is set to 5 seconds. If the page tends to take a long time to download, increase this value. In this case, use **100**, as shown in Figure 10.12.

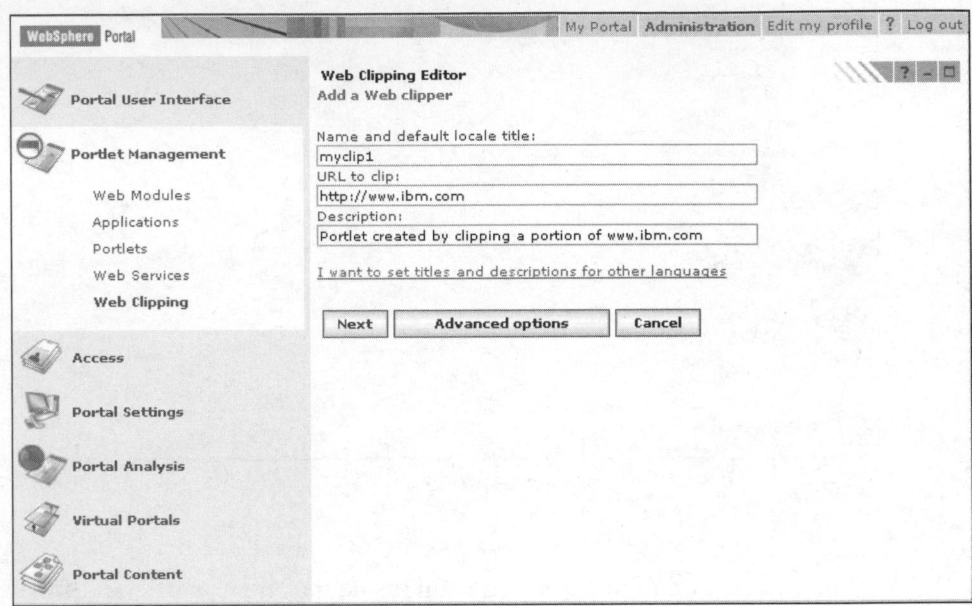

Figure 10.12: Details entered into the Web Clipping Editor portlet.

5. Instead of clicking Next to continue with the process, click the **Advanced options** button and then choose **Modify clipping type**. A screen appears, showing you the three ways of clipping, as shown in Figure 10.13.

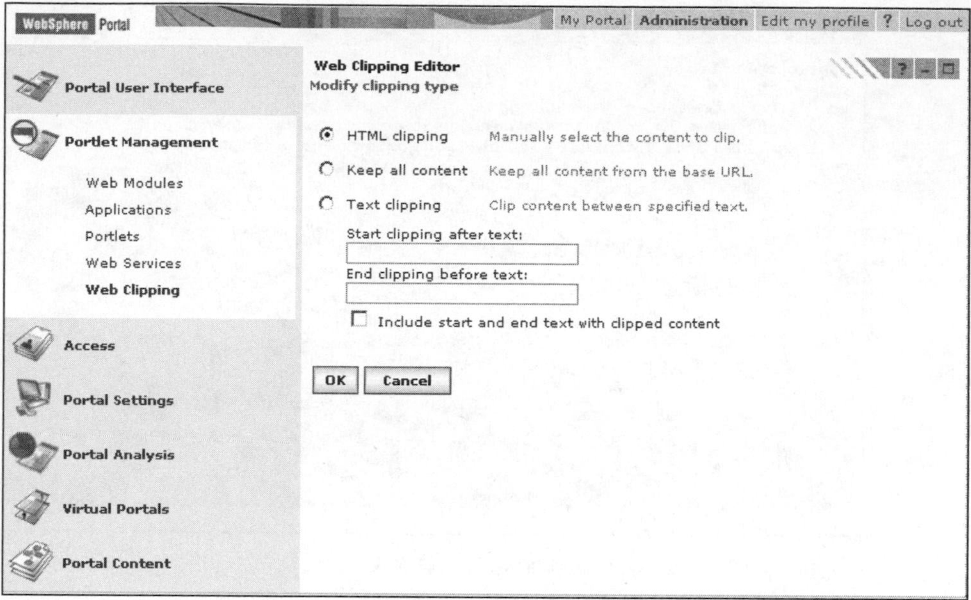

Figure 10.13: Screen showing the different clipping types.

6. The default is to Keep all content. Choose **HTML Clipping**, and click **OK**.

7. You should be back at the Modify Web clipper options page. Click **Next**. That should bring in all the content from the source URL.

8. Move your cursor over items in this URL—graphics, tables, and blocks of text. They are highlighted with a reverse background as you move over them.

9. Click to select content. In our example, we selected the main item. Click the **Preview** icon (eye glasses) to see what has been selected. This pops up a small preview window, as seen in Figure 10.14.

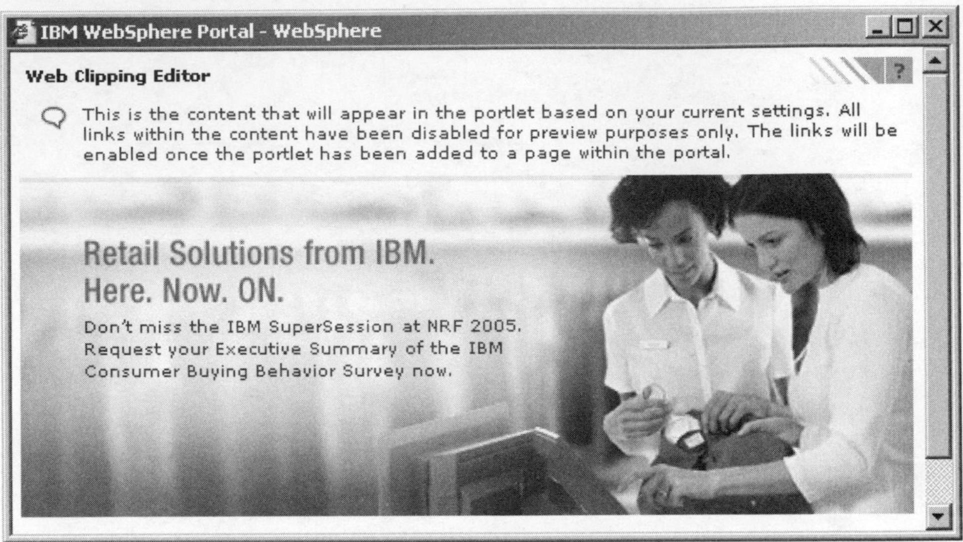

Figure 10.14: Web Clipping preview window.

10. If you are satisfied with what has been selected, close the preview screen by clicking the **X** button on the top right corner of the screen.

11. You may choose other items or click the **Back** button to start over. Click **Next** to continue; on the final screen click **Finish**.

12. If the Web clipper successfully creates the portlet, you will see it listed in the list of Web-clipped portlets, as seen in Figure 10.15.

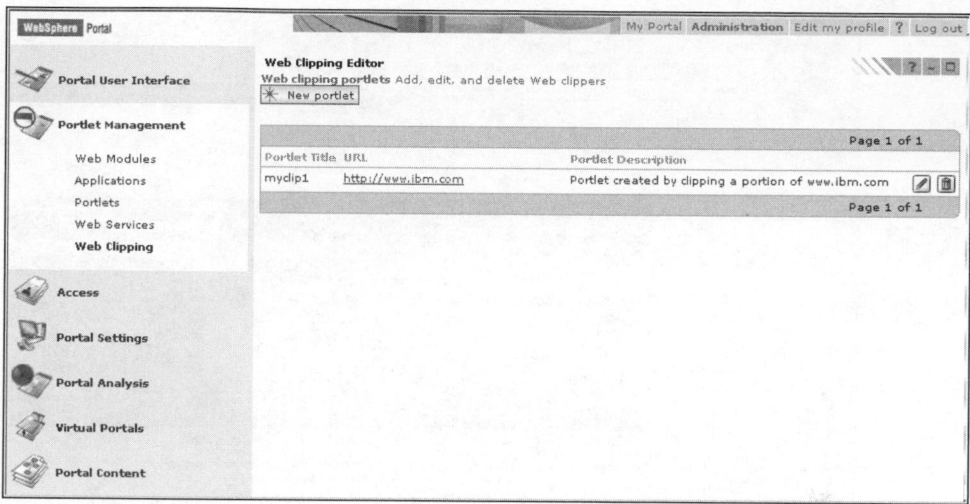

Figure 10.15: List of clipped portlets showing the newly created portlet.

13. You should now have a portlet called myclip1 that is installed and active. Verify this by going to Manage Portlets (**Administration → Portlet Managements → Portlets**) and searching for myclip1.

Example 2: Taking the Entire Contents of a Specified URL

The easiest way of generating a clipped portlet is configuring the clipper to bring in all the contents of a site. The following steps show you how to clip the entire contents of a specified URL:

1. On the Web Clipping page, click **Add**. If nothing was deleted, the Web Clipper box should display myclip1 from example 1.
2. Enter **myclip2** as the (mandatory) name for the portlet, and give it a description (optional).
3. Specify the URL to clip as http://www.ibm.com.
4. Because we know that Keep all content is the default, click **Next**.
5. All the contents from the source URL will be pulled in as one big portlet, as shown in Figure 10.16. Click **Finish**.

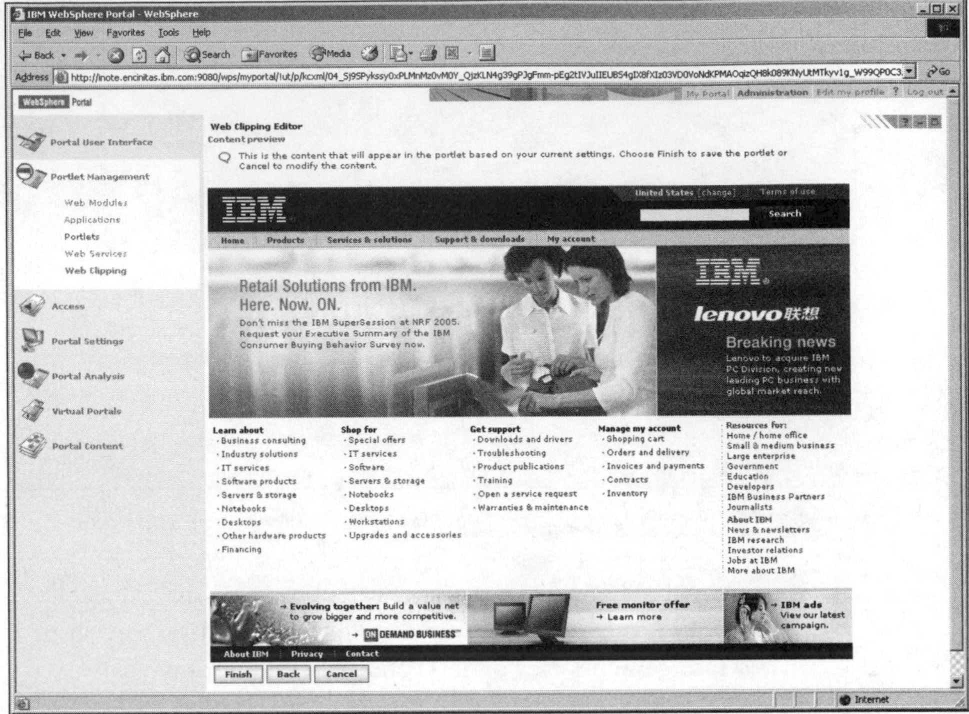

Figure 10.16: Web Clipper Content preview screen, displaying all contents of a URL.

6. You should now have a portlet called myclip2 that is installed, active, and ready for deployment.

Example 3: Using Tags to Take Specific Content from a URL

This is one of the trickiest methods of generating a clipped portlet because you need access to the HTML source. Using the clipper for this scenario becomes easier if the HTML source has good comments.

The following steps explain how to create a clipped portlet using tags or comments:

1. On the Web Clipping page, click **Add**. If nothing was deleted, the Web Clipper box should display myclip1 and myclip2 from examples 1 and 2.

2. Enter **myclip3** as the (mandatory) name for the portlet, and give it a description (optional).

3. Specify the URL to clip as http://www.ibm.com.

4. Click the **Advanced options** button. Select **Modify clipping type**. The screen showing the three ways of clipping is displayed.

5. Select **Text clipping**.

Note: Make sure you can view the source of the URL. Then, jot down the tags between which you want to clip. The HTML code between the tags should not be malformed.

---

6. For the purposes of this example, start clipping from the <table> tag, and end at the </table> tag, thus minimizing the chances of having malformed HTML. If more than one table exists, you will be given the option to choose the items.

7. In the Modify Clipping Type screen, enter the starting and ending HTML tags, as shown in Figure 10.17. Click **OK**.

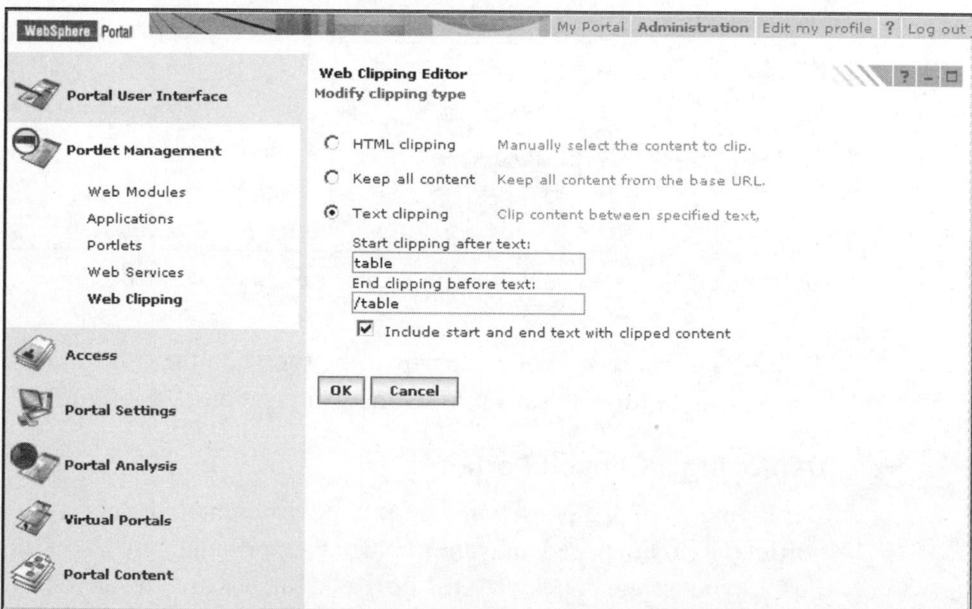

Figure 10.17: Screen to specify text clipping.

8. Click **Next**. All components that fall within those specified tags should be shown in the Content preview screen, as in Figure 10.16. If the tags are incorrect. you could see an error: *EJPHB1041E: No pairs of the start and end text <TAG1> and <TAG2> exist on the page.*

9. Check the item or items you want clipped and click **Next**. As shown in Figure 10.18, we chose the item with the IBM logo.

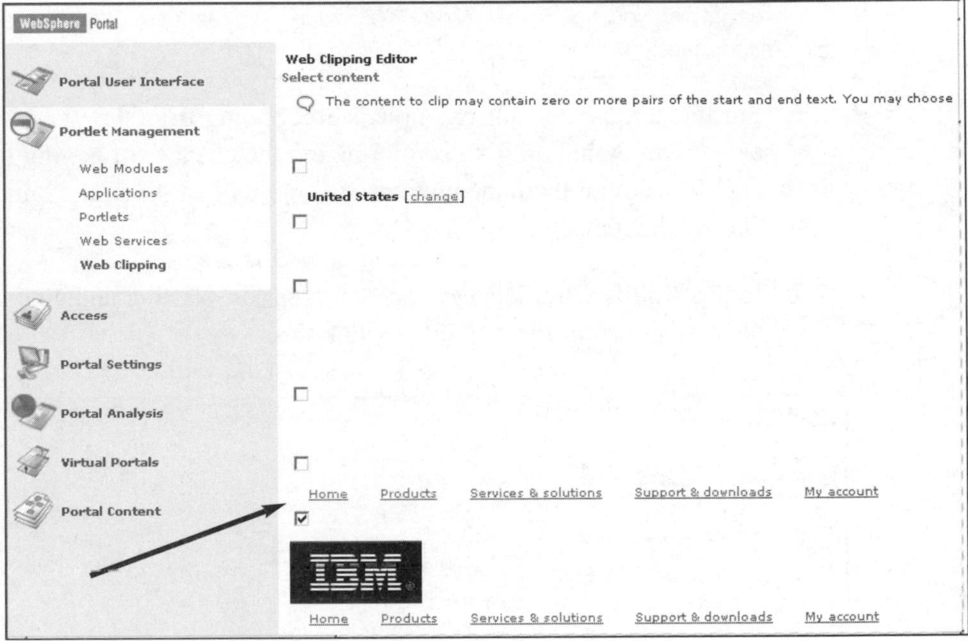

Figure 10.18: Content selection screen during textual web clipping.

10. The specified item or items will be shown in the Content preview screen. Click **Finish** to save it as the new clipped portlet, *myclip3*.

Deploying a Clipped Portlet

Deploying a clipped portlet on a page is no different than deploying any other portlet. Go to the page you want to place the portlet on, click on **Edit Page**. In the Edit Layout screen, click on **Add Portlets**. Then search for myclip. You should see the portlets that were created. Choose the one you want, as shown in Figure 10.19, and click **OK**. Click **Done** to view the portal page.

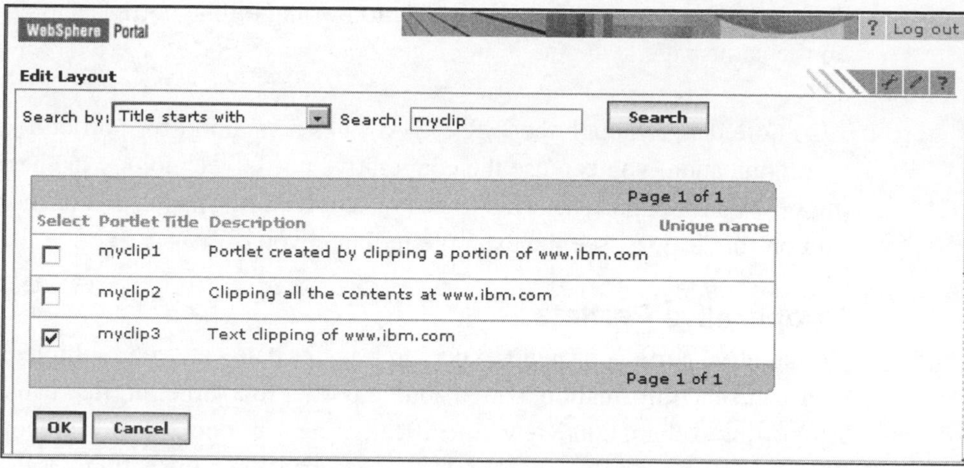

Figure 10.19: Choosing from among the clipped portlets.

Notes on Clipped Portlets

The beauty of clipped portlets is that, if the content on the source URL changes, the Web clipped portlets automatically change. As we just demonstrated, the newly created portlets are automatically installed and ready for deployment. You can select the clipped portlets and add them to a page as you would any other portlet. Furthermore, the titles of these clipped portlets can be modified as you normally would in any other portlet. The downside of clipped portlets is that if the source of the clipped portlet changes, then the portlet may not work anymore.

To delete a clipped portlet, go to the Web Clipping Editor Portlet, click the **Delete** icon (trash can) that pertains to the portlet. On the confirmation screen, click **OK**. If the portlet was deployed on a page and you deleted the portlet, there will be no trace of the clipped portlet on that page.

Portlet-to-Portlet Communication

Wouldn't it be nice if clicking in one portlet changed the view of another portlet? Well, WebSphere Portal Server provides this form of portlet-to-portlet communication in two ways: portlet messaging and cooperative portlets

Portlet Messaging

The Portlet API shipped with WebSphere Portal Server supports messaging between portlets. You can send a message to a particular portlet on a page, or to all the portlets on a page. The only restriction is that all the portlets should be visible on the same page.

Also note that, although the JSR 168 API has no support for portlet-to-portlet communication, you can use the cooperative portlet technology to enable messaging between JSR portlets. This topic was covered in Chapter 6. For more information on this feature, see the example in that chapter.

Cooperative Portlets

Cooperative portlets provides a way to transfer data between multiple portlets. A user can send information from a source portlet to a target portlet, causing the target portlet to change its view. Specifically, the user clicks a special icon in the source portlet and selects from a list of actions. When the action is selected, it causes the transfer of information to another portlet on the page. The target portlet consumes the information and changes its view accordingly.

For example, consider a portal page that displays stock information. The source portlet, A, shows a list of stocks. Target portlet B shows the trading history for the day, and target portlet C displays market news about the stock. A user clicks on the C2A icon next to a stock in portlet A and decides whether to display the trading history of this stock in portlet B or see related news stories about the stock in portlet C. This action could also be broadcast, which means both portlets B and C can display the information.

The transfer of properties between two portlets is initiated through either JSR 168-complaint portlets or IBM portlets.

JSR 168-Compliant Portlets

In the case of JSR 168-compliant portlets, portlets can be enabled for cooperation in one of two ways:

- *By using the Portlet Wiring Tool*. By using this tool, a user can create a persistent connection between two portlets, called a *wire*, which allows portlets to exchange properties. Currently, wiring support in the case of JSR-compliant portlets is available between two JSR-compliant portlets. A JSR-compliant portlet cannot be wired to cooperate with a IBM API-compliant portlet.

- You can programmatically enable cooperation between a JSR-compliant portlet and a portlet written using the IBM portlet API. In this case, the source IBM portlet can do a programmatic publish of properties to the broker when it determines that the property values have changed. These property values are transferred to target(s) only if wires have been created. For now, only IBM portlets have a programmatic API support.

IBM Portlets

Cooperation can be enabled between portlets written using the IBM API as follows:

- Using the Click-to-Action icon on the source portlet, a user can launch an event. The icon presents a pop-up menu containing the list of targets that could be the consumers of this data. After the user selects a specific target portlet, the property broker delivers the data to the target in the form of the corresponding portlet action, thus causing the target portlet to react to the action and display a new view with the results. The user also has the option to broadcast the property to all the portlets that have declared an action associated with the matching input property.

- While clicking the Click-to-Action icon, a user can hold the Ctrl key to have the action selection from the menu saved persistently. This will result in the property associated with the icon being wired to the target action. The next time the user clicks on the icon, no selection menu is shown but instead the wired action(s) will be automatically fired. These wires can also be created using the portlet wiring tool.

Cooperative Portlets Concept

Cooperative portlets subscribe to a model for declaring, publishing, and sharing information with each other using the WebSphere Portal property broker. Portlets subscribe to the broker by publishing typed data items, or *properties*, that they can share, either as a provider or as a recipient.

- The portlet that provides a property is called the *source portlet*.
- The properties that the source portlet publishes are called *output properties*.
- The portlet that receives a property is called the *target portlet*.
- The properties that are received by the target are called *input properties*.

Target portlets optionally provide actions to process the properties that they receive. Action processing in target portlets often does not need to distinguish between an action initiated within its own portlet area and an action initiated by the transfer of a portlet property value. Each action is also associated with a single input parameter and zero or more output parameters. Each parameter is associated with exactly one property. A parameter provides additional information about how the property value is transferred to or from the action. Parameters associated with input properties are called *input parameters*, whereas those associated with output properties are called *output parameters*. At runtime, the property broker matches the data type of output properties from a source portlet with the data type of input properties from one or more target portlets. If a match is determined, the portlets are capable of sharing the property.

Figure 10.20 provides a high-level architectural view of the cooperative portlets support in WebSphere Portal.

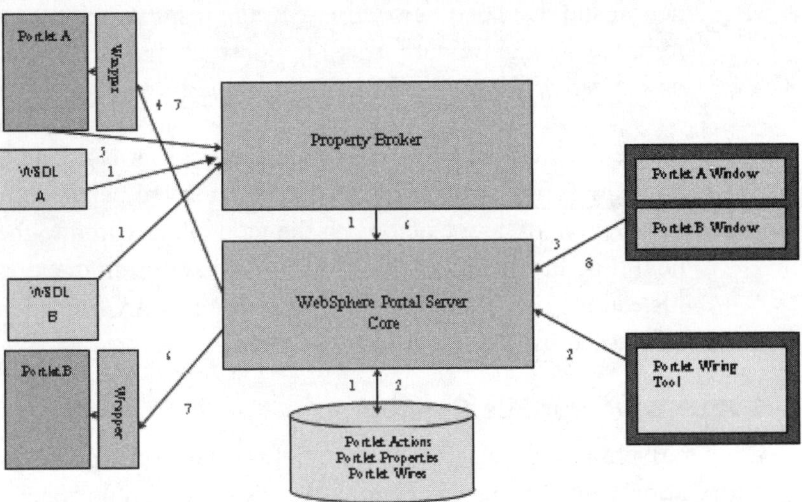

Figure 10.20: High-level WebSphere Portal architecture of cooperative portlets.

The Property Broker facilitates the exchange of similarly typed property values at runtime. The property broker runtime consists of a generic wrapper portlet, which is used to wrap each portlet that needs to be enabled for cooperation. The wrapper intercepts calls to the application portlet and interfaces with the broker appropriately to register actions supported by the portlet and to initiate data transfer between source portlets and target portlets using the property broker. The wrapper portlet is only used for portlets written using the IBM portlet API.

At the time of this writing, the wrapper portlet support is not available for JSR-compliant portlets. As such, the wrapper portlet is packaged in each cooperative portlet's WAR file, in the case of the IBM API. In the case of JSR-compliant portlets, the wrapper functionality is provided using a portlet filter that is part of the runtime.

The following series of steps correspond to a typical processing flow involving cooperative portlets.

Cooperative Process Flow in JSR 168-Compliant Portlets

1. During the deployment of the portlets, the Web Services Description Language (WSDL) file is processed and any actions and properties are registered with the portal runtime.

2. During the render phase of the request cycle, the portlet container requests markups from portlets and returns the resulting page to the browser.

3. An action is initiated by the user clicking on a Submit form button.

4. In the action phase, the request is received by the portlet container, and it calls the portlet's processAction() method, which may generate output property values.

5. The property broker transfers the property values to any wired targets by invoking the target actions associated with the wires.

6. The target portlet processes these property values. The above steps 4 through 6 may repeat as long as wires are transitively triggered.

7. After all action processing for all portlets on the page terminates, render processing begins. The portlet container calls the renderAction() method on each portlet, allowing them to generate markup.

8. After all the render callbacks are completed, the portal assembles the resulting response page and returns it to the client.

Cooperative Process Flow in IBM Portlets

1. During the deployment of the portlet, the WSDL file associated with the application portlet is processed, and actions and properties are registered with the portal runtime.

2. During the render phase of the request cycle, the container requests markup from each portlet. This may result in JSPs associated with the portlets being processed. Any click-to-action tags in the JSPs result in calls to the property broker, which determines matching actions on the page, based on the type information, and generates additional markup to display the icon used to invoke the pop-up menu.

3. After all the portlets have completed their render phase, the portal assembles the page and sends it back to the browser.

4. The end user may click a Click-to-Action icon and select one of the options from the menu with which he is presented.

5. A new request containing the chosen source and action information is generated and sent to the portal.

6. The portal core delivers the action to the target portlet. This is intercepted by the wrapper, which may interact with the broker to further process the request before delivering the action to the portlet.

7. Wires are triggered as in the previous flow.

Enabling Portlets for Click-to-Action

Click-to-Action enables end users to trigger the transfer of data or properties from one portlet to another one or more portlets using a pop-up menu–driven interface. These menus are constructed dynamically by the Property Broker. Source portlets provide property values to the Property Broker using tags from a custom JSP tag library. Target portlets declare actions and the properties they can consume in a WSDL file.

Enabling Source Portlets for Click-to-Action (C2A)

To enable a portlet to be a source, you insert custom JSP tags into the JSPs that are used by the portlet. These tags are part of the custom tag library shipped with

WebSphere Portal. To enable the C2A tags to be used in the JSP, all you have to do is put the following code at the top of the JSP file.

```
<%@ taglib uri="/WEB-INF/tld/c2a.tld" prefix="C2A" %>
```

One of the tags is <c2a:encodeProperty/>. For this tag, you specify the type, namespace, and value associated with the source. The namespace attribute groups related types together, so no conflict occurs between similarly named types in unrelated applications. The combination of type and namespace is used by the C2A runtime to match sources with compatible actions that can consume parameters of the same type. For the value attribute, you specify a string that contains the value to be transmitted to the target portlets.

A clickable icon is generated at the point where the encodeProperty tag is encountered by the property broker. When that icon is clicked, it generates a pop-up menu of actions compatible with the source. Advanced options on the tag allow the programmer to indicate whether a broadcast action is added to the menu or to scatter a set of property values to all portlets.

The <c2a:encodeProperty/> tag can optionally pass information to an enclosing <c2a:encodeProperties/> tag. This tag can be used to support the scattering of multiple sources to several actions at once. The code snippet in Figure 10.21 shows an example of using the encodeProperty and encodeProperties tags. This code is part of the shipping sample provided with the product. For more details on the C2A tags, refer to the product documentation.

```
<!– The following line includes the Click-toAction tag library -->
<%@ taglib uri="/WEB-INF/tld/c2a.tld" prefix="C2A" %>
 ......
<%
    Order[] orders = omb.getOrders();
    for (int i = 0; i < orders.length; i++) { %>

   <tr class="<%=((i % 2) == 0)?"wpsTableShdRow":"wpsTableRow"%>">

    <C2A:encodeProperties caption="Send.row.to.all" description="Send.row.data.to.all.portlets">

    <td>
    <C2A:encodeProperty name="orderId"
    namespace="http://www.ibm.com/wps/c2a/examples/shipping" type="OrderIDType" value="<%=
    orders[i].getOrderId() %>" broadcast="true" generateMarkupWhenNested="true"/>
    <%= orders[i].getOrderId() %>
    </td>

    <td>
    <C2A:encodeProperty name="customerId"
    namespace="http://www.ibm.com/wps/c2a/examples/shipping" type="CustomerIDType" value="<%=
    orders[i].getCustomerId() %>" broadcast="true" generateMarkupWhenNested="true"/>
    <%= orders[i].getCustomerId() %>
    </td>

    <td>
    </C2A:encodeProperties>
     .....
%>
```

Figure 10.21. Example of the encodeProperty tag.

Enabling Target Portlets for Click-to-Action

The target portlets associate their portlet actions with an input property that has been declared as an XML data type in a WSDL file. Web Services Description Language (WSDL) is a language that defines collections of abstract operations, together with the parameters (called *parts* in WSDL) for each operation. For more details about WSDL, read the WSDL spec at http://www.w3.org/TR/wsdl.

Associated with each action will be zero or one input parameters and zero or more output parameters. Each of those input or output parameters are associated with exactly one property, which is associated with an XML type. The input property's type is used for matching the action to the output properties that are produced by the portlets. These output parameters, which are produced as a result of executing the action, can be wired to other actions. In the case of portlets that already have action processing, very few changes have to be made. They simply have to declare their actions to the property broker using the WSDL without having to make additional source code changes.

The syntax used for declaring actions is standard WSDL. For IBM portlets, the base WSDL schema was extended with elements from a custom extension schema. You must use a custom binding section to specify how to invoke the declared operations on the implementing portlet. The custom binding syntax is illustrated in Figure 10.22 and described in detail in the instructions accompanying the product. The binding section maps each abstract operation to an action on the portlet. For each operation, the portlet action name must be provided. For each operation parameter, the action parameter name must be provided.

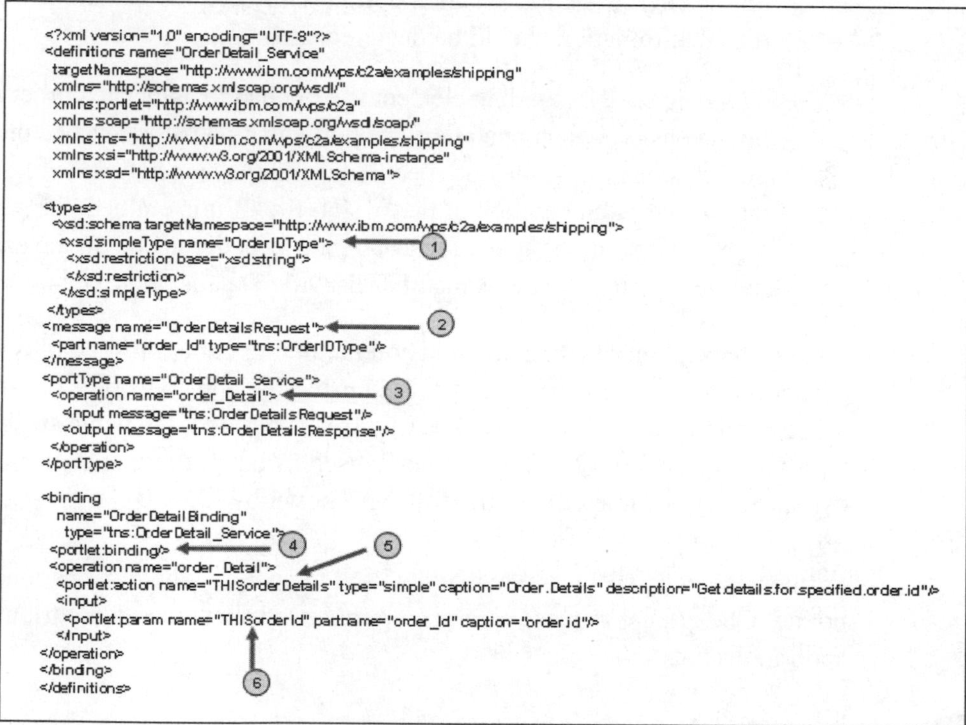

```
<?xml version="1.0" encoding="UTF-8"?>
<definitions name="OrderDetail_Service"
  targetNamespace="http://www.ibm.com/wps/c2a/examples/shipping"
  xmlns="http://schemas.xmlsoap.org/wsdl/"
  xmlns:portlet="http://www.ibm.com/wps/c2a"
  xmlns:soap="http://schemas.xmlsoap.org/wsdl/soap/"
  xmlns:tns="http://www.ibm.com/wps/c2a/examples/shipping"
  xmlns:xsi="http://www.w3.org/2001/XMLSchema-instance"
  xmlns:xsd="http://www.w3.org/2001/XMLSchema">

<types>
  <xsd:schema targetNamespace="http://www.ibm.com/wps/c2a/examples/shipping">
   <xsd:simpleType name="OrderIDType">        (1)
    <xsd:restriction base="xsd:string">
    </xsd:restriction>
   </xsd:simpleType>
 </types>
<message name="OrderDetailsRequest">          (2)
  <part name="order_Id" type="tns:OrderIDType"/>
</message>
<portType name="OrderDetail_Service">
  <operation name="order_Detail">             (3)
    <input message="tns:OrderDetailsRequest"/>
    <output message="tns:OrderDetailsResponse"/>
  </operation>
</portType>

<binding
   name="OrderDetailBinding"
     type="tns:OrderDetail_Service">
  <portlet:binding/>                          (4)
  <operation name="order_Detail">             (5)
   <portlet:action name="THISorderDetails" type="simple" caption="Order.Details" description="Get.details.for.specified.order.id"/>
   <input>
    <portlet:param name="THISorderId" partname="order_Id" caption="order.id"/>   (6)
   </input>
</operation>
</binding>
</definitions>
```

Figure 10.22: A portlet action described in a WSDL file.

Figure 10.22 shows an example of a WSDL file. The paragraphs that follow provide a brief description of how some of the WSDL extensions are used to support cooperative portlets.

- *<types>*—For cooperative portlets, this declares the data type of the data to be transferred. The data type is declared using XML Schema Datatypes (XSD, see the XSD specification). Multiple types may be defined in the document. Figure 10.22 shows an example of a type OrderIDType, indicated by ①.

- *<message>*—Input messages can contain only one part. In Figure 10.22, an example of the message element is indicated by ②.
- *<operation>*—This element provides an abstract definition of a click-to-action operation. Note that, in this example, we define an operation by the name of order_Detail, as indicated by ③.
- *<portType>*— Defines an abstract collection of operations. The operations must be defined in the document. One operation corresponds to each action on the click-to-action–enabled portlet. Only actions that are to be enabled for click-to-action should be declared (item ④).
- *<binding>*—The binding element is extended to associate portlet actions with operations. For each operation, the portlet action name must be provided. The portlet action name may be specified using the name attribute of the action tag in the binding section of the WSDL file. If it is omitted, the name attribute from the operation tag is used as the portlet action name. In the example, we define an action by the name of THISOrderDetails, indicated by ⑤

For each operation parameter, the action parameter name must be provided. The portlet parameter name may be specified using the name attribute of the param tag in the binding section of the WSDL file. If it is omitted, the name attribute of the part tag associated with the param tag is used as the portlet parameter name. In the example, that parameter is THISOrderID, shown by ⑥.

Further, the boundTo attribute may be used to specify where the parameter will be bound. Choices are request-parameter, request-attribute, session-attribute, or action-attribute.

Notice that the IBM custom extensions in the binding section have "portlet:" prefixed. The type attribute in portlet:action indicates whether this binding is for a portlet using the IBM API.

The actions on the portlet can be programmed following the normal portlet programming model. For portlet actions, simple action strings should be used instead of DefaultPortletAction class, which has been deprecated. Also, the action must expect a single input parameter delivered to it in the request object or as a request attribute or session attribute, as defined in the WSDL file. Figure 10.23 shows an example of the code in the actionPerformed method of the portlet.

```
public void actionPerformed (ActionEvent event)
  {
    ........
    String actionName = event.getActionString(); <----
    PortletRequest request = event.getRequest();

    //An action causes the state to be modified
     ShippingUtils.setLastModified(request);


    if (actionName.equals(ORDER_DETAILS)) {
      request.getPortletSession().setAttribute(ACTION_NAME, ORDER_DETAILS);
      request.getPortletSession().setAttribute(ORDER_ID, request.getParameter(ORDER_ID));
      //We do this as tracking id is an out param in the C2A WSDL file
      //We write the tracking id in the request so it can be published by
      //the broker in the same event cycle
      String orderId = (String) request.getPortletSession().getAttribute(ORDER_ID);
      OrderDetail od = ShippingDB.getOrderDetail(request.getParameter(ORDER_ID));
      request.getPortletSession().setAttribute(ORDER_DETAIL, od);
      if (od != null)
      request.setAttribute(TRACKING_ID, od.getTrackingId());

    } else if (actionName.equals(ORDER_ID_ENTRY)) {
      request.getPortletSession().setAttribute(ACTION_NAME, ORDER_ID_ENTRY);
    }
}
```

Figure 10.23: Code sample for processing the action.

As you can see, a simple action string is used. The portlet accepts the ORDER_ID parameter in its actionPerformed() method. This ORDER_ID corresponds to the input parameter defined for the action in the WSDL file in Figure 10.22.

Enabling JSR-Compliant Portlets for Cooperation

To enable JSR-compliant portlets for cooperation, you need to do the following:

1. Declare the exchange capabilities of the portlets using a WSDL file.
2. Program the portlet actions to provide information that can be transmitted through any wires that have been created, or to receive any information that has been transmitted by another portlet.
3. Modify the JSPs associated with the portlet to dynamically surface links that can be used to transmit information to other portlets.

These operations may vary slightly, depending on how JSR-compliant portlets have been implemented on your system. The process is best explained using code snippets from the shipping sample application that is shipped with the WebSphere Portal product.

Declaring Exchange Capabilities Using WSDL

Just as with IBM portlets, all the exchange capabilities of JSR-compliant portlets must be declared in a WSDL file. The same extension schema that is used for IBM portlets applies to standard portlets too. As we see next, some minor changes in the attribute values of certain extensions help identify the portlet as a JSR-compliant portlet rather than IBM portlet.

Figure 10.24 shows an example of a WSDL file associated with the Shipping sample.

```
<?xml version="1.0" encoding="UTF-8"?>
<definitions name="OrderDetail_Service"
  targetNamespace="http://www.ibm.com/wps/c2a/examples/shipping"
  xmlns="http://schemas.xmlsoap.org/wsdl/"
  xmlns:portlet="http://www.ibm.com/wps/c2a"
  xmlns:soap="http://schemas.xmlsoap.org/wsdl/soap/"
  xmlns:tns="http://www.ibm.com/wps/c2a/examples/shipping"
  xmlns:xsi="http://www.w3.org/2001/XMLSchema-instance"
  xmlns:xsd="http://www.w3.org/2001/XMLSchema">

<types>
  <xsd:schema targetNamespace="http://www.ibm.com/wps/c2a/examples/shipping">
   <xsd:simpleType name="OrderIDType">
    <xsd:restriction base="xsd:string">
    </xsd:restriction>
   </xsd:simpleType>
   </xsd:schema>
</types>

<message name="OrderDetailsRequest">
  <part name="order_Id" type="tns:OrderIDType"/>
</message>
....
<portType name="OrderDetail_Service">
  <operation name="order_Detail">
   <input message="tns:OrderDetailsRequest"/>
   <output message="tns:OrderDetailsResponse"/>
  </operation>
</portType>

<binding
   name="OrderDetailBinding"
    type="tns:OrderDetail_Service">
  <portlet:binding/>
  <operation name="order_Detail">
   <portlet:action name="orderDetails" type="standard" caption="Order.Details" description="Get.details.for.specified.order.id"
   actionNameParameter="ACTION_NAME"/>
   <input>
    <portlet:param name="orderId" partname="order_Id" caption="order.id"/>
   </input>
</operation>
</binding>
</definitions>
```

Figure 10.24: Sample WSDL file for a JSR-compliant portlet.

Although the WSDL syntax looks similar to an IBM portlet, some slight differences exist. First, the value of type attribute in the portlet:action element is set to standard for JSR-compliant portlets. This setting indicates that the action implementation to be used is the processAction method, instead of the actionPerformed method that is used with IBM portlets.

The second difference is the use of the actionNameParameter attribute. This attribute is used to specify the name of a request parameter that is used to store the action name. This is necessary because, unlike the actionPerformed method in the IBM portlets, the processAction method in JSR does not provide an action name explicitly. Therefore, JSR-compliant portlets must be programmed to store a distinguished request parameter to store the action name so that different action processing logic can be executed, based on different user-selected actions.

Program Portlet Actions

Figure 10.25 shows an example of the processAction method in the OrderDetailPortlet, which receives the property value. The input parameter in the WSDL file in Figure 10.24 specifies a parameter named orderId. In the action logic, the particular action that needs to be invoked is determined using the actionNameParameter value. The order ID value is extracted from the request parameter if the action name matches the name declared in the WSDL.

```
public void processAction (ActionRequest request, ActionResponse response) {
    ......
    String actionName = request.getParameter(ACTION_NAME_PARAM);
    if (actionName == null) {
       actionName = "";
    }
    .....

    if (actionName.equals(ORDER_DETAILS)) {
       String orderId = request.getParameter(ORDER_ID);
      if (orderId == null) {
          orderId = (String)request.getPortletSession().getAttribute(ORDER_ID);
      }

      if (orderId != null) {
          request.getPortletSession().setAttribute(ACTION_NAME, ORDER_DETAILS);
          request.getPortletSession().setAttribute(ORDER_ID, orderId);

     }
     ........
    } else if (actionName.equals(ORDER_ID_ENTRY)) {
       request.getPortletSession().setAttribute(ACTION_NAME, ORDER_ID_ENTRY);
    }
}
```

Figure 10.25: Example of processAction.

Figure 10.26 shows an example of how a portlet can obtain a reference to the service interface. This service interface is then used to invoke the Java APIs provided by the property broker.

```
boolean pbServiceAvailable = false;
PropertyBrokerService pbService = null;
public void init(PortletConfig config) throws PortletException {
   super.init(config);

  try {
      Context ctx = new InitialContext();
  →  PortletServiceHome serviceHome = (PortletServiceHome)
  ctx.lookup("portletservice/com.ibm.portal.propertybroker.service.PropertyBrokerService");
  →  pbService =
  (PropertyBrokerService)serviceHome.getPortletService(com.ibm.portal.propertybroker.ser
  vice.PropertyBrokerService.class);
      pbServiceAvailable = true;
  }catch(Throwable t) {
      getPortletContext().log("OrderDetailPortlet could not find property broker service!");
  }
 }
```

Figure 10.26: Code snippet for obtaining a reference to the property broker interface.

In this example, we use JNDI to obtain a reference to the portlet broker service. JNDI also allows us to get references to other services offered by the WebSphere Portal runtime. The use of the Boolean variable pbServiceAvailable allows this variable to be used to guard access to IBM-only services and also to make sure that portlet can function properly in environments where the service is unavailable.

Before we can invoke the JSP in the source portlet, the doView method sets an indication in the bean that is passed to the JSP. The bean indicates if the property broker service is available. This is shown in the code snippet in Figure 10.27. The use of the Boolean prevents the proprietary interface from being accessed in a non-IBM JSR 168 environment.

```
public void doView(RenderRequest request, RenderResponse response)
    throws PortletException,IOException
{
    ......
    OrderMonthBean omb = new OrderMonthBean();
    request.setAttribute(ORDER_MONTH_BEAN, omb);
   if (pbServiceAvailable == true) {←
      request.setAttribute(PBSERVICEAVAILABLE, "true");←
      request.setAttribute(PBSERVICE, pbService);←
   } else {
      request.setAttribute(PBSERVICEAVAILABLE, "false");
   }
    .......
}
```

Figure 10.27: The JSP is notified that the service is available.

Dynamically Generate Links in JSPs

Figure 10.28 shows a portion of the JSP used to display the orders for the month. First, it checks to see if the property broker service is available by checking if it has been set in the bean. Next, the areWiresActive method on the PropertyBrokerService interface indicates if dynamic links must be shown for the order IDs.

```
....
PropertyBrokerService pbService = null;
boolean pbServiceAvailable =
            "true".equalsIgnoreCase((String)renderRequest.getAttribute(OrderMonthPortlet.PBSERVICEAVAILABLE));
if (pbServiceAvailable)
            pbService = (PropertyBrokerService)renderRequest.getAttribute(OrderMonthPortlet.PBSERVICE);
OrderMonthBean omb = (OrderMonthBean) renderRequest.getAttribute(OrderMonthPortlet.ORDER_MONTH_BEAN);
......

Order[] orders = omb.getOrders();
boolean areOrderIdWiresActive = false;
boolean areCustomerIdWiresActive = false;

if (pbServiceAvailable) {
  areOrderIdWiresActive = pbService.areWiresActive(renderRequest, OrderMonthPortlet.ORDER_ID); <----
 }
 ......
<%-- If the output property "orderId" is wired with active actions, then set a link to trigger action--%>

<%
     if ( areOrderIdWiresActive ){
        PortletURL actionURL = renderResponse.createActionURL(); <----
        actionURL.setParameter(OrderMonthPortlet.ORDER_ID, orders[i].getOrderId());
        actionURL.setParameter(OrderMonthPortlet.ACTION_NAME_PARAM, OrderMonthPortlet.ORDERS_FOR_MONTH);
%>
        <A href="<%= actionURL%>">
         <%= orders[i].getOrderId() %>
        </A>
   <% }else {%>
     <%= orders[i].getOrderId()%>
   <% }%>

</td>
 ......
```

Figure 10.28: Surfacing links for wired properties.

The same action gets invoked whether a dynamically generated link is clicked or if the user clicks a Submit button on the form. The only difference is that additional parameters are passed for the dynamically generated links. These parameters could be an order ID, depending on the link clicked. These parameters are automatically located by the property broker and used to trigger any active wires with which they are associated.

Creating Wires Using the Portlet Wiring Tool

Once the portlets have been enabled for cooperation, you must create wires for cooperation to happen at runtime. For JSR standard portlets, the wiring tool is the only way portlets can be enabled for cooperation. Once instances of the portlet have been placed on a page, the Portlet Wiring Tool is used to view the exchange capabilities of the portlets on the page and create wires between compatible portlets. The Portlet Wiring Tool is launched by clicking **Edit Page** when viewing a portal page; it is located under a tab called Wires. This same tool can be used to wire IBM portlets also. More details about the wiring tool can be obtained from the product documentation or in other references on portlet cooperation listed at the end of this book.

Virtual Portals

Virtual portals (VPs) are among the newest features in WebSphere Portal V5.1. Simply put, virtual portals are virtual entities, each representing the logical behavior of a distinct WebSphere Portal instance running on a shared infrastructure. Virtual portals allow us to create additional portal instances on the same hardware without multiple software installations.

Virtual portals are very useful in situations in which a large enterprise has to preserve its brand entities, but needs a portal for each brand. Virtual portals running on a single instance of WebSphere Portal are the perfect option because they are easy to manage and relatively less expensive than designing separate actual portals. Virtual portals also are very useful for service providers that host and offer portal services to a large population. Figure 10.29 shows one of the most common VP configurations.

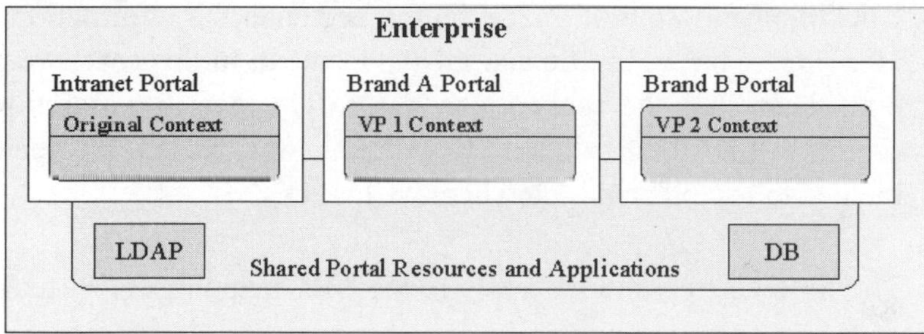

Figure 10.29: A common virtual portal configuration.

Creating a Virtual Portal

Typically, the portal administrator creates and manages VPs. Hence, the steps shown here must be performed when logged in as the portal administrator (wpsadmin). Under **Administration,** traverse down to **Virtual Portals → Manage Virtual Portals.** The initial virtual portal instance should be visible, as shown in Figure 10.30.

Note: The URL for any virtual portal created consists of /wps/portal/ + virtual portal URL context.

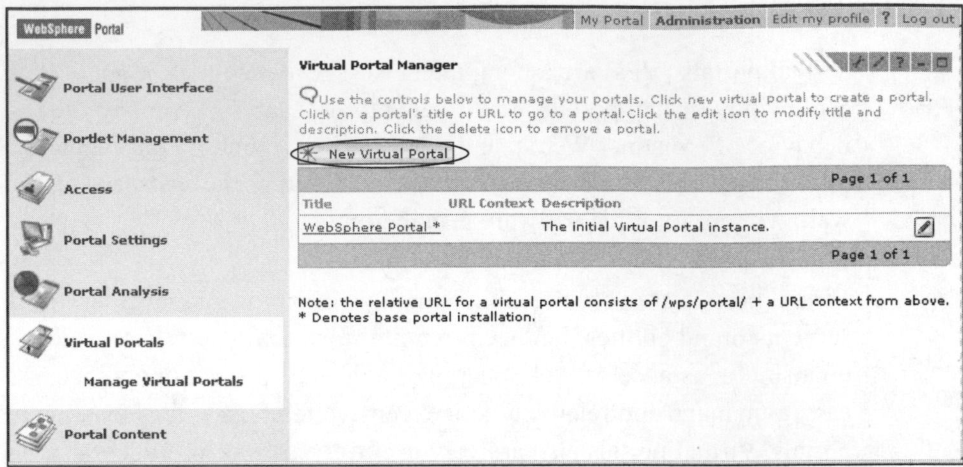

Figure 10.30: Virtual Portal Manager showing the initial instance.

Click the **New Virtual Portal** button and enter the information shown in Figure 10.31. Give the VP a title and a URL Context. In this case, we used ourCo for both. Then click the **Search** icon (magnifying glass) to search for Administrative groups in LDAP. The default, wpsadmins, was chosen. We decided to go with the theme we had created—ourTheme. Click **OK**.

The following conditions apply to the URL mappings of virtual portals:

- A one-to-one mapping exists between a virtual portal and its URL mapping. Each mapped URL points to the root content node of one virtual portal. You cannot use the same URL mapping for two different virtual portals.
- All URL mappings use the same context root and servlet name in the URL.
- You can use individual domain names for the virtual portals.

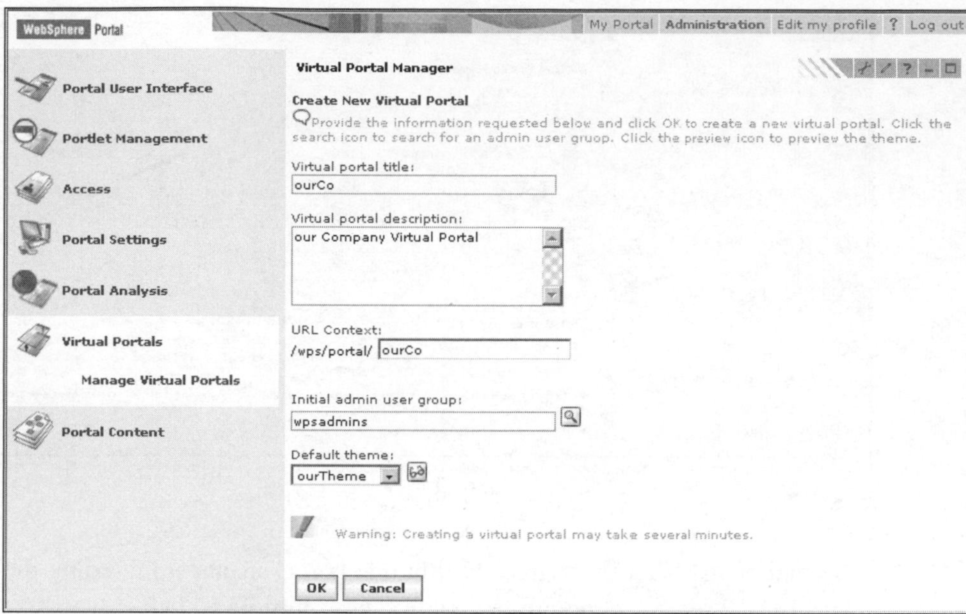

Figure 10.31: Creating a new VP.

After a couple of minutes, the new virtual portal named ourCo should be created and listed on the Virtual Portal Manager page. Look for the message *EJPAH2011I: Virtual portal ourCo has been created successfully*. You can now access this VP by opening a new Web browser and pointing to the following URL: http://<HOST_NAME>:9080/wps/portal/ourCo.

One icon appears on the Virtual Portal Manager screen that is new in WebSphere Portal V5.1. This is the Reinitialize icon, seen in Figure 10.32. If you click it, the existing virtual portal is brought back to its initial default state. This action is irreversible, and you will get a confirmation screen to OK or Cancel the intended action. Upon a successful re-initialization, you should see the message *EJPAH5001I: Virtual portal ourCo has been initialized successfully*.

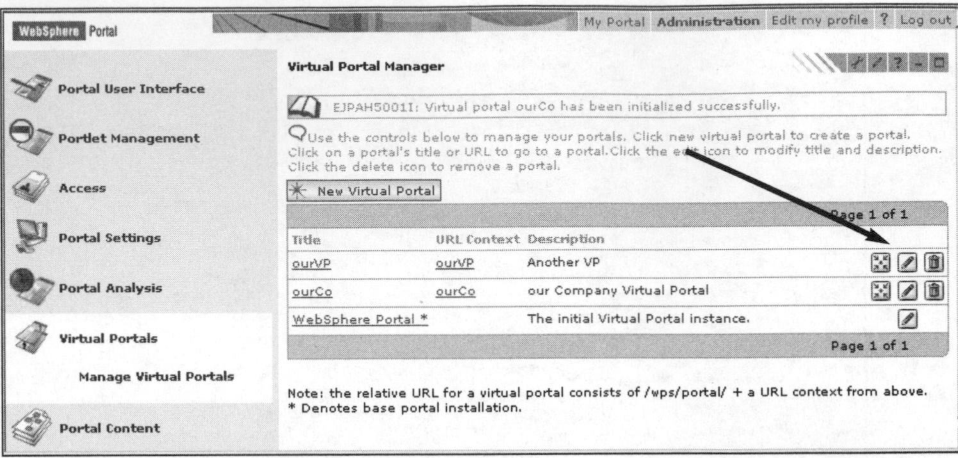

Figure 10.32: Creating a new Virtual Portal.

Virtual portals share resources within one portal instance, including the database and LDAP server. Although you cannot use multiple LDAP servers in a VP scenario, you can certainly create subtrees in the LDAP schema to obtain a limited level of user/group isolation. To illustrate that point, a new group called vpadmins was created in the LDAP structure. See Figure 10.33. This is the user group of subadministrators who would be able to administer the VP.

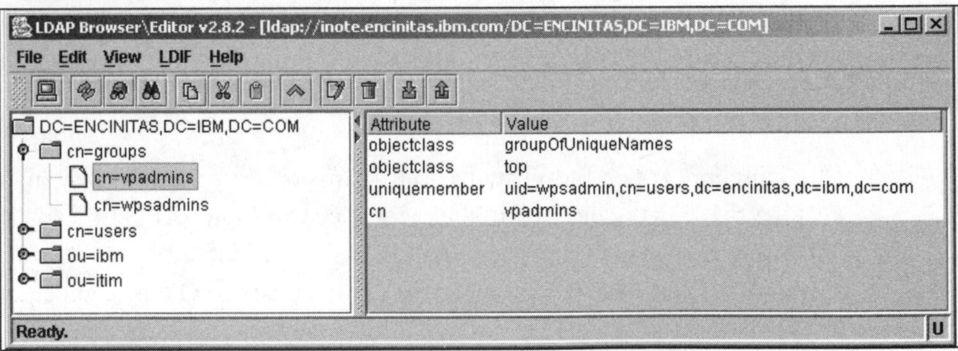

Figure 10.33: Virtual Portal Manager showing the initial instance.

A new virtual portal, called ourVP, was created using vpadmins as the Administrative user group. Make sure you search for “All available User Groups” and select vpadmins from the returned list. After the virtual portal is created, as shown in Figure 10.34, the VP is accessed via the following URL: http://<HOST_NAME>:9080/wps/portal/ourVP.

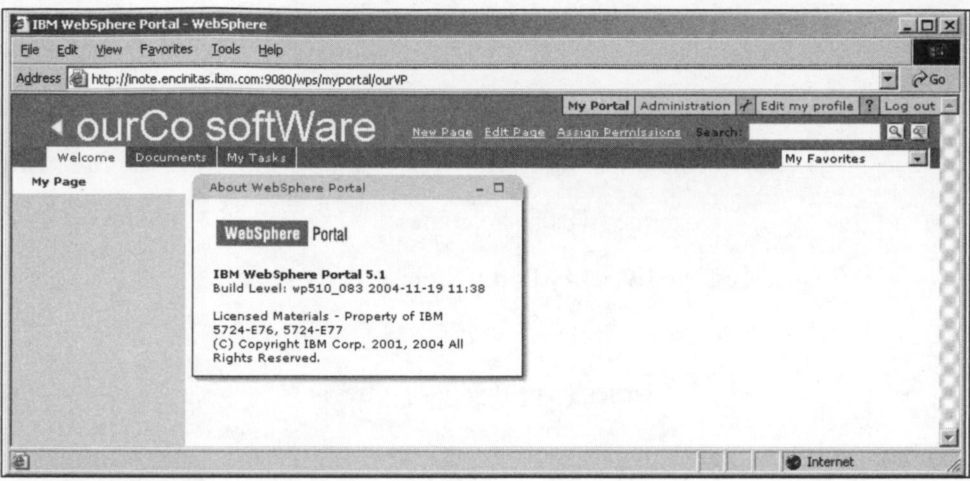

Figure 10.34: A virtual portal.

Notice that the VP has a subset of the parent's content. Even the administrator gets a subset of administrative functionality, all of which is configurable. Nevertheless, the MyTasks page is visible, which means users can still access their personal tasks and work on the tasks that are assigned to them.

(To state the obvious, if you stop the WebSphere Portal Server, all VPs also are stopped.)

Although the results are not obvious to the user, from a management perspective, the portal administrator can put users into different groups and manage them as they relate to these two different logical portals. These VPs have an individualized look and feel, using unique own themes, skins, and login and self-registration portlets.

Note: The VP has limited content. If you want to change or preconfigure the content, you have to modify the InitVirtualPortal.xml file found in <WAS_HOME>/installedApps/<NODE>/wps.ear/wps.war/virtualportal.

When a VP is created using the Manage Virtual Portals portlet, it invokes an XML configuration interface script that creates the initial content of the new virtual portal. By default, the initial content of a new virtual portal includes the pages and portlets listed here. This list also includes (in parentheses) the unique names that are used for the pages and portlets in WebSphere Portal Version 5.1.

- Content Root (wps.content.root). This includes the following pages and portlets:
- My Portal (wps.My Portal). This includes the Welcome and My Page page.
- Welcome (wps.My Portal.Welcome). This includes the following portlet:
    - Welcome (wps.p.Welcome)
- My Page (wps.My Portal.Welcome.My Page)
- Page Customizer
- Page Properties (wps.PageProperties)
- Organize Favorites (wps.Organize Favorites)
- My Favorites (wps.My Favorites)
- Search Center (wps.Search Center)
- Login (wps.Login). this contains the following portlet:
    - Login (wps.p.login)
- Enrollment/Selfcare (wps.Selfcare)
- My Tasks (wps.My Tasks)
- Administration (wps.Administration). This includes the following portlets:
    - Manage Pages (wps.p.Manage Pages)
    - Users and Groups (wps.p.Manage Users and Groups)
    - Resource Permissions (wps.p.Resource View)
    - User and Group Permissions (wps.p.User Group Permissions)
    - URL Mapping (wps.p.Url Mapping)
    - Custom Unique names (wps.p.Unique Names)
    - Manage Search Collections (wps.p.Manage Search Collections)
    - Portal Document Manager (PDM) (wps.p.Manage Doc Libraries, wps.p.Doc Picker, wps.p.Documents)
    - Enable tracing (wps.p.Enable Tracing)

The topic of Virtual Portals usage is huge—more than can be adequately covered here—especially in regards to setting up roles, management, degree of isolation, and shaping the user experience. Our closing recommendation is to provide user-friendly URLs for your users to access their VPs.

Web Services for Remote Portlets

Web Services for Remote Portlets (WSRP) was adopted as a standard by OASIS a couple of years ago. WSRP defines how to plug remote Web services into the pages of online portals and other user-facing applications. The OASIS WSRP standard simplifies the integration of remote applications and content into portals. Using WSRP, portal administrators can select from a rich choice of remote content and applications and integrate these into their portal with just a few mouse clicks and no programming effort. The WSRP specification defines a Web service interface for interactive presentation-oriented Web services. It allows users to perform the following tasks:

- Producers can provide portlets as presentation-oriented WSRP services and make them available to Consumers who want to use these services.
- Consumers can select from a rich choice of available Web services and integrate them into their portal.
- Users can then access the services and work and interact with them just as they do with local portlets.

Using WSRP to perform these tasks has the following benefits:

- WSRP becomes the means for content and application providers to provide their services in an easily consumable form to organizations that run portals.
- By virtue of the common, well-defined WSRP interfaces, all Web services that implement WSRP plug in to all WSRP-compliant portals without requiring any service-specific adapters. A single, service-independent adapter on the portal side is sufficient to integrate any WSRP services.
- Integrating content and applications into portals is made easier. No custom programming effort, using a variety of different interfaces and protocols, is required. Portal administrators no longer have to write interface code to adapt the WSRP services for their portal.

- Presentation-oriented services, as standardized by WSRP, allow Producer portals to deliver the requested data and their presentation to the Consumer portal. Previously, they delivered the data only, and the portal administrators had to provide the logic for how to present the data.
- Portal administrators do not have to keep the WSRP services code locally on their storage devices.
- The WSRP services appear and operate to portal users exactly like local portlets.

IBM is one of the founding members of the WSRP standards body. WSRP is supported in WebSphere Portal Server 5.0.2.1. Support is provided both as a producer and a consumer of WSRP services. Microsoft joined the WSRP body in February 2004, but has yet to provide WSRP support in their portal products (e.g., Web Parts are not consumable as WSRP remote portlets).

Enabling WSRP in WebSphere Portal Server

To use WSRP, you must enable the JSR 168 standard and then enable WSRP in your portal, because WSRP requires JSR 168 as a prerequisite. Specifically, the WSRP Consumer Client is implemented as a JSR 168 portlet.

Support for JSR 168 portlets is available in WebSphere Portal V5.1. By default, the support for both standards, WSRP and the Portlet API as defined by Java Standard Request (JSR) 168, is disabled in the WebSphere Portal. Thus, the portal as it is shipped does not support WSRP. On the Producer side, portlets cannot be provided as WSRP services. On the Consumer side, WSRP services cannot be integrated and used as portlets. As a result, commands of the portal XML configuration interface for tasks that are specific to the WSRP standard are rejected.

To enable WSRP, add the following two property keys to the file <WPS_HOME>/shared/app/config/services/ConfigService.properties and set them to true:

```
For JSR 168:   portal.enable.jsr168=true
For WSRP:     portal.enable.wsrp=true
```

After you make the changes and save the file, restart Portal Server for the changes to take effect.

WSRP Concepts

Portals that provide WSRP services are called Producers. The Producer part of the WSRP implementation provides an additional entry point into the Producer portal, enabling the portal to provide portlet applications or single portlets as WSRP services. The Producer is the "server" of the WSRP communication. A WSRP Producer provides one or more portlets as WSRP services for invocation by Consumer applications that reside at remote sites.

Producer

The Producer provides a set of interfaces as defined in the WSRP standard. The Producer can expose some or all of these interfaces to the Consumers, as appropriate. The interfaces are:

- *Service Description*—This interface is mandatory. It is the self-description of the Producer and its available portlets.
- *Markup*—This interface is mandatory. It is an interface for requesting and interacting with markup fragments.
- *Portlet Management*—This interface is optional. It grants access to the life cycle of the hosted portlets and to their persistent state.
- *Registration*—This interface is optional. It is not supported by the current implementation of WSRP in WebSphere Portal. However, the Consumer can handle Producers that support WSRP registration interfaces.

The Producer describes these WSRP interfaces in the Web Services Description Language (WSDL) document. The WSDL document provides general technical information about how the Consumer connects to the Producer and the related infrastructure.

The Producer portal receives the requests from the Consumer to the WSRP service and generates the markup accordingly.

Consumer

A WSRP Consumer is a portal that integrates WSRP services and consumes them. The Consumer is the "WSRP client." The Consumer selects the WSRP service and integrates it into the Consumer portal as a remote portlet. The Consumer portal receives the markup from the remote WSRP service and presents it to its users.

Example: Using WSRP in WebSphere Portal

Here, we demonstrate how to enable and use WSRP in WebSphere Portal through an example. We will expose the MyNews portlet on one machine (e.g. inote.encinitas. ibm.com) as a Web service and try to access it from another portal machine. The Producer portal is inote, and vishy2 is the Consumer portal. The following steps occur:

1. Provide the MyNews in the Producer portal (inote) as a WSRP Service so that Consumer portals can invoke them as remote portlets.

2. Configure the Consumer portal (vishy2) for integration of WSRP services as remote portlets

3. Integrate and use WSRP services as portlets in the Consumer portal.

These steps use the Portal administration portlets for the most part, but can also be performed using the portal XML configuration interface.

Producer Tasks

For a local portlet to be used as a remote portlet using WSRP, a Producer must:

1. Provide a portlet
2. Determine the group IDs and handles

In addition, the Producer can also withdraw a portlet.

WSRP Service Description

WSRP service Consumers need information about how to bind to the provided WSRP services. This information is described in the WSDL document of the Producer, and the Consumer can use this to bind to the Producer and retrieve further details about the Producer. When the Producer portal is also a WebSphere Portal installation, the WSDL can be accessed at the following URL: http://<producer_portal_hostname>:<port>/<context _root>/wsdl/wsrp_service.wsdl.

In our example, the URL used is http://inote.encinitas.ibm.com:9080/wps/wsdl/wsrp_service.wsdl. When the Producer is not a WebSphere Portal installation, this information must be obtained by the owner of the portal.

Providing a Portlet

A portlet is made available remotely to Consumers, once the portlet is provided on the Producer portal as a WSRP service. By withdrawing a portlet, the service is cancelled. Once a portlet is provided, Consumers can integrate it into their portals as a remote portlet.

The portlet can be provided in two ways:

- Use the Manage Portlets portlet
- Use the XML configuration interface

We document using the Manage Portlets here. The XML configuration documentation is available with the product documentation. Figure 10.35 shows a snippet of the generated XML file and the handle of the portlet that we will use in our example.

```
Select vi myxmlaccess.xml
                </portlet>
                <portlet action="update" active="true" defaultlocale="en" handle
="_5_00000000180G1CDM_1BQ" name="My Weather" objectid="_3_00000000180G1CDM_5B" p
rovided="true" servletref="_V_00000000180G1CDM_5A">
                    <localedata locale="en">
                        <title>My Weather</title>
                        <description>Displays weather condition data and forecas
ts for user-selected cities.</description>
                        <keywords>Weather,travel, MarketWatch</keywords>
                    </localedata>
```

Figure 10.35: Snippet of the generated XML file.

To provide the portlet using the Manage Portlets, perform the following steps:

1. Login to the portal as an administrator (wpsadmin).
2. Go to the Administration screens by clicking the **Administration** link.
3. In the Administration section, traverse down to **Portlet Management → Portlets**.
4. In the Manage Portlets screen, search for the portlet or portlets you want to provide and click the **Provide portlet** icon (star). In this case, the My Weather portlet is selected to be provided, as shown in Figure 10.36. Notice that the icon changes, and a check mark appears in the Provided column.

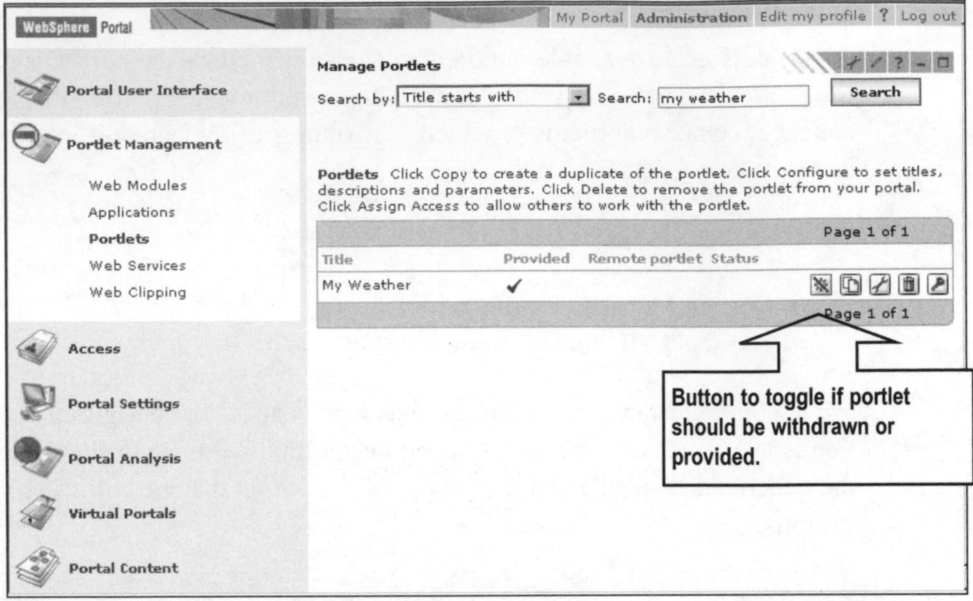

Figure 10.36: Screen showing a provided portlet.

Determining Group IDs and Handles

When a Consumer portal administrator must integrate a remote portlet into her portal, she will need the *handle* and *groupid* of the remote portlet. These must be provided by the administrator of the Producer portal.

If the Producer portal is a WebSphere Portal, this information may be obtained by exporting all the portlets being provided using the XML configuration interface. In the resulting XML file (Figure 10.35), look for those portlets that have the *provided* attribute set to true.

Consumer Tasks

For a Consumer portal to use a WSRP service as a remote portlet, it must:

1. Create a Producer instance
2. Consume the WSRP service to integrate it as a remote portlet

Create a Producer Instance

Creating a Producer in the Consumer portal makes the Web Service Producer known to the Consumer. Required registration must be done. Two scenarios can be used to create a Producer:

1. If you are online when creating the Producer, connect to the Producer, using the Web Service Configuration portlet or XML configuration interface.

2. If you are offline, XML configuration is the only option.

The steps to create a Producer instance online:

1. Click on **Web Services** under Portlet Management.

2. Click on the New Producer button and fill in the following information in the resulting screen:

   2a. *Title*—Give your instance a title.

   2b. *Description*—Enter a meaningful description.

   2c. *URL*—This is the URL for the WSDL service definitions of the Producer. This will be generally of the form http://<ProducerPortal Host> :<PortNumber>/wps/wsdl/wsrp_service.wsdl.

   2d. *Registration Handle*—The handle information will be in the exported XML file of the Producer portal.

These are the required fields, but other optional fields, such as user information and registration information, can also be filled in. See Figure 10.37.

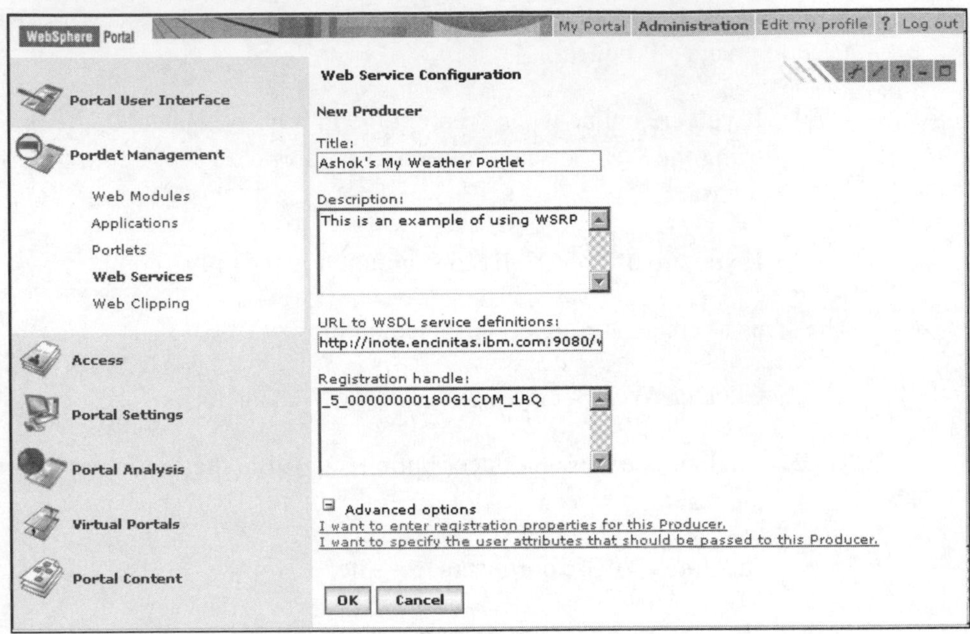

Figure 10.37: Creating a Producer instance.

3. Click **OK**. If the Producer instance is created, you should see the message *EJPAM1080I: Created the Producer successfully*. The newly created Producer portlet will be listed. Next step is to consume the WSRP service.

Consume a WSRP Service

Once the Producer instance is created, the WSRP services provided by that Producer can be consumed as remote portlets. To consume a WSRP service as a remote portlet, either the Manage Web Modules portlet or the XML configuration interface may be used. Here, we document the Manage Web Modules portlet example for consuming a WSRP Service:

1. Click on **Web Modules** under Portlet Management. Then click the **Consume** button.

2. In the Step 1 screen, choose the Producer. The Web Service Producers should be listed. If not, search for a particular portlet. Select a Producer Web Service from the list by clicking the link. We chose Ashok's My Weather Portlet.

3. In the Step 2 screen, select the portlet and click **OK**. See Figure 10.38. You should see a message *EJPAQ1801I: Web module(s) have been consumed.*

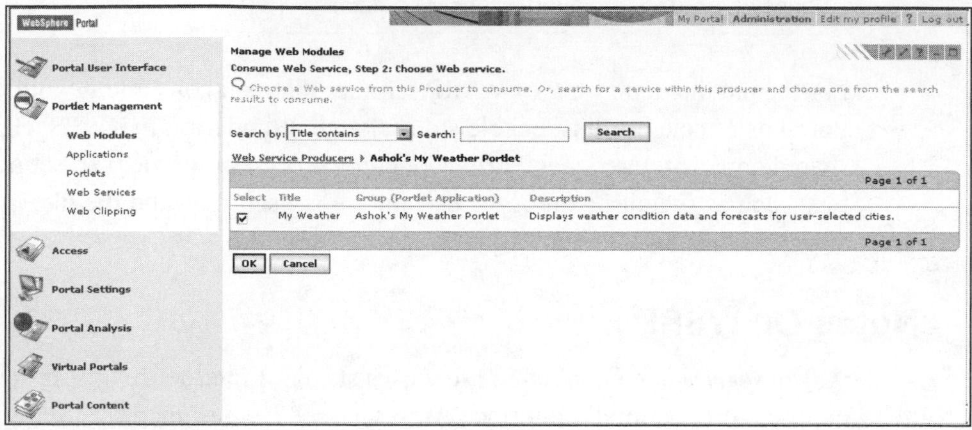

Figure 10.38: Selecting a Consumer web service.

Once these steps have been completed, the remote portlets (indicated by the suffix RP, as shown in Figure 10.39) are available in Portal Administration. Also notice the check box under the Remote portlet column. Remote portlets can be added to pages and handled in the same manner as other local portlets.

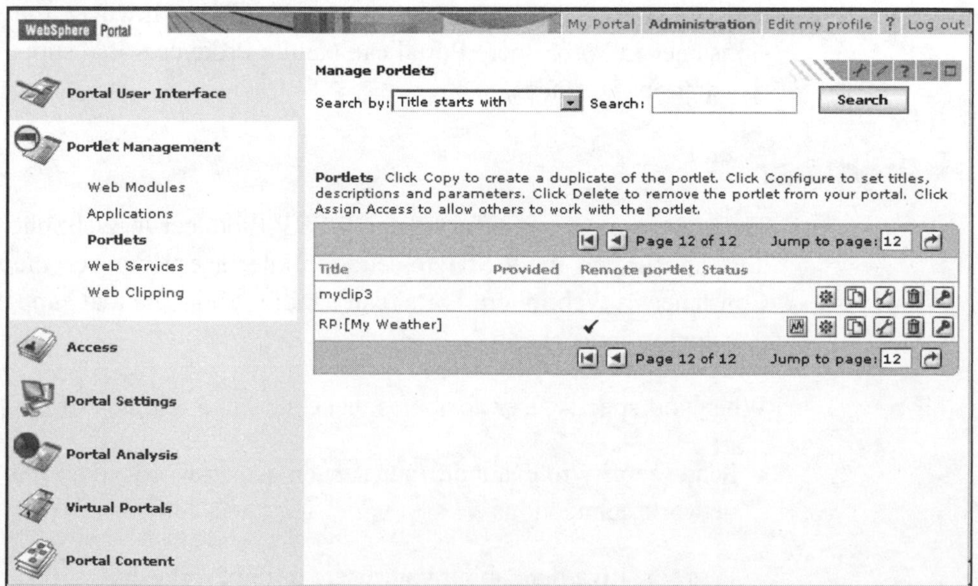

Figure 10.39: Remote portlet listed and identified by the suffix RP.

Note: If you add remote portlets to unauthenticated pages, switch on public sessions. This way you can benefit portal performance and avoid unexpected behavior resulting from the lost session data.

For the parallel rendering of WSRP services that you consume in your consumer Portal as remote portlets, enable std.useParallelRendering in <WPS_HOME>/shared/app/config/services/PortletContainerService.properties. To set other parameters, such as switching on or off caching, proxy settings, and the like, please refer to the product InfoCenter.

Notes On WSRP

A *Web service* is an application that uses standard Internet-related protocols to expose a programmatic interface. Web services are designed for use by other programs and applications like portlets, rather than by people.

- If you want to use WSRP with the IBM WebSphere Portal, you need to have WebSphere Application Server Version 5.1.1 Cumulative Fix 1 installed.
- The current implementation of the WSRP Producer in WebSphere Portal does not support the WSRP registration interface. However, the WSRP Consumer in WebSphere Portal can handle Producers that support WSRP registration interfaces.

Producer

- The current implementation of the WSRP Producer in WebSphere Portal does not support the WSRP registration interface. However, the WSRP Consumer in WebSphere Portal can handle Producers that support WSRP registration interfaces.
- When you specify user attributes make sure to avoid any of the following:
    - Send security relevant attributes, such as passwords, over unsecured network connections
    - Pass sensitive data about your users to the Producer.

Consumer

- You can consume a WSRP service only if you work online and can access the Producer's WSDL document.
- The WSRP implementation of WebSphere Portal does not yet make use of public WSRP services registries, such as UDDI, to discover and consume WSRP services. Instead, it uses the discovery mechanism of WSRP services, which is defined in the WSRP standard, to obtain a list and descriptions of the WSRP services that a certain Producer provides.
- An integrated portlet is always treated as a JSR 168 portlet.

Internationalization Support

WebSphere Portal customers in non-English speaking countries and multinational corporations need content in their native language. WebSphere Portal Server supports multiple languages by trying to match the user with a language preference. If the language preference is not specified, the portal tries to make a match based on the language of the browser. This capability also extends to any portlets that have been enabled for translation. Because the default language is English on any given page, any portlets that have the ability to show translated content will be shown in the language of choice; otherwise, they will be displayed in English.

Supported Languages

Currently, WebSphere Portal Server supports the following 27 languages:

- Arabic (ar)
- Czech (cs)
- Danish (da)
- Dutch (nl)
- English (en)
- Finnish (fi)
- French (fr)
- German (de)
- Greek (el)
- Hebrew (iw)
- Hungarian (hu)
- Italian (it)
- Japanese (ja)
- Korean (ko)
- Norwegian (no)
- Polish (pl)
- Portuguese (pt)
- Brazilian Portuguese (pt_BR)

- Romanian (ro)
- Russian (ru)
- Spanish (es)
- Simplified Chinese (zh)
- Traditional Chinese (zh_TW)
- Swedish (sv)
- Thai (th)
- Turkish (tr)
- Ukrainian (uk)

Selecting and Changing the Language

Let's look at the steps needed to change the language properties of WebSphere Portal Server into a language that is not on the supported list. There are various places and ways to change the language supported by the portal.

Installation

The installation program uses the default locale of the operating system to display the panels in the language supported by that locale. Once installation is done, this default language is stored in the LocalizerService.properties file in the <WPS_HOME>/shared/app/config/services directory. This file has three primary properties, as shown in the listing:

```
# Licensed Materials - Property of IBM, 5724-E76, (C) Copyright
IBM Corp. 2004 - All Rights reserved.

# ------------------------------------- #
# Properties of the Localizer Service #
# ------------------------------------- #

# Language, country, and variant settings for the default locale
#
# Default: <empty> [ = Locale.getDefault() ]
locale.default.language=en
locale.default.country  =
locale.default.variant  =

#
# List of BiDirectional languages separated by ',' or ';'
# Add ar,ur,yi,... when there are resources for those languages.
#
```

To change the default language and the locale supported, the locale.default. language and locale.default.country parameters must be changed. Sometimes, a locale variant exists; for example, to change to American English, the parameters should be set as follows:

```
locale.default.language = en
locale.default.country = US
```

A portlet can support one or more locales. All portlets must have their own default language specified in the deployment descriptor; otherwise, the portlet cannot be installed.

Changing Titles and Descriptions for Pages

1. Bring up the portal page and click **Edit Page** or, from the main portal, traverse to **Administration → Portal User Interface → Manage Pages**. Click the **Edit Page** properties icon for the selected page. In the Page Properties screen, expand the Advanced options and select *I want to set titles and descriptions*. This assumes you have the privileges to edit a page.

2. In the Page Properties screen, click the **Edit** icon (pencil) beside the Language you want to set. See Figure 10.40. Enter the title and description and click **OK**. The page will be displayed with its new "localized" name.

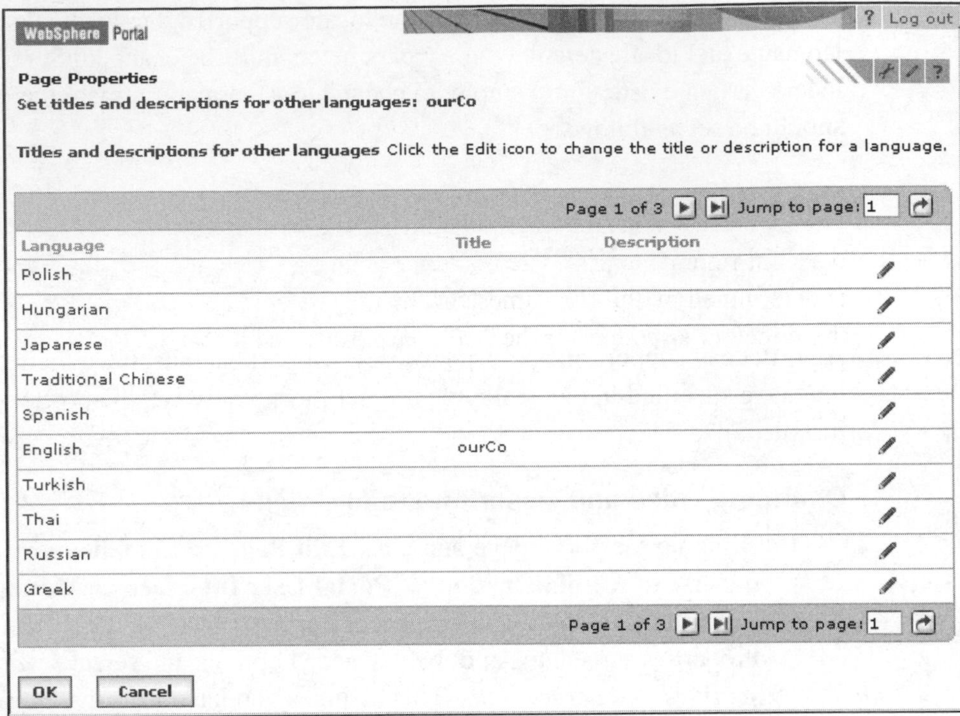

Figure 10.40: The screen to change the title and description of a page.

Language Selection by the User

A user can select a personal language preference for rendering portal content during the enrollment process. If the user later decides to change the locale, he can use the Edit My Profile portlet to specify the preferred language from the drop-down list. The list of languages supported in WebSphere Portal matches that specified in the language.properties file found in <WPS_HOME>/shared/app/config/ directory.

Language Selection by the Portal

The portal goes through the following sequence, during each user's logon process, to determine the language in which to render content:

1. If the user has logged in, then it uses the language specified by the user. (For anonymous users, the portal skips this step.)

2. If the user did not specify a language preference, then it uses the language specified in the browser.

3. If the browser's language cannot be determined, the portal uses the default locale of the portal.

4. If no supported language is found by the first three steps, then the portal uses the default language of the portlet.

The language then applies to the entire portal. If the portal or any component does not find the appropriate resource, a similar language is used. The language is determined by the file names for the resource bundles and the hierarchy of the directory structure for the JSPs. This search sequence applies to all portal components, down to the portlets. Thus, a portal can display individual portlets in different languages.

Depending on how a portlet is written, a portlet can support multiple locales. A portlet must specify the default language in its deployment descriptor; otherwise, the portlet won't be installed.

The character set for a language is stored in a database. The default encoding is UTF-8. The values in use for the various languages are shown in Table 10.3.

Table 10.3: Language Encoding in Use

Language	Encoding in Use
Japanese (ja)	Shift-JIS
Simplified (Chinese zh)	GBK
Traditional Chinese (zh_TW, HTML)	Big5
Traditional Chinese (zh_TW, WML)	UTF-8
Korean (ko)	KSC5601
All others	UTF-8

Supporting a New Markup Language

WebSphere Portal supports HTML, WML, and cHTML markup languages. If you want to define another markup language to support, you must ensure that you have portlets that provide markup for that language. In addition, you must create a subdirectory for the markup in each of the following locations—screens, themes, and skins – under <WAS_HOME>/installedApps/<NODE>/wps.ear/wps.WAR.

In the portal, the markup language must be modified following these steps:

1. Log into the portal as the Portal Administrator (wpsadmin). Under Portal Administration, navigate to **Portal Settings → Supported Markups**.

2. Highlight the markup you want to modify, as shown in Figure 10.41. Click **Edit selected markup**. If you want to add a new markup, choose Add new markup.

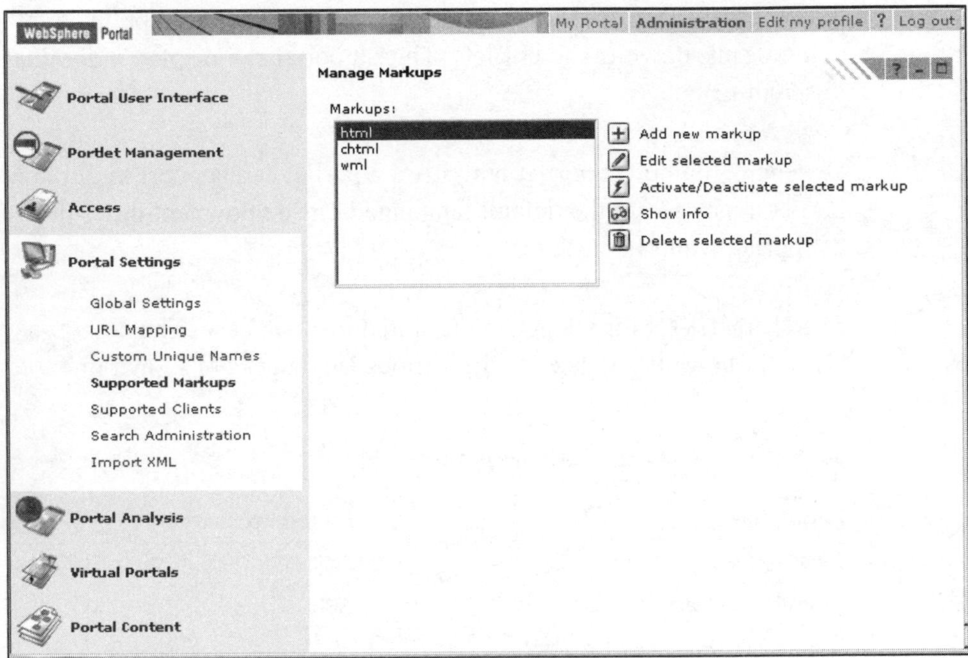

Figure 10.41: Selecting the markup to modify.

3. The Manage Markups screen shows the details of the current Markup, MIME type, and encoding as shown in Figure 10.42. Click **Set locale specific setting**.

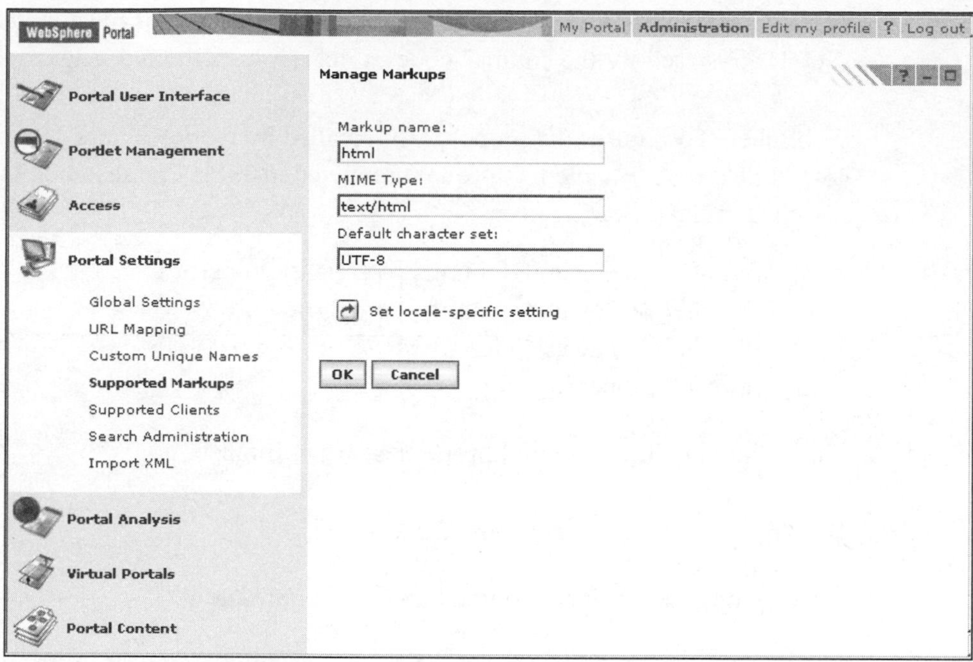

Figure 10.42: Markup details.

4. The following message will be displayed: *EJPAN0006I: the markup html has been modified,* and a screen showing all the languages and character sets will be shown. Select the language you want and click **OK**.

5. Click **OK** again to save the new markup.

Adding Support for a New Language

To support a new language, you need to add that language to the file language.properties. You do this by inserting resource bundles and adding JSPs for the new language, where applicable. Some JSPs use resource bundles, while others, such as help JSPs, are translated directly.

Resource bundles are located in <WPS_HOME>/app/Web/WEB-INF/classes/nls. They store text displayed in JSPs or in Java code. The naming convention for resource bundles is [bundle]_[language]_[country]_[variant].properties.

The ISO standard ISO-639 is used for the language codes of most languages, and ISO-3166 is used for the country codes. (Hebrew uses the old language code, iw.)

WebSphere Portal uses the properties file called by the Java class java.util.ResourceBundle to store text rendered in JSPs. The resource bundles are searched in the following order:

1. [bundle]_[language]_[country]_[variant].properties
2. [bundle]_[language]_[country].properties
3. [bundle]_[language].properties
4. [bundle].properties

The default bundles, [bundle].properties, are in English.

To add a resource bundle, follow these steps:

1. Copy an existing resource bundle and translate it.

2. Name the new bundle according to the naming convention for resource bundles.

3. Convert it into Unicode with the native-to-ASCII converter, native2ascii. It comes as part of the JDK and is found in <JAVA_HOME>/bin.

Here is a sample command to convert a Chinese text file, using UTF-16 encoding:

```
native2ascii -encoding UTF-16 helloWorld_zh.txt
helloWorld_zh.properties
```

JSPs that contain mostly static text are translated directly, which means the text is contained in the JSP instead of in the resource bundle. You have to copy and translate the existing JSP and store it in the appropriate location. The location of JSPs can be, for example, jsp/[mime_type]/[language]/[country]/[variant]/sample.jsp. The existing Help JSPs in WebSphere Portal are already translated and placed in the relevant [language] and [country] subdirectories.

Rather than create and use multiple JSP files, we recommend creating a single JSP file that contains the tags to load multilingual strings from the resource bundles. It is easier to maintain one JSP file than to keep multiple files in sync.

Door Closings

This chapter covered those features of WebSphere Portal that set it above the rest:

- Web clipping, one of the fastest ways to create a portlet
- Portlet-to-portlet communication, which has become very popular via C2A
- Web Services integration
- Portlets supporting multiple languages

While these powerful features are available out-of-the-box, they might not be available to the general portal user community. The portal architect or architecture committee should build a secure and practical design to get the most out of these features.

Appendix A
Installation Planning Worksheet

All WebSphere software products come with exhaustive online documentation; this is known as Information Center (InfoCenter). The WebSphere Portal Information Center includes introduction, planning, installing, configuring, administering, and developing topics. A ZIP file of the Information Center is provided, for each language, which you can copy to a local directory or to a server in your network.

1. Go to the WebSphere Portal library page on the Web at: http://www.ibm.com/websphere/portal/library.

2. Download the appropriate Information Center ZIP file for your language. The ZIP file is named language_ic.zip.

3. Copy the language_ic.zip file to a directory on your network.

4. Use a zip program to extract the Information Center from the ZIP file.

On a Windows system, if the Information Center was extracted in the WebSphere Portal folder on the C drive, then the access point would be:

```
C:\WebSphere\PortalServer\InfoCenter\index.html
```

It is important to gather the following information for the particular components you want to install *before* you begin installation. The planning worksheets list the information needed for installing the components. Fill in the table with values appropriate for your configuration, and do not assume the default values listed within the table are correct. Defaults are listed for the supported platforms: AIX, Linux, Solaris, and Windows. If the operating system is not specified, then the information needed is the same for all systems.

Use these worksheets to record any changes you make to the response file. No matter which installation type you use, you will need this information for uninstallation, so keep this worksheet for future reference. You will need to follow each component's directions for uninstallation, because one all-encompassing executable does not exist.

Data	Defaults	Write your values here:
IBM HTTP Server		
HTTP installation directory	C:\Program Files\IBM HTTP Server (Windows)	
IBM HTTP Server user name		
IBM HTTP Server group		
IBM HTTP Server password		
WebSphere Personalization		
Application Server name	WebSphere_Portal	
User name	wpsadmin	
Install directory	<WPS_HOME>/pzn	
Database type	cloudscape	
Database host		
Database port		
Database name	JCRDB FDBKDB LMDB	

Data	Defaults	Write your values here:
WebSphere Personalization		
Database ID	db2admin (Windows)	
Password		
Database URL	jdbc:db2j:jcrdb;create=true jdbc:db2j:wpsdb;create=true jdbc:db2j:lmdb;create=true	
Database driver	com.ibm.db2j.jdbc.DB2jDriver	
Driver location	<WPS_HOME>/pzn/shared/app/clouds-cape/db2j.jar	
WebSphere Application Server		
Installation directory	/usr/WebSphere/AppServer (AIX) /opt/WebSphere/AppServer (Linux/Solaris) C:\WebSphere\AppServer (Windows)	
WebSphere Application Server node name		
WebSphere Application Server user name		
Password		
LTPA password		
WebSphere Business Integration Server Foundation		
Installation directory	/usr/WebSphere/AppServer (AIX) /opt/WebSphere/AppServer (Linux/Solaris) C:\WebSphere\AppServer (Windows)	
Process Choreographer install directory	<WAS_HOME>/Process Choreographer	
Process Choreographerdatabase name	BPEDB	

(Continued)

Data	Defaults	Write your values here:
IBM SecureWay Directory		
IBM SecureWay installation directory	C:\Program Files\IBM\LDAP (Windows)	
Suffix	dc=yourco, dc=com (AIX, Windows)	
Administrative user	cn=root (all platforms)	
Password for administrative user		
TCP/IP port to use	389 (AIX, Windows)	
Proxy host	yourproxy.yourco.com	
LDAP server	ldapserv.company.com	
LDAP user distinguished name	an=ldapadmin	
LDAP user password	ldapadmin	
LDAP suffix	dc=yourco,dc=com	
Users DN prefix		
Users DN suffix	dn: cn=users,dc=yourco,dc=com	
Group DN prefix		
Group DN suffix	dn: cn=groupsdc=yourco,dc=com	
Administrator DN	uid=wpsadmin,cn=users,dc=yourco,dc=com	
Administrative group DN	uid=wpsadmin,cn=groups,dc=yourco,dc=com	
Lotus Domino Application Server		
User name	notes (AIX)	
Groups	notes (AIX)	
Password		

Data	Defaults	Write your values here:
Path for program files	C:\Lotus\Domino (Windows)/usr/lotus (AIX)	
Path for data files	C:\Lotus\Domino/data (Windows)/usr/notesdata (AIX)	
Domino name	host.yourco.com (AIX, Windows)	
Country code	US (AIX)	
Certifier organization	host.yourco.com (AIX, Windows)	
Certifier password		
Server name		
Host name	host.yourco.com (AIX, Windows)	
Administrative user first name	Domino (AIX, Windows)	
Administrative user middle name (optional)		
Administrative user last name	Admin (AIX, Windows)	
Administrative user password		
LTPA file		
LTPA password		
Token domain	.host.yourco.com (AIX, Windows)	
IBM Workplace Web Content Management		
Lotus Architect installation directory	c:\Lotus\Architect (Windows)	
Install directory	<WPS_HOME>/wcm	
Database type	cloudscape	
Database name	WCMDB	
Database ID		

(Continued)

Data	Defaults	Write your values here:
Password		
Database URL	jdbc:db2j:wcmdb;create=true	
Database driver	com.ibm.db2j.jdbc.DB2jDriver	
Portal Server		
LTPA password		
Install directory	/usr/WebSphere/Portal Server (AIX) /opt/WebSphere/AppServer (Linux, Solaris) C:\WebSphere\PortalServer (Windows)	
Host name	host.yourco.yourcom:##	
Base URI	/wps/portal	
Customized page	/wps/myportal	
Proxy host		
Proxy port		
Portal Server-LDAP		
LDAP server	hostname.yourco.com	
User DN	cn=Administrator,cn=users,dc=yourco, dc=com	
User password		
Suffix	dc=yourco,dc=com	
LDAP port number	389	
User object class	inetOrgPerson (TDS, Sun One)	
User DN prefix	uid (TDS) cn (Active Directory)	
User DN suffix	cn=users,doc=yourco,dc=com ou=people,dc=raleigh,dc=ibm,dc=com (Sun One)	

Data	Defaults	Write your values here:
Group object class	groupOfUniqueNames	
Group member	uniqueMember (AIX, Solaris) member (Linux)	
Group DN prefix	cn	
Group DN suffix	cn=group,dc=yourco,dc=com (TDS) ou=groups,dc=yourco,dc=com (Sun One)	
Administrative DN	uid=wpsadmin,cn=user,dc=yourco,dc=com (AIX) cn=wpsadmin,cn=users,dc=yourco,dc=com (Linux) uid=wpsadmin,ou=people,dc=raleigh,dc=ibm, dc=com (Solaris)	
Administrative group DN	cn=wpsadmins,cn=groups,dc=yourco, dc=com (TDS) cn=wpsadmins,ou=groups,dc=yourco, dc=com (Sun One)	
Portal Server-DB2		
Database name	wpsdb (AIX, Windows)	
Database user	wasinst (Linux)	
User password		
JDBC database driver	COM.ibm.db2.jdbc.DB2ConnectionPoolData Source (AIX, Linux, Windows)	
JDBC URL prefix	jdbc:db2	
JDBC driver library	/home/db2inst1/sqllib/java12/db2/java.zip (AIX) /home/wasinst/sqllib/java12/db2java.zip (Linux) C:\Program Files\SQLLIB\java\db2java.zip (Windows)	
Portal Server—WebSphere Member Manager Database		
Database name	wmmdb	

(Continued)

Data	Defaults	Write your values here:
Database user		
User password		
JDBC database driver	COM.ibm.db2.jdbc.app.DB2ConnectionPool DataSource (DB2) oracle.jdbc.pool.OracleConnectionPoolData Source (Oracle)	
JDBC URL prefix	JDBC:db2 (DB2) jdbc:oracle:thin:@hostname:1521 (Oracle)	
JDBC driver library	/home/wasinst/sqllib/java12/db2java.zip (DB2) /<ORACLE_HOME>/jdbc/classes12.zip (Oracle) C:\Program Files\SQLLIB\java\db2java.zip (Windows)	
Oracle Home	/opt/*databasename* (Solaris)	
Portal Server—Oracle		
Database name	wpsdb (Solaris, Windows)	
Database user		
Database user password		
JDBC database driver	oracle:jdbc.pool.OracleConnectionPoolData Source	
JDBC URL prefix	jdbc:oracle:thin:@hostname:1521	
JDBC driver library	C:\<ORACLE_HOME>\jdbc\lib\classes12.zip	
Oracle home	/opt/*databasename* (Solaris)	

In an environment that uses WebSphere Portal Extend components, these additional items should be noted:

Data	Defaults	Write your values here:
WebSphere Studio Application Developer		
Application Developer install directory	C:\Program Files\IBM\Application Developer (Windows)	
WebSphere Site Analyzer		
WebSphere Application Server	/usr/WebSphere/AppServer/SA (AIX) C:\WebSphere\AppServer\SA (Windows)	
Site Analyzer	/usr/WebSphere/AppServer/SA (AIX) C:\WebSphere\AppServer\SA (Windows)	
Name of server	Site_Analyzer	
WebSphere Application Server use name	wasadmin	
WebSphere Application Server password		
Site Analyzer administrative user name	saadmin	
Password		
Administrative database	saadmin	
DNS/IP database	sadns	
Project database	saprojct	
JDBC URL prefix	jdbc:db2:saadmin (DB2)	
Path to JDBC database driver	null/java/db2java.zip (Windows) /home/db2inst1/sqllib/java12/db2java.zip (AIX)	
Name of JDBC database driver	COM.yourco.db2.jdbc.DB2ConnectionPool DataSource	
Lotus Sametime (Windows Only)		
Server installation Directory	C:\Lotus\Domino (Windows with Domino)	
Home page	/portal	

(Continued)

Data	Defaults	Write your values here:
Customized page	/myportal	
Proxy host		
Proxy port		
Lotus Collaboration		
Discovery Server URL		
QuickPlace Server URL		
Domino Directory Server URL		
Sametime Server URL		
Sametime Server port		
WebSphere Portal Server root	/usr/WebSphere/Portal Server (AIX) C:\WebSphere\PortalServer\ (Windows)	
WebSphere Portal Server host name	host.yourco.com	
WebSphere Portal Server base URL	/wps	
Home page	/portal	
WebSphere Application root	/usr/WebSphere/AppServer (AIX) c:\WebSphere\AppServer\ (Windows)	
User name		
Password		
JDBC driver for database connection	COM.ibm.db2.jdbc.app.DB2Driver	
URL for database connection	jdbc:db2:wpsdb	
Driver location	*databasehome*\java\db2java.zip	
License Use Management		
License Server	host.yourco.com (Linux, Windows)	

Data	Defaults	Write your values here:
Remote LUM Server host name	host.yourco.com (Solaris)	
IBM Tivoli Access Manager		
Access Manager Installation Directory	C:\Program Files\Tivoli\Policy Director (Windows)	

Appendix B

References and Portal-Related Web Sites

Refer to the following Web sites for additional portal-related information.

Site Name	URL
WebSphere Portal	http://www.ibm.com/software/webservers/portal/
WebSphere Portal Library	http://www.ibm.com/software/webservers/portal/library.html
WebSphere Portal Support	http://www.ibm.com/software/genservers/portal/support/
DeveloperWorks WebSphere Portal Zone	http://www.ibm.com/developerworks/websphere/zones/portal/
IBM Support	http://www.ibm.com/support
DB2 Support	http://www.ibm.com/software/data/db2/udb/support.html
WebSphere Application Server Support	http://www.ibm.com/software/webservers/appserv/support.html
WebSphere Studio Application Developer	http://www.ibm.com/software/awdtools/studioappdev/

Site Name	URL
IBM Workplace Web Content Management	http://www.lotus.com/products/product5.nsf/wdocs/homepage
Lotus Extended Search	http://www.lotus.com/extendedsearch
IBM DB2 Information Integrator for Content	http://www.ibm.com/software/data/eip
Portlet Catalog	http://www.ibm.com/software/webservers/portal/portlet/catalog
DeveloperWorks Process Choreographer Zone	http://www.ibm.com/developerworks/websphere/zones/was/wpc.html
Rational Application Developer	http://www.ibm.com/software/awdtools/developer/application/
IBM Software	http://www.ibm.com/software/sw-bycategory/

Note: The IBM Support Web site may contain additional information about known defects and their workarounds. This site may also include supplemental information for topics covered in the WebSphere Portal documentation.

References

Product online documentation and all WebSphere Portal–related documents can be found at http://www.ibm.com/developerworks/websphere/zones/portal/proddoc.html.

Bruce Olson and Venkata Gadepalli. *Integrating WebSphere Portal and WebSphere Personalization Part 1: Building a Personalized Portlet*. April 2002.

Bruce R. Olson and Venkata Gadepalli. *Integrating WebSphere Portal and WebSphere Personalization Part 2: Building a Personalized Portlet Using WebSphere Portal content publishing V4.2.* June 2003.

Bruce R. Olson and Venkata Gadepalli, *Integrating WebSphere Portal and WebSphere Personalization Part 3: Writing Rules Based on Group Membership.* July 2003.

Amber Roy-Chowdhury, Shankar Ramaswamy, and Xinyi Xu. *Using Click-to-Action to Provide User-Controlled Integration of Portlets.* September 2002.

IBM WebSphere Portal for Multiplatform V5 Handbook, at http://publibb.boulder.ibm.com/abstracts/sg246098.html?Open

Marshall Lamb. Portlet Development *Best Practices and Coding Guidelines at* http://www-106.ibm.com/developerworks/websphere/zones/portal/portlet/portletcodingguidelines.html

Index

A

NOTE: Boldface numbers indicate illustrations or code listing; t indicates a table

B

C

D

E

F

M

W

X

Y

Z